Sicily '43

SICILY '43

The First Assault on Fortress Europe

James Holland

Grove Press
New York

For my oldest friend and best man, Giles Bourne

Contents

Part III: The Race to Catania

Part IV: The Conquest of Sicily

Note on the Text

Writing a campaign history such as this is a complicated undertaking. Although dealing with American, British, Canadian, German and Italian units across the armed services, I've tried to keep the numbers of unit names as low as possible. To help distinguish one side from another, I have used a form of vernacular, styling German and Italian units more or less as they would be written in German and Italian – not to be pretentious in any way, but just to reduce the potential for confusion. Having said that, it seemed to me that to describe a Tiger tank company as the 2. Schwere Panzerkompanie was perhaps taking this too far, so I have called it more simply 2. Heavy Panzer Kompanie.

For those who are not familiar with the scale of wartime units and the numbers involved, the basic fighting formation on which the size of armies was judged during the Second World War was the division. German panzer divisions were an all-arms formation of motorized infantry, artillery and tanks; panzer-grenadier divisions had fewer panzers – tanks – and more motorized infantry: a grenadier was simply an infantryman who was provided with motor transport to get from A to B. Infantry divisions had much less motorization by 1943 as fuel and other shortages were increasingly keenly felt within the Reich.

As a rule of thumb, a division was around 15,000 men, although some divisions could have as many as 20,000. Two divisions or more made up a corps, usually denoted in Roman numerals to distinguish them. Two corps or more constituted an army, and two armies or more an army group. Going back down the scale, American, German and Italian divisions were divided into regiments, while British and Canadian divisions were divided into brigades. Confusingly, the British did have regiments too, but in the case of infantry these were parent organizations and never fielded as a whole. US and German regiments and British brigades were much the same, each consisting of three core components, which in the case of an infantry regiment/brigade were battalions, although the Americans termed these 'regimental combat teams' or RCTs. An infantry battalion was around 850 men, divided into companies of some 120 men, each of which in turn broke down into three platoons and finally to the smallest formation, the ten-man squad, *Gruppe* or section, depending on nationality. I hope this helps.

List of Maps

Map Key

(See also the **Glossary of Terms and Abbreviations** on p. 501)

ALLIED UNITS □   ■ **AXIS UNITS**

STANDARD MILITARY SYMBOLS

I = Company	X = Brigade
II = Battalion	XX = Division
III = Regiment	XXX = Corps
	XXXX = Army
	XXXXX = Army Group

OTHER ABBREVIATIONS

Air = Airborne

Arm = Armoured

bde = brigade

bn = battalion

Br = British

Can = Canadian

CB = Coastal Battalion (Italian)

CC = Combat Command

CD = Coastal Division (Italian)

Cdo = Commando

FA = Field Artillery

Fall = Fallschirmjäger

GM = Gruppo Mobile

gp = group

HG = Hermann Göring (Panzer Division)

Inf = Infantry

It = Italian

LCI = landing craft, infantry

LST = landing ship, tank

LZ = landing zone

ME = Middle East

MG = Mobile Group

MT = motor transport

ops = operations

Para = Parachute

PG = Panzer Grenadier

Pz = Panzer

SRS = Special Raiding Squadron

TF = Task Force

TG = Tactical Group

US = United States

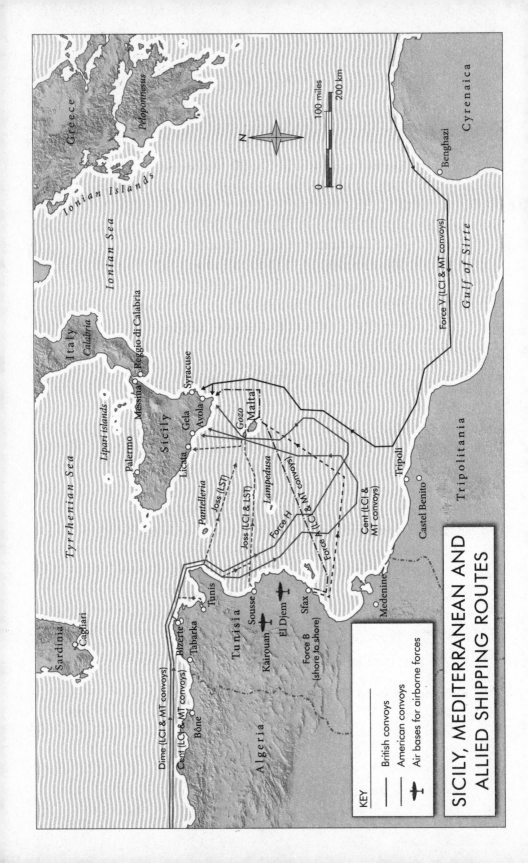

SICILY, MEDITERRANEAN AND ALLIED SHIPPING ROUTES

KEY
— British convoys
— American convoys
✈ Air bases for airborne forces

Greece

Peloponnesus

Ionian Islands

Ionian Sea

Cyrenaica

Benghazi

Gulf of Sirte

Force V (LCI & MT convoys)

Sardinia

Cagliari

Tyrrhenian Sea

Lipari islands

Palermo

Italy

Calabria

Reggio di Calabria

Messina

Sicily

Licata

Gela

Avola

Syracuse

Gozo

Malta

Pantelleria

Joss (LST)

Lampedusa

Joss (LCI & LST)

Force H

Force A (LCI & MT convoys)

Cent (LCI & MT convoys)

Tripoli

Tripolitania

Castel Benito

Medenine

Sfax

El Djem

Kairouan

Sousse

Tunisia

Tunis

Bizerte

Tabarka

Bône

Algeria

Dime (LCI & MT convoys)

Cent (LCI & MT convoys)

Force B (shore to shore)

N

100 miles
200 km

Planning in Lascaris, Malta

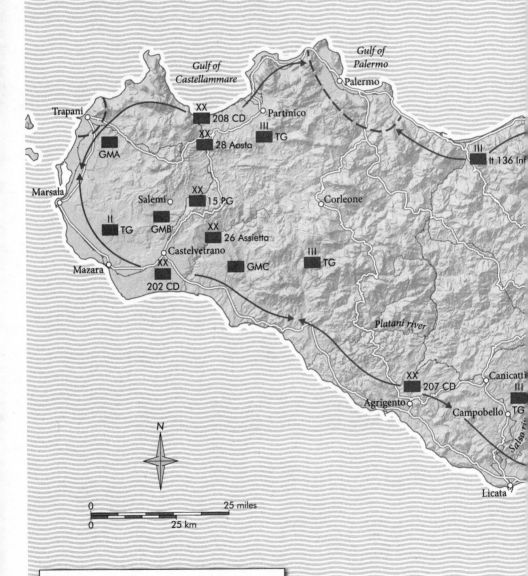

Gulf of
Castellammare

Gulf of
Palermo

Palermo

Trapani

XX
208 CD

Partinico

III
TG

GMA

XX
28 Aosta

III
It 136 Inf

Marsala

Salemi

XX
15 PG

Corleone

II
TG

GMB

XX
26 Assietta

Mazara

Castelvetrano

XX
202 CD

GMC

III
TG

Platani river

Agrigento

XX
207 CD

Canicatti

III
TG

Campobello

Salso riv

Licata

N

0   25 miles

0   25 km

KEY

- - - -   Approximate limits of port defensive areas
⟶   Coastal division defence sector

AXIS DISPOSITIONS
9 July

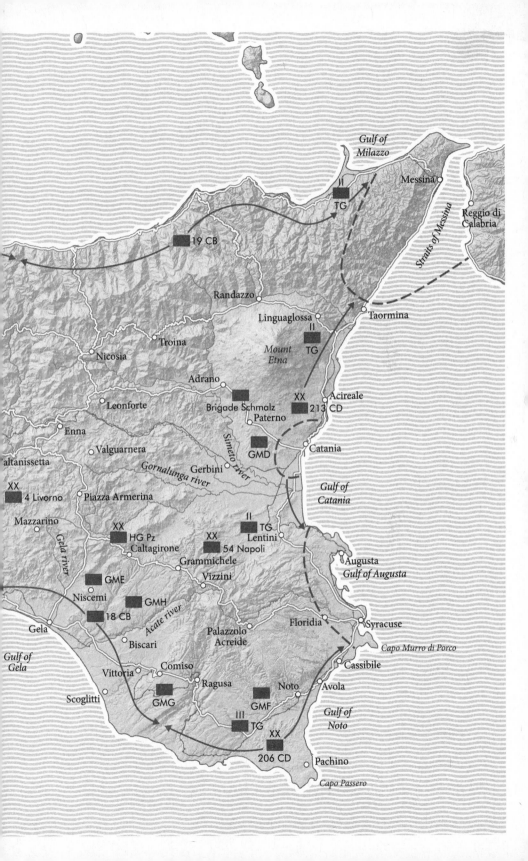

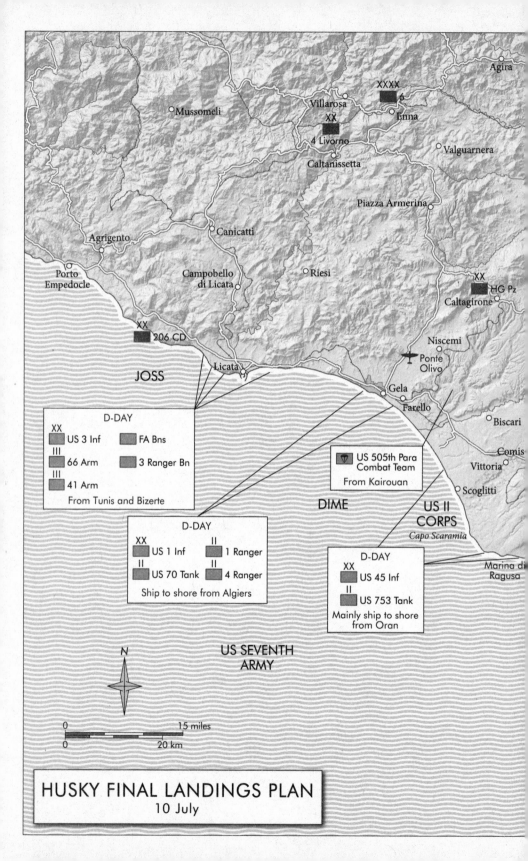

HUSKY FINAL LANDINGS PLAN
10 July

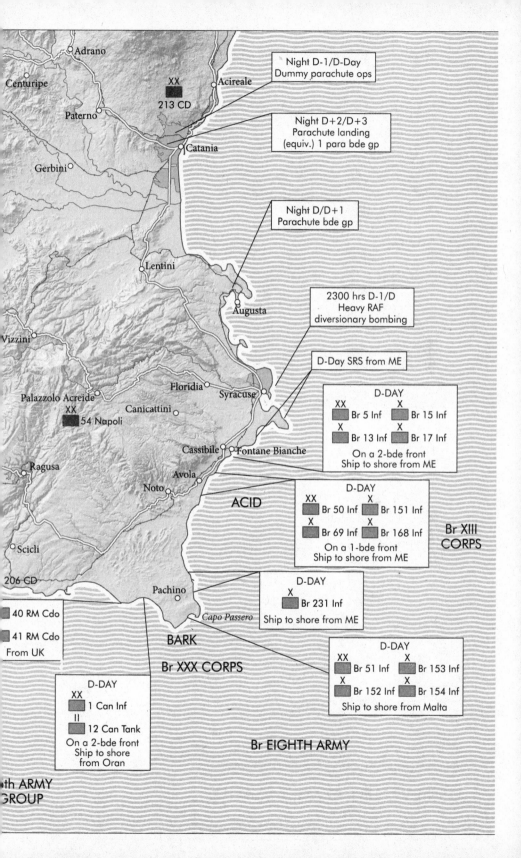

Adrano

Centuripe

Paterno

213 CD

Acireale

Gerbini

Night D-1/D-Day
Dummy parachute ops

Catania

Night D+2/D+3
Parachute landing
(equiv.) 1 para bde gp

Lentini

Night D/D+1
Parachute bde gp

Augusta

2300 hrs D-1/D
Heavy RAF
diversionary bombing

Vizzini

D-Day SRS from ME

Floridia   Syracuse

Palazzolo Acreide   Canicattini
54 Napoli

D-DAY

XX		X	
Br 5 Inf		Br 15 Inf	
X		X	
Br 13 Inf		Br 17 Inf	

On a 2-bde front
Ship to shore from ME

Cassibile   Fontane Bianche

Ragusa

Avola

Noto

ACID

D-DAY

XX		X	
Br 50 Inf		Br 151 Inf	
X		X	
Br 69 Inf		Br 168 Inf	

On a 1-bde front
Ship to shore from ME

Scicli

206 CD

Br XIII
CORPS

Pachino

D-DAY

X	
Br 231 Inf	

Ship to shore from ME

40 RM Cdo

41 RM Cdo

From UK

Capo Passero

BARK

Br XXX CORPS

D-DAY

XX		X	
Br 51 Inf		Br 153 Inf	
X		X	
Br 152 Inf		Br 154 Inf	

Ship to shore from Malta

D-DAY

XX	
1 Can Inf	
II	
12 Can Tank	

On a 2-bde front
Ship to shore
from Oran

Br EIGHTH ARMY

th ARMY
GROUP

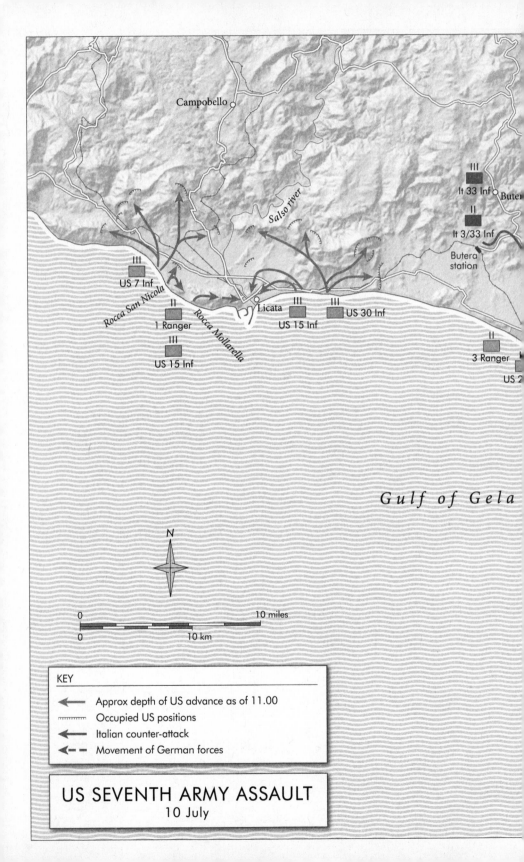

Campobello

It 33 Inf Buter

It 3/33 Inf

Butera
station

US 7 Inf

Salso river

Rocca San Nicola

1 Ranger

Rocca Mollarella

Licata

US 15 Inf

US 15 Inf

US 30 Inf

3 Ranger

US 2

Gulf of Gela

N

0   10 miles
0   10 km

KEY

← Approx depth of US advance as of 11.00

⌐⌐⌐⌐ Occupied US positions

← Italian counter-attack

◄-- Movement of German forces

US SEVENTH ARMY ASSAULT
10 July

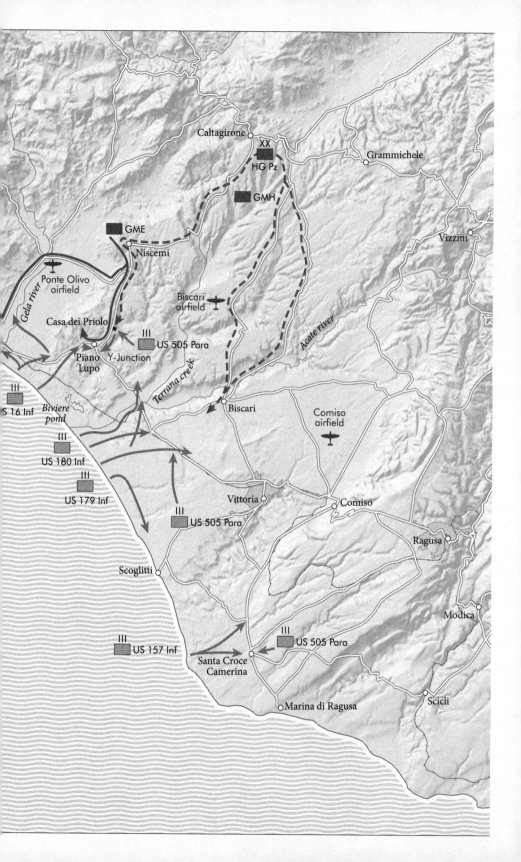

Patton on the
beach at Gela

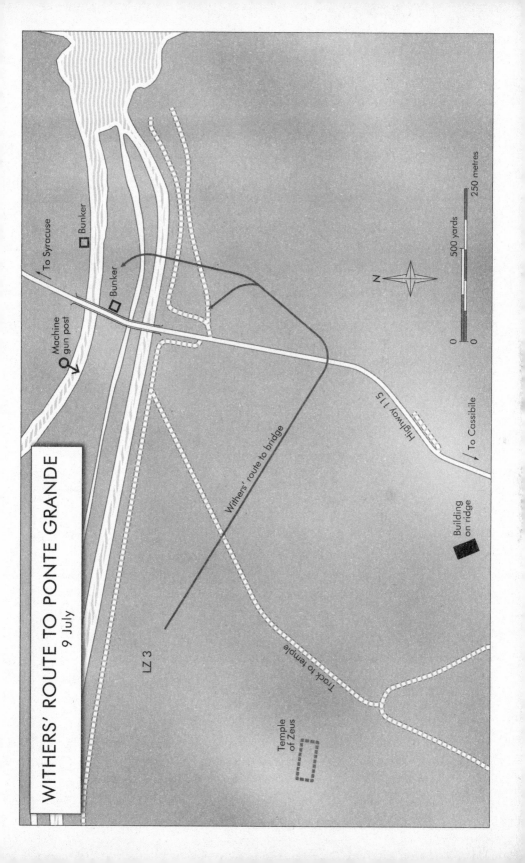

WITHERS' ROUTE TO PONTE GRANDE
9 July

To Syracuse

Bunker

Bunker

Machine gun post

LZ 3

Withers' route to bridge

Highway 115

To Cassibile

Building on ridge

Track to temple

Temple of Zeus

N

0   500 yards

0   250 metres

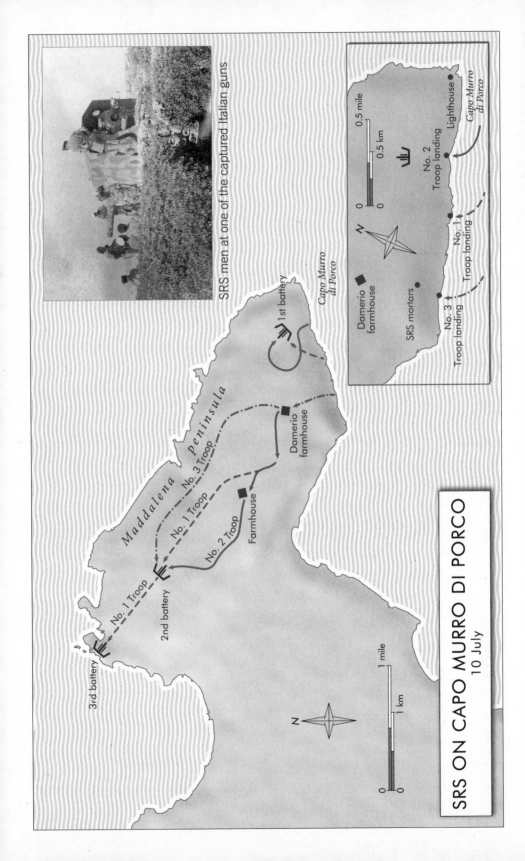

SRS men at one of the captured Italian guns

SRS ON CAPO MURRO DI PORCO
10 July

Maddalena peninsula

No. 1 Troop

No. 3 Troop

No. 1 Troop

No. 2 Troop

1st battery

2nd battery

3rd battery

Farmhouse

Damerio farmhouse

Capo Murro di Porco

N

0   1 km

0   1 mile

Lighthouse

Capo Murro di Porco

No. 2 Troop landing

No. 1 Troop landing

No. 3 Troop landing

Damerio farmhouse

SRS mortars

N

0   0.5 km

0   0.5 mile

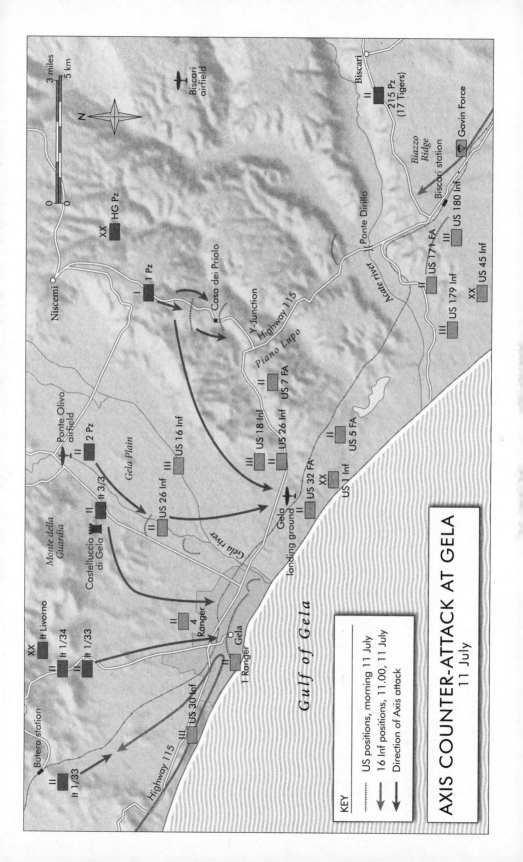

KEY

US positions, morning 11 July
16 Inf positions, 11.00, 11 July
Direction of Axis attack

AXIS COUNTER-ATTACK AT GELA
11 July

Gulf of Gela

3 miles
5 km

N

Biscari airfield

Biscari

215 Pz
(17 Tigers)

Biazzo Ridge

Biscari station

Gavin Force

US 180 Inf

US 171 FA

US 179 Inf

US 45 Inf

Ponte Dirillo

Acate river

HG Pz

Niscemi

1 Pz

Casa dei Priolo

Y-Junction

Highway 115

Piano Lupo

US 7 FA

US 5 FA

US 18 Inf

US 26 Inf

US 16 Inf

Ponte Olivo airfield

2 Pz

Gela Plain

It 3/3

US 26 Inf

US 32 FA

US 1 Inf

Gela landing ground

Gela

Monte della Guardia

Castelluccio di Gela

Gela river

4 Ranger

Butera station

It Livorno

It 1/34

It 1/33

US 30 Inf

Highway 115

It 1/33

Ranger

1 Ranger

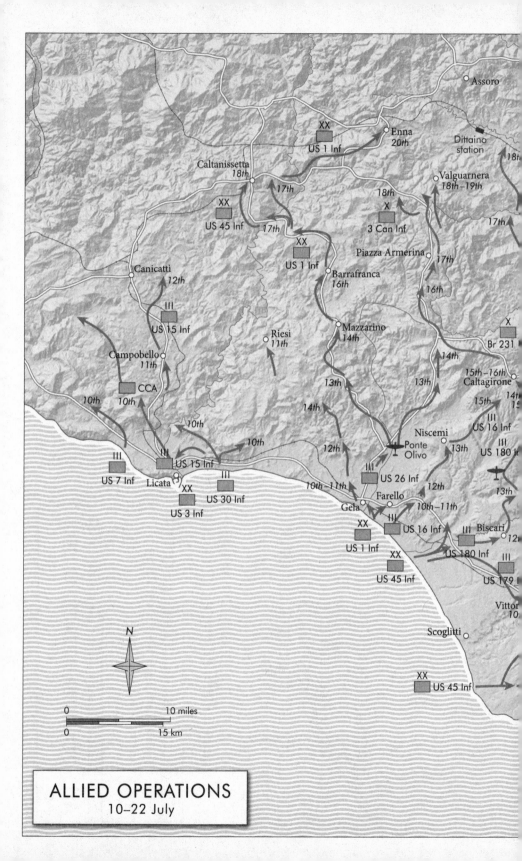

ALLIED OPERATIONS
10–22 July

Centuripe

Acireale

Catenanuova

Paterno

20th

Simeto river

Sferro

Misterbianco

19th–20th

Catania

17th–18th

Gerbini

19th–21st

18th–21st   *15th–18th*

Gornalunga river

Dittaino river

13th–14th

17th

15th

14th
X
Br 4 Arm & 151 Inf

X
Br 154 Inf

16th

X
Br 153 Inf

3 Cdo

Palagonia

X
Br 23 Arm

15th

Scordia

Agnone

Lentini
Carlentini

X
Br 4 Arm

Grammichele
15th

Francofonte
14th–15th

X
Br 69 Inf
13th–14th

13th–14th

Villasmundo

Augusta
12th–13th

14th

12th

13th

Melilli
12th

16th

Vizzini

X
Br 152 Inf

Sortino
13th

X
Br 69
Inf

Priolo
11th

13th

III
179 Inf

X
Br 153
Inf

13th *16th*

12th

Monterosso
13th

Buscemi
12th

Solarino

11th

Floridia

10th

Syracuse

III
US 157
Inf

Giarratana
13th

Palazzolo

10th–11th

Punta Caderini

2th

Chiaramonte
12th

X
Br 23
Arm

XX
1 Can Inf

X
Br 13 Inf

X
Br 17 Inf

Capo Murro
di Porco

III
US 180 Inf

Comiso
11th

10th

Ragusa
12th

11th–12th

X
Br 69 Inf

10th

Cassibile

XX
Br 5 Inf

11th

US 157 Inf

X
2 Can
Inf

*11th–
12th*

Noto

11th

Avola

XX
Br 50 Inf

X
1 Can Inf

Rosolini

12th

X
2 Can Inf

*10th–
11th*

10th

10th

X
Br 231 Inf

XX
1 Can Inf

10th

Pachino

Capo Passero

XX
Br 51 Inf

Correnti island

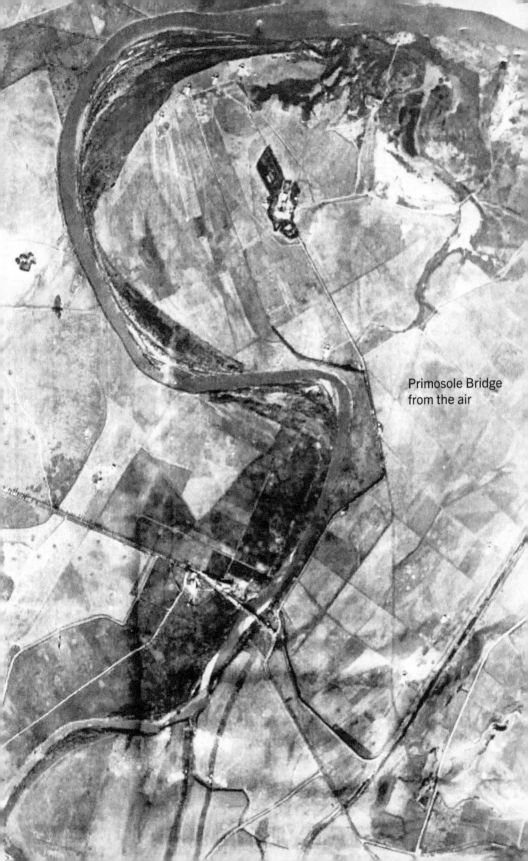

Primosole Bridge
from the air

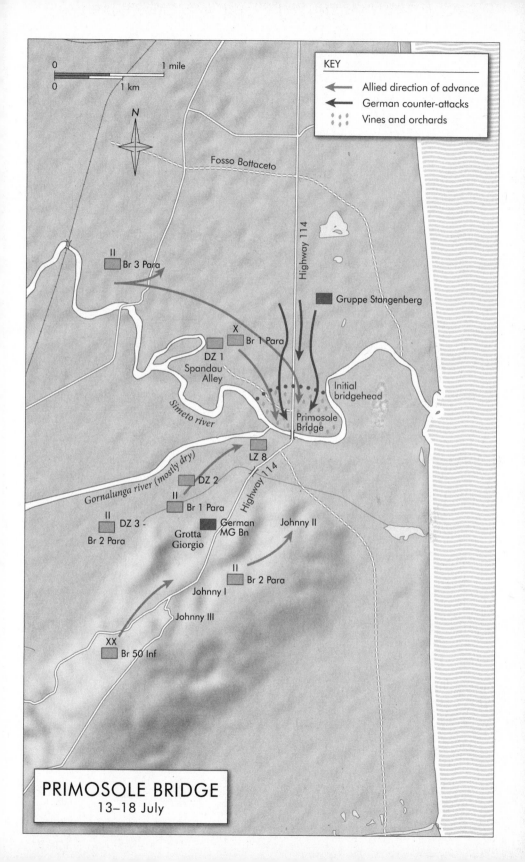

KEY

⬅ Allied direction of advance

⬅ German counter-attacks

⋮ Vines and orchards

0   1 mile

0   1 km

N

Fosso Bottaceto

Highway 114

II   Br 3 Para

Gruppe Stangenberg

X   Br 1 Para

DZ 1

Spandau Alley

Simeto river

Initial bridgehead

Primosole Bridge

LZ 8

Highway 114

Gornalunga river (mostly dry)

DZ 2

II   Br 1 Para

DZ 3

II   Br 2 Para

Grotta Giorgio

German MG Bn

Johnny II

II   Br 2 Para

Johnny I

Johnny III

XX   Br 50 Inf

PRIMOSOLE BRIDGE
13–18 July

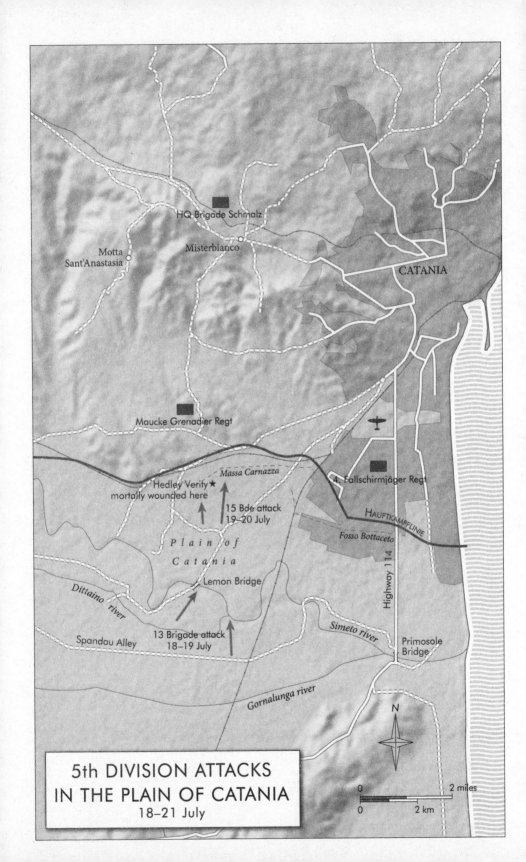

HQ Brigade Schmalz

Motta Sant'Anastasia

Misterbianco

CATANIA

Maucke Grenadier Regt

4. Fallschirmjäger Regt

Massa Carnazza

Hedley Verity ★
mortally wounded here

15 Bde attack
19–20 July

HAUPTKAMPFLINIE

*P l a i n   o f
C a t a n i a*

Fosso Bottaceto

Dittaino   river

Lemon Bridge

Highway 114

Spandau Alley

13 Brigade attack
18–19 July

Simeto river

Primosole
Bridge

Gornalunga river

N

5th DIVISION ATTACKS
IN THE PLAIN OF CATANIA
18–21 July

0   2 miles

0   2 km

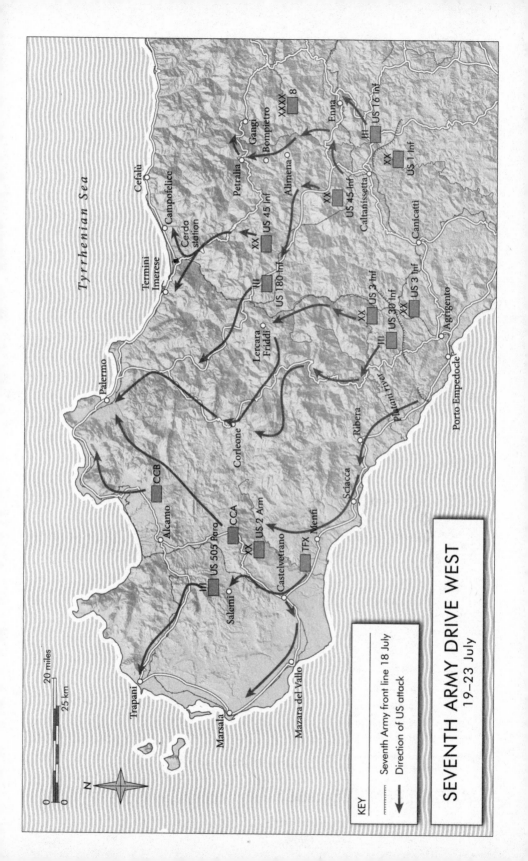

Tyrrhenian Sea

Cefalù
Campofelice
Termini Imerese
Cerda station
Palermo
Alcamo
Trapani
Marsala
Mazara del Vallo
Salemi
Castelvetrano
Menfi
Sciacca
Ribera
Corleone
Lercara Friddi
Petralia
Gangi
Bompietro
Alimena
Caltanissetta
Enna
Canicatti
Agrigento
Porto Empedocle
Platani river

XXXX 8
US 16 Inf
US 1 Inf
US 45 Inf
US 45 Inf
US 180 Inf
US 3 Inf
US 30 Inf
US 3 Inf
US 505 Para
CCB
CCA
US 2 Arm
TFX

KEY
.... Seventh Army front line 18 July
——► Direction of US attack

SEVENTH ARMY DRIVE WEST
19–23 July

N

20 miles
25 km
0

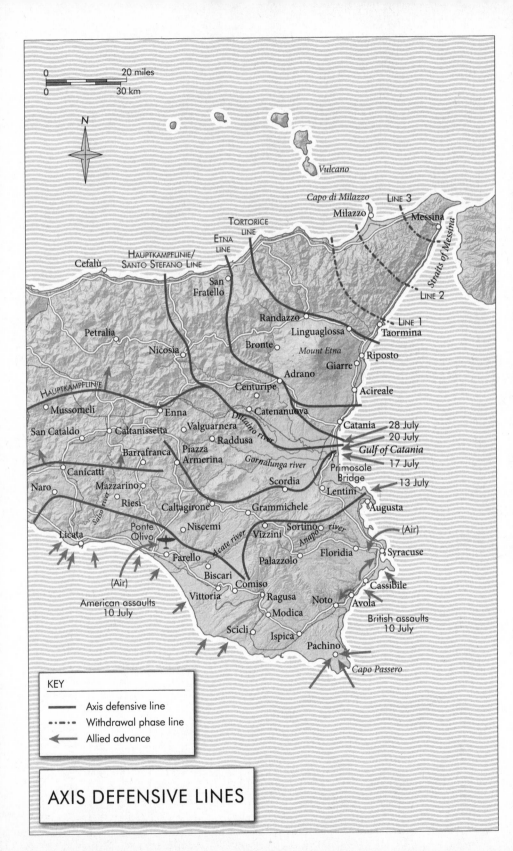

AXIS DEFENSIVE LINES

KEY

— Axis defensive line

- - - Withdrawal phase line

← Allied advance

Vulcano

Capo di Milazzo
Milazzo
LINE 3
Messina

Straits of Messina

LINE 2

LINE 1

Cefalù

HAUPTKAMPFLINIE/
SANTO STEFANO LINE

San
Fratello

TORTORICE
LINE

ETNA
LINE

Randazzo
Linguaglossa
Taormina

Petralia

Nicosia

Bronte

Mount Etna

Riposto

Adrano

Giarre

Centuripe

Acireale

HAUPTKAMPFLINIE

Mussomeli

Enna

Catenanuova

San Cataldo

Caltanissetta

Valguarnera

Raddusa

Dittaino river

Catania   28 July
              20 July
Gulf of Catania

Barrafranca

Piazza
Armerina

Gornalunga river

17 July

Canicattì

Mazzarino

Scordia

Primosole
Bridge

13 July

Naro

Riesi

Caltagirone

Grammichele

Lentini

Salso river

Licata

Ponte
Olivo

Niscemi

Vizzini

Sortino   river

Augusta

Farello

Acate river

Palazzolo

Anapo

(Air)

Biscari

Floridia

Syracuse

(Air)

Vittoria

Comiso

Ragusa

Noto

Cassibile

American assaults
10 July

Modica

Avola

Scicli

Ispica

Pachino

British assaults
10 July

Capo Passero

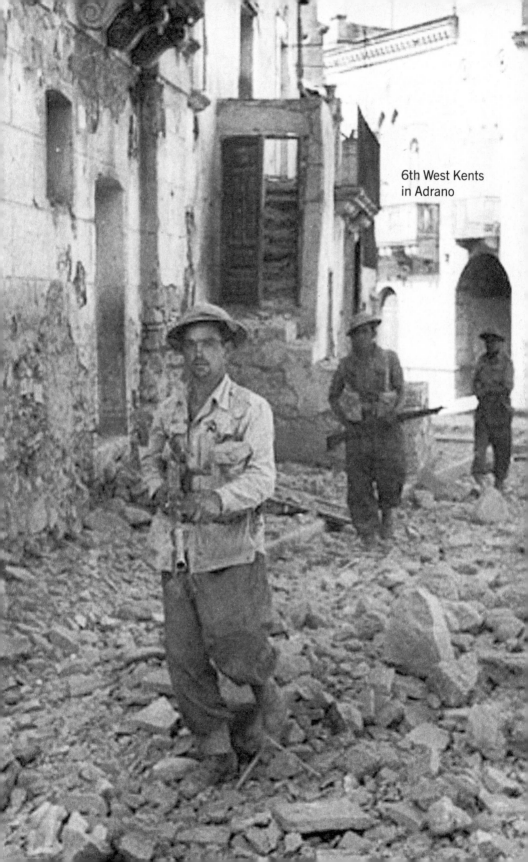

6th West Kents
in Adrano

Salso river

X
2 Can Inf

X
2 Can

27th–128th

Agira

25th–28th

31st

Regalbut

X
Br 231 Inf

2

XX
1 Can Inf

26th–28th

29th

1st

X
1 Can Inf

Mor
Tigl

23rd

31

23rd

X
Br 231 Inf

27
29

Dittaino
station

X
3 Can Inf

26th–27

Raddusa–Agira
station

Dittaino river

Libertinia station

RIDGELINE BATTLES
24 July – 7 August

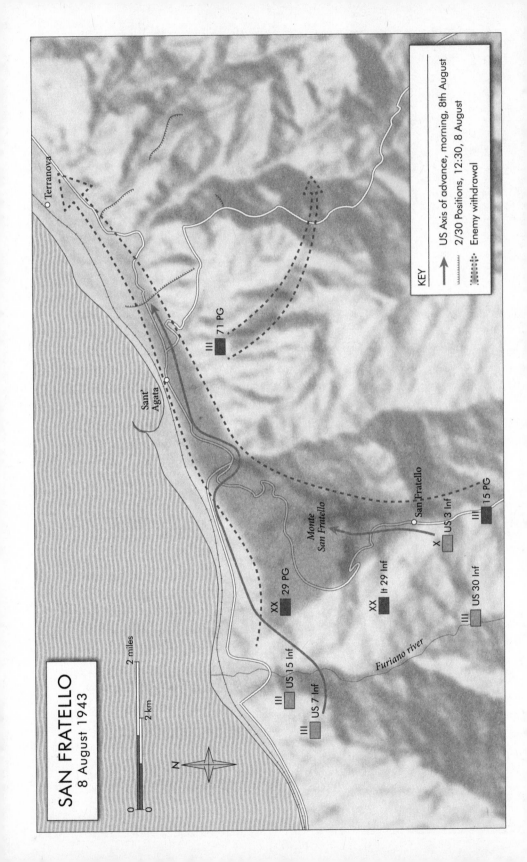

SAN FRATELLO
8 August 1943

N

2 miles
2 km

KEY

US Axis of advance, morning, 8th August

2/30 Positions, 12:30, 8 August

Enemy withdrawal

Terranova

Sant' Agata

71 PG

III

29 PG

XX

It 29 Inf

XX

Monte San Fratello

San Fratello

US 3 Inf

X

15 PG

III

US 30 Inf

III

US 15 Inf

III

US 7 Inf

III

Furiano river

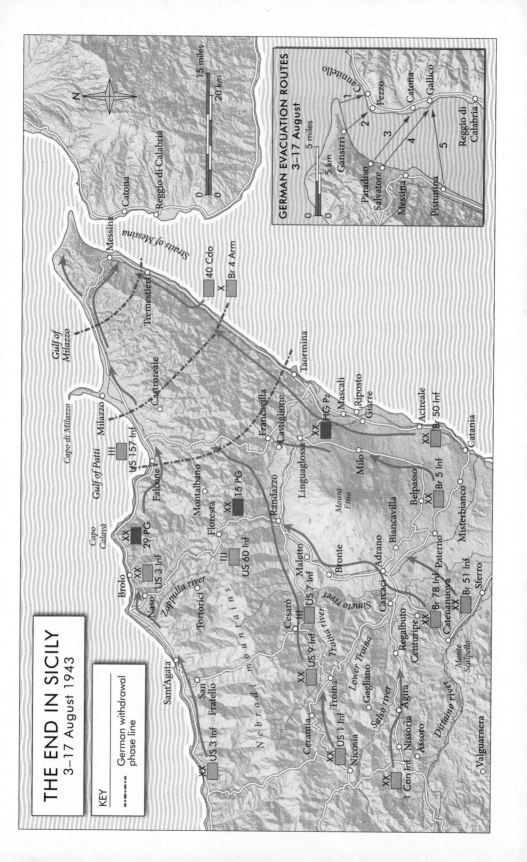

THE END IN SICILY
3–17 August 1943

KEY

--·--·-- German withdrawal phase line

GERMAN EVACUATION ROUTES
3–17 August

Cannitello

Gansirri
Pezzo
1
2
Paradiso
Salvatore
Catona
3
Gallico
Messina
4
5
Pistunina
Reggio di Calabria

Catona
Reggio di Calabria

Straits of Messina
Messina

Gulf of Milazzo
Tremestieri
Castroreale

40 Cdo
Br 4 Arm

Capo di Milazzo
Milazzo
Gulf of Patti
US 157 Inf
Falcone
Montalbano
Floresta
Capo Calavà
29 PG
Brolo
US 3 Inf
Naso
Zappulla river
Tortorici
US 60 Inf
15 PG
Randazzo
Maletto
Bronte
Cesarò
US 7 Inf
Simeto river
Troina river
Lower Troina
Adrano
Carcaci
Biancavilla
Sant'Agata
San Fratello
US 3 Inf
Nebrodi mountains
Ceramia
US 9 Inf
Troina
US 1 Inf
Nicosia
Gagliano
Salso river
Regalbuto
Centuripe
Paternò
Br 78 Inf
Catenanuova
Monte Scalpello
Br 51 Inf
Sferro
Agira
Nissoria
Assoro
Ditaino river
1 Can Inf
Valguarnera
Dittaino river

Francavilla
Castiglione
Taormina
Linguaglossa
HG Pz
Mascali
Riposto
Giarre
Milo
Mount Etna
Belpasso
Acireale
Br 50 Inf
Br 5 Inf
Misterbianco
Catania

N

15 miles
20 km

Principal Personalities

American

Major Mark Alexander
Commander, 2nd Battalion, 505th
Parachute Infantry Regiment, 82nd
Airborne Division

Staff Sergeant James Altieri
Fox Company, 4th Ranger Battalion

Lieutenant-General Omar M. Bradley
Commander, II Corps

Lieutenant John Mason Brown
Journalist and US Navy Reserve
officer serving on USS *Ancon*

Lieutenant James M. 'Jimmy' Bruno
Co-pilot, 99th Bomb Group

Harry Butcher
Naval aide to General Eisenhower

Lieutenant Max Corvo
Intelligence officer, Office of Strategic
Services

Lieutenant Charlie Dryden
Pilot, 99th Fighter Squadron

General Dwight D. Eisenhower
Supreme Allied Commander,
Mediterranean

Lieutenant Warren 'Bing' Evans
Company F, 3rd Battalion, Army
Rangers

Lieutenant Douglas Fairbanks Jr
Serving on USS *Monrovia*

Colonel James M. 'Jim' Gavin
Commander, 505th Parachute
Infantry Regiment

Private Eugene 'Breezy' Griffin
HQ Company, 2nd Battalion, 41st
Armored Infantry Regiment, 2nd
Armored Division

Captain Chester B. 'Chet' Hansen
Aide to General Omar Bradley,
II Corps HQ

Lieutenant Franklyn A. Johnson
Cannon Company, 3rd Battalion, 18th
Infantry Regiment, 1st Infantry
Division

Corporal Audie Murphy
B Company, 1st Battalion,
15th Infantry

Lieutenant-General George S. Patton
Commander, Seventh Army

Ernie Pyle
War correspondent for the Scripps
Howard syndicate

Sergeant Carl Rambo
1st Platoon, Company B, 70th Light
Tank Battalion

Lieutenant Charlie Scheffel
S-3 Staff Officer, 1st Battalion, 39th
Infantry Regiment, 9th Infantry
Division

Lieutenant-General Carl 'Tooey' Spaatz
Commander, USAAF North-West
African Air Force

Lieutenant Robert 'Smoky' Vrilakas
P-38 pilot, 94th Fighter Squadron, 1st
Fighter Group

British

General Sir Harold Alexander
Commander-in-Chief, 15th Army Group

Lieutenant-Colonel George Chatterton
CO, Glider Pilot Regiment, Airlanding Brigade, 1st Airborne Division

Corporal Bill Cheall
6th Battalion the Green Howards, 69th Brigade, 5th Division

Captain David Cole
2nd Royal Inniskilling Fusiliers, 13th Brigade, 5th Division

Air Marshal Sir Arthur 'Mary' Coningham
Commander, 2nd Tactical Air Force, RAF

Admiral of the Fleet Sir Andrew Browne Cunningham
Commander-in-Chief, Mediterranean, Royal Navy

Lieutenant Peter Davis
No. 2 Troop, Special Raiding Squadron

Corporal James Donaldson
Mortar Platoon, 2nd Devonshire Regiment, 231st 'Malta' Brigade

Wing Commander Hugh 'Cocky' Dundas
324 Wing, Desert Air Force

Lieutenant David Fenner
C Company, 6th Battalion Durham Light Infantry, 151st Brigade, 50th Division

Staff Sergeant Dennis 'Galp' Galpin
Pilot, Glider Pilot Regiment, Airlanding Brigade, 1st Airborne Division

Midshipman Peter Hay
Serving on HMS *Tartar*

Sergeant John Johnstone
2nd Parachute Battalion, 1st Parachute Brigade

General Sir Bernard Montgomery
Commander, Eighth Army

Lieutenant-Colonel Alastair Pearson
Commander, 1st Parachute Battalion, 1st Parachute Brigade

Major Peter Pettit
Second-in-Command, 17th Field Artillery Regiment, 78th Division

Sergeant Raymond Phillips
6th Royal Inniskilling Fusiliers, 238th Irish Brigade, 78th Division

Air Chief Marshal Sir Arthur Tedder
Air Officer Commanding-in-Chief, Mediterranean Air Command

Major Hedley Verity
Commander, B Company, 1st Battalion the Green Howards

Canadian

Captain Alex Campbell
Commander, A Company, Hastings & Prince Edward Regiment

Flight Lieutenant Irving 'Hap' Kennedy
Fighter pilot, 249 Squadron and 111 Squadron

Private Archie 'A. K.' Long
A Company, Hastings & Prince Edward Regiment

Lieutenant Farley Mowat
A Company, Hastings & Prince Edward
Regiment

Major Lord John Tweedsmuir
CO, Hastings & Prince Edward Regiment

German

Oberst Ernst-Günther Baade
CO, Division Kommando Sizilien, later
15. Panzer Grenadier Regiment

Oberst Hellmuth Bergengruen
Chief of Staff, Hermann Göring Panzer
Division

Kanonier Hanns Cibulka
Flak Regiment 7, later 31. Heavy Flak
Bataillon

Leutnant Karl Goldschmidt
2. Kompanie, 504. Heavy Panzer Bataillon,
Hermann Göring Panzer Division

Unteroffizier Bruno Kanert
11. Heavy Batterie, III. Bataillon,
Brigade Schmalz, Hermann Göring
Panzer Division

Feldmarschall Albert Kesselring
Commander-in-Chief, South

Oberfeldwebel Josef 'Jupp' Klein
2. Kompanie, I. Fallschirm-Pionier
Bataillon, 1. Fallschirmjäger Division

Oberstarzt Wilhelm Mauss
Senior Medical Officer, XIV Panzer
Korps Headquarters

Leutnant Martin Pöppel
1. Kompanie, Maschinengewehr
Bataillon, 1. Fallschirmjäger Division

Oberst Wilhelm Schmalz
Commander, Brigade Schmalz,
Hermann Göring Panzer Division

**Generalleutnant Fridolin von Senger
und Etterlin**
German Liaison Officer to General
Guzzoni, Sixth Army

Grenadier Werner Stappenbeck
1. Heavy Panzerjäger Kompanie, 104.
Panzer Grenadier Regiment,
15. Panzer Grenadier Division

Major Johannes 'Macky' Steinhoff
Commander, Jagdgeschwader 77

Generalleutnant Walter Warlimont
Deputy Chief of Operations,
Oberkommando der Wehrmacht

Italian

Tenente Melino Barbagallo
27° Gruppo Bombardimenti, Gela–
Ponte Olivo

Tenente Giuseppe Bruccoleri
8° Reggimento Genio

Generale Alfredo Guzzoni
Commander-in-Chief, Sixth Army

Vincenza La Bruna
Civilian living in Regalbuto

**Tenente-Colonnello Dante Ugo
Leonardi**
III° Battaglione, 34° Reggimento
di Fanteria, 4° Divisione 'Livorno'

Tenente Livio Messina
I° Battaglione, 33° Reggimento
di Fanteria, 4° Divisione 'Livorno'

Michele Piccione
Student sergeant, 4° Reggimento
Autisti

Mario Turco
Civilian living in Gela

Harold Alexander

Mark Alexander

James Altieri

Omar Bradley

Giuseppe Bruccoleri

Alex Campbell

Bill Cheall

David Cole

Arthur Coningham

Max Corvo

Peter Davis

Charlie Dryden

Hugh Dundas

Dwight D. Eisenhower

Warren Evans

Douglas Fairbanks Jr

James M. Gavin

Karl Goldschmidt

Alfredo Guzzoni

Chester B. Hansen

Hans-Valentin Hube

Franklyn A. Johnson

'Hap' Kennedy

Josef Klein

Farley Mowat

Audie Murphy

George S. Patton

Alastair Pearson

Raymond Phillips

Michele Piccione

Martin Pöppel

Ernie Pyle

Charlie Scheffel

Wilhelm Schmalz

Carl Spaatz

Johannes Steinhoff

Arthur Tedder

Hedley Verity

Robert Vrilakas

Walter Warlimont

Prologue

The Burning Blue

F RIDAY, 25 JUNE 1943. Morning, and another scorching day of soporific heat. Trapani on the western edge of Sicily was crowded with
aircraft: two more fighter groups had arrived that morning. Major
Johannes Steinhoff – 'Macky' to his friends – twenty-nine years old and
in possession of a lean, gentle face, blue eyes and fair hair, had been up
early, woken in the grey light of dawn and driven down to the airfield to
join the rest of I. and II. Gruppen of Jagdgeschwader – Fighter Wing –
77. Already, mechanics were furiously working on their Messerschmitt
109 aircraft, desperately trying to get as many as possible fit to fly despite
chronic shortages of parts – from simple bolts to electrical wiring to just
about everything complex machines like these needed.

Trapani lay on a dusty, sun-bleached, small coastal plain, and by the
time Steinhoff had planted himself in a chair in front of the wooden dispersal hut, the dawn light had been swept aside by the deep burning blue
of the daytime sky. Beyond, past the edge of the airfield, lay the vast
wine-dark sea. Crickets and cicadas chirruped. The heat grew palpably.

Steinhoff was exhausted. The previous day, General der Jagdflieger Adolf
Galland had arrived, having taken over from the sacked and disgraced
Generalmajor Theo Osterkamp, the former fighter commander – Jafü – on
Sicily. Galland had been commander of fighters back home in Germany,
defending the Reich, but had no experience of the Mediterranean and,
while a notable fighter wing commander earlier in the war, had had no
staff training and had been thrown in at the deep end to say the least. The
previous evening, he had summoned Steinhoff to the Trapani fighter
control base beneath the summit of Monte Erice, the mountain that

dominated the plain below. The route up there was a winding dusty road, one hairpin after another until, beneath a sheer wall of craggy rock, it reached a small plateau that extended outwards. Several buildings had been constructed, while pneumatic drills continued work on a shelter dug directly into the cliffs. From there, the whole western tip of Sicily could be seen stretched out before them – the white houses of Trapani town and its small port and then, further to the south, the airfield, and beyond that Marsala. It was nothing if not a stunning view. After briefing him on recent operations, Galland had then told Steinhoff he wanted to talk to the *Gruppen* and *Staffel* commanders, and so they had headed back down the mountain road to the airfield.

Sitting on stools and in deckchairs outside the dispersal hut beneath gnarled old olive trees, Steinhoff's commanders had listened in silence as Galland talked about the air defence of the Reich and the tactics that had been developed against the American four-engine heavy bombers. The key, he had told them, was to fly straight at them, opening fire at the nose of the bomber as close as possible then sweeping on over the top. The general also told them that against American heavy bombers, there was a 50 per cent chance of being shot down during a rear attack, and similarly poor odds for a side or flank attack too. It was hardly very cheering. On the other hand, a head-on attack greatly reduced the chance of being hit – but it did mean a pilot had only about two seconds of firing time, because it was only effective when really close, and with a closing speed of nearly 600 mph that didn't leave much margin for error. Steinhoff had watched his officers start to glaze over. When Galland had finished, not one had asked any questions.

'Very well then,' Galland had said. 'Until tomorrow.' And then he had driven back to Monte Erice. Steinhoff had barely slept, the general's words ringing in his ears: 'Get in close.' 'Don't fire too soon.' 'Lead them in head-on close formation.' Steinhoff knew one had to have nerves of steel to pull off these frontal attacks. He was not feeling confident, and in any case, he had already been a front-line fighter pilot for three long years – over France, during the Battle of Britain, over the Eastern Front and then in those difficult final days in Tunisia when suddenly it had become clear that the Luftwaffe was in deep and chronic decline and the Allies, with their shiny Spitfires and Lightnings, their Marauders and Flying Fortresses, had dramatically and decisively begun to wield the upper hand.

Steinhoff was fed up with fighting, fed up with the war, fed up with not having enough of anything. And he was utterly exhausted. The intensity, the constant fear, and now, here on Sicily, the blistering, energy-sapping heat.

Early that day, his III. Gruppe had arrived from their base in Sardinia, and then so too had III. Gruppe Jagdgeschwader 53, the Pik As, or Ace of Spades. This was all part of Galland's plan to show any Allied bomber formations that dared to fly over a heavy response by a mass of fighter aircraft; but with some eighty Messerschmitts now parked up around the airfield complex here at Trapani, Steinhoff was only thinking of the catastrophe that might unfold if they were heavily attacked by Allied bombers here.

The hours passed and the heat grew. Steinhoff wondered how many hours he had spent in a deckchair since the war had begun. 'A day seems very long when it is spent in waiting,' he noted, 'with nothing to occupy one's imagination except the war in the air.' He wondered whether he would be able to lead this huge formation of fighters into the bombers success-fully; it was no easy matter manoeuvring en masse because the distances on the inside of a turn were shorter than those on the outside. Leading a *Staffel* of, say, nine, was reasonably straightforward, but eighty . . . Then those other thoughts kept creeping into his mind – thoughts impossible to keep out: the raking fire of the Flying Fortresses' .50-calibre machine guns, the bailing out, the descent, the vainly hoping someone would spot the rub-ber dinghy on that vast dark Mediterranean Sea.

Then Oberst Günther 'Franzl' Lützow arrived, the new Inspector South for the Luftwaffe. An old friend of Steinhoff's, he had been the Luftwaffe's second pilot to amass a staggering one hundred aerial victo-ries. Steinhoff hadn't seen him since the Eastern Front the previous summer.

'I want to be here for your first big defensive battle!' called Lützow as he clambered out of his car. Steinhoff led him over to dispersal and to the mass of pilots sitting waiting under the shade of the olive trees. All this talk of big aerial battles was making Steinhoff feel increasingly on edge.

'Today's your big chance,' Lützow told the pilots. 'You must keep close together when you attack and dismiss from your mind any thought of mixing it with the Spitfires. The Fortresses are like a fleet of battleships and you can only get in among them if you break through their defensive fire in a compact phalanx.'

'For God's sake, Franzl,' Steinhoff snapped, 'spare me that awful pat-ter! For days now, advice and instructions have been raining down on our heads from on high. The General keeps dangling the gallant pilots of the Reich Air Defence as a shining example before our eyes.' It was, continued Steinhoff, enough to make all his men start to feel inferior. The reality was that, for some time now, the older veterans had been gradually, one by one, falling by the wayside, while the new boys being sent to him were short of hours and had had almost no tactical training – and, such were the fuel shortages, there was little opportunity to lick them into shape. 'You people don't know this horrible theatre yet,' he continued. 'It's mostly water and in the long run it gets us all. They'll wear us down by keeping us grounded and destroying our parks and workshops.' He was now in full flow. 'You don't, by any chance, do you, believe in the Teutonic superhero who, after a bombing raid, rises from his slit trench, shakes the dust from his feet and ascends on steely pinions into the icy heavens, there to wreak havoc among the Flying Fortresses?'

For a long moment, Lützow stared at him, as though suddenly he had accepted there was no longer any point keeping up the charade. Then he said: 'Yes, but how's it all going to end here?'

That was the question Steinhoff had been asking himself. It was what all the old-timers had been wondering. They'd lost Tunisia. It wasn't going well in the east. In western Germany, the Ruhr was being systematically bombed by the RAF each night and by the Americans each day. The Allies were getting stronger, while they were growing weaker. How *was* it going to end?

The discussion was suddenly silenced by anti-aircraft fire, followed by a deep rumble from the east, behind Monte Erice, getting louder with every moment. The pilots jumped up and ran for it. Steinhoff heard the whistle of bombs falling even as he fled towards the nearest slit-trench, then leaped for it, landing on the back of someone who had got there first. A carpet of bombs exploded in rapid succession, each one closer, the ground shaking, the noise immense. Steinhoff glanced across at Lützow, dust covering his head and at the back of his throat and in his lungs. Runnels of sweat pouring down his face marked lines through the dust on his skin. Steinhoff pressed his face to the ground as a bomb crashed horribly close, almost bursting eardrums, covering them in a swathe of grit and filling their lungs once more with choking smoke and dust.

And then the bombs stopped falling and the roar of aero-engines faded away. Slowly, unsteadily, they got to their feet and paused for a moment, legs dangling over the edge of the trench in case a second wave appeared. Ammunition from a burning plane was popping somewhere not far away. As they eventually got to their feet, Steinhoff saw splinters of glass; a little way away two ground crew, hands on hips, stood watching the burning wreckage of an Me109.

At the group hut, it turned out the phone line had been cut; soon afterwards a *Kübelwagen* appeared with a message from Galland asking Steinhoff to call immediately from one of the *Staffel* dispersal huts. Steinhoff hurried over to 1. Staffel, where the medical officer was tending a row of wounded ground crew. There, at least, the line was still working.

Galland apologized for the lack of warning. 'We didn't know the Marauders were on their way,' he said. 'They were so close to sea level that our direction finders didn't pick them up.' He told Steinhoff to be ready to scramble; radio traffic suggested bombers in Tunisia were starting to form up. It looked as though a big raid was on its way.

A little while later, and with the line from the group hut repaired, Galland rang again to say they were tracking an enemy raid that seemed to be heading for Naples. The fighters would be scrambled to catch them on the return leg. They most likely had an hour to wait.

But Galland was back on the line sooner than that. 'Take off straight away, Steinhoff,' he said. 'The bombers have turned south and attacked the port of Messina. You must hurry if you're going to catch them.'

Steinhoff put down the receiver and shouted 'Scramble!' at the operations clerk. Pilots ran to their machines, grabbing parachutes left on the wings, clambering up on to the wing root and hoisting themselves into the cockpit. A quick check, a signal to the ground crew, engine turning and bursting into life, then taxi out of the blast pen. Steinhoff checked his magnetos. The smell of oil, gasoline, metal and rubber, and a cockpit already hot as an oven. He glanced around, although the collar of his lifejacket restricted movement and his oxygen mask swung to and fro. Dust was being whipped up by the prop blast, making it hard to see, but with aircraft drawing up either side of him he opened the throttle and was off, rumbling forward, controlling the huge torque with opposite rudder. A routine performed hundreds of times; and then he was free of the ground and climbing high into the blue.

'Odysseus One to Eagle,' he said over the R/T – the radio – making contact with the ground controller below at Monte Erice.

'Pantechnicons withdrawing.' Galland's voice now in his headset. 'Grid reference Able two-two King. Steer zero-two-five.'

Steinhoff led his I. Gruppe, who closed in behind him as he circled Monte Erice. He had insisted on radio silence so all that could be heard was the background drone of the engine and the hiss of static in their headsets, interrupted only by the calm and precise instructions of General Galland from the fighter control room below.

'Odysseus,' Steinhoff heard him say, 'turn on to three-zero-zero, Pantechnicons at 20,000 feet heading west.'

As they climbed into the sky, the horizon and the sea below it slipped away. A high-pressure haze had settled around them, obscuring the land mass of Sicily and so blocking any fixed reference point that might aid navigation. More updates from Galland. The bombers – the 'pantechnicons' – were descending, now at 16,000 feet, but still being picked up by their Freya radar.

Then a further update. 'Odysseus, steer two-eight-zero. Pantechnicons presumably now at low level since the Freya has lost contact.'

Steinhoff looked around him. Down below he could see nothing. Either side, his pilots were starting to waver, rising and falling, as uneasiness grew. The haze seemed to thicken. Glancing behind, he could only see I. Gruppe behind him – the rest had disappeared from sight in the murk. He broke radio silence to tell them to close up, conscious they only had another ten minutes or so before it would be time to turn back.

'Pantechnicons right beneath us!' Steinhoff recognized Zöhler's voice. 'Right beneath us, lots of them, heading west!'

Steinhoff now saw them too, the desert yellow of their upper bodies standing out against the silvery grey of the sea, grouped in squadrons of nine or more aircraft. It was now around 1.30 p.m., and they were about 90 miles north-west of Trapani. The bombers had just pasted Messina, Sicily's biggest port, a mere mile from the south-west toe of mainland Italy. In all, 123 B-17 Flying Fortresses, mostly from the 97th and 99th Bomb Groups, had dropped nearly 2,000 tons of bombs on the docks, warehouses and railway marshalling yards. They'd caused considerable damage and had also had the good fortune to hit a 5,000-ton Italian steamer, the *Iris*, which was fatally crippled.

On paper, they were a very juicy target and blissfully free of fighter cover; but they were also low, very low, below radar, almost, it seemed, touching the waves. And they were, unhelpfully, heading in exactly the opposite direction, which meant there was now no time for a carefully worked-out manoeuvre. Steinhoff realized he needed to peel over immediately and begin his dive right away in a big arc so that he could emerge level with and hurtling directly towards them, not behind them. Even with the advantage of height and the greater speed of the Me109, there was not a moment to lose. He had to hope the rest followed. Steinhoff dipped the wing and the Messerschmitt turned and dived, building up speed so that in no time the altimeter told him he was now at just 6,000 feet. Glancing around he saw Strafer, Bachman and Berhard following tightly. Five thousand, four, three. The lower he got, the faster the bombers appeared to be flying.

He knew he had to get on to the same level as the bombers, but as he neared the closing speed suddenly seemed immense. Lining up on one, he aimed at the cockpit and opened fire. 'I pulled up my M-E to the same height as the bombers as though I had done it a hundred times before,' he noted. 'My task was to spray the gleaming cockpit with a hail of shot.' Tracer from his guns arced towards the bomber, while the luminous cross-wires of his gunsight shook from the recoil of the cannon and machine guns. Pulling back the stick, he climbed, g-force pressing him down in his seat. His stomach lurched, his mouth tasted bitter. Glancing back once more, he saw he was on his own – his *Geschwader* headquarters flight had dispersed in the attack – but his bomber had crashed into the sea. Over the R/T, pilots chattered – a mixture of excited cries and orders, but also many urgently saying they were low on fuel and pulling out. Looking down at his own fuel gauge, Steinhoff knew he had about twenty minutes' worth left, so turned and set off back for Trapani, a terrible sinking feeling growing in his stomach.

It had been a disaster, he was certain. It was not his fault they'd come across the bombers at the last moment before turning back, nor that among all the advice about how to attack a bomber over Germany at 18,000 feet no one had once suggested how to attack in haze over sea and at almost zero feet. 'Nothing,' he wrote, 'absolutely nothing, had favoured our attack.'

Looking around him, he saw the bombers had gone, vanished entirely, and that he was on his own, flying over the water, accompanied only by the growing anxiety that he might not have the fuel to get home. It was a familiar feeling – one he'd always hated, as almost all German fighter pilots hated it: a gnawing fear that had first gripped him while making repeated returns across the Channel during the Battle of Britain after dog-fights in southern England. The only difference now was that the Mediterranean was even bigger and their Messerschmitts, because of the dust and the shortage of parts, were less reliable. Over the radio, the chatter seemed to be getting ever more hysterical. With a rage born of frustration sweeping over him, he switched on to transmit and told everyone to keep their mouths shut.

But he did make it back. The familiar marker of Monte Erice came into view and soon after, with other single fighters also homing back towards Trapani, he came back into land. Engine off, the dust settling, and a sudden stillness. And the sinking feeling of disaster.

Clambering out, he was met by Hauptmann Lutz Burckhardt and Oberleutnant Gerhard Strausen, both from his headquarters flight. Although Strausen was enthusiastic about the Fortress Steinhoff had shot down, neither had had any success themselves, nor had they seen any other bombers disappear beneath the waves. Major Siegfried Freytag, commander of II. Gruppe, and a man with both a growing cynicism and a talent for calling a spade a spade, greeted Steinhoff as he approached the hut.

'That was a gorgeous balls-up, sir,' he said.

'Didn't your wing get any?'

'Not a single one,' he replied. He had lost sight of the headquarters flight in the haze, and then, when he did see the bombers, it was almost too late and they had had to attack from astern rather than head-on. 'And we botched it, really botched it.' It seemed the other two *Gruppen* hadn't even seen the bombers.

So there it was – as he'd feared. In all, just four had been shot down – one by Steinhoff, one other, as it happened, by one of Freytag's boys and two by the Ace of Spades. Not that Steinhoff knew it at the time. When, with a heavy heart, he phoned through to Galland on Monte Erice, he was able to report only his own single Fortress as confirmed shot down.

'But I told you in good time that they'd gone down low,' Galland replied. 'It really isn't possible – a hundred fighters and only one enemy shot down . . .'

An 88mm flak gun fired, shaking the walls of the wooden hut, and suddenly everyone was once again running to the slit-trenches, Steinhoff's call left unfinished as the telephone fell from its perch on to the floor. As he ran out of the door, the engines of the approaching bombers could already be heard. By chance he found himself once again crouching next to Franzl Lützow, who had earlier been with Galland at fighter operations on Monte Erice. Once more bombs started to whistle down and explode as the anti-aircraft guns boomed their response. Eventually, the raiders passed, and once again they dusted themselves down and wearily clambered out. Galland, Lützow told him, was seething with rage. 'Was there really nothing to be done?' he added.

Sensing a hint of reproach, Steinhoff turned on him. 'I'll be accountable to the general for everything,' he snapped, 'but what I do insist is that you finally get it into your heads that we're trying to do the impossible here!'

Lützow apologized – and assured his friend he was not reproaching him. 'But, my God,' he added, 'how's it all going to end?'

PART I

Command of the Skies

CHAPTER 1

The Long Path to HUSKY

IN THE LAST WEEK of June 1943, from Egypt across North Africa to Algeria and northern Tunisia, Allied troops were getting ready for what was to be the largest amphibious invasion the world had ever known. A pivotal moment in the war had been reached. On the Eastern Front, German forces were about to go on to the offensive once more, this time to try and straighten the Kursk salient following the retreat from Stalingrad back in February. In the Atlantic, the U-boats had been withdrawn after catastrophic losses, allowing Allied shipping finally to flow freely across that vast ocean for the first time since the start of the war. British and American bombers were attacking the Reich both day and night, while – after three long years of fighting – all of North Africa was now in Allied hands. And the future of Italy looked uncertain, to say the least, the Fascist state now reeling in the face of plummeting public morale, a string of military defeats and an economy in shreds.

There was a palpable sense that the noose was starting to tighten around Nazi Germany; and yet for the Allies to cross the sea and capture Sicily would be a mammoth undertaking. The challenges of such an operation, both logistically and in the levels of coordination needed between services and between coalition partners feeling their way in this war, were immense. Hovering over the Allies, too, was the knowledge that less than a year hence they would be attempting to cross the English Channel and invade German-occupied France; the last sizeable strike, at Dieppe in August 1942, had been an utter disaster. If Sicily went wrong, if it turned into catastrophe or even a long and bloody slog, then the ramifications would be enormous. The long road to victory would become even longer;

the cross-Channel attack might have to be postponed. Reverses, at this critical stage in the war, simply could not be countenanced. They were unthinkable.

The stakes, then, could hardly have been higher. The invasion of Sicily had to be a success. Yet for the senior Allied commanders far away across the Mediterranean, in Tunisia, Algeria and Egypt – from where the troops who would soon be attempting to land there were training – conquest of this ancient, even mystical, island seemed a very formidable undertaking indeed.

Most of the men now being put through their paces in North Africa were oblivious to such concerns. Training at Kabrit near the Suez Canal were the men of 69th Brigade, part of 50th 'Tyne Tees' Division, who would be part of the British landing force around Avola on the east coast of Sicily – not that Bill Cheall and the lads of the 6th Green Howards had any idea of that. 'We realised that we were going to invade somewhere,' noted Cheall, 'but, of course, how could we know where at that time?' The war had already been going on a long time for Cheall, a former greengrocer from Middlesbrough in north-east England. Joining the Territorial Army in the spring of 1939, aged just twenty-one, he had been mobilized on the outbreak of war that September, and had served in France with the 6th Green Howards. Escaping from Dunkirk, he'd then begun the process of retraining before being laid low with chronic sinusitis and so had not gone overseas with the battalion when they'd first been posted to the Middle East. Instead, he'd spent some time with the 11th Battalion, before finally being shipped overseas and rejoining his old unit at the end of March 1943. He'd been shocked by how few were left from the battalion that had escaped from Dunkirk, but after the Battle of Wadi Akarit, when Eighth Army had crashed into the Italians in southern Tunisia back at the beginning of April, he had begun to realize why. Being in the infantry was a tough, bloody, attritional business. Sooner or later, one was bound to come a cropper. One just had to hope it wouldn't be a fatal one.

They'd advanced to Enfidaville further north in Tunisia, then had been pulled out of the line. At the time, no one had the faintest idea why, but they were glad to be spared the final battles of the long North African campaign, which had not finally ended until mid-May. Back they went, some 2,000 miles, past previous battle sites, down into Libya, through Cyrenaica and then finally into Egypt once more. The carnage of war had been evident all the way: burnt-out tanks and vehicles, guns and the vast detritus of war. As they'd passed back through Wadi Akarit, Cheall had said a small prayer to himself. 'I imagined the faces of the pals I had lost,' he noted, 'and could see them just as they were before they gave their lives.' Eventually, they'd stopped at Sidi Bishr near Alexandria before moving again to Kabrit. Training continued, including Exercise BROMYARD in the Gulf of Aqaba, where they relentlessly practised amphibious assaults. The heat was intense and the flies as much a nuisance as they had ever been, but Cheall reckoned that by the beginning of July none of them had ever been fitter.

Not far away at another camp at El Shatt was their sister battalion, the 1st Green Howards. Unlike the 6th Battalion, the 1st had yet to see action, having spent the war so far training in England, Northern Ireland and, more recently, Palestine. The 1st Battalion would be part of 5th 'Yorkshire' Division, which was appropriate enough since the Green Howards hailed from that county of northern England, and were originally named after the landowner who had been the regiment's colonel back in the eighteenth century.

One of the officers, the commander of B Company, was quite a sporting celebrity. Major Hedley Verity was one of the finest spin bowlers ever to play cricket for Yorkshire and England, and in 1934 had taken fifteen wickets in England's biggest ever victory over Australia. Verity had considered joining up in 1938 during the Munich crisis, but Arnold Shaw, the colonel of the Green Howards and an old friend, suggested he first read some military textbooks and advised him to get in touch again should war break out. That winter, Verity had read voraciously during the England tour of South Africa before returning home for the final season before the war. Yorkshire once again won the championship that summer with Verity cleaning up Sussex, taking six wickets for 15 runs on Friday 1 September, the day Germany invaded Poland. On the Saturday, he travelled back to Yorkshire with the rest of the team, on Sunday Britain declared war, and on Monday Verity got back in touch with Colonel Shaw and joined up.

Quiet, unassuming and always generous towards others, he quickly showed a natural aptitude for military tactics. The best spin bowlers have both sharp intelligence and a tactical mind, and Verity brought these skills to soldiering. Unsurprisingly, his men and his peers all adored him, while in between training sessions he never tired of playing morale-boosting games of cricket. Since his arrival in the Canal Zone there had even been a match in which Lieutenant-General Miles Dempsey, commander of XIII Corps, had played. A keen cricketer since his school-days, Dempsey had been as overawed as most others to have the celebrated England player among his men. The chance to face the bowl-ing of this sporting star had been too good to pass over.

Not all British troops scheduled for Operation HUSKY, as the Sicily invasion was code-named, were in the Middle East. Some had been training in northern Tunisia, including much of Major-General Vyvyan Evelegh's 78th 'Battleaxe' Division, which was not to be part of the first wave of invasion troops but was to be kept in reserve, most likely landing a week or two later. Major Peter Pettit was second-in-command of the 17th Field Regiment, Royal Artillery, a lawyer from London who had joined the part-time ranks of the Honourable Artillery Company as a nineteen-year-old. During his twelve years of pre-war service with the HAC, he'd taken his soldiering seriously and had risen to acting major, and in March 1941 he had transferred out of the territorials and into the regular army by joining the 17th Field Artillery. A further eighteen months had been spent in England training until finally he and the regi-ment were posted overseas to Tunisia, where they'd been fighting with First Army in the north of the country since the previous November. The 17th had performed well in North Africa, but Pettit, now aged thirty-four, was not a man to sit on any laurels and took the business of being a gunner very seriously. Aware how vital the artillery had become in the British way of war, he thought deeply and carefully about how it could best support the infantry and armour, writing down his thoughts about the relative values of different types of barrages and fire support pat-terns, and ensuring there had been no let-up in training. 'Training from 0600 to 1200,' he wrote in his diary on 3 June, 'and training from 1700 to 1900.' In his next entry, he jotted: 'Gun drill for four hours, very hot.' Joint exercises were held with the Irish Brigade, one of three infantry brigades in the 78th. Combined all-arms training was vital because invariably infantry would be advancing with fire support from the gun-ners; and the more training there was, the more officers such as Major Pettit got to know their fellows in the infantry, all of which helped enor-mously when doing it for real.

While it was the infantry – and armour – who had to make the leap of faith and advance across ground if the enemy was to be overrun and beaten, both the British and the Americans put increasing weight on fire-power to bludgeon the enemy – and on the ground, at any rate, it was the artillery who could provide that support. Fire plans, barrages, counter-battery fire, the siting of forward observers – all required enormous skill and training, and since the 17th FA was the senior artillery regiment in 78th Division, Peter Pettit, for one, was determined his men should be up to the job. Very often, a skilfully executed fire plan could be the difference between living and dying for the infantry up ahead of them.

On 1 July, General Montgomery, commanding Eighth Army to which they were now attached, came to visit the officers of the division, assembled under a large canopy of old car hoods put together by the engineers, just a hundred yards from the sea. 'He said he planned on three principles,' wrote Pettit, 'that he would not move until he was ready, that objectives would be limited, and that he would not ask formations to do something they could not do.' Having been part of First Army in Tunisia, they'd not fought under Monty before, so this was their first proper sighting of their commanding general. Earlier, Montgomery had driven up to the men in the regiment and asked them to gather round. This had prompted something of a stampede, but Pettit knew the men had loved it, seeing this famous general – now their general – right there, in front of them, happily answering questions. 'He got right under their skins at once,' Pettit later jotted in his diary.

Meanwhile, at the coastal port of Oran in Algeria the US 1st Infantry Division had also been gearing up for this next phase of the war against Nazi Germany and its Italian ally. The men of the Big Red One – as the 1st Division was known – had been part of the initial TORCH landings at Oran and Arzew the previous November and had spent the most time in the line during the Tunisian campaign: 112 out of 132 days, which was a lot more than any other American troops. Second Lieutenant Franklyn A. Johnson had celebrated victory in North Africa with three days sleeping and loafing in Bizerte, but then the division had been transferred back to Algeria, and to a training camp at Mangin, 12 miles from the city of Oran. An officer in Cannon Company of the 18th Infantry Regiment, Johnson had survived the North African campaign with no further damage than a painful but not serious shrapnel wound to his hand, but he was tired after the long campaign and in need of some R&R. They all were; and, recognizing this, the divisional commander, Major-General Terry de la Mesa Allen, had announced a brief moratorium on training, plus unrestricted passes and trucks to take his boys into town.

Inevitably, after such a sudden release of steam, drunken mayhem had followed. The next morning, General Allen himself had gone down to the city's jails and bailed out the many men who had been locked up for over-exuberance the previous evening. The episode had cost Allen a severe dressing-down from Lieutenant-General George S. Patton, the commander of Force 343 for the upcoming invasion – what would soon become the US Seventh Army. Patton disapproved of his soldiers going on drunken sprees, and even more strongly of commanders encouraging such behaviour.

Frank Johnson had been among those assembled for a pep-talk by Allen a day or so later, by which time the holiday period was over and training had resumed. No mention was made of the drunken revelry in Oran. Instead, Allen had praised them all for their work in Tunisia, highlighting the GIs – the rank and file – above any of the officers. 'Do your job,' he finished. 'We don't want heroes – dead heroes. We're not out for glory – we're here to do a dirty, stinking job.' It went down well. 'We love and respect Terry Allen even more after he talks frankly to us at Mangin,' noted Johnson.

Johnson was from New Jersey, the son of a professor of Military Science and Tactics at Hamilton College, New York. With poor eyesight, he'd known he would not get a regular army commission, but at Rutgers University had joined the ROTC – Reserve Officer Training Corps – graduating in May 1942 and heading off to join the army for the duration immediately after. He had shipped to England in September and been posted to Cannon Company of the 18th Infantry Regiment, arriving in Algeria in November, just behind the invasion. More training had followed, and then they'd been sent into Tunisia to help stem the flow at Kasserine in February 1943, when the US II Corps had suffered a severe setback at the hands of a briefly resurgent Feldmarschall Erwin Rommel and his Panzerarmee. Johnson and the rest of the 18th Infantry had been in the thick of it throughout the rest of the fighting.

The cannon company attached to each infantry regiment provided a mixture of fire support – a platoon of tracked 105mm howitzers on a Sherman tank chassis known as a Priest, 75mm guns mounted on half-tracks, and anti-tank guns. Johnson commanded an anti-tank platoon and was very relieved to be giving up the 37mm pea-shooters with which they'd fought through Tunisia and getting his hands instead on the new 57mm, a gun of greater velocity and far superior range that packed a considerably bigger punch – essentially a British 6-pounder in all but name. At last, Johnson and his men had realized, they would be able actually to disable a German tank. That was quite something.

They had been working hard that June, training for village infiltration, firing upon towed targets and conducting invasion exercises. At one such landing exercise, General Patton had turned up to watch. Many of the men in the Big Red One thought little of Patton; he was too spick and span, insisting on the wearing of ties at all times and on being clean-shaven. They also suspected he was a glory hunter – and that he wasn't known as 'Old Blood and Guts' for nothing. Patton's approach to the military – that it was his life's mission and that appearances counted for everything – stood in sharp contrast to that of General Terry Allen and his Executive Officer, Brigadier-General Teddy Roosevelt, son and name-sake of the former president, who were decidedly more laissez-faire over such matters. Allen's and Roosevelt's approach inevitably flowed down-wards to the men. It also put Allen on a collision course with Patton, who had originally planned to leave the 1st Infantry Division out of the HUSKY order of battle. But the Big Red One was now comfortably his most experienced division in a force startlingly lacking in that most precious commodity. He needed them.

Johnson and his men had heard the sirens screaming before they'd seen Patton's cavalcade arrive. Then suddenly there he was, stepping out and inspecting them as they were hastily brought to attention. Johnson couldn't help but be impressed by the general's appearance: shiny leather boots and spurs, pink breeches, silver buckled belt and shellacked and star-studded helmet. 'After the aide signals that the inspection is over,' noted Johnson, 'we return to our work as someone mumbles. "Yeah, your guts and our blood."'

The Tunisian campaign had ended on 13 May, when the German General Jürgen von Arnim had surrendered all German and Italian forces – two entire armies, amounting to more than 250,000 men – on the Cap Bon peninsula, the north-eastern tip of Tunisia. Later that day, the Allied ground forces commander, General Sir Harold Alexander, commander-in-chief of 18th Army Group, had signalled to the British prime minister. 'Sir, it is my duty to report that the Tunisian campaign is over,' he wrote. 'All enemy resistance has ceased. We are masters of the North African shores.'

That North Africa was now teeming with American, British and Commonwealth troops seemed, on one level, rather bizarre; after all, it was a long way from Berlin, or France, or any other part of Nazi-occupied Europe. They were there, though, owing to a long and convoluted chain of events, whose origins could be charted back to June 1940. On the 10th of that month, when the French were staring down the barrel of defeat at the hands of the Germans and most of the British Expeditionary Force had already been evacuated back to Britain from Dunkirk, Benito Mussolini, the Fascist dictator of Italy, had declared war on both countries. It had been a massive gamble as his armed forces were underdeveloped, for the most part poorly equipped by modern standards and severely undertrained. Even the Italian navy, which was its most up-to-date component, lacked any aircraft carriers or any form of radar. Mussolini had gambled on both France and Britain being knocked out of the war, thereby giving him essentially a free hand in dramatically expanding his sphere of dominance in the Mediterranean and Africa. Libya and Abyssinia were already Italian colonies; next on the list were Malta, Egypt and Sudan – and the crucial Suez Canal, which would link them all neatly together. Also in his sights were Greece and the eastern Mediterranean.

Few of his senior commanders shared his enthusiasm, however – especially when it became clear that Britain had no intention of throwing in the towel. In early July, the Royal Navy sank much of the Vichy and Axis-backing French fleet at Mers el-Kebir in Algeria – hardly the action of a country soon to sue for peace. Then, in July, the Royal Navy's Mediterranean Fleet had clashed with the Italian navy, the Regia Marina, at the Battle of Calabria and had given the Italians a brutal taste of superior British seamanship. Even the tiny Mediterranean outpost of Malta, an island lying just 60 miles south of Sicily, had resisted Italian bombing and had been hurriedly reinforced by the British. All this had not augured well for Mussolini's ambitions.

By September 1940, with the RAF still successfully fending off all subjugation attempts by the Luftwaffe over southern England, men like Maresciallo Rodolfo Graziani, commander of the Italian Tenth Army in Libya, had begun to see the writing on the wall all too clearly. Land grabs in North Africa and the Mediterranean were one thing if the British were out of the war, but quite another if they were still fighting. It was reluctantly, and only under extreme pressure from Mussolini, that he advanced his men into Egypt on 13 September 1940; and then, having gone a few short miles, he stopped.

Already, Mussolini's plans were starting to unravel. In Germany, he had a bullying dominant ally with a raft of victories already under its belt, while his own generals appeared to lack any fire at all; and all the while, the British, whom he had supposed to be dead and buried, were getting stronger, not weaker. Mussolini had wanted a parallel war where the Germans kept off his patch and where Italian victories would be ludicrously easy; one that would make him and Italy look militarily strong and the leading world player he believed it was Fascist Italy's destiny to be.

By the end of that year such dreams had been completely dashed. The invasion of Greece at the end of October 1940 had quickly turned into a catastrophe as the Greeks unexpectedly resisted invasion and then fought back, while in December the British launched Operation COMPASS with its tiny Western Desert Force of 36,000 men. By February 1941, two Italian armies had been smashed, some 133,000 men taken prisoner and the remainder pushed back almost to Tripoli. Meanwhile, the British had also attacked through Sudan into Abyssinia and Eritrea, and by May had hammered the Italians there as well.

At this time, Britain's priority was keeping open the Atlantic sea-lanes and defeating the U-boat threat. From one perspective, North Africa and the Mediterranean theatre held little strategic importance for Britain, given that the Mediterranean – and hence the Suez Canal – as a shipping channel and short cut to India and beyond was already closed because Axis forces controlled the northern shores. Nor was Middle East oil especially important to Britain, because the world's leading oil producers at this time were America and Venezuela, and they were the sources of almost all Britain's domestic oil; Middle East oil supplied British Middle East operations and nothing more.

Rather, Britain's strategy in the Middle East and Mediterranean was largely opportunistic. This was a part of the world where Britain could easily concentrate the assets of the Dominions and the rest of the Empire – whether manpower or supplies – from India, Ceylon, Australia, New Zealand and South Africa. It offered a chance to defeat Italy, make it a liability for Germany and expose the Reich's southern flank, from which future operations might then open up. It was also the perfect testing ground for a British Army that needed to grow and develop rapidly following the fall of its ally, France, and the losses suffered on the continent. Britain also hoped to create an eastern Mediterranean bloc with Turkey, Greece and Yugoslavia, from which British and Commonwealth troops could also push into Vichy French Syria and influence Franco's Spain.

It was precisely for reasons of southern flank vulnerability that Hitler felt compelled to come to the rescue of his Italian ally. Generalmajor Erwin Rommel, one of the stars of the 1940 campaign in the West, was sent to Libya with two divisions, followed soon after by a third, while German troops swept into Yugoslavia, then mainland Greece, and then took Crete as well. This forced the British to siphon off troops from North Africa to support a failed cause in Greece and Crete, but in the long term the battles in the Balkans cost the Germans more, even though they won the day and sent the British scuttling back to the Middle East. This was because they took place immediately before the largest clash of arms the world had ever witnessed: Operation BARBAROSSA, the German invasion of the Soviet Union in June 1941. Germany had needed the dissipation of resources caused by being sucked into the Mediterranean like a bolt in the head. The diversion of even a handful of panzer divisions and the loss of vital transport aircraft and highly trained and motivated troops was keenly felt as, by late 1941, the German advance into Russia began to run out of steam. The aim of BARBAROSSA had been to annihilate the Soviet Red Army in a matter of three months at most, then feed off the booty gained. Instead, by the end of 1941, Germany had been sucked into an attritional and brutal campaign on the Eastern Front that was draining off ever more men and materiel, while at the same time pursuing a campaign in the Mediterranean that it could ill afford. Few in Germany had forgotten that fighting on two fronts for much of the First World War had done for them in that last major conflict.

Since there was absolutely no realistic chance of Britain invading Nazi-occupied Europe any time soon, and because they were now embroiled in North Africa and the Middle East, the British were compelled to keep fighting there until the bitter end. From June 1941 until the beginning of November 1942, the fighting raged across Libya, back and forth depending on the respective fortunes of the warring parties elsewhere. As a rough rule of thumb, when the Luftwaffe was on Sicily and pounding Malta, Axis fortunes in North Africa improved. When the Luftwaffe was needed elsewhere, however, as in the second half of 1941, then the British moved into the ascendancy, because Malta-based submarines, warships and aircraft were able to hammer Axis shipping convoys across the Mediterranean largely unchecked. When the Luftwaffe returned to Sicily en masse in the first half of 1942, Malta briefly became the most bombed place in the world. There had been discussions then about an Axis invasion of Malta, but it was eventually accepted that Rommel should push ahead with an offensive in Libya. Since that meant the Luftwaffe would be needed for support, most of Fliegerkorps II was transferred from Sicily to North Africa. At this point, Malta had been on its knees; but the easing of pressure and the arrival of more Spitfires allowed the island to get back on its feet. In North Africa, meanwhile, Rommel struck the British lines in late May 1942 and won a famous victory, with the garrison of Tobruk surrendering on 21 June and the British Eighth Army fleeing back to the Alamein Line, a mere 60 miles to the west of Alexandria in Egypt. For a brief moment, it looked as though Rommel's Panzerarmee Afrika might actually conquer all Egypt and push on into the Middle East.

There were a number of reasons why he was unable to do so. On Malta, the RAF managed to win back air superiority in short order. Then, when the most heavily defended Allied convoy of the war inched into Malta in mid-August, it threw the starving island a lifeline and the chance to bounce back swiftly. By this time, Rommel's men had hit a brick wall at the Alamein Line and couldn't burst through to snatch the final furlong to Cairo, Alexandria and the Suez Canal. To make matters worse, Axis supply lines were hideously long – the only decent-sized port available was Tripoli, over 1,000 miles away – which meant that half the available fuel was used up transporting it to the front, while British supply lines had shrunk dramatically and very advantageously. At the end of August, Malta-based aircraft sank six vital Axis tankers headed for North Africa, the Battle of Alam Halfa was lost, and the Panzerarmee Afrika was now on the back foot, while a reinvigorated Eighth Army was able to build up enough strength to ensure it never lost in North Africa again.

As this Mediterranean see-saw rocked back and forth, the United States had formally entered the war on 7 December 1941 following the Japanese attack on Pearl Harbor. In fact, America had tied its colours to the Allied mast far earlier, with senior men sent to London back in 1940 to observe the Battle of Britain and on 27 March the following year agreeing, in principle, that should the United States become embroiled in the war at some future point, defeating Germany would be the priority. This was reaffirmed at the Atlantic Meeting between President Franklin D. Roosevelt and Prime Minister Winston Churchill in August that year and swiftly confirmed during the ARCADIA conference in Washington between the American and British chiefs of staff – the first formal Allied conference, following swiftly on the heels of Pearl Harbor.

America had also been involved in the war materially long before the Japanese attack. Following the defeat of France, Roosevelt, who had won presidential terms in 1932 and 1936 on an isolationist ticket, had decided not only that he would stand for a historic third term in November 1940, but also that the Atlantic was no longer the barrier it had once been. His conundrum was how to successfully rearm on a massive scale while public opinion remained strongly against any involvement in European matters. Somehow, he had to pull off not only one of the biggest ever political voltes-face, but also win a third term – something no previous president had ever attempted.

In the event, he did both – by a combination of guile and political cunning, superb public relations and, perhaps most importantly, his superlative geopolitical understanding and clear vision of what needed to be done. Drawing around him a number of highly skilled technocrats and big businessmen as 'advisors', he began the process of kick-starting rearmament, using the argument that the best way to keep American boys out of the war was to help America's friends to use their young men to keep the wolves from the door themselves. By rearming, they could not only achieve this but help pull their economy out of the continuing effects of the Great Depression at the same time. Even better, a decent chunk of the cash to fund this initial push to rearm was coming from British coffers.

It is sometimes hard to grasp just how much the United States armed forces had been allowed to languish in the twenties and thirties. By 1935, the army had fallen to just under 119,000 men and even by September 1939 it stood at merely 188,000, which made it the nineteenth largest in the world, sandwiched between those of Portugal and Uruguay. Most units were operating at half-strength, and much of its equipment was obsolescent. Even by May 1940, there were just 160 fighter planes and 52 heavy bombers in the entire US Army Air Corps; only the navy had been kept up to date and given much investment. Back in 1918, the States had been the leading supplier in the world of TNT; by 1940 there were barely any manufacturers of explosives left in the country. So by the time Roosevelt pressed the 'go' button on rearming, the army and what would become the US Army Air Forces effectively had to start again from scratch. As a result, on 16 May 1940, Roosevelt asked for a defence budget increase not to $24 million, as had been originally mooted, but rather to $1.2 billion. The aim was to produce 50,000 aircraft a year and to have an army of 4 million by 1 April 1942.

This was rearming on an exponential scale and involved harnessing much of the United States' already advanced consumer industry – and, not least, making the most of its extensive automobile industry, cheap labour and isolated position, which meant there would be no threat of air raids or need for night-time curfews. Once America began producing armaments, it would be able, in theory, to keep on producing them, twenty-four hours a day, seven days a week. Even so, as Roosevelt was warned, this huge transformation could not happen overnight; it would take some six months or so to create the new machine tools needed for this huge manufacturing programme, then another six months to train up the workers and get the show on the road, and a further six months before the production lines would start to churn out materiel in meaningful numbers. That was eighteen months, which conveniently took America to the end of 1941 – precisely the time when the States formally entered the war. It is often assumed that by Pearl Harbor the United States had seamlessly emerged, fully formed, as the 'arsenal of democracy'; in fact, it was a fraught and dramatic process, and even though few in the summer of 1940 would have doubted America's armaments manufacturing potential, there had been a big difference between what might be possible and what was actually achievable.

None the less, the miracle was happening. Ships, tanks, guns, bombers and fighter aircraft were all starting to roll off the production lines, while the rapidly growing US Army, the result of the country's first peacetime draft, was emerging from camps all around the country and being put through vital training exercises – not just for the men but for the entire modus operandi of the army – at a series of large-scale manoeuvres in Louisiana in the late summer of 1941. Meanwhile, the US Atlantic Fleet had begun to play its part, helping escort British convoys across the ocean from early September 1941, and with orders to destroy any Axis vessel found in American waters or threatening its personnel or cargo. As it happened, the first US–German clash of arms happened the other way around, when a U-boat in the Atlantic sank an American destroyer, the *Reuben James*, in October 1941.

Although this caused public outrage in the States, Roosevelt continued to hold off entering the war until the Japanese attack on Pearl Harbor, and even then it was Germany that declared war on America, not the other way around. Once in the fight, however, Roosevelt and his military chiefs had been quick to express their desire to get into battle as soon as possible. Britain, lying off the European continent, was the obvious place to build up American forces with a view to launching a cross-Channel invasion later that year, 1942. The British, mustard keen to get the Americans ensnared in the fight against Nazi Germany right away, readily agreed, even though they knew perfectly well there was not the slightest chance either they or the United States would be ready for such an undertaking so soon. The following year, 1943, seemed a more reasonable bet.

Matters came swiftly to a head in the early summer of 1942 when Vyacheslav Molotov, the Soviet foreign minister, visited first London and then Washington in an effort to secure greater materiel support from the western Allies and also secure a pledge from them to launch a new front against Germany. It was clear the Germans were planning a renewed offensive on the Eastern Front, and Molotov stressed the Soviet Union urgently needed the Allies to draw off German troops as soon as possible. In London, Churchill told him that opening a second front in Europe simply would not be possible that year.

With this bombshell, Molotov travelled on to Washington. In the meantime, Churchill had reported the substance of his conversations to Roosevelt and reminded him of a suggestion he'd made the previous October: a joint Anglo-US invasion of Vichy French north-west Africa. This, he argued, would kill two birds, if not three, with one stone. It would speed up the conquest of North Africa and clear the southern Mediterranean; it might well hustle Italy out of the war; and it would give British and US forces a chance to operate together in an enterprise where victory was likely. As such, it could be a very useful test run for the cross-Channel invasion of Nazi-occupied Europe to which they had both pledged their commitment. In Washington, meanwhile, Molotov repeated the requests he'd made to the British – and this time, Roosevelt and General George Marshall, the US chief of staff, both confirmed that, yes, they would start a second front against Germany that year, 1942.

By this time, US men and materiel had begun arriving in Britain – the first troops, from the 34th 'Red Bull' Division, had reached the UK on 24 January 1942. To begin with, their training and organization were somewhat lackadaisical, to say the least, and Major-General Dwight D. Eisenhower, a protégé of General Marshall, was packed off to England to see US build-up preparations for himself. Returning with a fairly damning report, he unwittingly wrote himself into a job and was sent back to Britain as Commanding General, European Theater of Operations, with Major-General Mark W. Clark, another up-and-coming star, as his deputy.

In the summer of 1942, Eisenhower was still only a two-star general, but he had already shown plenty of signs of his remarkable talents. His upbringing could scarcely have been more humble. Born in Texas, he had been raised from an early age in the tiny rail halt town of Abilene, Kansas, in America's Midwest. Both studious and athletic, he had worked hard, won a place at West Point, the US Army Military Academy, and slowly but surely risen up the ranks by dint of hard work, a meticulous eye for detail, a highly organized brain and no small amount of charm and graciousness. Unlike contemporaries such as Patton or Mark Clark, he had not made it to the Western Front in the last war and had, by 1942, yet to command troops in battle, but had instead shown early promise as a highly competent staff officer.

After a stint serving with General Douglas MacArthur in the Philippines, he had returned to Washington and caught the eye of General George Marshall, who in September 1939 had become the Chief of Staff, the United States' most senior serviceman. Eisenhower had won further good notices for his part in organizing the Louisiana Maneuvers in 1941, the largest exercises of their kind up to that point, so that once America was in the war, he was an obvious candidate for higher command.

Eisenhower and Clark had reached London still believing their brief was to mount Operation SLEDGEHAMMER. This was to be a cross-Channel invasion of France, to capture a key port, establish a bridgehead and then use it to break out with a bigger operation – ROUNDUP – in 1943. Yet it soon became clear to them that, despite promises to Molotov from Roosevelt and Marshall, the British had no intention of attempting such an undertaking. That there were still two entirely different strategic agendas as late as July 1942 underlined the gulf between the British and the Americans, who – though widely referred to as 'the Allies' – were at this point still only coalition partners rather than bound by a formal alliance. Both Britain's and America's war leaders had to feel their way into this new relationship. And, for all the Americans' gung-ho enthusiasm to strike swiftly at the heart of the Reich, there was no doubt the British had a point. There was a lack of shipping, they argued, and also a shortage of landing craft – new vessels were being built but there were not yet enough. What's more, no American troops had ever fought against a German panzer division, and many US infantrymen had not even seen a tank yet, let alone trained with one. Failure would have a disastrous knock-on effect for ROUNDUP the following year.

By mid-July, SLEDGEHAMMER had been scrapped; but the promise made to Molotov hung over the Americans, and so Churchill once again raised the prospect of a joint Anglo-US invasion of French north-west

Africa. On 24 July, with Roosevelt's approval, this was agreed in principle: it meant the Americans could keep their promise to the Soviets, the operation would not need as many landing craft or warships as a cross-Channel invasion, and it could, as Churchill had earlier suggested, give the new coalition partners a fairly safe opportunity to test the water of joint operations. An overall Allied commander would be needed for the entire operation, and General Alan Brooke, the British Chief of the Imperial General Staff, suggested it should be an American. The Brits also proposed that the landing operations in Algiers and French Morocco should be led by US troops, partly as an additional sop to the Americans and partly because Vichy French antipathy to Britain was still very strong after the sinking of the French fleet at Mers el-Kebir back in July 1940. This was all agreed, and so the new operation, codenamed TORCH, was now on. Eisenhower became the natural choice for overall commander, and was duly appointed with a promotion to lieutenant-general. Planning was carried out from Eisenhower's headquarters in London and with a joint Anglo-US planning team getting down to the nitty-gritty.

As a first foray into mounting such operations, TORCH certainly ticked the boxes outlined by Churchill when he first suggested it, and it was agreed it would take place on 8 November 1942, as a second punch following Eighth Army's main attack on the Panzerarmee Afrika at Alamein on 23 October. By this time, General Bernard Montgomery, who had taken over command of Eighth Army in early August, had built up overwhelming strength, although the battle still turned out to be a bloody and attritional affair. None the less, by 3 November it was all over, Rommel's forces fleeing back across the desert with the British in pursuit, and this time for good.

Superb planning, led by General Mark Clark, ensured that TORCH was a success. Clark himself had made a clandestine visit to North Africa for pre-invasion talks with the Vichy French, which had gone some way to ensuring the opposition to the landings was extremely light. Even so, it was no small feat to land three separate invasion forces, two from Britain and one directly from the United States, pretty much on time and pretty much where they were supposed to after just two months' planning. Having subdued the Vichy French, who sued for terms within four days of the invasion, the plan was to make straight for Tunisia: the British First Army, which included the US II Corps, would drive in from Algeria in the west, while Eighth Army, from the east, sped as quickly as possible across Libya to trap Rommel's forces in a pincer movement.

After the success of the TORCH landings and the victory at Alamein, however, the Allies had not found the going in North Africa quite as good as they'd hoped. Northern Tunisia was, in places, further north than Sicily, it was not the flat open desert of Libya, and by late November 1942 winter had arrived and bad weather began to slow down the advance of the British First Army.

The second spanner in the works was Hitler's decision to send massive reinforcements to Tunisia. As soon as the Führer heard about the Allied invasion, he ordered the total occupation of France – much of the south had remained unoccupied since the armistice back in June 1940 – and told the Oberkommando der Wehrmacht, the German general staff, that a bridgehead was to be created around Tunis. There were those who suggested to Hitler that this wasn't the best idea, but he was having none of it. He had always been obsessed with the Mediterranean, because of the threat from the Allies striking the soft underbelly of his southern flank, which was why he'd insisted on earlier interventions in North Africa, the Balkans, Greece and Crete.

Of all the places on the long North African coastline, Tunisia was the closest to Sicily – and Europe – and so the easiest for German troops to reinforce. Hitler hoped to avoid any Italian collapse, and saw the build-up of men and supplies there as the means of keeping the southern flank secure. It was to be held at all costs. The Luftwaffe was sent south once more, as too were panzer divisions, some even equipped with the new giant Panzer Mk VI, better known as the Tiger.

This build-up of troops had enabled the Axis forces to check the advance of the British and Americans racing to Tunis, while it had taken time for Eighth Army and the RAF to shift themselves 1,200 miles west. In January 1943, Churchill, Roosevelt and the Joint Chiefs of Staff had met at Casablanca for a strategy conference. By this time, Rommel had around 80,000 men in his Panzerarmee Afrika, while General Jürgen von Arnim's 5. Panzerarmee now amounted to some 65,000 – and growing – in northern Tunisia. Eisenhower actually offered to resign over this setback, but Marshall, Brooke and the chiefs of staff recognized that he was now carrying too much responsibility. Instead, he was made Supreme Allied Commander, which allowed him to concentrate on political and wider operational issues, and a new deputy and overall field commander was brought in under him. This was General Sir Harold Alexander.

On 21 January, Eighth Army took Tripoli, and while Montgomery waited for the rest of his forces to catch up, Rommel took the opportunity to sweep into southern Tunisia, where he attacked with his old dash and flair on St Valentine's Day 1943, his panzers smashing into the unprepared and still green US II Corps in what became the ten-day Battle of the Kasserine Pass. The US 1st Armored Division, with losses of some 1,400, was hardest hit, but overall the Allied casualties at Kasserine had been serious rather than disastrous, and the American defeat was not really the catastrophe that is so often depicted – more a short-term tactical gain for the Axis forces than a victory of much strategic value. It had shocked the Americans, none the less; but for troops new to battle, sometimes there is more to be learned from defeat than victory, and that was certainly the case in this instance.

In any case, the reverse at Kasserine was checked in fairly quick order, leaving Rommel's Panzerarmee in the south once again overextended and needing urgently to turn back to face Eighth Army's advance from Libya. In March, the Allies fought back. Eighth Army pushed the Panzerarmee Afrika back at Medenine in southern Tunisia, after which Rommel, now sick and exhausted, left Africa for good, handing over command of his forces, now increasingly made up from Italian units, to Generale Giovanni Messe. Eighth Army then attacked the strong defensive Mareth Line between the coast and the Matmata Hills, while the New Zealand Corps outflanked the position by making a 200-mile trek around the back of the mountains. By the beginning of April, Eighth Army had turned north; while they were briefly halted by the Italians at Wadi Akarit, II Corps and the rest of First Army advanced from the north and west against von Arnim's 5. Panzerarmee. The Allies were closing in, the Axis bridgehead becoming ever smaller. The final offensive, in the Medjerda valley west of Tunis, was possibly the best-executed battle the Allies had yet launched, smashing the last resistance and ensuring that by 13 May victory had, at last, been secured in North Africa.

While all this had been going on, the Allies were busy planning their next move: the invasion of Sicily and the first assault on Fortress Europe, an operation of mind-boggling complexity and one that presented what had first appeared to be insuperable challenges.

CHAPTER 2

A United Front

B Y LATE JUNE 1943 the Allies were almost ready, and in Algeria the US 9th Division was among the American units training for the forthcoming invasion. Since the end of the Tunisian campaign, they had been based in the middle of the rocky desert 30 miles south of Sidi bel Abbès, an ancient walled oasis town south of Oran. The 9th Division, like all those American ground units that had fought in Tunisia, had learned the hard way and learned fast; well aware by now there was no room for any kind of complacency, they had, since arriving back in Algeria, been training hard.

Within the division, the 39th Infantry Regiment had been adopting a number of British tricks of the trade, thanks to 24-year-old Lieutenant Charlie Scheffel, who had spent time attached to a British brigade in England and then more recently, during the Tunisian campaign, at the battle schools set up under British instructors in Algeria. Since victory in Tunisia back in May, Scheffel had been promoted from platoon commander to first lieutenant, and was now 1st Battalion S-3 staff officer – plans and operations. After imparting the benefits of his fast-growing experience to the whole of the battalion, Scheffel had been asked to do the same for the other two battalions in the division. In the 39th, as elsewhere, there was a hunger to learn and get better; after all, it didn't take a genius to realize that the better the soldier, the better the chances of survival. Combine that with dramatically increased amounts of supplies and there was every reason to think the US Seventh Army would soon be a formidable outfit. No one, though, could expect this to happen overnight. Apart from the fifty US Army Rangers who had taken part in the ill-fated Dieppe Raid the previous August, it was only since November that American troops had been in combat on the ground in the western theatre and, for the vast majority, only since the turn of the New Year that they'd been fighting the Germans and Italians. That wasn't very long, yet very soon the Americans would be providing an entire army to help re-enter Europe and capture Sicily. It was a big ask, to put it mildly, in this still early phase of their part in the war against Germany and Italy.

Raised in the small town of Enid in Oklahoma, Charlie Scheffel was the son of a German and a Swedish immigrant. His parents had reached America with little but had done well; after briefly serving in the US Army, his father had had first the insight to set up a filling station and then the entrepreneurial flair to start prospecting for oil. By the summer of 1929 he had a number of highly successful wells, plenty of money and a brand new Studebaker, in which the family drove to California for an unforgettable and wonderful holiday. Then, in October, everything had come tumbling down around them with the financial crash. First the oil business collapsed, and then Scheffel's father, always so strong and vital, contracted pneumonia; three months after the Wall Street Crash he was dead, aged just fifty. 'All of a sudden,' noted Scheffel, 'we were alone in a world that seemed increasingly uncertain. I was scared.'

The Great Depression that hit the United States after the crash brought untold hardship to millions. It is extraordinary to think how many of the young men like Charlie Scheffel, now fighting in the war, had grown up deprived of one, if not both, parents. Undoubtedly it made them tougher and, generally speaking, better able to cope with the challenges and adversity flung at them now America was at war. The Scheffel family, cruelly shorn of a husband and father as well as their livelihood, had somehow to pull themselves together and play with the cards they had been dealt – a prospect made even tougher by the dwarfism suffered by Scheffel's younger brother, Stanley, in an era when physical differences were a considerable handicap.

Charlie himself grew up physically strong and athletic and won a sports scholarship to Oklahoma A&M University, where he played tennis, basketball and, especially, baseball. He also joined the college ROTC, which provided him with a useful few extra dollars. In the summer he played semi-pro baseball for a dollar a day; and back home in Enid he had a girlfriend, Ruth, with whom he was smitten, so life had been looking up. In the fall of 1940, the draft was introduced and the college ROTC began recruiting for the advanced course; signing up for this meant he would not be conscripted before completing his college degree, and also that later he could join the army directly as a second lieutenant.

The Japanese attack on Pearl Harbor on 7 December 1941 changed everything. With the United States now irrevocably at war, Scheffel had returned to college expecting to be sent off to the army full time right away, but was given a reprieve to complete his degree the next May. With the future suddenly so uncertain, Scheffel asked Ruth to marry him; after their wedding at the end of March 1942, they spent their honeymoon in a dollar-a-night room above a garage. 'We had no time to go anywhere else,' Scheffel recalled. After graduating, he was offered a place in the Finance Corps, but spurned the chance of an easy war and instead joined the infantry. 'A surge of patriotism made me want to get to the SOBs who had attacked us,' he wrote. 'I was also young and needed to prove myself as a man.'

Sent to Britain as part of a replacement unit, he bade farewell to his mother, brother and new wife, and set sail across the Atlantic. He and the rest of his provisional company were initially attached to a British brigade, most of whom had already fought in France back in 1940. This was an early experiment to see whether British and American troops could operate and fight literally side-by-side, and although Scheffel soon realized there were a lot of cultural differences, he learned much from his new comrades. British officers, for example, had batmen – soldier-servants. This was not for the maintenance of some antiquated class division but rather because an officer needed a personal assistant, not least to dig a foxhole when first in the line. 'If you're an officer in command,' he was told, 'you're going to be so damn busy figuring out how to get out of the mess you're in, you'll never have time to dig your own slit.' Scheffel also learned it was far better to dig a foxhole for two men than for one, as he'd been taught back home. Two men could support each other, watch backs, one staying awake while the other slept. They could provide more warmth, and emotional as well as physical support.

He learned much more besides, and even went off to war on an all-British ship as part of Operation TORCH. Soon afterwards, though, the novelty of being with the more experienced British began to wear off. He and his fellow Americans, still part of a provisional company, seemed to be given all the worst tasks – endless night patrols and night duties – and Scheffel, for one, wanted to be back with his own kind. 'I think we got the shit details because we were rookies,' he noted, 'and the Brits didn't trust us much.' After a few days, he asked the brigadier if he and his men could rejoin the US Army – and the very same day, they were on their way: half, Scheffel among them, sent to join the 39th Infantry Regiment in the 9th Division, and the other half to join the Big Red One, the 1st Infantry Division.

While the Big Red One had fought alongside the British in northern Tunisia, the rest of the US II Corps had suffered its bloody nose at Kasserine Pass. The perceived humiliation of being so badly overrun by Rommel's Panzerarmee cut deep, but was none the less an important stepping stone in the development of the US Army. The British had suffered their fair share of setbacks too, having also begun the conflict with a tiny standing army. It was inevitable. Training was, of course, vital, but required battle experience to be truly valuable; route marches, map reading and rifle firing only took the raw recruit so far. The Americans were growing their army exponentially, mobilizing more men at greater speed than even the British, and for much of the time so far had had insufficient equipment with which to train and few instructors with any experience whatsoever. The lessons of modern combat had to be learned, absorbed and applied.

Scheffel had seen plenty of action in Tunisia, and like many Americans who survived the early fighting in that campaign, he had emerged a considerably better soldier – and officer. After Kasserine, a number of the American units had been rotated through the battle schools that had been set up in Algeria on the model of those originally established by the British following the evacuation from Dunkirk in 1940. These were the brainchild of General Sir Harold Alexander, who had the idea of training conscripts in simple battle drills to which they would react automatically in times of stress – orders, such as 'Down, crawl, observe, fire!' Alexander had also recognized that some kind of battle inoculation was needed before green troops were subjected to the terrors of dive-bombing, shelling, mortaring and machine-gunning. This could only be done using live ammunition. Finally, he also realized that it was essential that all troops were battle fit. For the time, such training was quite innovative, and battle school soon became a key part of a young conscript's training.

Despite his earlier time with the British, Scheffel was one of those packed off to battle school. He reckoned he had been pretty lucky to have made some mistakes and yet lived to tell the tale, so had paid keen attention to all he had been taught. While there, he spent an evening with a group of junior British officers in a mess tent drinking local wine and shooting the breeze. Most didn't think they had much chance of surviving. 'We sat there giving coarse opinions on the war,' recalled Scheffel. 'We gave everybody hell – Patton, Eisenhower, Churchill, Montgomery, Alexander – we didn't miss anybody except ourselves. We were the only good guys in the war, serving at the mercy of fools.'

They'd been grousing a while when the tent flap opened and in stepped a trim British officer whom all recognized immediately, the American included. Hastily they got to their feet and saluted. The visitor addressed Scheffel.

'You're an American?'

'Yes, sir,' Scheffel replied. 'Oklahoma.'

'I've been to Fort Sill,' he said, then motioned to the group – 'Sit down, gentlemen' – before joining them. He confessed he'd heard some of what they'd been saying, but swiftly allayed their fears. He, too, had been a young officer once. He understood their concerns, and reassured them a corner had been turned. Eventually, ready to leave, he stood. 'I want you to remember this,' he said. 'Gentlemen, the Boche are beginning to lose this war. If you think it's bad on our side, just be glad you're not on theirs.'

Their visitor had been none other than General Alexander himself, at the time newly arrived in Tunisia to take command of 18th Army Group.

Alexander – or 'Alex', as he was always known – was really a rather remarkable character, although not one ever to blow his own trumpet. In the world of high command, where ego and personal ambition often went hand-in-hand, Alex was notable for having very little of the former and almost none of the latter. Certainly, there were few people more prone to self-deprecation. Such unassuming modesty had been drummed into him during a childhood in which he had been brought up to respect notions of honour, duty and impeccable manners in all things and at all times.

His had been an aristocratic upbringing: a large estate in Northern Ireland, school at Harrow, then a commission in the Irish Guards. Charming, well connected and with no small amount of dash, he effortlessly excelled at all sports, was a highly talented artist and even took up motor racing at Brooklands. The four long years of the First World War developed him as a soldier. He quite openly enjoyed it, despite – or rather, because of – spending almost the entire war with fighting troops. At the First Battle of Ypres in November 1914 he was seriously wounded in the thigh and hand and invalided home. Recovering well and determined to get back to the front as soon as possible, he walked 64 miles in one day to prove to a cautious doctor that he was fit enough. Sure enough, by February 1915 he was back, and later that summer led his company at the Battle of Loos. His reputation had grown rapidly, notably for exceptional personal courage, but also for extraordinary imperturbability and the gift of quick decision. Always leading from the front and with no regard to his own personal safety, he soon had the complete devotion and respect of all those who served under him.

Though wounded twice more, Alex survived the carnage of the Somme, Cambrai and Passchendaele, and in 1917, aged just twenty-five, became acting lieutenant-colonel commanding the 2nd Battalion. By the Armistice, he had earned a DSO and bar, an MC and the French Légion d'Honneur, and had been mentioned in dispatches five times. Nor did his combat record stop with the end of war. In 1919 he was sent to command the Baltic Landwehr, part of the Latvian Army, in the war against Russia. Since most of the men in this force were of German origin, he was unique among the current Allied commanders in having led German troops in battle. Staff college and staff appointments were followed by stints of further action along the North-West Frontier between India and Afghanistan, where he was one of very few guardsmen to command a brigade. By the outbreak of war in 1939, this gilded officer was one of the army's youngest major-generals and commanding 1st Division. He went with them to France, and after the British retreat in May 1940 was left behind to supervise the final withdrawal of British troops. Alex, in fact, was the final British soldier to be evacuated – the last man out of Dunkirk.

Remaining in England for the next two years of war, Alex realized that the vast majority of infantry troops under his command were simply not ready for battle, and it was at this point that he instigated the battle schools. It was also during this time that he particularly came to Churchill's notice. The prime minister was certainly influenced by Alex's easy charm and illustrious background, but also by his calm control and a military record that was second to none. Even when sent to oversee the retreat from Burma in May 1942, Alex had impressed with his unflappable ability to make the best of a bad situation. And he looked the part, too: although by early 1943 a rather shabby military chic had developed with Eighth Army, Alex always looked immaculate. There was a bit of sartorial flair to his style. 'As calm and serene as a lecturer in a college,' noted the American war correspondent John Gunther. 'Everyone calls Montgomery "Monty" but Alex is General Alex.'

By early 1943, there was no British commander with a greater reputation, not even Montgomery. Now a full general, Alex was also unique in having commanded men in battle at every single officer rank. He never swore and never really lost his temper – not publicly, at any rate – and also somehow managed to speak German, French, Italian, Russian and even Urdu fluently. He had also developed a very sound sense of judgement and, perhaps even more importantly, an understanding of the men under his command, including the recognition that confidence and good morale were absolutely vital ingredients for success – especially with largely conscript armies. And this in turn meant that the approach to battle – the preparation and the removal of potential stumbling blocks – was the key to victory.

This stood him in good stead as Eighth Army began to claw their way back across North Africa in the summer and autumn of 1942. Although Alamein is seen as Montgomery's victory, Alex – appointed C-in-C Middle East at the beginning of August 1942, and so Monty's boss – deserves every bit as much credit for that crucial turning point in British fortunes. It had been Alex who had first made clear there would be no more retreats. It had also been Alex, arriving at Alamein in the middle of the battle with matters not going entirely according to plan, who subtly suggested a different approach to his army commander.

When Alex had been appointed commander of the newly formed 18th Army Group after the Casablanca Conference, his brief had been to finish the battle in Tunisia as quickly as possible. Reaching Tunisia immediately following the setback at Kasserine, he had hurtled up and down the front to see the situation with his own eyes, and spent the first week swiftly reorganizing his forces into greater concentrations, plugging gaps and then counter-attacking. Within ten days of his arrival at the front, the Kasserine defeat had been reversed, allowing Alex breathing space to lick his forces into shape and to develop a new plan to complete the Allied victory in North Africa. Raw and undertrained units were whisked off to the battle schools in Algeria, while Alex himself spent as much time as possible at his tactical headquarters camp near the front and visiting as many troops as he could – including Charlie Scheffel, on whom he had certainly made an impression. 'I had great respect for Alexander,' he noted. 'Maybe my meeting him had something to do with that opinion . . . but General Alexander inspired me and I know I was a better officer for having met him.'

In this still new situation of coalition warfare, a deft touch was needed to ensure the Anglo-US partnership worked on the battlefield. Alexander was ideally placed to provide this steer and soon won over his new American subordinate commanders, including Major-General Omar Bradley, who at the end of March 1943 was soon to take over command of US II Corps. Initially put out that his corps were not to be used in the final drive on Tunis, Bradley had braced himself for a confrontation, only to be swiftly disarmed. Alex had listened and assured him II Corps would be part of his plans. 'We were impressed with Alexander,' noted Bradley's aide, Captain Chester B. Hansen. 'He was a striking and possessed individual who simply exuded an air of confidence.' Later in the campaign, once II Corps had been sent to northern Tunisia and Bradley had taken over, Alexander had visited his headquarters. Bradley had shown him the current map and his dispositions and planned movements, of which Alex did not entirely approve. 'By a brilliant piece of diplomacy,' noted Harold Macmillan, then the British political advisor to General Eisenhower as Supreme Allied Commander in North Africa, 'he suggested to his subordinate commander some moves which he might well make. He did not issue an order. He sold the American general the idea, and made him think that he had thought of it all himself.' It was a command style particularly suited to coalition operations.

Alex was far too polite ever to have looked down upon his new peers and comrades in arms; and moreover, a sense of unity of purpose, of working together, side-by-side, hand-in-hand, was stressed over and over by the Joint Chiefs of Staff and was personally championed with religious zeal by Eisenhower. It was a firm policy that stood in stark contrast against the naked contempt with which Nazi Germany regarded its allies.

Certainly, it would have been a crime had the chiefs of staff allowed Eisenhower to resign back in January 1943. While not all had run smoothly on the battlefield, there was no doubt he had handled the extremely difficult political situation, with the Vichy French leadership coming in from the cold, as well as the myriad different personalities under his command, with admirable deftness and diplomacy.

Eisenhower – or Ike, as he was widely known – understood that given the cultural differences, and given that Britain had been fighting the war for far longer than the Americans and had a more entrenched military tradition, it would be all too easy for their new British colleagues to appear superior and to look down their noses at their new Johnny-come-lately comrades in arms. Equally, it was every bit as important the Americans did not develop unhealthy chips on their shoulders about

British snootiness or perceived standoffishness. National pride and competitiveness – tribal instinct – were one thing; Anglophobia and Americaphobia, quite another. 'I do not allow, ever,' Eisenhower made clear, 'an expression to be used in this Headquarters in my presence that even insinuates a British versus American problem exists. So far as I'm concerned, it doesn't.'

'In his current efforts to improve British and American relationships,' noted Eisenhower's good friend and naval aide, Harry C. Butcher, in March 1943, 'I see in Ike something akin to a fireman atop an observation tower watching a forest for smoke or flame. He has to put out some fires by logical argument that to win the war the Allies must stick together.'

Eisenhower warned all his US senior commanders that any American preaching anti-British sentiment would be sent home. Alexander was similarly impressed upon to do the same with British commanders, as were the other British top brass. Publicly, Alex certainly made sure the Americans got their due deserts following victory in North Africa. The 34th 'Red Bull' Division were a case in point. They had arrived in North Africa having never even seen a tank, let alone trained with one, and their first engagement at Fondouk in Tunisia in February had been a disaster. Sent to battle school, they had then returned and in April had captured from the Germans and held a vital high point, Hill 609, despite repeated enemy counter-attacks. In recognition of this, Alex had insisted the Red Bulls lead the subsequent victory parade in Tunis.

And while a host of varied factors had contributed to that huge Allied success, there was no question that Alex, as the overall Allied battlefield commander, had gripped the situation swiftly, acted with tact, charm and sound judgement, and played a key role in making sure the fighting in Tunisia was brought to a rapid and successful conclusion. Equally, it was Eisenhower who had led from the front in terms of forging the coalition. There were disagreements, naturally, but there were many new – and lasting – friendships being developed too, and these relationships were ensuring that the Allies were indeed working together towards one united goal: the eventual unconditional surrender of Nazi Germany, as had been agreed at the Casablanca Conference back in January; and with it, victory.

Sicily, however, would be very different from Tunisia, for both men. For Eisenhower, the challenges of preparing for Operation HUSKY were gargantuan, especially since planning had been taking place concurrently with the campaign in Tunisia. The responsibility, too, for overseeing the Allied re-entry into Axis-controlled Europe was on an entirely different level from the campaign in North Africa, carrying a hugely increased weight of importance. Alexander, for his part, also found himself in uncharted territory. Up to this point, he had repeatedly been brought in to salvage a situation that had gone badly awry. Now, for the first time, he was commanding a multinational force that was in the ascendancy, and at this stage in the war it was essential that Allied fortunes remained that way. Under him were two army-sized forces: the brand new and comparatively inexperienced US Force 343, which would become Seventh Army, and the battle-hardened and experienced British Eighth Army, still code-named Force 545, both with commanders whose experiences mirrored those of the men they commanded. Yet those two men – Patton and Montgomery – were also strong-willed and highly divisive characters and would need careful handling. In fact, the entire operation would need careful handling, to put it mildly, for the pressures now were even greater. Failure was not to be countenanced. It was simply unthinkable, and yet the risks remained huge. No one could say for sure how the enemy would react. Would the Italians fight as they had in Tunisia? Would the Germans throw more men and materiel into the island as Hitler had so dramatically reinforced Tunisia? No amphibious operation on this scale had ever before been attempted. There was, unquestionably, much that could still go wrong.

CHAPTER 3

The Problem of Planning

P LANNING FOR HUSKY WAS an extremely daunting challenge for the Allies, for a whole host of reasons. Winning in North Africa, where the Axis forces had had very difficult lines of communication, was one thing. Breaking into *Festung Europa* was quite another. Operation TORCH the previous November had been an astonishingly successful undertaking, but it had been an amphibious landing against poorly trained and equipped Vichy French troops – and in any case, political machinations beforehand had paved the way and ensured the 'enemy' forces opposing them came to heel in quick order and barely put up a fight.

Operation HUSKY, by contrast, was an altogether much bigger undertaking, and the Allies' first attempt at re-entering Europe since the withdrawal of 1940. The last time the Allies had undertaken a major European amphibious assault had been at Gallipoli in the First World War, and no one needed reminding how badly that had gone. Alexander, who had studied the campaign at staff college and had walked the ground back in 1922, was all too aware that only by very close cooperation between the Allies, and between their collective air, land and naval forces, could the risks of such a massive undertaking be kept to reasonable proportions. What's more, now that they had a great victory behind them, it was absolutely inconceivable that HUSKY should fail. Militating against failure trumped all other considerations. All.

The decision to invade Sicily had been made during the Casablanca Conference in January 1943. It had been back in December 1942, at a time when they had been expecting a swift end to the campaign in

Tunisia, that Roosevelt and Churchill had agreed to meet with their chiefs of staff to plan future strategy; but then bad weather and unexpected heavy reinforcements by the Germans had put paid to any such rapid outcome, so that long weeks – months even – of fighting were still to come before the Allies would finally win the North African battle for good.

None the less, the meeting had been planned and organized for January, the Allies still needed to thrash out the next moves, and there were fundamental differences of opinion between the American and British chiefs of staff as to what those moves should be. The British approach was largely opportunistic. They would continue to build up strength, see how matters turned out, and respond to what opportunities presented themselves. The Americans, by contrast, preferred to look at Berlin and draw the straightest possible line to the closest launch point, which was Britain. The invasion of north-west Africa had been reluctantly accepted by the American military because of Roosevelt's support for the plan, but now the US chiefs of staff, headed by General Marshall, had arrived in Casablanca wanting to pin down, first and foremost, how and when they were going to cross the English Channel and get into France. The British, for their part, better prepared for the conference and still, at this stage, the dominant partner when it came to land warfare, argued that by continuing operations in the Mediterranean they would be hastening Italy's exit from the war and possibly even prompting Turkey to join the war on the Allied side.

In the sunshine of Casablanca, the Joint Chiefs, with Roosevelt and Churchill as the great overseers, thrashed out a way forward. In the end, the Americans agreed on a joint assault on Sicily in part because a great Allied force had already been amassed in North Africa and in part because of the shipping issue. As the American chiefs accepted, shipping was the biggest obstacle to their favoured strategy of a cross-Channel invasion of Nazi-occupied France. The drain on supplies caused by the fighting in North Africa had been startling. Both Britain's and America's war effort had suddenly and massively increased, which meant shipping was in considerably greater demand. After all, it wasn't just the growing scale of operations in the Mediterranean, nor even the ongoing build-up in Britain, that had to be supported; there was also the war in the Pacific and in the Far East being prosecuted in parallel.

As things stood, the eastern Mediterranean remained closed, which meant shipping to the Far East was still heading all the way around

South Africa, a long route which in turn caused a further drain on this precious resource. Capturing Sicily would open up the Mediterranean, enabling Allied shipping to use the Suez Canal and so save considerable time and effort. In other words, the British argued, by invading and taking Sicily, the Allies would be moving closer to making the cross-Channel invasion possible. In any case, argued General Sir Alan Brooke, the British CIGS, it was doubtful Germany could be sufficiently weakened to allow a successful cross-Channel invasion that year. The Dieppe Raid of August 1942, in which half the attacking force had been lost, had been a disaster and a salutary lesson. Yet the Soviet Union still needed diversionary support. Reluctantly, the American chiefs accepted that a cross-Channel operation in 1943 was not practicable; yet the political and military pressure to continue ground operations that year following the end of the North African campaign, not least to relieve pressure on the Soviet Union, was immense. Taking Sicily would help in forcing the Germans to spread their weakening resources still further, especially if, as hoped, the Italians were knocked out of the war. General Marshall and the US chiefs conceded there should be ongoing operations in the Mediterranean – but only on the non-negotiable condition that the British back a cross-Channel invasion of Nazi-occupied France in 1944.

And so it was settled, on 23 January 1943, with a directive issued to Eisenhower. Although Sardinia had been discussed, Sicily was the only realistic target. It was a far greater political and military prize, but also considerably more manageable now that Malta had been transformed from the most bombed place on Earth into what was in effect a stationary aircraft carrier just 60 miles south of Sicily. Everybody accepted there could be no invasion without fighter cover, which ruled out southern Greece and, realistically, Sardinia too.

Agreeing that Sicily should be the next focus was, however, the easy part. Eisenhower had announced his three service chiefs on 11 February – Alexander as land commander, Air Chief Marshal Sir Arthur Tedder as air commander and Admiral Sir Andrew Browne Cunningham as naval commander. In terms of experience and seniority it made perfect sense for them to all be British – but just three days later had come Rommel's strike against the Americans at Sidi Bou Zid that opened the way for the defeat at Kasserine. Suddenly Alexander was being diverted to take charge of the crisis in Tunisia, and clearly this was his first priority, demanding that he devote much of his time, and his mental and physical energy, to touring the front and making the necessary dispositions.

None the less, by this stage Alexander had already concluded that the secret to the Allied way of war was to draw together more closely than ever before the three elements in which it was conducted: land, air and water. 'Army, Air Force and Navy must become a brotherhood,' he said. This mantra held especially true for HUSKY and was the starting point for planning for the invasion. From the outset, it was agreed that two invasion forces would be needed for HUSKY, one British and one American, and these, for the time being, were allotted code numbers. Force 545 was to be British, commanded by General Montgomery, and would sail for Sicily from Egypt. For planning purposes, Force 545 was based in Cairo, 1,400 miles away, even though Montgomery was still commanding Eighth Army in Tunisia. The American Force 343 was to be commanded by General Patton, known as a firebrand and an armour expert, and currently based in Algeria. Its headquarters was at Rabat in Morocco, over 1,000 miles from Tunis – but soon Patton, too, was pulled into the Tunisian battle to take command of II Corps after the sacking of the hopeless General Lloyd Fredendall. The air commanders also had their hands full with the Tunisian battle, leaving only the Allied navies with any kind of time to plan, although even they were caught up in anti-shipping operations against Axis convoys. Absentee landlordism was to be a major feature of the planning of HUSKY, but part of the reason for agreeing to Sicily was that most of the forces – including their commanders – were already in the Mediterranean theatre. Bringing in a new and untested team would rather defeat the point of the object. Even so, and to make matters more complicated, there was a planning team in London and also ostensibly another under Alexander in Bouzarea, near Algiers: Force 141, so named for security reasons but also after the main room used in the St George Hotel in which the team were housed.

There were at least certain prerequisites on which everyone was agreed. Air superiority was essential, so too was naval superiority, and so too was a sufficient speed with which ground forces could be landed and reinforced compared with the likely rate of Axis reinforcement. Naval superiority was more or less a given, since the Italian fleet had not been to sea since the middle of the previous year, but air superiority was not yet assured and there was a huge question mark over how effectively the Allies could build up their strength once ashore.

The geography of Sicily hardly helped. Messina was the ultimate goal, as the city closest to the toe of the Italian mainland and the access point through which enemy supplies would principally flow. It was also comfortably the largest port on the island, with a daily handling capacity of some 4,500 tons. However, it was in the north-eastern corner of the island, which was dominated by the mighty volcanic mass of Mount Etna. 'It was strongly defended,' noted Alexander, 'difficult of access and well out of range of air cover.' As an invasion point, it was a non-starter. Away to the west along the northern coast was the second largest port, Palermo, with a daily capacity of 2,500 tons; but near to Palermo was the Trapani–Castelvetrano complex of airfields. Along the central eastern coast, some 150 miles from Trapani, was Catania, the third largest port, and south of that, Augusta and Syracuse. Catania had an airfield, and a little further inland was the Gerbini airfield complex, while on the southern coast there were further airfields at Gela and Comiso. When planning began, there were nineteen airfields on Sicily – no small number – but by the end of June there were thirty.

Planners reckoned they needed to be unloading some 3,000 tons of supplies a day initially, rising rapidly to 6,000 as the invasion strength grew. Operation TORCH, although a major amphibious landing, wasn't a huge amount of help in terms of lesson learning because the Vichy French had had no air forces, the enemy strength had been known and the ports had been swiftly captured. For HUSKY, hastily developed landing craft could deliver a certain amount of supplies directly on to beaches, but this was considered a temporary measure at best. The swift capture of ports was recognized to be essential.

Yet in this respect the island was poorly served, despite its long history as a maritime base. Shipping had grown massively in recent decades and so had armies, yet Sicily, still centuries behind the times in many ways, had not caught up. Without Messina, it was estimated the east coast ports could manage around 3,400 tons a day, while western harbours – Palermo plus Trapani and a couple of other smaller ones – could collectively cope with around 4,700 tons. The tiny southern coast ports together could handle possibly as much as 1,400 tons each day. And that was assuming the ports had not been wrecked first and would be open for business almost immediately.

A horrible planning conundrum was very quickly rearing its ugly head. Key to success was air power, and yet a mass of enemy airfields were stretched along both sides of this awkward triangular and really quite large Mediterranean island. Fighter aircraft from Malta could cover the eastern side of Sicily, but not the west. From Cap Bon in Tunisia, Palermo was at the outer reach of effective fighter cover. The much-needed ports were in both the west and the east, which implied the need for landings at the geographical and logistical extremes in both directions. That was all very well, but risked the two invasion forces being effectively independent of one another and therefore not mutually supporting, and so being exposed to defeat in isolation. Since planning was taking place from February – and starting at the very moment of a reversal in fortunes in Tunisia – it was impossible to know what enemy strength they might face when they finally landed in Sicily. It was anyone's guess in February 1943, and even more so by the beginning of May when a plan was finally agreed. It made the entire operation the most terrible risk.

Historians have not been kind to the Allied planners for HUSKY. Everyone, it seems, has had it in the neck from those sitting in the comfort of their armchairs many decades after the events took place. Eisenhower has been accused of being too weak, Alexander for not gripping the process, everyone else for being at one another's throats, and Montgomery, especially, for being brash, arrogant and selfish. Really, it's been extraordinary how deep the criticism has run; yet because most of the key decision-makers already had their hands full fighting a bitter battle in Tunisia, it's hard to think of a more challenging set of circumstances in which to prepare such an enormous undertaking.

A different point of view on the planning of HUSKY is that it was always going to be a mind-bogglingly difficult operation to prepare, and that an evolving plan was entirely normal and understandable for such an enterprise in such challenging circumstances. Furthermore, what is remarkable about the HUSKY planning is not the levels of discord involved, but rather, how well the new coalition partners were operating and rubbing along together.

It is all too easy to be seduced by a choice one-liner in a diary taken in isolation. The journals and letters of these senior commanders need to be read and understood within the context in which they were written: by men with overwhelming amounts of responsibility and as a means of letting off steam as much as to set down a record for posterity. Most people, at some point in their lives, have argued vociferously for something they care about, whether with colleagues, friends or family. So it was with the Allied commanders, but for them the consequences of making the wrong decision were potentially catastrophic – including the loss of many young men's lives – so of course, at times, matters grew heated. It was to be expected. But this really does not mean the coalition was crumbling at the seams. Far from it; that the senior commanders could debate such matters so openly was both healthy and a demonstration of how much they cared about the mission they had been given.

In this new partnership, Eisenhower was the chief executive answerable to a board of Joint Chiefs, President Roosevelt and Prime Minister Winston Churchill. Alexander, Tedder and Cunningham were the CEOs of subsidiary arms. The difference was that their results would be judged not in terms of share price, but in success in battle and numbers of casualties.

Alexander wrote to General Brooke on 5 April from his tactical headquarters near the Tunisian Front. Despite having to give much of his attention to current operations, he had, he told the CIGS, been giving time to the study of HUSKY. 'I think we are on a good wicket,' he wrote, 'provided certain obvious conditions are fulfilled – such as air and naval superiority and not too many good German formations in the way. The latter we cannot prevent, but the former we can influence and I want to put it quite plainly. The margin between success and failure is small. If the Navy and the air forces, especially the latter, will go all out 100% in their backing the Army, we should pull off a great victory.' He was keen to use the airborne forces being assembled in helping to secure the beachheads. Alex was also aware of the shortfall in shipping caused by the continued and growing battle in Tunisia. 'LSTs are short – other shipping is short,' he acknowledged. 'But it must be found, even if people at home go short. Half measures or half-hearted measures will spell defeat for certain – <u>we must go all out 100% for a win.</u> RN, RAF and Army.'

What he meant was, HUSKY was not the operation on which to take any avoidable risks. Stalingrad, Tunisgrad – as it was now being called – the start of the all-out strategic air offensive against Germany by Bomber Command, and the battle against the U-boats in the Atlantic which was about to reach a peak in favour of the Allies: all pointed to a dramatic reversal of fortunes for the Axis. It was on its knees and there was, realistically, no way back now for Nazi Germany. What was uncertain was how much longer the war would continue and how many more lives would be lost in the process. For the Allies to attack Sicily and be thrown back into the sea would not mean losing the war but it would be a terrible setback. It would also unquestionably push back OVERLORD, the cross-Channel invasion that had been agreed for 1944. Far better to cover all bases, cut out as much risk as possible and make sure HUSKY was a success. Alexander's assessment was spot-on.

The date for HUSKY had been set for early July when the moon was favourable, and although both Churchill and Marshall repeatedly urged Eisenhower and Alexander to bring it forward a month if at all possible, as time marched on, and the Tunisian campaign continued, it became increasingly clear they would have to stick with the July date. This was because even once victory had been won in North Africa on 13 May, time was needed to properly train the assault battalions and also the airborne forces who were seen as a key component of the invasion. So Eisenhower stuck to his guns. The day of invasion, D-Day – *the* day – would be Saturday, 10 July.

The British chiefs of staff in London had already developed a speculative plan, which they passed on to Alexander's Force 141 in Bouzarea. With Alex off at the Tunisian front, it was left to Major-General Charles Gairdner, his new chief of staff, to oversee the multinational planning team and try to make some sense of the complex issues that faced them. One particularly ominous line in the London plan warned: 'We are doubtful of the chances of success against a garrison which includes German formations.' Alexander felt this was massively overstating the threat but made clear to Gairdner, in the brief moment he was able to give it his attention, that the first plan was a starting point only. None the less, at this early stage of the planning, it seemed a good idea to try and find a way to make landings in both the east and the west, possibly staggered, so as to both knock out key concentrations of airfields and also swiftly capture Palermo as well as Catania, Augusta and Syracuse, and so solve the issue of how to build up strength rapidly.

'The month of February and the early days of March were the most critical periods in Tunisia,' noted Alexander, 'and it was impossible for me to give the plans for Sicily any detailed attention.' That was more than understandable, albeit far from ideal; but even so, he was able to make some suggestions and modifications to the plan. His biggest concern with the early drafts was the distance between the divisions and brigades that were landing – they were clearly too far apart, not mutually supporting and in danger of being picked off in isolation. Nor were the burgeoning airborne forces of paratroopers and glider troops being concentrated enough. In fact, the early drafts lacked any kind of concentration of force, a military tenet to which Alexander was rightly wedded.

Alex even considered sending both task forces to the south-east of Sicily, but this plan hit a wall of opposition elsewhere because it was still felt the quick capture of Palermo was essential. At this time it was estimated –

or guessed – that there would be at least eight enemy divisions in Sicily. Alex had ten divisions earmarked for the invasion in total.

In between periods of commanding at the front, Alex and the other key commanders met for planning conferences whenever they could, although the constraints on their time and the distances they had to travel to be in the same place meant that Eisenhower, Alexander, Tedder and Cunningham were very rarely all together. It really was far from ideal. Geography dictated where the British and American landings would be focused. Because most of the British forces would be sailing from Egypt and the Middle East, they would be landing in the eastern part of Sicily. Similarly, because the Americans would be setting off from Tunisia, logic suggested they should be in the west. Furthermore, because the eastern parts of the island were closest to Messina, it seemed likely this side would be the more heavily defended. Moreover, the Gerbini airfield complex, close to Catania, clearly held the key to the defence of the island, and both the port and the surrounding airfields had to be the overriding number one initial target priority. On this, Eisenhower and Alexander were united. Montgomery demanded an extra division for his landings around Avola, just to the south of Syracuse, and one was eventually found. As Easter approached, it seemed that a plan of sorts was emerging upon which everyone was agreed.

Then, on 24 April, a brusque and damning signal arrived from Monty, in which he called the proposed HUSKY plan a 'dog's breakfast' that had no chance of success. 'Unless someone will face up to this problem,' he told General Brooke in London, 'there will be a first-class disaster.' Needless to say, this caused consternation elsewhere. Both Tedder and Cunningham were seething at Montgomery's proposed front-loading of the Eastern Task Force to focus on the Avola area because it meant moving the planned British force that had been due to land around Gela and Licata on the central southern coast. Their task had been to overrun the airfields at Comiso and especially Gela–Ponte Olivo, which had recently grown in size and sophistication. Tedder felt they posed far too great a risk to be left in enemy hands, and so too did Cunningham. 'I'm afraid Montgomery is a bit of a nuisance,' wrote Cunningham to Admiral Sir Dudley Pound, the First Sea Lord. 'He seems to think that all he has to do is to say what is to be done and everyone will dance to the tune of his piping. Alexander appears quite unable to keep him in order.'

The real gripe for Tedder and Cunningham, though, was less that Montgomery was unhappy with the plan as it existed, more the way in which he demanded changes. It was, after all, only right that individual commanders should air concerns if they had them. Perhaps Alexander could have given Montgomery a lesson in manners, but Monty had always been forthright and outspoken; and he had Brooke's unwavering support. In any case, he was the primary assault commander and it was essential he was carrying out a plan that had his backing. Montgomery had repeatedly proved himself a highly competent operational commander and was, by some margin, the most famous and lauded British general of the war to date. He instinctively understood what could and could not be achieved by largely conscript armies whose personnel would no longer be shot at dawn should they decide they didn't want to go into battle after all. His big failing was his total inability to show any kind of sensitivity to others. He cared not a jot about rubbing people up the wrong way, and seemed to have no awareness of his appalling rudeness.

Much has been made over the years of tensions between the British and the Americans, but the spats that did occur rarely ran on national lines; they were nearly always over matters of differing tactical approaches or doctrine, or basic clashes of personality that had nothing to do with nationality. Almost all the senior commanders loathed Montgomery; that didn't make him a bad commander, but it did complicate matters, especially when there was quite enough pressure and tension to deal with as it was. Even in a time of coalition warfare and diplomatic singing from the same hymn sheet, Monty steadfastly proved incapable of abiding by the rules.

His scathing critique of the current favoured plan was, on the face of it, all the more remarkable because he had earlier appeared reasonably happy. What had changed his view had been the fighting in Tunisia. After the Battle of Wadi Akarit at the beginning of April, Montgomery's Eighth Army had swept up the coastal plain confident of bursting through the next obvious defensive position around Enfidaville, which was held by what had once been Rommel's Panzerarmee Afrika but was now a mostly Italian force commanded by the Italian Generale Messe. Instead of a swift victory, Eighth Army had hit a brick wall. Takrouna, a particularly well-defended strongpoint, proved an especially stubborn and hard-fought battle. It made Montgomery realize, with stark clarity, that on the home soil of Sicily the Italians might well not prove the pushover being predicted. 'Planning so far', Monty wrote to Alex, 'has been based on the assumption that the opposition will be slight and that Sicily will be captured relatively easily. Never was there a greater error. The

Germans and also the Italians are fighting desperately now in Tunisia and will do so in Sicily.' Montgomery might have been overstating matters, but HUSKY was not the time to throw caution to the wind and gamble. It went back to the most vital of all considerations: HUSKY could not be allowed to fail.

Expressions of caution over the likely strength of enemy defence had prompted caustic signals from Churchill, who seemed to be forgetting Gallipoli back in 1915, when the Allies had landed against what had been assumed to be comparatively weak Turkish troops. In any case, Monty's bombshell chimed with nagging doubts as to the current plan shared by both Eisenhower and Alexander. By the end of April, however, it was clear the Tunisian campaign was nearly over and so there was now time to give HUSKY more detailed consideration. The picture was beginning to clarify. 'It must be remembered when considering the frame of mind in which we set out on this expedition,' noted Alex, 'that this was the first large-scale amphibious operation in the war against a defended coastline and opponents equipped with modern weapons ... No care was too great to ensure our first landing in Europe should be successful beyond doubt.'

While Alexander and Eisenhower now accepted Montgomery's demand for greater strength around Avola, that did not mean they had completely accepted his plans; after all, there was the question of what to do about the airfield complexes at Gela–Ponte Olivo and Comiso. Failing to neutralize thirteen enemy airfields that could threaten shipping and landings was every bit as unacceptable as attacking under strength at Avola.

Montgomery's planning team went back to the drawing board and on 1 May he flew in person to Algiers, where he met with Major-General Walter Bedell Smith, Eisenhower's chief of staff, and suggested abandoning the western assault altogether and instead directing Patton's Western Task Force to the southern coast at Gela and Licata. Bedell Smith was sold on this idea but initially Eisenhower refused to discuss it further without Alexander being present. Bad weather prevented Alex from reaching Algiers the following day, although a conference was held then after all. By the time Alexander finally reached Allied Forces HQ on 3 May, Ike had come round to Montgomery's proposals.

By now Alexander had needed little persuading. He'd already proposed such a plan early on, and only the accepted need for Palermo's port had persuaded him otherwise. Both Tedder and Cunningham seemed content, although Tedder decidedly grudgingly so; he had long since grown weary of Montgomery – and could hardly be blamed for that. Only two concerns troubled both Ike and Alex. One was unloading directly on to the very extensive beaches around Gela; but this, it seemed, was being solved in part by the arrival of DUKWs. Pronounced 'ducks', these were ingenious amphibious vehicles developed by the Americans that could swim from larger vessels and then drive straight on to the beach. Large orders had been placed on 22 March with an understanding they would be available for HUSKY.

The second concern was the perception that the Western Task Force, or more simply US Seventh Army as it was about to be renamed, should somehow be playing second fiddle. Its commander, General Patton, was as forthright as Montgomery and not known to mince his words or hide his displeasure if slighted. But when this new and final plan was presented to him, Patton was as good as gold. 'It is an impressive example of the spirit of complete loyalty and inter-Allied co-operation', wrote Alexander, 'which inspired all operations with which I was associated in the Mediterranean theatre.'

CHAPTER 4

Hitler's Gamble

G ERMAN COMMANDERS IN THIS war were not widely known for their eccentricities, but the senior army officer on Sicily that May certainly stood apart from his peers. Partial to wearing a tartan kilt and a claymore sword slung by his side, Oberst Ernst-Günther Baade had been something of a legendary figure in Rommel's Afrika Korps, known for his fearlessness, immense charm, wonderful sense of humour and penchant for tapping into British telephone conversations and having a chat in his flawless English with whoever was on the other end of the line. Another favourite trick was calling in to misdirect artillery fire.

Born to wealth in Brandenburg in 1897, Baade had grown up an avid horseman, roaming widely on his family estates. Clever, and intellectually curious, he was immensely well read and spoke not only excellent English but fluent French as well. With a thirst for adventure, he enlisted in the cavalry the moment Germany went to war in 1914, even though he was still just seventeen. Somehow, he survived four years on the Western Front before being gassed very near the end in August 1918, albeit not too severely. He had been making a good recovery by the time the Armistice was signed that November.

It had been Baade's intention to remain in the army, but with the great cuts in size after the war there was no place for him and so instead, still aged only twenty-two, he had settled on one of the family estates in Holstein in northern Germany, where he became a notable horse-breeder. His ambitions for an army life had not been blunted, however, and just a few years later, in 1924, he was accepted back – into the 14. Cavalry

Regiment. Between army duties, he and his wife continued to breed horses and became quite celebrated as international show-jumpers.

Remaining in the cavalry, he served in Poland, then France, and when the Wehrmacht's last cavalry division was disbanded in 1941, he took over command of the 4. Maschinengewehr Bataillon on the Eastern Front. In April 1942, he was sent to North Africa and soon after took command of the 115. Gewehr Regiment, just in time to join Rommel's offensive against the British at Gazala at the end of May and personally leading the assault that ended Free French resistance at Bir Hakeim – wielding his claymore as he did so. On one occasion, Baade found himself caught in a British minefield, but persuaded a captured English sapper to lead him through the gap. Once safe, Baade shook the man's hand, wished him luck and let him go. In the desert he won a Knight's Cross and a reputation as a superb commander who led from the front; in that, he was cut from the same cloth as Rommel. His men were devoted to him and although higher up the chain his eccentricities – not to say wackiness – and his insistence on old-fashioned military chivalry ruffled feathers, his performances and the esteem in which he was held by Rommel and others ensured he was safe enough. Perhaps unsurprisingly, Baade was no great fan of Hitler and the Nazis.

Severely wounded at the Battle of Alamein, he returned to duty in December 1942, but was not deemed fit for combat and so was posted to a staff position at the Italian Comando Supremo, the Italian high command, and then, in April, to Sicily to try to salvage and organize some German units from those returning from Tunisia or those who had been sent south as replacements but had been held back as defeat in North Africa loomed. Division Kommando Baade was the starting point, although by the time of the Axis surrender in North Africa on 13 May, he had formed just one four-battalion panzer-grenadier regiment. Had the Allies been able to hustle their way across the Mediterranean and land right away, the door would have been wide open. Instead, Baade was able to continue building up German forces on the island; by 14 May he had about 30,000 troops, now redesignated Division Kommando Sizilien, and more were heading his way.

Among those moving south were a number of supply and support troops and also flak units, including several batteries drawn from Flak Regiment 7, with a mixture of 88mm anti-aircraft and four-barrelled quick-firing Flakvierling 38s, 20mm cannons. These flak units were veterans of the Eastern Front and had already seen considerable action during the war. One of them included 22-year-old Kanonier Hanns Cibulka from Jägerndorf in Upper Silesia – when he was born, part of the new Czechoslovakia, but now within the German Reich once more.

Cibulka was something of an intellectual and a poet, but in the German army he was a wire man, responsible, within a small team of three, for ensuring the batteries were all connected to battalion headquarters with field telephone wires. Travelling with their wiring equipment in a truck rather than on foot or by horse-drawn cart, the column wound slowly down through Italy. On 14 May they had been south of Rome, but it wasn't until two days later that they finally reached the Straits of Messina. It was 3 a.m., still dark, and both sides and the water in between seemed to be still, quiet and devoid of life. A ferry was waiting ready; first to load were the headquarters company, including the wire team and their truck. An hour later they pushed off.

The sea was dead calm, but a cold breeze blew gently over them, dawn breaking in the east. As they pushed further out, the water began to swell, splashing on to the wooden deck. Then the sun rose, glistening, dispersing the fog – and suddenly there was Sicily, at first a narrow blue strip and then, as they drew closer and the morning mist cleared, so Messina seemed to rise up and, behind the city, the grey hills. 'In the coastal waters, colourful sails,' wrote Cibulka in his diary, 'at the pier a few men are sitting and fishing, on the beach promenade trees stand in joyful green. The air that blows over from the land is warmed by the sun, but on the tongue, I don't know where from, a salty, bitter taste.'

An air raid siren rang out and moments later, they saw them: four-engine bombers, thundering over ponderously in close formation, their shapes clear against the steel-blue sky. Cibulka and his comrades stood on the pier watching, waiting apprehensively for the bombs to start falling, but the Flying Fortresses moved on in the direction of the mainland. The anti-aircraft gunners along the heavily defended straits opened fire, the sky suddenly full of clouds of bursting shells. The noise was immense – the guns, the explosions, the roar of engines. Suddenly there was a bright flash, an explosion. Cibulka and his friend Arno stood by the truck, their heads craned skywards, watching as a wing plunged down into the sea in a slow, sloping arc. 'So this is what death by air looks like,' he thought to himself. 'What is left of the ten-man crew is a single parachute that descends slowly and pendulously over the waterway.' And then, in what seemed like no time at all, the Straits of Messina were empty again. So, this was Sicily. Cibulka remembered a line from

Goethe's *Italian Journey.* 'Italy without Sicily makes no picture in the soul: here is the key to everything.'

Cibulka and his comrades had no idea where they were headed, although news from North Africa had reached them by now. German plans at this moment were still very uncertain, the German high command disconcerted, to say the very least, by the disaster that had just occurred in Tunisia, following hot on the heels of the catastrophe at Stalingrad. Urgent plans needed to be made to try to repel the next enemy onslaught – wherever that might be – while also working out what to do about Italy, an ally that was clearly on the ropes.

A striking feature of Nazi Germany was the truly appalling way in which it treated its allies, with the possible exception of the Japanese, whom they largely ignored apart from a bit of intelligence sharing. All Germany's other allies, whether Romania, Hungary, the Balkan states, Bulgaria or even Finland, were browbeaten and bullied and treated with little more than contempt. Only the Axis alliance with Italy, first signed in 1936 and then militarized with the Pact of Steel in May 1939, had begun on reasonable terms, not least because initially Hitler had been rather inspired by the Italian dictator Mussolini, and the two had struck up something akin to a real friendship.

That, however, soon turned sour when Germany began planning for the invasion of Poland without any prior consultation with Italy whatsoever. The cynical Molotov–Ribbentrop Pact with the Soviet Union of August 1939, also made without Italy's knowledge, which paved the way for the outbreak of war that September, chilled the mood further. Indeed, although Germany was prepared to help Italy materially, it was on the basis of a clear quid pro quo. Germany would fight to expand its borders and pursue its own aggressive foreign policy without the need for Italian military assistance. Italy, for its part, would expand its own empire and sphere of influence in the Mediterranean without the involvement of German troops. This suited Hitler because he had always been paranoid about fighting on multiple fronts – that Germany had done so in the previous war had been one of the major factors in its defeat in 1918. The last thing Hitler wanted to be worrying about was his southern flank – the soft underbelly of Europe. Italy's role in Hitler's master plan was to ensure the south was kept safe and secure from enemy influence.

But that simple plan had gone terribly awry from the moment the Italians first tried to assert themselves over the British in the Mediterranean.

The brief glimpses of triumph – especially after the fall of Tobruk in June 1942 – had proved an illusion; yet such had been Hitler's obsession with his southern front that he'd poured not just men but huge amounts of materiel into Tunisia, so that what had begun with a couple of divisions in February 1941 had ended up swelling to two German–Italian armies. By the time the Axis forces surrendered on 13 May 1943, some 250,000 men were in captivity in North Africa. In the final battles, more than 300 tanks had been lost, while the three battle-hardened divisions of Rommel's old Afrika Korps, the 21. and 15. Panzer Divisions and 90. Light Division, had been wiped out: every man killed, wounded or put in the bag, along with all their equipment and invaluable combat experience. For the Luftwaffe, the picture was every bit as grim: from November 1942 until the end of the campaign, a staggering 2,422 German aircraft alone – not including those of the Italian air force, the Regia Aeronautica – had been lost in the Mediterranean theatre. These were crippling numbers.

For the OKW – the men trying to plan and shape Germany's war while also acting as Hitler's mouthpiece – the loss of Tunisia had far-reaching and decidedly grave consequences. No longer was the war in the south restricted to the arm's-reach safety of the North African coast-line; it now encompassed the entire sweep of the Mediterranean.

Deputy Chief of the OKW Operations Staff was Generalleutnant Walter Warlimont, a 48-year-old career soldier and former artilleryman who had served on the operational planning staff since before the war. This had given him almost daily access to Hitler and the largely unenviable task of trying to put the Führer's wishes into some kind of action. It also meant that right now, with North Africa lost, some serious plans needed to be made and in quick order. Warlimont's staff soon produced figures to suggest that by reopening the Mediterranean and the Suez Canal the Allies had freed up around 2 million tons of shipping for the movement of troops and supplies, which was certainly not good news.

Worse, though, was the realization that the Allies now had vast armed forces in the Mediterranean and were almost certain to send them across the sea for an assault on a major Axis stronghold in the southern theatre. It was Warlimont's job to try to work out where that might be and to prepare for such an eventuality. And it was also the task of his team to consider what the Germans might do about their Italian ally, an appreciation they set to work on immediately. The 'Survey of the Situation Should Italy Withdraw from the War' was prepared on Hitler's direct instructions and was an extraordinary admission of just how low relations between the two allies had sunk.

Hitler's view was that the most likely target for further Allied action in the southern theatre was the Balkans. His lack of geopolitical understanding repeatedly hindered German strategy; he was utterly incapable of looking at any situation except through the prism of his own worldview. The Balkans were the part of the southern flank he feared losing most; so that was where the Allies would strike. Whenever he tried to put himself into the Allies' shoes, he merely transposed his own thoughts on to their situation. The reason for this obsession with the Balkans was because this route into Europe led directly to the Romanian oilfields, some of Nazi Germany's most prized assets, as well as to critical supplies of bauxite, copper and chrome that came from the area. With much of the Balkans, from Greece to Yugoslavia, now in revolt against their German occupiers, the region seemed ripe for the Allied plucking – along with the fact that long stretches of its coastlines were poorly and thinly defended by Italian troops who had not been given any updated equipment since 1941. That there might not be anything like enough beaches or ports, or half-decent internal infrastructure, or that it was way beyond Allied fighter cover – an absolute non-negotiable prerequisite for any major amphibious landing – does not appear to have swayed him from his conviction that the Balkans were now the Allies' major goal. The Balkans, he announced on 19 May, were 'almost more dangerous than the problem of Italy, which, if the worst comes to the worst, we can always seal off somewhere.'

Warlimont, though, was aware, as were others, that the Allies would need a stepping stone in crossing the Mediterranean, and that Sicily, Sardinia or even Corsica were the most likely targets. Clearly, it was essential to keep the Allies as far away from the southern Reich as possible, and this meant sending reinforcements into Italy and also the Balkans. These would have to come from the Eastern Front but could also be drawn from France, since it now seemed unlikely the Allies would attempt a Channel crossing any time soon.

Hitler broadly accepted Warlimont's appreciation, although he seems to have become convinced that the first stepping stone would be Sardinia, not Sicily. This was in large part due to Operation MINCEMEAT, a rather ghoulish intelligence wheeze by the British Secret Intelligence Service and their XX 'Double Cross' Committee, who had had the idea to take the corpse of a Welsh down-and-out who had killed himself with rat poison, dress him up as an officer and dump him from a submarine just off the southern Spanish coast. No longer would the dead man be Glyndwr Michael; he was now (Acting) Major William Martin of the Royal Marines. No small detail was overlooked: about his person were letters between 'Martin' and his fictitious girlfriend, receipts, and various other seemingly innocuous details that lent verisimilitude to the whole elaborate scam. Most importantly, though, he was carrying documents relating to Allied plans to make landings in southern Greece at Cape Araxos and Kalamata. There was also a reference to 'sardines', which was supposed to be perceived as a possible coded clue to an operation against Sardinia. The body was prepared to look as though the man had died in a plane crash, and was dropped close enough to the Spanish coast to ensure that it would be washed up on the beach and picked up by the Spanish authorities, who would pass all the information on to the Germans. 'Major Martin' was put into the sea in the early hours of 30 April and everything went exactly according to plan, so that by 14 May British cryptanalysts had decoded German ciphers warning that an Allied invasion was expected in the Balkans.

MINCEMEAT was certainly ingenious, but one of the reasons it worked was because it reinforced a conclusion upon which Hitler had already decided. What's more, it wasn't the only piece of intelligence chicanery employed by the British. The Axis were also led to believe a Twelfth Army had been established in the Middle East, ready to invade Greece, even though in reality it was every bit as fictitious as Major Martin and simply a cover name for Eighth Army. In Greece itself, Operation ANIMALS was carried out by a British Special Operations Executive (SOE) mission led by Brigadier Eddie Myers, a quiet and methodical engineer turned sabotage maestro. In just over three weeks between 29 May and 23 June, Myers and his team carried out some forty-four acts of sabotage in Greece, cutting telephone wires, blocking roads, blowing railway lines, destroying the Asopos viaduct and blocking the Métsovo pass, all of which was supposed to make the Axis believe the Allies would be landing in Greece, and possibly Sardinia, but certainly not Sicily.

Clever as all these elaborate deception plans were, however, they couldn't obscure the fact that Sicily was just such an obvious choice, despite Hitler's view to the contrary. It was the only target that afforded realistic fighter cover, and it was very obviously the target that promised the most bang for the Allied buck. Certainly, Feldmarschall Kesselring remained convinced Sicily would be the Allies' target – and so too did

Mussolini, for what it was worth. At any rate, neither MINCEMEAT nor any of the other deception plans were responsible for changing the entire course of the Second World War, as has often been claimed by film-makers' and publishers' hyperbole. What does seem clear is that Hitler had already decided on the Balkans and possibly Sardinia as the targets, intelligence scams or no, while those who were convinced, rightly, it was going to be Sicily were not dissuaded by any washed-up corpse or blown-up viaduct.

Far more corrosive for Axis fortunes in the Mediterranean was the growing toxicity of the alliance, for wherever the Allies struck it was absolutely clear by now that neither the Germans nor the Italians trusted the other one inch. Germany was actively planning for life without its Italian ally, while most senior Italian commanders were wondering how they could extricate themselves from the war with the minimum amount of German retribution, which, for obvious reasons, was feared might be terrible indeed.

With the loss of North Africa, Hitler accepted the writing was on the wall for Italy but – perhaps because of a lingering affection for Mussolini – he did not want to accept that Il Duce might now stab him in the back and take Italy out of the war. Instead, the Führer had become convinced that Mussolini was in poor health and now, at sixty, too old to hold on to the reins of power with his former iron grip. After all, Il Duce was not the absolute leader that Hitler was; Italy was still a monarchy, and because of that there were checks on his power.

'Do you think', Hitler asked Grand Admiral Karl Dönitz on 14 May after the latter's return from a seven-day visit to Rome, 'that the Duce is determined to go all the way with Germany right to the end?' Without Mussolini, Hitler knew, Germany's partnership with Italy would be over; it had always been the two leaders' personal relationship that had glued their nations together. Despite the catalogue of catastrophic errors Mussolini had made, Hitler had remained curiously loyal to his old Fas-cist friend. He had even offered to send five German divisions to Italy, but in early May Mussolini had declined the offer; perhaps he had thought it would make too much of a dent in his prestige, or that it was too dangerous to have too many German troops in Italy should the tide turn against him at home.

At any rate, less than a week later, on 20 May 1943 at the Wolfschanze, Hitler's field headquarters in East Prussia, a conference was held to dis-cuss the deteriorating situation with Italy. Those present included

Feldmarschall Wilhelm Keitel, chief of the OKW and Hitler's number one lackey, as well as Warlimont and also Rommel, who had recently been appointed commander of Army Group B, formed to defend northern Italy should the worst come to the worst. Also attending was Sonderführer Konstantin Freiherr von Neurath of the SS, the Reichsprotektor of Bohemia and Moravia, who had just returned from a diplomatic mission to Rome. While there, von Neurath had had a number of conversations with Generale Mario Roatta, who had been commander of the Italian Second Army in Yugoslavia before taking over on Sicily. He had recently returned to Rome as he was due to take over from Generale Vittorio Ambrosio as chief of staff of the Italian armed forces.

It was Sicily that had been of particular interest to von Neurath, and Roatta had told him he had little faith in the Italians' ability to hold the island, should it ever be attacked. Already the Allied air forces were shooting up railways and other lines of communication. There was, he reported, just one ferry operating across the Straits of Messina. The others were being saved for 'more important purposes'. What were these? Hitler asked.

'Well, my Führer,' von Neurath replied, 'at one moment the Italians say, "When the war is over" – that's a very frequent expression – at another moment they say, "You never know what's going to happen."' German troops von Neurath spoke to told him the ferries over the straits were there and in working order but that the Italians were holding them back. German troops already in Sicily were deeply unpopular. 'Once the English arrive, that's the end of the war,' von Neurath continued. 'That's the general opinion in Southern Italy – that once the English come the thing will be over quicker than if the Germans are still there making life unpleasant.'

As the discussion continued, Hitler and the rest of those attending increasingly began to work themselves into a lather about Italian treachery. The Allies were flattening Palermo but not Cagliari in Sardinia, another sign they were intending to land on the latter and use its port facilities. Generale Roatta was known to have a number of pro-English staff officers under him; some were even married to English wives! 'Personally, in so far as I know him,' added von Neurath about Roatta, 'I wouldn't trust him further than I could kick him.' He had always been rather a fox. Hitler agreed; Roatta was a spy! A completely spineless spy! That Roatta had come to be known as the 'Black Beast of Yugoslavia' for the brutality with which he dealt with Communists and partisans, a ruthless approach earlier much admired by the Germans, was forgotten. That was then; now the filthy weasel was clearly up to something and planning to stab them in the back. The Italian leadership, too, was feckless, spoiled and corrupt – they were always bleating to the Germans they never had enough supplies, and yet continued to party hard in Rome like overindulged playboys.

'I am quite clear in my mind,' Hitler then announced. 'A certain section in that country has consistently sabotaged this war from the beginning. From the beginning!' Back in 1939, if Italy had declared war on Poland at the same time as Germany had, then France and Britain would never have entered the conflict. 'Every memorandum I sent to the Duce', he continued, 'was immediately transmitted to England.' Treachery was clearly lurking at every turn. They now wondered whether they shouldn't get the Hermann Göring Panzer Division out of southern Italy. Rommel suggested perhaps they should demand the Italians send more troops to Sicily instead. The last thing anyone wanted was for their own troops to be isolated, surrounded and betrayed. Rommel had so little faith in the Italians he even questioned whether they should be sending any German troops into Italy at all.

'The great question for me is what's the Duce's state of health?' Hitler said, returning to a now familiar theme. 'That's the decisive factor with a man who has to take such important decisions. What does he reckon the odds are, if for instance, the Fascist revolution goes under?'

The truth was, Mussolini would not have been able to give Hitler an answer to his question even if he had been standing before him. Mussolini had got himself into power back in 1922 as the world's first fascist dictator through energy, drive and force of character. To a war-weary, poverty-stricken nation where democracy seemed to do little for the ordinary citizen, Mussolini had offered something brash and bold and exciting. He had restored some much-needed pride and yes, the trains had improved – as had employment, and as had Italy's wider reach, with Libya, and then Abyssinia, drawn into a burgeoning empire. Many Italians, especially the young, had loved the marches, the militarism, the snappy uniforms. Vast crowds had cheered when Mussolini had stood on the balcony of the Palazzo Venezia in Rome on 10 June 1940 and announced that Italy had declared war on Britain and France. 'Vinceremo!' he had promised, his jaw set, chin jutting upwards with resolute bombast. 'We will win!'

Not quite three years later, his dreams of a new Rome with himself as its Caesar had long been punctured. Even the might of Nazi Germany and Hitler's panzers and Messerschmitts had not been able to stave off disaster. And Hitler had been right about one thing: Mussolini was feeling ill. The previous July he'd gone to Libya expecting to lead the triumph into Cairo. He had returned with the Axis armies stuck at Alamein and with a stomach problem he couldn't shift. Whether it was psychosomatic or not, it was eating away at his resolve. At the Council meeting in Rome the previous November, his appearance had shocked his ministers; he'd looked like a dying man about to collapse at any moment. 'From October 1942,' he wrote, which was when Montgomery had launched the Battle of Alamein, 'I had a constant and growing presentiment of the crisis which was to overwhelm me. My illness greatly affected this.' Or perhaps it was the other way around.

At any rate, he was certainly aware the vultures were starting to circle. Most within the Italian establishment – those very same Roman elites that had prompted so much contempt from Hitler and von Neurath – had been wondering how Italy might extricate itself from the war ever since the disastrous defeat at Alamein. The loss of North Africa had merely brought the question into sharper focus. Perhaps, some wondered, Mussolini might ask for Hitler's consent to conclude peace with the Allies? This was, of course, a vain hope, but conversations were had and meetings held, although nothing much seemed to come of them – not least because it was obvious that if Italy did somehow make peace with the Allies, the country would most likely be invaded by Germany. The payback, inevitably, would be appalling. Italy found itself between a rock and a hard place.

Mussolini knew it too. He wrote a long letter to Hitler pleading with him to sue for terms with Stalin and turn his attention closer to home, in the south. The Führer simply ignored it; obsessed though he was with his southern flank, Hitler's ideology and that of National Socialism was wedded to the struggle against Bolshevism and racial battle in the east. None the less, in Rome the plots continued to thicken, and although none of them seemed to get much beyond the conversational stage, conspiracy, as von Neurath had discerned so palpably, was in the air.

In February, Mussolini had had a clear-out, sacking those he thought most likely to be plotting and the most outspokenly pessimistic. One of those to go was his son-in-law, Count Galeazzo Ciano, one of the playboys Hitler had scorned, but a clever man, who had far greater geopolitical awareness than his master and who had seen the writing on the wall a long time earlier. Ciano, a serial philanderer, was made Ambassador to the Vatican. 'The ways which Providence chooses', he wrote in one of his last diary entries, 'are indeed sometimes mysterious.'

The change of team at the top made little difference. Mussolini had become isolated; he was sick and alone. He held no reciprocal affection for Hitler, who seemed to rant at him whenever they met. When more German troops were proposed to help shore up Italy and Sicily in May, Mussolini turned down the offer, fearing further humiliation and ulterior German motives. Hitler felt betrayed by Italy; Mussolini felt betrayed by Hitler, also dating back to 1939, for embroiling Italy in a war for which it had clearly not been ready. Neither man was prepared to consider his own culpability for the disasters that now faced their respective countries.

Wracked with stomach pains, surrounded by men he could no longer trust, Il Duce began to go a little mad on occasion. In early June, Carlo Pareschi, the minister for agriculture, admitted during a meeting that the harvest so far had not brought the yields hoped for. Mussolini suddenly cut in. 'A few days ago,' he said, 'I was in the countryside and I saw what the birds get up to. They land on the stem, and their weight bends the ear of the wheat so that they remain hidden. Then they eat the grain.' His solution was to kill the birds. 'Kill them all!' he exclaimed.

In many ways, the immediate fate of Mussolini was in the hands of King Vittorio Emanuele. Tiny of stature and pretty tiny of mind too, the King had sanctioned Fascism and had sanctioned a catastrophic war; now he seemed less concerned about the fate of his people, and more about the fate of the monarchy and whether it would survive any peace with the Allies. He also worried whether it would survive an invasion by the Germans. Whatever course it took, the future looked far from rosy, and if the King was considering removing Mussolini he did nothing about it. For the time being, Mussolini would remain Il Duce.

Meanwhile, across Italy, civil strife grew worse. The country was being bombed – not, perhaps, with the same city-flattening treatment that was starting to be meted out on Germany, but by the end of 1942 some 25,000 homes had been destroyed in Turin, while more than half a million people had been evacuated from Milan. Food shortages were really beginning to bite, especially in the cities – most people were living off less than 1,000 calories a day, which was not enough – and other commodities were in short supply too. There was little petrol. Corruption and black marketeering were rampant, making life even more miserable for the masses. Hundreds of thousands of young men were now locked up in Allied or Russian prison camps.

And nowhere was the misery of war felt more keenly than in the south – and especially in Sicily, the island off the toe of the mainland that was part of Italy but also not part of it. On Sicily, for centuries home to a mass of impoverished, beaten-down peasants, life was especially tough. It was soon to become a lot tougher.

CHAPTER 5

Air Power

O N THURSDAY, 22 APRIL 1943, two Spitfires from Takali airfield on
the tiny island of Malta took off at first light and, banking, turned
and headed north in the direction of Sicily. A year earlier, the Luftwaffe
and Regia Aeronautica had done their level best to crush the island and
pummel it into the sea. Lying 60 miles to the south of Sicily, Malta lay
directly in the path of any Axis shipping heading to North Africa. From
this island, torpedo bombers, fighter aircraft, submarines and warships
could all operate against the Axis supply line. The most successful Allied
submarine of the war, HMS *Upholder*, had operated from Malta. So too
had Force K, two cruisers and two destroyers that had played havoc with
Axis shipping, so much so that in November 1941, 77 per cent of all
Rommel's supplies crossing the Mediterranean had been sent to the bottom. A few weeks later, his forces were driven back across Libya.
Feldmarschall Kesselring, newly appointed C-in-C South, realized that
Malta needed to be neutralized: its port facilities wrecked, its RAF contingent destroyed, its airfield made unusable, its harbours inaccessible
for both warships and submarines. Luftflotte II, an entire air army, had
been sent to Sicily for the purpose.

In April 1942, 6,728 tons of bombs had been dropped on the island,
sixteen times the amount that had destroyed the English city of Coven-
try back in November 1940. Some 841 tons had been dropped on Takali
airfield alone, and a similar amount on neighbouring Luqa. On five separate days that month there had been just one serviceable fighter left for
the RAF to fly, and on one day, 14 April, there had not been a single one.
Malta had been a brutal place to be back in April 1942.

Kesselring had not been able to finish the job, however. Malta had been on its knees, but his Luftwaffe were needed across the sea in North Africa to support Rommel's planned offensive at the end of May 1942. More Spitfires had reached the island and the fightback had begun in the air, and very successfully too, but by June the island – and the fighter pilots – were beginning to starve. By July the situation was desperate. And by August, the shortages were so dire it had seemed that Malta might have to surrender after all. One last effort was made to save the island with the mounting of the most heavily defended Allied convoy of the entire war: Operation PEDESTAL. The Allies were determined the convoy should get through, the Axis were equally set on ensuring it failed. A mighty battle raged the length of the western Mediterranean as bombers, U-boats and fast torpedo boats were all flung at the convoy. Of the fourteen vessels that set sail, just five made it, including the one tanker, the *Ohio*, which despite being hit ten times and even having a crashed Stuka dive-bomber land on its decks, managed to limp in, woefully low in the water and with two destroyers lashed either side because its engines had stopped. It reached Grand Harbour on 15 August 1942, the Feast Day of Santa Maria, the most important *festa* in Malta's calendar. A miracle had occurred. Malta had been saved.

In October the same year Kesselring had made one more effort to extract this thorn in the Axis side, but by then the island was bristling with fighter planes and his air forces were shot down in droves. Now, a year on from the height of the Malta Blitz, the island was still looking bashed and beaten, rubble still lay in the streets and life was tough for the Maltese, many of whom had been made homeless, but it was also awash with Allied fighter aircraft. How the tide had turned.

The two Spitfires taking off that early morning were from 249 Squadron, a Battle of Britain veteran fighter unit that had been operating from the island for more than two years, since the spring of 1941. Pilots had been rotated in and out, however, and the two now heading north had both been on Malta a few months only. One was the newly promoted Squadron Leader John J. Lynch Jr from Alhambra, California, just twenty-four years old; the other was even younger, twenty-year-old Flying Officer Irving 'Hap' Kennedy, from Cumberland, Ontario.

Since the outbreak of war, the RAF had attracted – and welcomed – pilots and aircrew from all around the world, and certainly the fighter pilots on Malta had always been a fairly polyglot bunch. Johnny Lynch really should have been flying with an American outfit, but having joined the US Army Air Corps – as it had then been – before the war, he had become impatient for some action and so had taken himself north to Canada and signed on the dotted line for the RAF instead. Although he'd wound up in one of the all-American Eagle Squadrons in England, he had then accepted an overseas posting to Malta in September 1942. Seven months on, he was not only still on the island but had taken command of the squadron and was in no especial hurry to join his fellow Americans now serving in the USAAF. Lynch liked 249 Squadron just fine.

Hap Kennedy had arrived on Malta just a month after Lynch; at the height of the siege, three months was considered ample time for a tour on the island, but throughout the Mediterranean theatre aircrew were carrying out longer tours now, as it was recognized that the more experienced the pilots were, the better the Allied air forces would be. Malta remained a physically tough posting and was still short of many of the creature comforts of home, but it had been transformed in recent weeks.

Both men were carrying auxiliary fuel tanks that could be discarded once the fuel they carried had been used. The idea for this flight had been Lynch's; he'd spent a fair amount of time at Lascaris, the operations and fighter control rooms dug into the rock underneath the island's capital Valletta, studying patterns of behaviour by the Luftwaffe and Regia Aeronautica, and realized they would often fly transport planes bringing in supplies early in the day. He hoped to catch some this morning.

Flying low over the sea, they were soon past Capo Passero on the south-east tip of Sicily and continuing on their way, Avola and then Syracuse off to their left. Just north of Catania, near the coastal town of Riposto, Kennedy spotted an aircraft heading south towards them and inland, presumably to land at either Catania or Gerbini. He wondered whether he should break radio silence, because it was clear Lynch hadn't seen it. He decided he would – after all, it might be the only aircraft they saw.

'Tiger Green One,' he called over the R/T. 'Aircraft eleven o'clock ahead, same level, proceeding south. Over.'

Lynch still couldn't see it.

'Green One. Aircraft is now at nine o'clock,' Kennedy said. 'Might be a Junkers 52.'

After a pause, Lynch replied that he still couldn't see it, so Kennedy told him he was going after it before they lost the aircraft entirely. Opening the throttle and banking away to the left, he soon caught it, creeping up directly behind as close as he could. Aiming at the port engine, he gave it a quick burst of cannon fire and saw the engine burst into flames and the aircraft immediately plunge down into the sea, before turning again and quickly catching up with Lynch once more.

On they flew, Mount Etna on their left, up through the Straits of Messina swiftly before anyone could fire at them and then turning to port along the north Sicilian coast. The sun was now up and behind them, which was ideal, and up ahead Kennedy soon saw three small specks of light, which at first he thought might be birds but then realized had to be aircraft. Once again he warned Lynch, who, still struggling to see, asked him to take the lead. Kennedy gave the Merlin engine extra boost and felt the Spitfire surge forward. Much to his delight, he saw the three aircraft were not fighters, as he'd first thought, but bigger.

'Green One,' he called. 'The three aircraft dead ahead are twin-engined. I'm opening up a little more. We must catch up more quickly. Over.'

Lynch followed, and together they soon caught their quarry at barely 200 feet above the surface of the sea. In fact, they were three-engined Ju52s – transports, just as Lynch had hoped. Kennedy drew in close towards the nearest and, seeing the machine gun of the mid-upper gunner pointing upwards, realized the man was snoozing in the morning sun. It had been the perfect stalk – with the sun directly behind the two Spitfires, the German crews could not see them at all. Kennedy opened fire and, once again, the plane flipped over and dived into the sea. 'I reckon that woke him up,' he thought. Only now was Lynch catching up. Kennedy hammered the second of the three, and once again saw smoke billow from the port engine. Lynch now drew right up behind the third and blasted it into the sea, before turning to the second and finishing it off.

'Green Two,' said Lynch, 'Green One here. Let's go home.'

They climbed as they flew over Sicily then dived down low over Comiso in the south, at zero feet, watching men on the ground scattering in all directions. 'We were rubbing it in,' noted Kennedy.

Back at Takali, they landed safely. Lynch was a serious, quiet fellow, and the ground crews called him 'Smilin' Jack' because he rarely did. But he was smiling now.

'What are you going to claim?' he asked Kennedy.

Kennedy thought a moment. He wanted the CO to take him on another trip like that. He'd begun the day with three confirmed kills to his name, so the two he'd shot down alone gave him five and that made him an ace. It seemed a little churlish to demand he share the Junkers they both hit.

'What about sharing even, two each?' he suggested.

'Sounds reasonable,' Lynch replied. Six days later, Lynch shot down another Junkers 52 on a similar early-morning sweep, although that time he hadn't taken Kennedy. It was the 1,000th enemy aircraft destroyed by Malta-based units since the start of the war. That was a lot of enemy aircraft. Malta had been revitalized, and so had its pilots, now flush with experience, confidence and plenty of aircraft. The tables could not have been more blatantly turned.

In his letter to Brooke back in early April, General Alexander had stressed that HUSKY required the all-out commitment of the Allied naval and air forces – especially the latter – to support the army. He had not been disappointed. At the end of May both Brooke and the prime minister had visited Algiers to see for themselves how preparations were coming along, to provide a bit of a morale boost for the men and, of course, to confer with the senior commanders. On Monday, 31 May, Churchill and Brooke sat down with Eisenhower and the three service chiefs for HUSKY; and Tedder, as overall Allied air commander, was able to report that his men had been blasting Axis communications for weeks and were already exerting considerable pressure on the enemy's windpipe. A few days later, at Eisenhower's villa, Tedder reported to Churchill that they were attacking relentlessly, bombing communications centres, airfields and the enemy's main bases. A Daimler-Benz factory near Naples, producing engines not just for the Messerschmitt 109 but also the Italian Macchi 202, had been hit on 30 May; airfields at Bari in southern Italy had already been hammered and so they had now turned on Foggia further up the leg of the peninsula. Intelligence showed the Italians had moved some units further north still from Foggia all the way up to Piacenza. 'Our bombing of ports and railways,' Tedder told him, 'was interfering effectively with shipping and supply lines.'

There were now almost 3,500 Allied aircraft in the Mediterranean, a huge fleet and well over double the size of the Axis air forces in the theatre. Air power had always been at the heart of British and then American strategy, a central part of the 'steel not flesh' principle designed to keep the numbers of young men fighting at the coal-face of war as small as possible. Unlike the Axis, the Allies were truly fighting on air, on the sea and on land, and coordinating their operations very effectively, despite ongoing grumbles in certain quarters – gripes that were generally made through ignorance and a lack of understanding rather than reflecting real deficiencies.

Really, the development of Allied air power was quite remarkable. Although Britain had developed the world's first fully coordinated air defence system before the outbreak of war and had used it superbly during the Battle of Britain in the summer of 1940, the RAF's performance in France beforehand had shown up just how little thought had been given to tactical air power – supporting the army in their operations on the ground. Bombing capability had also been far short of what had been confidently hoped. The United States, on the other hand, had merely had the US Army Air Corps rather than a fully fledged air force. By May 1940, at a time when Messerschmitts were marauding at will over northern France, the Americans had just 160 fighter aircraft and fifty-two heavy bombers. Since then, not only had production of aircraft in both the United States and Britain risen urgently and dramatically, the means of operating them had been transformed too, and it had been in North Africa, over the desert sands, that Allied tactical air power had been born.

Air Chief Marshal Tedder had certainly played his part. Lean, thin-faced, with dark, keen eyes and a pipe never far from his mouth, he was sharply intelligent, forward-thinking and driven by belief in the huge possibilities air power might yield. So too had Air Marshal Sir Arthur Coningham. An Australian by birth who had been brought up in New Zealand, he had arrived in Egypt in the middle of 1941 and taken over command of what became the RAF's Desert Air Force. Known to all as 'Mary', derived from 'Maori' – a nickname that, curiously, he rather liked – he was a tough and charismatic figure, bristling with ideas and energy; he devoutly believed air power was vital not just for strategic bombing and defence but also for achieving victory on the ground.

Tedder had understood that improving technical maintenance in the field had been a first step, but had also overseen the development of new methods – or doctrine – as Army and RAF together strove for a clearer understanding of the role of close air support in a land battle. Army commanders wanted to have the air forces at their beck and call, but Tedder – and Coningham – rightly resisted this. Air commanders, they argued, were best placed to judge when and where air power should be used. An army commander would always want permanent air cover almost directly above his troops, but while an air commander would certainly help take out specific targets, he would also direct his aircraft to destroy enemy air forces or supply columns before they reached the front. Fortunately, Tedder and Coningham had Churchill's support and a new directive, based on the concepts of air support that had been outlined by Tedder, had been issued back in September 1941.

By the early summer of 1942, Coningham had honed his tactics further, thanks to his collaboration with his number two, right-hand man and administrative chief, Air Commodore Tommy Elmhirst, a diminutive and altogether quieter fellow as well as the owner of incredibly bushy eyebrows. Coningham might have been the visionary but Elmhirst was the enabler, implementing greatly improved management of supplies and maintenance, as well as better ground control and a system of leapfrogging. Landing grounds were established all along the coast from the main airfields around Cairo to the front. Stores and supplies were built up at each, which meant forward units could keep as close to the fighting front as possible. If they needed to retreat suddenly, the aircraft could take off and the ground crew shuttle back to the next landing ground. The aircraft would then join them on their return from operations over the front. This enabled Coningham's fighters and bombers to harry the enemy almost constantly, and after the fall of Tobruk on 21 June 1942 and with Eighth Army in full and desperate retreat, it was the Desert Air Force that very probably saved it from annihilation, hammering the pursuing Axis forces without let-up.

The pause that followed between Rommel's defeat at Alam Halfa at the very beginning of September that year and the Battle of Alamein in the third week of October had allowed Coningham and Elmhirst to develop their forces yet further. Piecemeal units were kicked into touch and replaced by groups of fighters, divided into three wings, each with its own administrative staff. This centralization of administration allowed wing and squadron commanders to get on with the job of leading their men and fighting the enemy rather than worrying about paperwork and logistics. It also meant the pilots could train harder and better. Gunnery techniques were improved and the hours in logbooks increased. Coningham didn't want his pilots thinking about flying; that was to be automatic. He wanted them thinking about how best to shoot down the enemy or destroy targets on the ground.

Like Tedder, Coningham also firmly believed the aim of a tactical air force should be to win air superiority over the battle area. Once that was achieved, more direct support could be provided for the troops on the ground. In other words, while the Desert Air Force could offer close air support to Eighth Army, it could do much more than that; but although it was obviously vital to form close working relations with the army command, it was also essential that the air commander be left to command his force how he, as an airman, thought fit. Sometimes, for example, he could best help troops down below not by responding to a specific target request, but by neutralizing a threat further back behind the enemy.

Coningham had also learned from the enemy, and while he had been impressed with how effective dive-bombing could be, he had also realized how vulnerable the Junkers 87 Stuka was as it emerged from its dive to any Allied fighter waiting to pounce, and that generally it was simply too slow in all forms of flight. Instead, he increasingly used fighters, especially the rugged US-built P-40 Kittyhawks, as fighter-bombers, not least because they could out-dive the latest Messerschmitt 109s and Macchi 202s. The 'Kittybombers' soon became an incredibly effective weapon, and increasingly so as the pilots gained in experience. Able to hurtle towards a target at speed, which made them harder to shoot down, they could drop their load and speed on out of the fray. The results were quickly felt. Not only did the RAF save Eighth Army's bacon, it contributed to the victory at Alamein every bit as much as the troops on the ground – as Montgomery, to be fair to him, freely acknowledged. And Monty also accepted and understood the importance of working hand-in-hand with the air forces, gladly agreeing to joint tactical HQs as Coningham had proposed.

Coningham's developments, backed up by Tedder and combined with the authority to act independently from the army commanders conferred by Churchill, transformed close air support in North Africa and laid down the basis of future doctrine not just for the RAF but for the USAAF as well – which was significant, because with the TORCH landings had arrived burgeoning US air forces, including a bevy of bright, dynamic and hugely competent airmen only too happy to learn, improve and develop the very exciting and ever-growing potential of air power.

Prominent among them was Lieutenant-General Carl 'Tooey' Spaatz, who had first reached North Africa soon after the TORCH landings as USAAF Theater Commander. Spaatz was fifty-one, with a resolute jaw, trim silver moustache, intelligent eyes and a natural air of charisma and authority. An experienced airman with combat experience from the First World War, he had risen up the ranks of the Air Corps during the 1930s to become Chief of Plans. A close friend and colleague of General

Henry Harley 'Hap' Arnold, C-in-C of the USAAF, Spaatz had been at the forefront of modernizing America's air forces. Energetic, open-minded and forward-thinking, he oozed competence and good sense from every pore. Sent to Britain in 1940 as an observer, he had swiftly – and correctly – concluded the Luftwaffe had little chance of winning the Battle of Britain. A bomber man first and foremost, he recognized that weight of numbers, both of aircraft and of bombs, counted, and that the Luftwaffe simply didn't have enough of either. But he'd also been impressed by RAF organization, and had returned to Britain earlier in 1942 to take command of the fledgling US Eighth Air Force.

US involvement in North Africa meant that no sooner had he begun to lay foundations for the Eighth than he was needed in the Mediterranean instead. He had arrived in Algiers in November with a number of misgivings, not least the depletion of Eighth Air Force, which lost some fourteen units of fighters, bombers and transports to the Mediterranean.

There had been a further concern, however, and that was doctrinal. The Eighth was a strategic air force designed to operate on its own, and they had worked out and agreed their doctrine for daylight operations in coordination with, but separate from, RAF Bomber Command. The duties of Twelfth Air Force in North Africa, however, were very different: part strategic, part coastal and part tactical in support of ground operations. For this he had good numbers of aircraft, but inexperienced crews, an untested logistical organization and no doctrine at all for close air support. What's more, unlike the RAF, which was an independent armed service, the US air forces were part of the army. Eighth Air Force could operate without interference from the army ground forces, and were already doing so; but North Africa was already proving a different kettle of fish.

As if to complicate matters further, there had been no unified command. The Americans were doing their thing in Twelfth Air Force, and the RAF were doing theirs – and were also split up between Eastern Air Command in Algeria and Tunisia, and the Desert Air Force and other units of RAF Middle East. The set-up had been designed in this way to support the landings and on the assumption that Tunisia would be swiftly captured; but by the end of 1942 it was clear that this had been wishful thinking. Spaatz, quite rightly, had felt that the dispersal of command and total lack of any coordinated close air support doctrine had been threatening to undermine the material strength being thrown into the theatre.

But everything the Allies had been doing in Tunisia in terms of air power had been new. Even in Libya, where Mary Coningham had been developing his Desert Air Force into a finely tuned tactical force offering close air support, he and his men had still been feeling their way and working out methods on the hoof. What's more, they only had Eighth Army to support, whereas in north-west Africa there were the American, French and British ground forces to support, all new to fighting and each with different structures and attitudes to air power. Joined-up thinking on air power was decidedly lacking. Yet if they were feeling their way, it was hardly surprising. After all, just three years earlier the United States had only had an air corps amounting to a handful of fighter planes; it had already come an incredibly long way in really no time at all.

Clearly, unifying the Allied air forces in the Mediterranean had been essential; and it had been done, as part of the shake-up in February 1943 in which Eisenhower had been made Supreme Allied Commander and Alexander put in charge of 18th Army Group. Tedder had become C-in-C Mediterranean Air Command and so the overall Allied air commander. Under him fell RAF Malta, RAF Middle East and also the new North African Air Force, which was by far the largest single command now in the Mediterranean. This was given to Spaatz, and directly under him was now the Northwest Africa Strategic Air Command headed by another American hot-shot, Major-General Jimmy Doolittle, a celebrated aviation pioneer and a household name back in the States. In the same reorganization, all Allied tactical air forces were handed over to Coningham, first as Air Support Tunisia but then renamed North African Tactical Air Force, which also fell within Spaatz's command. Coningham's new deputy was Brigadier-General Larry Kuter, who had helped write the USAAF's strategic air doctrine; he too was supremely competent and forward-thinking, and was eager to hone this exciting and rapidly developing weapon every bit as much as Tedder, Spaatz, Coningham et al. Nor was that all. Also under Spaatz's umbrella were coastal air operations against Axis shipping and the all-important training command.

It was notable how well these commanders, different people all, and suddenly thrown together, seemed to get on. A pioneering spirit welded them together. For sure, ruffles occurred along the way – including a fairly major spat between Coningham and Patton in March during the latter's command of US II Corps. Patton, with no understanding at all of the new doctrine being developed for close air support, had angrily demanded a permanent umbrella of fighter cover for his operations in southern Tunisia. Coningham and Kuter had told him this was not possible, prompting ire from Patton and an increasingly heated exchange that ended with Coningham accusing the American of crying wolf. Tedder had been furious with Coningham for threatening Anglo-US relations, while Alexander had thought Patton had rather deserved it. On Tedder's insistence, however, Coningham was forced to apologize and visited Patton in person. They shook hands and lunched together, and, as Patton noted, 'We parted friends.'

At the start of the Tunisian campaign, Allied soldiers on the ground had grumbled that the Luftwaffe appeared to roam at will above them; by the end, there were no such complaints. Day by day, week by week, the Allied air forces began increasingly to dominate the skies. The American and British contribution in terms of numbers, logistics and effort was simply immense. By the last days in Tunisia, some three thousand Allied aircraft were dominating barely three hundred of the Axis. This level of commitment produced more than a hundred new airfields in the theatre, and all-weather ones at that, which required labourers, concrete, graders, bulldozers and other plant – almost all of which had to be shipped from the United States or Britain. After Kasserine, five new airfields were built around the nearby town of Sbeitla – all within seventy-two hours.

Meanwhile, in the skies, increasingly confident and more experienced airmen were winning the day. On Palm Sunday, 18 April, intelligence reached Coningham's air forces that around a hundred Ju52 transport planes were approaching Tunis. It was late afternoon and in all, four squadrons of Kittyhawks and eighteen Spitfires climbed into the air to try to intercept the fleet of enemy transports. In what became known as the 'Palm Sunday Turkey Shoot' no fewer than seventy-four Luftwaffe aircraft were shot down.

No matter that on the ground, US troops were still a little green and learning the ropes, or that British forces were still working out an effective way of war; in the air, in a matter of months, the Allies had transformed their offensive capabilities.

CHAPTER 6

CORKSCREW

'F OLLOWING THE LOSS OF Tunisia,' wrote General der Flieger Wolfram von Richthofen, C-in-C Fliegerkorps II, on 23 May, 'the island chain comprising Sardinia–Sicily–Crete represents the advanced defence line of Southern Europe. Should the enemy succeed in gaining a foothold in one of these islands, he will have achieved a penetration into Fortress Europe which would signify a grave threat to the defence of the mainland. Every last man and weapon must be rallied to prevent this happening.' Von Richthofen made the point that at the moment of assault the enemy would be at his weakest because he would be in landing craft and devoid of cover. Therefore all Luftwaffe personnel, unless servicing aircraft or directly employed in flying operations, would be issued with weapons and given training, and would be expected to help repel the enemy in the event of an invasion attempt.

It was all a bit desperate and smacked of panic. It would, of course, have been far better that Hitler, recognizing there was now no reasonable chance of winning the war, threw in the towel right away and saved a huge amount of carnage, but that was never going to happen. To start with, the Nazis already had too much blood on their hands; and secondly, Hitler had always been a black-and-white kind of person. There would be the Thousand Year Reich or there would be Armageddon, but no half measures. Tragically for Germany and for all those fighting the war, Armageddon now looked a dead cert. The only question was how long it would take.

Von Richthofen now had his air forces spread to the four winds in an attempt to counter every eventuality. One of the features of the glory days of the Blitzkrieg – and indeed of earlier German and, before that,

Prussian, successes – was the concept of the *Schwerpunkt*: literally a 'heavy point', meaning a concentration of forces to deliver a maximum punch. These days, though, the Luftwaffe, like every other part of the Wehrmacht, were on the defensive and thinly spread. As a result, there were Luftwaffe units in Greece, in southern Italy and on Sardinia as well as Sicily, where there were now three *Gruppen* of JG 53, the Ace of Spades, each with three *Staffel* or squadrons; there was also one *Gruppe*, the second, of JG 27; and there were two *Gruppen* of Macky Steinhoff's JG 77, with the third based on Sardinia.

The air defence was supposed to be a joint effort by Germany and Italy, but the Luftwaffe and Regia Aeronautica were like an estranged couple reluctantly still cohabiting but barely speaking to one another. Certainly there was no shared doctrine or even common operational orders. The Luftwaffe had radar on the island and ground controllers, for example, but the Regia Aeronautica did not and the Germans were not about to share it – a bizarre state of affairs. They would pass on information if asked, but that was about it. As it happened, the Italians rarely did ask.

There were still a number of Italian bombers and torpedo bombers and seven *gruppi* of fighters on Sicily. Among the bombers were the Cant Z.1007s of the 27° Gruppo Bombardimenti at Gela–Ponte Olivo: three-engine bombers that could each carry a rather underwhelming 1,200kg of bombs. Reasonably quick and with good visibility for the crew, the Z.1007 none the less suffered from poor reliability and was woefully underarmed, with just four machine guns. Nor did it particularly help that the fuselage was mostly made of wood.

Among the aircrew at Ponte Olivo was 22-year-old Melino Barba-gallo, part of an air force unit called Carro 1000, a radio service group named after the 1,000-watt radio they used on the ground to communicate with aircrew. Very often he would be sent up into the air as a spare radio operator and technician; since joining the Regia Aeronautica, he'd been up on a number of different bombers and missions. A native Sicilian, born and raised in Catania, from an early age he had dreamed of becoming a pilot but had left school at sixteen without either the right academic qualifications to be accepted for flying training or a wealthy enough father to pay for it. Even so, he still managed to join the air force rather than the army or navy, and was sent to Milan to train as a radio operator. From there he was posted back to Sicily, and to Gela–Ponte Olivo. He had been thrilled – at last he was able to see up close many of the various aircraft of the Regia Aeronautica. He was soon carrying out operations against Malta and against Allied shipping, including attacks on the Allied PEDESTAL convoy. 'I was really passionate about the war,' he said. 'I wanted to defend my country and I really wanted to take part in the war until the end.'

The Italian air forces would soon be leaving the island, but the German fighter boys were staying put, for the time being at any rate. Macky Steinhoff felt weighed down by a constant feeling of impending doom he couldn't shift, made worse by the knowledge that as commander of an entire fighter *Geschwader* he was responsible for the men under his charge. Most of the pilots were still boys – there were a few old-timers, *Experten* with more than twenty-five victories to their name and Knight's Crosses dangling round their necks – but the majority were no older than twenty-one at most.

He had taken over command of JG 77 in Tunisia in the latter half of March, having been given some leave following a long tour in the Caucasus and Crimea, on the southern Eastern Front. It had been good to spend some time with his wife, Ursula; but then had come a call from General der Jagdflieger Adolf Galland offering him a choice of commands: either France or North Africa. He chose the latter. 'I had never been there,' he admitted, 'and I think the adventure appealed to me.'

Steinhoff's predecessor at the head of JG 77 had been Joachim Müncheberg, one of the legends of the Luftwaffe's fighter arm and a commander much loved by his men. In 1941, from Sicily, Müncheberg had led a fighter group against Malta that in two months had shot down forty-three Hurricanes for not one loss of their own; Müncheberg had claimed twenty of them. By the time he died on 23 March 1943 in a mid-air collision with an American Spitfire, he had 135 aerial victories to his name. His loss seemed to symbolize a terrible realization that the Luftwaffe's glory years lay behind them. 'I knew him,' said Steinhoff, 'and he was a great pilot, good man, great sense of humour and a fine gentleman.' Müncheberg's shoes were hard to fill, but Steinhoff had a pretty impressive record himself, having shot down some 152 Soviet aircraft over the Eastern Front. As he had quickly discovered, however, Allied fighter pilots were of a different calibre from those of the Red Army: on one of his first missions in Tunisia he had had his radiator shot out by a Spitfire, forcing him to crash-land in the desert. Despite this, he'd soon won the trust and respect of his airmen – and also that of the ground crew, whom he arranged to fly out to Sicily without his superiors' knowledge.

JG 77 had escaped to Sicily by the skin of their teeth, landing at

Trapani on 8 May. Their Messerschmitts had been covered in bullet holes and hadn't been serviced for days, but in the fuselage of each one had crouched a mechanic with whatever tools he could carry. It had been dangerous, but the gamble had paid off. None the less, to a man, from Steinhoff down to the most junior pilot, they knew they'd been whipped. Everyone was physically and mentally exhausted, and they all realized there was little chance of their fortunes improving any time soon. General von Richthofen might have issued memos about Luftwaffe personnel readying themselves to fight on the beaches and instigating training programmes, but Steinhoff wasn't playing ball. Nor did he stand on ceremony. His men, unshaven, wore a range of odd uniforms and non-regulation clothing, with sandals on their feet and a variety of scarves, headscarves and hats on their heads. 'Let me just say,' Steinhoff commented, 'we had developed the beach mentality.'

The day after their arrival, Kesselring drove over to see them, appearing just after Allied bombers had been over and given Trapani a pasting. The field marshal was less shocked by the ambulances screaming past hither and thither than he was by the state of the pilots.

'Steinhoff,' he exclaimed, 'do your men know that there is a war on?'

'Yes, Herr Feldmarschall,' Steinhoff replied, 'we have been fighting it for about four years now.' Kesselring, ever the optimist, liked to appear cheerful and was known as 'Smiling Albert' but he was certainly not smiling now.

'Tell your men to at least pretend that they are German soldiers. This is a disgrace. What if the Reichsmarschall had come here and seen this?'

'I do not think we have a chair that would support his weight, Herr Feldmarschall,' replied Steinhoff with all the insolence of a man at his wits' end. Around him the men started to snigger. Kesselring ordered them to stand to attention, then asked Steinhoff a number of questions. How were things going? Rotten, Steinhoff replied; he had just forty aircraft and right now, not one of them was serviceable. So no, they were not combat ready. And no, they did not have enough aircraft or ammunition. He implored Kesselring to allow his men a brief rest.

'Sir,' Steinhoff pleaded, 'the group is no longer a battle-worthy unit. Its combat value is precisely nil. Do, please, believe me when I say that after coming through the murderous defensive battles in North Africa and Tunisia my pilots are absolutely all in. The heavy casualties have utterly demoralized them. May I therefore request that they have a few weeks off operations?'

'The overall situation demands that your group remain operational,' Kesselring replied icily. Then he got into his car and left to go and see the troops arriving at the tiny port of Marsala. The next day, however, while conferring at a house near the harbour where he had stayed overnight, it was hit by a bomb during an air raid. Lucky to survive, he managed to escape by sliding down a rope to the street below, burning his hands in the process. At least he was alive, which was more than could be said for his ADC. Later, he appeared back at Trapani and, before flying out, told Steinhoff his *Geschwader* could move to Bari in southern Italy for a few weeks. 'But be quick about it,' he added. 'I shall want the group back in Sicily soon, fit for action.'

Steinhoff's men were not the only ones having a bit of downtime. So too were the Allied Tactical Air Force. Air Marshal Mary Coningham was determined to enjoy the recent victory, having spotted a luxury villa overlooking the sea at Hammamet which he had decided would make a splendid new HQ. As he pointed out to Tommy Elmhirst, they had roughed it ever since arriving in North Africa and most likely would be roughing it again soon. Elmhirst had been packed off to get Alexander to sign a piece of paper confirming the Villa Sebastian was allocated to C-in-C Tactical Air Force. Alex had looked at him 'a bit sideways' as he knew one of the divisional commanders was already occupying it; on the other hand, the army were about to move, so he signed it. Coningham had his villa.

Many visitors would call in at the Villa Sebastian over the coming weeks, from Alex to the prime minister to the King, who even rather gamely joined in for a skinny-dip in the sea as no one had trunks. Not all the visitors were VIPs, however. One was Hugh 'Cocky' Dundas, who at just twenty-two was the youngest wing commander in the RAF. A veteran of Dunkirk and the Battle of Britain who had already commanded a wing of Typhoons, he had been sent to North Africa to take command of 324 Wing only to learn that the existing Wingco, George 'Sheep' Gilroy – nicknamed for his former life as a Scottish shepherd – had recovered from a minor wound in the arm and was carrying on. So Dundas joined as supernumerary wing commander. After the end in Tunisia, Gilroy had been promoted to group captain and so Dundas had expected to take over 324 Wing after all. He was as pleased as anyone about the recent victory and, like many others, had driven out to see the POWs in one of the many temporary camps. He'd been shocked to see tens of thousands of them, dirty, disarmed and dejected. 'Well, fuck 'em all, I thought,' he noted. 'They were the defeated ones, but they were safe. That was more than could be said for me and my friends. We had won; so we had to go on and start all over again.'

Dundas was impressed by Coningham's villa – he honestly believed he had never seen a more beautiful place – and was treated to fresh coffee and brandy followed by a delicious lunch. They chatted widely, Dundas wondering why he'd been summoned, but eventually Mary got to the point. Air Vice-Marshal Harry Broadhurst, the current commander of the Desert Air Force, didn't want him as commander of 324 Wing. It was no reflection on Dundas' capabilities or leadership, Coningham emphasized. 'You know Broadie,' he said. 'He likes to choose his key men. And I have always let him do so.'

Although this meant he could very possibly take a safe desk job for a while, Dundas couldn't help feeling both deeply disappointed and ashamed. Coningham explained: apparently, Dundas had once clashed with Broadhurst over a matter of tactics; the superior officer had sided with Dundas, and Broadhurst had taken a dim view of being trumped by a junior officer. Coningham tried to placate the young pilot; he would find him a good post outside the Desert Air Force, and more immediately, he wanted him to fly one of two Typhoons that had arrived for trials from Casablanca to Cairo; but for Dundas, it was by far the most shattering experience of his short but celebrated career to date.

While the tactical air forces were training and refitting, the strategic air forces were as busy as ever. After the Tunisian victory Tedder and Spaatz had immediately sat down to work out a clear and comprehensive plan of action for the Allied air forces to support HUSKY. They envisaged four major stages: they were to neutralize the enemy air forces as far as possible before the invasion, so that whatever airfields they could not immediately capture on the ground would be unable to offer much resistance; they were to destroy enemy communications; they were to isolate the expected battlefield by making it as difficult as possible for enemy ground forces to rapidly deploy troops towards the Allied bridgehead; then, once the invasion had taken place, they were to offer close air support to the ground forces. In addition, Allied air forces were to support naval operations, provide convoy cover, deliver airborne troops, protect base areas and offer ample air–sea rescue. In other words, the demands were both many and varied.

Between now and the invasion, however, it was the bombers who would be expected to do the heavy lifting, albeit supported by fighters operating from Cap Bon and Malta. Already, as early as 7 May, just a few days after the final HUSKY plan was agreed, Spaatz had sent General Jimmy Doolittle, commander of the US Strategic Air Forces, orders to pummel the western part of Sicily. Palermo, Marsala and Trapani were all to be hit 'as critical points in the enemy's lines of communications.' The aim was to deny the enemy the use of the ports and any other facilities that might be of use to the Axis – railway lines, warehouses, vehicles or roads. 'A high degree of destruction is therefore indicated,' added Spaatz. 'It is desired that you critically analyse the size and distribution of your effort and the types of bombs and fuses to be used, in order to insure the complete demolition of areas attacked.'

Now the Allied air forces had their foot on the Axis throat there was to be no release of pressure; this was emphatically underlined by Spaatz's tough, severe and uncompromising orders. And Doolittle was swift to respond, with Palermo and Trapani hit heavily on both 9 and 10 May – which was when Kesselring was visiting Macky Steinhoff and the men of JG 77. Among those flying over Palermo on 9 May was Lieutenant Jimmy Bruno, co-pilot on a B-17 Flying Fortress of the 99th Bomb Group. Bruno had not been alone in groaning inwardly during the briefing that morning after photo reconnaissance revealed that Palermo was now bristling with anti-aircraft guns. Their task was not to hit the harbour on this occasion but to fly over it and try to knock out as many anti-aircraft positions as possible. This, they all knew, would make it easier for them to return in future; but it only took one well-aimed shot to bring down a bomber and its crew. In any case, they could hardly expect to destroy all those flak positions in one raid.

Bruno had been brought up near Waukesha, Wisconsin, and had decided he had to become a pilot after seeing the pioneering aviator Charles Lindberg fly over the family farm back in August 1927, when he had been eight years old. 'Aviation is in its infancy,' he had later written in his high school yearbook; 'the opportunities are unlimited.' Just over a decade later, in 1939, he'd taken his first flying lesson, in a Piper Cub, and a short while after that he and a friend bought an OX-5 Curtiss Pheasant biplane for $175 – a small fortune for the two young men, but as far as they were concerned a bargain for the dream it enabled them to fulfil. Another couple of years on, in September 1941, having brushed up his academic qualifications, Bruno applied to join the US Army Air

Forces and was accepted, beginning his flying training the following February. So rapidly was the new force expanding that entire bombardment and fighter groups were being formed as one, and Bruno's entire Class 42-1 were all posted to 99th Bombardment Group, newly formed on 23 January 1943. Two months later they'd flown to North Africa, where they were sent to the newly completed air base at Navarin, near Oran in Algeria, arriving at their tented home on 27 March. Four days after that they flew their first mission, to bomb Villacidro airfield in southern Sardinia. Since then, Bruno and the rest of Lieutenant Blaine Bankhead's crew had completed seven missions.

On this eighth mission, they reached Palermo without a hitch and flew low over the city, their bomb-bay doors already open. Flak was bursting all around them but they dropped their bombs and managed to get clear away without damage, although Bruno saw one Fortress come down. 'This particular mission was extremely discomforting to me,' Bruno admitted, 'and I sensed the other men on my plane were equally uneasy about it.' They made it back to Navarin safely, only to head back the following morning to hammer Trapani.

Once the Tunisian battle was finally over, Tedder and Spaatz agreed a timetable for HUSKY. From 16 May to 6 June, bombers would range widely over the Mediterranean area without focusing especially on Sicily. Between 6 and 13 June, the key islands of Pantelleria and Lampedusa would be the focus, before normal strategic bombing ops would resume. Finally, from 3 to 9 July, heavy and systematic attacks upon Axis air bases on and close to Sicily would be the priority.

The swift smashing of Pantelleria was to be another early test of the Allies' new-found dominance of the skies. Lying almost halfway between Sicily and Tunisia, some 63 miles to the south-west of the former and 53 miles from the latter, it had been an Italian military zone since 1926; and it contained a key airfield, one that would be very useful for the Allies to capture before HUSKY as a base for Allied fighters, which would then be within range to support the Americans when they landed at Licata and Gela on the southern Sicilian coast.

Capturing Pantelleria, though, was potentially a very tricky proposition. It was well defended, with over three hundred concrete gun emplacements and a plethora of pillboxes built into the cliffs; an amphibious assault had just one small beach to land, and had also to cope with vicious offshore currents and an unusually high surf for the Mediterranean. There were also some twelve thousand Italian troops crammed into this 10-mile-long bean-shaped island. For Operation CORK-SCREW, Eisenhower asked Admiral Cunningham to provide a powerful naval striking force and also earmarked the British 1st Division for a landing. First, though, Allied bombers would blitz Pantelleria and reduce its defences as much as possible. 'I want to make the capture of Pantelleria a sort of laboratory to determine the effect of concentrated heavy bombing on a defended coastline,' Eisenhower wrote to Marshall. 'When the time comes we are going to concentrate everything we have to see whether damage to materiel, personnel and morale cannot be made so serious as to make a landing a rather simple affair.'

Conscious this was to be an important test for Allied air power not just in the Mediterranean but more generally, Spaatz recruited a British medical doctor and research anatomist to help him. Professor Solly Zuckerman had been brought into Combined Operations, Admiral Lord Louis Mountbatten's commando and raiding organization, and had been introduced to Spaatz that March when the air chief had briefly been back in England. The two had hit it off immediately. 'They were men who were learning,' wrote Zuckerman of Spaatz and his staff, 'as I was learning, and unlike some professional military people whom I had met, there was no assumption of superior knowledge and no assurance that they knew how Germany was going to be defeated.' In May, Zuckerman was asked to come to North Africa, and since he was between jobs he readily accepted, arriving on the 22nd. After being briefed by Tedder he was sent straight to Spaatz's headquarters with the challenge of applying his scientific and analytical techniques to the feasibility of an assault on Pantelleria. After two days of studying intelligence data on Italian morale on the island and also the island's defences, Zuckerman concluded it was certainly possible. Spaatz, who was always looking for new ways to advance air power and very happy to think outside the box, brought Zuckerman into his staff and asked him to prepare a detailed bombing plan.

This was delivered to Spaatz on 2 June, using not only intelligence on Pantelleria's defences but also data previously gathered about the effectiveness of various bombs. No one had ever applied this level of number-crunching data analysis to the bombing of a specific target before. Neutralizing strongly prepared defensive positions by air power alone, Zuckerman admitted, had previously been considered next to impossible. 'In so far as the task has never before been attempted on any large scale,' he wrote, 'Operation CORKSCREW thus becomes a test of the tactical possibilities of this form of air attack, and an exercise in the most economical disposal of the available air strength.' It was no wonder the Allied commanders were going to follow CORKSCREW with a mixture of excitement and nervous apprehension. It felt, understandably, like a big moment in the Allies' journey with air power.

It was also an operation that required not only strategic bomber forces but also the Coastal Air Force and the medium twin-engine bombers of Coningham's Tactical Air Force, as well as his fighters for escort duty. The organization and administration of such an operation fell squarely within Air Commodore Tommy Elmhirst's remit; Coningham had never been one for paperwork, which was why Elmhirst had always been such an invaluable sidekick. Elmhirst, however, had been in Algiers helping to prepare detailed plans for HUSKY. Arriving back at the villa after three weeks away, he was told they were on forty-eight hours' notice for CORKSCREW. Hurriedly phoning round the bomber wing commanders, he asked whether they had enough bombs and fuel. To a man, they replied that they did not. After managing to secure a loan of a hundred army trucks, he arranged for them to set off at dawn the next morning for their ammunition dumps 50 miles behind the old front line. 'My situation was saved!' recalled Elmhirst. 'But my staff for once got the rough edge of my tongue.' Coningham's and the Tactical Air Force's blushes had been spared.

With a naval blockade of the island already in place, bombers had already begun to strike before Zuckerman had delivered his detailed plan to Spaatz. Heavy bombers flew over the island on 1 June. Also flying that day were the 99th Fighter Squadron, the first all-black air unit to see action in the war. Racial segregation was still a feature of the US armed forces, although a growing number of more enlightened senior commanders, not least Tooey Spaatz, were working to use African-American troops at the front line. Spaatz had inspected the 99th FS at Oujda in Morocco on 19 May, meeting the men and talking with their commander, Lieutenant-Colonel Benjamin O. Davis, the son of the first black US general. 'Lieutenant-Colonel Davis impressed me most favourably,' he noted in his diary, 'both in appearance and intelligence.' Colonel Davis was remarkable for having graduated from West Point despite suffering four years of racism and silent treatment, largely shunned by his contemporaries. Indeed, all the men in the 99th Fighter Squadron were impressive because all had had to overcome so much to be there.

Among them was Lieutenant Charlie Dryden from New York. Dryden had wanted to fly for as long as he could remember – 'aeroplane', or a childish version of it, had been almost the first word he'd spoken – and although he had worked hard at school and had managed to secure a place on one of the Civilian Pilot Training Programs, his dream of flying for his country in the US Army had so nearly been thwarted time and time again. The son of British Jamaicans, he had feared he wouldn't get accepted in the first place because neither of his parents had ever got around to applying for US citizenship. Once as a boy he'd been arrested for trying to get on the New York subway using a fake dime, and when asked whether he'd ever fallen foul of the law at his air force interview had wrestled with himself over what to say. He'd decided to tell the truth – and it turned out they'd known all along; they had wanted to test his honesty. And although he'd already got his civilian pilot's licence, he quickly discovered once he'd arrived at Tuskegee Campus in Alabama to begin his military training that whatever flying hours he already had in his logbook counted for next to nothing.

Of the eleven men who had joined Dryden in Class 42-D, only three had gained their coveted wings. Dryden himself had been warned numerous times he was within a whisker of being washed out. The moment the silver wings had been pinned on his chest, Dryden had scarcely been able to believe the moment had actually come. 'My heart was racing so fast I feared I might pass out from excitement,' he recalled; 'for now, at last it was over. All the hurdles that could have killed my dream were now, themselves, washed out.' At the time, he and two of his classmates had been three of only eight black officers in the United States Army Air Forces. To get to that point they had had to be better than their white colleagues at every stage of the training programme. Most new pilots heading to England or North Africa had around 350 flying hours in their logbooks, but by the time Dryden was posted overseas on 2 April 1943, some twenty-six months after the formation of an all-coloured air force unit had been first authorized, he had accrued some 538 hours, including 207 on the P-40 Kittyhawk and not including the 90 hours from his civilian pilot training programme.

In fact, that the 99th FS was going to war at all was something of a miracle as Jim Crow had attempted to throw a spanner in the works at every opportunity. General Hap Arnold had thought it would take too long to train both aircrew and ground crew to be of any value in the war, and had recommended the 99th FS be posted to a backwater in the Caribbean. It was Eleanor Roosevelt, wife of the president, who had done much to overcome such barriers. Visiting a polio clinic in Tuskegee and seeing aircraft flying overhead, she was told they were flown by coloured pilots and introduced to some of the key personnel; she had even been given a flight. Back in Washington, she had urged the president to intervene; and the squadron, with just twenty-eight pilots, had finally been posted overseas.

The 99th had left Oujda on 30 May in two flights of fourteen, headed for Tunis. Dryden was in the second flight but soon after they'd taken off his wingman, Willie Ashley, began having problems with overheating and so they decided to turn back, Dryden accompanying him to make sure he made it all right. This set them back a good while, and when they finally reached the staging post of Blida the following day, the second flight had already taken off again for Fardjouna airfield near Tunis. And by that time the first flight, led by Colonel Davis, had already taken the 99th FS into action over Pantelleria.

Dryden finally flew his first combat sortie on 4 June, as the air bombardment of Pantelleria continued. With a 500-pound bomb slung underneath his Kittyhawk, he dived down, following his flight leader, red tracers streaking past his cockpit. He was concentrating so hard he didn't have time to feel scared; only as he pulled up from the bomb run did it cross his mind the enemy below had been trying to shoot him. 'Only then,' he admitted, 'did I tweak a bit.'

He was back over Pantelleria again on 9 June, which was when he ran into the Luftwaffe for the first time. This time, he'd been leading a flight of six when a number of Me109s had been spotted flying above them. The German pilots had tried to manoeuvre with the sun behind them, but Dryden and his flight were able to perform a tight 180-degree turn towards the enemy. The Messerschmitts swiftly scattered. Although none had been shot down, Dryden felt elated and relieved. 'When I saw the swastikas on those Me109s and felt the urge to go get 'em,' he wrote, 'I knew that I had conquered my fear of possibly turning yellow and turning tail at the first sign of enemy.'

The pounding of Pantelleria continued remorselessly, in conjunction with heavy naval bombardments. On the evening of 8 June, a naval force of four cruisers and six destroyers departed Malta to join the assault on the Italian island early the following morning. 'It was a perfect dawn we saw breaking this morning,' jotted Midshipman Peter Hay, 'but the whole atmosphere was rather tense.' Hay was just nineteen and had become a midshipman the previous year, joining the battleship *Nelson* and taking part in Operation PEDESTAL, the convoy that had relieved Malta in August. He had sat his midshipman's exams in March and passed with a second – as had most of his fellows – and had then been posted to HMS *Tartar*, one of the Tribal class that were designed to be fast and agile, with a greater emphasis on fire-power than torpedoes. *Tartar*, for example, could not only travel at 36 knots – around 41 mph – but was armed with eight quick-firing 4.7-inch guns, one four-barrelled light anti-aircraft gun and two quadruple quick-firing 5-inch guns, which for a ship of 125 yards in length was quite a lot of fire-power and quite a lot of speed.

Their force of warships was joined by HMS *Whaddon*, which, Hay learned, had General Spaatz aboard as an observer. Having closed up at action stations, they saw the bombers fly over. 'There were literally hundreds of them,' noted Hay, 'and we saw Fortresses, Baltimores and Mitchells, to say nothing of the Lightnings, Spitfires and Kittyhawks.' The naval forces split up at around 11 a.m.; a quarter of an hour later, 'Battle Ensigns were broken at the yard' and the cruiser *Euralyus* opened fire on the coastal defences from 15,000 yards. *Tartar* sped back and forth while the bombers started to do their work, then closed in at 30 knots. Peter Hay watched the bombs falling, first into the sea then creeping up on to the beach and inland. Meanwhile, *Tartar* opened fire with her guns, along with the rest of the force. 'At first our shots could be seen falling,' jotted Hay, 'but very soon the smoke and dust from the bombs obscured the target. During all this time I had seen no firing from Pantelleria except a little at the bombers.' They closed further to around 3,500 yards then sped parallel to the coast, firing continuously. The enemy did reply, but at first their shots were far too high; then a shell landed just ahead of *Tartar*, producing a huge spume of water through which the ship ran. Everyone out on the fo'c'sle, Hay included, was soaked. A second fell close again, drenching them once more – but that was it: suddenly the enemy guns fell silent. The whole action, Hay reckoned, lasted around forty-five minutes, by the end of which Pantelleria had largely disappeared behind a pall of smoke.

Tartar returned with the rest of the force to Malta, but was back again on 11 June, the day of the planned invasion by the British 1st Division. Also attacking this time were a number of small, fast motor gun boats – MGBs – that sped towards the harbour, raking it with fire. There were some sixteen Italian shore batteries that might have fired back at the MGBs, but only three did so and not with much heart. The will of the defenders, after such a sustained pounding, was beginning to break. Of the town of Porto di Pantelleria not much remained, and especially not after the night-bombing of 10–11 June, which had been heavy and sustained.

By morning on the 11th, the Italian garrison commander, Contrammiraglio Gino Pavesi, had lost the will to continue; many of his men had already deserted. The Allies, he signalled to Rome, had plunged the island into 'a hurricane of fire and smoke'. The situation was so desperate there was no further means of resisting. At 9 a.m. on the 11th, D-Day for 1st Division's amphibious invasion, Pavesi issued the order to surrender, just as waves of B-17 Flying Fortresses were coming over. *Tartar* was a mere 3,000 yards off shore. 'We could distinctly see them coming down,' wrote Hay, 'and a few seconds later saw great clouds of black smoke and rubble – mixed a moment later with brown dust.'

They and the rest of the naval forces soon joined the bombardment, unaware that the surrender had already been signalled – a message that had not reached the assault commander either, so that the British came ashore as planned at around 11.55 a.m. Less than half an hour later, what remained of the town was secured and by the end of the day over eleven thousand Italian troops had been taken prisoner, along with some eighty-four enemy aircraft. Despite the force of the assault, casualties had been surprisingly low, with fewer than two hundred Italians killed and the same again wounded. But the shattering mental effect of having some 6,200 tons of bombs dropped on to their positions had very effectively broken the will of the Italian defenders.

Spaatz was elated; so were all the Allied commanders. 'Pantelleria', noted Tedder, 'was the first defended place to be reduced to surrender in the Second World War as a result of air and naval bombardment alone.' That was true enough; but more than that, for HUSKY it meant another airfield under Allied control closer to Sicily. It also suggested the Italians might not fight as hard in the coming battle as some had feared. No one was feeling complacent. But the Allies could now look towards the invasion with a little more confidence than they had before. CORKSCREW had been a resounding success.

CHAPTER 7

Man of Honour

THE PRE-WAR BAEDEKER GUIDE to southern Italy and Sicily warned that under no circumstances should the traveller attempt to visit Sicily during the months of July and August because of the appalling heat and prevalence of disease. The Allied planners were not taking any heed of that, but they were preparing a booklet for the Allied soldiers about to take part in HUSKY, which was to be issued to every single serviceman and included a brief history of the island and an outline of what they might expect when they got there, from climate to the living conditions of ordinary Sicilians, along with a handful of useful words and phrases. 'The Island,' the *Soldier's Guide to Sicily* stated matter-of-factly on page 1, 'has a long and unhappy history that has left it primitive and undeveloped, with many relics and ruins of a highly civilized past.' Sicily in 1943 was an island that had been rather left behind; the Allies might have been about to re-enter Europe, but this wasn't a Europe many of them would recognize: parts of Italy – Sicily in particular – were very different from the modern, industrialized and increasingly urban worlds of Britain, the United States and Canada.

Shaped not unlike a stone-age flint arrowhead, with the point facing west, Sicily was, in many ways, trapped in a world that had barely changed in a thousand years: it was a place where agriculture dominated the economy and class dominated society, and where the peasants, which meant most of the population, were as poor, downtrodden and oppressed as they had ever been. In winter there could be vicious soaking downpours, which often did more harm than good as there were no dams or reservoirs to make the most of the rainfall, causing mudslides that could block roads to and from the hilltop towns for weeks. In the spring and early summer, Sicily would be briefly bathed in soft green and a multitude of wild flowers; but then came the long, volcanically hot summer, baking the hilly and mountainous interior into a brutal, bleached landscape that became more desert than farmland. In high summer, the air would be as still as the inside of an oven one day but the next whipped by dust storms brought on the North African *scirocco*.

Nor was this tough landscape improved by the dominating presence of Mount Etna, Europe's most active volcano, looming high over the north-east corner of the island and on clear days visible from even distant parts. It was like an all-seeing god, standing sentinel, occasionally with volcanic steam hanging over the top like a white cap. Sometimes, of course, it would erupt. Back in 396 BC, an eruption had stopped the Carthaginians in their tracks; another in 122 BC had destroyed much of Catania, lying just to the south-east of the mountain. Catania was nearly overrun again in 1669, while almost all of the town of Mascali, lying on the coast to the east of Etna, was swamped by lava barely more than a decade before the war in 1928.

Volcanic eruptions were one threat to the livelihoods – and lives – of Sicilians; earthquakes were another. At 5.20 a.m. on 28 December 1908 a massive quake hit Messina, swiftly followed by a 40-foot-high tsunami along the coastline. More than 90 per cent of Messina was destroyed and tens of thousands killed – possibly as many as a hundred thousand.

Along with natural disasters and a savage climate, Sicilians over the centuries had also had to deal with marauders and invaders. It was an island with an astonishingly rich history. Those modern, twentieth-century troops who had been taught Latin and Greek during their schooldays would have remembered that Sicily was the place where Daedalus, the first aeronaut, landed – according to the myth – and where, in Homer's tale, Odysseus tricked and blinded the Cyclops.

Sicily had always been a bridge, or stepping stone, from one world to another – first to the ancient Greeks, then to the Romans and Carthaginians. Over time it was occupied by Vandals, Goths, Byzantines, Arabs and Normans, before becoming a vassal to the Bourbons of the Holy Roman Empire, then to Napoleon, then back to the Bourbons once more. Over and over, successive powers arrived in Sicily, imposed themselves and ruled with an iron rod until usurped by someone else. The one constant was the appalling treatment of the native Sicilians. At the same time, the island was subjected to regular raids by pirates from Arabia, from Africa – from all over. This turbulent history gave rise to one of Sicily's characteristic features: the lack of villages or isolated settlements. It was never safe to live in small communities, and so most Sicilians lived in towns, more often than not perched high on a hill for safety. Daily, the menfolk would leave the town and head down into the fields to eke out a pitiful living, then, the backbreaking day done, trudge back up to their homes.

Even by 1943, Sicilians for the most part were still living lives of appalling poverty. There was an electricity grid, but by no means all homes were connected, certainly not in the more remote towns of the mountainous interior. Only around two-fifths of the population had access to running water and those were mostly in the cities – the majority of the island's towns, perched atop hills and mountains, were dependent on wells and rooftop water tanks, just as they had always been. This also meant modern sanitation was the preserve of the elites only. Most people simply threw effluent into the street.

Mario Turco lived in the coastal town of Gela. Thirteen years old, he was from a working-class family but they were better off than many. His father and uncle ran a construction business – in fact, one of their jobs had been to put up some wooden buildings for the Regia Aeronautica at the nearby Ponte Olivo airfield. Mario was one of five children, which was not at all unusual. There was no luxury and very little spare cash; life was simple. Turco was happy enough, however. 'I had a good childhood,' he said. 'My father made sure we had everything. We all went to school.' Food was simple, too: milk for breakfast, pasta for lunch, vegetables and fish for supper, meat once a week. 'During the war,' he said, 'meat was scarce and expensive or it wasn't available at all.' Not only was there severe rationing in Italy, often it was impossible to get even what little was supposed to be available – increasingly so on Sicily as the war progressed, primarily because the transport system was on the point of collapse due to the loss of shipping and, more recently, Allied air attacks on the railways.

There were hardly any vehicles in Gela – just a few cars for the most senior town officials, but no trucks, although that had been the case before the war too. 'People used to move on farm wagons,' said Turco, 'on donkey-drawn carts.' There was a cinema in town, and a public radio in the town club – a kind of community centre – where people could hear the news. Otherwise, contact with the outside world was minimal; for Mario Turco, Gela was his entire world.

In contrast, sixteen-year-old Vincenza La Bruna, who lived in the town of Regalbuto in the eastern centre of the island, not far from the foot of Etna, lived a life of grinding hardship. There were nine crammed into their family home – her parents, her grandmother and six children. Vincenza went to school for just three years, and much of the rest of her time was spent working. 'At home,' she said, 'but there was also work to do in the fields. At home there was a donkey and mule to look after too, and some chickens and a pig to feed. There was no lack of work.' The family even had to make their own shoes – simple wooden clogs – although much of the time they wore nothing. 'We were barefoot,' said Vincenza, 'like slaves.' Despite the animals and chickens, food was short, increasingly so as the war progressed. Boiled wheat berries became the staple.

Mario Turco was healthy enough as a boy, helped no doubt by swimming almost daily in the sea, but disease was rife on Sicily. In the plains in the west near Trapani, on the southern coastal strip and in the larger, low-lying Catania plain, malaria was an ever-present threat – but it could be caught in the mountains too. Vincenza La Bruna had had it as a child, which interrupted her time at school; by the time she'd recovered, her mother insisted she stay at home and help look after her younger brothers. And malaria was only one threat to health. Throughout the island sandfly fever, dysentery, typhus and typhoid were all prevalent. 'The insanitary condition of the island,' noted the *Soldier's Guide* dryly, 'is one of its best defences against an invader.' While it was true that Sicilians had built up a level of immunity to many of these diseases, life expectancy was still way below the national norm.

Public services and facilities were rudimentary or absent. Some 40 per cent of the islanders remained illiterate, and what public education there was remained basic in the extreme. Although the state roads, the *strade stato* – the ones that crossed the island and ran along the northern and southern coasts – were asphalted, the vast majority of the island's thoroughfares were *strade bianche* – made of dirt and stone. Outside the cities there were few vehicles; Sicilians depended on donkeys, mules and their own two feet to get around, much as they had always done.

More than half the adult male population was involved in agriculture. Cereals, vegetables, olives, citrus fruits and also almonds as well as wine were all produced on the island, although with tools that had barely changed over the centuries and with the majority wedded to a system that went back to medieval times and beyond. Millennia ago, in the time of the Phoenicians, the land had been divided up into latifundia – effectively, large estates – which were then leased to local notables, who in turn forced locals into slavery, or even brought in slaves from elsewhere, to work the land. It was a system that continued right through the period of Arab rule; then, when the Normans arrived and swept out the Arabs in the tenth century they brought with them their feudal system, which was not so very different from the system of latifundia, except that instead of explicitly being slaves, Sicilian peasants now worked like slaves but at least got to take home some of what they produced, while the barons kept the rest. This baronial class stayed in place even after the Bourbons arrived to rule Sicily. The old latifundia were now known as *feudi* – large tracts of land of at least 5,000 acres each, of which several might be owned by a single baron. Increasingly, though, the last thing any self-respecting baron wanted to do was spend his time in some godforsaken spot getting baked alive when he could live off the proceeds more comfortably in a large town house in Palermo or Naples – or even Rome or Florence. This meant overseers were needed to keep an eye on things and make sure the share-croppers tending the soil – the *contadini* – were keeping their side of the bargain. Violence and systematic exploitation were part and parcel of the system.

The feudal system officially ended in 1812, although, as with the switch from latifundia to feudalism, the actual differences were – for the hapless *contadini* at any rate – rather slight. Instead of answering to armed guards, share-croppers now had to deal with a *gabellotto* – a kind of steward, who rented the entire *feudo* and paid the absentee landlord a guaranteed income, while continuing with his henchmen to grind the peasant class into the dust, screwing them for everything they possibly could. Armed revolutions in Sicily in 1820 and in 1848 loosened the power of the old aristocratic baronial class yet further, as did the Risorgimento of 1860, in which the Bourbon dynasty was finally overthrown and Italy became an independent and – notionally, at least – unified state. Yet even though Sicily had been at the centre of Garibaldi's battle for freedom, the Sicilians, typically, suffered badly from its success, because the island did not fit into a one-nation brand of political rule. Italy may have been the most Catholic country in Europe, but it had more regional dialects and patois than any other, and even after unification remained more of a geographical concept than a nation-state. Not that the central government in Rome accepted this. New taxation laws were introduced along with across-the-board conscription, which prompted outrage among the Sicilians. Theirs was both an agricultural and a highly patriarchal society; men worked on the land, women stayed indoors and tended the home. Conscription meant fields would not be tended and people would starve and die. To avoid it, young men fled to the hills, recruiting officers were lynched and rural Sicily – especially the western half – became ever more lawless as these outlaws evolved into bands of brigands roaming the countryside. Now, Sicilian peasants no longer feared pirates from across the sea, but they did fear being rustled or robbed. Within a couple of decades of the Risorgimento, the murder rate on the island was ten times higher than it was in northern Italy.

It was into this melting pot of poverty, misery and growing violence that the Onorata Società – the Honoured Society – began to emerge as a dominating factor in Sicilian life. At the most basic level, it was a protection racket; but it also had a complex set of codes that revolved around respect, outward devotion to family life and, above all, loyalty. These 'men of honour' were also known more simply as the Mafia.

It's hard to pin down the origins of the word conclusively, although it may well have come from an Arabic word of similar sound that means 'place of refuge', as safety, or protection – of a kind – is what the Mafia were offering. On the other hand, in the Palermo patois, *mafioso* was another word for 'beautiful' and 'self-confident'. So a person described as *mafioso* came to mean someone attractive and self-assured.

The men of honour were none other than the *gabellotti*, who, after a period of years looking after the *feudi* and making money, were starting to acquire enough wealth themselves to invest in land of their own, putting them in a position to turn against the absentee landlord by refusing to pay up, threatening him – or worse, if he did appear on the doorstep – and eventually coercing him into selling up. By this time, the *gabellotto* had developed into a man of immense local power. He now had land he needed to protect on his own account, and a workforce and subsidiary interests that also needed safeguarding. Protection of the workforce was offered with guarantees and at a price. Those who refused to pay up would be 'warned'. They might find their olive grove felled or livestock rustled – this was what they could expect if they didn't have protection. If they still didn't play ball, then blood would be spilled, often fatally. Bandits would either be paid off or warned off. If a life had to be taken, so be it. The rule of central government counted for nothing in these backwaters of Sicily because everyone, from the police to the politicians to the local parish priest, was in the pocket of the local man of honour.

Gradually, these men of honour began to respect different fiefdoms – there was, after all, some safety in numbers – and so a code began to develop: a code of honour that transcended any normal human loyalties, including those of blood relationship. There were strict lines that no man could cross with impunity. The rules were understood and they were accepted; if they were broken, blood would be shed and dishonour brought down on the perpetrator and sometimes those around him too.

Between the turn of the century and the outbreak of the First World War, in a great exodus fuelled by the Messina earthquake of 1908, some 1.1 million Sicilians – a huge number, amounting to roughly a quarter of the entire population – had emigrated in search of a way out of the grinding oppression and poverty of life on the island. Some went to Britain, France or even South America, but most – around 800,000 – headed to the United States. Yet more left in the 1920s, and among them were many *mafiosi*, fleeing Fascist clamp-downs. The very notion of having much of central and western Sicily run by a secret organization that was uncontrollable by central government was anathema to Mussolini. He was Il Duce, the dictator, and he was in charge, not some so-called 'man of honour'.

Determined to stamp out the Mafia once and for all, Mussolini dispatched a hard man, Cesare Mori, to sort it out. Mori, a tough and uncompromising policeman from Pavia in northern Italy, had first been posted to Sicily before the First World War and had made a name for himself for catching the notorious bandit Paolo Grisalfi; he had also used strong-arm tactics against banditry again immediately after the war when still serving on the island. Although he had since retired to Florence, Mussolini now persuaded him to return to duty and posted him back to Sicily as the prefect of Trapani with the sole task of destroying the Sicilian Mafia. 'Your Excellency has carte blanche,' Mussolini told him; 'the authority of the State must be absolutely, I repeat absolutely, re-established in Sicily. Should the laws currently in effect hinder you, that will be no problem. We shall make new laws.' Mori set about his task with an iron fist, smashing bandit gangs, imprisoning *mafiosi* without trial, and humiliating men of honour publicly with parades and show trials to try to dispel their mystique. Not for nothing was he known as the 'Iron Prefect'. By the time he was brought back to mainland Italy by Mussolini in June 1929, he had arrested more than 11,000 *mafiosi*, most of whom continued to languish in prison without having ever had a trial. Very publicly, it was announced the Mafia had been destroyed.

That had been something of an overstatement. Still, rampant banditry, cattle rustling and small-time *mafiosi* had definitely been crushed. Mori's successors in the 1930s turned away from show trials, preferring to send many *mafiosi* into internal exile on Sicily with the threat of further strong-arm tactics if they erred. What remained were a handful of Mafia groups, now operating more quietly and subtly. Perhaps a better way of describing matters would be to say the Mafia were lying dormant in Sicily; but there was definitely a sense that by the outbreak of war in 1939, their era of dominance was over.

In fact, the Mafia had rebooted itself into the United States, profiteering first from dominating the lemon trade and then from prohibition and a host of other protection rackets, and while there were plenty of Italian-American gangsters who did not hail from Sicily – Al Capone and Vito Genovese, to name but two – a large number of Sicilian *mafiosi* not only moved to and began operating in the United States, they also maintained firm links with the old country. *Mafiosi* always thought of themselves as a breed apart, and as men of honour that meant living and operating outside the normal rule of law. And yet the normal rule of law did exist; and having a foot in two different countries could be extremely useful.

In the central west of Sicily, lying on the edge of the province of Caltanissetta between Palermo to the north and Agrigento to the south, stood the small town of Villalba, home to around three thousand people. This was particularly harsh countryside, surrounded by low mountains, connected to the outside world by remote winding tracks, its thin, stony soil baked the colour of sandstone in the long summer. The town itself was built on a slope, looking northwards towards the Madonie Mountains, and laid out on a grid of thirteen streets by six around a town square, the Piazza Madrice, dominated by the Chiesa Madre – the Mother Church. Away from the church, the handsome stone houses around the piazza and along the central streets very quickly gave way to hovels and squalid one-room dwellings, or *bassi*, with compacted mud floors, effluent in the gutters and no running water.

This small, unremarkable and impoverished town was home to Calogero Vizzini, a 65-year-old man whose only sign of wealth was his paunch, a conspicuously rare feature on an island where very few fat people existed. With his spectacles, moustache and greying, receding hair, he looked otherwise nondescript; there were certainly no bespoke clothes, his usual outfit being a short-sleeved shirt and trousers with braces.

Born in the town back in July 1877, Vizzini had been the first son of a labourer and *contadino*, although his mother was slightly higher in the social hierarchy with the additional prestige that came from having a member of her family in the priesthood. While Vizzini's two younger brothers took to their studies and later went into the Church, he had remained illiterate, deciding instead to make his way in the world in a different manner by trading in the *cancia*, the barter of wheat for milling into flour, which enabled him to take a cut at both ends as well as demand a transport fee. The men in this trade effectively acted as intermediaries between the peasants who needed their wheat milled and the mills that produced the flour – and the mill, in the case of Villalba, was 50 miles away along tracks that were impossibly dangerous and controlled by bandits.

Vizzini got around the travel risk by coming to an arrangement with the biggest bandit in the region, Paolo Varsalona. Together they ran the *cancia* very much to their own profit. Along the way, Vizzini was accused of robbery and murder and twice arrested, but acquitted on both occasions for lack of evidence, protected by the barrier of *omertà* – the Mafia's sacred code of silence. Through a combination of guile, intelligence, ruthlessness and daring, by the outbreak of the First World War Vizzini had won respect and authority and had become a *gabellotto*. Unsurprisingly, he managed to duck war service and instead made a packet through the black market, supplying horses and other animals for the army through a combination of theft, bribery and threats. When he was eventually investigated, all those who had originally testified against him suddenly retracted. Nine of them were then accused of perjury and imprisoned; all nine took their sentences without so much as a further squeak. The episode only served to enhance Vizzini's prestige as a man of honour.

Vizzini had become a *gabellotto* more powerful than the landowner, and so was able to buy his own *feudo* at auction at a ludicrously low price because there were no other bidders. Such was his rising influence and power. On another occasion, a young *mafioso* from Villalba named Lottò committed a very badly planned murder, so blatantly that his arrest and conviction seemed to be foregone conclusions. Not so. Certainly, men of honour did not simply murder people – there was a process to be gone through, and authority had to be given; and Lottò had breached the rules. And yet, for men of honour it was unthinkable that punishment should be left to the state. To have allowed this to happen would have caused Vizzini a loss of respect, and so he took matters into his own hands. First, Lottò was transferred to an insane asylum where, soon after, he 'died'. His 'corpse' was then removed in a specially ventilated coffin and 'buried'. Meanwhile, the very much alive Lottò was given false documents and some money and smuggled to the United States. Arriving in New York, he was met by 'friends', and identified himself by producing a yellow silk handkerchief on which was embroidered a single 'C' – C for Calò.

Vizzini continued to accumulate wealth and expand his interests, entering into a partnership with some Fascists to develop sulphur mines in the Caltanissetta region. Although he was strongly anti-Fascist, it suited him to keep in with the Church and the Fascist Party, and he skilfully managed to do so without the slightest loss of prestige as a man of honour – which was one of the reasons he escaped the fate of many other *mafiosi* during the regime of Cesare Mori. This didn't stop him from repeatedly being charged with criminal conspiracy, but every time, without fail, he was acquitted due to lack of evidence, either because key witnesses clammed up or because vital papers mysteriously disappeared. In 1935 he declared himself bankrupt and from then on the authorities left him in peace; but by June 1943 he was as rich, powerful and unscrupulous as he had ever been, and while the Mafia might have been lying low, Don Calò, as he had become, was the most senior *mafioso* in all of Sicily, with contacts not just across the island but in the United States as well.

Don Calò had every interest in making sure Mussolini and the Fascist regime came to an end, because the Fascists had waged war against the Honourable Society and that needed to be avenged. Moreover, whenever there was political chaos there was opportunity, and that needed to be exploited too. Another Sicilian who was every bit as eager to see the back of Mussolini and Fascism, but for somewhat different reasons, was Lieutenant Max Corvo, now a citizen of the United States of America, who until the age of nine had lived in Melilli, a town perched in the hills overlooking Augusta and Syracuse in the east of the island. His father, Cesare, an outspoken critic of Fascism, had been forced to emigrate to the States ahead of the rest of his family, a separation that affected Max deeply. A keenly intelligent and determined young man, Max Corvo grew up fired by the same strong liberal political views as his father and, with the onset of war, was determined to play his part both for his adopted country and for the island of his birth.

While still in training as a conscript, Corvo wrote a paper he called his 'Plan to Overthrow the State in Sicily', outlining the kind of work US intelligence might carry out to undermine the Fascist regime. Managing to get it into the hands of the right people, Corvo eventually caught the attention of Earl Brennan, then head of the Italian Section of Secret Intelligence, a department of the Office of Strategic Services, or OSS, which had been established in June 1942 to train and deploy secret agents to gather intelligence and operate behind enemy lines, and to work alongside army and navy intelligence as well as the Counter Intelligence Corps (CIC). Corvo's theory was that the dissatisfaction many Sicilians felt with the war and with their lot in general could be exploited and that, as someone who could speak the local dialect and had an intimate knowledge of the island's customs and cultural quirks, he was well placed to help with this.

Brennan was impressed, and employed him to draw up a detailed plan and to start recruiting agents and operatives among the large network of Sicilians now in the United States and their connections back in Sicily. Corvo soon managed to gather around him and Brennan a team of men, ranging from eminent anti-Fascist exiles to young liberal firebrands, who, it was planned, would infiltrate into Sicily as soon as possible. Once Sicily itself became a target for the Allies, the intention was to send these agents in with the invasion troops so that they could rapidly begin the process of undermining Sicilian resistance to the Allies. However, Corvo and Brennan agreed at an early stage that no attempt should be made to establish contact with the Mafia or any other form of organized crime, even though several attempts were made by other OSS sources to arrange a meeting between Corvo and Lucky Luciano, a Sicilian gangster in prison in New York for running a prostitution racket. Despite being locked up, Luciano had continued running his businesses via another Italian-American, Vito Genovese, and had maintained links with associates not only in the States but also back in Italy – including Sicily. Corvo had resisted these approaches. 'I explained to Brennan that we could gain nothing from such a tie,' he noted, 'and that the relationship might prove embarrassing in the future.' In any case, as far as he was concerned, the Mafia had been practically stamped out. They were nothing.

Corvo had set off for Algiers on 20 May 1943, flying via Cuba, Guiana, Brazil and then across to West Africa. Even with a week's delay en route while his plane was repaired, that gave him and the agents of the Italian Secret Intelligence section of the OSS around six weeks to finalize plans for their infiltration and to put the 'Corvo Plan' into action.

*

Corvo had been right in his view that the majority of Sicilians had been instinctively against Fascism, although plenty had cheered Mussolini when he'd first declared war. Images of Mussolini were everywhere – black-painted stencils of his helmeted head and the Fascist slogan *Credere, ubbedire, combattere* – 'believe, obey, fight'. Giacomo Garra remembered when Italy entered the war in 1940. At the time he was the youngest of six children in a large and comparatively well-to-do family in Caltagirone, towards the south-east of the island, and his older brothers were all in the army. His family had embraced Mussolini and so had he, albeit through the naïve prism of a young boy. They had all been utterly confident of victory. 'How could we not win the war?' he'd thought. The British were viewed as utterly despicable and inept, even though they would repeatedly crush the Italians in the opening years of the conflict.

Nearby in Gela, Mario Turco had been at the town club at the time war was declared, and Mussolini's speech had been broadcast on state radio. 'There was only one radio in Gela,' he said, 'and it was at the Nobles' Club right in the centre of town.' He had been excited by the prospect of war. 'We believed', he added, 'that we were the strongest nation in the world.' It was hardly surprising; as a young boy in Fascist Italy he had joined the Fascist Youth, starting with the Figlio della Lupa – She-Wolf's Child – at the age of just six, then at eight moving up to the next stage, the Balilla, and on to the Balilla Moschettieri at eleven. Like so many others, he had been indoctrinated. 'I used to believe all the things they taught us.' He enjoyed it well enough, because his mates also did it and there were lots of sports. One time, he missed a weekly Saturday muster and was threatened with having his junior membership taken from him. 'And do you know what it meant not having the membership card any more? It was like the end of the world,' he said. 'At my age, it meant being isolated, no more friends, and not even being allowed to go to school.'

Another who had cheered the declaration of war on 10 June 1940 was Livio Messina, who back then, aged eighteen, had applauded excitedly alongside crowds of others in the Piazza Plebiscito in Naples, where he'd been brought up, though born in Sicily. He'd then looked around him and had noticed an elderly lady beside him with tears running down her cheek. Catching his eye, she raised a hand and touched his face. 'My son,' she said, 'you don't realise what is going to become of us.'

At the time, Messina had thought little of it. He had wanted war because he was fiercely patriotic and wanted Italy to be a great nation; he believed it was only right that Italy should expand and create a new Roman Empire. Patriotism – nationalism – had been drummed into him in the Balilla and Fascist youth organizations. At university he'd then taken a course in Colonial Studies and had never had much cause to question what he'd been taught. Now, three years on, he was back on the island of his birth and a *tenente* – a lieutenant – in the signals platoon of the 4° Divisione 'Livorno', and still young enough and naïve enough to be taking in his stride everything that life threw at him. An uncle had been killed during the fighting in Albania, which had shaken him, and the reverses of fortune in the war had dented his confidence a little, but when he'd been called up at the age of nineteen he'd set off for officer training with no small amount of pride. His father had been to see him off at the station and had given him a razor, brush and soap as a parting gift – even though, fair-haired and baby-faced as he was, he'd barely needed them, which he'd felt as something of an affront to his manhood. So far, though, the war had treated Messina fairly well. He'd been passed from pillar to post but, now aged twenty-one, was yet to go into action. Even after arriving in Sicily with the division the previous November, that prospect still seemed to him a remote one.

Not all were as naïve as Tenente Livio Messina, however. Tenente-Colonnello Dante Ugo Leonardi was commander of the III° Battaglione of 34° Reggimento in the same Divisione Livorno, and although he was doing his best to prepare his men for the invasion he felt certain was to come on Sicily, he was doing so with a heavy heart. Leonardi did not share either Messina's more laissez-faire approach to soldiering or his youthful enthusiasm for war. Rather, he was convinced that most Italians had entered the war with little conviction and that, despite Fascism, as a nation they had simply never had the aggressive spirit or hatred of their enemies to justify taking the terrible step to armed conflict. In fact, he reckoned they had never really thought through the consequences of going to war at all.

There was a lot in this view. It resonated with Graziani's reluctance in invading Egypt in September 1940, when it had become clear Britain had no intention of giving up the fight. Suddenly, Italy had found itself woefully ill-prepared. The country had even fewer natural resources than Germany. Compared with the leading powers, it was backward, too. Italy's military was not modern enough, not well equipped enough, not organized enough and – as Colonnello Leonardi knew – not committed enough to win the war. Now, in June 1943, Italy seemed finished – most certainly so if what he'd discovered on the island was anything to go by. 'The conditions on Sicily,' he noted, 'were abject.'

When he had first arrived in November 1942, Leonardi had toured the entire island and had been horrified by the lack of any kind of centralized defensive organization. Rather, the various units had been left to pursue their different approaches and differing ideas of how best to organize themselves. Some coastal units were even speaking entirely different dialects, which, of course, was hardly ideal for any kind of coordinated defence. The coastal divisions were made up of poorly armed and poorly trained men, most of whom had been hurriedly conscripted and showed not the slightest interest in fighting. They were also horribly stretched in certain parts of the coastline, with battalions of some six hundred men each defending stretches of up to 30 miles. 'For example,' he noted, 'the Battaglione 435 had thirteen men per kilometre. The best case scenario was the Battaglione 388 with sixty men per kilometre spread over ten kilometres.' Nor was there any naval artillery outside the main ports. 'None!!'

Matters had improved significantly with the arrival in February 1943 of Generale Roatta to command Sixth Army on Sicily. Contrary to what Hitler and von Neurath believed, Roatta was not a spy, spineless or otherwise. Having made a name for himself in the Balkans as an utterly ruthless hard man, willing to wage war against Yugoslavian insurrectionists with the utmost brutality, he had come to Sicily determined that Italy should fight and do its very best to repel the invasion which, like Kesselring, Mussolini and others, he felt certain would be directed at the island. In expressing his views to von Neurath, whom he had known for some time, he had been merely speaking frankly; such, though, had been von Neurath's – and Hitler's – paranoia, they had not taken Roatta's warning in the spirit in which it had been made.

Roatta had been as appalled as Leonardi by what he had discovered on Sicily. At the time, Sixth Army had only partial control over Italian anti-aircraft defences, and none at all over the militia units or navy or Regia Aeronautica. Leonardi was right – there was no joined-up approach to the defence of the island at all. Clearly, this could not be allowed to go on; and, since Roatta was a wily operator, he managed to secure a decree from the Italian general staff, the Comando Supremo, that made him overall Armed Forces Commander, Sicily, a post that gave him control of some seven military and nine civilian defence agencies on the island. The only parts of Sicily's defence that eluded him were the three naval fortress areas of Messina–Reggio in the north-east, Trapani in the west and Augusta–Syracuse in the east.

With the vastly increased power and authority that came with his new title, Roatta had set about licking Sicily's defences into shape. Both troops and locals were drafted in to build bunkers, lay mines and wire, and create anti-invasion obstacles along the island's beaches. Frustratingly for Roatta, however, many of the resources earmarked for Sicily ended up being sent to Tunisia, where they were lost for ever, either sunk en route or taken by the Allies. The general had demanded and had been promised some 160,000 tons of cement a month. Only around 7,000 tons had ever reached him.

On 13 May, the very day North Africa was lost, Ammiraglio Arturo Riccardi, the head of the Regia Marina, the Italian navy, held a conference in Rome. The report on Sicily made for grim listening. Allied bombing was causing mayhem and had cut off almost all coastal traffic, which was principally how Sicily was supplied. By May 1943, almost all of Italy's merchant fleet was at the bottom of the Mediterranean; in fact, between November and the middle of May, Allied aircraft had sunk over 170 Axis ships and damaged a further 120, while Allied naval forces had sunk several hundred thousand tons of shipping too. Unlike the Allies, whose shipyards in the United States and Britain were building new vessels at an unprecedented rate, neither the Italians nor the Germans had any means of either building or bringing into the Mediterranean any more freighters. They were simply running out of shipping, which was why there were just forty small vessels left for maritime supply of Sicily. This meant that the population, already underfed at the best of times, was suffering even more severely from food shortages – and this went for the military as well as the civilians. It also meant there was little chance of Roatta getting the cement he needed – or much else besides, including boots, the shortage of which had repeatedly and bizarrely plagued the Italian army ever since it had gone to war. Many of the men in the coastal divisions were now wearing sandals or going barefoot – and so disabled by this that training had been affected. As it happened, there were warehouses full of boots; but they were all far too big and so had remained where they were.

The failure of Roatta's attempt to provide Sicily with adequate defences also explained why, at Gela, some bunkers were now being made of cardboard instead of concrete. Tenente Giuseppe Bruccoleri was an engineer whose particular task of setting up barrage balloons around Italy had

exempted him from overseas service; then his mother, who had a connection to Mussolini, wrote to Il Duce explaining that she had already
lost her husband to war in 1917, and needed her son back home in Gela.
Incredibly, Mussolini personally agreed to post Bruccoleri to Sicily,
where he was to oversee the elevation of barrage balloons at Augusta but
then could return to Gela – although he was to take his balloon company
with him and set up a telephone switchboard in his house, and help with
the preparation of local defences. This he did; and, since there was not
enough cement, he and his men made fake bunkers out of cardboard.
The idea was to fool the Allies into thinking Gela had stronger defences
than it did. Bruccoleri's story reveals one of two things: either Mussolini
really was going a little mad, or the Italian army had by now become so
institutionally broken that an officer could be sent home because his
mother had the influence to demand it and end up overseeing the construction of cardboard pillboxes. Whichever was the case, it was certainly
no way to fight a war.

Generale Roatta did his best, but even for a mover and shaker like
him, the current shortages and endless difficulties now facing the Italians were insurmountable. In the middle of May, he made a speech which
was thought to be just a little bit too disparaging about the Sicilians and
questioning their patriotism. The Comando Supremo, nervous that the
gulf between Sicily and the rest of Italy was already dangerously wide,
recalled him, appointing him to the top job in place of Ambrosio – which
was why he was in Rome talking to von Neurath, reflecting on the invidious situation in which they now found themselves.

The decision to push Roatta upstairs also revealed the stark limits to
Fascism's power; no German general would have been removed for fear of
worrying the locals, after all. In his place arrived Generale Alfredo Guzzoni, sixty-six years old and retired since May 1941 after a long career that
had begun in the Italo-Turkish War of 1911. Small, heavy-set and with
little obvious enthusiasm for the posting, he had never once before set foot
on Sicily. Nor had his new chief of staff, Colonnello Emilio Faldella, who
was much younger and more obviously energetic. In fact, Faldella and
Guzzoni had never met one another before either, so their appointments
were curious ones. It was now June, and as the Axis were all very well
aware, an Allied invasion, wherever it fell, could not be long in coming.

On 22 June, Generalleutnant Fridolin von Senger und Etterlin was summoned to see Hitler at the Berghof, the Führer's home in Berchtesgaden

in the Bavarian Alps. Recently returned from commanding 17. Panzer Division on the Eastern Front, von Senger had been enjoying a very rare stint of leave; now, on joining Hitler, Keitel and Warlimont at their daily situation conference, he was told he was being sent to Sicily as German liaison officer to the Italian Sixth Army. His brief was somewhat loose. Hitler talked at length about the possibilities of defending Sicily, should it come to that, but was still undecided about how many German units he should commit. Baade's newly constituted Division Kommando Sizilien was already there and a second division, the Hermann Göring Panzer Division, was also on its way. Others were potentially waiting in the wings. Generalleutnant Hans-Valentin Hube, one of Hitler's favourites, was also now in southern Italy. Due to the machinations of the Italian royal court and general staff, he reported, it was likely the Italians would soon defect and be out of the war – although it was felt the Allies had already missed the boat by not invading Sicily immediately after their landings in north-west Africa.

Afterwards, von Senger lunched with Warlimont, who believed that in the event of a major Allied attack on Sicily, it would be best to transfer the mass of Axis troops to the mainland. 'This appreciation and definition of my task,' noted von Senger, 'were not in line with those of Hitler.'

Von Senger was precisely the kind of military aristocrat Hitler loathed. The feeling was mutual. 'I detested him,' wrote the general, 'for all the misfortune he had brought upon my country.' Born near the Swiss border in 1891, Frido von Senger had been educated in part at Eton College in England and then as a Rhodes Scholar at Oxford, which had helped give him a slightly broader world-view than many of his peers. A fine military career had followed, initially in the First World War, then between the wars and now in this current conflict, where he had proved outstanding, both a deep student of warfare and also a compassionate and highly regarded general. A fine, indeed world-class, equestrian like Baade, he was also a devout Catholic, a cultured intellectual and, along with Kesselring, less prone than many senior Germans to regarding all Italians as feckless Latin types deserving only of deep contempt. This made him an ideal choice to play the go-between with German and Italian forces, regardless of what Hitler thought of him personally.

Three days later, von Senger was in Rome meeting with Kesselring, who talked far more optimistically about the chances of preventing an invasion of Sicily. The Allied assault on Dieppe back in August 1942 had been easily repulsed, he pointed out. Von Senger was not so sure; he felt the Allied victory in North Africa marked an entirely new phase of the war that did not augur well. On the other hand, he agreed that German forces could not fight two opponents – both the Allies and the Italians, should they defect. Von Senger would need to tread sensitively and carefully, Kesselring warned him; Sicily was a tinderbox, and the Germans would disregard the primacy of Guzzoni on the island at their peril. While Kesselring and von Senger were singing from the same hymn sheet with regard to relations with their Italian comrades in arms, the same could not be said of General von Richthofen, who told von Senger, in no uncertain terms, that the Luftwaffe was going its own way. Unlike Kesselring, Guzzoni or Mussolini, he was convinced Sardinia was the most likely target for the Allies and so had already begun moving his air forces there. 'All this revealed', commented von Senger, 'a regrettable divergence of views.' It also put Allied planning disagreements into perspective.

Once actually in Sicily, the first stop for von Senger was Enna, an ancient town perched on a flat mountaintop right in the geographical centre of the island. Viewed from the west, Enna was silhouetted against the sky like a fairytale medieval bastion, Etna looming beyond; it was here that Guzzoni had his headquarters. Accompanied at this first meeting by Kesselring, von Senger found Guzzoni realistic and candid. The coastal divisions were next to useless and could not be relied upon; the four regular divisions were better equipped but still not up to standard, although the Livorno was in the best shape with some motorization and half-decent officers and commanders. It became clear, however, that there was a divergence of views as to how best to repel the enemy if he did come. Guzzoni was for keeping the coastal batteries intact and out of range of large naval guns, but the German view was that it was far better to have as much fire-power forward as possible. The time to repel an invasion was right away, while the attackers were exposed, under strength and devoid of effective cover. Let the Allies secure a bridgehead and it would be all over. This difference of views was not resolved, while Kesselring's continued optimism also contrasted markedly with Guzzoni's more sceptical view. At least the meeting remained cordial. None the less, there was still much to iron out – not least exactly where the German divisions should be located.

Time, though, was running out. Unbeknown to the Axis officers as they sat in Guzzoni's palazzo up in Enna that day in late June, the Allies would be assaulting the island in just two weeks' time. The countdown was on.

CHAPTER 8

The Glitch in the Plan

O N FRIDAY, 11 JUNE 1943, at around 4 p.m., an American C-47 transport touched down at Luqa airfield on Malta. On board were two colonels of the 52nd Troop Carrier Wing, as well as two battalion commanders of the 505th Parachute Infantry Regiment and the regiment's commander, Colonel James M. Gavin. It had already been quite an eye-opening journey. The party had travelled from the 82nd Airborne Division's training base at Oujda in French Morocco, first to Tunis, where wrecks of German aircraft were still scattered all around the city's edge; from there they headed out low over Cap Bon, the site of the final Axis surrender on 13 May, and down the east coast to Monastir. There they met with their British counterparts, who seemed to possess an insouciance Gavin found both impressive and unnerving. 'We are sweating, tense, trying hard at everything we attempt,' he jotted in his diary. 'They are relaxed, appearing indifferent at times, no pressure, and everything seems to be getting done in tip-top shape.' Sleeping on their C-47 that night, they were up early the following morning to fly on to Tripoli, en route crossing over the Mareth Line, the scene of more fighting back in March. Briefings received and clearance given, they then headed on to Malta, via Pantelleria, which had fallen to the Allies that very same day.

On Malta they switched planes, boarding several Mosquitoes – the 'wooden wonders' of the RAF, multi-function aircraft capable of flying at over 400 mph. Since there was only room for two in a Mosquito, including the pilot, Gavin had to take on the role of navigator. Once dusk had fallen, off they went, hurtling over the sea towards Sicily, following the route his troops would take on 9 July, in four weeks' time, and simulating the same night-time conditions by flying at just 600 feet off the deck. As temporary navigator, Gavin found the drop zones – DZs – easily enough; then they flew inland towards Niscemi, a town perched on a ridge looking down over the Gela Plain towards the sea, before turning back and speeding by Ponte Olivo airfield, one of the key Allied targets for D-Day on Sicily. Flying separately in different Mosquitoes, his two battalion commanders, Lieutenant-Colonels Krause and Keens, sped directly over Ponte Olivo and were both shot at by flak. 'No one hit,' noted Gavin. 'We are all pleased with the results of our reconnaissance.'

Gavin and his men were to be the first American troops on Sicily, and had been given the mission of parachuting in ahead of the seaborne landings to capture and secure the Piano Lupo – the Plain of the Wolf – an upland area to the east of Gela – and both prevent the enemy from using it and also use it to their own advantage; it was always good to control the high ground. They were also to disrupt enemy lines of communication and then, on D-Day itself, help the attacking 1st Infantry Division in taking first Gela and then the Ponte Olivo airfield. The men, he knew, were well trained and physically fit and ready; but none of them had ever been in action before, and Gavin, outwardly confident, calm and collected, none the less worried privately. No person really knew how they would respond to being under fire until they faced this challenge for the first time. Doubts were inevitable. So too was fear. On 5 July, Gavin would find a man from the 2nd Battalion with a rifle across his knees and a bible in his hand, contemplating suicide. 'Said he was going to be killed anyway,' noted Gavin. 'So it goes.'

Jim Gavin was thirty-six years old but looked younger. He had formed the 505th Parachute Infantry Regiment from scratch, using training programmes he had devised, and applying tactics and operational techniques he had developed himself. Ambitious, extremely driven and a deep thinker about all aspects of modern warfare, he was a progressive officer hugely respected by his superiors, his peers and the men under his command. That he was a regimental commander at all was all the more remarkable because of his extremely humble beginnings. An orphan, he had been adopted at the age of two and brought up in the coal-mining town of Mount Carmel, Pennsylvania. It had not taken him long to realize a career as a miner was not for him, even though he had left school at just twelve years old and needed to get a job to help with the family coffers. At seventeen he had run away to New York, where he managed to blag his way into the army, even though he was under age. Posted to Panama, he read prodigiously and caught the eye of a senior NCO, who took the young man under his wing and encouraged him to apply to a local army school – an opportunity for Gavin to better himself, because from there the brightest and best students were encouraged to try for West Point. Catching up on his lost schooling in quick time, Gavin duly won a place at the army school in Corozal in the Canal Zone, and from there a place at West Point. In the land of opportunity, this orphan was grabbing it firmly with both hands.

In June 1929 he graduated as a second lieutenant in the US Army, continuing his studies as his fledgling career got under way. Stints in the infantry at home and then out in the Philippines were followed by a posting back to West Point and specifically to the Tactics faculty. He was still there when war broke out in Europe and, studying German operations in great detail, quickly became an advocate of airborne warfare. When the US Army decided to form its own parachute school at Fort Benning in June 1940, Gavin was among the early volunteers, eventually released from West Point in February the following year and soon making a name for himself. He was asked to write the airborne field manual, *FM 31-30: Tactics and Techniques of Air-Borne Troops,* which not only gathered together lessons from his studies of German – and also Soviet – airborne forces, but also drew on his own tactical studies and included information about how such troops should be structured and organized, and how and when they should be deployed. Far from a carbon copy of German doctrine, Gavin's vision was very much his own.

A stint at the US Army Command and General Staff College marked Gavin out for higher command and sure enough, in August 1942, he was made the first commander of the newly activated 505th Parachute Infantry Regiment (PIR). By April 1943, he reckoned he had licked his men into pretty good shape: they were physically and mentally tough, able to think on their feet, experienced at jumping out of aircraft and at a more advanced state of training than any other regiment – which was why they were sent to North Africa to join Major-General Matthew Ridgway's 82nd Airborne Division. Ridgway had it in mind that Gavin's 505th would spearhead the US airborne operations for HUSKY.

Gavin and his men had landed at Casablanca on 10 May and from there been posted to Oujda for further training. It had been accepted from an early stage of the HUSKY planning that airborne troops would play a key role in the invasion as a whole, not just the American sector.

Both paratroopers and glider-borne troops were, however, new elements in Allied planning. It's fair to say that both American and British war leaders had been somewhat dazzled by the cut, dash and sheer chutzpah of German airborne operations. Germany's glider troops had captured a seemingly impregnable Belgium fort, Eben Emael, back in May 1940, while their paratroopers had taken key bridges; later, German paratroopers had helped to capture Crete in May 1941. These airborne formations were regarded within the Wehrmacht and by their opponents with a certain amount of awe as highly trained special forces – an elite of shock troops that offered tactical flexibility in attack.

While the Allies quickly latched on to the successes of the German airborne forces, less analysis was given to their shortcomings. On 10 May 1940, at the start of the attack on France and the Low Countries, the Luftwaffe had lost a staggering 353 aircraft, most of which were delivering the airborne spearhead; this was the worst single day of losses for the Luftwaffe in the entire war to date, but was never much considered by Allied planners. Nor was the fact that a battalion of paratroopers was destroyed at Dombas in Norway in April 1940 by the Norwegian army, who were not widely recognized as being especially well equipped or well trained at the time. Nor was much attention paid to the fact that, for the most part, German airborne operations had been against low-quality troops, or that half the force of paratroopers sent to the assault on Crete had been lost over the island, despite the Germans' subsequent victory there.

The British, with Churchill as one of the loudest advocates, had quickly put plans together to create an airborne brigade of five thousand men; that had soon swollen to double the size. In October 1941, the 1st Airborne Division had been created and more recently, in April 1943, a second division, the 6th, was also formed. In the United States, the first airborne formation had been the 501st Parachute Infantry Unit; in March 1942 the 82nd Airborne Division had been formed, followed in August the same year by the 101st, and in May 1943 by two more airborne divisions. Both the British and American armies were also developing glider-borne and parachute units concurrently. A huge amount of time, effort, money and training had gone into creating forces that so far had not really been tested in battle. Airborne troops had been dropped as part of the Allied invasion of north-west Africa, but that had been a total fiasco, while a British paratrooper operation to capture an enemy airfield in Tunisia had also achieved absolutely nothing except the loss of a few good men and a very long and risky walk back to friendly lines. In terms of glider operations, there had been just one, by the British, into Norway in November 1942. All the men aboard had been killed, or captured and subsequently executed.

Much discussion had taken place over exactly how these rapidly growing airborne forces should be used for HUSKY. In the early plans, the British and Americans were to land one after the other, which had meant all transport aircraft would be available to lift airborne troops for both. That all changed once the final plan had been accepted, at which point a certain amount of frantic jockeying for position had taken place. General Ridgway, concerned his airborne forces might have to play second fiddle to the British because of a shortage of transport aircraft, went straight to Patton, who, as he had hoped, demanded and was given a paratroop jump ahead of the seaborne assault.

Ridgway's concerns had been understandable. The British, who had taken the top spots in command of all three services for HUSKY, had also, from early May, secured the senior airborne command too. This was given to Major-General Frederick 'Boy' Browning, dapper, dashing, and married to the best-selling novelist Daphne du Maurier. Browning had been commander of the British 1st Airborne Division, but had since been bumped up to become Airborne Advisor to Allied Forces Headquarters; for all Alexander's incredible experience, airborne operations were entirely new to him and almost as new to Eisenhower too. Clearly, airborne forces were a growing element in Allied plans, and there was also an implicit understanding they would be used to spearhead the cross-Channel invasion the following year too, so Browning's role was an important one.

The trouble was, no one had much idea about how airborne operations should best be used. Young, ambitious commanders were inevitably drawn to the new airborne forces precisely because they were new, at the cutting edge of war. There had also been an understanding from the outset that airborne troops were special – an elite force. All these men were volunteers, not conscripts thrown together. They trained harder, were physically fitter and, crucially, were highly motivated, which meant they were far more likely to be able to use their initiative, an essential attribute that particularly marked out the better troops from the rank and file. Unlike the vast majority of soldiers fighting in the Allied armies, who simply longed to keep their heads down and get through, airborne soldiers wanted to be fine soldiers. They wanted to be the best, and generally speaking thought of themselves in such terms. Their commanders understood this attitude, and the prestige and accolades that would potentially follow from it. Ambition was not a fault; but it did mean there was a level of competitiveness among the airborne forces that was, perhaps, more prominent than in other parts of the armed services, pitting one regiment against another, paratroopers against glider-borne troops, British versus American. Ridgway's concern had been that with Browning, a Brit, as the new senior airborne advisor, it would be the British 1st Airborne, rather than the US 82nd Airborne, who would get first dibs at the precious C-47 fleet.

As it happened, however, he need not have worried, because Boy Browning's replacement at 1st Airborne was the newly promoted Major-General George 'Hoppy' Hopkinson, a man of enormous charm and voracious ambition, but less for paratroopers than for glider-borne operations. Before taking command of 1st Airborne, Hopkinson had been commander of the 1st Airlanding Brigade, and to say he was messianic about glider operations would be an understatement. Hopkinson had always been a man in a hurry. Twice he had resigned from the army because of a lack of opportunity and because the rate of peacetime advancement had been too slow. He liked being in charge and leading new units – such as the specialist GHQ unit, codenamed 'Phantom', that was supposed to be the British Expeditionary Force commander Lord Gort's eyes and ears on the ground back in 1940. After Dunkirk, Hopkinson lobbied hard to be allowed to develop Phantom into a permanent unit; he got his way and it became the GHQ Liaison Regiment, although after the invasion scare had evaporated, Hopkinson himself lost command. Then came another opportunity with the development of airborne forces and in particular, for him, of gliders. Relentless ambition and a gift of the gab unquestionably helped him move swiftly into the top job at 1st Airborne in early May 1943, and with this promotion he was determined to become the champion of glider-borne forces. The trouble was, so tunnel-visioned had he become in his enthusiasm that he had failed to realize his force was not remotely ready for deployment.

By this point, Britain had been at war long enough to have sorted much of the wheat from the chaff when it came to generalship. The Americans, too, after North Africa, were starting to work out who was good and who needed sending home. The airborne forces were still so new, however, and those making the decisions on fresh appointments had their eyes on so many other matters besides, that it was not hard for an individual like Hopkinson, who talked a fantastic game, to get a divisional command in an untested arm. The same factors explained why he was able to convince those who might have known better – had they really thought about it rationally – that it was a good idea to send very badly trained glider pilots across a huge expanse of sea, at night, in gliders they were not used to operating, to land very close to the sea on ground that was both rocky and contained a lot of stone walls.

It's clear that from the moment Hopkinson was appointed commander of 1st Airborne he did all he could to avoid being in a room with Browning, because the latter, when still commanding the division, had strongly advocated using paratroopers on the night of the invasion to capture a key bridge south of Syracuse, the Ponte Grande, and then storm the city itself. Instead, rather as Ridgway had done with Patton, Hopkinson managed to secure a face-to-face audience with Montgomery and persuade him instead to use glider-borne troops both for this key objective and then to attack a second bridge further north, at Augusta, the following night. Paratroopers, he cautioned, would not be able to drop with the concentrated accuracy needed; what's more, only with gliders could the invaders achieve the kind of tactical surprise needed to capture a bridge intact before the enemy realized what was happening and blew it up first. Paratroopers would be better used for a later objective, the Primosole Bridge, which led into the Plain of Catania – by which time the cat, of course, would be already out of the bag.

He might have had a point had there been plenty of the right gliders available, along with lots of highly skilled and trained pilots, and had he himself any experience of mounting such an operation. But not a single one of those criteria had been met. As it happened, the Glider Pilot Regiment had a new commander in Lieutenant-Colonel George Chatterton – the previous CO having been lost in the ill-fated Norway venture the previous November. Competent, intelligent and, above all, a realist, Chatterton had been tearing his hair out in frustration since being warned earlier in the year to get his men ready for overseas deployment. The unit was still new; and although the British had developed the Horsa glider, there had yet to be enough of them for his small force to train adequately. It was all well and good being sent overseas, but what about training? And what about the gliders that would be needed? His questions were met with obfuscation or, worse, silence.

On 3 April, Chatterton had finally been told the regiment were to be posted to North Africa. Still no one could tell him how many gliders might be available, and he boarded their ship with his men none the wiser. Most of his pilots had between six and twelve hours' flying time logged over the previous six months; it was as though the British had returned to the bad old days of the last war when they'd sent young pilots up in their Sopwith Camels with just a handful of hours in their log-books. They reached Oran in Algeria on 22 April after two weeks at sea. 'I was full of foreboding,' said Chatterton. 'There was indeed a great gulf between those in authority and myself as to our proper role in battle.' That was something of an understatement.

In Algeria, Chatterton discovered to his horror that there were still no gliders, which meant his 240 pilots had now not flown for at least three months. It was a ludicrous situation, and makes Hopkinson's manic lob-bying of Montgomery all the more bizarre, because by 7 May, when he had his audience with the Eighth Army commander, he would have been well aware of how deplorable the state of glider pilot training was and also of the total lack of any gliders with which to hurriedly lick them-selves into shape. Neither factor was mentioned to Monty. As far as Montgomery was concerned, airborne forces were to be used, and here, in front of him, was the commander of the 1st Airborne Division advis-ing him on how best they should be deployed. It did not occur to him that Hopkinson could be so woefully reckless as to promote something for which his men were ill-prepared and unequipped.

Within a day of his meeting with Montgomery, Hopkinson had briefed Chatterton and shown him photographs of the planned landing zones, with their rocks, walls and almost total lack of any kind of flat and open ground.

'You know, sir,' Chatterton interjected, 'that the pilots have had no flying practice for at least three months and little or no experience of night flying at all?'

Hopkinson brushed aside his concerns. The Americans were going to provide both tugs and gliders.

'American gliders?' Chatterton asked.

'Yes, what difference will that make?' Hopkinson replied.

'Difference, sir?' Chatterton answered, scarcely believing what he was hearing. 'Why, they hardly know our own gliders, let alone American!'

Hopkinson then warned Chatterton that if he didn't start playing ball, he would be sacked and sent home. After a short consideration, Chat-terton decided, with a heavy heart, that it would be better to stand by the men, even though he thought Hopkinson's plan insane.

When the American Waco gliders did eventually turn up, they were in crates spread over a number of different ports, and when they were unpacked, it was discovered many had suffered damage during the crossing. Key assembly tools were also lacking – as was any sense of urgency. At Blida, for example, assembling the gliders was sixth priority, and the task of putting together the twenty-five crated gliders delivered there was given to one officer and twenty GIs, none of whom had any previous glider assembly experience. By 25 May, a little over six weeks before HUSKY D-Day, only thirty gliders had been assembled. Eventually, as it was at last realized a crisis was looming, glider assembly was given greater priority, so that by 13 June some 346 gliders had been put together and delivered to the airfield at La Sénia. Many were then damaged by strong winds and so grounded for repairs, causing further training delays. By 30 June, most of the gliders had developed weaknesses in the tail wiring, and so all were grounded yet again for a further three days.

In addition, thirty-six Horsa gliders, which were quite different and with which the British pilots were familiar, were being flown out from England twelve at a time by A Flight, 295 Squadron, using ageing Halifax bombers. From the outset, the operation was beset with problems. First, 295 Squadron did not fly Halifaxes and so the pilots and crews had to convert in quick order. Three pilots didn't cut the mustard in time and a fourth crashed in bad weather. Towing the Horsas all the way from England to North Africa took around seventy-seven hours for each Halifax and crew, an amount of flying time that meant the Halifaxes required a huge amount of servicing; but the stores for this, although sent ahead, had not arrived in North Africa when the Halifaxes turned up with their Horsas. Then there was the added problem of extreme turbulence while flying over the Atlas mountains, which did nothing to improve the state of either the Halifaxes or the gliders they were towing.

In all, one Halifax and Horsa were shot down en route, another pairing disappeared entirely, one Halifax crashed, one Horsa became detached and fell into the sea, another was brought back and another had to be written off on arrival. One pilot suffered six engine failures during the six weeks of ferrying flights, others experienced several – and almost all were due to oil leaks. As one of the ferrying pilots, Flight Lieutenant Tommy Grant, noted, 'An oil leak may easily force the Halifax to jettison his glider, and two oil leaks on a long sea journey may cause complete loss of the Halifax.' One of the Horsa pilots – Chatterton's adjutant, Captain Alistair Cooper – had been attacked over the Bay of Biscay by Focke-Wulf Condors, released himself from the tug and ditched in the Atlantic, been picked up, sailed back to England, collected another Horsa and ferried it out to North Africa. By the time he walked into Chatterton's Nissen hut, it was almost time to fly to Sicily. Although an extremely competent pilot, he had zero hours' night-flying experience.

The net result was that by the beginning of July only nineteen out of the thirty-six Horsas had been delivered, and there was almost no time at all for training in flying them loaded even by day, let alone by night. Nor had there been much training on the Wacos. Chatterton had first flown one on 14 May, and on the basis of this a rough training syllabus was prepared. His men flew as much as they could, but that was not saying very much. By 9 July, Chatterton's glider pilots each had an average of 1.2 hours of night flying and just four and a half hours of flying time in Wacos. It was nowhere near enough. But the die had been cast.

A further operation was being planned for the early hours of 10 July, and that was to take out an Italian coastal defence battery on Capo Murro di Porco – the Cape of the Snout of the Pig – which lay on a peninsula that stretched out into the sea directly south of Syracuse. This battery, which contained four guns of what appeared from aerial photographs to be at least 150mm calibre, posed a serious threat both to the invasion beaches immediately to the south and to an assault on Syracuse. It was essential they were destroyed, and in quick order, before the landings occurred.

The men given this task were some of what had been 1 SAS – the Special Air Service – who had caused havoc against the enemy the previous year in Libya. Operating independently and deep behind enemy lines, they had made a series of daring raids on enemy landing grounds, supply columns and other targets. However, since their maverick commander, Lieutenant-Colonel David Stirling, had been captured in January in Tunisia, an environment not so well suited to such hit-and-run tactics, the men of the SAS had been at something of a loose end, sent back to their training camp at Kabrit in Egypt, their future uncertain.

Among those wondering whether he would ever see any action was 21-year-old Lieutenant Peter Davis. He had been posted to the Middle East straight from officer training back in England the previous autumn, and after being sent to the vast Infantry Base Depot next to the Suez Canal at Geneifa had volunteered to join C Squadron, 1st Special Service Regiment, which despite its name had in fact been at the time the only squadron in this still embryonic unit. Set up the previous summer, initially to help develop guerrilla warfare on the Syrian border with Turkey in case Rommel's forces should reach the Suez Canal, it too had been at a loose end and so had eventually been merged into 1 SAS. By March 1943, however, rumours were flying around that the SAS would be broken up entirely. Stirling was a prisoner of war, while his right-hand man, Major Paddy Mayne, had gone on a drunken spree in Cairo, had had one too many fights and bust up one too many bars, and had ended up in a cell.

Davis had first met Mayne soon after he'd been released and had returned to Kabrit. Already, Mayne was something of a legend – a former rugby international for both Ireland and the British Lions, he was known for his utter fearlessness, stamina, and imperturbability in the face of extreme danger. Davis had been struck first by Mayne's sheer size. 'His form seemed to fill the whole tent,' he noted. 'Standing well over six feet, every part of his body was built on a proportionately generous scale: his wrists were twice the size of those of a normal man, while his fists seemed to be as large as a polo ball.' At the time, he had been wearing a reddish beard and had looked at Davis with keen, piercing blue eyes – but then had spoken in a soft voice, with a hint of an Irish brogue, that was totally at odds with his immense physicality. Davis thought he seemed rather shy, albeit perfectly courteous and charming.

As it happened, Davis was about to see a lot more of him because 1 SAS was then split into two, 250 of them – including himself – joining the newly created Special Raiding Squadron under Mayne's command, and the remaining 150 making up the new Special Boat Squadron under Major George Jellicoe, another desert stalwart and son of the First World War admiral. Both units were to take part in HUSKY: the SBS to launch diversionary raids on Sardinia, the SRS to attack the battery at Capo Murro di Porco – not that any of them knew that then. The idea was for the SRS to parachute into battle, and the SBS to get there by sea.

The SRS was, from the outset, Mayne's unit, although on paper they were answerable to a colonel commanding HQ Raiding Forces, who arrived at Kabrit and gave a speech that impressed no one very much. 'It hardly mattered,' noted Davis, 'as we hardly saw anything of him. To all intents and purposes Paddy was the boss and took no orders from anyone.' Mayne's mission was to shape this new unit and train it as he saw fit, so long as the training involved stifling heat, endurance, scaling cliffs, close-quarters fighting and firing mortars. He decided to divide his men into three troops of three sections each, which were divided down again into half-sections and then three-man teams. Davis was put in No. 2

Troop under Captain Harry Poat, whom he liked and respected immediately. In fact, he liked all his new fellows.

On 20 March, Mayne had briefed his men in a soft, faltering voice that
could barely be heard. They were, he told them, in for a very intense period
of training – for what, no one knew, not even he; but it was going to be
important. Within a week, after one last drunken party, they set off for
Palestine, where they began training with a 45-mile march in oven-like
heat. Over the next two months, there was no let-up; at the beginning of
June, by now physically honed, they boarded the converted Irish Sea ferry
HMS *Ulster Monarch* to begin a month of intensive training in seaborne
assault, involving getting ashore in LCAs – landing craft, assault – climbing cliffs and carrying out night-time research assaults; plans for a parachute
assault had been quietly dropped. That this was the kind of operation for
which Jellicoe's SBS had been established was never mentioned. At the end
of June came further endurance marches and experiments with Benzedrine, an amphetamine – 'speed' – that was trialled on No. 3 Troop. Mayne
had been quite impressed with its effect: the men had been dragging their
heels, but after taking the drug perked up enormously, picking up their feet,
swinging their arms and singing merrily. Finally came their last training
exercise: a mock assault on a British anti-aircraft battery 2 miles or so from
where the *Ulster Monarch* was docked. 'The attack', noted Peter Davis, 'was
an outstanding success in every way. I do not think it any exaggeration to
say that those gunners were completely at a loss.'

By early June, then, the Allies had a decent number of supremely
well-trained and highly motivated troops. There were also British Commandos, created and designed for raiding operations. Really, these men
were among the very best soldiers anywhere in the world at this time. It
was in the delivery of these troops where differences emerged, for while
the SRS and Commandos were in pretty safe hands with the navy, the
same could not be said for Allied paratroopers, whether those under
Gavin's command or the British training for later operations on the
Primosole Bridge; for while the state of glider training was absolutely
deplorable, training for the troop carrier commands was hardly sufficient either. In part this was because delivering paratroopers into combat
was just one of their many roles; transports were constantly busy, especially given that the Allies were preparing for HUSKY from bases
stretched as far apart as Palestine, Malta and French Morocco.

It meant, though, that troop carrier aircrew simply had not had the same levels of combined training as had those being delivered into battle by the navy. This amounted to a grave flaw in the development of the airborne arm: that while so much thought had been given to training the elite troops themselves, the same concentration had not been applied to those charged with delivering them to the battle zone. The British had not developed a troop transport, and while the Americans had success-fully developed the DC-3 into the C-47 – called the Dakota by the British – some important adaptations had not been made, such as pro-viding the military aircraft with self-sealing fuel tanks, which helped prevent the fatal spread of fire should one of them get hit. Furthermore, the cream of the crop among pilots and navigators tended to fly fighters or bombers, not transport aircraft. This led to the paradoxical situation where some of the very best troops were being delivered into combat by among the least trained and least skilled pilots. There were, of course, exceptions; but 52nd Troop Carrier Wing, who would be delivering the 505th Parachute Combat Team into Sicily, had conducted only two night-time parachute drop exercises. Of these, one had become badly dispersed while the second went rather better; it was hard to know what could be gleaned from these results, but even an optimist could only conclude they now had a fifty–fifty chance of getting it right on the night. A better option would be to have the troops dropped in daylight, but that simply wasn't possible. The invasion fleet needed to approach the coast under cover of darkness because of the threat of enemy aircraft and coastal batteries, which meant the invasion had to be launched at very first light. The whole point of the airborne operations was to take out strongpoints and secure ground before the landings. And that meant dropping in darkness.

Colonel Jim Gavin had wavered continually during this training and waiting period. Jump exercises on to the hard, stony desert near their training base in Morocco had led to one too many injuries, which was frustrating. His men were in fine fettle; but despite this, one moment he felt confident, the next dark doubts crept into his mind. 'I feel quite cer-tain that I will also get an opportunity for advancement if I survive,' he confided to his diary. 'I may not. I am going to keep the parachute tradi-tion in mind. Chances will be taken, risks run, and everything ventured. If I survive, well and good. If I am killed at least I have been true to myself, my convictions . . . At the moment, I haven't the slightest fear.'

He worried, too, about his subordinate commanders. One in particu-lar, Major Gray of the 2nd Battalion, troubled him. Gavin just didn't feel he was cutting it. Despite these concerns, he'd not thought to relieve him before the assault; but then Gray had gone AWOL for a few days. As it happened, he had been on a legitimate fact-finding operation – but for Gavin it was enough to wield the axe. 'More bad judgement than AWOL,' Gavin had conceded. 'I should have replaced him in the States.' Gray had been one of just three battalion commanders in the 505th, and Gavin had to feel totally confident in all of them. Major Mark Alexander, the highly competent battalion XO – deputy – took over the command on 21 June. Despite Gavin's doubts, Gray had been popular with the men, making Alexander's task, just a couple of weeks before the jump into action, an invidious one. 'It really put pressure on me,' said Alexander, 'as I had a lot to do to get on top of things. There were a lot of good men in the battalion, but some of them were still Gray's men and I had to fight that issue because they didn't understand why he was being relieved.'

None the less, Alexander, at thirty-one, was older than most, tall and athletic, and had a natural aura of authority; he was also, like Gavin, the kind of man who would never dream of asking any of his men to do something he would not do himself. Gavin gave him a very able West Pointer, Captain Jack Norton, as his new XO, and together the two men swiftly got the battalion back on an even keel. Even so, Alexander had not been too happy with how the night exercises had gone, and so had spoken to the commander of the troop carrier group that would be taking them to Sicily. No matter where they were dropped, Alexander emphasized, he wanted to make sure the battalion was dropped together. That way, they would at least have the opportunity to organize themselves and fight as a battalion. It was hardly a resounding vote of confidence in the Troop Carrier Wing.

Then there was the time it took to move everyone and all their equipment up to Tunisia. The move from Oujda in western Algeria had begun on 16 June, by which time Gavin had once again been racked by doubts. It was too late for any more practice jumps, however, as the move was not expected to be completed until 3 July. By that time they were bivouacked about 20 miles north of the ancient city of Kairouan and 10 miles south of Enfidaville, where just a couple of months earlier there had been fierce fighting. Battle debris was still strewn all over the place. 'The loneliest sight in the world,' Gavin jotted in his diary, 'is to come across a lone grave in the desert marked only with a simple wooden cross and a rusty helmet.' He was keenly aware that one day very soon, that could easily be him.

CHAPTER 9

Crescendo in the Air

TENENTE LIVIO MESSINA'S LIFE had improved dramatically in recent weeks: he now had a woman to sleep with regularly. Ever since arriving on Sicily, he'd attended dances and chatted up as many girls as he could but, maddeningly, there had always been some chaperone or other to get in the way – a mother, or brother, or cousin. To make matters worse, some of his fellow officers, billeted with families where the men were away with the war, were boasting of their conquests. In the end, he'd decided to pay for it instead. Prostitutes were tolerated within the camp on the unwritten understanding that such visits were discreet and that there was no trouble. The men were still expected to treat the prostitutes well and with courtesy.

So he was thrilled when, having forked out a fee for a night in his tent with a lady from Calabria, she came back for a second night at no further cost. And then another night. Soon she was visiting him several times a week, ensuring that he was having some fun of an evening but was not a ducat worse off as a result. It had been making him tired, though, which had not escaped the notice of his battalion commander, Tenente-Colonnello Osvaldo Alessi, a veteran of the last war.

'What do you do at night?' he asked Messina one day. Messina replied that he slept. 'That's not true,' Alessi told him. 'Make sure you get some proper sleep.' Messina later learned from his lover that she charged everyone else, including Colonnello Alessi; but she continued to sleep with him for free.

While Messina spent more time thinking about his sex life than any prospective invasion, others on Sicily – and beyond – were confronting the growing might of the Allied air forces and the destruction they were bringing. The reach of the bombers extended well beyond the island; aerial bombardment was also hitting the northern industrial heartlands of Milan and Turin hard. There were shortages of absolutely everything from soap and medicines to fuel, shoes and food, especially in the cities. The southern cities such as Naples and Taranto were also suffering badly, while now that the bombing of Sicily was escalating, the levels of destitution in Palermo, Catania and Messina were appalling.

Magda Ceccarelli de Grada was a poet living in Milan, married to a brilliant but rather unsuccessful artist, Raffaele de Grada. She had been to Palermo the previous September to see her son, who was stationed there, and she was shocked. 'Palermo has things of indescribable beauty,' she recorded in her diary, 'but they are all in streets of irredeemable filth; and the ragged people that stream by put the loveliness in the shade for me, because the grimness, the disease and the poverty evident in their rags is totally overwhelming.' What particularly distressed her were the number of emaciated children, dressed in tatters, ribs showing but with bloated stomachs. And forced to beg. 'There were tears behind my glasses,' she wrote, 'and my heart ached.' To her disgust, the Germans she saw looked well fed and healthy.

Giacomo Garra was also increasingly aware how Italian fortunes had plummeted. Although he was still too young to fight himself, his brothers and cousins wrote of the hardships and in their letters hinted at the terrible trauma of being on the receiving end of bombing – one brother, Vincenzo, was in Naples, and another, Alfio, was in Messina. At Christmas his cousin had visited, having returned from Russia. Giacomo had asked him whether they were winning the war. 'I would not say so,' his cousin had replied.

Palermo, along with Catania and Messina, looked considerably worse now. The city was to be hit 69 times in all; Messina, 58; Augusta, 43; Trapani, 41; and Catania an incredible 87 times. Rubble littered the streets, electricity barely functioned at all, and night after night the civilian populations were forced to take to the growing numbers of public shelters. Poverty, homelessness, hunger and a growing lack of medical supplies were all taking their toll.

One town that had escaped much of the bombing was Avola on the south-eastern coast, a small fishing port of only a few thousand people – among them Michele Piccione, just eighteen years old, who had been called up into the Italian army and posted to the 4° Reggimento

Autisti – the 4th Driver Regiment. However, he was classified as a 'student sergeant' and so on 12 June was posted home to study for and sit a series of exams. His father, a policeman, was away serving in Brindisi; Michele worried for him and for his whole family, especially now that the number of Allied aircraft flying over was so obviously increasing. There was definitely something in the air. One night, he saw a red light a short way out to sea, and the following morning soldiers found two small boats abandoned on the beach. 'These kinds of happenings,' he noted, 'together hearing shooting going on and so on, were making us feel increasingly tense.'

Meanwhile, it was up to the Axis air forces to try to stop the bombing, although the Luftwaffe on Sicily were still in bad odour with the high command. Following the disastrous attempted attack on the low-flying American bomber formation on 25 June, it wasn't only the General der Jagdflieger, Adolf Galland, who had blown his top. So too had the commander-in-chief of the Luftwaffe, Reichsmarschall Hermann Göring. Major Macky Steinhoff had been asleep when Galland had rung, his voice now placatory and even apologetic. He had, he told Steinhoff, just received a teleprint from Göring. He wasn't to get agitated. 'Take no action for the moment,' Galland said, 'but I've got to inform you.' The missive stated that earlier that day the fighters had failed in their duty. 'One pilot from each of the fighter *Geschwader* taking part', Galland read out, 'will be tried by court martial for cowardice in the face of the enemy.'

Cowardice in the face of the enemy. Steinhoff had barely believed what he'd been hearing. Soon after, having gathered as much composure as he'd been able to summon, he'd spoken to his pilots. There had been stunned silence as they'd looked at him in equal disbelief. Then Major Freytag raised his glass. 'Well, well,' he said. 'Let's drink to that.' Steinhoff could have hugged him.

What little faith the senior pilots had once had in Göring had been lost a long time before; but to be here, in Sicily, beleaguered, abandoned by the top brass, undersupplied yet expected to achieve miracles, and then to receive this appalling slap in the face seemed to Steinhoff an insult too far. Not one of his pilots was older than him, and he was still only twenty-nine. Nor had it helped that two dozen Italian fighters that day had confidently claimed shooting down seven Fortresses for certain and probably two more. That in reality only five had suffered damage and none had been shot down was apparently neither here nor there.

As it happened, the court martials never took place; Galland saw to it that once Göring's ire had been spent, the matter had been quietly forgotten. There were, at least, some small advantages of being far away from Berlin. In any case, Luftflotte II needed every pilot it had. Even so, the Jagdwaffe – the fighter force – all got to hear of this grave insult and morale, already low, sank further. This grievous slight had also been a humiliation for many men who had been flying almost without respite since the start of the war. The fighter pilots had been the shining knights not just of the Luftwaffe but of the Third Reich itself – and yet now seemed to be the whipping boys for the failures of Göring and the Nazi leadership.

The changes at the top had been disruptive, too. Theo Osterkamp had been a popular commander of fighters, so much so that he'd been affectionately known as 'Uncle Theo'. Galland had an incredible reputation as a combat leader, but he had no experience of the Mediterranean air war, and while he might have been instinctively sympathetic to his fighters, he had been given a stern talking-to by General von Richthofen, who was as hard as steel, utterly ruthless, and also new to the theatre and to commanding Fliegerkorps II. 'Discussed the whole fighter problem with Galland,' he noted in his diary on 30 June. 'Agreement, Galland has dealt sharply with fighter pilots who recently have attacked poorly or not at all.' A newer, tougher, less *sympathisch* Jafü was really not what the fighter pilots needed right now, while the demands of his new role also threatened to take the shine off the high esteem in which Galland had been held as a free-thinking and outspoken fighter pilot.

Part of the frustration of the Luftwaffe command arose from the powerful effect the increasingly dominant Allied air forces were having on their operational capability. Increasingly impotent, they had yet to accept the massive change in shape of this Second World War that had come first with the Allies' naval dominance in the Mediterranean and now with their command of the skies. In the Blitzkrieg years, it had been the German army, in tandem with the spearheaders of the Luftwaffe, that had ruled the roost; but the subtle change that had occurred over the Western Desert during the summer of 1942 had become a huge and decisive shift in power by the time of the Axis defeat in Tunisia. For Göring and the Nazi leadership, and for senior commanders like General von Richthofen, it was easier to point the finger of blame at pilots than it was to accept that the war was now going catastrophically badly because of appalling decisions and errors at the very top.

Certainly, the sustained air attacks were being badly felt by the Axis. On 22 June all Luftwaffe bombers were moved from Sicily to mainland Italy and Sardinia; the Regia Aeronautica had already moved theirs. This meant bombers now had further to travel if they were to strike back at the Allies, which in turn made them less effective. Now, only fighters remained on Sicily, although, unlike the Regia Aeronautica, the Luftwaffe was still replacing aircraft that were being lost. More than 40 per cent of German fighter production in May and June was sent to the Mediterranean, and more aircraft were drawn from the Eastern Front and sent south. It still wasn't enough, though; and for fighter commanders like Steinhoff, a bigger issue was the shortages – of properly trained new pilots, of ground crew and of spare parts. Aircraft alone were not enough to stem the tide that was flowing against them.

A big factor in the shortage of parts was the pasting the Axis lines of supply were taking. Because fuel was running short, German and Italian forces were heavily dependent not only on shipping but also on railways; and the rail links in Sicily had been badly hit. In Palermo, the marshalling yards had been smashed, with seven locomotives destroyed and a further twenty damaged. The repair sheds had also been hit. At Caltanissetta, past Enna on the main line from Catania, all lines had been put out of action. Catania itself, from where lines ran to the north, south and west, had also been hammered. Rail traffic there had almost ground to a halt, while bottlenecks had built up at Messina.

By the beginning of July, the pre-invasion air plan was in its crescendo, the Allied air forces about to embark on the final phase – smashing Axis airfields, especially on Sicily, as hard as possible. Mary Coningham's Tactical Air Force had been rested after Pantelleria but was now back on operations along with Doolittle's Strategic Air Forces, while Malta was packed with fighter squadrons. Two new strips had been built on Malta itself, while American engineers had hacked out an entirely new airfield in just seventeen days on the smaller neighbouring island of Gozo.

Also now in Malta was Wing Commander Cocky Dundas, who after safely delivering his Typhoon to Cairo had been ordered back to see Coningham and had been told he was to rejoin 324 Wing after all as 'Acting Wing Commander, Flying' until a permanent replacement had been found. Flying out to the island on 11 June, he'd discovered the four squadrons of the wing had been joined by a fifth. In all, there were some twenty Spitfire squadrons, five night-fighter squadrons and various reconnaissance and transport aircraft, and that was not including the

Americans now on Gozo. Despite this density of aircraft, the Axis air forces made no attempt to attack Malta. What had been a daily occurrence the previous year had dwindled to nothing; after all, how were Axis air forces supposed to attack an island bursting at the seams with radar, anti-aircraft guns and, especially, hundreds of fighter planes?

Meanwhile, over in Tunisia, the 99th Fighter Squadron were busy flying escort missions for Spaatz's day bombers. On 2 July, they were sent over to Sicily to cover the backs of bombers as they pasted the Axis airfields at Castelvetrano. It was a crystal-clear day, with no sign of the haze that often shrouded Sicily, and Lieutenant Charlie Dryden could see the island spread out before him, then the airfields below. For some reason Dryden couldn't fathom the bombers circled the airfield before dropping their bombs, by which time he could see the tell-tale clouds of dust as enemy fighters scrambled 8,000 feet below him. He could feel himself tense as he watched them take to the air. Soon, he felt certain, he would be facing their fury, and in combat, pilot against pilot, for the first time. He felt himself begin to sweat.

Dryden was flying wingman to Lieutenant Bill Campbell. As a whole, the task of the fighters was to circle the bombers in a wide loop then, once they'd delivered their loads, to cover their return and prevent any enemy fighters from trying to attack or chase after them. But his specific task was to stick to Bill Campbell like glue – and because they were flying comparatively low, it wasn't long before the enemy fighters were among them. Desperately trying to keep off Campbell's port wing while also scanning the sky, he spotted two Me109s bearing down on them from behind and called out over his radio for Campbell to break.

To his horror, Campbell appeared not to have heard him. With no time for call signs, he yelled, 'Campbell, break right, NOW!' Still no reaction; so Dryden pushed open the throttle and turned into the tightest turn he could manage to face their attackers. Red streaks of tracer zipped past his cockpit, but as soon as he had a bead he opened fire himself, and saw from his own tracer that some had hit home. It did the trick – the two Me109s broke off their attack, their bellies flashing past him – but it meant Dryden had left his wingman and now he realized he was on his own – something they had all been warned to avoid at all costs. Pulling into a tight left turn, he swiftly scanned the sky and, spotting a lone P-40 some 500 feet below, dived down to latch on to him instead.

As he did so, he realized his new friend was also under attack from two more Me109s. 'Here's a chance to save a Yank, get one, maybe two victories,' he thought to himself, 'and be the first of the 99th to down a Nazi in aerial combat.' With a surge of adrenalin, he dived, allowed for deflection and opened fire, peppering the rear of the two aircraft, even though he'd intended to hit the lead one. In the heat of the moment, however, he'd briefly forgotten his own tail and suddenly saw tracer whizzing past him again. Another tight left turn; but his pursuer was skilled and had now positioned himself to fly outside Dryden's own turn, having taken his first shot, and was pushing him around the sky, so that in quick time, because of the geometry of their different turning circles, he had him in his sights again. Now Dryden saw the pilot was flying a Macchi 202, not a Messerschmitt. Suddenly there was a bang, and the aircraft juddered as a cannon shell took a bite out of his port wing. Dryden quickly prayed to God and it seemed He answered because a moment later another P-40 was climbing and opening fire on the Italian fighter, who broke and turned away.

That was not the end of it, however, for as Dryden and his new-found flying buddy flew clear of Sicily and headed back to Cap Bon they were attacked again, this time by Messerschmitts on their tail. They turned in towards the Me109s, and so began a game of cat and mouse as the Kittyhawks circled again and again, but with Dryden and his new mate inching ever closer to home all the time. After about ten minutes of this, another Macchi 202 – or was it the same one? – joined in. 'Twisting and turning,' noted Dryden, 'breaking left then right to defend against each pass, then running west, balls to the wall, until the next pass, we finally reach Pantelleria.'

So relieved was Dryden as he approached their airstrip that he had a huge urge to perform a victory roll. At the last moment, he decided against it, and back on the ground was glad good sense had won, as the aileron on his damaged wing was hanging by a thread – one that would surely have snapped under the pressure of such a manoeuvre. 'Needless to say,' wrote Dryden, 'I thank God for my deliverance and for the "something" that had told me: just land the plane – don't show off.'

Back on Malta, Cocky Dundas was having a little bit of trouble with the 111 Squadron CO, George Hill, a tough and aggressive Canadian who was always eager to get stuck into the enemy the moment he saw them. Dundas, however, had learned that a wing formation of several squadrons together was only really effective if held tight together so the wing commander could direct them from the air into battle at the right moment. Tearing off broke that cohesion and could potentially jeopardize an advantageous position. 'In this way,' noted Dundas, 'the thirty-six planes in a wing could not only impose the maximum damage on the enemy but also on occasions be able to reform as a unit after a fight and so remain an effective force both for attack and defence.'

The previous night, 1 July, there had been a party for AVM Broadhurst at which, with the drink flowing, Hill had challenged Dundas and told him he didn't like his way of doing things, although he put it as a criticism rather than an insult. At any rate, now they were flying fighter cover for the bombers, and over Sicily were heavily attacked by Me109s, which duly broke up the wing into small formations fighting separately. Dundas managed to disengage and was heading back with his wingman, Flying Officer Young, when they were attacked again, but as they were already crossing the southern Sicilian coast, this time the Messerschmitts pulled away. Young's Spitfire had been hit, however; it was streaming the white smoke of coolant and his engine temperature was already rising – though at 16,000 feet, there was a good chance he'd make it back.

They were halfway home to Malta when George Hill called up on the R/T. He was circling a pilot in a dinghy a few miles south of Capo Passero and asked for some company; there were, he added, some Me109s joining him. Checking his fuel tanks, Dundas saw he had 20 gallons left and, with Malta now in sight, he passed on the message to the air–sea rescue boys, told Young to carry on but to bail out if his engine rose above 125°, then turned back.

Diving towards Capo Passero, he called up Hill for a precise position and was told he was under 500 feet off the water and there were now six Messerschmitts above him.

'Hold on,' Dundas told him. 'I'll be with you in a couple of minutes.'

Fortunately, he spotted Hill's aircraft quickly and, as he came nearer, saw one of the enemy fighters dive down to attack. As Hill turned to face the Messerschmitt, Dundas opened his throttle wide and hurtled down towards them, flying through the Me109s, firing as he went, and to his surprise this seemed to do the trick. With Hill climbing to attack as well, the Messerschmitts all pulled away and sped off to the north. Both now dangerously low on fuel, they turned and hot-footed it back to Malta.

'Thanks, sir,' said Hill as they both wandered back to dispersal having safely landed.

'Don't mention it, Old Boy,' Dundas replied.

*

The Fourth of July, Independence Day in the United States, had seen heavy attacks on Gerbini; and they were even more concentrated the following day, Monday, 5 July. The pilots of JG 77 took off from Trapani at first light and flew straight to Gerbini in an effort to strengthen the fighter defence there. It seemed to Major Macky Steinhoff that he had always been firefighting, sent in wherever action flared; but never had his men been expected to do the job with supplies so short. Using a different airfield as a forward base meant splitting up ground crews, of which he was already short because those lost in North Africa had still not been replaced. The only thing to do was to send a truck over the night before with whatever spare parts were available, but it was the best part of 180 miles to Gerbini by road from Trapani.

Steinhoff landed amid swirling yellow dust so thick he could see nothing, aiming in the direction of the hut and trees he'd seen on coming into land. Coming to a halt, he pushed open the canopy, the wings of his Messerschmitt now coated in dust. 'It was unbearably hot,' he wrote. 'Not a breath of wind disturbed the humid air; my shirt, dripping with sweat under my harness, clung to my body. The sun had made the cockpit like an oven.'

Jumping down, he headed for the hut to make contact with Franzl Lützow, the new Inspekteur der Jagdflieger Süd under Galland, and find out what the hell was going on. The murderous heat beat down on his head. Inside the hut it was blisteringly hot, even hotter than out in the open. The single room contained two iron beds, a narrow table opposite the door and, connected by wires stretching through the window from the olive tree outside, a brown box that contained a field telephone, map and teleprinter. News had already reached them: Comiso had been attacked half an hour before.

Back outside, the pilots languished in the heat, trying to stay in the shade of the olive tree. The perimeters of Gerbini were now rammed with aircraft from JG 51 and JG 53 as well as their own from Trapani and a *Gruppe* of FW 190 fighter-bombers. Most had been dispersed under olive trees, but that was not going to protect them much if the bombers came over. 'This complex of airfields', jotted Steinhoff, 'was an ideal target for the Fortresses with their carpet-bombing technique.'

They were also keenly aware that Malta was now bristling with Spitfires. Steinhoff's II. Gruppe commander, Siegfried Freytag, had flown over eighty missions to Malta during the Luftwaffe's blitz of the island. 'One time,' he told the others, 'I was pulled out of the water close to

Valletta harbour just as the British rescue launches were coming up.' Steinhoff noticed Freytag was still wearing sandals even though he'd warned him not to – boots were far more fireproof. He couldn't be bothered to chastise him, though; there seemed little point.

'How's it all going to end here, sir?' Freytag suddenly cut in. It was a question often asked in recent weeks. 'They'll be landing on the island soon.' That the invasion would target Sicily seemed blindingly obvious to them; as fighter pilots, they understood what Hitler and even von Richthofen seemed not to grasp: that fighter range was paramount. There could be nowhere else. 'In a day or two,' Freytag continued, 'we won't have a single aircraft left to fly. And they'll leave us behind in Trapani. No-one's going to get us out of here. This time the trap's going to close with a snap.'

Steinhoff promised him he would make sure every man made it back to the mainland. By hook or by crook.

The Allied air forces were certainly out in numbers that day, flying in wave after wave. First came the B-25 Mitchell medium bombers, accompanied by the P-38 twin-engine fighters; these were followed by a second batch, and both had hammered the Gerbini I airfield in turn before the pilots from JG 77 had arrived. It was around mid-morning that Comiso was hit by yet more Mitchells, flying in low and dropping their loads with great accuracy. Gerbini was hit again while JG 77 were airborne, while B-26 Marauders then struck at Gerbini Satellite 7, followed swiftly by twenty-four Fortresses. For the defenders, it was like a continuous rolling assault – bombers and fighters appeared, bombs fell, bullets flew, and then, when the dust and grit and smoke had settled, over came another wave.

The biggest attack of the day, however, came in the form of seventy-six Fortresses, all headed for Gerbini. Among those flying were Lieutenant Bankhead's crew, part of the 347th Bomb Squadron in the 99th Bomb Group, flying for the first time since 25 May. For all their new-found dominance in the air, the Allied air forces were still suffering plenty of casualties themselves – whether from flak or from enemy fighters. For Bankhead's crew back on 25 May, it had been a combination of both. They had been bombing Messina and were moments from releasing their load when a burst of flak hit the starboard wing, sending the no. 4 propeller spinning out of control, despite all attempts to feather it. Somehow, they managed to keep in formation until the bombs were away, but they couldn't keep it up for long as their over-speeding prop was causing terrible drag and they, in turn, soon began to lag. An isolated and wounded bomber was always the most vulnerable, and sure enough, before too long eight Messerschmitts began attacking. As co-pilot, it was Lieutenant Jimmy Bruno's job to direct the fire, and he told the gunners to hold off until the enemy were clearly within range. 'Under no circumstances,' he noted, 'could we afford to waste precious ammunition.'

A continuous battle now opened up as the crew unleashed their .50-calibre guns. Slow and cumbersome compared with the agility of a fighter, the B-17 none the less had thirteen heavy machine guns on board, which offered a good deal of fire-power; it was why they were so feared by Axis fighter pilots. And the crew's guns were striking home, one Messerschmitt exploding, another going down soon after and then a third, before the rest scarpered.

With the no. 4 prop still out of control, they set course for North Africa and their base, still more than 600 miles away. They'd not gone far, however, when a deafening vibration began in the right wing and suddenly the cowling for no. 4 engine flew off. It was a heart-stopping moment: Bruno feared the entire starboard wing might shear away.

'Prepare to bail out!' Bankhead called out over the intercom, just as the propeller, now red-hot, severed and disappeared under the wing, slicing the aileron in half. Both pilots reacted instinctively by applying full left rudder and aileron to keep the stricken Fortress under control. 'I do not know what thoughts the other nine men had swirling around their brains,' wrote Bruno, 'but . . . I prayed to see one more sunset as the sun was going down to the west.' They were now rapidly losing height and Bankhead warned them to prepare to ditch. Anything loose was thrown out, including spare ammo and even a pair of shoes. Bruno was calling out the airspeed as they flew ever lower over the water. A normal touch-down speed was around 90 mph, but they were about to come down on the water in a 24-ton bomber. Then had come a glimmer of hope. Down at sea level, the remaining three engines were now working more efficiently and more smoothly.

'Give us a course for home,' Bankhead called to the navigator. 'We're going to try and make it.' As the engineer began pumping fuel from no. 4 engine into the tanks of the other three, a twin-engine aircraft appeared in the distance. At first they thought it might be an RAF Beaufighter come to guide them home, but when it began diving on them and then opened fire, they realized to their horror that it was a Messerschmitt 210.

'He can do 400 miles per hour,' muttered Bruno. 'I'm not going to enjoy being a clay pigeon for this guy.' Moments later, a cannon shell struck the B-17 a few inches above Bruno's head, hitting the compass correction card mounted in a metal frame that also held a picture of his wife, Merlyn, and sending a splinter into Bankhead's knuckles. Bruno motioned to take over, but grimly Bankhead kept flying.

Fortunately, the bombardier had saved one box of ammunition, which was hurriedly brought up to the top-turret gunner, while every time the German dived, Bankhead pulled back on the throttles, called Bruno for 20 degrees of flaps and pulled up to turn inside the fighter, prompting the enemy pilot to pull up and fire over them. Behind them, most of the men huddled in the radio compartment – after all, there was only ammo for one gun. On another pass Fred Manship, the radio operator, was hit in the back. The rest did what they could for him but he was in a bad way and losing blood.

The German made one last pass, but this time without firing, his own ammunition clearly exhausted. Bruno watched him, grinning at them, then waggling his wings and flying off. All thoughts of reaching their home base had been discarded, but they hoped they might make Cap Bon in Tunisia, and sure enough, after what seemed like an eternity, they finally made out the North African coastline, spotted a fighter airfield and came in, although they almost ran out of runway, finally coming to a halt 15 feet short of a high embankment at the far end.

Miraculously, nine of the crew survived that mission, with only Blaine Bankhead wounded. Fred Manship, although still conscious as he'd been taken away in an ambulance, died later that night. Since then, the others had been sent to a rest camp. 'If we had any battle fatigue,' noted Bruno, 'we were not aware of it. However, none of the crew objected to the resort where we were to spend the next ten days.'

Now, on 5 July, they were back, in a brand new B-17, and all of them were anxious to get on with the job, finish their remaining thirty-four missions and go home. Climbing up to 20,000 feet, the twenty-eight ships of the 99th rendezvoused over the Mediterranean with the rest of the bombers and with their fighter escort from Malta, which was led by Cocky Dundas. Then Sicily loomed up and they were turning in over the coast for the bomb run.

At Gerbini, Major Macky Steinhoff had been going through an explanation of tactics; but he knew they'd be horribly outnumbered and that if they tried to tie up the enemy fighters, that would allow the bombers to get through. They were on a hiding to nothing when the numbers were so far against them. He was still talking when suddenly they were scrambled and everyone was running towards their aircraft. Steinhoff burned his hands as he clambered into his, the metal was so hot. The cockpit was like a furnace. He started the engine, dust, leaves and straw swirling from the prop blast. As he moved out, he saw silhouettes of other Messerschmitts through the dust. Throttle pushed open, the aircraft gathered pace. Tail up, airspeed indicator to 60 and then he was airborne, and out of the corner of his eye he saw Burckhardt and Strausen were too. It was a relief to be off the ground, to feel cool air once more.

'Odysseus One, Comiso bombed,' he heard in his headset. 'Pantechnicons flying north, very high. Watch out for Spitfire escort.'

Salty sweat ran down his forehead under his flying helmet and into his eyes, so he closed them and wiped the lids with the back of his glove; it smelled of fuel. At 3,000 feet they rose out of the haze encircling Etna. The bombers were now 20 miles south of Catania. Steinhoff turned north to gain height. He had some twenty-five aircraft with him. That was all. As they cleared Etna he saw the mountains of Calabria rise up beyond in the toe of Italy. Freytag's group was on his right and his own headquarters flight was still with him. 'Nevertheless,' he noted, 'you were alone, very much alone in your thundering glass-topped box, a prey to the thoughts and temptations that war brings.' He was conscious of the immensity of the sea, and the mountains below him, and began to question what possible chance he had of surviving. And if he did survive this mission, he would only be sent up again on another, and another. And another.

He was still thinking such thoughts when the enemy was spotted, and moments later the Spitfires were flying right through them. 'And suddenly,' he wrote, 'the old bitter taste was back on my tongue again and my mouth went dry.' Then there were the bombers, down below, in their stepped-up formation. Mayhem on the R/T – warnings, shouts, screeches. And then Steinhoff was in a steep dive heading towards two Spitfires – something he had done instinctively without conscious thought. Both opponents were in his sights, but then one flipped his aircraft on its side and began turning in towards him – the other now lost from view – so that now Steinhoff and the one Spitfire were in a tight-turning circle. Steinhoff was pulling so tightly the wing slats jumped out, while the shaking of the stick told him he was in a heavy buffet and on the point of stall. Slowly but surely, though, he was gaining on the Spit, so that in one more circle he reckoned he would have a clear shot. 'Like one possessed,' he wrote, 'I rode this carousel, the final phase of the duel in the air.' And then a crack and he turned his head to see another Spitfire in a steep turn right on his tail. Tracer arced lazily towards him and then his engine spluttered. A clatter of bullets hit the armour plate behind his head, the cockpit filling with the stench of cordite.

In their new B-17, Lieutenant Bankhead's crew flew straight on towards Gerbini. 'Long before the target was in sight,' noted Jimmy Bruno, 'swarms of Messerschmitts were ready to defend their base.' Excited chatter filled the airwaves, among it some complaints that Spitfire bullets were hitting them. All around them fighters swirled and tumbled, tracer zipping and criss-crossing over the sky. The Fortresses continued on their way, dropping height for the final run-in – and then the bomb bays were opened and the bombs tumbled out, plastering Gerbini just as Steinhoff had predicted. Bruno always felt a tremendous sense of relief once the bombs had gone and they began their diving turn off the target; but now the rear of the formation came under attack and the last three of 348th Bomb Squadron were all shot down. Bruno could hear the crews frantically trying to bail; he hoped they had done so. In fact, on the first, *Dee Zipi Zip*, six bailed but five – they had carried eleven – were killed; the pilot of *Dirtie Gertie* was also killed, as were four others, but five managed to get out; while the pilot of *Rambling Wreck* also died, along with five of his crew, but four bailed. All those who came down were taken prisoner.

Other aircraft were falling out of the sky too, including that of Maggiore Franco Lucchini, the commander of 10° Gruppo and one of the leading aces of the Regia Aeronautica with twenty-two victories. Lucchini was killed; but Major Macky Steinhoff was still trying to make sure he survived. Having been hit, he pushed his Messerschmitt into a classic escape manoeuvre – a spiralling dive, the aircraft oscillating, stick sluggish in his hand, milky coolant smoke gushing past his canopy. At 6,000 feet, with no one shooting at him any more, he flattened out, then cut the engine, and looked for a field in which to land. He saw one – narrow, between trees, sloping up towards Etna. A belly-land, wheels up – and only as he hit the ground, bending the prop blades, did he see just how stony this patch of Sicily really was. A lurch and he was flung forward; the canopy hurtled off, and for a moment Steinhoff thought the aircraft might somersault, but then, on the point of tipping over, it fell backwards with a crash. Coming to, he could hear nothing but the faint hum of static from his radio. Otherwise silence.

Clambering out, he realized how much his back hurt. Easing himself down on to a rock, he gingerly unstrapped his Very pistol and cartridges from around his lower leg and fired. 'Shading my eyes,' he noted, 'I looked up at the sky and saw there, gradually dispersing, the pattern of the air battle described in the innocuous-looking white tracery of condensation trails.'

The flare had not attracted anyone, except some Sicilians who tried to steal his parachute. Getting on to the radio, he called for help, then sat down in the shade of an olive tree to wait. Eventually, a Fieseler Storch buzzed him then came in to land – it was Burckhardt and his chief mechanic, come to pick him up. They were heading back when Burckhardt yelled in his ear: 'They're attacking Gerbini! They're bombing—'

Plumes of earth were rising into the air over the fighter-bombers' strip but their own was also now shrouded in smoke and dust. There was only one thing for it: to head on to Trapani. They flew on, and Steinhoff, overcome with fatigue, began to worry he would fall asleep at the controls; he would have been better to let Burckhardt fly. None the less, he kept going and landed at Trapani to find a number of his pilots already there and I. Gruppe about to land. Six Fortresses had been shot down; two of his own wing were missing. Back at the hut, in the heat and amid the chirruping crickets and cicadas, Steinhoff had to report in to Lützow and managed to tell him the essence of what had happened before the line cut out. It had been an exhausting few hours. 'We were tired,' wrote Steinhoff, 'worn out and dispirited.'

CHAPTER 10

Countdown

I T HAD BEEN THE middle of the afternoon on Thursday, 1 July, that the loudspeaker on the troopship HMT *Derbyshire* had crackled and, in a clipped English accent, the officers were asked to assemble in the ship's main lounge. Lieutenant Farley Mowat, a platoon commander in Able Company of the Canadian Hastings & Prince Edward Regiment, got up from his seat beside a pile of ammunition boxes and hurriedly made his way through the heaps of kit bags and packs crowding the decks to join a crowd of young men eager to discover whether their destination would finally be revealed. They'd already been at sea for two weeks and although they'd guessed it would be somewhere warm, everyone had had their opinion. Mowat thought it would be Italy, because a divisional staff officer had hinted knowledge of a bit of 'wop lingo' might be useful. Corporal Hill had bet on Greece. Others thought Istanbul and some even French West Africa.

All the 1st Infantry Brigade staff appeared to be there, as were a group of British Commandos, a small number of nonchalant-looking Desert Air Force pilots, some navy sub-lieutenants and even a couple of American liaison officers. 'But all of these', noted Mowat, 'were as the plums and raisins in a pudding composed mainly of khaki-clad officers wearing the insignia of the infantry, artillery, tank, engineer, medical, signals, ordnance and service corps.' Mowat had been saved a chair by his friends and fellow A Company officers Alex Campbell, Al Park and Paddy Ryan. Park surreptitiously passed him a mug of rum and lemon under the table. Then a brigadier cleared his throat, the assembled mass hushed, and the briefing began. They were to be part of Operation HUSKY. 'It is my great pleasure to inform you,' said the brigadier, 'that at dawn, July 10, you will land on the south-eastern tip of Sicily where you will join battle with the enemy in this first dagger-thrust into Fortress Europe.' Mowat noticed some artillery officers exchanging coins; one of them had bet wrong.

In the manic activity that had marked the next few days at sea, Mowat had attended endless 'O' groups: orders groups, where briefings were given, maps studied, pamphlets handed out – including the *Soldier's Guide to Sicily* – and they learned of their initial objective, which was Pachino and its airfield. Plaster relief maps were laid out and Mowat and his fellows tried to memorize every hill, nook, lane and cranny. Reconnaissance photos and maps with enemy defences marked up were also studied in painstaking detail.

The Hasty Ps – as the Hastings & Prince Edward Regiment were known to all – were part of the 1st Canadian Division, which had been added to Eighth Army's roster for HUSKY only on 23 April. This was its first overseas posting since its troops had disembarked in Scotland back in December 1939; and even now it was only steaming towards Sicily at all because of a personal plea by William Mackenzie King, the Canadian prime minister, and the lobbying of the minister of national defence, James Layton Ralston. Churchill had eventually given way, although he had wanted to keep the whole of the First Canadian Army – all 170,000 men of its five divisions – together in southern England, ready for the cross-Channel invasion when it finally took place. That had also been the wish of the First Canadian Army's officer commanding, General Andrew McNaughton. In the last war, the Canadians had stuck together, and McNaughton, who had earned his spurs in that conflict, firmly believed the same principle should hold in this war too. On the other hand, they had been a long time training in Britain and needed to be tested to gain crucial experience; for although Canadian troops had made up the bulk of the personnel for the ill-fated Dieppe Raid, that had been just a one-day dash across the Channel and back again, leaving half their number in France, either dead or prisoners. With political pressure mounting from Canada, however, and with the support of General Brooke, McNaughton had been overruled and Churchill persuaded. The British 3rd Division, Montgomery's old command back in 1940, which had earlier been earmarked for Sicily, would remain behind, and the 1st Canadian Division, plus a tank brigade, would be sent out instead. Farley Mowat was excited at the prospect, as were most of his fellow officers.

'Oddly,' he wrote in a letter to a girl back in Canada, 'I don't feel the least bit scared. Maybe that will come later, but at the moment, I can't wait for the show to open.'

As the Allies sailed towards Sicily, the German troops and commanders on the island were frantically trying to organize themselves. Oberst Baade, having created Division Kommando Sizilien, had then been posted back to Italy to continue his staff duties. In his place had come Generalmajor Eberhard Rodt, a highly competent commander who through no fault of his own had seen his panzer division decimated on the Eastern Front. The remnants had been posted to Italy to recuperate and refit, and were now the backbone of Division Kommando Sizilien, redesignated 15. Panzer Grenadier Division on 29 June in honour of 15. Panzer Division of the old Afrika Korps. Its individual units were also renamed after the old 15. Panzer numbers, which meant that Hanns Cibulka, who had arrived in Italy with men of Flak Regiment 7, had found himself in Flak Bataillon Sizilien, then 315. Flak Bataillon and now 31. Heavy Flak Bataillon. It was all a little confusing; but for all the name changes, Cibulka had not moved since reaching the small town of Catenanuova, 25 miles west of Catania and just in the foothills climbing from the very edge of the Catania Plain. Headquarters was an old, falling-down farmhouse, but although from time to time Cibulka and his team had looked up and seen Spitfires flying over or masses of bombers, they'd soon laid all the wires and linked up the batteries, and so the rest of the time he, for one, had been rather enjoying himself, going for walks, doing maintenance, reading his Goethe and admiring the views. They were overlooking the River Dittaino, which ran east all the way to the sea. 'The whole valley resembles a huge garden,' noted Cibulka, 'orange and lemon groves . . . In the middle of the valley, an unmanageable olive grove, fig trees and peach plantations, here and there a flat farmstead, brown quarry stone, in between a few dwellings, whitewashed, bright spots in the landscape where the sandy brown colour of the soil dominates.' He had marvelled at the immensity of Etna, seen a scorpion up close for the first time and become friends with an elderly Sicilian called Gabriele Struzzi, who could speak German, having been taken prisoner by the Austrians in the last war. Struzzi had fought at the Isonzo; Cibulka's father had fought on the same front, at the Piave.

The guns were set up to help defend Gerbini and they would open up increasingly frequently. On 5 July, during the big air raids on the airfield complex, Cibulka had been alone at the farmhouse when he had heard what he first thought was the rumble of a tank. Then the ground underneath had begun to vibrate. Going outside, he had looked down the road, but it was empty. Pulses were throbbing through the ground; he could hear the entire farmhouse crackle and feel the invisible swaying of the walls. It had been the heavy bombers attacking, 10 miles away.

Among the new German troops on Sicily was 21-year-old Werner Stappenbeck, a former Afrika Korps anti-tank gunner in what had temporarily been the 'Schnelle Abteilung Sizilien' – or Rapid Deployment Battalion Sicily – but now that 15. Panzer Grenadier Division had been set up had become the 1. Heavy Panzerjäger Kompanie, in the 104. Panzer Grenadier Regiment. Stappenbeck was by no means match fit, suffering from a slow-to-heal foot wound, but he was otherwise able-bodied and had experience of fighting the Allies; and so he was brought back into the line in the hope that by the time the Allies attacked – if indeed they did attack – he would be better. He and his comrades were in no doubt at all that Sicily would be the Allied target, and as he had travelled across the Straits of Messina on 30 May, he had been conscious of a palpable tension in the air. Stappenbeck also felt as though the Italians had let them down. 'If the Italians had shown more energy, the battle in North Africa would have ended differently,' he wrote. 'The Italian soldiers were battle weary.' He wondered what had happened to the eight million bayonets Mussolini had boasted about at the start of the war. His toe was hurting more each day, which was not improving his mood; but on the bright side it enabled him to hitch a ride on a SdKfz 6 half-track – a 5-ton gun tractor for towing artillery which also had three rows of bench seating. It was thirsty for fuel but, Stappenbeck discovered, surprisingly smooth and comfortable.

They had initially made for Enna and set up camp among some olive groves; here Stappenbeck had spent the next few weeks in the medical tent, struggling with the intense heat. It had been hot in North Africa, but at least they had been near the coast. Here in the centre of Sicily it was different: endless flies, mosquitoes, the constant sound of crickets and no refreshing breeze off the sea. And here they remained, in their camouflaged encampment, the men training and reconnoitring, while Stappenbeck slowly but surely started to recover – at least to the point where he could be given light office duties.

Meanwhile, the Hermann Göring Panzer Division had begun reaching Sicily in numbers from 20 June. Originally set up the previous

November, its formation had never been completed because its first units had been shipped to Tunisia and almost all lost there. Although very often referred to as the 'elite' Hermann Göring Division, they were most certainly not. However, because they were carrying the *Reichsmarschall*'s name, Göring had made sure they were given the cream of what equipment was available; it may well have helped, too, that Kesselring had been made a field marshal of the Luftwaffe, not the army. At any rate, also on the island were the seventeen Tiger tanks of the 2. Heavy Panzer Kompanie, in need of a home. 'Now a tug of war began,' noted Leutnant Karl Goldschmidt, a platoon commander, 'between the two divisions and somewhat higher places about who should get our Tigers.'

Goldschmidt, still only twenty-one, was from Brücken, in the Saarland in western Germany. Lean, blond, blue-eyed and every bit the panzer poster boy, he had initially served in the infantry before transferring to the panzers, and was among the first to be posted to the new heavy panzer battalions. The 504. Heavy Panzer Bataillon had been formed at Fallingbostel back in January, and soon afterwards the 1. Kompanie had been hurried to Tunisia, where they had confounded the British who had come up against them. One of their tanks, Tiger 131, had been knocked out by three hits, the first melting a groove in the turret so it could no longer traverse and the second damaging the barrel elevation. The crew had bailed out and the tank had been captured almost intact – a mighty beast tamed, and regarded by the British with something close to awe.

Goldschmidt and the 2. Kompanie, however, had reached Sicily just before Easter, their tanks taken from Germany by rail all the way to Marsala in the western side of the island. The intention had been to send them across the Mediterranean too, but there had not been the shipping available and so they had stayed put. That was a considerable loss to the Axis forces in North Africa, but a commensurate gain to Oberst Baade: suddenly, here on Sicily, he had an entire company of Tigers, which, given their size, armour and 88mm high-velocity guns, were comfortably the biggest and most powerful tanks now in the Mediterranean. Needless to say, it was the Hermann Göring Panzer Division that now laid claim to these precious monsters.

They were now on the move too, heading from the west to the centre of the island – and the hard way, by road, as the railways were kaput. This was not good news: the Tigers were spectacularly complex and equipped with a hydraulically controlled semi-automatic pre-selector gearbox designed by Ferdinand Porsche that was very easy to break, so the less time they spent on the road the better, particularly now they were on Sicily with very limited access to spare parts and heavy lifting equipment. At least they still had their gantry crane, an indispensable piece of kit for any Tiger heavy tank company.

The reason for the move was the ongoing deliberations about where exactly the 260,000 Axis troops now on Sicily should be deployed – or rather, where the four Italian infantry and two German divisions would be best located. Generale Guzzoni was unwavering about his plan: the coast, he insisted, could not be defended, and so he wanted to create an inner triangle based around the two German divisions and the Livorno, which was his best, all of which would be gathered in the central south-east of the island; the coastal divisions would provide what opposition they could and, hopefully, buy time, but expectations for them were not high. Guzzoni, like Oberst Wilhelm Schmalz, commanding part of the Hermann Göring Panzer Division, had concluded the Allies would most likely land in the south-east of the island. The other Italian divisions would try to keep the Allies at bay until the two German divisions and the Livorno could mount a concentrated counter-attack and kick the Allies back into the sea.

Kesselring accepted the German divisions should be kept as a mobile reserve; but he still felt the threat from a landing in the west needed countering and, through a combination of charm and persuasiveness, managed to get Guzzoni to fall in with his plan. As a result, rather than placing the German divisions near Gela and Catania as Schmalz had argued, the 15. Panzer Grenadier Division was shifted to the west and the Hermann Göring Division was moved into the central south-eastern part of the island around Caltagirone in their place.

There were two massive flaws in this final plan. The first was that the German divisions would no longer be mutually supporting. While 260,000 men might have looked a lot on paper, more than half were men in weak coastal divisions. As a consequence, they simply did not have enough troops to cater for all eventualities, and there was a very strong argument for doing as Schmalz had suggested and concentrating in the centre and south-east of the island – especially since one detachment from 15. Panzer Grenadier had already been posted west and so was already keeping an eye on any threat from that quarter. These men could have been left there to firefight should there be a landing in the west, and, because they were comparatively small in number, could also quickly extricate themselves if need be and fall back to the eastern side, as the smaller the number, the easier it was to move swiftly. The rest of the division could – and should – have been left exactly where they already were.

And this was the second flaw: it made no sense whatsoever to move 15. Panzer Grenadier from ground with which they were already familiar and with which the Hermann Göring were not. Understanding the local terrain was an advantage over any attacker – it meant troops knew the narrowest or widest roads, the dips in the land, key features that commanded the best views and so on. Any advantage should have been grabbed with both hands and made as much of as possible. The 15. Panzer Grenadier Division had already done their local reconnaissance in the Caltagirone area. Now, in the first week of July, both German divisions would be moving into parts of the island with which they were barely more familiar than the attacking Allies. It simply made no sense whatsoever; and yet, although von Senger disagreed strongly with Kesselring's movement of these two divisions, it was presented as a fait accompli. 'The fact is,' noted von Senger, 'that things were being arranged behind the scenes.'

At any rate, this was why Werner Stappenbeck and the rest of his Panzerjäger company were taking down their camouflage nets, folding away their tents, loading up and moving out, with all the unnecessary use of extra fuel such a deployment involved. Stappenbeck was now even more convinced the Allies were coming. 'Was the island's crew strong enough to thwart a landing?' he wondered. 'By the number of divisions, in my opinion, yes. But here again it was the Italian divisions whose combat value we were aware of, and unfortunately in a negative sense.' The convoy chugged slowly west, winding its way through various Sicilian towns with their narrow streets.

Pausing in the town square of Sciacca, a small port in the south-west of the island, they became aware of a faint roar, getting rapidly louder. Blinded by the sun, they squinted up, unable to tell whether the aircraft above them were friends or enemies. But then they were diving straight towards them, all twenty-seven of them, dropping their bombs on the tiny port and jetty. Stappenbeck threw himself under a truck in the hope he might at least be protected from splinters. Not for long: as a building nearby was hit and collapsed, the driver of the truck under which Stappenbeck was sheltering explained that since it was full of ammunition, he needed to move it quickly. Deprived of his cover, Stappenbeck crouched as grit, splinters and shrapnel fizzed and ricocheted worryingly close to him.

As soon as the bombers had gone, they all set off once more, Stappenbeck safely back in the same Opel Blitz, and eventually reached their destination near Castelvetrano after dark. The next day they began reconnoitring their new area. 'A lot of fuel was consumed during these necessary reconnaissances,' he noted. 'The equipment had visibly suffered from the stony ground. Vehicles and weapons were overhauled.'

Stappenbeck's company were not the only ones urgently preparing for an Allied invasion. So too were all the German units now they had been given their new dispositions. Much of the Hermann Göring Division left a lot to be desired, despite its new Tiger company, but Oberst Schmalz, for example, had now cobbled together a half-decent brigade, or battlegroup, with an infantry regiment of three battalions, each of around 900 men, under Oberst Wolfgang Maucke, made up from men pulled out of leave, former Afrika Korps veterans recovered from wounds and other convalescents, an assault gun company of tracked anti-tank guns and artillery, some flak units, which could double up as anti-tank guns if necessary, and also an Italian light tank battalion. Defensive positions were being dug and prepared along a line that ran from Catania through Misterbianco to the towns of Paterno and Belpasso and along the lower slopes of Etna. With the volcano now at their backs, they held commanding views across the Plain of Catania. Nothing would be able to move there without them seeing it. As a defensive position, it really wasn't at all bad. From here, Schmalz reckoned he could move south if needed – and he had the motor transport to do so – but could also pull back behind this prepared position.

Meanwhile, General von Senger was trying to get to grips with exactly what was and what was not available; it was all so last-minute and ad hoc. Touring around, he soon discovered there were actually more stores on the island than he'd thought, although most were in the west, far from Messina – placed there in anticipation of being shipped to Tunisia. There was, however, a shortage of vehicles: neither the HG Division nor the 15. Panzer Grenadier had their full allocation. This meant that moving ammunition, stores and other equipment, not to mention men, had to be done using a shuttle service, which was far from ideal and yet another reason for not moving two divisions at the same time. Finally, there was also a shortage of signals equipment. Von Senger had an inadequate staff of one general staff officer and no attached signals unit, and so no clean link to Kesselring's HQ in Rome. There was a Luftwaffe telephone system, but at Enna, where he too was now based, von Senger had neither radio nor land-line to German headquarters in Rome, while his only links with German units in Sicily were via the Italian land-line network.

In his final briefing with his commanders, Kesselring told them that the moment an invasion fleet arrived, they were all to go into action immediately.

'If you mean to go for them,' replied Generalmajor Paul Conrath, commander of the HG Division, 'then I'm your man.' It was just the kind of fighting spirit Kesselring liked to hear. 'I returned home,' he noted, 'feeling pretty confident.'

Kesselring might have been feeling upbeat but there was no denying that Nazi Germany was on the back foot, and not just here in the Mediterranean. Germany's cities, and especially the Ruhr industrial heartland, were being bombed nightly by the RAF and now in daylight by the USAAF as well. On the Eastern Front, by the beginning of March, the Germans had been thrown back between 200 and 450 miles, and although they had in turn counter-attacked around the city of Kharkov, the advance had since come to a halt, leaving a major bulge around the town of Kursk. Hitler had demanded this salient be cleared and the line straightened, as it added an extra 150 miles to the front line, tying up some eighteen divisions. Preparations for Operation ZITADELLE had been under way ever since, but its launch had been repeatedly postponed. One of the problems facing General Warlimont at the OKW had been that many of the units earmarked to be sent to the southern front were also the core attacking forces for ZITADELLE. On 18 June, with the eastern attack already delayed, and with an Allied assault in the Mediterranean clearly imminent, the OKW had advised scrapping the Kursk operation altogether. Defending in the south, they concluded, was of greater strategic importance than going on the offensive in the east.

Hitler had taken these recommendations calmly but had insisted ZITADELLE be carried out as planned, on either 3 or 5 July. The trouble was, the Red Army had been preparing a truly gargantuan defensive system, which included no fewer than seven defensive lines, each one formidable. As Hitler's staff at the OKW were well aware, although they had amassed huge forces for ZITADELLE, these were still unlikely to be enough to win the day – not against the defences now arrayed against them, and against a Red Army at Kursk which had even more men, tanks, guns and aircraft than the Germans. Despite this, Hitler stuck to his guns. ZITADELLE was launched in the early hours of 5 July. 'Victory at Kursk,' the Führer pronounced, 'will be a beacon for the whole world.' His only concession was that if the Allies landed in the Mediterranean during ZITADELLE, he would immediately call off the offensive. As to where and when the Allies might land, however, there was still no clear intelligence. 'So far as Italy is concerned,' the Japanese Ambassador to Germany reported back to Tokyo, 'Sicily and Sardinia are at present regarded as places where enemy landings will be attempted. Feeling, however, that the Italian mainland may also be attacked, and bearing in mind the possibility that the enemy might even carry out simultaneous operations against Crete, Peloponnesus and Albania, the Germans and Italians are rushing their preparations for all they are worth.' Reading this deciphered signal, the Allied war leaders would have been delighted.

Across the sea, in ports from Algeria to Egypt, loading had been under way for the invasion throughout this first week of July 1943. To see the ports of Bizerte or Sfax or Algiers was to witness a new scale to the war as the vast armada assembled – the biggest the world had ever seen. Any Axis troops would have wept to see the huge parks of guns, trucks, other vehicles and lines of tracked armoured fighting vehicles, from row upon row of Sherman tanks to half-tracks, tank destroyers and tracked artillery. This was industrialized warfare on a massive scale – and all the more remarkable since just three years earlier both the United States and Britain had been forced to have an entire rethink about strategy and rearming. The fall of France in June 1940 marked the dramatic defeat not only of Britain's ally but of a world superpower, and of an army of millions that held twice as many tanks and guns as Nazi Germany. Britain's tiny standing army had been evacuated from France but nearly all its equipment had been left behind, and while its navy and burgeoning air forces had been enough to halt any German dreams of an invasion, if Britain were ever to go back on the offensive it would have to go right back to the drawing board. This meant creating a sizeable army – one far larger than had ever been anticipated before the war had begun. Britain's war chiefs had agreed it should have a strength of fifty-five divisions, each of around fifteen thousand men, although this was still small compared with the forces fielded by Germany, the USSR and Japan. Fighting power, however, was to be achieved by effectively combining air, sea and land power together and using as much mechanization as possible in order to keep to the bare minimum the number of young men forced to lay their lives on the line. This in turn could only be achieved, first by harnessing Britain's considerable global reach and access to the world's resources, its own merchant fleet, and the merchant vessels of other, friendly countries, which in sum amounted to around 80 per cent of the world's freighters; and second, by growing industrial power, the rapid building of ever more factories and the development of cutting-edge technology. Already, for example, twenty new aero-engine factories had been built in Britain, and over a hundred new airfields had been completed or were under construction with all-weather runways for RAF Bomber Command alone.

For the United States, the transformation in three years had been even more astonishing. Since his drive to rearm back in the summer of 1940, Roosevelt had changed key men at the top, harnessed big business to the military imperative, nullified stifling laws and turned the United States into the biggest and fastest-producing armaments industry on the planet, able to fight a global war in Europe and the Pacific concurrently. On 12 November 1942, four days after the Americans landed in north-west Africa, a new 10,000-ton freighter was completed after just four days, fifteen hours and twenty-six minutes. What a truly incredible achievement that was. Of course, it had been a publicity stunt; but Liberty ships, as they were known, were now regularly being built within a couple of weeks. America was as wedded to the 'steel not flesh' mantra as Britain, and anyone flying over the docks preparing for HUSKY would have been dazzled by the array of shipping and masses of vehicles on display, and by the fleets of aircraft flying overhead.

This staggering growth was truly exponential – and yet only during the fighting in Tunisia had the still-new Anglo-American coalition had much of a chance to work together in a major campaign. If there were teething problems, that was only to be expected, and these should never take away from the absolutely incredible achievement of both nations in getting to this point. To be able to mount an operation on the scale of HUSKY three years after ground zero was astonishing.

HUSKY D-Day, 10 July, would see 160,000 men delivered on to Sicily, along with 14,000 vehicles, 3,500 aircraft flying in support and a staggering 2,590 vessels. Admiral Cunningham had split his naval forces into two: a predominantly American Western Task Force under the US Vice-Admiral Henry Kent Hewitt, and the Eastern Task Force under British

Admiral Sir Bertram Ramsay, the commander of the Dunkirk evacuation. In all, there were some 6 battleships, 15 cruisers, 2 aircraft carriers, 128 destroyers, 36 frigates and corvettes and 42 minesweepers, as well as anti-aircraft ships, gunboats, 243 fast motor torpedo and motor gun boats, 237 merchant vessels and troopships and 1,734 landing craft. All were attached to different US task forces or Royal Navy forces or to troop convoys, both fast and slow. The routes, the timings, the coordination – all involved mind-boggling organization and immense levels of training, made all the more complicated because of the enormous spread of planning teams across the length of the Mediterranean.

One of the complications was how to get troops from both Britain and the United States into the Mediterranean and to join the Western Task Force at the right time, for although the plan had been to use forces already assembled in the Mediterranean for HUSKY, reinforcements had been called for, ranging from the Canadians to the US 45th Infantry and 2nd Armored Divisions. Task Force 85, for example, was carrying and escorting the 45th Infantry Division, the 'Thunderbirds', which had left from Hampton Roads on the US east coast back on 8 June. Aboard the USS *Ancon*, a former Panama Railroad Company passenger and cargo vessel converted into a grey camouflaged troopship, was Lieutenant John Mason Brown, a former journalist for the *New York Evening Post* who now, in a time of global conflict, found himself not only in the US Navy but a junior officer on the flagship of Rear-Admiral Alan Kirk, commander of TF85.

By 3 July, Mason Brown's forty-third birthday, they had been in Algiers almost two weeks, having unloaded the 45th Infantry and paused to refuel, revictual and join up with other ships of the Western Task Force. The following day, 4 July – Independence Day for him and his fellow Americans – he was feeling contemplative. 'I cannot help remembering at such a time,' he mused, 'when – thank God – the British are our friends, when we – thank God – are theirs, and when two of His Majesty's warships are gathered peaceably in our midst, how smileable are the twists of history.' Right now, he realized, was not the time to celebrate tea parties in Boston Harbour or victories over a former enemy. Rather, Mason Brown preferred to think of his Shakespeare and Henry V's rousing address to his troops before Agincourt – glorying in the band of brothers they had become and glad to be a part of something noble.

Not that on this Independence Day Mason Brown had any clear idea yet of where they were headed. Like the vast majority of Allied servicemen earmarked for HUSKY, it was not until they were out to sea and en route to Sicily that he would finally hear their destination. On the *Ancon*, it was announced on the bulletin board by Admiral Kirk in a message that was copied around the entire task force. They were heading to Scoglitti, south-east of Gela, where they were to deliver and protect the 45th Infantry Division. 'If you don't get all the news don't worry,' Kirk told them. 'You will be doing your job to the limit; so will everyone else. We have bad news to deliver, but we are saving it, this trip, for Benito Mussolini.'

On 6 July, HMS *Tartar* was still at Malta, in Marsaxlokk on the southeast of the island along with a number of other Royal Navy warships. In all, there were some 1,614 British vessels massing for HUSKY. 'It is obvious now that the "Big Op" is coming off very shortly,' noted Midshipman Peter Hay. 'Several officers are in their cabin working away frantically at this and that with notices on the doors saying, "Knock and Wait" so as to give them time to hide the secret papers away.' The truth was finally revealed to him and his fellows later that afternoon. For a nineteen-year-old like Hay, it was rather dizzying to be told he was to be part of the biggest such operation ever mounted in history. It was also thrilling to know that Generals Eisenhower, Alexander and Montgomery were all on Malta along with Admiral Cunningham and other top brass – giants all to a lowly midshipman.

Alexander had established an operations room at Lascaris, the underground complex dug into the limestone beneath Valletta. Outside the sun blazed down, but in Lascaris it was like living in a fridge. Everyone here wore sweaters and jackets, promptly stripping them off the moment they stepped outside. It was good to have all the senior commanders, Eisenhower included, together at last, rather than spread to the four winds. By this time, Ike and Alex had developed a growing friendship. 'Alex seems to have a genius for getting people to work for him,' Eisenhower wrote in a letter to Brooke on 3 July, 'just because they want to get a pat on the back from their commander.'

The naval commander, Admiral Sir Andrew Browne Cunningham, had also reached Malta from Algiers aboard the cruiser HMS *Uganda* in early July. Cunningham – or 'ABC' as he was widely known – was a lionhearted sailor who had fought and sailed the length and breadth of the Mediterranean most of his professional life. A destroyer captain in the First World War, he was unusual in having achieved flag rank without having spent much time early in his career on the larger battleships and cruisers; and it was as Rear-Admiral Destroyers in the Mediterranean between the wars that he had been able to develop an unrivalled understanding of the tactics required in operating these smaller, agile warships in narrow seas. In May 1939, he'd been promoted to Commander-in-Chief, Mediterranean Fleet, a post once held by Nelson and one of the most prestigious in the Royal Navy. Since 1940, much of Britain's land fighting had been either side of the Mediterranean, and so ABC had been at the forefront of tri-service operations: supporting landings and evacuations on Greece and Crete, providing offshore naval fire-power all along the North African coast, helping to bring precious convoys to Malta, taking on the Italian fleet, whether by launching torpedo strikes from aircraft carriers against the vessels at harbour in Taranto, as in November 1940, or more traditionally on the open seas, as at the Battle of Cape Matapan in March 1941. Under Cunningham's decisive command and aggressive eye, Axis convoys had been harried and sunk from below the surface and above, the Italian navy had repeatedly been bested and indeed neutered, and British naval supremacy in the Mediterranean – despite taking significant blows along the way – had never faltered.

Now sixty years old, Cunningham was short, trim and fighting fit, with the ever-present gleam in his eye of a man who relished the drama and thrill of a fight, and deeply scored crow's feet at the edge of his eyes showing that humour was never far away. Tough, shrewd and with an unrivalled reputation, he was highly respected and liked by both his men and his peers, having forged very good relationships with all the senior Allied commanders now assembled for HUSKY – not least Eisenhower, with whom he had worked very closely for Operation TORCH and the subsequent Tunisian campaign.

Malta was an island ABC knew extremely well. It had been both his base and his home through much of the 1930s, when it had also been home to the Mediterranean Fleet, and he had witnessed with mounting dismay its destruction at the hands of the Axis air forces. Now he was back – and at Admiralty House, too, a magnificent baroque palazzo in the heart of Valletta, which had mercifully survived the Blitz. Settling in on the ground floor, with his immediate subordinates on the floors above, he was also a mere stone's throw from Lascaris. This network of tunnels and subterranean offices, impervious to bombs, had been the control room for the island's air forces during the siege and was now bustling as the command centre for HUSKY. It might have been cooler than the outside world, but it was none the less not the most hygienic of environments, stinking of sweat and a hotbed of sandfly fever – the sandflies had been disturbed by the recent expansion of the bastion and a number of those working there had been struck down – an inconvenience that had done nothing to ease the enormous pressure facing the expanding staff there.

There were two operations rooms, one with a map table for the RAF and another with a giant wall map for the navy. 'Looking at that chart showing the carefully synchronized movements of hundreds of vessels in convoy,' wrote Cunningham, 'all steaming through certain points at their pre-arranged speeds, I often found myself wondering what might happen if things went wrong.' U-boats were still lurking in the Mediterranean and had already struck three troopships in the slow convoy; although no soldiers had been lost, equipment had. There was still much that could go wrong, even though he had implicit faith in their planners. Planning time had been so short; an error of calculation might literally mean the difference between success and failure. And although HUSKY was a tri-service team effort, ultimate responsibility for delivering the landings rested on his shoulders. 'It is hard to describe one's feelings at such a time,' he noted, 'but idle to suggest that one did not feel anxiety on the eve of a great operation. So much depended upon success in this, our first invasion of enemy territory in Europe.'

'The Spitfires have not flown as low as they have today for a long time,' noted Hanns Cibulka in his diary on 9 July. 'It looks as if they want to fly under the treetops.' Their guns stayed silent, though, so perhaps they still hadn't spotted the German positions. Even he could tell the enemy's air superiority had been growing; as a precaution, the battalion staff HQ had moved over a quadruple 20mm Flakvierling light anti-aircraft gun as protection. Just as well: an hour later, they were attacked from the air. '3. Batterie reports', he noted, 'heavy attack on the positions. Two *jabos* shot down, two guns down, three dead, four wounded. Need ammunition.'

By the end of that same day, the Luftwaffe on Sicily, Sardinia and southern Italy had just 165 serviceable fighters left in all, and only 78 on Sicily. Since 16 May, the Germans had lost 323 aircraft and the Italians a similar number, including 105 destroyed on the ground. Macky Steinhoff and his beleaguered band of brothers had been moved from Trapani and were now based for the day's operations at a tiny landing strip hastily found and established as a temporary satellite a few hours earlier. 'The things we did with our Messerschmitts on this tiny path of earth we called an advanced landing ground', noted Steinhoff, 'bordered on the realm of acrobatics.' Desperate times called for desperate measures.

Every airfield, every landing strip, on Sicily was littered with shattered and twisted and burned-out aircraft. The hangars that had existed stood smashed and skeletal, the ground pockmarked. Marshalling yards were strewn with twisted tracks and buckled and derailed locomotives and wagons. In all, of the thirty airfields and landing strips Sicily had had by the end of June, only Sciacca and Milo were still serviceable. The Allies had paid a price for this level of destruction – some 250 aircraft had been lost since 16 May – but that cost had not even slightly disrupted the round-the-clock hammering that had risen to a peak on Sicily in the last few days. Early in the planning, concerns over still-operable enemy airfields had been central to heated discussions over just where the ground forces should land; since then, the methodically planned and executed air assault had, it was confidently hoped, eased many of those concerns. No one, though, in the Allied command was taking anything for granted. The real test would come the following day – D-Day for Operation HUSKY.

PART II

Invasion

CHAPTER 11

Airborne Assault

EARLY ON 8 JULY, Generale Guzzoni had placed all troops on Sicily on invasion alert; but twenty-four hours later he had lifted it, and so that morning, Friday, 9 July, Tenente Livio Messina had volunteered to help a company of engineers rescue any injured and clear up the rubble from the bombing the previous night. It had seemed likely that the Allies had been targeting their camp, just a mile away. Walking by a house that had lost a part of its front wall, he pushed open the door and walked in, to discover a dead girl, possibly about eighteen or so years old, lying naked on a bed. She had an ugly gash on her chest and had clearly been hit by shrapnel. Messina guessed she must have been naked because of the heat. She was beautiful, but her skin was now pale and waxy. She was the first dead person he'd ever seen. Hastily, he pulled the sheet up over her and ordered his men to remove the body.

Meanwhile, far away in East Prussia, at the Führer's daily conference, reports of Allied convoys steaming through the Mediterranean had reached the OKW. Hitler and General Jodl, the OKW's chief of staff, were confident they were heading for Greece. It was one of the main reasons why some 60,000 troops had been placed on Crete alone. For all Hitler's certitude, at about 1.30 p.m. the OKW was handed reports of some 150–180 ships in five convoys, and nearly two hours later, around 3.20 p.m., the Luftwaffe reported the convoys steaming east just to the south of Pantelleria. Then, at 4.30 p.m., came confirmation: the convoys, Kesselring's headquarters were informed, were headed towards Sicily. Within ten minutes, Kesselring had alerted all troops on the island.

*

General Eisenhower reckoned his stomach felt as though it were like 'a clenched fist'. 'It is no small event,' noted his naval aide Harry Butcher, 'to be sending 150,000 men on a highly dangerous landing on an enemy coast highly fortified with mines in the water and on land, shore batteries, U-boats, and worst of all, close air bases for havoc-wreaking fighter bombers.' Ike was also feeling a little bit impotent; before TORCH, he'd had direct control of all operations, but for HUSKY the real responsibility lay with Alexander, Tedder and Cunningham. Eisenhower's role was that of referee if disagreements or spats needed sorting – or if someone had to make the decision to call the whole thing off.

Everyone was apprehensive. Lying awake at night at Admiralty House in Malta, Admiral Cunningham had been able to hear the distant rumble of bombs falling and anti-aircraft guns firing as the air bombardment continued to pound Sicily. It hadn't been the crump of explosions that had been keeping him awake, however, but the weather. Winds were on the rise, and he knew from long experience that the capricious *khamseen* from across the sea in North Africa could make life very difficult, creating a vicious and increasing swell. Sure enough, once he was up and about on the morning of Friday, 9 July, it was clear the weather was deteriorating. He had earlier warned Eisenhower that up to twenty-four hours before zero hour, set for 2.45 a.m. on the 10th, he could still call back the many convoys now at sea. After that, come what may, the invasion would have to go ahead and they would have to face the consequences.

ABC and his staff watched the weather all morning. Privately, they reckoned they could still reverse the decision at midday, but noon came and went. The convoys continued on their way, two enormous task forces, while out to sea around Malta white breakers could be seen forming on the waves. By mid-afternoon, the weather was bad, winds whipping across the sea from the south-west. Eisenhower was with Cunningham when the meteorologists brought in their latest forecasts. The winds, they reckoned, would start dying down in the early hours of the following day, D-Day, and in any case, on the eastern side of Sicily, in the lee of the winds, the British landings were unlikely to be affected. It was going to be a choppy ride for the Americans and Canadians landing on the southeast, however. Some landing craft might well get swamped. 'So with rather fearful hearts,' noted ABC, 'we decided to let matters take their course.' Even so, watching the landing-craft flotillas setting off from Malta that afternoon, spray flying over them as they bucked over the breakers, it was hard to feel sanguine. Eighty-odd miles in flat-bottomed boats on those treacherous seas was going to be a bumpy ride, to say the least.

Eisenhower had also been trying to smooth Patton's ruffled feathers over the question of air power – concerns that had been stoked by Major-General John Lucas. Lucas had been sent out by General Marshall to be Eisenhower's deputy, but instead Ike posted him to Patton's headquarters; he wanted an experienced officer he trusted to keep an eye on his flamboyant subordinate. Lucas was likeable, intelligent, an old friend of Patton's, and by background an artillery man who had commanded a number of units from regiments to divisions and had also held a large number of staff jobs. Although only fifty-three, he was balding, wore round, wire-rimmed spectacles and often smoked a pipe, giving him a kind of avuncular appearance and demeanour. As an artillery man, Lucas was immediately concerned about fire support on the beaches. 'I could not find', he noted, 'that a great deal of air power had been allocated to immediate support of the infantry.' As he pointed out to both Patton and Eisenhower in turn, their task was to get ashore and take the Gela–Ponte Olivo airfield complex as soon as possible; and yet, in his humble opinion, they were not being given the air support to help them achieve this swiftly. It was only natural that every commander would want the maximum fire support possible; but it was also important to understand the limitations of air power, and this was something many ground commanders were still failing to grasp – including Patton and, so it seemed, Lucas. This was understandable, because Lucas had spent much of the past two decades in the United States and had not witnessed the rapid development of tactical air power at first hand. But in raising the point now, he had fanned the flames of a doctrinal argument that should have been put to bed some time previously.

And so, despite having had modern tactical air power explained to him in some detail, Patton was still chuntering on about the lack of control as he prepared to lead American troops on to Sicily. No matter that the Allied air forces had been operating round the clock, hammering at enemy targets near and far; Patton felt he had not been told enough about the air plan to support his troops. This was because neither Tedder nor Coningham, whose Tactical Air Force would be providing direct close air support on D-Day, were in a position to tell him at exactly what time their aircraft would be over the beaches. They could promise support, but the distances from Malta were too great to be able to provide constant cover – and, in any case, as Coningham had explained back in Tunisia, it was for the air commanders to decide where and when they used their aircraft, because there might well be something beyond the horizon that needed dealing with and took priority over anything within a commander like Patton's immediate sphere on the ground.

Eisenhower continued to do everything within his power to ensure smooth relations between the coalition partners, but privately Patton bristled and complained and felt he was getting a raw deal. 'We have a pro-British straw man at the top,' he scrawled in his diary. Spaatz too, Patton reckoned, was a 'straw man', too willing to dance to the British tune. 'I cannot see how people at home don't see it. The US is getting gypped.' This was nonsense. Both Eisenhower and Spaatz were perpetually fighting those corners that needed fighting, and always considering national interests as well as those of the coalition. Much of the time, the two sets of needs reinforced one another rather than conflicting. Patton's Force 343 had become I Armored Corps; then in mid-May Eisenhower had agreed it should have army status, according Patton equal billing with Montgomery. Spaatz had even ensured Coningham had a new American deputy in Brigadier-General John K. Cannon, and it had been agreed that the HQ of XII Air Support Command, the US fighters attached to Coningham's Tactical Air Force, would be attached directly to Patton's HQ once they were on Sicily. But Patton was proud and hot-headed; he believed he was right on most things to do with fighting battles, and absolutely that it was his destiny to achieve greatness. Anyone – anything – that got in the way of that caused him immense frustration. His diary was an outlet for those frustrations.

He was, unquestionably, an extraordinary man. Independently wealthy, he had been born to serve in the US Army – his grandfather and great-uncle had served in the Civil War, he had grown up reading vast amounts of military history and had never considered any other career. Commissioned in 1909, he had first seen action in the Pancho Villa Raid in New Mexico in 1916, before shipping out to France and the Western Front, where he was wounded. Between the wars, he had written many pamphlets and articles about the future of warfare – including a prophetic piece on the possibility of a Japanese attack on Pearl Harbor. While the US Army shrank and stagnated, he was one man who tried to buck the trend. During the Louisiana Maneuvers in 1941 he had run rings around his opponents. A true pioneer of armoured warfare, Patton was an obvious choice to take over the command of US II Corps after the setback of Kasserine, and he had done well, although repeatedly restrained by Alexander, who feared this firebrand was in constant danger of overreaching himself, of being too aggressive. Now, on the eve of a great invasion, he was leading a force of 90,000 men, soon to swell further – a force that would become Seventh Army as soon as the clock passed midnight into the morning of 10 July. Admiral Kent Hewitt, on whose flagship, the USS *Monrovia*, Patton was travelling, had presented him with a Seventh Army flag; and at five minutes to midnight, the I Armored Corps flag would be lowered and replaced with the new standard. 'Born at Sea, Baptized in Blood' was the motto.

A man of many parts – and contradictions – Patton cut an imposing figure. He was tall, and always dressed immaculately, invariably in breeches and cavalry boots with a brace of ivory-handled revolvers at his hips. His eyes were pale and fierce, his rather high-pitched voice totally at odds with his character and bearing. A noted horseman, champion swordsman and former Olympic pentathlete, he was also something of an amateur poet, God-fearing, utterly devoted to his wife and family, and obsessed with fears of failure and his own mortality. On the journey across the Mediterranean, he had listened to officers talking about looking forward to returning to peacetime life when the war was over. 'I don't,' noted Patton bluntly, in his somewhat manic scrawl. 'I look forward to fighting, here, in Japan, or at home, for the rest of my days.'

Yet his thirst for war, his impatience to make his mark, even his bravura could not hide the fact that Patton lacked the combat experience of many of the British commanders. He could chunter all he liked, but it was an undeniable fact, because the US Army had joined the fight twenty-eight months after the British. He wasn't even the most experienced of the American generals. His stint commanding II Corps had been short-lived; Bradley had commanded them for longer in combat and in a greater variety of scenarios in Tunisia. Terry Allen had more experience than either of them, having commanded the Big Red One during the TORCH landings and right through to the very end in North Africa. National pride – and especially personal pride – might have bridled at playing the support role to Eighth Army, but Monty's men had been in the game a lot longer. So too had the British airmen and sailors; the development of tactical air power had been forged the hard way, through blood and guts in the heat and sand of the Western Desert, when Patton had been nowhere near any front-line action. Yet really, there was no reason for him to feel any slight at all. He and his men still had much to learn. No one was doubting their capacity to do so, and they had already demonstrated this brilliantly in the final battles in Tunisia; but there was no substitute for experience, and right now, on the eve of the invasion, the British had more of it.

Now, on the USS *Monrovia*, Patton was nearing Sicily along with the rest of the invasion force. The ship was crowded and rolling a fair amount, but Lucas reckoned the waves were no more than 3 feet high. 'Why have we not been attacked?' he wondered. 'Our air is either doing a bang-up job or the enemy is unbelievably short.' At 8 p.m., the chaplain arrived at the large cabin Patton shared with Lucas and together they prayed. Then the man who was about to become Seventh Army commander read a detective novel until 10 p.m., and turned in.

By this time the airborne operation was already under way, with tugs and gliders having taken off from six airstrips along the eastern coast of Tunisia in what was code-named Operation LADBROKE. In the latest episode of the somewhat haphazard planning and preparation, three extra Wacos had become available at the last minute, but because there were not enough aircrew, three Americans were drafted in thirty-six hours beforehand as co-pilots. In all, over two thousand men were to be flown over in 147 gliders – eight Horsas, each with a 28-man platoon and two pilots, towed by seven Halifax bombers and one ageing twin-engine Albemarle, and 139 Wacos, each carrying thirteen men and two pilots, towed by the C-47s of the 51st Troop Carrier Wing. Although lightly armed, as all airborne troops were, the force included mortars, machine guns and even some 6-pounder anti-tank guns. It was hoped these would be enough for the tasks they'd been allotted.

Lieutenant-Colonel George Chatterton had driven down to the airstrip in his jeep at around 6 p.m., accompanied by the commander of the Airlanding Brigade, Brigadier Pip Hicks. Thirty C-47s – or Dakotas, as the British called them – and their Waco gliders were lined up, gleaming in the early evening sun, which continued to bear down oppressively. Chatterton's was Glider No. 2, and he clambered into the cockpit along-side his co-pilot, Peter Harding. 'It was a tense moment,' noted Chatterton. 'There was a strong wind blowing, the light was hard and brittle and great waves seemed to leap into the air at the far end of the runway.'

At 6.48 p.m. they were off, hurtling down the runway, dust swirling all around them – and then they were airborne and climbing, the Waco above the Dakota tug and the sea, with its white horses, below both of them. Immediately the glider was being thrown about, jumping up and down and lurching from side to side in the wind, so that in no time Chatterton's arms were aching badly. Wacos were straightforward to fly, their controls laid out in much the same way as any aircraft, but the pilot had to keep the glider above or below the tug or else the effect of turbulence would be too great. There were no hydraulics or pneumatics, and this meant that in a stiff wind of the kind they were now experiencing, keeping the glider in formation and at the right altitude was a physically draining task. After a while he handed over to Harding, but his co-pilot was struggling with terrible airsickness and so Chatterton took back the controls himself and tried his best to relax. Some seven Wacos had failed to get airborne but, glancing back, Chatterton now saw an extraordinary sight. 'Stretching back in the evening light was a great armada of well over two hundred aircraft,' he wrote. 'It was a great moment, one not to be missed, and all the hazards, risks and difficulties still to be faced seemed to dissolve into thin air.' He couldn't help wondering whether enemy fighter planes might suddenly appear. What sitting ducks they were! As dusk gave way to darkness, however, and there was still no sign of the enemy, a sense of relief swept over him that they'd got away with it.

It was at 8.05 p.m. that the seven Horsas took off, later because their Halifax tugs were faster than the C-47s, the Dakotas. Among them was Glider No. 133, with Staff Sergeant Dennis 'Galp' Galpin as first pilot and Sergeant Brown next to him. Their tug was flown by Flight Lieutenant Tommy Grant, who had reached Kairouan in Tunisia only four days earlier. Grant and his fellows of A Flight, 295 Squadron, had been confronted by stultifying heat of 125° Fahrenheit – 51° Celsius – and had then been expected to put up their own tents, dig slit-trenches and manhandle 50-gallon fuel barrels. By the evening of 9 July, they had all been utterly exhausted.

On board Glider No. 133 were Lieutenant Leonard Withers and 15 Platoon in C Company of 2nd Battalion South Staffordshires. They were to take part in Phase One of LADBROKE, a *coup de main* assault by eight of the larger Horsas carrying men from A and C Companies of the 2nd South Staffs. This entailed landing on what had been designated LZ 3 – landing zone 3 – next to the all-important Ponte Grande bridge, a mile or so south of Syracuse, then swiftly storming the bridge, codenamed 'Waterloo', and capturing it intact. This was crucial, because it was the only bridge that could realistically be used by the men of Eighth Army landing to the south and pushing north into the city. The plan was for Ponte Grande to be in the hands of the South Staffs by 11.15 p.m. that night.

Following them, in Phase Two, would be the main force, lifted mainly in Wacos and landed at LZ 1 about 3 miles south of the bridge. They were due to be on the ground by 1.15 a.m. Finally, in Phase Three, the rest of the Wacos would land next to LZ 1 in LZ 2; their troops, mostly men of the 1st Border Regiment, would hurry north while 2nd South Staffs held on to and defended the bridge, pushing on into Syracuse and, with luck, capturing the city by 5.30 a.m. Special black and white 'moonlight maps' had been produced and all the surrounding enemy strongpoints identified, marked up and given code names, either of biting insects or towns in the Midlands. Walsall, for example, was a strongpoint just to the south of Ponte Grande, which would have to be taken out before any troops from LZs 1 and 2 could get near the bridge; Mosquito and Gnat were gun positions. Since the operational orders had only been issued three days earlier, there had been much feverish work to learn all these features, and to memorize as much detail as possible from the array of maps and photographs. Lieutenant-Colonel Chatterton had been having sleepless nights as the wind had started to blow, because the gliders were heading in an easterly direction first, then dog-legging at Malta, turning due north and finally due west for the final approach. It was this last bit that was going to be the biggest challenge because they would be gliding directly into the gale. So at what height should they be releasing? And should they be cutting the cord closer to the coast? In the end, he left it right to the last minute, then agreeing with the commanders of the 51st Troop Carrier Wing and the RAF 38 Wing that the gliders should be released 500 feet higher than initially planned.

At Generale Guzzoni's headquarters in Enna, Kesselring's message warning of an imminent invasion, sent at 4.40 p.m., was not received until 8.05 p.m., although the Italian commander had ordered a partial alert at 7 p.m.

At Avola, Michele Piccione and his brother Enzo had decided to go for an after-dinner stroll. They headed to the piazza where they met some friends, then set off towards the town hall and the public garden around it. A horse-drawn cart approached and then stopped beside them as anti-aircraft gunners began opening fire and they all stood to watch what was going on. Then suddenly an enemy bomber approached, swooping in low in the direction of the railway station. Michele started to run, his brother and friends following, then dived for cover behind the gate of a house on the corner of Corso Umberto and Via Gaetano d'Agata. They heard the roar of the aircraft, the whistle of bombs and then explosions, all worryingly close by. The balcony of the house where they were sheltering collapsed. 'Its pieces of concrete landed very close to us,' said Piccione, 'and so we jumped clear away, and ended up lying on top of each other.'

Once the bomber had gone, they all dusted themselves down and Michele and his brother hurried back home, past piles of rubble and through clouds of dust and grit; on the way they passed a man who, unhinged by what was happening, was now raving nonsensically. At the family home, they discovered their mother and sister had been thrown over by the blast, and although they were all right, everyone was shocked and frightened. The family had a small house out in the countryside, clear of the town and close to the beach, and they decided they should all head there for the night, their neighbours included. It was not far to walk. Once there, they divided themselves between two dormitories, one for the men and one for the women. In one room went his mother, sister, great-aunt and daughter, their neighbour and her two-year-old daughter; in the other, himself, Enzo, his great-uncle and his uncle. It was quite a squeeze, but the cramped conditions were the least of Piccione's worries. 'I couldn't sleep,' he said. 'I couldn't stay calm.'

On Malta, General Eisenhower had finished dinner with Admiral Lord Louis Mountbatten, the commander of Allied Combined Operations. Together, they drove to the south-east edge of the island to watch the first tugs and gliders go by. It hardly inspired confidence to see the planes and gliders behind bucking in the wind as they flew over. Ike had offered up a prayer; then they'd returned to the Lascaris War Rooms where, still dressed, the Supreme Commander had tried to get some sleep.

By this time, many of the glider force were floundering. One glider had even landed at Luqa airfield on Malta, the men hurriedly jumping out just as a jeep drove up and pulled over. Believing they were on the LZ in Sicily, they were nonplussed to be told to get off the runway and to pull the 'bloody glider' clear too. Another had landed near the Mareth Line in southern Tunisia. Chatterton, the other side of Malta, was having a torrid time, the glider having become even more difficult to control. His arms were aching terribly, his eyes were stinging with fatigue and his head throbbed from the constant concentration needed. At one point, as they'd turned over the island, the glider was flying on a loose line

side-by-side with the C-47. Chatterton felt physically sick with apprehension. Somehow, however, the glider then miraculously righted itself,
and they began climbing towards Sicily, ready for the cast-off.

Around a quarter to eleven, Chatterton was able to pick up the vague
dark mass of the Sicilian coastline and then saw flak rising from around
Syracuse.

'Can you see the release point, Peter?' Chatterton asked his co-pilot,
straining his eyes in the inky darkness.

'Another five minutes,' he replied, then almost immediately said:
'There it is!'

A moment later, the C-47 tug began to turn and dive. This was it.
Chatterton pulled on the release lever and suddenly they were on their
own, the glider dramatically smoother after all the rough handling of
the tow. But now Chatterton could not see a thing. It was as though a
great wall of darkness had risen up to meet him, blocking out the quarter moon entirely. Unbeknown to Chatterton, this was a cloud of dust
that had been whipped up by the wind, and it meant he was now flying
blind. Of the way point of the Capo Murro di Porco, there was no sign.

What could he do but turn into the dark and hope? Doing so, in what
he prayed was the direction of the coast, he was startled by a sudden raft
of tracer bullets hurtling upwards through the murk and raking his
wing. The Waco jerked, fabric tore from the wing and although he managed to straighten up they were now rapidly losing height, plunging
downwards, the glider's capacity for lift as shredded as the wing. The
dust pall clearing, he saw the sea rush towards them. Frantically trying
to level out, they hit the surface with a mighty splash, water came up over
his head and he was conscious of shouting as he desperately fumbled
with his straps.

Someone hauled him out and on to the fuselage. Fortunately, the
Waco was still afloat, and everyone aboard managed to get out and cling
to either the wings or the fuselage. A searchlight swept from the shore
and Brigadier Hicks shouted at everyone to lie flat. Moments later,
machine-gun bullets spat past them above their heads.

'It's no good staying here,' Chatterton said to Hicks. 'Shall we swim
for it?' The brigadier agreed, and, having ditched their weapons and
equipment, they all dived in. They had only just reached the shore when
there was a deafening explosion, bombs dropped in the sea all around
them and then an aircraft hit the water with a mighty crash, setting the
surface of the sea on fire where, moments earlier, they had been

swimming. 'I lay there,' wrote Chatterton, 'paralysed with fear and shock watching the flames lapping the shore.' Strangely, he couldn't help but think of burning brandy on a Christmas pudding.

Around the same time, Glider No. 133 was finally approaching Sicily after a somewhat fraught journey. Although a very experienced pilot, Flight Lieutenant Grant had never towed a glider at night before and never at all on an active mission. What's more, his Halifax was already a bit battered, with a faulty compass and an unserviceable auto-pilot. To make matters worse, soon after take-off he had developed engine trouble and so turned around, intending to fly back to base. Then, inexplicably, the trouble seemed to rectify itself; so Grant banked the Halifax and they set off again, behind the rest of the leading gliders, but heading for Sicily all the same.

Staff Sergeant Galpin wasn't too concerned – they might have been behind schedule, but he wanted to do as he'd been commanded, get Lieutenant Withers and his men down on LZ 3 and then join them in the assault on Ponte Grande. By this time it was getting dark, although he had seen some Wacos climbing and heading out over the sea. Despite the buffeting wind, they reached Malta, made the dog-leg without a hitch and continued north, the navigator calling out the courses and land-marks to Flight Lieutenant Grant, which Galpin could hear through the intercom. 'This was a great help,' said Galpin, 'as I knew exactly where we were and how long it would take to reach the objective.' As Sicily loomed up, he saw anti-aircraft fire, tracer and criss-crossing searchlights illu-minating the sky. Suddenly, Grant's Halifax was caught in the searchlights; there followed in quick succession stabs of light anti-aircraft fire. They were all being rocked and knocked about not by the wind but by the violent bursts of flak. Despite this, and with astonishing sang-froid, Grant told Galpin over the intercom that he would bring them in closer than prescribed due to the strength of the wind. Now Galpin spot-ted the shape of Capo Murro di Porco, just as it appeared in the photographs and on the map. Grant banked to the right and gave Galpin the signal to cast off – and then they were on their own, the Halifax heading northwards and out of the fray. Down below, it was now hard to see anything much through the night sky – there was, after all, only a quarter moon, while the searchlights were a little way to the north.

Using the predetermined compass setting, Galpin and his co-pilot set off, hoping for the best. Fortunately, he suddenly recognized where he was – he had flown too far north and was over Syracuse itself, which was not a healthy place to be – so he turned to where he hoped he might soon find LZ 3. Sure enough, from 2,000 feet he spotted it, and was just congratulating himself when they were caught in searchlights and tracer began arcing towards them. Taking violent evasive action, Galpin then soon realized he was back out over the sea, which was absolutely not where he wanted be. Turning, and with still enough lift, he decided to fly in low, parallel to the river and canal, knowing that this way they'd soon reach the bridge again. 'The searchlight followed my glider right down to the deck level,' said Galpin, 'and as I was crossing the coast, it very kindly showed me exactly where the field lay, lighting up the bridge at the same time.' Pulling up the nose to reduce speed, he applied full flap and then shouted back to Withers and his men to brace themselves; it was the moment to lock arms ready and raise their boots off the floor for the crash-landing of a largely wooden aircraft – always a hazardous moment in glider operations. Moments later, they hit the ground, sliding along the field and finally coming to a halt in a cloud of swirling dust. Galpin celebrated with his co-pilot by sharing a tot of whisky, while the men clambered out. Withers had managed to sprain an ankle but otherwise the men were in one piece. More disconcerting was the lack of any other gliders, because Withers reckoned that after the false start, they ought to have been the last Horsa down; and yet they were the only one. He began to doubt whether they were even at the right place.

They were still getting their bearings when the silhouette of another glider appeared in the sky above them. Unbeknown to them, this glider contained 17 Platoon and also their own C Company commander, Major Edwin Ballinger. Galpin and the others were looking up, watching it circling, when a burst of machine-gun fire opened up, tracer stabbing upwards, raking the Horsa. For a moment it appeared to stop mid-air, perhaps 300 yards from the bridge; and then suddenly there was a bright flash of an explosion and the flaming glider fell to the ground by the canal bank. Clearly, tracer must have hit some of the explosives they had been carrying. Stunned by the vivid and shocking loss, the men of 15 Platoon none the less had to get a hold of themselves and consider how best to take the bridge, and in quick order. Meanwhile, Galpin and Brown hurried to the wreckage, which had come down in the same field on their side of the canal. They found a scene of utter carnage; miraculously, there were three survivors, but all were in a bad way. Galpin and Brown gave one horribly wounded man a big shot of morphine, but with no more gliders in sight, it now seemed pretty clear they were on their own. Of eight gliders for the *coup de main* operation, the single most important objective for the Airlanding Brigade that night, only one appeared to have successfully made it to the LZ. Of Chatterton, of the battalion commander and of A Company, there was no sign. Some 254 men had been reduced to just thirty.

Lieutenant Len Withers was only twenty-one years old. It was now a little after 11 p.m., very dark, and there were enemy strongpoints a couple of miles to the south and either side of the Ponte Grande bridge. The entire area was part of the Augusta–Syracuse Fortress area commanded by Ammiraglio Primo Leonardi; immediately around them were the men of the 206° Divisione Costiera, troops protected by bunkers, armed with machine guns, mortars and rifles. Quickly, Withers gathered his men around him and drew up a plan. It was essential they capture the bridge and so he decided to attack from both sides. He would lead five men across the canal and river, which here ran parallel to one another, and then mount a diversionary attack. With a bit of luck, this would distract the enemy; then the rest of the platoon would storm the bridge from the south.

Withers had been right to act, because no other gliders were heading their way. A number had been cut adrift too early; three of the four Horsas carrying A Company lost too much height too soon and came down in the sea; although the gliders were made largely of canvas and wood, and so had a fair chance of staying afloat, fourteen of the men on one were drowned as it ditched, while a second sank and killed all thirty on board. The fourth managed to reach the coast but landed too far away from the bridge. Two more of C Company's gliders also landed on Sicily, and they were too far away to help Withers now. Phase One of LADBROKE had been a disaster.

Fortunately, no Italians appeared. Ahead, trees lined the southern bank of the canal, while off to their right, perhaps 200 yards away, was Highway 115 and the earthen ramp of the approach to the bridge. Withers knew from his photographs that the pillbox on the northern bank was also on the western side of the bridge, so despite his sprained ankle, he led his small section to the road, cautiously crossed it, then worked his way to the southern edge of the canal, which was lined with trees. The canal was neither wide – around 15 yards across – nor deep, and they managed to wade through it, weapons held aloft, then scramble quietly up the other side, down into the river and up again on to the northern bank, where they paused, and then crept stealthily towards the pillbox. Still they had not been seen; so, drawing near, Withers opened fire with his submachine gun, his five men following up with grenades and bursts from their own weapons. Incredibly, the defenders were caught completely by surprise. Now the assault group charged from the south. In moments, the stunned defenders of the bridge had laid down their weapons and surrendered, crying out and emerging from their pillboxes with hands raised. Neither Withers nor any of his men had suffered so much as a scratch.

Immediately, he set up his men ready to defend the bridge while the two sappers, with the assistance of the platoon's medical orderly, set about cutting any wire that looked like detonator cable and began the search for demolition charges on the bridge. Against the odds, they now had the bridge, the objective of the entire operation, after all; but they were all keenly aware there were not very many of them to keep hold of it. They had to hope and pray the second and third phases of gliders – bringing the main force – would have greater success reaching the bridge than those in the *coup de main* assault.

While Withers and his men had been storming the Ponte Grande, and the rest of the main glider force were heading to Sicily, the 3,405 men of the 505th Parachute Combat Team were also on their way. The first C-47s of the 52nd Troop Carrier Wing had begun revving up their engines and moving out from their airfields in northern Tunisia at around 8.15 p.m. In all, there were 226 of them, most carrying twenty-eight men, each man weighed down by around 80 pounds of equipment and heading off to battle for the first time. There was no going back – not for anyone; Colonel Jim Gavin had made that crystal clear. Jump refusals would not be tolerated. Whatever nerves, whatever feelings of anxiety any man might feel, he had to overcome them. All were volunteers, and all were highly motivated and highly trained for this moment. Gavin reckoned they were ready.

Leaving the ground, the aircraft had climbed, forming into vics – 'V' formations – of three and then into larger formations of nine. In all, it took around half an hour for them all to get airborne, by which time the dust swirling around the airfields was so thick it could be seen more than 5 miles away. After circling to form up they had headed off, a sizeable air fleet, crossing over the North African coast and heading due east to Malta; here they would turn to head for the south-east corner of Sicily, then westwards along the coastline to the drop zones, or DZs, around Gela.

Visibility was the toughest challenge for the pilots and navigators, most of whom had had precious little night-flying training or experience. There was only a quarter moon, and the wind, at around 30 mph, was twice the maximum considered safe to jump. Furthermore, because they were flying low, at only around 500 feet, some pilots were struggling with salt spray over the cockpit windscreens. On the other hand, the B-17s sent ahead to jam enemy radar appeared to have been successful and the first flight of troop carriers, reaching their objectives at 11.32 p.m., had achieved total surprise. Although tracer soon began arcing up towards them, not one of the first formation was hit. That was the good news. More worrying was that on an already dark night of strong winds, the DZs were mostly covered by smoke and haze from earlier bombing, and while the first wave were dropped reasonably accurately, those flying further back in an armada some 100 miles in length had gone increasingly off course.

Colonel Gavin was in the fourth group in order of flight, along with Regimental HQ and the 456th Parachute Field Artillery Battalion. Having memorized the route exactly, he knew they were a little behind schedule, but around midnight he saw Sicily. What troubled him was that none of it was recognizable from the studies he'd made. What's more, they were now alone, the aircraft either side of them having disappeared from view. He was starting to become increasingly troubled – but then, up ahead, flashes from the pre-invasion bombing could be seen. That meant they were definitely over Sicily, at any rate. Soon the red warning light came on; it was time to get up ready to jump. On the ground, the anti-aircraft gunners had become fully alert. Tracer was hurtling towards them, stabs of light arcing upwards. Down below they couldn't see the DZ, so the pilot asked if they wanted to go around again. But with the amount of tracer in the sky, they decided they'd better not risk it. On came the green light and Gavin led his stick by jumping first. Blast from the prop, brief free fall and then the sudden hard jerk as the parachute blossomed, while suddenly there was a burst of light as a C-47 not far away was hit and consumed by flames.

Major Mark Alexander and his 2nd Battalion were in the second group; as he'd hoped, their transports had managed to stick together and so the men were dropped as a battalion, although for a brief moment that had looked as though it was going to be straight into the sea. Standing by the open door, Alexander had seen the green jump light had come on but also that they were still over water. He immediately blocked the door, but some of his men were so keen to jump they tried to push past him.

'Get back, dammit!' he yelled. 'We're still over the water! Get back!' Once he'd calmed them down he had hurried forward to the cockpit, where the pilot confessed his co-pilot had got nervous and pressed the green light too early.

'He sure as hell did!' Alexander growled.

They had droned on, soon with anti-aircraft fire coming up towards them; once over the coast, the green light came on again and out he jumped, hitting the ground more quickly than he'd anticipated. As he landed, his chute pulled him backwards and he hit his head against a stone wall. Tracers were being fired above him. Carefully getting up and rubbing his head, he looked around. It was a little hazy as well as dark, but he saw a figure with a rifle and bayonet pointing at him.

'George!' called out the man.

'Marshall!' Alexander replied, responding to the agreed password. It was his orderly, Trooper Sanders.

It was noisy. The sound of guns and small arms could be heard from almost every direction. Gathering a handful of men around him, Alexander could see they were on some high ground, but whether it was their objective, the Piano Lupo, was not clear. Up ahead, above them, was a farmhouse. Here, when the first soldier – one of the sergeants – approached, the door had opened and the sergeant had immediately opened fire on the man who stood there. It turned out he had just been an elderly civilian, killed in the heat of the moment through fear and adrenalin. 'I could have brought charges against him,' Alexander said later, 'but it wouldn't have been a good idea. Everybody was all keyed up because it was their first time in combat. Things happen and you wish they hadn't.'

Alexander now realized they were not on their planned DZ, although where the hell they actually were he had no idea. As more and more men arrived, it swiftly became apparent that they had landed next to a series of five mutually supporting Italian pillboxes around a road intersection. Wild firing was rapidly revealing the enemy's positions; the farmhouse was above the nearest pillbox and clear of the arc of fire. Making the farmhouse his temporary command post, he left Captain Jack Norton in charge, and headed out to command the attacks on the Italian defences.

One pillbox was destroyed by a single trooper lobbing grenades through the embrasure; Alexander hurried forward with a machine-gun team to attack a second, larger, round one. As they poured machine-gun fire towards the slits, Corporal Eider, the assistant machine-gunner, cried out that he'd been hit. Quickly examining him, Alexander saw he'd been shot in the neck, but incredibly the bullet had passed right through without hitting an artery or anything else vital. The tiny-calibre bullets being used by the Italians had saved him. 'I wrapped a bandage around his neck,' said Alexander, 'and he continued to fire his machine gun.'

The paratroopers now had some mortars firing and, while their machine-gunners continued to hammer at the slits of the pillboxes, others crawled forward with grenades. Soon the surviving Italians waved a white flag and surrendered. With the immediate threat sorted, Alexander hurried back to the farmhouse to confer with Norton as yet more of his men appeared. They might have been some way from the DZ, but it did seem that most of the battalion had landed together, and that was something.

Meanwhile, Jim Gavin had also touched down, although the landing had been hard and he had hurt his leg. None the less, having freed himself from his parachute he was able to walk about all right and so, ignoring the pain, he hurried off in the direction the aircraft had come from looking for the rest of his stick. It was, he thought, one of the most significant moments in his life; at long last, he was in combat, facing the test he had trained for over so many years. Soon he found some of his men and in pretty quick time had collected around twenty, but it was clear they were nowhere near their DZ. In the distance, as much as 20 miles away, he saw tracer and the flickering light of explosions, and so he decided they should head in that direction, leading the way at a blistering pace. Gavin was bitterly disappointed; it was not how his first taste of action was meant to be. After an hour they came across a drunken Italian soldier; Captain Ben Vandervoort, one of his staff officers, rushed the man with a knife and revolver, but Gavin pulled him back; he felt they might be able to get some useful information out of him. 'I still had some doubt,' he noted, 'as to whether we were in Sicily, Italy or the Balkans, although the odds strongly favoured the first.' When Vandervoort put his Bowie knife to the man's crotch, he screamed loudly, fearing the stories of Allied troops' brutality were true; then grabbed the knife and, despite cutting his hand, pushed Vandervoort to the ground and fled into the night. The only information they had gleaned was that he was definitely Italian. It was something, but not much.

At 11.15 p.m., General Frido von Senger received a message from Guzzoni: 'We anticipate an attack at dawn against Catania and Gela.' This signal was issued to every single unit on Sicily, although it wasn't until 1 a.m. that Tenente Livio Messina, on duty, was awoken by the dispatch rider reaching the entrance to their camp near Mazzarino. Plenty of aircraft had been flying over and a number of officers had already abandoned their billets in town, but Messina wasn't especially concerned. The dispatch rider now strode into the battalion HQ tent and handed him an envelope. 'This battalion to place itself immediately on alert for possible utilization,' he read. 'Further instructions will follow.' It was, thought Messina to himself, bound to be another pointless drill. There had been so many.

Away to the south-east, near Avola, Michele Piccione was feeling considerably less laissez-faire. He'd managed to drift off to sleep, only to be woken again by more aircraft overhead. Standing up and peering out of the window, he saw a plane flying terrifyingly close. 'I stood still,' he noted, 'fear got me completely frozen.' Getting a grip of himself, he then woke everyone. Just a hundred yards or so away there was a natural cave in the escarpment that rose up overlooking the coast. It would be sensible, he suggested, for them all to spend the night there. Once again they packed up their things and stepped out into the dark; then, huddling down in the cave, prayed they would be safe.

CHAPTER 12

Early Hours of D-Day

D-DAY FOR HUSKY, a little after midnight on Saturday, 10 July 1943. H-Hour, the hour of hours, the moment when the landings would begin, was set for 2.45 a.m. in the British sector: only around a couple of hours away. On board the transport *Winchester Castle* were the men of the 6th Battalion, the Durham Light Infantry. It had been the fate of the Durhams to find themselves pretty much wherever the fighting had been since the war had begun, and so it was no surprise that they found themselves not only with orders to land on Sicily, but in the very first wave too. Lieutenant David Fenner and his men in 13 Platoon, C Company, paraded in the mess along with the rest of the assault troops, ready to clamber into the LCAs hung from davits on the side of the vessel. Earlier, they had had a cooked meal, which they had grimly termed 'the last supper'. Fenner had looked around his fellows and wondered which of them might get the chop in the battle to come.

David Fenner was twenty-one and had joined the Durhams nine months earlier, in time to fight through the Mareth Line and beyond, so he'd already experienced his fair share of action and had quickly realized that fighting in the infantry was a bloody business and expensive in men. Already, though, he felt deeply proud of the regiment of which he was part, even though he'd been born in India and wasn't a northerner at all. After his mother had died when he'd been just three years old, his father, serving in the Indian merchant navy, had sent him back to England to be raised by an aunt. At eighteen he'd joined the British merchant navy – but had decided it wasn't how he wanted to spend the war. So he transferred to the army, and after gaining a commission had been posted to the 6th DLI.

There were only twenty-three men in his assault platoon – rather than the normal thirty-seven – plus three sappers, whose task was to blow gaps in any enemy wire using anti-tank mines and fuses. Now that the hour was at hand, Fenner was quite calm, as were his men, who reached their allotted LCA and clambered aboard in good order despite the heavy loads they carried. Then they sat there, suspended. The wind had begun to die down, but they were still swinging, a foretaste of what was to come once they hit the water. At 1 a.m. the ship's engines stopped and the first LCAs began to be lowered into the sea – and then it was their turn. The waves were smacking against the sides as the cables were released, spray covering them all so that in moments they were soaked. And then they were off, into the inky darkness, the flat-bottomed LCA rolling and pitching on the swell.

While the first wave of Durhams were setting off, Lieutenant David Cole lay on his bunk, half dressed, trying unsuccessfully to get some sleep. Someone nearby was playing a mouth organ. Others were actually laughing. 'I looked at the electric light and the basin and the bunks,' he noted, 'and wondered how long it would be before I knew such comforts again.' It struck him as an odd way to go into battle – on a great water-borne hotel with hot and cold taps. A subaltern in the 2nd Inniskilling Fusiliers, he was part of 5th Division and would, around dawn, be landing on the beaches south of Syracuse near Cassibile, in the central zone of a stretch of the south-eastern coast code-named 'Acid'. He felt reasonably confident about the outcome but, as a signals officer, was anxious about whether his platoon's radio sets would work properly and how he would conduct himself once shells started falling. He'd not been in action before. It was what he didn't know that was troubling him.

One person who had seen plenty of action despite his youth was Midshipman Peter Hay aboard the destroyer HMS *Tartar*. The previous evening, he'd been on the bridge as Etna had come into view, although his eyes had been straining to see not the volcano but the enemy bombers which they all felt certain must appear any moment – but did not. The only aircraft they'd seen were Dakotas towing gliders later on. Then, a little after 1.30 a.m., they turned towards the coast, leading the first columns of troopships in towards the shore until they were around 7 miles out. Lying a couple of miles off the shore were British submarines, which had laid sonic buoys of different frequencies. The idea was for the naval forces to pick up the right one for their area on their Asdic – the ship's sonar – and so fix a position, enabling them to give the landing craft the correct course to their sector. Now, though, for some reason they could not fathom, they could not pick up the buoys at all and so had to use dead reckoning instead.

HMS *Tartar* was part of Force A supporting XIII Corps' landings in the northernmost stretch of the invasion front. The Yorkshiremen of 5th Division would be landing around Cassibile; on their left flank would be the 50th 'Tyne Tees' Division, which included David Fenner and the 6th DLI. Commanding Force A was Rear-Admiral Thomas Troubridge, who made a good pairing with Lieutenant-General Miles Dempsey, the corps commander. The two were well known to each other – they'd been friends at Shrewsbury School and had played cricket together for the 1st XI; it was a small thing, but it did help if commanders from different services already had an established relationship.

The Acid area was further split into four beach sectors – King, Jig, How and George, running south to north. *Tartar's* sector was Jig, and as it happened, the darkness and the swell and perhaps the inevitable confusion attending such a massive landing operation conspired to ensure their covey of landing craft did not pass them as they'd been expecting. 'At least,' jotted Hay, 'only about 8 or 10 boats did – the others apparently had got lost.' *Tartar* closed to within 1½–2 miles of the beach looking for them but then, seeing nothing, returned to their previous position.

They were braced for action, knowing the moment first light crept over them they would be engaging enemy targets and also potentially fending off enemy bombers, but dawn was still some hours away yet. In the meantime, Hay could see plenty of activity further to the north around Syracuse: the sound of guns, distant explosions, searchlights, the sky patchily lit by flares and then illuminated as if it were already day. At 2 a.m., Allied bombers flew over Syracuse and began dropping their loads, sending distant crumps and flickers of light pulsing through the air.

Further to the south, in the area code-named 'Bark South' around Capo Passero, the 51st Highland Division, part of XXX Corps, were getting ready to land, while the 1st Canadian Division, part of the same corps, were due to do so on the far side of the cape, around the western edge, on beaches designated Queen, Roger and Sugar. On board the troopship *Derbyshire*, the men of the Hastings & Prince Edward Regiment – the Hasty Ps – were being called in their serials to their designated boat station over the ship's tannoy. Lieutenant Farley Mowat was already hot and sweating from the combination of the kit he was carrying and being cooped up with too many other men within the narrow confines of the ship. He'd also just stopped one of his men from trying to shoot himself in the foot. 'You don't get off that easy!' he'd hissed in the man's ear, grabbing the rifle from him at the same time.

Mowat and his platoon were serial 67. 'My bowels', he noted, 'began to constrict' as he thought about the waiting enemy cannon and machine guns, Junkers 88s and Savoia-Marchettis. It was now about half-past midnight. The men shuffled down dark corridors, getting ever hotter; then they were out on the deck and into cooler air. Then the clambering into the landing craft, the uneasy suspension and the lowering into the water with a resounding smack. The noise of winches, of LCAs clanging against the edge of the mother ship, was enormous, so that Mowat felt certain the enemy would be able to hear them in Pachino. There were, out at sea, now some four hundred vessels of all sizes bobbing about in the dark as they set off. 'Standing in the bows beside the coxswain's cubbyhole,' wrote Mowat, 'I could just manage to peer over the high gunwales. The night was full of looming shadows, and the heaving waters were patterned with the glimmering phosphorescent wash of unseen boats.'

Out at sea off the southern coast, Task Force King, part of the Western Task Force, was approaching the stretch of coast either side of the small fishing port of Scoglitti, code-named 'Cent', where the US 45th Infantry Division was due to be landing. On board USS *Ancon*, Lieutenant John Mason Brown was out on deck watching the start of the invasion. 'A great wave of planes – our planes – has swept over us,' he recorded. 'They were our transports coming out. Although only a few of them could be seen, all of them could be felt and heard.' The trouble was, Mason Brown shouldn't have been able to hear quite so much noise. The aircraft he was hearing were more than a hundred that had dropped over half the paratroopers – Mark Alexander's 2nd Battalion included – in the Cent area around Scoglitti, rather than in their target zone further up the coast near Gela. Inexperience, lack of training, enemy flak, unexpectedly high winds and darkness had conspired together to ensure woefully few transports dropped their loads anywhere near the correct DZs.

Also aboard the *Ancon* was General Omar Bradley, commander of US II Corps, which included the 45th Infantry Division headed for Scoglitti, and the Big Red One and two Army Ranger battalions due to land at Gela. Bradley, however, was confined to his bunk, already sick with a bug of some kind and worse for the weather and rolling of the ship. Captain Chet Hansen, Bradley's senior aide, had got his head down around

10 p.m., but had been woken again at 1 a.m., as instructed, and staggered out on to the deck, having learned the American landings at Scoglitti had been delayed by an hour to 3.45 a.m. Huge fires were visible on the coastline, now some 8 miles away. The largest, he reckoned, was blazing around Comiso airfield. So far there was no enemy fire from the shore. 'Apprehension now and much of it,' he jotted, then added: 'But still the battle is detached, a million miles away.'

Soon after, the loudspeaker on the neighbouring ship called the assault platoons to begin loading on to the landing craft just as a searchlight from the shore switched on and began scanning the sea. But no enemy firing. Hansen could not understand it. 'And still no enemy bombers to molest our convoy,' he noted.

Meanwhile, in the centre of the US invasion front, code-named 'Dime' and centred on Gela, was Task Force How, including Admiral Hewitt's flagship, the USS *Monrovia*. Among the ship's officers was Lieutenant Douglas Fairbanks Jr, before the war one of Hollywood's leading stars, known above all for his swashbuckling adventure movies. Joining the navy before the US entry into the war, he had already seen plenty of action both in the Atlantic and in the Mediterranean, when, serving on the aircraft carrier USS *Wasp*, he had helped get Spitfires off from her decks to help the besieged island of Malta.

Soon after that operation, Fairbanks had been posted to England on an officer exchange programme and joined his old friend Admiral Lord Louis Mountbatten, who was then commanding Combined Operations, which oversaw British Commando raids – harassment and sabotage missions. Although primarily a staff officer, Fairbanks had undergone the rigorous Commando training programme and had even taken part in several raids across the Channel, all of which made him think there was a place for a force within the US Navy that could carry out similar raids, but primarily for deception purposes.

Back in the States, he put his suggestions to Admiral Kent Hewitt, then training for operations in the Mediterranean. Enthused by the concept, Hewitt asked Fairbanks to prepare a paper, which was then passed to Admiral Ernest King, the head of the US Navy. On 3 March 1943, King approved the creation of a new force of 180 officers and 300 enlisted men. Volunteers had to meet certain criteria: no seasickness, experience of handling small boats, enough electrical knowledge to be able to fix a radio, and basic knowledge of celestial navigation. 'The Navy,' the notice added, 'is requesting volunteers for prolonged, hazardous, distant duty for a secret project.' Much to Fairbanks' frustration, he did not have the rank to take command of his idea himself; but he was given the task of developing, organizing and supervising the formation, and in June 1943 he was posted to Algiers to join the rest of the staff of Beach Jumpers Unit 1 as they prepared for HUSKY. The aim was to use smoke and mirrors – or rather, radios and a lot of noises – to create a diversionary raid far to the west of the main US landings.

Fairbanks, still chafing at not being part of the Beach Jumpers' operations himself, was now an officer on *Monrovia*, with the slightly ambiguous task of keeping an eye on planned Beach Jumper operations and helping the beach masters manage the landings at Gela once the landing craft had actually reached the shore. As it happened, the weather was considered too poor for the small, fast air–sea rescue vessels with which the Beach Jumpers were operating and so the mission was postponed – but Fairbanks himself was, at least, soon due to be landing on Sicily. Earlier the previous evening, he'd been summoned to see Patton. The general had been working on an inspiring message to give to the men and wanted Fairbanks' help and the benefit of his theatrical experience. Standing before him, Fairbanks listened as Patton, in his odd, high-pitched voice, read out his message. 'I said I thought it was wonderful,' he wrote. 'And I suppose it was, in a rather corny, melodramatic way.'

In Gela itself there had been much activity all night, of which Mario Turco was very conscious. First, early the previous evening, there had been the noise of people outside the family house in the Capo Soprano, in the western part of the town, and his father had hurried out to see what was going on. He had soon learned that much of the seafront area was being evacuated and now entire families were moving out. It seemed the army was standing by to blow up the jetty to deny it to the enemy.

Mario's father and uncle had urgently discussed what they should do. Should they flee too? His uncle suggested they head to Butera, a village 12 miles inland to the north-west, but Mario's father, who had survived the First World War, felt they would be better off simply heading up the hill behind their house and sheltering on the leeward side. There, he said, they would be safe from any naval shelling, and they could get there a lot more quickly. Soon after, the whole family set off together and were hunkered down behind some rocks when at 2.50 a.m. the jetty was blown. A huge explosion seemed to rip the sky apart and the ground convulsed.

So powerful was the blast that it destroyed not only the jetty but much of the central piazza in Gela.

'A terrible explosion up by Gela and moments later a huge carrump,' noted Captain Chet Hansen aboard the *Ancon*. 'Wondered what it was, not a tanker or ammunition ship we hope.' By this time, H-Hour was getting near – less than an hour away at Scoglitti. Around the *Ancon*, all seemed calm. Hansen could hear other ships' tannoys and the sound of pulleys as landing craft were lowered. The searchlight beam from the shore continued to swing around out to sea, but the fires set off by the RAF's bombers were dimming. At sea, landing craft were heading to the shore, bumping their way through the swell and drenching the men.

Hansen was now startled by two flashes of fire from one of the US warships, a sheet of flame and two tracers hurtling through the sky towards the shore, followed by the sound of a distant explosion. Moments later more guns opened fire as destroyers rushed towards the shore, guns blazing. From the coast, the searchlight came on again, silhouetting the ships with an eerie light. Hansen felt apprehensive – the enemy had found them for certain – but the reply he was expecting from the coastal guns never came. Fire was pouring towards the searchlight and it quickly went out again. 'Fire increasing in intensity,' noted Hansen. 'The shore is a morass of exploding shells.' Now, further out at sea, the cruisers and heavy gunboats began firing broadsides, the flash of their muzzles vivid, the din terrific. Shells could be heard manically screaming overhead.

Back at Gela, the first US troops were heading towards the shore. These were the Army Rangers, attached to General Terry Allen's Big Red One and, together with some engineers they had with them, given an assault name of 'X Force'. Commanding was Lieutenant-Colonel William O. Darby, the founder of the Rangers – a new special force within the US Army that had been formed the previous year in England and originally based on the British Commandos. Like airborne forces or the SRS, they were all volunteers, highly motivated, supremely fit and competent, each man able to think on his feet. In North Africa they'd performed brilliantly, so much so that they'd been expanded: to the 1st Battalion had been added the 3rd and 4th for HUSKY, with the 2nd training back in the United States. Already they were known as the 'Spearheaders', and now were being sent forward ahead of the rest of the 1st Infantry Division here at Gela and the 3rd at Licata, further west up the coast.

Tough they might be, but that didn't mean they weren't a little scared. Platoon staff sergeant in Fox Company of the new 4th Battalion was

James 'Al' Altieri, one of Darby's originals who had been among the first intake back in Britain and had passed the test at the Commando school in Achnacarry in Scotland. Now twenty-three years old, he'd earned his spurs in Tunisia and with them, promotion. He was one of the stalwarts on whom Captain Walt Nye, Fox Company commander, was depending. In the past few days, they had been over and over the plan: 1st Battalion would land on the left of the pier and assault the Italian coastal battery at the Capo Soprano, while the 4th Battalion would land on the right, eastern, side of the pier and head straight up on to the rocky bluff on which the town was built and clear it. They had memorized aerial photographs, marking up every wire entanglement, pillbox, gun position and machine-gun nest.

Now, heading to the shore, their British-crewed LCA pitching violently in the swell, the Fox Company Rangers crouched, tight-lipped and tense-muscled, Staff Sergeant Altieri chewing a ball of tobacco to try and keep his nerves in check. Fortunately, they were still a way off out to sea when the Gela pier was blown at 2.50 a.m. Coastal searchlights were sweeping the sea and seemed to catch them all too frequently, although the swell was helping to hide them. From the shore, green and blue tracer was already being fired out to sea, while mortar shells exploding threw up momentary and dazzling flashes. On the ridges beyond the town in the distance, the red glow of fires could be seen. Unbeknown to them, these had been lit by the few members of the 505th Parachute Combat Team who had actually landed on the Piano Lupo.

Five miles from the parent ship an LCS – landing craft, support – drew up alongside them and Colonel Darby called out. They were ahead of the rest of the flotilla and were to stand by until the rest caught up.

'Right, sir!' yelled back Captain Nye.

'Good luck,' called out Darby. 'Have a good shoot!' Suddenly, the swell lessened, so that now the LCA was bobbing on the water as it idled rather than being pitched up and down – which meant it was easier for the searchlight to spot them.

'Hey, Al,' called out Private First Class Hoffmeister, 'how about dousing that light with a good spit of chaw terbaccer!'

'Don't do it, Al,' someone else called out. 'Save the juice for the pillbox guys 'case we run out of ammo.'

It was now getting on for 3.30 a.m. and, the rest of the landing craft having caught up, they were on their way again, machine-gun fire now hissing and spitting around them and mortars exploding. One landed painfully close to Altieri's LCA, lifting it up out of the water; as it smacked back down again, the metal buckled and the men were hurled into one another. Altieri was winded and, worse, they seemed now to be locked in the beam of a searchlight. At this point the USS *Shubrick*, a destroyer, closed towards the shore and began firing, smothering the searchlight with cannon fire until the light went out. 'We couldn't restrain ourselves,' noted Altieri. 'A cheer of relief erupted from our hoarse throats.' On they surged, Altieri racked by doubt and growing fear that a mortar would land inside their craft. Another explosion nearby shook them again. He glanced at Captain Nye, who looked calm, resolute. Altieri knew the new boys were also looking to him for assurance and that he needed to appear as steadfast as the captain, even if he wasn't feeling it. 'It's against Rangers regulations,' he told himself, 'to fraternize with fear, even when you're smothered by it . . .'

Ahead, in LCIs – landing craft, infantry – were their engineers, ready to clear a path through the wire and minefields. One of their landing craft hit a sandbar and began to capsize. Believing themselves to be in shallow water, the men started jumping off – but the water was much deeper than they thought and, loaded with equipment, many quickly sank before they could struggle free from their packs. Desperate shouts from drowning men plucked Altieri from his inner fears. He wondered whether Nye would agree to picking them up or whether they would plough on. To his relief, and at the suggestion of the coxswain, they pulled over.

'Help, help!' one man was shouting. 'We're going to drown!' Leaning over, they grabbed the struggling men and pulled them aboard. Seventeen, however, had already drowned, pulled down to the seabed by the weight they carried.

That delay of several minutes, as bullets continued to ping and mortars explode around them, meant they were no longer in the van of the Rangers landing in the 4th Battalion's sector of what had been named Green Beach. Instead it was men from Dog Company who were first on to the beach at 3.35 a.m., headed by Lieutenant Walter Wojcik. Newly promoted from sergeant following the reorganization, Wojcik was much loved by his men, indeed all who knew him, and had already gained a well-deserved reputation for fearlessness. Running as fast as he could, exhorting his men to follow, he led the way as they rushed the beach – straight into a minefield. The first explosion blew Wojcik to pieces, then others tripped wires: the 1st Platoon lieutenant was blinded by shards of fizzing metal; four other riflemen were killed instantly. First Sergeant Randall Harris was badly hit and blown backwards but, getting back on his feet, heard yells from another sergeant who had found a route through.

After helping the rest of the men out of the minefield, Sergeant Harris noticed he had a gaping seven-inch wound in his abdomen; he could feel his intestines slithering around in his hand. Clearly in need of urgent medical attention, he also knew the men now lacked their leader. Pushing his guts back in, he lowered his belt around the wound, tightened it and took over command, leading the rest of Dog Company up the cliffs and along a dirt road that had been cut into the rock, running just below the pillboxes that were still spitting bullets and cannon shells down on to the beach. The pillboxes were not one of Dog Company's objectives but, recognizing they could decimate Fox Company, now approaching the shore, Harris and another of his men took it in turns to run along the road hurling grenades through each of the apertures, silencing them one by one.

Now the ramp was down on Altieri's LCA and he and the rest of the platoon were clambering out into the water, which was right up to his crotch. Getting wet was the least of his concerns, however: a stench of brine and burnt gunpowder filled the air, and he waited for more tracer and bullets to stream down upon them. Thanks to Sergeant Harris, however, there was nothing, and soon they too were off the beach, through the gap in the minefield and up on the track beneath the still smoking pillboxes, now reeking of cordite and sharp, acrid smoke.

Up on the top of the cliffs on which much of the old town of Gela was built, they paused by a stone warehouse. There they waited for 2nd Platoon to catch up; but when, after five minutes, there was still no sign of them, Captain Nye told them they would press on towards the main piazza, their next objective. Off they moved, heading cautiously down the street towards the town's church, the crash and rumble of battle raging all along the beachfront behind them, and slipped into the main piazza.

To the south-east of Sicily, British troops were now heading towards the beaches too. The most northerly of them, and the closest to Syracuse, were the 287 men of the SRS. At around 2 a.m. they had been ordered to prepare to embark. Lieutenant Peter Davis had given his equipment one final check and then had hurried out on deck. During the journey, he'd had moments of deep apprehension and had wondered how many of them would survive the next few days. 'The uncertainties and dangers of the coming D-Day filled our whole horizon,' he noted, 'and caused us more mental torture than any hardships of battle.' Once he clambered on to the LCA, however, such worries began to melt away. They'd practised this so often now that it still felt like a training exercise rather than the real thing. Down the side of the *Ulster Monarch* they went and smacked into the sea, then circled the ship while waiting until all the LCAs had been safely launched.

Although they were all swiftly drenched, after half an hour or so the endless bucking eased as the wind began to drop off and they neared the shore with the shelter it offered. A searchlight was sweeping the coast here too, and Davis worried they would be spotted and all surprise lost. Another potential fly in the ointment was the number of downed glider crews, who, clinging to wreckage, were yelling at them to be rescued. One LCA stopped and picked up a handful of men, but most doggedly continued towards the shore. They had a mission to fulfil – one they had been told was of the utmost importance.

A few hundred yards from the shore, the LCAs cut their throttles and coasted almost silently. Peter Davis could hear the wind whistling and the waves smacking against the front of the vessel. Up ahead was Capo Murro di Porco, the rock rising from the sea. The cliffs were 60 feet high at their south-eastern tip below the lighthouse and in places quite sheer; but further west, along the lower part of the pig's snout, they dropped away a little and the ground rose in rocky steps that, from the photographs they had all studied intimately, looked easier to climb. Running roughly parallel to this southern stretch of the peninsula and perhaps a third of a mile inland was a road that led to the battery and buildings and then on to the lighthouse. The plan was for No. 3 Troop to land furthest west, clamber up the rocks and cut the road to the west of the battery. Captain Harry Poat's No. 2 Troop – Davis included – were to land on their right, hurry inland too and move around behind the battery and attack from the north, while No. 1 Troop, further to the right, would head straight to the battery and attack. Captain Alec Muirhead, in charge of the mortars, would set up his team between the road and the coastline to the west of the battery. Paddy Mayne's idea was to completely confuse the defenders; in the darkness and early dawn, it would appear as though they were being attacked from both behind and the side in a kind of pincer movement.

Davis and his men were still a few hundred yards from the shore when they suddenly heard more shouting and saw the dark shape of something on the water followed by flashes of torches. His first thought was that they'd been rumbled by an enemy torpedo boat, but then he realized the voices were English. Heaving to, they found the crew of another glider, and so hauled them aboard – not least to shut them up: Davis wondered why on earth the enormous racket they had been making had not alerted the enemy.

Soon after that, they finally hit the shore with a gentle bump and clambered out, just as they had numerous times during training. It was around 3.30 a.m., the first troops having landed a quarter of an hour earlier. At the foot of the rocks they came across yet more men from the glider force – they were, in fact, Lieutenant-Colonel Chatterton, Brigadier Pip Hicks and other members of the Airlanding Brigade HQ who had been on the lead glider. They had been sheltering at the foot of the cliffs and now, although without weapons, joined the men of No. 2 Troop as they began assembling for the attack. The early morning of D-Day was certainly not panning out as Chatterton had imagined.

Peter Davis found the climb far easier than the photographs had suggested it might be. Reaching the top, he quickly made contact with his commander, Harry Poat, who told him to stay put while he rounded up the rest of the troop. Minutes passed. Davis was still in the same spot, waiting for further orders from Poat, when he and his men heard the tell-tale sound of mortars whistling overhead. A moment later there was a crump and a small cry of pain behind him as one of his men was nicked on the hand by a splinter. Clearly, Alec Muirhead and his mortar team, having not stopped to pick up any glider pilots, had landed ahead of them, hurried up the rocks on to the headland and found their planned mortar position. What was worrying, though, was why, if Muirhead was in the right place, a mortar shell was falling anywhere near them. While they were pondering this, a second mortar whistled down and landed perfectly on an ammunition dump just a couple of hundred yards or so in front of them. A huge explosion tore the night apart – and also set the surrounding grass on fire. Suddenly, the entire battery was conveniently lit up.

This made plain that No. 2 Troop had landed further east, towards the lighthouse end of the snout, than they'd planned. No matter how well trained they were or how thoroughly they had studied their maps and photographs, it was down to the navy to drop them; still, in the almost pitch dark of the approach it was a very easy mistake to make, especially along a stretch of coastline where, from the sea, distinguishing features were hard to make out. Now, at least, Davis could see everything clearly enough – and there, vividly silhouetted directly in front of him, was the steel pylon they had identified as a marker, half a mile to the east of where they were supposed to have been.

Miraculously, there was still no reaction from the enemy. Davis could not understand it. Away to their left, a Bren gun began hammering, presumably from No. 1 Troop, while mortars continued to whistle over regularly. And then, from somewhere close by, they heard someone begin to wail pitifully. 'The sound of this voice crying in the wilderness,' noted Davis, 'cheered us up immensely.' Clearly, panic was setting in among the defenders; against all the odds, they had achieved the surprise that had been at the heart of their assault plan.

Even so, the plan of attack had already gone awry because of No. 2 Troop's landing further east than planned. This made it difficult for them to move across the headland and then cut back and attack from the north, because to do so would now mean cutting across No. 1 Troop's axis of attack. Fortunately, the opposition seemed so weak it hardly mattered. Davis waited at the top of the cliffs for ten minutes or so, wondering what had happened to Poat, then decided to loiter no longer but take his section straight for the battery. The ground was uneven, covered in a dense coastal vetch, and rose up towards the gun emplacements and network of concrete bunkers; the whole area was surrounded by entanglements of wire. Here he bumped into Johnny Wiseman's section from No. 1 Troop. There was healthy competition between the three troops; and so, rather than assault together, as soon as the No. 1 Troop men were over the wire they disappeared off into the murk; in his hurry to catch them, Davis managed to tear the seat of his trousers.

Only once all his section were across and they were advancing did the fireworks really start. Red tracer from the SRS men began streaking and criss-crossing through the air up ahead, pouring on to the site, and although there was now some Italian green tracer as well, the response was half-hearted to say the least. Davis was all for dashing forward, restrained only by the sober voice of Corporal Mitchell, a desert veteran, cautioning against such recklessness. Bursts of grenades and shouts of SRS men could be heard over the din from small arms. By now the mortars had stopped firing, and soon after that the fighting seemed to lessen too. The very first glimmer of light was creeping over the headland and, from the defensive position he had set up directly south of the battery, Davis saw figures wandering around and heard occasional bursts of a Tommy gun ringing out. Hearing the voice of 'Chalky' White, a sergeant in No. 1 Troop, he called out the password, 'Desert Rats?'

'Kill the Italians,' White replied, which seemed as good a cue as any for Davis and his section to scramble up and join the rest. By now the shooting had stopped; the battery had been taken. SRS men mingled around the bunkers and gun positions, Paddy Mayne wandering among them looking pleased with himself. Realizing that No. 2 Troop had landed in the wrong place and that the opposition was weak, he had decided to unleash Major Bill Fraser's No. 1 Troop pretty much on their own, and Fraser's men had been responsible for clearing much of the battery. Now Mayne turned to Davis and asked him where Poat was. 'It was unpleasant having to answer that I did not know,' Davis recalled. 'But he did not seem to mind and decided to call them by sending up the local success signal of three green Very lights.' Poat and his section appeared a short while later, having stuck to the original plan of attack. This, however, had involved a wide detour to get clear of No. 1 Troop's attack; by the time they were finally in position, the battle was already over.

Huddles of Italians stood about in groups, watched over by nonchalant SRS men. The prisoners looked a sorry sight, and included women and children who had obviously been sheltering in the bunkers for the night. Davis was shocked. 'They were a poor lot, dirty, shabby and ill-equipped,' he noted, 'ingratiating and fawning, they formed a startling contrast to the mental picture we had formed of the tough, experienced and fanatically patriotic defenders we had expected to come up against.'

Davis and his section sat on the edge of the circular well of one of the guns, legs dangling over, smoking cigarettes and watching the dawn light spread over the headland. It was only around a quarter to five; first light had been 4.39 a.m. Mayne decided they needed to get a shift on. The guns had to be destroyed and prisoners organized, and then they needed to get away, clear of the destroyed battery. Swiftly organizing themselves back into their troops, the SRS men moved clear of the guns while their engineers put charges in each of the breeches with a five-second time fuse and then dashed for cover. A series of explosions and a rain of shrapnel, and each of the guns was soon put out of action for good. Curiously, the four main coastal guns were all British manufactured 6-inch varieties, presumably left over from the last war when Britain and Italy had been allies. Also destroyed were three 20mm light anti-aircraft guns, a range finder and a number of machine guns.

While this had been going on, Peter Davis had looked out towards the sea as the sun had begun rising, and had spotted more than a dozen black shapes floating on the surface. With dismay, he realized they were gliders. Clearly, the ones they had seen earlier as they'd sped towards the shore had by no means been exceptions. In fact, out of the 147 gliders that had been finally earmarked for the operation, 10 never left North Africa, 5 returned early without having ever successfully cast off, 69 ditched into the sea and a further 9 had vanished entirely, leaving just 54 that had made land. As the men waited for further instructions and began to look around, they realized there were more gliders everywhere, crashed and wrecked against the abundant stone walls and rocky ground. 'Heavens, they were all over the place,' noted Davis. 'What a massacre!' He was also now aware that a number of men in red berets had joined their number and saw Hicks and Chatterton introducing themselves to Paddy Mayne.

The contrast between the two methods of attack could not have been greater. Both the battery at Capo Murro di Porco and the Ponte Grande bridge – as well as the city of Syracuse – were right next to the sea. The SRS, despite being parachute trained, had landed with comparative stealth by boat and had destroyed their objective completely without a single person killed and only a couple of men slightly hurt with superficial wounds. In contrast, the glider force of ten times their size had been decimated. Just four gliders had landed on their designated LZs and only one at the key spot next to the bridge. The British – and Americans – had developed airborne arms and so felt an obligation to use them, even though the system of air transportation to the battle zone was nowhere near ready to be deployed. It would have been far better to use these highly trained and motivated troops in precisely the same way as had been done with the SRS. Politics, misunderstanding, hubris and the sense of needing to test this airborne force had conspired against better sense. The result had been an utter fiasco. Tragically, it was a fiasco that was soon to become even worse.

At 5.20 a.m., Mayne fired green flares to signal the battery had been destroyed, then moved up to a farmhouse called Damerio, captured earlier by No. 3 Troop, and set up a temporary command post there as he pondered what to do next. His orders from General Dempsey, written after seeing his men in training, had charged the SRS with destroying the battery at Capo Murro di Porco and 'any subsequent action at discretion of OC squadron'. Davis and his men assumed they would be returning to the *Ulster Monarch* – but then a sudden boom from a short distance away stopped any such plans in their tracks. Davis and his fellows were braced for an incoming shell, but a few moments later they saw a large spume of water rise up from the sea. At any rate, Mayne now decided they would push on to the second battery marked on their maps, which had begun firing, destroy it, then join up with the main force. The SRS's operations were not over yet.

CHAPTER 13

Landings

IN THE CAVE BY the beachfront house near Avola, Michele Piccione had struggled to sleep. The sounds of aircraft, of battle – of invasion – had been too close and too intense. Everyone was huddled together, terrified of what unknown horrors might be going on. Then, at 4 a.m., he heard engine noise coming from the sea and what sounded like amphibious vehicles. Soon after, some men opened the gates to their house and approached the well, which was no more than a few yards from the steps that led up to their cave. Piccione lay there, frozen, barely daring to watch. Weapons were placed on the edge of the well; the Tommies shot a few rounds at the house and then yelled, 'Italians, c'mon, Italians!' Several men entered the house, then two others found bicycles and began riding them round the well, ringing the bells. Piccione couldn't help fearing what would happen if they saw the steps up to the cave; but soon afterwards, they left. 'Thankfully, God saved us on that occasion,' he noted. 'We were safe once again.'

After they'd gone, everyone in the cave wanted to move again; it was now first light and they would soon be spotted, so it was best to get going quickly. They were already too late, however: more men and supplies were being dumped on the beach in front of them, while a soldier stood watch by the gate. It was Piccione's neighbour, Giuseppina, who was first down the steps; the rest of them followed. Moments later the soldier spotted them and, slowly walking towards them, then indicated he was thirsty by pointing at the well. Piccione quickly filled up the bucket and brought it to him; he wanted one of them to drink first, which Giuseppina's daughter did. After this, more Tommies came over and began filling their bottles and drinking from the bucket.

On the beach, guns were being brought ashore, while a tent with a large red cross on it was being set up. It was all rather bewildering for Piccione and his family and neighbours. Nothing much had ever happened in Avola in Piccione's lifetime; now, suddenly, over the course of one memorable and terrifying night, the invasion was here, the sea was thick with ships, the beaches of Avola were already crowded with men. At least, though, along their corner of the coastline, the firing had stopped – for the moment.

All along the invasion front, as first light crept over Sicily, Allied troops were landing along a 105-mile stretch of the south-east and central southern coastline. The heavy swell and the darkness as the first troops headed to the shore had inevitably brought with it a fair amount of confusion. In the most northerly invasion sector, code-named Acid, from Avola up to Fontane Bianche a little south of Syracuse, General Dempsey's 5th and 50th Divisions of XIII Corps had been due to land side-by-side, the 50th on the left at Avola, the 5th on the right. Lieutenant David Fenner and the 6th DLI had been scheduled to land on Jig sector just to the south-west of Avola, pretty much where Michele Piccione and his family were. The journey with his C Company platoon to the coast had not begun well, however, when the coxswain of their LCA had cheerfully told him the compass light was unserviceable, which meant they were effectively travelling blind. Fenner, not much amused, irritably told the coxswain that he should have found that out beforehand and that from now he was to stick closely to the other LCAs carrying the battalion. It seemed these instructions had cut little ice, for Fenner had soon realized they were veering badly north. Drawing alongside another LCA, they found out it was carrying men of the King's Own Yorkshire Light Infantry, part of 5th Division, not 50th to which they belonged. 'I then took a firm line with the coxswain,' noted Fenner, 'and got him heading in the right direction.' In correcting his course, however, the coxswain then rammed another LCA, which turned out to be carrying another platoon from their own battalion. Fortunately, no lasting damage was caused, and at least they now had the shadowy shape of an LCA they could tag along behind. In their own LCA there had been about a foot of water by this time in which were swilling various vomit bags. Fenner had passed around the rum in the hope that a snifter might improve morale. Few had the stomach for it, however.

As they neared the shore, mortar shells began landing nearby and machine-gun bullets zipping and fizzing past. A searchlight was switched on and swept the sea. Then the coxswain came forward and told Fenner he'd accidentally dropped his anchor too soon, which meant he couldn't beach the LCA. Really, the coxswain was having a shocker, and the men now began to 'comment freely' about his ineptitude. Fenner told him to go forward as far as he could then lower the ramp. Down it went; Fenner waved his pistol over his head and, urging his men to follow, jumped out, splashing through the shallows only to be stopped on the beach by a continuous double apron fence of barbed wire. Hastily calling up the sappers in their assault platoon, Fenner watched them hang a pair of anti-tank mines on the wire and fix igniters and a fuse before they all rolled back down the beach to avoid the blast. Glancing around as enemy fire continued to stream towards them, Fenner saw he was lying next to one of his corporals, now dead. It was a shock; but the firing, though continuous, wasn't very accurate.

Moments later, the mines exploded – but in the process a bag containing explosives caught fire. Hurriedly, the sappers threw sand over it and managed to put out the flames before they were all blown to smithereens; then Fenner jumped up and led his men through the gap in the wire they'd just blown. He kept running, vaguely wondering whether they were crossing a minefield, and only stopped when he came to a railway embankment. Hurrying up behind him was Corporal Elson, who, panting and badly out of breath, asked him to slow down as the rest of them were struggling to keep up. Fenner, meanwhile, was puzzled by the embankment, as it shouldn't have been there. Clearly, they'd landed at the wrong beach.

Since there was little option but to cross it, that's what they did, and soon met up with men from 14 Platoon. After a brief confab, they agreed they were most likely 4 miles south, not north, of where they should be, which meant they were to the south-west of Avola. 'We should have been approaching this from the north,' noted Fenner, 'not from the diametrically opposite compass point. At this time, we had no idea where our OC, Company HQ and 15 Platoon were.'

Ironically, Private Bill Cheall, in the 6th Green Howards, who had clambered into his LCA several hours after Fenner, had managed to reach Jig Beach near Avola pretty much as planned at around 8 a.m. Even though he and his mates were not in the first wave, they'd still been keyed up for action, so were surprised to find themselves landing with so little opposition. They all wondered what had happened to the Italian defenders.

Further to the north, meanwhile, the first troops of the 1st Green Howards had successfully touched down on How Amber beach just to the south of Fontane Bianche at 6.15 a.m., followed by Major Hedley Verity and the rest of B Company at 7.40 a.m., by which time passages through wire and mines had been secured; despite persistent but largely unthreatening shelling, resistance was remarkably light. The 1st Green Howards flushed out some pillboxes, the Italians being quick to wave white flags. In one they found an American paratrooper who had come down among the enemy and been captured. Despite the poor state of the Italian defenders, they really were squandering an excellent defensive position. From the beaches there were good opportunities for hiding troops and, more importantly, mortars and artillery. The railway embankment also offered strong cover, while towering behind them in the Acid assault area was the high escarpment where not only guns but especially observers should have been placed, helping to create a devastating kill zone. Fortunately for the British, it seemed these coastal divisions really had no stomach for a fight.

Further to the south, the 231st 'Malta' Brigade, independent of any division, landed just to the north of Pachino. The Devons, Dorsets and Hampshires, all regiments from the south-west of England, had spent the past three years on Malta, playing their part in ensuring it got through the worst of the siege. Suddenly, on 30 March, they'd been told they were leaving the island, and found themselves in Egypt training for HUSKY along with the rest of Eighth Army's invasion force. Rather like the RAF on Malta, beleaguered defenders had dramatically become attackers.

Among those in the 2nd Devons was 23-year-old James Donaldson, a corporal in the battalion mortar platoon and originally not from south-west England but from Leith, near Edinburgh. He'd been a whaler, then a quarryman, and had been working in Devon at the outbreak of war. Two days later, he'd gone to the recruiting station in Exmouth and joined up. Now his wartime journey was taking him to Sicily – although he'd only realized that was their destination when he'd seen Etna in the distance the previous evening.

Crossing the Mediterranean in a landing ship had been hellish for most on board, especially once the wind had got up, but Donaldson was all right, probably because of his whaling days when he'd developed sturdy sea legs. At any rate, he and the mortar platoon were to land on a small island a couple of hundred yards off the coastal fishing town of Marzamemi, just north of Pachino. There they were to set up their mortars and provide fire support for the landings. They had been told that the island was occupied by a professor and his beautiful daughter, so Donaldson and his mates were rather looking forward to getting ashore.

In the event, they never had a chance to meet this reputed Sicilian beauty, because the Malta Brigade not only landed right on schedule, they did so achieving complete surprise. One Sicilian gun crew 50 yards from the beach was still asleep when they landed, and only one battery managed to fire anything at all – directly at the little island. 'They started belting away,' said Donaldson, 'and we had to wade back off the island to our salt pans. Their shells were just bouncing off the rock.' It hadn't lasted long, however, and before any introductions could be made to the island's two inhabitants, the mortar platoon was ordered off and taken to the shore of the main island. By noon, the Malta men were inland and had reached the Pachino–Avola road heading north.

On the Malta Brigade's left flank were the 51st Highland Division, part of XXX Corps, who landed without too much difficulty and with almost no opposition at all; in fact, a few days before the landings, aerial photographs had showed a number of local women swimming from one of the landing beaches, which suggested they didn't need to worry too much about wire and mines. So it proved, and by first light they already had some tanks and anti-tank guns ashore.

Further around on the western side of Capo Passero were the Canadian landing beaches. Here, the sea was more choppy and Lieutenant Farley Mowat and the rest of his men were having a grim time. They were all soaked, and vomit filled the flooded bottom of the LCA; one of his men even threw up all down Mowat's back. Then, to make matters worse, and after some time moving shorewards, the British coxswain pulled him aside and said, 'We're fucking well lost, ducky! Can't find no bleedin' marker buoy. Wot yer wanter do?' Mowat had felt panic engulf him. There was no one to call on for help, and they were crashing around in a vomit-drenched tin can. The faint light of dawn revealed the dim shapes of a couple of LCAs up ahead, and so he said, with as much authority as he could muster, 'Steer 340 degrees!' This, he knew, was the right course – but only if followed from the right departure point. Moments later they came under fire.

Fortunately, soon after that and before anything had hit them, HMS *Roberts* began the naval bombardment with a deafening broadside from its two 15-inch and eight 4-inch guns. Mowat and his men cowered, hands clutching their ears, at the sound of this immense and deafening thunder. Once the salvo had exploded on the shore, Mowat looked up and saw the coastline perhaps a mile up ahead emerging in the early dawn light. Desperately he scanned it for anything recognizable from the photographs and maps he'd studied. A spit of land away to their right seemed familiar, so he ordered the coxswain to head for it just as another salvo from *Roberts* screamed overhead. Now, as the coxswain opened the throttle, Mowat saw two other craft heading in the same direction, which was reassuring, and then spied standing in the bows of one of them his company commander, Captain Alex Campbell, firing bursts at the shore from a Bren. Mowat, meanwhile, stayed crouched by the ramp, clutching his revolver and waiting for the LCA to hit the beach and the ramp to drop down.

Then came a violent, juddering crunch and a drenching fountain of water. Mowat had jumped at the explosion, cracking his knuckles against the ramp. Moments later they hit a sandbar, and, just as a salvo of shells from their own warships hit the beach on which they should have been landing, the coxswain let down the ramp. This was the moment to which Mowat's time in the army so far had been leading. Tommy gun over his shoulder, still gripping his revolver, he shouted: 'Follow me, men!', stepped off – and fell into 8 feet of water, dropping like a stone. Fortunately, he was so shocked by this he forgot to thrash and flail and instead walked forward until his head emerged and then his shoulders and finally he was out of the water – and rather thrilled to realize he was the first ashore from all their landing craft. Machine guns sputtered up ahead, kicking up sand, and he dropped to the ground, only to be pushed forward by a wave breaking over him. Glancing back, he saw one man standing by the ramp – Tiny Sully, the man who'd been so scared he had contemplated shooting himself in the foot the night before. Mowat watched Sully screw up his eyes and jump, but as he did, a volley of mortars exploded around him, killing him instantly.

'Somebody blow that wire!' yelled Sergeant-Major Charlie Nutley, dropping down beside Mowat. 'Where the hell's the bangalores?' At this Alex Campbell came, charging up the beach, yelling, and slid a bangalore torpedo – a long tube through which an explosive charge could be detonated – under the wire; the explosion created a gap, and they were all on their feet to dash through; all except Nutley, who lay still on the beach, dead, with a bullet through his throat. Beyond the wire were clumps of bamboo and sand dunes, and for a moment no one was quite sure what to do or where to go next until they saw Captain Campbell standing at the top of the dunes shouting at them, oblivious to the blood spurting from one arm. Rushing over, Mowat caught his arm – a bullet had gone clean through the muscle without him realizing. While a medic quickly bandaged it up, Campbell yelled at them again to attack the house behind. Rushing through the canes, Mowat led his men into a little field below a small, low hill on which stood a cluster of farm buildings. A mortar was quickly set up in a drainage ditch and a number of smoke bombs were fired, while the rest of the men charged forward. No one seemed to be hit; Mowat couldn't understand it. Then more wire stopped them, so they lay down and continued to fire at the house until Campbell's voice bellowed out at them to stop.

'Fix bayonets!' Mowat called out, and once they had, they scrambled over the wire, tearing shorts, shirts and legs as they went, and charged recklessly up the hill. Only as they reached the top did he at last see why no one had been firing. Unbeknown to Mowat and his men, the Commandos, who had landed on their left, had already taken the strongpoint from the other side.

'Cor!' said a Commando sergeant to Mowat, once they had calmed down. 'You chaps did look loverly! Just like the Light Brigade. Never seen nothin' like it 'cept in that flick with Errol Flynn.'

The sandbar that had almost done for Farley Mowat was one of many facing those landing on the southern shores of Sicily, especially the Americans going ashore around Gela and Scoglitti. The beaches along this stretch of the coast sloped gradually but with numerous false beaches, and between these sandbars and the actual shore there were a number of runnels, which could be fatally deep, as one of the LCIs bringing in the engineers of X Force had discovered off Green Beach at Gela. The Americans had surveyed the beaches beforehand, so they were forewarned, but this was why the two jetties at Gela and Scoglitti were so important for their chances of swiftly unloading significant amounts of materiel. Both had been destroyed, however; it wasn't just the one at Gela that had been blown on Generale Guzzoni's instructions.

The weather was also significantly worse in the American zone, especially in Cent sector around Scoglitti where the 45th Division were coming ashore, and the strong currents and lack of many significant landmarks, as well as the heavy surf, sandbars and runnels, all conspired against an orderly and cohesive landing. The 180th Infantry were the worst hit, some of their landing craft veering wildly into the Big Red

One's sector and others far to the south. This meant men were landing in entirely the wrong places, badly disorientated and therefore unable to storm inland with quite the concentrated punch that had been intended. For all the training that had been going on prior to HUSKY, no one in North Africa had attempted landings in such conditions. The naval crews in action here were new to landing men into a real combat zone and most definitely lacking experience of handling flat-bottomed vessels in the dark, and in conditions for which they were not trained and the craft they were operating were not designed.

On the other hand, they had also been lucky, because overlooking the 157th Regimental Combat Team's landings at Capo Camerina had been the 206° Divisione Costiera, armed with coastal guns that could have caused untold trouble. Their guns, however, were captured French pieces, and while the troops manning them had plentiful stacks of ammunition it was all of the wrong calibre. And so they remained silent. Not for the first time in this war, the Italian quartermasters had bungled matters.

Further west, around Gela, 16th and 26th RCTs of the Big Red One had landed, to the east of the town in the Dime sector, and to little waiting opposition. Waiting in reserve offshore was the 1st Division's 18th RCT, which included Lieutenant Frank Johnson and his Cannon Company aboard the troopship *Château Thierry*. 'The rising sky of dawn reveals the level, hazy plain of Gela,' he noted, 'partially obscured by smoke, dust, and flaming bursts of shell fire.' He was mesmerized by the cruisers' heavy shells hurtling over, some solid shot, others with streaks of flame, curling towards the coast and exploding.

If the 1st Division at Gela had a comparatively easy landing, they could thank not just the impressive fire support from the navy, but also the work done already by the Rangers who, having overcome the beach defences, had systematically begun clearing the town. Even so, the defending 429° Battaglione Costerio had not rolled over, and bitter fighting had been going on throughout the town. The 1st Ranger Battalion, landing to the left of the wrecked pier, had initially hit heavy enemy fire – an entire platoon had been killed or wounded – but had soon cleared the beach defences and by dawn were storming the battery on the Capo Soprano, near where Mario Turco and his family had their home. There they had captured three 77mm guns, which for some reason had not once been fired. Although the Italians had removed the gunsights and elevating mechanisms, there were plentiful piles of ammunition and the guns were still capable of firing. Captain James

B. Lyle, who had led the assault, now turned the guns around so they faced out towards the Gela Plain that ran inland towards the Ponte Olivo airfield. Defences were hastily set up straddling Highway 115, the coastal road towards Licata, and an OP – observation post – was established on the second floor of a house next to the battery.

The 4th Battalion had fought their way through the town street by street. One man in James Altieri's platoon had been firing his Browning automatic rifle alongside another man only to discover his new companion was an Italian. When they both realized, the Italian had dropped his weapon and promptly surrendered. Yet it hadn't been easy: each street had had to be cleared, and snipers had been taking pot-shots. As a purplish dawn had spread over the town, Altieri had met up with Captain Walt Nye outside the main church, the Duomo of Santa Maria Assunta. Inside were some Italian soldiers who weren't giving up; Nye had casually ordered Altieri to clear them out.

Altieri had felt a little uncomfortable about having to fight inside a church, but figured it wasn't the time to have a moral debate. With several of his platoon behind him, he kicked open the main door, flung in a grenade, pulled back until it exploded, then rushed back in and fired eight shots towards the corners of the Duomo. His men then rushed past, killing two Italian soldiers in the sacristy, and together the Rangers bounded up the winding stone steps to the tower and captured a further three.

By 6 a.m., the Duomo and surrounding piazza were quiet, and some 450 prisoners had been taken in and around the town. Soon after, however, in the main square, civilians began venturing out. Two old ladies crouched down beside the bodies of two dead Italian soldiers by the Duomo. Another young Italian lay dead in a pool of blood just to the right of the entrance to Santa Maria. A young woman rushed over to him and, burying her head in his chest, began weeping, urging him back to life. Altieri had had enough. 'I couldn't take any more of this,' he wrote. 'It is bad enough for a soldier to be compelled to kill; but to witness the bereavement of the enemy's women is an anguish too torturous to endure.'

For the civilians caught up in this battle, the experience was utterly terrifying. Tenente Giuseppe Bruccoleri had been living at home with his family while manning a military telephone switchboard with some of his men in a part of his house. When it became clear the invasion was about to begin, he had persuaded his men to ditch their uniforms and weapons – hiding them in his uncle's granary – and put on civilian clothing instead. The house was accessed on the street side by an arched entrance that then led through a 15-yard tunnel into a courtyard. To the left was a large barn; behind that was the house. Believing the tunnel was the safest place to be, Bruccoleri had built a kind of shelter here for his family, with mattresses, chairs, first aid and other supplies. When the shelling had started he had brought all his family out there for the night, and there they had remained, huddled together, scarcely able to comprehend what was happening to their quiet little coastal town.

In the morning, they had gone back into the house to get some breakfast and had been still in their nightclothes and dressing-gowns when the American Rangers arrived, pushing open the door to the dining room and pointing Tommy guns at them. Bruccoleri told his family to keep calm and not to speak or move.

'Put your hands up,' said one of the Rangers, 'and woe betide those who move.'

Bruccoleri spoke to his family and, while one American kept his weapon pointed at them, others went upstairs, taking a number of valuables as loot, and then rounding up the men who had been holed up in the switchboard room in a different part of the house. Eventually they left, taking the men with them as prisoners of war, despite their civilian dress. Bruccoleri and his wife, although heavily pregnant at the time, were also taken, although they were released and sent back home soon afterwards.

By 9.00 that morning, the Rangers had secured Gela. The bodies of dead Italian soldiers and civilians lay in the streets as the sun continued to rise in the sky. The 429° Battaglione had suffered 45 per cent casualties in the fighting, including nearly two hundred dead or wounded and a further two hundred taken prisoner. The fighting had been bitter; it was no wonder Giuseppe Bruccoleri's family had been terrified.

Some 18 miles further up the coast, near Licata, the 3rd Ranger Battalion had also gone in ahead of the main assault force, in this case the 3rd Infantry Division, and had attacked a series of Italian coastal defences on and either side of a jutting outcrop, the Rocca Mollarella. Rising more than 80 feet, with commanding views to either side, it was an obvious strongpoint and, sure enough, aerial reconnaissance photographs had identified a number of concrete pillboxes and coastal defences, both on the Rocca and on the high ground that rose to the east of the beaches.

Two companies had attacked east of the Rocca and two to the west. It was Lieutenant Bing Evans' Fox Company that had landed furthest east, at the edge of a small, curving bay. Their task had been to get quickly off the curving sickle-shaped beach to the right of the Rocca and up and on top of the rocky cliffs that overlooked the little bay from the east.

Tall, athletic and with film star good looks, Evans, from South Dakota, was also blessed with a fine voice that had earned him the nickname 'Bing' after Bing Crosby. During training in Scotland the previous year, he'd stood out as exceptional and had even been singled out for the press as the 'typical American Ranger'. He'd more than lived up to his billing in Tunisia, demonstrating natural leadership, humane concern for his men and a complete disregard for his own safety, and had been rewarded with a commission and command of Fox Company in the new 3rd Battalion.

On the journey in Evans had done his best to calm his men, many of whom were struggling with seasickness, but it was clear as they neared the coast that the enemy were very much alert. Soon tracer was pouring towards them and a number of LCAs were hit by small-arms fire. Despite this, they successfully reached the shore and charged the beach. Evans had already discovered that in the heat of combat his mind went into a kind of vacuum. 'You don't know fear, you don't know apprehension,' he said. 'You just do your job. It's a fatalistic approach.' He felt this now as he and his men had hit the beach. He knew what he had to do: keep his men moving, get them off the sand and through holes in the wire blown by assault engineers using bangalore torpedoes. With Easy Company on their left, they managed to knock out one machine-gun nest and then a second, barely stopping as they clambered up the rocks, tracer zipping over their heads, attacking each machine-gun post and mortar pit in turn with Tommy guns, bazookas and grenades. The long hours studying photographs and maps on the journey had paid off. It meant that when the 15th Infantry of the 3rd Division began their landings here, almost all resistance had already been effectively destroyed.

The first transports of the 52nd Carrier Wing had landed back in Tunisia at 1.25 a.m., while the last had limped in at 6.20 that morning. Initially, aircrew reported positively and assured intelligence officers they had dropped the paratroopers with what appeared to be 80 per cent accuracy, but in fact the troops had been spread far and wide. Some thirty-three sticks of paratroopers had been dropped in the British area away to the east, while 127 had been dropped in the 45th Division's area, including Mark Alexander's 2nd Battalion of the 505th Parachute Combat Team. In all, just fifty-three aircraft had managed to reach the rough area designated, and only nine sticks actually landed on the Piano Lupo and the other assigned DZs. By daylight, Colonel Jim Gavin had discovered there were just six men in his small group, and not long after that they ran into an enemy strongpoint as they crested a hill. One of his troopers was killed in the firefight, so too was an Italian officer, and it quickly became clear that on this occasion the better part of valour was to pull back and try to find a different route.

Fortunately, the Italians they'd run into made no effort at all to pursue them, and so they managed to get out of the field of fire, work around the position and keep going. Clearly, moving around in daylight in the middle of enemy territory was going to be difficult, so Gavin told himself they just had to survive until dark and then they could use the night finally to get some miles under their feet and reach the high ground of the Piano Lupo. 'And there, with the help of God,' he noted, 'I hoped to find troopers and an enemy to fight. For that is what I had come three thousand miles and thirty-six years of my life for – the moral and physical challenge of battle.'

The people of Caltagirone had always thought they were immune from bombing, but the RAF had been over Sicily in force that night of the invasion. Mosquitoes had been sent from Malta on intruder patrols over enemy airfields in Sicily, southern Italy and Sardinia, while other Mosquitoes and Beaufighter twin-engine fighter-bombers had been sent to patrol the invasion beaches. Wellingtons, meanwhile, had been sent over not only to plaster Syracuse and Catania – yet again – but also to bomb an Axis landing ground at Caltagirone, one of the new emergency strips that had been hastily developed in response to the repeated bombing of the main airfields on the island.

Inevitably, there had been stray bombs and the town itself had been hit. Giacomo Garra's grandmother's house had been struck and partially destroyed by a bomb, as had that of his Uncle Rosario. Early in the morning, the family had decided to pack up some vital belongings and essential food and head to a house they owned in the countryside at San Mauro, a couple of miles to the west of the town. Packed into a horse-drawn buggy, they set off down the snaking road from Caltagirone, only to find themselves soon caught up in the movement of a column of

German troops and tanks from the Hermann Göring Division, including the Tigers of the 504. Heavy Panzer Battalion. Using loudspeakers, the Germans repeatedly ordered the flood of refugees to get out of the way. 'My father drove the buggy,' noted Garra, 'and more than once we had to stop so as not to get in the way of the Tigers.'

Roads clogged with refugees was exactly what the HG men did not need. On paper, General Paul Conrath, the divisional commander, had placed his troops reasonably well – 25 miles inland, out of range of any of the invasion forces, and only an hour or so from both Scoglitti and Gela. The trouble was, thanks to marauding American paratroopers cutting telephone lines, he was cut off from Generale Guzzoni at Enna and so had not received the latter's orders. Instead, it had been Feldmarschall Kesselring, in Rome, who had rung through to Conrath's HQ and told him to strike towards the American landings and knock them back into the sea. The upshot was a lack of coordination with the rest of the Italians in Guzzoni's planned counter-attack.

Another big problem was the unfamiliar terrain. Because they had only just completed their move to the Caltagirone area on 5 July, they had barely had time to reconnoitre the area, let alone test the roads for the weight, scale and size of machinery that was now rumbling forward. Conrath and the senior divisional staff had driven around looking at the network of roads and the surrounding land, but the men themselves had not yet had the chance. What's more, since the HG Division had been roughly cobbled together during the previous weeks, they had not had much opportunity, if any, to train – and certainly not together. The key principle of *Kampfgruppen* – battlegroups – was flinging infantry, artillery, armour and combat engineers together quickly and then hurling them at the enemy, but that required experience, something conspicuously lacking in many of the HG Division's units – along with much else. True, the Hermann Göring Division did include among its number some highly competent and experienced men and some half-decent kit – the company of Tiger tanks included – but there were also many who were ill-trained, clueless and, frankly, incompetent. It was a cocktail of forces that lacked any kind of cohesion whatsoever. 'At this point,' noted the division's chief of staff, Oberst Hellmuth Bergengruen, 'it should not be concealed that, with few exceptions, the troops were not up to the task of their position.' Leutnant Karl Goldschmidt was of the same mind. 'Things were very confused,' he noted. 'It was clearly noticeable that the units were not yet homogeneous, not well coordinated.'

Nor did Conrath have an entire division at Caltagirone – rather, it was roughly equivalent to an American regimental combat team or a British or Canadian brigade, because half the division was under Oberst Wilhelm Schmalz's command near Catania. However, since there were two separate American landings in their area that needed confronting, and because the roads certainly could not cope with the whole formation moving together, Conrath split the remainder of his force into two. Kampfgruppe Rechts – Right Battlegroup – was made up from the division's smaller, Mk III and Mk IV panzers, along with the reconnaissance company, artillery and engineers, while the Tigers were part of Kampf-gruppe Links – Left Battlegroup – and had with them the only two available battalions of mobile infantry, as well as some mobile artillery. This left Kampfgruppe Rechts a bit light on infantry, troops that were essential to panzer operations; the two needed to work hand-in-hand, the tanks offering fire support and protection for the infantry, the infantry the eyes and ears for the tanks. But what could Conrath do? He was trying to use one division to counter-attack in three places at once: on the east coast under Schmalz, and in two thrusts in the south against the Americans. 'And so,' noted Goldschmidt, 'the Tigers started their mission.'

That the Tigers and Conrath's two battlegroups were heading off to meet the enemy on their own was in no small part down to the American paratroopers. However frustrated Gavin might have been feeling, the scattered drop had not only thrown the defenders into some confusion but also given them the impression that many more had been landed than was actually the case. When British troops began pushing into Avola, for example, they were surprised to discover the town was already in the hands of seventy-five Americans from Mark Alexander's 2nd Battalion of the 505th. For his part, Alexander found that by first light he had 475 of his own men, and because he had managed to work out they were on the high ground south-east of Scoglitti, decided to take them off to Marina di Ragusa. Aware that part of the 45th Division were landing nearby, Alexander sensibly accepted he was far too far from his given objective to pursue the original plan, and so decided instead to support the 157th RCT now landing a little further to the west. Swiftly over-whelming the Italian defenders at Marina di Ragusa, they then headed to the high ground to cover and disrupt the coast road.

At Enna, Generale Alfredo Guzzoni was desperately trying to make sense of what was going on: the reports coming in, as well as the amount of Allied aircraft overhead, seemed to suggest an invasion far bigger than he'd imagined. Broadly, though, he had guessed Allied intentions correctly. At 1 a.m. he had already ordered all units into action to try to repel the invasion; half an hour later he had told his XVI Corpo commander, Generale Carlo Rossi, to be ready for landings around Gela, and had given instructions to blow up the pier not only at Gela but at Scoglitti too.

By four in the morning, Guzzoni had a clear enough picture to order his forces to counter-attack without delay, although this involved a series of reassignments of units that, frankly, could have been agreed beforehand, especially since the Sixth Army commander had believed the Allies would land exactly where they were now doing so. As a result, Rossi's XVI Corpo was, in the early hours of 10 July, given the Divisione Livorno out of reserve, alongside the half of the Hermann Göring Division that was based around Caltagirone. They were to counter-attack, striking back towards Scoglitti and Gela with all speed. The independent armoured mobile group Gruppo Mobile E was also ordered to get moving, and fast.

Not one of these units had seen action before, although there were a few men among their ranks who had been in combat. The same, of course, could be said about the new Rangers battalions, the 45th and 3rd Infantry Divisions and the Canadians, but there was a big difference: all the Allied formations were very well equipped, they were well trained, their communications were good, and by 10 July they were all in pretty good order. The same could not be said for any of these Axis divisions, including the HG Division.

The Italian Gruppo Mobile E, for example, was equipped with Renault 35 tanks, which were small, underarmed has-beens with a 37mm machine gun; the Germans had captured them from the French back in 1940 and handed them over to the Italians because they hadn't wanted them themselves. Bolstering their numbers were sixteen 3-ton L3/35 tanks, which were little more than tracked machine-gun carriers; these had a role but weren't up to much.

The Divisione Livorno, meanwhile, was also split. Tenente Livio Messina and the rest of the 33° Reggimento were at Mazzarino, while Tenente-Colonnello Leonardi's III° Battaglione of the 34° Reggimento was at a camp near Caltanissetta, some 45 miles from Gela. Leonardi and his men had been put on alert at 1 a.m. just like everyone else, the men roused by the camp bugler. The different companies swiftly got themselves together and trucks soon began moving out. Leonardi watched them, many still half-asleep, stumbling with their weapons and packs, others laughing and joking. 'I would have laughed too,' he noted in his diary, 'if my spirit was as young as theirs. My spirit got old because of the weight of responsibility I was constantly carrying.' Yet once everyone was loaded up, nothing else happened. Leonardi had been told to get his men ready and to await further orders. Minutes passed, then hours. As dawn broke, Leonardi moved the men under the shelter of trees so as not to be spotted by enemy aircraft. But still no orders came. Having been revved up for battle, now his men began to settle down again, lying in the shade of the trucks or by the trees.

Meanwhile, their sister regiment was on its way from Mazzarino. By 6.30 a.m., their column of trucks was heading down a *strada bianca*, kicking up huge swirls of dust. Either side of them were wheat fields; glancing at the surrounding countryside, Tenente Messina saw men harvesting, cutting the wheat with their scythes. Some of them waved, doffing their caps. It all seemed so tranquil.

Not long afterwards, however, Messina's reverie was broken by knocking on the roof of the truck's cab.

'Lieutenant, sir!' said one of his men. 'Planes, planes, planes!'

Messina hurriedly leaned out to look. A dozen or so, but friendly, he thought, judging from the rondels on their sides.

'Don't worry,' he called back. 'They're Italian.'

But he was wrong about that. Machine-guns were hammering and men leaping from the trucks. Messina jumped out and scrambled down the embankment at the side of the road. The column had been well and truly caught out, all in a line, kicking up dust, as they were curling around an exposed hill. American P-38 Lightnings were swooping down, guns blazing, spurts of bullets getting closer and closer to where he lay, then at what seemed like the last moment, one of the planes thundered past and he felt something thump his shoulder. He immediately thought he'd been hit but then realized it was just an empty cartridge case.

Back the Lightnings came again, raking the column. Messina lay where he was, rigid, helpless and shocked by the awesome power of these machines. Then they were gone, and the men dusted themselves down and surveyed the damage. All in all, it could have been worse: just one man dead and a handful wounded. None the less, it had been a devastating lesson in Allied air superiority. Clearly, moving around by day was going to be a very dangerous business.

*

While Guzzoni hoped the Livorno and HG Divisions would quickly push the Americans back off the island, he knew he needed to strike every bit as swiftly against the British and Canadian landings, so ordered the Divisione Napoli to counter-attack and sent a signal to Oberst Schmalz to head south too. As for the naval fortress of Syracuse–Augusta, that was not directly under his command; he hoped Ammiraglio Leonardi's men would make a decent fist of things there. That stretch of the coast was, after all, the most heavily defended on the island, with the exception of the Straits of Messina.

For Oberst Schmalz, however, the decision to move his brigade from their position in the foothills of Etna near Misterbianco had prompted some soul-searching. His own armoured radio cars, already further south, had reported back sightings of the enemy invasion fleet. Although he, like General Conrath, had not received any message from Guzzoni at Enna, he had managed to make radio contact with divisional headquarters, and then he and his Brigade Schmalz were on their own, heading south quite independently. He hoped he'd made the right decision, but was conscious he might have fallen into a trap carefully laid by the British: an assault in the south, drawing forces there, and then a second assault around Catania, when there were no German troops left to defend it. 'These are the commander's decisions,' he wrote, 'about which so often are spoken and written. Outsiders make easy judgements, but decisions such as these are infinitely difficult when one has to bear the responsibility oneself.' On the other hand, he couldn't just sit there, waiting for a trap to be sprung that might not even exist. 'Better to do something, even if it's wrong,' he told himself, 'than wait until it's too late.'

Unlike the rest of the division, however, Schmalz's men had already been fully prepared by their commander. All knew exactly what they had to do. In the early hours of Saturday, 10 July, Brigade Schmalz was already on its way south to meet the enemy.

CHAPTER 14

Foothold

MAJOR MACKY STEINHOFF HAD been woken by the sound of guns firing from out to sea with particular intensity, so that the crash of the shells shook the floor and ceiling of the grotto where they had taken to spending the night. Soon after, the telephone started ringing. First it was the Monte Erice monitoring section giving an update, then the operations room and then a call from his I. Gruppe, now based at Sciacca. So that had been an end to any thought of more sleep. At first light, Steinhoff and the rest of his headquarters team dragged themselves up from their camp beds. Two Me109s were needed for a dawn reconnaissance flight down to Cap Bon and Pantelleria, and another two over Gela and the south coast to see what was going on there. The rest of JG 77, Steinhoff was informed, would begin air operations once they'd moved from Trapani to their temporary landing strip in a clearing among the hills a little further inland.

By around 6 a.m., the *Geschwader* was coming into land, Steinhoff leading. He and Hauptmann Burckhardt had reconnoitred the site the previous day in the Storch – a bleached meadow beside a dried out river-bed and surrounded by hills thinly covered with oaks. There was also a farmhouse, which could double up as the dispersal hut. Having landed the Storch, they'd then paced it out and concluded there was room – just – for an Me109 to land and take off, but to play it safe they'd put down a yellow cloth, which was the point where the pilots had to touch down. Any further, and they'd overshoot – and crash.

Now, though, as he circled the low hills, the scrubby field looked much smaller; but with neither a breath of wind nor a hint of turbulence, he managed to touch down without mishap, which was precisely the example he'd hoped to set to the pilots following behind, and then come to a halt. Only then did he realize that if a pilot misjudged his landing, he would have only a half-moment in which to decide to go round and try again; any dithering and he would fly into the slopes at the far end. Taking off and landing a Messerschmitt 109 was difficult at the best of times, because of the immense torque, high wing-loading and comparatively narrow undercarriage which could make it unstable; on a short runway, it was even more challenging.

Steinhoff remained in his cockpit, radio leads still plugged in, but everyone seemed to be managing OK, and although one decided to go around again, he made his decision in time. 'There were the usual dust clouds,' noted Steinhoff, 'the crescendo and diminuendo of engines, the taxiing aircraft, the refuellers moving up, the bustling mechanics: a kaleidoscope of war invading this peaceful valley with explosive force.'

Amid all this activity, Steinhoff had been watching and occasionally speaking to Freytag's group as it came in on his machine's R/T. He'd just switched off and unplugged when he heard increasingly agitated cries as one pilot was coming in too steeply and too far to the left. Moments later, he saw a 109 touch down beyond the yellow marker, going too fast. Everyone stopped to watch, braced for what was to follow. Steinhoff thought it would smash into some trees, but before it reached them the tail reared up; the plane balanced momentarily on its prop, then somersaulted over, its undercarriage pointing skywards.

Vehicles raced towards the plane and in no time a number of airmen and ground crew were around the tail, trying to lift it and the stricken pilot clear. There was a fuel leak, someone shouted.

'It's probably one of the new officers,' said Burckhardt, now standing beside Steinhoff, then added, 'Christ – d'you hear that? The generator's still running. That means the ignition is still switched on.'

The men were desperately trying to get the pilot clear. Steinhoff saw arms appear, then a head, and finally the entire body. Others had extinguishers at the ready. 'Pull him clear!' someone shouted and then the pilot was on his knees, but banged his head against the edge of the wing. Suddenly, with a loud *whoof!* the aircraft erupted into an angry orange ball of flame and everyone was running. 'We were out of the danger area when we saw a running figure, blazing like a torch,' noted Steinhoff. 'It was the pilot. After a few yards he halted and suddenly collapsed.' Extinguishers were emptied over the stricken figure, the flames swiftly put out, but by the time Steinhoff reached him the pilot was in a terrible state – still alive but screaming, an appalling stench rising from the burnt flesh around his head and upper body, his hair melted and his face a mass of blackened blisters. Someone found some morphine to calm him, while someone else desperately tried to keep the flies off him. The Storch was summoned from Trapani, but as they were all aware, the chances of survival were slim. Burckhardt had been right; he had been a new boy. He'd not yet even flown an operational sortie. 'For a long time,' wrote Steinhoff, 'I was unable to shake off the impression of what had just happened. In between telephone conversations and aircraft state reports, the boy's face kept reappearing before me and I thought I could detect the stench of burned flesh.'

A couple of hours later, at 8.22 a.m., they were scrambled – although they then sat in their cockpits at readiness for a quarter of an hour before finally ordered to take off. Bombers were approaching, and they were to try to intercept them as they reached the coast. As they climbed into the bright morning sun, Steinhoff looked out over southern Sicily stretching away before him. He thought it looked like a rather lovely watercolour. Down towards the south coast and there, like a white smudge, was Gela and huge numbers of vessels. Soon after, they were warned that enemy aircraft should be crossing any moment – and then there they were: two waves of Boston medium bombers, thirty-five in all, escorted by forty Kittyhawks, heading for Sciacca. Steinhoff attacked one bomber, but his cannons jammed, leaving him only machine guns with which to fire. None the less, bullets seemed to strike home – he saw a shower of sparks as they hit the metal – but then he had to pull up and over and, because of his diving speed, shot well past the bomber, although now Burckhardt was attacking in turn. By then, the bomber was a wreck, but still flying as it turned south-west, fuel streaming behind it. Steinhoff couldn't understand how it wasn't on fire. But time was running short already, and so he ordered his men to break and head for home and that devilishly tricky short landing ground.

The men of JG 77 were not the only ones feeling outnumbered, undersupplied and underappreciated. So too were the other German fighter units still on Sicily – downcast not least by the scale of the invasion that met them as they climbed into the sky that morning. 'The entire sea was covered in ships, large and small,' said Leutnant Alfred Hammer, of II. Gruppe JG 53. 'Anyone who had seen this could not imagine any favourable result of the war any more.' Even so, and despite the numbers being so heavily against them, Axis aircraft had got through and had attacked the invasion fleet from the moment first light had crept over Sicily. Ju88s and Italian bombers as well as Me109s had dropped flares and attacked a number of ships. The minesweeper USS *Sentinel* was hit by a dive-bomber and later sank, while the destroyer USS *Maddox* was also struck by a lone Ju88. The bomb hit one of the ship's magazines and it disappeared under the water in just two minutes, although seventy-four men were saved. US Navy spotter planes were also shot down – six in all. These float-planes, or seaplanes, were easy pickings, which was why the Royal Navy had, for the most part, got rid of them, preferring to send in forward observers with the first wave of troops instead.

For those on the ground and out at sea, even these few incursions were far too many; yet really, the Axis air response was proving negligible. The immense aerial campaign by the Allies in the run-up to HUSKY had been incredibly successful. In the final week, from 3 to 10 July, German air strength alone on Sicily – not including the Regia Aeronautica – had been reduced by 100 aircraft, half of which had been lost over Sicily. On 3 July there had been 185 fighters on the island; a week later, on the dawn of the invasion, there were just 78. All Focke-Wulf 190s had been moved to southern Italy, the bombers had gone too, while Allied attacks on Sardinia had reduced strength there by 65 per cent. The Regia Aeronautica had, of course, already left Sicily. So, by the time the Allied invasion began, the Axis air forces had been massively weakened. True, the total strength in the Mediterranean theatre was still well over a thousand aircraft, but not all were serviceable – and in any case, they now had to travel to reach the battle zone, thus sacrificing the all-important home advantage and eating up both vital fuel and combat time in the process. Fighter aircraft now based around Naples, for example, had to travel 200 miles out and 200 back, reducing their time on target to a matter of just ten minutes or so. To make matters worse for the Axis air forces, the Sicilian-based fighters like those of JG 77 had to defend their airfields as well as harry the invasion, and it was difficult to do both, as Macky Steinhoff had appreciated on his first combat sortie that morning. What's more, because of the complete lack of any kind of cooperation and coordination between the Luftwaffe and Regia Aeronautica, what sorties they did mount were piecemeal and hesitant.

Arrayed against them, by contrast, were Allied air forces that were well led, well prepared and operating with cohesion. Even so, Allied air commanders were taking absolutely nothing for granted. While the air operations in the build-up to HUSKY had been pretty successful, neither Tedder nor any of the senior commanders were entirely sure what the Axis air response might be. The Americans and XXX Corps had been given airfields as their prime objectives: Pachino, Comiso and Ponte Olivo were all to be swiftly captured and secured, both to deny them to the enemy and to get Allied aircraft on to them just as soon as possible.

Air Chief Marshal Tedder and General Tooey Spaatz were overseeing this next phase of the air effort from La Marsa near Tunis. Tedder had been slightly put out that the three service chiefs did not have their headquarters together, but Malta was the traditional home of the Mediterranean Fleet and had operations rooms side-by-side with the tactical air forces operating from the island, so it had made sense for Cunningham to base himself there – and close to Sicily, where key decisions about weather could be best made. Alexander needed to be next to ABC for the same reasons, which was why he too was on Malta. There simply wasn't room to house Tedder and Spaatz and the staffs of the strategic air forces there as well, however, so they were all in Tunisia. Mary Coningham flew over to Malta for the actual invasion. It wasn't ideal, but it was just one of the many problems of trying to plan and execute the biggest invasion ever in the history of the world across the Mediterranean. 'The absence of Alexander was indubitably a handicap,' noted Tedder, 'especially as he took all his heads of branches with him.' On the other hand, Tedder was able to keep an aircraft on permanent standby at La Marsa, so it was possible for him to be in Malta within two hours if needed. At any rate, Allied command was far tighter and more coordinated than that of the Axis on Sicily.

One of the challenges was how to support the landings. Those out at sea or moving on the beaches were never happy to see any Axis aircraft overhead or skies above them empty of their own air forces, but, of course, few of those sailors and soldiers were aware that the Allied air forces had other tasks as well, such as hammering airfields, shooting up any enemy inland that was seen moving – such as Livio Messina's column, for example – and blitzing Axis lines of communication. The sphere of operations for the air forces was not just the invasion front but spread far and wide over all of Sicily and beyond to southern Italy and Sardinia. In fact, Spaatz's strategic air forces were also out in strength, with more than fifty Flying Fortresses hitting Gerbini yet again and medium bombers pounding not just Sciacca but also Milo in the far west of the island and the marshalling yards at Catania in the east. American Mustangs and Light-nings were also dive-bombing Axis communications in the centre of the island too.

Despite these wide-ranging demands, the Allied air forces planned to keep as much of an air umbrella over the beaches and bridgeheads as possible. The challenge, of course, was how to do this when even Malta was 60 miles away and Cap Bon 100. None the less, the planners on Malta had worked out how to maximize coverage during the sixteen hours of daylight. There would be continuous air cover for the first hour and a half of daylight and the last hour of light in the evening, provided by an umbrella of a squadron strength – twelve or sixteen aircraft. Each invasion sector had been allocated to a US fighter group or RAF wing – effectively the same – and there would never be more than occasional half-hour breaks in cover. It wasn't a 100 per cent permanent air umbrella, but it was pretty impressive all the same and, much to Tedder's relief, it seemed not one vessel in the troop convoys had yet been hit.

Among those flying that morning were the US 99th Fighter Squad-ron, still based in Tunisia, who were covering the landings at Licata. They'd all sensed something big was up when, a few days before, they'd been visited first by Eisenhower and then Mary Coningham, who had briefed them about RAF standard operation procedures. Charlie Dryden had been undergoing some soul-searching over the past few days, his recent first few experiences of air combat prompting him to wonder just what his motivations were. He knew he wanted to prove that men of colour were as willing as any other citizens to defend the United States against its enemies. But what did they expect in return? 'We expect to help defeat domestic enemies back home,' he noted. 'Jim Crow attitudes and practices in government, schools, jobs, churches – everywhere!' It was, he knew, a tall order. Now, though, he had other thoughts on his mind as he flew over the southern coast of Sicily and saw the invasion under way: to protect those men down below and to then get back to base safely.

On Malta, meanwhile, Wing Commander Cocky Dundas had been up and about since long before dawn. Outside his little house near the Hal Far airstrip, he had felt the breeze and seen white-capped waves out to sea. As he'd shaved and drunk down a mug of tea, he had wondered how the flotillas of landing craft had been faring. His wing had been allocated the Acid sector where 5th Division were landing. Sheep Gilroy, the former CO of 324 Wing and now group commander, had decided to lead the first patrol. Each squadron was to fly thirty-five minutes over the patrol line marking their designated sector – no more – and then head home, with the replacement squadron arriving straight away.

'There was an unforgettable atmosphere of tension and excitement at the dispersal points that historic morning,' noted Dundas. 'The Spitfires of five squadrons stood ready, silhouetted against the lightening sky, engines crackling to life and exhausts showing red as the mechanics warmed up the engines and tested the magnetos.' While he waited for the off, Dundas toured the squadrons, talking to each of the COs and pilots, making sure they understood the timings. If one squadron allowed themselves to get out of sync, there would be a domino effect that would knock the entire day's operations off kilter.

Dundas set off with 43 Squadron at 5.25 a.m., accompanying his housemate at Hal Far, Squadron Leader Micky Rook. Dundas was particularly tall at 6 feet 4 inches, but Rook was reputedly the tallest man in the RAF at 6 feet 6½ – and because he also had very large feet, he always wandered about in bedroom slippers, leaving his flying boots permanently wedged into the rudders of his Spitfire; as he clambered on to the wing, he would toss his slippers to his ground crew and somehow fold himself into the cockpit.

Taking off, they flew north, and soon saw the great armada. Reaching their patrol line, Dundas checked in with Sheep Gilroy who reported all had been calm with no sign of the enemy at all. 'Beneath us,' noted Dundas, 'our ships were everywhere, landing craft were still chugging into the beaches, looking like swarms of little swimming beetles. Cargo ships stood offshore, surrounded by smaller boats taking off supplies. Destroyers rushed back and forth like sheepdogs flanking their flock.' Even from 10,000 feet up, he could also see the wreckage of many gliders, and guessed there had been a disaster.

Despite the injunctions to adhere strictly to timings, Sheep Gilroy insisted on staying a little longer than the allotted span, so they were still there when 111 Squadron arrived for the third shift. Dundas now turned for home, having seen no action but grateful to have witnessed the extraordinary scale of the invasion below. As he was landing with the rest of 43 Squadron behind him, he heard Gilroy come over the R/T and announce he was coming into the circuit, so Dundas told the rest of 43 Squadron to hold back and let Gilroy and the rest of first patrol land ahead of them. Clambering down from his own Spitfire, he paused to watch them come in. One, he now saw, was approaching with an engine already dead for lack of fuel. Gliding in, the pilot made a slight turn to line up the runway, but he was going too slowly for the manoeuvre, however small, and the Spitfire stalled, flicked over and crashed into the sea. It was their only aircraft lost that morning.

Meanwhile, on the ground, the invasion was progressing: more men and materiel coming ashore through still rough surf with every passing hour, Guzzoni's reserve limbering up for a counter-attack, firefights taking place where coastal troops were still resisting, columns of Italian prisoners rapidly growing elsewhere. Offshore, naval warships never let up their fire. Wrecked gliders littered the countryside and sea south of Syracuse while American paratroopers continued to try to coalesce.

A handful of them were doing just that near the Piano Lupo. Among the very few to land close to the designated DZs were men of Company A of 1st Battalion, 505th Parachute Combat Team, including the company commander Captain Edwin M. Sayre, albeit with Italian machine guns firing at them from nearby as they landed and tried to organize themselves. In fact, they had come down not on the Piano Lupo, but on another stretch of higher ground a little further to the north beside the road that led south from Niscemi, and about 3 miles from Gela to the south-west. As Sayre quickly realized, scampering around between olive trees and other vegetation, the machine guns needed to be silenced, and quickly.

Hastily assembling a dozen men, he led them forward, creeping as close as they could, the enemy MGs easy to spot from the tracer they were using, and then hurled grenades. From the light of the explosions, he saw they had been attacking a concrete pillbox. Pulling back, he decided to hold off attacking again until first light, when he could get a clearer picture of what the enemy defences were. By around 4.30 a.m., he'd gathered some forty-five men and, as dawn crept over them, Sayre realized the Italians were dug in around a prominent villa, a square, two-storey building with a number of pillboxes in the grounds. Behind them, the ground dropped away quite sharply to a Y-shaped junction between the roads from Niscemi and Scoglitti from which a single road led on to Gela. The Piano Lupo rose up from the southern side of the Y-junction, and the idea had been to secure this area of high ground and use it as a firm base from which to create a blocking position against any enemy thrust from either Niscemi or Scoglitti.

Sayre launched his second attack at 5.30 a.m., with an assault from the

front and on the flanks using mortars, bazookas, machine guns and grenades they'd managed to gather together from the jump. All went
according to plan as they laid down heavy fire and stormed the villa.
Very quickly, its occupants surrendered, and then so did all the others
in the strongpoint, a haul which amounted to forty Italians and ten
Germans from the HG Division, who under questioning confessed
they were part of a forward outpost of a *Kampfgruppe* due to be heading
their way. This was Conrath's Kampfgruppe Rechts.

The capture of the strongpoint brought Sayre's men a bounty of
50,000 rounds of machine-gun bullets and twenty Italian machine guns,
which would come in very handy for the lightly armed paratroopers.
Matters improved further with the arrival of the 1st Battalion commander, 28-year-old Lieutenant-Colonel Arthur 'Hard Nose' Gorham, a
tough and inspirational commander in whom Gavin had enormous
faith. Gorham had landed a few miles to the east, near the Ponte Dirillo,
a bridge where a long straight road crossed the River Acate. Protecting
the road on the western, Gela, side as it snaked up through rising bluffs
was a well-sited Italian strongpoint of two pillboxes with four heavy and
six light machine guns, two anti-aircraft guns and one artillery piece. At
its foot were a long barn and farmhouse that had housed some sixty
men. Gathering around thirty men of his own, Gorham had attacked the
position at around 2 a.m. and, despite the Italians' advantage in weaponry, had overrun the entire strongpoint in a textbook attack – an
achievement all the more remarkable because it was carried out not only
at night, but using men hastily gathered together in their first taste of
combat.

By the time Gorham had made his way to Casa dei Priolo, the villa
just captured by Sayre's group, he had brought with him a further thirty
men and quickly they set up a blocking position on the road from
Niscemi, using the high ground to dominate the shallow gorge that cut
down towards the Y-junction just to the south.

There were now two enemy columns heading towards them – the left-
hand part of Gruppo Mobile E and Kampfgruppe Rechts. Fortunately
for Gorham and Sayre, the two Axis forces were not even in contact with
one another, let alone working together. Sure enough, the Italians
appeared around 7 a.m., led by outriders on motorcycles and a single car.
Allowing them to come on, the paratroopers then opened fire, killing
them all and stopping the rest of the column dead in its tracks. Infantry
jumped out of trucks and began fanning out to attack. Again, the

paratroopers let them come on before cutting the Italians to pieces with the twenty captured machine guns.

Earlier, Sayre had sent a patrol to reconnoitre Objective Y – the road junction behind Casa dei Priolo. These men had now returned, reporting the junction was defended by around twenty Italians in several pillboxes. With Gruppo Mobile E now bringing forward an assault gun and starting to shell the paratroopers' position, Gorham decided to pull back and secure Objective Y and the Piano Lupo to the south of it, which was, after all, their main task. As they were pulling out, however, six Italian tanks appeared on their right flank. Gorham and Sayre now feared the worst, but suddenly one of the tanks burst into flames, then a second, and at that the remaining four promptly beat a hasty retreat. They'd been hit by bazooka fire from another group of marauding paratroopers who had been trying to reach the DZ when they'd seen the tanks moving nearby.

Their attack had come in the nick of time, allowing Gorham's men to pull back to another area of high ground overlooking the Y-junction. By this time a naval spotter plane was circling overhead, trying to direct offshore gunfire against the Italians, but as he was doing so, the pilot was pounced on by a single German fighter plane and shot down. Despite having no radio link to the navy out at sea, Gorham ordered an Italian prisoner to head down to the pillboxes and demand their surrender; if they didn't, Gorham told him, they would direct the navy to destroy them. The Italian, unaware Gorham had been bluffing, did as he was told, approaching the pillboxes carefully under the eye of the watching Americans. Soon after, the Italians all threw in the towel. Objective Y was taken; although as with the Ponte Grande, the question was how long it could be held without reinforcements.

On board *Monrovia*, General Patton was receiving a flurry of messages and also listening in to radio traffic to keep up with events on shore. He was reasonably happy with how things were developing. General John Lucas was also encouraged, having been on deck to watch the first waves of landing craft return with no wounded that he could see. He then went ashore himself, heading off at 7.30 a.m. and landing to the east of Gela to find a mass of confusion. Fuel cans and all manner of equipment were piled chaotically all over the place. Trucks were stuck in the sand, while surf rolled over upturned landing craft. Debris and detritus were strewn everywhere. The navy beach master was struggling to make himself heard over the din of the breaking waves and, with no megaphone, was at a loss as to what to do. Newly landed infantry were sitting in the dunes waiting to be given orders. 'Get the hell out of here,' Lucas growled at them, 'and move against the enemy.'

Also coming ashore was Lieutenant Douglas Fairbanks Jr. From *Monrovia*, Blue Beach looked to be completely empty, while others, as Lucas had witnessed, were starting to clog up. Efforts to contact anyone on shore to get an explanation had proved fruitless, so Fairbanks and the British liaison officer, Lieutenant Commander Gerald Butler, had been told to go and investigate. A little while later, their landing craft scrunched on to the beach, the ramp went down, and Fairbanks and Butler jumped into knee-high water and waded on up to the beach. It was deserted except for one abandoned LCT, and so they began waving at the beach master at Yellow Beach, a hundred yards or so to their right. The response was a wave urging them to come to him. Then there was a scream above and a shell hurtled over, sending both men falling flat on their fronts into the sands as the explosion erupted behind them in the sea.

Dusting themselves down, they now strode towards Yellow Beach, anger rising at the stupidity of the landing parties in leaving this virgin beach untouched, so that when they reached the beach master, they let go with a stream of invective. The man looked aghast and interrupted them.

'Sir! Thank God you're okay,' he said. 'You've just walked over a minefield!'

In Gela, meanwhile, the men of Fox Company in the 4th Ranger Battalion had now set up an OP in the top storey of a house on the northern edge of the town. Around 9 a.m., Staff Sergeant James Altieri and his platoon commander, Lieutenant William A. Branson, were peering through field glasses out over the Gela Plain. Altieri could see scattered houses roofed with terracotta tiles, ripe wheat fields and, beyond, the bluish hills and mountains rising out of the plain. He reckoned it was the kind of view that would make a good travel poster. It was a beautiful day, the sky deep blue, the sun beating down. Now, though, they saw some black dots that appeared to be moving towards them. A few moments later they realized they were tanks – not German, but French Renaults. This was the second Italian column, the Gruppo Mobile E. Picking up the field telephone that had already been set up by the wire men, Branson dialled into battalion headquarters to call up some fire support.

Around the same time, the 1st Ranger Battalion had reported the advancing tanks from their new OP at the battery at the Capo Soprano and also asked for support. There was no artillery yet ashore, but the navy would help; and sure enough, soon after USS *Shubrick* closed near to the coast and opened fire, as did the Rangers themselves with the recently captured 77mm guns. The more accurate shells from *Shubrick* swiftly knocked out several of the tanks, but the remaining nine pushed on through the smoke and began speeding down the road towards Gela.

Wasting no time, Altieri and Lieutenant Branson spread the word to the men to get ready, as the tanks were heading straight for them. BARs – light machine guns – were set up at key points, bazookas primed and positioned and their 60mm mortars zeroed. Cursing the lack of air support, they watched the tanks hurtling towards the town. Soon after, they were working their way down the streets of Gela towards the central piazza and Duomo. Branson ordered the platoon to fall back to the buildings around the square and to fight off the tanks; while he covered the move with his bazooka, Altieri led the platoon across the street just as the lead tank turned into view and fired: the 37mm shell smashed into the corner building just behind them. Swiftly, Altieri ordered his men to take up positions in the three-storey stone buildings around the edge of the piazza, urging them to get as high as they could, beyond the reach of the tanks' guns at full elevation. As soon as they saw the tanks, they were to shower them with everything they had.

Just as he had finished issuing these instructions, Colonel Darby himself and his XO, Captain Charles Shundstrom, tore into the square in a jeep and, pulling over beside Altieri, demanded to know what was going on.

'All right,' growled Darby after Altieri had explained about the tanks, 'we'll give them a fight! They won't get through, is that clear?'

Altieri assured him they wouldn't, then ran back into the building and sprinted up two flights of stairs to rejoin his men. Not very long afterwards, one of the Italians' Renaults began turning into the piazza, spitting bullets from its machine gun. The Rangers shot at it and threw grenades, prompting it to pause before continuing its turn into the square. At the same moment, a jeep hurried in at the far side of the piazza, towing a 37mm anti-tank gun. Out hopped Darby, bareheaded and with his sleeves rolled up, and Shundstrom. Swiftly, they unhooked the gun just as the tank begun rumbling towards them. Darby jumped back into the jeep and, standing behind the .30-calibre machine gun, began spattering the tank with bullets, at which it stopped and fired two rounds in quick succession, both shwooshing straight over Darby's head. By now the 37mm was ready, so, leaping down again from the jeep, he pushed a shell into the breech and Shundstrom peered through the sights. The gun bucked backwards with the recoil, but the shell hit the tank squarely, knocking it backwards a few feet before it burst into flames. 'We cheered wildly,' wrote Altieri. 'Even as the drama unfolded before my eyes, I couldn't believe it.'

Now Rangers were jumping from behind corners with bazookas or creeping up and lobbing grenades, while one group dropped dynamite from their rooftop position right on top of the turret of another tank. In all, four of the tanks were knocked out, while the crew of a fifth surrendered. The rest turned and withdrew, although each one had suffered some kind of damage. It was now around 10.50 a.m.

There was more to come for the Italians. Livio Messina's column might have been held up, but the 800 men of the III° Battaglione were still on the move. Moving down the road from Butera, they marched straight into the waiting men of the 1st Ranger Battalion, positioned around the Capo Soprano to the west of Gela. Had these infantrymen moved forward with the tanks of Gruppo Mobile E, they might have given the Rangers a run for their money, but instead they were met with a hail of bullets and mortars and naval shelling and cut to pieces. When the dust and smoke cleared, the survivors were seen staggering about, while the dead and wounded lay strewn over the open fields either side of the road. Four hundred men were captured. The III° Battaglione had been completely destroyed.

At the Ponte Grande, a few more men of the Airlanding Brigade had started to join Lieutenant Len Withers and his platoon, and Staff Sergeant Dennis Galpin, for one, was pleased to see a few of his fellow pilots too. Had all gone to plan, the mass of the brigade would have reached them at 8 a.m. and then pushed on to Syracuse, but there was no sign of them. Those at the bridge, Galpin among them, guessed the glider drop had not gone entirely well, but at the time neither he nor anyone else knew that more than half of those who had taken off had ended up in the sea, or that the rest had crash-landed so far from the landing zones.

Even though it was now broad daylight, their small band were holding on to the bridge quite comfortably, although being regularly harassed by enemy machine-gun fire and sniping. 'We used some of our precious mortars,' noted Galpin, 'in attempting to neutralise the nearest and most troublesome ones.' It seemed to work, as for a while afterwards the enemy was far quieter. And all the while more men kept arriving, from all branches of the brigade, so that by around 9 a.m. there were some eighty dug in around the bridge and covering both sides of it; it was better than the thirty men they had begun with, but it would not be enough should the Italians make a concentrated and heavy attack – and in any case, a soldier was only any good while he had a weapon to fire and ammunition to put in it. They had simply to hope they could hold on until reinforcements arrived.

A matter of a few miles away, on the Capo Murro di Porco, the SRS had continued to wreak destruction. The moment more guns had opened fire, Lieutenant-Colonel Paddy Mayne had decided they should take the next gun battery out as well. First, though, they had moved away to the isolated Damerio farmhouse, half a mile or so from the first coastal gun battery on a patch of higher ground. As they'd headed towards the farmhouse, Lieutenant-Colonel George Chatterton had been helping escort the prisoners, now armed with a British rifle. Approaching them were a number of other prisoners; as they drew near, a crack of a rifle rang out and Geoff Caton, one of the SRS men from No. 1 Troop, collapsed; a bullet had hit him in the top of the thigh, catching an artery. Momentarily, everyone was stunned – the prisoners looking around them, the SRS rushing to Caton and looking for the sniper. Suddenly, one of the No. 1 Troop men pushed through the prisoners and, without a word, swung his rifle at one of the Italians, smashing in his skull.

'Why on earth did you do that?' Chatterton asked him, barely believing what he'd just witnessed.

'Didn't you see the bastard?' he replied. 'He shot my chum,' he explained, 'and then dropped into the column. I happened to turn round just as he dropped.'

As the SRS approached the Damerio farmhouse, most of the Italians there fled, although those that remained were swiftly dealt with. It turned out the site had been used as an OP, so Mayne paused to get his bearings and to make a plan to take the next battery, which stood on the north side of the peninsula across the bay from Syracuse. Then, as Chatterton was marvelling at the scale of the fleet out to sea, shells started whistling over from offshore – clearly the navy had seen the shelling from the Italian guns and felt some counter-battery fire was needed. Fortunately, since Mayne had been accompanied by a naval forward observation officer, they were able to make radio contact and swiftly tell them to stop before anyone got hurt.

Nor was anyone hit when spasmodic firing opened up from a neighbouring farmhouse. After laying down some mortars, the occupants promptly surrendered, only to reveal themselves as glider-borne troops. 'They were firmly convinced that we were Ities,' wrote Peter Davis. 'We were the only troops who wore khaki berets, and these, with the sun shields over our backs and our blue Indian shirts, did give us a rather foreign appearance.' The South Staffs men were relieved and ashamed in equal measure.

The men of the three SRS troops now pushed forward along different routes and in bounds, confidence growing quickly. Davis and his men kept pausing to pick up the small orange tomatoes that were growing all around them, eating some as they went and stuffing more into their pockets. 'Our sections just pressed forward,' he wrote, 'ignoring completely the mild and spasmodic opposition with which they were occasionally faced.' From one farmhouse or building after another would come the zap or whine of a badly aimed bullet or two, then they'd spot one or more enemy soldiers and Davis and his men would respond with a clatter of heavier and better-aimed fire, prompting some to flee and others to emerge with their hands up.

Eventually reaching a church, they were greeted by a priest who, in perfect English, asked them to spare his church and the women and children sheltering inside. This they reassured him they would do – then realized the battery was now behind them. Hurrying back towards it, Davis and his men got there only to discover it had already been captured and a further five anti-aircraft guns destroyed, along with one range finder and several mortars and machine guns. The SRS men had been utterly ruthless, and anyone who dared cross them had been brutally dealt with. Earlier in the day, a pocket of Italians had been spotted sniping at South Staffs troops clinging to their wrecked glider. 'Needless to say,' said Sergeant Albert Youngman, 'they didn't see their families again.' Snipers had been pursued and dealt with; any who dared resist were slaughtered. George Chatterton witnessed Paddy Mayne shoot an Italian officer at point-blank range after he fired a shot as other officers were surrendering. 'There was no more trouble,' noted Chatterton.

In the south-east corner of the island, Pachino airfield, a vital objective for the Allies on this first day of the invasion, fell before midday. Just one bullet was fired in defence; then the defenders either surrendered or melted away. The biggest discomfort for Lieutenant Farley Mowat and the rest of A Company of the Hasty Ps was the heat. The Pachino peninsula was a particularly unforgiving part of an unforgiving island, rising from the sea into a sun-baked arid plateau, almost featureless except for the network of stone walls, dirt roads and occasional small towns like Maucini and Pachino. It turned out they'd landed quite a way further west from the rest of their brigade, and so had climbed up from the sea into empty fields shimmering in the heat haze.

Even as he marched, Mowat had been nodding off with the combination of fatigue and stultifying heat when he was suddenly jolted back into full consciousness by a brief exchange of fire around the corner up ahead. Hurrying forward with his men, he saw two wooden-wheeled First World War-era field guns that had veered off the road, an ancient truck steaming from a shattered radiator and a handful of Italians huddled in the middle of the road, their arms aloft. Holding them at gunpoint were Paddy Ryan's platoon. Three Italians lay dead by the side of the road. Mowat went over to take a look and saw one of the men staring up at him. 'His eyes were open and as yet undimmed,' he observed. 'And they were blue, like mine. This was no alien, this youth who must have been about my own age.' Like Mowat, the dead man had also tried to grow a rather thin blond moustache. His skin was rapidly draining of colour as the blood spread, dark and horribly, from a chest punctured by bullets from Ryan's Tommy gun. These were men from the 54° Reggimento di Artiglieria of Divisione Napoli, part of the main counter-attack supposed to throw the Allies back into the sea. Collecting the Italians' horses and gathering the prisoners, the Canadians continued on their way towards Pachino, hot, hungry, tired and increasingly thirsty.

On the east coast, in 5th Division's sector, Acid North, Lieutenant David Cole and his signals platoon of the 2nd Inniskillings had landed around mid-morning – and on the right beach: by now, the coxswains had got used to ferrying troops from the ships and could see what they were doing. As they'd neared the shore one of his men had started quietly humming 'Oh I do like to be beside the seaside', while others were vomiting as they bounced on the still choppy seas. Inland, he had heard 25-pounder field guns already booming and the distant chatter of small arms. Once landed, they had moved off the beach along lanes through the wire and mines already marked with white tape, while off this track more sappers were clearing other mines. Ammunition boxes were scattered around; a wrecked glider lay broken and smashed, as did a shattered gun emplacement. Telegraph poles stood at savage angles and craters pockmarked the ground. Reaching a dusty *strada bianca*, lined by a high stone wall either side, they saw a shuffling mass of Italian prisoners.

'Where are Mussolini's twenty million bayonets now, chum?' Cole heard one of the Inniskillings say to the men. He was shocked to see such slovenly, unshaven and poorly dressed men. Most seemed only too happy to have been captured. Behind them came a party of civilians. 'Viva inglesi,' said one woman.

Cole and his men pushed on towards Cassibile, which was already in British hands. More stone walls lined the road into the town, stencilled with 'Viva il Duce' and 'Vincere', which Cole thought now seemed absurd. Cassibile was a long, linear town, a place of pale stone and terracotta roofs, many of the houses, churches, workshops and other buildings lining the main road now battered and smashed. They came across two burning Italian tanks and a dead Italian in the middle of the road, a pool of blood spreading from underneath him.

Further west across the south coast of the island, meanwhile, Licata, the westernmost town on the invasion front, had fallen to the Americans by 11.30 a.m. with losses to the 3rd Division of only a hundred men. Among those put ashore here was Private First Class Audie Murphy, of B Company in the 1st Battalion, 15th Infantry, feeling deeply frustrated at having landed more than three hours after the rest of the battalion because of confusion during the run-in. 'If the landing schedule had not gone snafu,' he wrote, 'we would have come ashore with the assault waves. That was what I wanted. I had primed myself for the big moment.'

Murphy was just eighteen years old and appeared even younger, with his teenage good looks and big brown eyes. Like so many working-class Americans, his upbringing in the Depression-hit States had been tough. One of nine kids – two of whom had died young – he had still been a child when his father had walked out on them, while his mother, worn down by poverty and the burden of raising a brood of seven on too little, fell ill and died when Murphy was sixteen. His three youngest siblings went to an orphanage, while the rest scattered. To Audie, the army offered an obvious substitute for the family he was missing and he joined as soon as he could, although he was considered too scrawny for his first choice, the US Marine Corps. Then he tried the Airborne, but they thought him underweight too. Eventually he was accepted by the infantry. 'I was not overjoyed,' he wrote. 'The infantry was too commonplace for my ambition.' Murphy was a young man in a hurry and with a huge amount of pent-up anger inside him just bursting to get out. Combat was to be his release, but he'd arrived in Tunisia too late; and now, on HUSKY D-Day, the shooting match was apparently all over before he'd had a chance to fire a single shot. He was mad as hell.

Major-General Lucian Truscott, the divisional commander, was altogether more sanguine, however. He had been able to come ashore at the town's small harbour a little after midday; also ashore were men of the 2nd Battalion of the 41st Armored Infantry Regiment, part of 2nd Armored Division. Although they were part of the floating reserve, Truscott had ordered them up to help rapidly expand the bridgehead. 'Amazingly,' noted Private Eugene 'Breezy' Griffin, 'our LCI went right to the dock.' Weighed down by full field pack, ammo belt around his waist, two more bandoliers across his chest, rifle and a mortar ammo carrier, he trudged off the landing craft on to the quayside and milled around with his fellows waiting for orders.

Soon after, they were formed up on the quay and told to march out in a column of four. Griffin had scarcely been able to believe what he'd heard, for all through training it had been drummed into them that they were always to look to disperse, yet now, on the first day of the invasion, they were marching out as though on parade. 'Everybody was scared to death that we were going to get clobbered because we presented such an inviting target,' he noted. 'Why we didn't is anybody's guess.' They didn't because the enemy at Licata had already surrendered, but he was right to be wary of marauding enemy fighter aircraft; there might not have been many in the sky, but the Allies still didn't have total control of the air space.

At Gela the 26th Infantry was pushing inland, as was the 16th Infantry on their right; by late morning they had created a bridgehead and were pushing towards the Piano Lupo to meet up with the airborne forces. They, too, were finding that resistance was rapidly crumbling with dusty, dishevelled prisoners appearing in droves. What they didn't realize, however, was that only a handful of paratroopers now had a foothold on the Piano Lupo and that two columns of German battlegroups were heading into the fight.

CHAPTER 15

Night Attack

M ARIO TURCO'S FATHER AND uncle had ventured into Gela early on the morning of 10 July to see what was going on, and later Mario had left their shelter and headed into town too, curiosity getting the better of him. 'And that's when I saw one of the American soldiers,' he said. 'He offered me a chocolate bar but I refused it.' He also saw a number of dead Italian soldiers lying in the streets – and knew they had been defeated. For a boy who had grown up with the Fascist youth organizations it was hard to comprehend; he had believed Italy was invincible, yet now they were the losers. 'All that pride had vanished, we were nothing!' he said. 'It was a disappointment.' He was also truly amazed by what was being delivered from the landing craft – guns, jeeps, other vehicles and, what particularly struck him, pneumatic impact wrenches, which engineers were using to tighten bolts on to newly delivered trackways. Nothing like this had ever been seen in Gela. 'Everyone in Gela worked and built everything by hand,' he said. 'Suddenly we saw these giants.'

What he was witnessing was the arrival of the first LST straight on to the beach at Red 2. Because the pier had been destroyed, and because General Allen was insistent tanks and other vehicles be unloaded as soon as possible, it was vital the pontoon causeway carried by LST 338 was fixed up right away. Rigging the causeway began just after 8 a.m., while shells were falling around and the swell was still strong. Three Me109s swooped in low at around 10 a.m. and dropped bombs, but all missed. Half an hour later, some 63 vehicles and a further 300 troops had been unloaded from the landing ship. LSTs also landed bulldozers towing sleds loaded with sections of the prefabricated beach covering that were needed for wheeled vehicles to get off the soft sand beach. Six sleds were enough to offload some 400 yards of this PSP – perforated steel plating – trackway, which was bolted together using the pneumatic equipment that had so dazzled Mario Turco. Also in operation for the first time were DUKWs, each capable of carrying some 3 tons. Beetling back and forth, they were bringing ashore ammunition boxes, rations, medical supplies and more, delivering them to rapidly growing stockpiles.

While Mario Turco watched with amazement what was happening on the beaches, a few miles inland at Ponte Olivo, Melino Barbagallo and all the ground control units that had remained were now getting ready to leave. Having seen and heard the pyrotechnics of the early hours, they'd then listened with mounting alarm to the fighting developing in Gela and watched the advance of the Gruppo Mobile E. They had been wondering what they should do when they received orders to pull out. 'There was a lot of confusion,' said Barbagallo, 'but we organised the retreat for those of us left on the ground.' There were a few trucks, so they loaded them up with their precious radio and radar equipment and got going. He was able to get a ride in one of the trucks, but many were left to walk.

Meanwhile, the two-pronged advance of the HG Division finally got under way around 2 p.m., some thirteen hours after the division had been put on alert, ten hours after being ordered to advance, and with a conspicuous lack of tactical chutzpah. In truth, the narrowness of the roads, combined with a lack of familiarity with the area, frequent skirmishes with pockets of American paratroopers and a complete lack of any cohesion among the units ensured an entire dearth of impetus. Several times General Conrath himself had to go forward and give his men a kick; at one point he even relieved the commander of Kampfgruppe Rechts and took over himself.

Oberst Hellmuth Bergengruen, the division's chief of staff, had joined Conrath and soon caught up with the vanguard as it neared Casa dei Priolo – where Captain Sayre's Company A of the 505th had attacked Italian positions earlier. The sun was dazzling and, despite his field glasses, Bergengruen struggled to see anything very clearly. Even so, on paper, at any rate, Kampfgruppe Rechts was a fine combination of mobile all-arms, with tanks, mobile assault engineers and reconnaissance troops taking the infantry role, and also mobile artillery. Yet as they pushed off the ridge and down towards the Y-junction, the lead reconnaissance and assault engineer troops were cut to pieces by Lieutenant-Colonel Gorham's paratroopers, reinforced by men of the 16th Infantry who had pushed inland from the beaches east of Gela. The panzers now moved forward too – but the Americans were able to direct naval guns at them, their shells thundering over in a devastating barrage, stopping the Germans in their tracks and then prompting them to fall back.

General Conrath, his fury and disgust at his men rising with every passing hour, ordered them to renew their attack at 3 p.m., but again the combination of American mortars and small-arms and naval fire-power outfaced the panzers. 'The young panzer regiment,' noted Bergengruen, 'failed completely.'

Some miles to the east, the left-hand punch wasn't doing much better either, although the mobile artillery had pushed further forward than the rest. The company of Tiger tanks had barely got anywhere. These were Kampfgruppe Links' best asset and, together with the two battalions of panzer-grenadiers, should have made hay, but Kesselring's decision to move the division into the Caltagirone area just days before the invasion was now really working against them as they trundled south along roads and through countryside with which they were woefully unfamiliar. The left-hand column was using two roads south towards Biscari, neither of which was asphalted. The 20-mile journey might not have looked very far on a map, and the distance was far less as the crow flew, but the roads were narrow and passed through several small towns – towns lined with narrow streets, first laid out and built back in the days when the biggest vehicle to pass through was a horse-drawn cart. Even now, in July 1943, Sicilians still used the same ways of getting around, and while smaller trucks and armoured vehicles could just about weave a route through, the same could not be said for the vast Tiger tanks, each nearly 12 feet wide, more than 20 feet long and with a huge gun extending out beyond the front. Several times that day the Tigers found themselves getting stuck and having to reverse and find alternative routes.

The Panzer Mk VI, better known as the Tiger I, was the biggest tank in Sicily, with immensely thick armour of up to 120mm – 4.7 inches – impervious to most Allied anti-tank shells, and a powerful high-velocity 88mm gun that could hurtle a shell through the air at just under 3,000 feet per second – and over far greater ranges than any Allied tank and anti-tank gun save the British 17-pounder. Those confronting them quite understandably found the Tiger terrifying. It was not designed, however, for operating in places like central Sicily, with its web of narrow and underdeveloped roads. Now, as they pushed southwards, they were struggling badly in the dust and manoeuvring along roads not built to take the weight of such a 56-ton beast. Tigers were also incredibly complex pieces of machinery and mechanically nothing like as robust as their outer shell, a vulnerability exacerbated by the shortage of supplies and infrastructure on Sicily. Surrounded as they were by hills, curves in the road, hidden peaks, terraces climbing above and dropping away from them, and plenty of olive and citrus groves, progress was painfully slow. A far better decision would have been to place them in Kampfgruppe Rechts, heading out from Niscemi, where they could make good use of the ideal tank country offered by the Gela Plain.

It was perhaps not surprising, then, that the main thrust of the left-hand battlegroup was not going very well. Oberst Bergengruen was, it seemed, the only man in the HG Division moving at speed that day: having handed over to General Conrath at Casa dei Priolo, he then dashed back to Caltagirone and then down the Biscari road towards the Biazzo Ridge beyond to see what was going on with Kampfgruppe Links. When he reached the vanguard at around 4.30 p.m., he found the infantry commander of 1. Panzer Grenadier Regiment lying next to his adjutant with their heads ducked down behind a rock as American bullets zipped and whined overhead and mortars rained down from the far, western side of the River Acate valley now stretching away to their right. 'He could hardly lift his head,' noted Bergengruen. 'He'd already been there an hour and so couldn't properly command.'

Bergengruen was not impressed, and rightly so. The entire Kampfgruppe Links had been stopped in its tracks by a handful of Americans from the 180th Infantry who had advanced inland with no artillery or armour supporting them. Bergengruen also quickly discovered the II. Bataillon of grenadiers had not even been deployed and only one battery of artillery was in position. The reason why the commander of the panzer-grenadier regiment was so inept was that he was a former Luftwaffe bomber pilot who had been grounded because of combat stress and who had no ground combat experience whatsoever. Not only were his nerves shot to pieces, he was completely clueless as a battlefield commander. It was hardly surprising he'd fallen at the first hurdle.

Now in contact with Conrath via radio, Bergengruen made his report. Furious at the lack of progress, Conrath sacked the commander on the spot, replacing him immediately with Bergengruen, whom he ordered to press forward the attack. Summoning up the II. Bataillon, Bergengruen now ordered his entire battlegroup to go for an all-out assault towards the Ponte Dirillo, captured the previous night by 'Hard Nose' Gorham and his men, and now held by men of the US 180th Infantry.

Although still without the Tigers, this time the battlegroup showed considerably more gumption, overrunning the thin forward units of the 1st Battalion of the 180th Infantry and capturing its commander and a number of the troops as the rest hurriedly fell back towards the coast. With their tails up, the HG men might have pushed them back all the way to the sea, had it not been for the arrival of the 3rd Battalion, 180th Infantry, who dug in firmly along the southern side of Highway 115 and then stood their ground.

Suddenly, and for no obvious reason apart from a spontaneous mass panic born of combat inexperience and inadequate training, the German infantry began to cut and run, falling back in wild disorder and ending any further thoughts of a counter-attack that day. In consultation with General von Senger via a radio link, Conrath agreed they would attack again alongside the Italians early the following morning.

Away to the east, the British and Canadian landings were still going well, while not only had Paddy Mayne's SRS completely destroyed two vitally important coastal batteries, but No. 1 Troop had gone on to attack a third. This had left Lieutenant Peter Davis and the rest of No. 2 Troop lolling around the second battery, sitting in the shade of olive and almond trees and getting their prisoners to scavenge nuts and other edibles for them. Of the 287 men who had landed, they were, incredibly, still only one man down after Geoff Caton had bled to death. While this pause was very welcome for Peter Davis and his fellows in Nos 2 and 3 Troops, it was none the less something of a wasted opportunity, as they were less than 4 miles away by foot from the Ponte Grande, where the beleaguered few of the Airlanding Brigade were struggling to hold on to the bridge.

From around 11.30 a.m., shelling of the bridge had increased once more. One direct hit on a pillbox killed a number of Italians being kept prisoner there, while around the bridge the defenders were strung out, dug in along both sides and to the north and south. They were a mixed bag of men: sixteen glider pilots – including Dennis Galpin and two Americans, Flight Officers Sam Fine and Roderick MacDonald, who had been drafted in for the operation at the last moment – and perhaps sixty others from a mixture of companies. The challenge for the defenders was to keep the enemy at bay while taking care to be very sparing with precious ammunition.

As morning had given way to afternoon, so the Italian counter-attack had begun to intensify. Mortars, artillery and sniping were taking their toll, so that by a little after half-past two there were only around fifteen defenders still unscathed. One man had a lucky escape when a sniper's bullet knocked his mug of tea out of his hand, but plenty of others were not so fortunate. With growing confidence, the Italian infantry began pushing forward. Galpin and the others now found themselves attacked on all sides – from Syracuse, from the south, and from along the river and canal – in a situation that was becoming increasingly desperate. The help of the SRS men at this moment would have been a godsend; so too would even a fraction of the two and a half thousand glider-borne troops originally detailed for LADBROKE. As it was, the only men coming to their rescue were those of the 2nd Royal Scots Fusiliers, leading the way for the 5th Division. In fact, they were reasonably close, no mean achievement by the early afternoon of the first day ashore, since Ponte Grande was some 8 miles from their landing beaches. It was precisely because of this distance that the Airlanding Brigade had been sent in to secure and hold the bridge; yet none of those in the planning, with the possible exception of George Chatterton, had contemplated such a paltry number making it to the bridge.

Soon after, at around 3 p.m., the Italians won a foothold on the north of the bridge. 'It was not long before we ourselves were completely overrun,' admitted Galpin, 'and lost the bridge we had tried so hard to hold.' By about 3.30 p.m., with ammunition exhausted, those defenders still standing had no choice but to make a run for it. The wounded, meanwhile, could only surrender. Sam Fine had been one of those to put his hands in the air; he'd had no choice, as by this time he had been wounded twice, in the right shoulder and neck, and had just two rounds left in his pistol.

The battle for Ponte Grande was not over, however. Sam Fine was among the walking wounded marched north along the road to Syracuse. They'd not gone far when a British officer jumped out from behind a tree and shot one of the Italian officers. In the alarm and confusion this prompted, Fine grabbed a couple of rifles off the panicking Italians and threw one to a trooper next to him; the pair of them shot as many Italians as they could, while the rest of the guards scarpered into the woods next to the track. Together with some miraculously appearing British reinforcements – glider men who had come down some distance away and who had been working their way to the bridge – they turned back to finish the job they'd started.

Meanwhile, to the south, Galpin and others then ran into the lead elements of 17th Brigade, working their way northwards following the capture of Cassibile. Once again, the tables were swiftly turned, with captors becoming the captives. Galpin was among those who now took his guards prisoner and then began hurrying back to the bridge along with the men of the Royal Scots Fusiliers. Seeing the Tommies arriving, the Italians at the bridge then fled – and, crucially for the British, did so before their sappers had finished laying the charges to blow it sky high. It was now around 4.15 p.m., and, despite the fiasco that had been LADBROKE – despite the appalling lack of glider and tug training beforehand and the woeful waste of manpower – the operation had achieved its objective. The bridge had been captured, then lost but now taken again intact. It meant the road to Syracuse, a D-Day objective, now lay open.

Among the Americans now ashore at Licata was the war correspondent Ernie Pyle, a slight figure, prematurely grey, prematurely balding and something of a manic depressive. Despite this, the 43-year-old was a revolutionary journalist, having made a name for himself before the war touring the United States meeting everyday folk and writing up his encounters in a novel conversational style, informed by a razor-sharp eye for detail and a poetic turn of phrase. His columns, written for the Scripps Howard syndicate, were read from east coast to west and everywhere in between. Since the beginning of the war he had acquired a new celebrity status, covering the conflict first from England and then in North Africa. Pyle had always been interested in the ordinary people rather than the big cheeses, and since there were so many ordinary people now caught up in this extraordinary global war he was determined to tell their story, name-checking those he encountered and with whom he had conversations along the way. Needless to say, every soldier, sailor and airman around wanted to get a write-up from Ernie Pyle.

He'd sailed with the Western Task Force on the USS *Biscayne*, the Task Force Joss flagship for 3rd Division's landings around Licata, and had got a ride on a landing craft at around 8 a.m. Even by then, the beach was teeming with activity: men, vehicles, piles of supplies. 'Our organisation on shore took form so quickly,' noted Pyle, 'it left me gasping.' By mid-afternoon it seemed to Pyle that the countryside far and wide was now full of men and vehicles of every kind. Even Breezy Griffin and his fellows in the 41st Armored Regiment now had their trucks and half-tracks. Jeeps beetled about; phone wires had been laid and CPs – command posts – set up in olive groves and citrus groves. 'The Americans worked grimly and with great speed,' he noted. 'I saw a few officers who appeared rather excited, but mostly it was a calm, determined, efficient horde of men who descended on that strange land. The amazed Sicilians just stood and stared in wonder at the swift precision of it all.'

He was also amazed at the paucity of the Italian defences. The invaders had all been keyed up for battling through thick minefields and wire entanglements, grappling with stubborn defenders determined to fight for every yard of their homeland, but Licata had been almost too easy – so much so that Pyle sensed a palpable disappointment among some of the men he met. Unpacked boxes of mines had been left on the quayside, while the roadblocks out of town were laughable. 'They wouldn't have stopped a cow,' he wrote, 'let alone a tank.'

Pyle was also impressed by how quickly POW camps had been set up. Within a couple of hours, a large area had been ringed off by thick barbed wire entanglements, and by the time Pyle visited there were around four hundred people there, all sitting quietly on the ground – a couple of hundred troops and about the same of civilians. He noticed that some Sicilians had even brought their goats with them. Nor did he see any dejected Italians; on the contrary, he thought they all looked really quite cheerful, as though they'd just been liberated rather than conquered.

Further east down the coast at Gela and Scoglitti, the Americans were having a tougher time of it, although even there the invasion had gone better than expected despite the swell and the difficulties of getting ashore. 'Still no enemy air and we are mystified that he hasn't come,' noted Captain Chet Hansen aboard the *Ancon* off Scoglitti that morning. 'The friendly air cover continues to surround us and it is comforting to look up and listen to the friendly whistle of the Spitfire.' Bradley was starting to feel a little better and impatient to get ashore, so early in the afternoon Hansen volunteered to head to the beaches to see what was going on and report back, for although messages had been arriving thick and fast there was no substitute for eyes on the ground. His landing craft was one of swarms now heading to the shore, and although the wind had died down in the early hours and the sea had been dead calm by midmorning, it was now picking up sharply once more, and Hansen's craft was cresting and diving as it smacked against one wave after another. From the shore, shelling could be heard, but nothing came their way.

When Hansen finally scrambled on to the beach it was to be confronted by an extraordinary sight. Abandoned landing craft, some swamped, some pitched over, were scattered along the shore. On the beaches were sleds stacked with ammunition, piles of ration boxes, medical supplies, radio boxes, bedding rolls, insulators, tools, guns and discarded lifejackets. A teeming mass of men were straining to get these rapidly stacked supplies safely off the beaches as a procession of yet more landing craft and DUKWs drew on to the sand. Anti-aircraft guns were being set up and men digging in. It was, thought Hansen ruefully, a wonderful target for the enemy.

Getting off the beach, he snagged a jeep and went looking for the II Corps CP – command post – but after a while without result abandoned his quest and headed back to the beach, where he picked up a ride back to the *Ancon*. 'Breaking into the breakers and wind we are tossed about wildly and completely wetted to the skin,' he noted. 'I can hardly see the front of the boat for the salt in my eyes.' Back on board, and wringing wet, he reported to Bradley, who told him to get the command cars ready to head onshore that night.

At Avola, Michele Piccione and his family had been taken to another of the hastily established camps springing up along the invasion front. Inside the wire, guards had been placed at the corners armed with machine guns. The mass of people confined here included civilians, disarmed Italian troops, police officers and Carabinieri. Piccione's uncle was a police officer and had been asked to hand over his wristwatch, which initially he refused to do. 'When they pointed a gun at his head,' noted Michele, 'he immediately changed his mind.' They were all ordered to sit down and be still. If anyone needed to relieve themselves, they had to ask permission and then be escorted to a tree now acting as camp urinal.

Further north, the British continued towards Syracuse along the roads that led beyond the town to Augusta and Catania. The 2nd Inniskillings were now 6 miles inland beyond Cassibile on the road to the town of Solarino, in a blocking position near a bridge over the River Cavadonna should there be any enemy counter-attack. Lieutenant David Cole had come forward with the battalion commander, Lieutenant-Colonel Joseph O'Brien Twohig, and was dug in by the bridge along with Lieutenant Johnny Duane's 10 Platoon of B Company. The heat was stultifying, the hot air shimmering on the road ahead. Butterflies were in abundance, flitting lazily in the dry heat. Apart from the occasional distant thump of guns, Cole thought it like a peaceful summer's day.

Then, towards 4.30 p.m., around a bend in the road just up ahead, a number of Italian troops on bicycles appeared, ambling towards them with no obvious sense of urgency. A moment later a Bren gun opened fire, spraying them with bullets. The Italians fell and jumped from their bicycles, which clattered on to the road. Cautiously, from the ditches beside the road, hands began to be raised; then one after another they got to their feet, weapons abandoned, and walked towards the waiting British, where they were met, searched, then shuffled to the rear.

Not long after that an Italian motorcyclist appeared, skidding to a halt right by the Inniskillings' roadblock, followed by a column of armoured cars and trucks. This time they let the column reach the roadblock and watched as it halted, toe-to-bumper, and men began getting out of their vehicles and shouting at one another as though it were rush hour in central Rome. Only then did the waiting Bren gunners open fire. 'What had looked, a moment before, like an Italian traffic jam,' wrote Cole, 'now seemed more like a battlefield, with some limp forms lying lifelessly between the deserted vehicles and the sound of wounded men calling and groaning in the ditches.'

Despite these losses, the Italians managed to set up a Breda machine gun and began firing back until one of the Skins – as the Inniskillings were known – crawled forward and then charged the MG single-handedly, killing the Italian gunners with his Tommy gun. In the meantime, two other platoons from B Company worked their way around the back of the enemy column and so trapped the lot. A white flag was produced and a number of officers appeared. Looking immaculate, in contrast to their men, they smiled affably, relieved their war was over, and surrendered along with some seventy men. B Company had suffered just one man wounded.

These Italian troops had been from the Divisione Napoli, who had been supposed to coordinate their actions with Oberst Wilhelm Schmalz's group. But Schmalz, setting off with most of his men and equipment early that morning, had been unable to make any contact at all with his counter-attacking partners. An Italian ordnance officer had contacted him with further orders from Generale Guzzoni to attack immediately with the Divisione Napoli towards Syracuse. This, Schmalz had patiently pointed out, was impossible without knowing where the Italians were or what, precisely, were their plans. 'I asked him to find out urgently,' noted Schmalz. 'He then came to me twice more during the day to report he had not found the Divisione Napoli.'

Schmalz's orders had been quite explicit: the coastal divisions would defend for all they were worth and then, together with the Napoli, he was to counter-attack. On the other hand, he had absolutely no confidence whatsoever in his Italian allies, had already convinced himself that Guzzoni had no proper plan to offer much resistance, and was well aware from the regular reports coming in from his leading scout troops operating in armoured cars equipped with radio sets that the coastal divisions were surrendering in droves. Even worse was the wholesale abandonment of the Syracuse–Augusta naval fortress area that afternoon. Schmalz had ordered a German mobile flak battery that had been near Syracuse back to join the rest of his battlegroup now moving south from Catania under Oberst Maucke. This withdrawal had prompted mass panic among the naval fortress troops – after all, if the Germans were pulling out, they convinced themselves, then the situation really must be dire. Although no British shells were hitting them and no bombs dropping, a strange mass hysteria rapidly spread, so that in no time the pulling out of one small German unit had translated into massed retreat. Such events did happen – men of the French 55th Division, for example, had fled from positions overlooking Sedan back in May 1940 on the basis of an entirely false rumour that German panzers were about to overrun their positions.

The Panic of Syracuse took hold now as Italian troops began destroying their guns, blowing up ammunition dumps and fuel stores. Crews of an armoured train even destroyed their four 120mm guns. Apart from Messina, this was the most heavily defended stretch of the Italian coast, with twenty-three coastal batteries, five light anti-aircraft and anti-airborne batteries, a mass of pillboxes and bunkers, wire entanglements and mines, all manned by some twelve thousand troops. Some of the defences had been destroyed by enemy action, such as those in the firing line of the SRS and the Airlanding Brigade, but most of the defenders simply deserted because of the rapidly spreading panic. The 2nd Royal Scots Fusiliers reached Syracuse that evening, General Dempsey's men having marched 10 miles to take their D-Day objective. Apart from the occasional sniper, they found Syracuse devoid of troops and the harbour left intact, so anxious had the Italians been to get away. Floridia, another town on the main road to Catania, was also taken by 5th Division later that evening.

Learning of this flight, Schmalz, quite understandably, made his own decisions. 'The planned counter-attack,' he noted, 'now had no chance of success.' Reconnaissance and the study of his maps told Schmalz that his best option now was to delay the British advance for as long as possible. From Syracuse, there was a low and narrow coastal road that wound its way northwards; a few miles inland, as the hills rose up from the sea, there was a second road, a *strada stato* or highway, that linked a number of towns such as Melilli; and 5 miles or so further inland there was a third road that ran through Sortino then northwards. All three roads came together just to the north of the town of Lentini before dropping down into the Plain of Catania and across the one bridge to Catania itself, the Primosole. Here, the three rivers that cut down from the mountains into the Plain merged into one, the Simeto. This made Primosole Bridge absolutely vital, because here, and only here, was where the three roads heading north and the three rivers flowing in from the west all converged.

Schmalz knew he had to defend all three roads south of Lentini, but because historically Sicilians had learned not to loiter near the coast but instead to build their settlements on higher ground from where they had clear views of their enemies coming from across the sea, it was the Melilli–Lentini road that presented both the best opportunity and, Schmalz recognized, the key route to defend as the British tried to push north. It was here, on ground that favoured defence, that he planned to send his strongest troops under Oberst Maucke.

Meanwhile, General von Senger, still based at Enna and out of touch with most of the German troops, agreed with Guzzoni that 15. Panzer Grenadier Division should be moved back into the centre of the island – notwithstanding a message from Kesselring at 6.41 p.m. warning against pulling all troops out from the west. 'C-in-C of Italian 6. Army feels that he cannot alter his decision to withdraw 15 Pz Div back into the centre,' von Senger signalled Kesselring at 11.45 p.m. 'The division has accordingly begun its move.'

One of those in 15. Panzer Grenadier was Werner Stappenbeck, who, at his camp near Salemi in the west of the island, was wondering what on earth was going on. Late the previous evening, the 1. Heavy Panzerjäger Kompanie had been ordered to move. The vehicles had been loaded up and guns hitched, and off they had gone, leaving behind nine men, including Stappenbeck and five others still not fully combat fit, to guard what remained. 'All that was certain,' he wrote, 'was that we had received rations for three days and that we were to look after the equipment entrusted to us and await further orders.'

Now, twenty-four hours later, in the evening of 10 July, one of their trucks showed up again and, though already full to bursting, picked up six of the men. Stappenbeck and the two others he was left with – Gerhard

Dybeck and Gerhard Preller, both from Thuringia – were promised another couple of trucks would be along shortly to collect them, the last of the equipment, and a further seven men at a different camp a mile and a half away. They would then be taken to the Enna region to rejoin the rest of the company. All travelling, though, had to be done by night because with the enemy controlling the air space, driving by day was impossible. Stappenbeck couldn't help feeling a little abandoned.

Meanwhile, at the farmhouse command post near Catenanuova, further to the east, Hanns Cibulka and the men of the 31. Heavy Flak Bataillon had spent the day picking up messages about the Allied invasion. There was talk of the Allies landing with three thousand troop transporters and seven hundred warships. Naval fire-power was, apparently, holding back German and Italian units along the coast. As a keen student of history, Cibulka couldn't help thinking about all the previous times Sicily had been invaded – something that had happened repeatedly over the centuries. 'On a day like this,' he jotted in his diary, 'you can look history straight in the throat.'

Out at sea, as that first day of invasion turned to night, the Allied navies were still busy. Earlier, the slower convoys had arrived with a mass of second-wave troops and supplies, so that the coastal waters were thick with vessels. On HMS *Tartar*, Midshipman Peter Hay had spent much of the morning waiting for the Axis air forces to turn up, but he'd seen nothing, which had allowed them and other warships to go in close to the coast and pummel enemy batteries instead. It was another benefit of the spectacular work the Allied air forces had done in the days and weeks before the invasion. There was also a far greater number of their own fighters overhead than Hay had expected – in their Acid sector, those from Cocky Dundas' 324 Wing. 'We had Spitfires above us nearly all the time,' Hay noted in his diary, 'though we had been warned previously that the fighter cover would not be first class until we could get Sicilian airfields.'

At 11.30 a.m., Hay was allowed his first sleep since a ninety-minute cat-nap earlier the previous morning, only to find himself woken again just an hour after collapsing, exhausted, into his cot, needed back on duty. Soon after that, the big troopships of the first assault convoy began leaving, and an hour later were disappearing over the horizon. He was still wondering where on earth the enemy air forces were when, later in the afternoon, he saw explosions near Syracuse. With the ship's alarm ringing, they sped closer just in time to see a dozen Ju88s fly in from the north and drop a number of sticks of bombs among some merchant vessels there. The dive-bombers then sped towards *Tartar* and the dozen or so vessels they were protecting.

Their ship's guns opened fire with everything they could. The A, B and Y guns – the main deck guns – couldn't get sufficient elevation, but tracers from the Oerlikon 20mm cannons shot up towards the aircraft and flak bursts from quick-firing four-cannon 40mm pom-poms seemed to do the trick: the formation split up as they were overhead. Even so, bombs were soon falling. Hay could actually see them drop, the first few among the merchantmen, then the fourth, fifth, sixth and seventh getting ever closer to *Tartar*, until the eighth whistled down and hit the sea just 15 yards off the starboard side abreast the ship's bridge. Hay fully expected the next to hit them but it went over, landing 10–15 yards off the port side. 'We carried on firing 'til they were out of range,' jotted Hay, 'just to relieve our feelings and then got ready for the next attack.' Fortunately, however, that was it – no more bombs fell, although the spumes of water around them were immense. When the sea had subsided and the bombers gone, they looked around and were relieved to discover not a single ship had been hit. Luck had been with them.

On the Cent beaches to the west of Scoglitti, Captain Chet Hansen was now ashore once more with the command cars and looking for the II Corps CP, whose location had been selected during the planning back in North Africa. Movement was slow, but he saw plenty of Sicilian civilians, many of whom gave the victory sign with their fingers when they passed, and very few dead of either side. 'We passed many abandoned shore defence positions,' he noted, 'trenches and pill boxes, artillery pieces and the like.' Eventually, he found the CP only for it to come under enemy shellfire, so moved a few hundred yards further back before setting off again to find Major-General Troy Middleton's 45th Division CP so he could send a wire back to the *Ancon*. Now he saw plenty of wounded men streaming back from the earlier fighting with Kampfgruppe Links, and even stopped to give aid to one struggling soldier and take him to a dressing station. By the time he finally reached the 45th Division CP it was dark. 'Crawl in slit trench, which is their message center,' he noted, 'to write message under the canvas tarp thrown over the hole with light of flash lamp.'

Following the attack by the Junkers 88s over the Eastern Task Force and the appearance of several other lone enemy fighters, two Spitfires of

92 Squadron had been shot down by trigger-happy naval gunners; one of the pilots was picked up, but the other was killed. As the day had worn on, the number of enemy air alerts had increased, which meant Midshipman Peter Hay had had to miss his supper entirely. By this time, he'd had two and a half hours' sleep in the past thirty-six. At dusk action stations later that evening, they laid smokescreens around their convoy, although this could not cover the three hospital ships that were further out to sea. Painted white with red crosses on the decks and sides, they were also lit up so as to identify them more clearly. Hay was out on deck keeping watch when the first night attack struck, further to the south. For about a quarter of an hour he watched, almost transfixed by the tracer from the flak, which began white, then turned to green and then red, while at the same time orange and yellow flares rose up and cast umbrellas of light, while shells burst with an orange and red glow. 'They really formed an attractive sight,' noted Hay, 'if you didn't think too hard of the reason for it all.'

Then it was their turn to face the enemy bombers. It was now around 10 p.m. Their guns hammered away and bombs fell, but because of the smokescreen it was hard to tell how bad the attack had been. Only once things quietened down and the smoke drifted away did Hay notice that one of the hospital ships, SS *Talamba*, had all but a few of her lights out. At first he thought it must be some air raid precaution but then realized she was down in the water by her stern. In fact, *Talamba* had been hit twice by an Italian bomber. *Tartar* now hurried to her aid, and as they neared they saw lifeboats in the water and people jumping for it, and heard shouting. They sailed carefully over to the port side of the stricken ship, picking up survivors as they went, until the vessels were just 20 feet apart. The injured were lowered into boats, while nurses, doctors and the largely Indian crew clambered down ropes flung over the sides of the damaged vessel. Drawing alongside, *Tartar* and *Uganda* lowered nets and also whalers to help pick up those now in the water. By now the *Talamba* had begun to list, and soon it was clear she was about to go. *Tartar* moved away. 'With a crackling, hissing sound,' jotted Hay, 'her stern went under, her bows reared up and she began to slide under – still 2 or 3 people were jumping off her sides. As she disappeared, her 2 after funnels were wrenched from their positions and forced up to the surface again, only to sink a moment later in the boiling, hissing water.'

For the next half-hour they picked up survivors along with several other ships, so that they soon had a further two hundred on board, including ten nurses. At 11 p.m. they went alongside the armed merchant cruiser HMS *Bulolo* and transferred the lot. They'd done good work: in all, some four hundred were rescued and only five men went down with the ship.

The rest of the night was quiet for *Tartar*, but not for her fellow destroyer HMS *Wallace*. First lieutenant on board *Wallace* and, at twenty-one, one of the youngest to hold that position in all the Royal Navy, was Philip Mountbatten, grandson of George I of Greece and nephew to Admiral Lord Louis Mountbatten. Despite this lineage, Lieutenant Mountbatten had achieved his post firmly on merit, having repeatedly displayed courage, leadership and highly skilled seamanship since the start of the war. Now, as this first day of HUSKY neared its end, *Wallace* was patrolling off Syracuse when the sound of an aircraft drew nearer, followed by the scream of its engine as it dived towards them. Then the whistle of bombs and a stick of them hit the water, the closest 200 yards off their starboard side.

It was a bright clear night and, despite the blackout, any enemy aircraft could see the ship's wake, which glowed with a strange phosphorescence that could be seen from the sky. A conference was held on the bridge and Mountbatten suggested that, if there was another attack, he should fire a flare in the direction from which they thought it was coming so that their guns could then fire a barrage in that direction. Sure enough, another bomber neared them around half an hour later, but despite the flare being fired as planned and the guns unleashing all the rounds they could, the bombs still whistled down, this time far closer.

It seemed likely they would be attacked again and next time with fatal accuracy, so Mountbatten now suggested to the skipper, Lieutenant-Commander Duncan Carson, a plan to create a decoy. On the upper deck, the men now hastily built a wooden raft on to which was fastened a smoke float, which was activated the moment it was lowered and hit the water. Swirls of smoke and bursts of orange flame made it look rather like burning debris. Quickly steaming away from it, the captain then ordered the engines to be stopped. On the bridge, the officers waited, listening intently. Soon, the faint hum of engines could be heard, becoming louder as a bomber roared over the raft and dropped a further stick of bombs.

The ruse, it seemed, had worked, for the bomber turned and disappeared and did not come back.

It was now early morning, Sunday, 11 July, the second day of the invasion.

CHAPTER 16

Counter-Attack at Gela

NONE OF THE AXIS commanders had slept much that first night after the invasion. Guzzoni, von Senger and the various corps and divisional commanders had spent it trying to make sense of the situation and come up with a coordinated plan of action for the following day, though broken communications networks continued to cause problems; the Allied air forces and errant paratroopers had done their jobs well. For Generale Guzzoni, the situation already looked fairly bleak; although he was certainly not prepared to throw in the towel yet, he had been shocked by how far the Americans had got at Licata, with reports reaching him that the enemy had penetrated as much as 14 miles inland. The particular worry this raised was that 15. Panzer Grenadier and the rest of the Italian XII Corpo might be cut off and even Enna, his headquarters in the centre of the island, threatened; it was only around 55 miles from Licata. Another regiment from his reserves was hurriedly sent west to plug the gap where the coastal division there had been.

As midnight chimed, Guzzoni had still thought the greatest threat lay from the southern central thrust. Von Senger had earlier warned him that Syracuse had fallen, but the Sixth Army commander had dismissed this as a fantastical exaggeration, and so instructed Generale Rossi, the XVI Corpo commander, to counter-attack towards Gela early the following morning. Meanwhile, Conrath had already concluded the Americans were too strong to boot back into the sea, telling Oberst Bergengruen that they would need at least two more divisions – and he meant German ones – to defeat the invasion on the south coast. The best he reckoned they could hope to achieve now was a strike to contain the enemy bridgehead.

Soon afterwards, he was summoned to see Generale Rossi, along with Generale Domenico Chirieleison of the Divisione Livorno. At Rossi's headquarters in Enna, the two men were ordered to attack Gela in three columns each, the HG Division from the north-east, the Livorno from the north-west. This was to get going at 6 a.m. There were to be no more uncoordinated, piecemeal attacks of the kind that had been so haphazardly executed the previous day. Conrath accepted these orders, only to find on returning to his CP direct instructions from Kesselring telling him to attack on the Gela Plain, where his panzers would be better able to manoeuvre. Given that his men were already split into their two battlegroups, Conrath chose to follow Kesselring's instructions only partially, instructing Kampfgruppe Rechts to advance south from Niscemi towards the Y-junction, while Kampfgruppe Links would head south from Biscari.

That was all well and good, but at 3 a.m. Guzzoni finally learned the terrible truth about the fall of Syracuse. This put a different spin on matters, because clearly Catania was now under serious threat, and if that vital city fell and the British and Canadians swarmed across the Plain of Catania, then the road to Messina would be open and everything would be lost. And so, with the countdown already on for the counter-thrust towards Gela, Guzzoni now issued new orders. Once Gela had been taken, the HG Division was to turn east and threaten the rear of Eighth Army, while the Livorno, with help from 15. Panzer Grenadier Division – currently in transit – was to turn west towards Licata.

Where the battle plan for the counter-attack on Gela won points was in bringing disparate forces together, converging in a *Schwerpunkt*. This latest adaptation, by contrast, dissipated these forces, spreading them apart again. Not for the first time over the past few months, Axis commanders found themselves facing a persistent problem: that they simply did not have enough men and materiel for the task in hand.

In sharp contrast, the Allied senior commanders had cause to sleep well. Eisenhower had hit the hay straight after dinner and slept in until 5 a.m. 'So far,' signalled Ike early that morning to the Joint Chiefs of Staff, 'the operation has proceeded almost exactly according to plan.' Casualty figures hadn't yet been received, but were unquestionably light. Enemy air attacks had been greater over the American front because Allied air forces had had greater difficulty in meeting them there than over the south-east, where the invasion force was closer to fighter bases on Malta, but even further west they had been light.

General Alexander was also able to give an encouraging picture to Churchill. Some 81,500 men in Seventh Army, along with 7,100 vehicles, 360 tanks and 835 guns, were due to be successfully landed by midnight that Sunday, 11 July. For Eighth Army, the figures were much the same, except that the tanks numbered 294 and the guns 1,000. That was quite something: 163,000 men in all. 'General situation to date,' signalled General Alex, 'very satisfactory.'

General Montgomery had also turned in early, as was his way. A commander had to give himself time to think; and to think well, he was convinced, one needed rest, so he was off to his quarters at 9 p.m. sharp every **night; no** gadding about in the early hours making frantic telephone calls or holding conferences for him. Monty had been on Malta for HUSKY D-Day but that evening, accompanied by Admiral Lord Louis Mountbatten, he had boarded HMS *Antwerp*, a former liner brought into the navy back in 1940 and now flag and operations ship of the commander of the Eastern Task Force, Admiral Sir Bertram Ramsay. After a far calmer crossing than those on the same route had experienced the previous night, Montgomery, with Mountbatten in tow, landed at Capo Passero in the XXX Corps sector at around 7 a.m., already aware they had massively overestimated the strength of the Italian resistance in Sicily. 'I was wrong,' he admitted, three words that had rarely, if ever, come out of his mouth before.

It was, of course, always better to overestimate the enemy's strength than underestimate it, especially when launching the biggest and most complex amphibious invasion ever attempted, which could not be allowed to fail under any circumstances. For the Allies to be driven back off Sicily was simply unthinkable, an outcome with long-term consequences too grave even to contemplate. This was why so much emphasis had been placed on the role of air power before the invasion; this was why such an immense armada had been assembled. And it was also why Montgomery had insisted on landing with two corps, four divisions and a raft of subsidiary units, from airborne forces to Commandos to the SRS. Now, on D plus 1, that approach had been proved over-cautious. Historians have sharply criticized Montgomery for this, ignoring the fact that during the planning debates it was not an excess of caution that any of the other senior commanders had been grousing about. On the contrary, what had prompted those arguments was one party or another worrying about being caught short.

Monty had unquestionably made the right decision to insist on the weight of forces he'd been given, especially since the HUSKY plan had been agreed even before the North African campaign was over. Yet however correct the logic and however sound the decision-making process, there were now, potentially, consequences. Infantry, guns and ammunition had been given priority over motor transport, which meant that although Eighth Army was 100 per cent mechanized, now, and for the next few days, many of the men would have to advance on foot, which was not only exhausting for them but meant they could not go hell for leather for Catania with the weight of force they might have done had the assault divisions landed with all their transport. They could only hope that, despite this potential handicap, the roads north would be largely clear. Getting bogged down by enemy blocking and delaying tactics was the last thing Eighth Army needed.

None the less, vehicles and supplies were continuing to be unloaded – and more troops too, as the previous evening Patton had decided to throw in his floating reserve to make up for the shortfall in paratroopers, who were still widely scattered. Although one part of 2nd Armored had already landed at Licata, the rest of the division was to head for the beaches to the east of Gela, as was the 18th Regimental Combat Team, the Big Red One's third infantry component. Among those making for the shore in the early hours of Sunday, 11 July, was Lieutenant Frank Johnson of Cannon Company in the 18th RCT. That night, before boarding, he'd watched the astonishing spectacle of heavy naval shells hurtling overhead. 'Some are solid flame,' he wrote, 'some intermittent, but all are dynamic and graceful as they lace the sky.'

At first light, the shore at Green Beach looked utterly chaotic as far as Johnson could see. A hundred yards off, he saw a still-smoking barge at the water's edge, detritus everywhere, the skeleton of a burnt-out aircraft, and beach masters hurrying·men out of the sea as they waded in. His own landing craft ground to a halt on yet another sandbar, but after yelling at the top of their lungs to a passing DUKW, they were able to transfer and finally land on European soil. Despite the weight of his pack and equipment, Johnson soon realized they needed to get off the beach quickly. An enemy fighter swooped in low, machine guns and cannons blazing, while enemy shells were also exploding uncomfortably close.

His orders were to get his platoon to the CP of the 18th RCT, which had landed ahead, but no one seemed to know where it was. Clearly, though, they needed to push inland without delay. Getting his column of men in some kind of order, he then led them off, his sergeant beside him at the head. 'We do not know quite where we are going or what we shall find,' he noted, 'and I try to appear confident. But inside, I am lonely and apprehensive.'

Getting infantry on to the shore was one thing; dealing with the arriving armour of Combat Command B of the 2nd Armored, quite another. Yellow and Blue beaches had still been off limits until finally cleared in the early hours, so initially the armour had been directed to Red 2, where there was already congestion. As the day dawned, enemy shelling, increased numbers of German fighter-bombers, and beaches whose sand was simply too soft for heavy vehicles all conspired against them. General Terry Allen, the Big Red One's commander, was urgently demanding tanks and artillery, but the ten Shermans that had come ashore in the early hours had become stuck in the sand. By the time day dawned, the night's unloading had yielded four more infantry battalions, including one from 2nd Armored, but no more armour and precious few guns.

The battle for Gela was now under way. Conrath's headquarters had not been able to make any radio contact whatsoever with his Italian allies, but all six columns had managed to trundle forward overnight to their starting positions, and between 6 and 6.30 a.m. the fighting had begun.

Among those now marching across the Gela Plain was Tenente-Colonnello Dante Ugo Leonardi, whose III° Battaglione of the 34° Reggimento di Fanteria had had a fraught journey south from Caltanissetta the previous evening, attacked three times by Allied aircraft. Fortunately, casualties had been light: two dead, twenty wounded and four damaged trucks. 'The enemy could have destroyed us,' he noted. 'Instead, our drivers managed to accelerate and surprisingly, the enemy aircraft went away.' By 11 p.m. they had reached Ponte Olivo – but still had no detailed orders. All Leonardi had been told was to get ready to attack the Americans the following morning. No timings had been given, nor any appreciation of the enemy, nor any indication of what fire support they might expect. So, in the meantime, he and several other officers had set off on foot on a fact-finding mission. Leonardi had been struck by the silence that hung like a shroud over the plain; he felt vulnerable, alone and in the dark, actually and metaphorically. Eventually they came across Tenente Franco Girasoli, commanding a company of motorcycle marksmen who had been caught up in the fighting earlier that day. Having told Girasoli about the Americans in Gela, Leonardi decided to join him in the lee of Monte Castelluccio, an outcrop topped by the remains of a solid rectangular twelfth-century Norman castle, a little way to the west of the airfield and at the edge of the plain.

Finding his men where he had left them, he now ordered them south on foot to their jump-off position at Castelluccio. As they tramped on in silence, Leonardi wondered what the men walking beside him were thinking. For over a year, they had lived and trained together, and in just a few hours they would be going into battle. The weight of responsibility weighed heavily upon him. 'I knew that many of us would never return,' he wrote, 'because war is made of blood, not words!'

By dawn his men were ready, although there was still no sign of any supporting artillery. Leonardi had scrambled up to the top of Monte Castelluccio, where the ruins of the old castle still stood, and had looked out over the plain towards Gela, spotting his first enemy troops some 800 yards away, in a blocking position on Highway 117, which ran directly from the airfield into Gela. Ahead, the wheat fields had been freshly cut, so – apart from a few ditches – they would be completely exposed as they advanced over the open ground. In the distance was Gela, perched on its promontory – and beyond that, a sea thick with Allied ships.

At long last, a captain from divisional headquarters arrived with details for the attack. On their left, there would be a column of German armour across the plain to the far side of the highway; beyond that, a second German armoured column was to attack down the road from Niscemi. Leonardi's own battalion was now joined by the remnants of the Gruppo Mobile E, so badly mauled the day before. Meanwhile, on their right, using the road from Butera as its axis, were two more Livorno infantry battalions and then a further battalion using the railway line from Butera station to Gela. Further to the east, attacking from Biscari, was Kampfgruppe Links. So, six thrusts in all, converging on the coast like spokes on half a wheel.

Among those preparing to attack from Butera were Tenente Livio Messina and the men of the I° Battaglione of the 33° Reggimento. The night before, he'd listened to a briefing from the battalion commander, Tenente-Colonnello Alessi. They would be attacking at 6 a.m., he told them, and unfortunately, that meant in daylight. 'Tomorrow,' he had said, 'I will be at the head of the battalion. We must throw the Americans back into the sea.'

The Americans were actually further forward around Gela than the Axis forces had realized. General Allen had always been a great advocate of night operations – as was Patton – and insisted his men train for them, so from midnight men from the 26th Infantry had been pushing out of Gela towards Ponte Olivo and were now holding the blocking position Leonardi had seen from the Castelluccio, while others from a battalion of the 16th Infantry had joined Lieutenant-Colonel 'Hard Nose' Gorham's paratroopers on the Piano Lupo. Together, they had moved up from the Y-junction towards Casa dei Priolo, where Captain Sayre's men had fought in the early hours of the previous day, and then beyond, setting up two blocking positions. The newly arrived 18th Infantry, meanwhile, had taken up positions a couple of miles north of the coast between the men of the 26th and 16th on the eastern edge of the Gela Plain.

Although ordered to start his attack at 6 a.m., when the time came General Conrath was once again out of all contact with his Italian allies, and so fifteen minutes later told his men to get going. The right-hand panzer battalion began to move off from their overnight positions at Ponte Olivo, heading for the 26th Infantry's first blocking position on Highway 117 to Gela, while his other panzer battalion began moving down from their jump-off point a couple of miles south of Niscemi.

On Conrath's right-hand flank were Leonardi and his III° Battaglione; but they too had had no word from any superior, whether Italian or German. Leonardi was becoming increasingly frustrated; they had been ordered to attack at 6 a.m., following an artillery barrage ten minutes earlier, but the minutes had passed and there was still no sign of any guns, which were supposed also to have been moved forward the previous night to a point just a mile and a half to their rear. Really, he had very little idea of what was going on. He wasn't in communication with any of the other attack columns because he had no radios. The attack was supposed to be synchronized, but it most certainly wasn't. What to do? He had his orders to attack; and yet without artillery, advancing over the plain in clear sight of the enemy would be little short of suicidal. 'In these situations,' wrote Leonardi, 'you can only rely on God!'

It was now 6.30 a.m., half an hour after they should have set off. The sun shone down on the plain, the sky a clear, beautiful blue. Gela and the vast fleet out at sea twinkled in the clear morning sunshine. They had no artillery so would have to improvise, providing their own fire support from mortars and machine guns. It was time to go, so they set off from behind the shelter of Monte Castelluccio, Leonardi thinking of the lines of the poet Vittorio Locchi:

> *In the frontline nobody said a word*
> *Feeling their hearts beating like never before*
> *As drops of blood, the terrible minutes*
> *That measure the time remaining*
> *Before the beginning of the assault.*

As they emerged on to the open fields, the air filled with the sound of battle. Mortars and shells exploded, bullets hissed and whipped past them, yet Leonardi felt strangely calm. Glancing at his men, seeing the first ones fall, it seemed more as though they'd stumbled rather than been shot; it seemed too unreal to think of them dead and dying. Capitano Dante Capello was among the first to be hit, wounded by shrapnel, but kept urging his men forward. Thirty yards from Leonardi, another of his men, Rino Tarini, was almost decapitated, his head nearly completely detached from his neck as he stood for a moment before crumpling. 'The ground was vomiting fire and steel,' wrote Leonardi. 'The air was dropping fire and steel. The ocean was sending fire and steel!'

In Gela, the Rangers were watching the enemy advancing. While the 1st Battalion up on and around the Capo Soprano faced the Italians advancing from Butera and Butera station, the 4th looked out upon the Gela Plain. From his platoon's position on an upper storey of a building at the northern edge of town, Staff Sergeant Al Altieri peered through his binoculars, squinting into the bright morning sun. They'd known there were enemy tanks out there somewhere, but when he first saw the columns he couldn't help feeling a combination of fear, awe and astonishment: lots of Panzer Mk IIIs and IVs moving forward across the plain in small groups of three or four, grenadiers following behind them.

'Must be a hundred big babies out there!' whistled his platoon commander, Lieutenant Branson. Altieri now went around to their men, warning them to conserve ammo and, when the moment came, to make sure they fired back from the windows, not leaning out. However terrifying the spectacle, he told them, they had plenty of armour on the way to help too. It wasn't as bad as it looked.

'How do you like that?' exclaimed Sergeant Green. 'A hundred tanks we see coming at us, and he says it's not as bad as it looks! Shall I tell my men it's a mirage?'

'No,' Altieri told him. 'Just tell 'em to forget the tanks and keep score on the infantry they hit!'

His advice was all well and good – and he found the experience of watching the enemy advance curiously mesmerizing, as though he were a privileged spectator with a grandstand view – but when a shell hit the house next to them, killing three civilians and wounding a Ranger, his mind snapped back into proper focus. It was now 6.35 a.m. Twelve Italian bombers swept in and attacked the ships out at sea, hitting the troopship USS *Barnett* and damaging two others. One bomb fell close to the *Monrovia*. Hot steel fragments from the furious naval anti-aircraft gunners rained down on the Rangers' houses. They wondered where their own air support was; unbeknown to them, the fighters were currently grounded at Malta by fog, although that would soon lift and normal service resume.

German tanks were sweeping in an arc across the plain and also heading down the road from Niscemi, where they crashed down upon the men of the 16th Infantry and Gorham's paratroopers. With only some bazookas and small arms, the Americans fought back, supported by some field artillery and a handful of anti-tank guns that had been earlier brought up. General Conrath himself was personally commanding the assault down the Niscemi road and, concentrating his forces, attacked again, his panzers and grenadiers moving to outflank the Americans on both sides. Those up beyond Casa dei Priolo now had little choice but to pull back.

Around the same time, Alessi's I° Battaglione of the 33° Reggimento were cresting a hill on the road that led down into the Gela Plain from the west. Livio Messina could now see the battlefield spread out before him: there was the town, and beyond it the ships in the sea. Hundreds of them.

'Tenente-Colonnello, what good are we going to do in Gela?' he asked Alessi. 'It's full of our ships!'

'Would to heaven that were true,' Alessi replied. 'Those are all enemy ships.'

Messina was stunned. He'd no idea the situation was quite so bad; and now they were advancing into this maelstrom. The heat was already oppressive, and he was struggling to keep his men, with their heavy packs and equipment, in good order. They marched on, as though on parade. He thought of his family back in Naples. Soon they would be out of the hills and on to the plain, a matter of a few miles from Gela. And they would be sitting ducks. It was hard to keep calm; the men alongside him looked tense.

A little further east, by around 8 a.m., the lead elements of Leonardi's force had managed to reach and overwhelm the American outposts around 3 miles north of Gela. At this moment, Leonardi had thought victory was within their grasp; but he quickly realized they had merely punctured the outer skin of the American defences and that up ahead was a second blocking position. 'The crucial moment of the battle,' he wrote, 'still lay ahead.' Then suddenly, artillery fire from behind them rained down on the enemy positions; it was two hours late, but at last, and in the nick of time, they had some fire support. Now, though, in answer, came the rush and scream of enemy naval shells combined with machine-gun fire and ever more mortars exploding. Leonardi's three companies continued to press forward, men crouching and running, then ducking down, before pushing on. As Leonardi looked through the thickening smoke, he saw dead and wounded lying all around. The advance was now slowing, but he desperately wanted his men to keep going, in part to overcome the enemy but also so they could reach safety.

Reports continued to reach him at regular intervals from his attacking companies. By around 8.30 a.m., all the officers in 9a Compagnia were dead or wounded, although Capitano Capello was still urging them forward. One young second lieutenant, Enrico Zupo, had been wounded once, but got back to his feet and had continued to advance into the fire. Hit a second time, he shouted, 'Advance! Long live Italy!' then collapsed and died. Others in 10° Compagnia were also suffering, while Leonardi himself and several others from battalion headquarters were pinned down by an American machine gun – until Sergente Ezio Benassi suddenly jumped up and, with his sub-machine gun, charged the position, dodging bullets, and managed to silence it: an act of heroism that seemed to inspire the men. Although 10° Compagnia was decimated and 9a stopped in its tracks by its losses, Leonardi's remaining men now found some inner reserves and charged the second outpost of the 16th Infantry, which, also coming under attack from the 2. Panzer Bataillon, now hurriedly pulled back.

This gave Leonardi's men a chance to pause. Approaching the survivors of 10° Compagnia, he felt momentarily lost for words. 'We looked at each other for a long time, silent,' he noted. 'No-one dared speak. Our eyes, however, were tearful with emotion at the memory of so many fallen comrades.'

It was around this time that Lieutenant-Colonel Gorham and his paratroopers, along with some of the men from the 16th Infantry, began pulling back, although because much of Conrath's Niscemi force had begun sweeping around in a flanking move, the retreating Americans were able to hold the higher ground overlooking the Y-junction. While they were clinging on, the Germans were moving past, straight towards the coast and the 18th Infantry, only just arrived earlier that morning. In fact, the 18th were now facing both the main panzer force from Niscemi and also those driving south from Ponte Olivo. The two HG Division columns were converging, as had been planned.

Soon after spotting the first enemy tanks, Lieutenant Frank Johnson hurried forward to the 18th RCT command post, where he was given the lowdown from the S-2, the operations staff officer, who told him they still had very little heavy equipment except a few 105mm howitzers. The anti-tank company was nowhere to be seen. Johnson crawled back to his own position with this sobering news as the panzers pressed forward towards the beaches to the east of Gela. Clearly, the enemy was now aiming to cut the road, Highway 115 from Biscari and Vittoria, and reach the sea, then disrupt the landings. From his ditch, it looked to Johnson a pretty bleak picture.

Not long after this the regimental commander, Colonel George R. Smith, appeared running, with the rest of his CP staff, all looking somewhat ludicrous with their bedrolls and blankets under their arms. Johnson couldn't understand what had come over them to make them flee so ignominiously until a communication sergeant rushed over and breathlessly told him and his men that over a hundred armoured vehicles were up ahead trying to isolate the entire regiment.

It was now around 9 a.m., and 4 miles away in Gela, General Patton came ashore on Red Beach amid scenes of chaos but looking as immaculate as ever, his riding boots polished, necktie perfectly in place and shirt freshly pressed. About his waist were his twin revolver pistols. Nearby were two destroyed DUKWs; as he was looking at them, shells screamed over and hit the water some 30 yards behind them. Patton barely flinched. 'It's all right, Hap,' he said, turning to his chief of staff,

Hobart Gay, 'the bastards can't hit us on account of the defilade afforded by the town.'

After his command car had been de-waterproofed, Patton intended to head out along the coast road east to find the Big Red One's HQ, little realizing it was now in danger of being completely overrun; but as they drove up into the town, he noticed Colonel Darby's flag and so changed his mind and headed off to see him first – which was just as well, because only about ten minutes later German Panzer Mk IVs were crossing the highway east of Gela along which he would have been driving. As Patton drew up at the Rangers' CP on the Capo Soprano to the west of the town, the sound and smell of battle was heavy in the air as Gela came under heavy attack from all sides.

Darby asked him which part of the enemy attack he wanted to see and then led him to the observation post on the top storey of a building 100 yards from the Capo Soprano. Darby's captured 77s were still firing, while a chemical mortar company,* his two Ranger battalions, a company of the 26th Infantry and a company of engineers, whose half-tracks had been hastily converted to mobile artillery with machine guns fixed up and mounted, were all primed and ready. The engineers were patrolling the perimeter, both firing and moving almost constantly. Patton, when he saw them beetling about, was most impressed. None the less, Darby's garrison in Gela were now entirely cut off from the rest of the 1st Division.

With Leonardi's force still battling the 26th Infantry's outposts in the Plain, the most immediately pressing attack from the west was suddenly from the Italians now approaching, but Darby had his mortar teams ready for them, having given them instructions to hold fire until the enemy were only around 2,000 yards away.

This was the column to which Tenente Livio Messina was attached. Alessi's men had begun crossing the cut wheat fields of the plain when the first shell hurtled over, bursting somewhere behind where Messina and his men were marching. Flinging himself on to the ground, Messina looked up to see gun muzzle flashes from a warship out to sea. This was the USS *Savannah*, a light cruiser, firing its fifteen 6-inch and eight

---

* A chemical mortar company was one that had mortars that could fire traditional high explosives but also chemical, gas and smoke canisters if necessary. The Allies never fired chemical weapons deliberately in the war, but did always have them on standby in case the enemy decided to use them.

5-inch guns; it had been called upon to help by Captain Lyle from his two-storey CP in Gela just as Darby's men had also opened up with their mortars. Messina writhed on the ground as more shells exploded around him. The intense din was deafening, while the whole earth seemed to be shaking and rippling with the force of the explosions. Lying there, help-lessly, Messina felt his body trembling. Smoke began billowing as the stubble caught fire. He was already hot and thirsty, and now the smoky air made his throat feel even more desperately parched. Around him, there was simply no shelter at all – he saw no walls, no trees, not even a ditch. Nor could he see any of his men. Where were they? Clearly, he had lain prostrate too long, immobilized by shock and fear, and now found himself abandoned. Whether they had pulled back or all been killed he didn't know, but ahead he saw the railway line and so, as shells continued to fall, he crawled towards it, praying he would make it there safely and hoping that if he did he would find his friend Tenente Nino Ciabattoni, the son of a general, whose scout platoon had been due to deploy there ahead of their column. All the time mortar shells went on raining down while the guns of the *Savannah* continued to thunder, sending their lethal loads screaming over. In all, the cruiser would fire some five hun-dred rounds at the men of the Divisione Livorno.

General Patton, who was still at the Rangers' CP, watched the onslaught. Turning to Captain Lyle, he growled, 'Kill every one of the goddam bas-tards.' Further to the north of the town, Al Altieri and the 4th Rangers had also watched the Livorno crossing the plain. 'I knew', recalled Altieri, 'I was about to witness one of the most futile and lost-cause attacks in the history of warfare.' As the shells had screeched over and exploded, he had seen men hurtling into the air and blown to pieces. The two battalions of the Livorno had been decimated.

While the Italians were being pummelled to the west of Gela, to the east the shelling of the beaches had also intensified. The Rangers had landed on Red and Green beaches right in front of the town, but the main 1st Division assault beaches were several miles to the east, the far side of the Gela river: Yellow, Blue, Red 2 and Green 2. Then Yellow Beach was closed down, first because of mines and then because of shelling, and landing craft were diverted to Blue Beach instead. Then Blue Beach became too dangerous and so that was closed too, with a further diver-sion to Red 2. Enemy shelling and the rapid advance of the two panzer columns then made Red 2 unusable, leaving Green 2 as the only beach still viable for unloading. The leading panzers, now across the main road and only a mile or so from the beaches, began liberally firing at supply dumps and spraying anything they could with their machine guns. At this point, Conrath was informed that an Allied signal had been picked up claiming the Americans were now re-embarking. This he sent to Sixth Army headquarters at Enna.

It was just about the only radio signal contact the HG divisional HQ managed to make, and was picked up by an ecstatic Guzzoni, who, after consultation with von Senger, issued orders for the second part of the plan to be carried out. The panzers were now to wheel eastwards into the tail of Eighth Army. Considering the generally woeful level of communication among the Axis forces, and how long it had taken to get the columns to Gela from Caltagirone, 25 miles away, not to mention the comparative paucity of their fighting strength and combat experience, this was wishful thinking to say the least. The Axis thrust that morning had pushed the Americans back and driven a wedge between their forces, but they had not actually reached the beaches, and the Americans were certainly not re-embarking. Whether the signal Guzzoni received was a mistranslation of American radio chatter or simply misinformation is not clear, but the Axis were deluding themselves about the levels of success achieved.

Nor had unloading completely stopped: the 32nd Field Artillery Battalion, coming ashore from a DUKW on a reopened Red 2, hurriedly moved straight into the dunes above the beach. The first gun ashore immediately began firing on the leading panzers, swiftly followed by others. Shortly after, four of the Shermans got going, while the frenetic defence of the beach was also reinforced by the welcome arrival of the 16th Infantry's Cannon Company. Unloading stopped briefly as shore parties were hastily brought into a firing line along the dunes. The impressive speed with which these deployments were made stopped the panzer thrust in its tracks. The leading German tanks began moving back and forth, uncertain where to go, what to do and how to get across the highway. From his position in the rising hills just to the north-east of the road, Frank Johnson and the men of the 18th Infantry had grandstand views and could see the first of the 105mm howitzers firing from the dunes. Johnson also saw one of the leading panzers get hit and start to burn. As a second tank began to cross the road, this too was hit, then two more. Soon after, the rest began to manoeuvre back, pursued by several of the Shermans that had finally got off the beach. 'The beachhead, at least momentarily,' wrote Johnson, 'is safe, thanks to an old burned-out 105 and its battered crew.'

The offshore warships had held their fire on the panzers during this fight for fear of hitting their own side, but now they began shelling the retreat and also the Niscemi road – the cruiser USS *Boise* fired a thirteen-minute barrage from 9.50 a.m. and then again for over an hour continuously from 10.40 a.m., along with the destroyer USS *Glennon*, shell after shell screeching over relentlessly. Cruisers and even smaller destroyers could provide an enormous weight of fire, and without attack from the air, there was absolutely nothing any Axis forces around Gela could do to stop them. In all, with *Savannah* shelling the Livorno to the west of Gela, these three ships alone brought together twenty-one 130mm and thirty 150mm guns. It was no wonder Livio Messina had been lying on the Plain of Gela cowering with terror.

It was the same sustained 62-minute barrage from *Boise* and *Glennon* that slammed into Tenente-Colonnello Leonardi's battered battalion and the remaining Italian mobile group. Leonardi had just finished reorganizing the survivors into new companies with the intention of digging into new and better forward positions when the shells suddenly screamed over and began exploding around them, although most were directed towards the Germans as they pulled back on their left. His batman, Saverio Bensi, was hit in the arm by shrapnel; Leonardi patched him up as best he could with field dressings. 'I'm glad to shed blood,' Bensi told him. 'Now I really feel like a soldier.' Leonardi was losing yet more men. When the shelling finally subsided, he sent a runner back to Colonnello Martini, the regimental commander, urgently asking for more men, weapons and ammunition so they might exploit their earlier success. This, of course, was a vain hope: no reinforcements were going to turn the battle now.

'The Italian advance,' noted Patton in his diary, 'seemed to stick about 1130.' News also arrived that the third Italian column, advancing from Butera station, had been stopped by a patrol from 3rd Division, which had pressed down the coastal road from Licata, 18 miles away, then turned back up the route of the Italian advance. Despite being only a company-size patrol of little more than a hundred men, they'd inflicted heavy casualties on the Italian column of eight hundred, who had then fallen back to play no further part in the counter-attack.

General Patton now returned to Darby's CP to see what was going on to the right, where the Germans had been attacking. Soon after his arrival, a couple of shells hit the building. 'No one was hurt,' jotted Patton, 'except some civilians. I have never heard so much screaming.' Not long after, an officer from the 3rd Division arrived with ten Shermans; then a further two tanks that had been unloaded at Red 2 also reached Darby's headquarters. By now Patton, relishing every moment, had taken personal control of the battle. The gap between the town and the men of the Big Red One out to the east was to be closed up while Darby's Rangers, along with the newly arrived tanks, were to counter-attack against the shattered Italians.

In truth, there wasn't much to counter-attack against. Leonardi's III° Battaglione had been reduced to under two hundred men by the morning's fighting and were now digging in around the former blocking position of the 26th Infantry 2 miles to the north of the town, while the men in the second column were dead, wounded or, like Livio Messina, trying to crawl their way to some kind of safety or lying low in ditches or any other cover they could find. A lot of men were behind the railway line, built on a shallow embankment that ran across the north of the town and so offered a modicum of shelter.

Needless to say, those who survived surrendered in droves, too dazed and too shocked to offer much more resistance. The Rangers were rather horrified to find bits of Italians scattered among the branches of trees just to the west of the town. It seemed that more than 50 per cent – an incredible proportion – of the attacking force had been killed or wounded.

Some, however, didn't surrender and avoided capture – among them Livio Messina. It had taken him an age to crawl his way across the fields, through the dead bodies, past the wounded screaming and shouting, in between debris and through choking smoke, but eventually he found his friend Nino Ciabattoni sheltering by the shallow embankment of the railway line. Ciabattoni had lost a number of his men – some killed, some wounded, some taken prisoner. He himself had been captured but had just managed to escape again. He was now determined to get help for his wounded comrades, although how they were to do that was not clear. Messina, still in shock, could not think clearly at all, and so mutely agreed, and together they half-crawled, half-ran to a solitary farmhouse some 200 yards away. Once there, Messina paused, only to realize he was drenched in sweat and so physically and mentally shaken he could barely stand. From a different part of the building an Italian gun now began firing.

'We've got to move,' Ciabattoni told him, realizing the farmhouse had become an obvious target. 'Now.'

Ciabattoni told him they should make for a deep irrigation ditch, which meant scrambling through their own barbed wire, Messina cutting himself and shredding his uniform in the process. Shells continued to fall, bullets zipping and snapping nearby, smoke filling the air. No sooner had they clambered down an embankment the far side of the farmhouse than a huge explosion boomed directly behind them, followed by the clatter of stone and rock. The farmhouse had been hit. They were now on the southern side of the railway and near the main coastal road to Licata, Highway 115. The irrigation ditch was on the far side: Ciabattoni said he would make a dash for it first, then Messina was to follow. Ciabattoni, still half-crouching, ran and safely made the ditch as machine-gun bullets raked the road. When the firing stopped, he signalled to his friend, and Messina took his own leap of faith; as he neared the ditch he tripped over the trailing strap of his map case and fell, just as bullets whipped above him at chest height. Ciabattoni reached up and, grabbing his belt, pulled him into the ditch. Messina had been lucky; had he not tripped, those bullets would have cut him to pieces.

By around midday, whatever brief crisis the Americans had faced at Gela was over. With it had gone the Axis forces' last chance of pushing the Allies back into the water. The battle was far from over, even on this central southern front, but – despite the poor weather, despite the fiasco of the airborne drops, despite the immense complexity of the entire operation – the Allied landings had succeeded. They now had a foothold in Europe.

CHAPTER 17

Fightback at Gela

A S NIGHT HAD FALLEN on the first day of the invasion, Colonel Jim Gavin and his small entourage had used the hours of dusk and then darkness to continue their journey, finally making contact with an outpost of the 45th Division from Scoglitti at around 2.30 a.m. on the morning of Sunday, 11 July. Then, at last, he learned where he was: a little way to the south-west of Vittoria, which already had been taken by the 45th late the previous day. Pushing on to the edge of the town, Gavin was able to pull rank and commandeer a jeep; then, with Captains Ben Vandervoort and Al Ireland, he sped off down the main Highway 115 in search of other paratroopers, having been told some had been seen the previous day.

Around dawn, they came across a large number of 3rd Battalion troopers of the 505th dug into the tomato fields either side of the road to Gela. Gavin was startled to find Lieutenant-Colonel Ed 'Cannonball' Krause, the battalion commander, sitting on the edge of his foxhole, his feet dangling down, looking in no hurry at all to get moving. Gavin asked him what his battalion had been doing; Krause told him he'd been rounding up his men and now had some 250 with him. That was good news, but Gavin wanted to know why they had spent the night in a tomato field rather than heading with all speed to their objective. Krause told him there were a lot of Germans up ahead and so he'd stayed where he was.

Gavin was shocked. It was not the aggressive, gung-ho attitude he'd expected from a battalion commander, and it crossed his mind to relieve Krause on the spot. On the other hand, if the Germans were close at hand, they would soon be in a fight and this was probably not the time to sack officers. Instead, he told him to get his men moving and in quick order; they would be heading towards Gela right away. Back in his jeep, Gavin drove on, and after a couple of miles found a further twenty airborne troops – engineers under Lieutenant Ben Wechsler – and around forty soldiers from the 45th Division, who told him the Germans were a little way up the road along a ridge that overlooked the Acate river valley. No one seemed very eager to take on this force, but Gavin was having none of their reluctance. Their task was to get to Gela, and if there were Germans in their way, then they should destroy them. And so, with the twenty paratrooper engineers, and with Ireland and Vandervoort still in tow, he pressed on, although this time on foot and very much on alert.

They hadn't gone far when around a kink in the otherwise straight road a German motorcycle and sidecar appeared. Immediately they pointed their weapons at the two men, at which the Germans quickly surrendered, although the man in the sidecar pointed to his medical insignia and suggested he should be allowed to go free. 'We weren't about to release him,' noted Gavin. 'He was the first live German we had ever seen in combat and we noticed he had hand grenades in the sidecar.' Telling a couple of men to take their Germans to the rear, they pushed on. It was now around 8.30 a.m. The encounter had proved what they'd been told – that a German force was up ahead. Clearly, Gavin reasoned, the ridge was key ground; and, come what may, he was set upon taking it and then holding it.

Captain Chet Hansen had been having a tricky time that morning down near Scoglitti. Soon after dawn the II Corps CP had come under fire again, and in the confusion the beaches looked like the biggest shipwreck in history, with vehicles stuck in the sand and half submerged, and ammunition boxes on the water's edge being gently lapped by the waves. Their own anti-aircraft guns were pounding away, but Hansen couldn't tell if they were firing at friend or foe. And while there were plenty of people scurrying about, none of their activities seemed very organized. Uncertainty – even anxiety – hung heavy in the air. There were also now around two hundred landing craft that had been abandoned after burning out their engines trying to get off the sandbars. Hansen thought he'd better get back to the *Ancon* to report to Bradley, but even when he found a ride the landing craft he was in then also blew its engine trying to get off the beach and eventually had to be towed off.

On board were four wounded men who certainly didn't need this extra delay and difficulty; Hansen gave them cigarettes, but it wasn't much of a consolation for their extreme discomfort.

When he finally reached the *Ancon*, it was to discover that Bradley, now recovered, had already headed for the beaches – so back Hansen went again. Once ashore, he soon found a sergeant and jeep from HQ, and off they went to Scoglitti town to find Bradley, along a road littered with Italians killed the day before. 'Refugees simply pass the dead by, walking around them,' he jotted. 'Make no attempts to bury them.' They passed a long column of prisoners and stunned-looking civilians; then he saw an Italian officer sitting on the steps of the town hall, weeping. Inside, he found Bradley, in a bad mood because they'd been kept waiting for transport and he wanted to get moving and get a grip on the situation. Nor were they in communication with the rest of the corps' units. A DUKW they had earlier set up as a mobile communications centre had not yet reached Scoglitti, but a radio jeep had been spotted half submerged back on the beach, so a bulldozer was ordered to pull it out and engineers were told to try to get it back in order quickly.

Meanwhile, Hansen was sent off to find the 53rd Signal Company, which was apparently near the original CP that had been set up early on the previous day. After a long, tortuous drive, he found them in a citrus grove; ordering them to leave their belongings under guard to be picked up later, he told some to get walking while he began shuttling the rest back to Scoglitti. Such were the challenges facing Corps headquarters that second morning of the invasion.

This second day also promised to be another big one of air operations, both for the Axis, who were well aware the chances of stopping the invasion in its tracks would soon slip out of their grasp for good, and for the Allies, who knew they had to make sure that did not happen. Major Macky Steinhoff, however, was flying away from the maelstrom that morning – briefly, at any rate. At around 5 a.m. he'd taken off from Trapani, where JG 77 had returned the previous evening, and, climbing, headed north-west. He was on his way to Cagliari on Sardinia, to see his III. Gruppe, check how they were faring and give them a report on the situation on Sicily. Although still under his command, the III. Gruppe had often been detached from the rest of the wing and had been sent to Sardinia to help protect the island from attack from Allied bombers. He'd had little sleep, as Trapani had been attacked again and then he'd had to stay up attending to the paperwork that was part and parcel of the CO's job, no matter how the battle was going. Utterly exhausted, he none the less felt his tension easing as he left Sicily behind and flew out over a vast blue empty sea. For this short flight, he was alone.

As he flew away from the island, though, so his fatigue began to catch up with him, and he had to shake his head and move his shoulders to keep himself awake. It was also now bitingly cold in the cockpit, the earlier sweat on his shirt now freezing on to his back. He wondered what he was going to say to the men; he knew no one would be impressed by platitudes or by reassurances that General Galland would be speaking to the *Reichsmarschall* on their behalf. Ahead, Sardinia emerged from the haze, an island quite different from Sicily; to start with, it didn't look so bashed about. As he flew into land, he even sensed an air of calm order among the rows of tents and untouched buildings around the airfield.

'The sirocco started blowing today,' Major Kurt Ubben, the III. Gruppe commander, told him as Steinhoff clambered out of his Messerschmitt. 'It's over a hundred in the shade.' The hot wind seemed to have turned the sky yellow. As they walked over to the dispersal tent, Steinhoff said, 'I'd better have a word with the pilots.'

With a glass of lemon tea in his hand – warm, strong and unsweetened – and the men gathered around him, he decided to give them the unvarnished truth as he saw it: the attacks on the airfields by day and night, the hopelessness of trying to destroy the bombers. The best they could do, he told them, was to force the enemy to divert a proportion of his strength to deal with them. That might help the defence of the island. Steinhoff knew nearly all of these men by name, and all but the greenhorns understood the situation was bleak, that there was no chance of any improvement and that their task was to stay alive without being overly cautious. Euphemisms had crept into their orders, such as, 'diverting to advanced landing grounds' or 'flexible in our operations' and 'concentration of our remaining strength'. No one was fooled by such terms, however. The Luftwaffe was in a desperate situation. Somehow they had to try to survive in the face of their growing weakness, by improvisation and experiment – and with a massive dollop of luck.

By dawn that Sunday, the Tigers of 2. Kompanie, 504. Heavy Panzer Bataillon had finally got into position after a long and frustrating day in which they'd been able to play no part at all in the fighting experienced by Kampfgruppe Links. At least now, gathered together up in olive groves to the north of Biscari, they no longer faced a 20-mile advance down winding narrow roads to get to their jump-off positions. None the less, the battlegroup as a whole was not in the best of shape, having had its commander summarily sacked the day before and with Oberst Bergengruen still acting commander of a disparate bunch of inexperienced grenadiers, artillerymen and engineers – and the seventeen Tigers, whose crews, although attached to the Luftwaffe, were still part of the army. With poor radio communications and a terrible lack of combat leadership, getting Kampfgruppe Links together as a coordinated force with which to attack was proving challenging, to say the least. And so the Tigers, although ready to head into action, were kept waiting as the leading elements of the column galvanized themselves and pushed south from their overnight positions to the north-west of Highway 115 between Gela and Vittoria. Eventually, as the morning wore on, orders reached Oberleutnant Hummel, the Tiger company commander, to move towards Gela, where the main bulk of the division's panzers were making their thrust and finding themselves under pressure. The plan was to attack along Highway 115 towards what the Americans had labelled the Y-junction.

Initially, just the 1. Platoon was sent forward, but after a couple of hours, by which time it was mid-morning, Leutnant Karl Goldschmidt and the rest of the Tigers were also ordered to move out. Heading down the road that wound its way from Biscari into the Acate river valley, Goldschmidt then experienced his first taste of Allied air superiority. 'At first,' he noted, 'we waved to the double-fuselage aircraft, assuming they were Focke-Wulfs. But they were Lightnings and they heated us up quite a bit with their bombs and weapons.' His own Tiger was hit, cannon shells and machine-gun bullets holing his smoke dischargers, so that when he attempted to release some smoke to give them much-needed cover, it went straight back into the tank. 'We almost suffocated,' he added.

None of the tanks was completely knocked out, however, although one man was badly wounded, and so they trundled onwards, pressing further towards the Ponte Dirillo and the highway to Gela and eventually linking up with Leutnant Heim's 1. Platoon. At this point, Oberleutnant Hummel halted his thirsty panzers for refuelling, then led three Tigers off on a reconnaissance patrol. They'd not gone far when his tank was hit on the hatch by an anti-tank round, wounding Hummel badly in the knee. Panicking, his driver tried to get their Tiger off the road but then got stuck. Firing forward with their main 88mm guns and machine guns, they swiftly drove off the enemy, but when a second Tiger tried to pull out Hummel's stricken beast, it broke its steering mechanism in the process. Exactly the same happened when a third Tiger tried to haul him out, so that now three of these very precious tanks had been immobilized entirely because of mechanical failure.

With Oberleutnant Hummel now *hors de combat*, Leutnant Heim took over and further split the remaining Tigers as counter-orders now arrived to head to the main Highway 115 then turn east towards Vittoria, not west to Gela. While Heim pressed forward down the eastern fork in the road towards Biscari, Goldschmidt was ordered to take his 3. Platoon, clear the road to Gela of any remaining enemy troops and then recover the three Tigers. Seeing nothing at all on the way, they reached Hummel's Tigers where Goldschmidt, leaving his men to start trying to recover them, clambered up to some high ground on foot – and despite the reservations of his crews – to get a better eye on their surroundings. There was no one around, although some 2 miles away he saw what looked like a company of infantry – around a hundred men at least. Branches got in the way of a completely clear view, though, and he simply couldn't tell whether they were German, Italian or American. Heading back, he was relieved to discover his men had managed to set up some welding equipment and were busily trying to repair the tanks. Even better, they had rounded up half a dozen American paratroopers as prisoners. On the other hand, eleven Tigers were now tied up, stationary, way behind the rest of Kampfgruppe Links, and achieving nothing but some frantic mechanical repairs in the field.

The left-hand flank of Kampfgruppe Links, meanwhile, was being drawn into a fight on the Biazzo Ridge, which rose up from the Acate river valley and through which the main Highway 115 ran towards Vittoria. It was here that Colonel Jim Gavin had attacked a little after 9.00 that morning. With his small band of airborne engineers he had pushed on from a railway crossing up towards the ridge, which lay about two-thirds of a mile beyond. The road, lined with olive trees either side, continued straight after the bend from where they'd captured the German motorcyclist, the grass fields either side burned yellow in the scorching Sicilian sun. Using the olive trees to cover their advance they neared the top of the ridge, then came under fire with machine-gun bullets tearing through the leaves and branches above their heads. Lieutenant Wechsler was hit, as were several others.

Not long after this, Gavin's small fighting force was finally joined by the 250 men of Krause's 3rd Battalion as well as a company from the 180th Infantry, part of the 45th Division that was also fighting from the coast in the valley below. Even though Gavin still had no idea in what strength the enemy was present on the far side of the ridge, he led them forward and past what turned out to be thin enemy outposts. By this time, it was around 11 a.m.; Gavin now ordered his men forward again, but as they pushed on beyond the ridge, so the enemy fire became intense. 'We were going to have a very serious situation on our hands,' he noted. 'This was not a patrol or platoon action.' He was right about that, because heading their way were not only one of the Kampfgruppe Links grenadier battalions but also artillery and Leutnant Heim's six active Tigers. Gavin's men soon came under artillery and mortar shelling, and he realized that while the 45th Division were on the left down towards the coast, his right flank was completely exposed, with nothing to stop the enemy working their way up over the ridge a short distance to the northeast and then around and behind them. Unfortunately, he could do little more than send a patrol out on their right flank and keep a watch for any enemy movement there.

On the ridge either side of the main road, meanwhile, the battle raged. By midday, a 75mm pack howitzer and crew had joined Gavin's band of troopers, followed by a second. Other paratroopers, drawn by the sound of fighting, had also reached them. Gavin tried to dig himself a foxhole, but on the rocky ground his entrenching tool was useless and so he tried using his helmet instead. Mortar fire was very effective on such ground as the explosions chewed up the stone, spraying razor-sharp shards all around.

Never in one place for long, he hurried first to the right flank to check the situation there, then back again to help drag up another 75mm pack howitzer. In between, when a new salvo of mortar shells came in he found himself lying prostrate on the ground, being bounced up and down from the concussion. Captain Al Ireland now offered to hurry back to 45th Division CP to get help. 'It was the best idea I had heard all day,' noted Gavin, as the rumble and squeak of tank tracks could now be heard. Up ahead, beyond a vineyard about 400 yards to their right, were a group of buildings, and it was here that Gavin saw first a tank track appear around the corner of one of the stone houses, then the gun swivel in their direction. 'A Tiger tank,' he wrote, 'is an awesome thing to encounter in combat.'

The men beside him on the pack howitzer decided they should chance their arm, even though the weapon had never been designed for use as an anti-tank gun and lacked the necessary velocity. Gavin, a keen student of history, was reminded of Major John Pelham firing his lone artillery piece at the Union line at the Battle of Fredericksburg in 1862. Back then, however, the Union had not had a Tiger tank with which to reply. Suddenly, there was an explosion in front of the gun, the blast knocking everyone like ninepins, Gavin included, as an 88mm shell hit the ground a little in front of them. By some miracle, not one man was hurt, and the gunners quickly got back to their howitzer and fired a single round that hit the Tiger. Although it merely ricocheted off, it was enough to force the tank to pull back. It was a small victory, but one that was swiftly superseded by the arrival of the other five of Leutnant Heim's panzers. As casualties swiftly mounted and with no answer to these behemoths of the battlefield, Gavin pulled his men back off the ridge.

It was not, however, a full-scale retreat. Rather, Gavin hoped that by falling back on the reverse slopes, they would be shielded from the line of fire of the Tigers' big 88mm guns, and that if the panzers did press forward, they would expose their more vulnerable undersides as they crested the ridge. It was a gamble, however, and others, Major William Hagan and Captain Vandervoort included, urged Gavin to pull back further. He was obdurate. 'We are staying on this goddamned ridge,' he shouted at them, 'no matter what happens!'

By midday, on the western end of the island, Major Macky Steinhoff had arrived back at Trapani. Taking off from Cagliari, he had soon been utterly overwhelmed by fatigue, and so had felt in his knee pocket for a packet of Pervitin pills he'd been given by the MO, Dr Sperrling, but had never used. They were supposed to keep him awake, Sperrling had told him; so he pulled out one, then a second and then a third, and chewed them up. He had no idea such pills were methamphetamines. They tasted revolting, but he had hoped they would keep him awake. And so they had – and more. As he flew south he started to have an out-of-body experience where he thought he was floating above the aircraft and looking down at it. For a brief few moments he remembered what he'd long ago forgotten: how joyful it could be to fly.

Despite having just taken a huge dose of speed, Steinhoff made it back to Trapani, landing after yet another raid had just pasted the place, and bursting a tyre on a piece of shrapnel as he taxied across the battered field. Jumping down into the oppressive heat, he walked to the remains of the hut. Seeing Dr Sperrling, he asked him about the Pervitin, wondering what on earth was in them. When Sperrling heard he'd eaten three, he had a fit and forbade him from flying again that day.

General Bradley, meanwhile, had taken a DUKW down the coast to see Terry Allen and the 1st Division that morning; satisfied the threat there had been seen off, he returned to Scoglitti in the afternoon. Emerging from the water, they had driven into town, where a GI called out to the general from the side of the road.

'Better watch your step, General,' he said, 'there's a Kraut sniper in town.'

'Thanks, son,' Bradley replied, arming himself with a carbine. If there was a sniper about, it would be an Italian rather than a German; in any event, as Bradley approached the steps of the town hall, he handed his carbine to Captain Hansen. As his aide took the weapon, however, he accidentally touched the trigger and a shot rang out across the piazza. 'Sniper!' shouted someone as soldiers all dropped to the ground.

'Chet,' Bradley said, 'be careful with that damn thing, please.' Hansen was not having a particularly good day.

However, by this time, at least, radio communications were up and running, with the radio jeep repaired and the Signals Company and radio DUKW having arrived. Bradley's chief of staff at II Corps, Major-General William Kean, was waiting for him with a signal from Seventh Army HQ. General Matt Ridgway was going to bring in the 504th Parachute Infantry Regiment that night. 'Notify all units,' Bradley read, 'especially AA that parachutists 82d Airborne will drop about 2330 tonight July 11–12 on Farello landing field.' This was the unused satellite landing ground east of Gela.

In fact, Ridgway had been against the move, but it was Patton who'd insisted on bringing in the 504th PIR. The 82nd Airborne commander had felt very dispirited by the 505th's drop. He himself had not parachuted in, but instead had headed to Sicily on the *Monrovia*. Fully aware that a night-time drop had never been attempted before, he'd landed early on 10 July and straight away headed to see General Terry Allen at his freshly established CP. Allen had heard no news whatsoever from any of the 505th Combat Team who had been dropped. Ridgway and his aide, Captain Don C. Faith, had then walked on but had seen no one; he thought it seemed as silent and forbidding as the moon. Climbing up a grassy knoll off the plain, he looked around towards the Piano Lupo and in the direction of the Y-junction, but still saw nothing. Eventually, he'd flagged down Brigadier-General Teddy Roosevelt, Allen's deputy, who was passing in a jeep, but he hadn't seen any paratroopers either.

Eventually, he met a few small groups of 505th troopers, but certainly no concentrated number. Back at the Big Red One's CP, Ridgway had repeatedly tried to raise Gavin on the radio, but to no avail, and so headed back to the *Monrovia*. Patton was all for sending over the 504th that night, but Ridgway dissuaded him, worried as he was both that the 505th's drop had failed and that the planned drop zone for the 504th, the Gela–Farello airstrip, was not yet fully secure. By the next morning, however, 11 July, Patton had changed his mind and wanted the 504th to land that Sunday night. Ridgway was still worried, although now his biggest concern was the safety of the carriers, who would have to fly low over the US invasion fleet. This was a concern he had repeatedly raised in the weeks leading up to HUSKY D-Day, since the 504th had already been lined up for a follow-up drop and he was well aware that by the time they were brought in, the sea off the Gela coast would be swarming with warships and anti-aircraft guns and gunners. In the dark, a low-flying aircraft would be all too easy to mistake for the enemy. Ridgway had repeatedly asked for reassurances from the navy there would be no friendly fire, but no such assurance was given. They could vouch for their warships, they said, but not for the mass of landing craft, troopships and AA gunners already ashore. Ridgway wasn't happy, despite warning messages from both Eisenhower and Patton to all naval commanders that airborne troops would be coming over that night. In an effort to ensure his men's safety further, Ridgway spent much of the afternoon back on shore personally telling the crews of every AA gun now dug in on the dunes what was afoot that night. He had to hope it would be enough, because the die had been cast: Colonel Rube Tucker's 504th PIR would be dropping that night.

While senior American commanders made decisions and preparations for the second drop of the 82nd Airborne, to the north-east of Gela the Axis leadership was becoming increasingly confused, with differing appreciations and contrary orders crossing over the airwaves as the situation rapidly evolved. Early that afternoon, realizing that the Americans were not, after all, re-embarking, and with their troops now pushing eastwards from Scoglitti towards Vittoria and the vital airfield at Comiso, Generale Guzzoni ordered Rossi's XVI Corpo to call off all offensive action and start pulling back to the centre, just as he'd envisaged before the invasion had begun. This order was issued at 1.15 p.m., but once again, never reached General Conrath or his HG Division headquarters. Just under three hours later, von Senger received a signal from Conrath announcing that Kampfgruppe Links was still pushing towards the coast to the north of the Acate river. 'Strong enemy forces in the region of Vittorio–Comiso,' ran the message. 'Enemy is apparently turning away to the east.'

Von Senger now hurried down from Enna to see the situation for himself, driving in a smaller vehicle that made light work of the roads that had caused the monstrous Tigers so much trouble. He found the fighting raging around the Acate and up on the Biazzo Ridge, much as had been claimed by the HG Division's signal. In other words, it seemed as though they were doing quite well; and, with this in mind, he ordered them to press on eastwards towards Comiso. With luck, they might save the airfield, and if not, at least they could make a thrust into the enemy's exposed flank. In giving these orders to Bergengruen's *Kampfgruppe*, however, von Senger was going directly against the orders of Guzzoni. Nor did his instructions take into account the American forces still on the Biazzo Ridge.

Back in the Plain of Gela, by early afternoon Tenente-Colonnello Leonardi had begun to wonder whether the promised reinforcements would ever arrive. The shelling had largely quietened down, while ahead nothing seemed to stir. As the hours passed, he felt increasingly that a golden opportunity to exploit their earlier success was slipping through their fingers. All those losses, that terrible sacrifice, had to have been for something. He had no appreciation of what had happened elsewhere in the battle for Gela – that the rest of the division had been sent packing or slaughtered out on the western side of the plain, or that the Germans had been forced to pull back after significant losses. Then, later in the afternoon, word reached them that reinforcements really were finally on their way. 'A wave of new hope enveloped us,' he wrote. 'Hearts swelled, because all our thoughts were by now focussed on Gela, so close . . . By taking the town, we were convinced we would win!' Some time later, however, they learned the promised reinforcements were a mere mortar company. It was not enough for a further attack on the town. Not remotely enough.

Away to the west, meanwhile, Livio Messina was still crouched in the irrigation ditch just the other side of Gela. Early in the afternoon, a jeep sped past him and other survivors on a mopping-up operation and sprayed the ditch from a mounted machine gun. Bullets had hit the earth precisely where Messina had been moments before. In response, an Italian MG team had opened up and the jeep had swiftly pulled back. Moments later, mortars had rained down upon them with uncanny precision, killing the machine-gun team and an officer. When it quietened down again, Messina saw half the officer's face had been blown clean away. Then more mortars fell. Messina pressed himself into the earth and prayed he would be spared.

On the Biazzo Ridge, as the afternoon wore on, Gavin's men were still holding out on the reverse slopes as more paratroopers, drawn by the sound of battle, had arrived and joined in the fight. Together they had managed to see off three separate attacks despite the presence of the six Tigers. In the meantime, Captain Al Ireland had arrived at the 45th Division CP to find General Bradley there with General Middleton. Immediately recognizing the significance of the threat Ireland reported, Bradley ordered Middleton to send whatever heavy artillery support he could. Realizing this might take too long to organize, Ireland grabbed a three-man navy forward observation team and hurried back in a jeep, reaching Gavin at around 4 p.m.

Immediately, the forward observers got on to their radio and began directing offshore naval fire, something that concerned Gavin as he wasn't precisely sure where he and his men were. He needn't have worried, however. The first shell screamed over and hit exactly where a tank had been spotted. This ranging shot brought down a concentration of fire delivered with devastating power and accuracy, stopping the German assault dead. Suddenly, the enemy was pulling back.

A thick, heavy pall of smoke hung heavy over the ridge. Within an hour more troopers had reached them and then, just after seven o'clock, some Shermans arrived. 'I decided it was time to counter-attack,' said Gavin. 'I wanted to destroy the German force in front of us.' He also wanted to be able to recover the dead and wounded on the far side of the ridge. Jumping off at 8.45 p.m. that evening, as dusk was starting to fall, his improvised battlegroup finished off the HG men, the remainder of whom now cut and ran. The final column of the Axis counter-attack had been repelled; and this time, the Biazzo Ridge was in American hands for good.

CHAPTER 18

Expanding the Bridgehead

W HILE THE AMERICANS HAD had a tough but ultimately successful day around Gela and Scoglitti, General Lucian Truscott's 3rd Division had also had considerable success at Licata. Opposing his landings to the north and west were the Italians of XII Corpo, on their own and without the support of the 15. Panzer Grenadier Division, who were already on the move to the centre of the island. Sensing an opportunity, and having had a better time of it unloading than the Americans at Gela or Scoglitti, Truscott ordered his division to attack in a wide arc around his front to rapidly expand his bridgehead.

This had finally given Audie Murphy a sharp taste of action, first when a shell had killed one of the men in his platoon on the evening of the 10th and then again the following day, when they'd attacked towards Campobello, some 10 miles to the north of Licata. While advancing on the town, they'd come under machine-gun fire from the far side of a railway track. The sound had made Murphy's flesh creep; it stopped when they took cover, but clearly they were going to have to attack and destroy it. They would have to take that leap of faith and get up and make the charge.

'When you get the signal,' the order was passed down in hoarse whispers, 'make a run for it. Stop for nothing until you find cover on the other side of the track.' Murphy waited for the sign and then there it was – the hand raised in a wave. Scrambling to his feet, he began running, the renewed sound of machine-gun bullets filling his ears. Two men jerked backwards and fell, then there was a blast of a grenade. Murphy leapt in to a shallow gully and another man, Private Joe Sieja, originally from Poland, dropped in beside him.

'Did they get the machine gun?' Murphy asked him as the shooting quietened.

'They get it,' Sieja replied. 'But the sonsabecches knocked over two of our men.'

Campobello fell soon after, as the Italians of Gruppo Schreiber, part of the Italian mobile reserve, swiftly fell back.

While Murphy and his fellows in the 15th Infantry were still moving inland on their own two feet, Breezy Griffin and his fellows in the 2nd Battalion of the 41st Armored Infantry were delighted to have been swiftly reunited with their M3 half-tracks. 'Boy, we were glad to see them!' enthused Griffin. 'They were our home, our protection, and our transportation.' As far as Griffin was concerned, they also rode a lot better than a truck, with two comfortable benches in the back and room to stash gear – personal and general – as well as plenty of ammo, mines, grenades and a .50-calibre machine gun. Their armour plate was not thick enough to stop any major warhead, but it would keep bullets out and offer blast protection. The M3 was a very well-designed and highly flexible armoured fighting vehicle.

None of the constraints facing the Big Red One and the Thunderbirds – German troops, a semi-coordinated counter-attack, and insufficient unloading of artillery and armour – were present on the 3rd Division's front. Griffin's 41st Armored Infantry were now part of Combat Command A, which by D plus 1 had all its elements intact. The speed with which this sizeable armoured all-arms force of tanks, mobile infantry and mobile artillery had been assembled really was astonishing. It was no surprise that, full of confidence and bristling with weaponry, they swiftly brushed aside the poorly trained, poorly equipped and poorly motivated Italian troops. By evening, CCA was nearing the town of Naro, some 15 miles from Licata.

They had also been helped by marauding American fighters, especially the twin-engine P-38 Lightnings, which had the range and fire-power to be incredibly effective in this western half of Sicily, shooting up any Italian column that dared show its head. Since most of the roads were not asphalted, the clouds of dust caused by anyone moving along them made them incredibly easy to see from the air.

In fact, this second day of the invasion had been one of heavy activity in the air on both sides. Allied fighters had flown their protective air umbrellas over the invasion fronts, but there had been considerably more effort from the Axis air forces too. Both the Luftwaffe and the Regia

Aeronautica had flung everything they had at the invasion, even though, for the most part, that meant sending aircraft all the way from central and southern Italy. Charlie Dryden and the 99th Fighter Squadron had been flying over Sicily, as had 324 Wing from Malta, getting into a number of tussles. The American Spitfires of the 31st Fighter Group, for example, had attacked a formation of eleven German Dornier bombers and two Focke-Wulf 190 fighter-bombers over Scoglitti just before seven in the morning, shooting down one of the Dorniers, while several lone Ju88s were hit too. The squadrons of 324 Wing had also claimed a number of enemy planes shot down, while their own losses had been light: just six RAF and eleven USAAF all day. Despite this overwhelming dominance in the air, inevitably some Axis aircraft were getting through and causing damage; and this gave the impression to those on the ground and out at sea that their air forces were not supporting them quite as well as they might have done. This, though, was simply not true. Before the invasion, Allied naval forces had expected to lose as many as three hundred vessels; in fact, they'd lost just twelve in all, and in a large part that was due to the heroic efforts of their air forces before and during the invasion.

None the less, on this second day of the invasion, despite continued maximum effort from the Allied air forces, the beaches, under attack from enemy shelling during the morning, came under increasingly heavier air assault as the day wore on. By mid-morning, so urgent was the need for armour and artillery that landing ships had been ordered right in, but by this time only one pontoon had been successfully rigged, at Red 2. Landing ships had come in one after the other, the first offloading its cargo of sixty-three vehicles and three hundred men by around 10.30 a.m. despite being attacked by three Me109s carrying bombs. Fortunately, all had missed. As the first LST had moved out, so another took its place on the lone causeway that had been hastily fixed up. More LSTs had continued to unload through the afternoon alongside the DUKWs that tirelessly ran on and off the beaches.

Inevitably, though, some of the attacking aircraft hit their marks. At 3.40 p.m., as many as three dozen Ju88s managed to get out over the sea off Gela at a moment when there was a gap in the air umbrella. As their bombs fell among the transports, the Liberty ship *Robert Rowan*, part of the follow-up invasion convoy, was hit. Ammunition on board started exploding and, all firefighting attempts having failed to douse the flames, the ship was abandoned. Fortunately, every man aboard was safely taken off. At two minutes past five, the ship exploded with a single, massive blast that could be seen and heard for miles. The *Robert Rowan* simply disappeared in a massive eruption of smoke and millions of fragments.

Then, at just after half-past six that evening, a single Me109 swooped in from the west with the setting sun behind it and dropped a single bomb on to LST 313, which was crammed with fully fuelled trucks, jeeps, half-tracks and ambulances, as well as guns, ammunition and mines. In moments the whole ship was a raging inferno. Amazingly, about eighty men were saved from the fantail when the skipper of the neighbouring LST – a young reservist – manoeuvred alongside the stern so they could leap to safety. Even so, these losses, so visible to all out at sea and on the beaches, gave rise to a feeling that their air forces were not giving the same level of air support they had the day before. And naval gunners, conscious that more and more enemy aircraft were getting through, started to feel a little twitchy.

For the beleaguered Axis air forces, however, flying at their own maximum capacity, operating over the beachhead or indeed anywhere over the island was proving dangerous in the extreme. That day the Luftwaffe would lose thirty aircraft, and the Regia Aeronautica fourteen – numbers far higher than those of the previous day. Among those to be shot down was Leutnant Karl-Heinz Messer from I. Gruppe JG 53, based at Gerbini, who appeared at Trapani late in the afternoon.

Macky Steinhoff had still been feeling the effects of his triple hit of Pervitin and failing to get the sleep he so badly needed when the phone rang to warn him Leutnant Messer would soon be joining them, having bailed out over Corleone, some miles to the east. Hobbling in with the help of a stick, Messer had been grilled about his experience by Steinhoff – though in fact he had needed little encouragement to talk. He had, he told them, been flying over Gela and, having dropped his single bomb, had then climbed up out of the fray, clear of the murderous fire of the Allied ships' flak gunners. Then he'd been clobbered by a gaggle of P-38 Lightnings who'd apparently been waiting for him and the others in I. Gruppe. He'd dived and sped off, weaving through the valleys, but his pursuers had stuck to him like glue and started scoring hits. 'But before they could finish me off completely,' he told them, 'I pulled her up and jumped.' He'd been pleasantly surprised not to have been shot while floating down, and although he'd hurt his leg he had been swiftly picked up by an Italian truck. 'There are Italian army lorries all over the place with odd-looking civilians on board,' he said. 'In other words, the glorious Italian Sixth Army on its way home to mum.' Gerbini, he reported, was in a terrible state. Aircraft had been ploughed up as though they were part of the harvest. Carpet bombing had plastered the entire complex. Steinhoff's pilots were due to head over there first thing in the morning and he asked Messer whether they'd be able to get in. Overnight, Messer explained, labourers would fill in the craters and make it just about usable again, so if they arrived at first light they should, he thought, be all right.

Messer explained they'd been planning to assault the invasion force with a massed attack, each fighter carrying 500 pounds of bombs. 'We would certainly have sent a few to the bottom if we hadn't been picked off one by one,' he told them. 'By the time the enemy landed on the island, my group was already done for, smashed on the ground.'

Out in the Plain of Gela, meanwhile, by dusk, the survivors of Dante Ugo Leonardi's battalion were starting to lose heart. No further reinforcements had arrived, but news of the disaster to the rest of the division had. Trucks had turned up with warm rations, but Leonardi, for one, felt barely able to eat. As darkness fell, he was startled by the sound of shots and small-arms fire ringing out from the direction of his 9° Compagnia. Hurrying across, Leonardi almost tripped over the dead body of one of his men, then found two more. Clearly, an American fighting patrol had been probing forward; and although it had melted back into the darkness, this brief firefight did not augur well. 'The event confirmed the gravity of the situation that was taking shape,' he noted. 'Only the arrival of reinforcements could have saved us from encirclement that night, for sure.'

A few miles away and still keeping his head down in the irrigation ditch, Livio Messina had started, by dusk, to feel ill and soon after, became gripped by a fever; earlier, he'd been so thirsty he'd drunk some brackish water, something he now bitterly regretted. His friend Nino Ciabattoni had meanwhile scampered off to try to round up some more survivors of the day's slaughter. Returning triumphantly with around thirty men, he began plotting their escape. Unfortunately, soon after, five Shermans moved forward and halted only 100 yards or so away. Gripping his stomach and by now shivering, Messina wondered whether the time had come to surrender.

'No,' Ciabattoni replied. 'Officers must never surrender, we have to go on fighting as long as we can.' He told Messina he was going to try to get past the tanks; whether Livio came too or stayed was his choice. Turning to the rest of the small band of survivors, Ciabattoni now offered them all the same choice. 'It's up to you,' he told them. 'If you're coming, get on my left; if you're staying, get on my right.' About half chose to try their luck with Ciabattoni, Messina among them. There was a gap of about 30 yards between two of the tanks; they headed for this, crawling slowly. The Shermans looked enormous to Messina, but silhouetted against the sky he saw the hatches were down, so with luck the crews were asleep; certainly, he could not hear any sound from them.

Past the tanks. A small feeling of relief. Then, about a hundred yards further on, suddenly there was shouting from behind him and moments later a machine gun opened up. Seeing a base plate of a mortar sticking up, he quickly cowered behind it, but no bullet hit close by and after a number of bursts the MG was silent again. Messina waited a while longer, then began his crawl once more, until he felt it was safe to get up and start walking. The others were still with him and suddenly a delicious silence and stillness shrouded the edge of the plain. No guns, no explosions, no aircraft. It had been his first day in battle and, he realized, he had not fired a single shot. The day's fighting had shown up tragically the shortcomings of the Italians. Those Italian troops that had performed well in North Africa had done so largely through learning the hard way and assimilating battlefield experience, but the Italian military machine itself was rotten to the core. Messina, as an officer, had been woefully prepared for modern combat, as the days before, during and immediately after the invasion had starkly revealed. His ignorance of the wider situation, of what to expect, and his inadequate training were symptomatic of an Italian military that was simply not fit for purpose.

While Messina was slipping away to freedom, Dante Ugo Leonardi received orders to pull back to Monte Castelluccio, the base from which they'd started their attack nearly eighteen hours earlier. Leonardi was devastated. 'Leaving those positions, fought for tooth and nail, stained with the blood of so many wounded and the sacrifice of so many dead,' he wrote, 'meant renouncing forever a page of pure glory and the cry of effort of the previous day. It meant saying goodbye to our fallen loved ones, although they had believed in victory until the last moments of their lives. It meant leaving the best part of ourselves on those clods of earth that had felt the desperate beats of our hearts during the battle!'

As they marched back, no one spoke. Leonardi, for one, could not stop thinking about all his men who were no more and the defeat that now seemed certain. And, as if to add weight to the sense of impending doom now hanging over him, even before they reached Monte Castelluccio they were attacked again by another enemy patrol. None of his men were trained in night fighting – it simply had never been part of their tactical doctrine; now this vulnerability added to the growing sense that the enemy were creeping up on them in the shadows of the night, closing in around them. The end, Leonardi knew with a broken heart, was near.

Disaster for the Livorno – and disaster too, was about to follow for the 504th Parachute Infantry Regiment. With the enemy counter-attack at Gela stalled and the situation on the Biazzo Ridge ending in victory for Gavin's men, there was now no need to drop the 504th in at all, certainly not under cover of darkness. If Patton still wanted them, they would most probably be able to land at Ponte Olivo airfield within twenty-four hours. At the very least, it would have made more sense to drop them the following morning, in daylight, and under the cover of a specially organized air umbrella. The Axis air forces might have put up a good effort on the 11th, but they would not be throwing in that weight of aircraft again because, for all those that had got through, plenty more had not; even the attack on the *Robert Rowan* cost the attackers four Ju88s shot down. Their numbers were depleting fast.

Yet undoubtedly there had been far greater enemy air activity over the invasion beaches that day, and especially as the afternoon had progressed. The 144 C-47s of the 52nd Troop Carrier Wing bringing in the 504th were following exactly the same route that Gavin's 505th had taken, which meant a long stretch flying low off the coast. At night, in the dark, C-47s sounded and looked rather like twin-engine enemy bombers. It seemed like a perfect storm, as Patton now realized. 'Went to office at 2000 to see if we could stop the 82nd Airborne lift,' he noted in his diary, 'as enemy air attacks were heavy and inaccurate Army and Navy anti-air were jumpy. Found we could not get contact by radio. Am terribly worried.'

He had reason to be, and, frankly, should have thought about this earlier. Although the first few arrived over the DZ near Gela at around 10.40 p.m. and dropped their sticks of paratroopers without any dramas, as more and more transports flew over suddenly one Allied anti-aircraft gun opened fire, then another, prompting a domino effect. Recognition signals frantically flashed from the transports as they turned in towards the coast had no effect whatsoever. Aircraft began to explode or come down in flames. Other pilots took dramatic evasive action, so that many men of the 504th were as scattered across Sicily as the 505th had been. That night, twenty-three C-47s were knocked out of the sky and a further thirty-seven were badly shot up. The 52nd Troop Carrier Wing suffered 90 casualties, of which 7 were killed and 53 missing, while the 504th lost 81 dead, 132 wounded and 16 missing: around 10 per cent of their number, and all caused by fire from their own side.

The decision to fly them in was a terrible one on so many different levels, not least because the navy commanders, with their refusal to give sufficient assurances, had given ample warning of their suspicions that such a tragedy was likely. Ridgway himself had declared his reservations, and by the evening even Patton had realized it was a mistake. Why they hadn't trusted their gut instincts, especially after the airborne fiascos of two nights earlier, is hard to understand – especially since by around 11.30 a.m., as Patton himself had testified in his diary, the crisis at Gela had passed. The drop could have been cancelled or moved at that stage; it could still have been stopped later in the afternoon, since the transports didn't take off until later on that evening. To attempt it that night, in the dark, at the end of D plus 1, had been completely unnecessary. The Americans had brilliantly won the day: the Divisione Livorno had been effectively destroyed, while the largest part of the HG Division had been forced into retreat and its formations badly mauled. The reputation of the navy, who had performed such a vital and heroic role over the past couple of days, was badly tarnished that night; yet for some reason the commanders making the decisions have largely escaped criticism, even though they were more to blame for the fiasco than anxious young gunners new to combat who had faced a difficult and nerve-stretching day. The tragedy of the 504th's drop was a bad end to two otherwise exceptional days for the Americans, who had showed considerable mettle in the air, on the sea and on land, both operationally and at the sharp end.

The end for Tenente-Colonnello Leonardi's battalion came at dawn. Through the early hours he'd been unable to sleep, his ears tuned to every sound or movement. Then, at first light, naval shells had screamed over, smashing into the castle and all around them, rock splinters and shrapnel hissing and spinning, the ground quaking as though repeatedly hit by a giant hammer. When the shelling subsided the Americans attacked, frontally at first, but gradually working their way around their flanks and then to the rear. 'So at dawn, on the memorable 12 July, 1943,' wrote Leonardi, 'we were encircled by superior forces.' Superior in number, superior in equipment and superior in training. Leonardi's men fought on bravely – there had never been any doubting their courage – but by 7 a.m. it was all over as they fired their last shots and threw their final grenades and then surrendered. The survivors were rounded up and marched back down the road to Gela, finally reaching the town they had set out for – but as defeated men, not victors. Some civilians were crying and offered them bread and water, while others shouted abuse. As they were herded into a wire holding camp, Leonardi felt as though they had become the slaves of Rome, about to be fed to the circus. Later, they were led out again and on to landing craft to be taken to a troopship and then to Africa. 'We were leaving ideals, affections, hopes and dreams. Our hearts bled,' he wrote. 'The torment of imprisonment had begun.'

The Americans' night-time thrusts had been part of the US 1st Division's plan to straighten the line again north of Gela and so establish a clear lodgement from which unloading could continue without fear of enemy shelling. Rangers had taken the higher ground to the west of the plain, while the 26th and 18th Infantry had pushed towards Ponte Olivo, still one of the key HUSKY objectives. Yet the fighting around Gela was not over, despite Conrath's orders of the previous evening for all his forces to retreat towards Caltagirone. Overnight, not all his troops had been able to pull back; it is hard to understand why, although perhaps the persistent problem of poor radio communication had led to confusion.

Among those moving forward into battle at around 5.30 a.m. on Monday, 12 July were the remaining serviceable Tigers of the 504. Heavy Panzer Bataillon. During the night, Leutnant Karl Goldschmidt and his men had been busy. Despite the risks of using highly visible welding equipment in the dark, they had received nothing more than a couple of harassing shells, which passed harmlessly over them, and so were able to get on with attempting to repair the damaged tanks. Before first light, they had two working again, although Hummel's was still kaput and had to be blown up to avoid it getting into enemy hands.

However, they did not now drive back to Caltagirone, because they'd not received any such orders to retreat. In fact, the previous evening they'd been joined by Hauptmann Weber, one of the HG panzer-grenadier battalion commanders, and around a hundred men. According to Weber, he had orders from HG Divisional HQ to advance towards

Gela as far as the Niscemi junction – the same Y-junction the American paratroopers had recognized as a key feature in the Gela battleground. Weber, who outranked the officers of a platoon of Tigers, told them they were now under his command and ordered them to be ready to get going at 4 a.m. The idea was to conduct limited operations to buy time for the rest of the division to fall back, although why they hadn't simply all swiftly retreated to the Caltagirone area the previous evening is not clear. The orders still swilling around were becoming increasingly mixed and contradictory: Guzzoni had ordered a general retreat to the centre of the island, but von Senger had told Conrath to keep pushing east; Conrath had gone against von Senger's direct instructions and pulled back, but had then ordered limited operations to block any American attempt to harry their tails.

The trouble was, Conrath risked throwing too few troops against too many, and while he might delay the Americans, the cost of doing so could easily outweigh any potential gain if those left behind for this task weren't very careful. A defensive blocking operation was one thing, but going on the offensive was quite another. Goldschmidt, however, had no qualms about accepting Weber's command. After all, his platoon, despite having six of the most powerful tanks on Sicily, had so far contributed very little. As far as he was concerned, it was time to change that.

They'd duly moved out at 4 a.m., the grenadiers riding on the tanks, Weber beside Goldschmidt on the turret of his Tiger, and had rumbled down Highway 115 in the direction of Gela. It was about 5.30 a.m. as they approached the Y-junction, where they paused to shoot up machine-gun nests and pillboxes now occupied by the Americans, the grenadiers working in parallel with the tanks by jumping down and playing the infantry role. The Americans responded with their 57mm anti-tank guns and a 75mm pack howitzer but made little impact against the Tigers, which blasted them and then simply ran them over, crushing the dead and wounded gun crews to a pulp as they pressed on. A little later, several Shermans appeared up ahead. Goldschmidt gave the order to the lead Tiger to shoot, but for some reason he couldn't fathom, it didn't – and then nor did the second – and neither made any response on the radio. Goldschmidt realized their radios must be out of action, and opened fire from his own Tiger. 'The Sherman tank is about 2,300 metres,' he noted, 'and burns after the first shot.' A second Sherman tried to pass it and Goldschmidt's tank fired again, with the same result; at that range, the Sherman's 75mm gun could not even dent a Tiger, whose

Left: A B-17 flies over Messina, which was attacked 58 times.

B-17s head towards a target, while (**below**) Castelvetrano is carpet-bombed.

AIR POWER

Air power played a vital role in the invasion of Sicily, not least in the months and weeks leading up to the invasion, when bombers hammered communications networks by pounding ports and airfields, and fighters took on the enemy in the air.

Left: Smashed remains of Messerschmitt 109s beside wrecked railway rolling stock.

Below left: Pantelleria under attack. The island surrendered, overcome by the combined weight of air and naval power.

Below right: British troops march through the shattered town of Porto di Pantelleria on 11 June 1943.

Left: The Luftwaffe were horribly exposed all over Sicily. Here an Me109 is partially hidden beneath olive trees.

Below: One of JG77's Me109s at Trapani. Behind is Monte Erice.

Below left: An American P-38 Lightning – as flown by Smoky Vrilakas. These were particularly effective ground-attack aircraft.

Below right: Two Me109s destroyed on the ground lie amid the churned-up earth at the Gerbini airfield complex.

Bottom: More abandoned and captured Luftwaffe Messerschmitts and Regia Aeronautica Macchis.

GETTING READY

Left: The Allied commanders for HUSKY. *From left to right*: Eisenhower, Tedder, Alexander and Cunningham.

Below left: Benito Mussolini, the Fascist dictator of Sicily – clinging on to power by his fingertips by the beginning of July 1943.

Below right: Kesselring (*left*) and von Senger.

Below: The RAF operations room in the underground Lascaris bunker complex on Malta.

Right: British troops loading LSTs for Operation HUSKY.

Above: Allied materiel might had grown exponentially since 1940 – here rows of LSTs line up at Bizerte as US troops march aboard.

Above right: The invasion fleet under sail.

Below: British glider-borne troops load up in Tunisia.

Above right: Night-time airborne operations ahead of the seaborne invasion were a key part of the plan – but while the troops themselves were very well trained, the same could not be said for those flying them to Sicily. US paratroopers aboard this C-47 would soon lose their grins once over the island.

Below: A very rare photograph of a Horsa glider en route to Sicily.

Above: Very rough seas off Licata on D-Day.

Above right: The British XIII Corps invasion, with the high escarpment looking down on the invasion beaches.

Left: British Tommies coming ashore, while (**above**) a near miss sends a fountain of water high into the air near Avola.

Below: The 231st Malta Brigade coming ashore on D-Day.

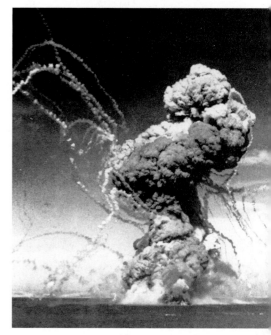

Above: The Allies were prepared for the loss of 300 vessels but in the end only twelve were destroyed by the enemy, including LST 313 at Gela, and (**right**) the Liberty ship *Robert Rowan*.

The Allies harnessed naval power not only with huge numbers of jam-packed transport vessels (**above**) but also with immense fire-power from warships, such as the light cruiser USS *Brooklyn* (**above right**).

Right: British troops move through Cassibile.

Above: The Americans faced heavier attacks from the air on 11 July, the second day of the invasion, as the explosions here at Gela show.

Above right: An Allied bomber flies over Gela.

Right: US troops move on out of the town.

Above: The destroyer HMS *Tetcott* firing on Augusta while the SRS, on board the *Ulster Monarch*, close in to assault the town.

Left: Italian POWs in the main piazza in Scoglitti, while US (**below left**) and Canadian (**below right**) infantry push inland.

SICILY

The view out over the Plain of Catania (**above left**). Sicily was a brutal place to be in high summer – blisteringly hot and dry. It was also pretty primitive, with widespread poverty and disease, few vehicles and much of the island lacking either running water or electricity.

Right: The Mafia chief Don Calogero Vizzini.

Below: The landscape around Mount Etna.

Above left: Melilli after its bombardment from the sea; both newly homeless civilians and men of the 1st Green Howards gather by the church.

Above right: The Italian strongpoint at Ponte Dirillo, taken in swift order by 'Hard Nose' Gorham and his men of the 505th Parachute Combat Team on D-Day.

Above left: One of the mighty Tigers of 2. Kompanie, 504. Heavy Panzer Bataillon.

Above right: Well-positioned German machine-gunners with a powerful and rapid-firing MG42.

Right: Monty addressing Canadian troops early in the campaign.

Below: US infantry moving forward as they start rapidly expanding the bridgehead.

Left: Italian dead and the remains of their antiquated truck near the south-east of the island.

Above: German *Fallschirmjäger* moving forward. Highly motivated, well trained and with considerable combat experience within their ranks, they were also equipped with twice as many machine guns as the ordinary infantry.

Above left: The scene of the Battle of the Gorge on the road between Melilli and Villasmundo.

Above right: A knocked-out German 88mm of the kind that caused the advancing 15th Brigade such problems.

Right: British paratroopers of the 2nd Parachute Brigade.

Above left: Captured British paratroopers and Tommies taken during the Battle of Primosole Bridge.

Above right: An American half-track struggles through the narrow Sicilian streets – designed for horses and carts, not the materiel might of the Allies.

Above left: German dead on Highway 114 running north from Primosole Bridge.

Above right: Men of the Durham Light Infantry keeping their heads down amid the cactus around the bridge.

Below: Wrecked Shermans after the Battle of Primosole Bridge.

Above: German machine-gunners well camouflaged (**left**). Sicily's terrain certainly favoured the defender. A German *Kubelwagon* (**right**) needs a change of wheel as a Sicilian boy watches. The sudden influx of huge numbers of vehicles was a novelty for most of the island's civilians.

Below: The Allies captured tens of thousands of prisoners, mostly Italian, such as these at Enna (**left**), but plenty of Germans too. Germans of the Hermann Göring Division talk to their captor (**right**).

Above: A Spitfire comes into land at a newly captured airfield in the south-east of the island, while the harvest continues.

Right: A British sapper clears one of the many mines the Germans left whenever they pulled back.

Above: American troops of the 2nd Armored Division pass through cheering crowds in Palermo on 22 July (**left**), while yet more Italian prisoners are led from the city (**right**). The Americans captured a staggering 53,000 Italians in five days during their sweep west.

Above: British tanks of the County of London Yeomanry cross the Plain of Catania, Etna looming up ahead (**left**). Sicilians walking through the ruins of yet another smashed town (**right**).

Below left: Shoeless Sicilians watch an American medical auxiliary attend to a wounded GI. **Below right**: Generals Alexander (*left*) and Patton.

Above: 6th Royal Inniskilling Fusiliers marching from Catenanuova towards Centuripe (**left**); troops on the slopes near Centuripe (**right**).

Left and below: Centuripe the day after it fell. Both Centuripe and Troina were mountain-top towns, incredibly difficult to attack and bitterly contested.

Right: The shattered remains of Regalbuto after the successful assault by the Canadians and Malta Brigade.

Below: A *Fallschirmjäger* anti-tank gun crew. The Germans fought both bravely and extremely effectively as they fell back.

Above left: Major-General Vyvyan Evelegh of the 78th Division (*far right*) and Colonel George R. Smith of the 39th Infantry (*second from right*) meet on the road near Randazzo.

Above right: Artillery of the 78th Division passes Italian dead in the ruins of Paterno.

Above: A British 25-pounder in action.

Right: The astonishing bridge-building effort by American 10th Engineer Battalion at Capo Calavà.

Below: US troops enter the wreckage of Messina (**left**). The narrow Straits of Messina, the toe of Calabria beyond (**right**).

THE BATTLEFIELD TODAY

Above: The view from Assoro on the narrow plateau held by the Hasty Ps. Beyond, in the middle distance to the left, is Agira, and beyond that, Mount Etna.

Below: Centuripe – the prostrate man (**left**). Gela beach – the pier long since repaired after being blown up in the early hours of D-Day (**right**).

Left: Troina – the highest town in Sicily and scene of so much carnage in early August 1943. **Below left**: The still-ruined church at Troina. **Below**: The fighter operations rooms on Monte Erice. The entrance to the bunker, dug into the sheer rock face, can still be seen.

88mm gun had more than the force needed to destroy the American tanks.

Goldschmidt saw the other Shermans furiously trying to back up, and shot up a third and then a fourth before rumbling on. Weber had told them that when they reached the Y-junction, they would be meeting a column from the HG Panzer Regiment – and there, sure enough, coming down from Casa dei Priolo towards them, was a Panzer Mk IV: but, rather than hailing it as a friend, one of Goldschmidt's other tanks promptly destroyed it with a single round. Goldschmidt yelled at its commander over his radio for being such an idiot, but again got no response.

Confusion now reigned. In reaching the junction, Goldschmidt's six Tigers had driven deep into the American positions held by Hard Nose Gorham's band of paratroopers and the 16th and 18th Infantry. Gorham himself tried to take on the Tigers by running out and aiming at one with his bazooka. Shrugging off the blast, the Tiger killed Gorham instantly with a single shot; so died a fearless and brilliant young airborne commander.

Around the same time, the rearguard of Kampfgruppe Rechts had met the advancing Americans on the Niscemi road and had responded by trying to push them back. So now American and German shells and bullets were fizzing around the junction, with Goldschmidt's six Tigers caught in the middle and unable to communicate with anyone. Despite repeatedly calling over the radio, Goldschmidt was unable to raise Weber, who had disappeared from view entirely, or any of his other tanks. Firing recognition flares made no difference, so Goldschmidt pushed on, off the road and down towards the Gela Plain. 'We roar into the area,' noted Goldschmidt, 'with the strongest expressions the German soldier knows.' Still fire from the Niscemi road seemed to follow them; so, grabbing the swastika flag kept in the turret of every German tank, the loader jumped out and waved it frantically from the turret – and at last the shelling stopped. 'Finally,' exclaimed Goldschmidt, 'the idiots have realized we're Germans!'

In fact, Goldschmidt had been mistaken, unaware that the remaining German troops on the Niscemi road had already pulled back, and that the bulk of the HG Division around Gela had retreated the previous evening. This meant they were now on their own; the swastika-waving had not stopped the shelling, but rather had coincided with a pause as the Americans brought up reinforcements. The 16th Infantry's Cannon

Company was now hurrying into the action, as were both the 5th and the 32nd Field Artillery Battalions. Then more tanks joined the fight.

'Sherman tanks at nine o'clock!' Goldschmidt heard in his headphones from Unteroffizier Fred Günther, one of his Tiger commanders still in contact. At the same time, Goldschmidt's Tiger was hit on the turret. 'Rivets fly around our ears,' he noted. 'Thank God, no shot came through.' In fact, some eight Shermans had joined the fray and began peppering the Tigers, hammering them with shots. Even Tigers had weak spots, especially in their tracks and rears, and the two lead panzers were disabled, the crews bailing out and scampering for cover.

These two knocked-out Tigers now blocked Goldschmidt's retreat. On his left was a deep and impassable valley, while on the right the ground rose, possibly too steeply for a Tiger to handle. With no other option, he ordered his driver to try the steep slope and up they went, tilted so far that Goldschmidt worried they would somersault backwards. Luckily for them the 56-ton beast made it back on to the road, and with a fourth Tiger now knocked out, that left just two of them: his own and that of Fred Günther.

Back down Highway 115 they went, speeding out of the fray as quickly as they could and with no obvious sign of the Americans following. Then the radiator on Günther's Tiger began to boil and they had to stop. Goldschmidt ordered two of Günther's crew, Werner Hahn and Eugen Grün, to go and get some water from a large house 100 yards further on, while the two surviving Tigers were driven into cover off the road. Clambering down, Goldschmidt discussed the situation with his men and assessed the damage. 'It looks bad,' he noted. 'My Tiger has about 110 hits.' That was not all. The Tiger's complex and sophisticated six-speed gearbox was in no way designed to cope with the kind of aggressive combat action it had just been through. The automatic shift now only worked between second and fifth gears, while the engine had also suffered damage. 'Only now,' he wrote, 'do we realize we are over thirty-six hours without sleep.'

By noon, this last action by the HG Division was over, although the US 16th Infantry had also been badly battered by three days' fighting. The rifle companies were down to half strength and the 2nd Battalion had been reduced to just two hundred men from nine hundred, including the last of Gorham's paratroopers. Not only had Gorham himself been killed, the 16th's 1st Battalion commander had also been shot and evacuated. The 18th Infantry's Cannon Company were among those sent forward to shore up the weakened 16th; Lieutenant Frank Johnson, along with one other man, was ordered to carry out a forward reconnaissance patrol of the hills in this eastern part of the Gela battlefield to make sure the Germans really had gone. He soon passed two of the German tanks that had threatened the beaches the previous day, now burnt out and abandoned, but then further on found one of the anti-tank guns that had been crushed flat by the Tigers, the dead crew sprawled around it. Around the Y-junction, smashed pillboxes stood broken and destroyed. Pushing on, Johnson and his companion came to a dried-up river-bed, the eastern flank of the 16th Infantry, and here they saw three blackened and smoking Shermans, those first shot up by Karl Goldschmidt earlier that morning. Flames still crackled in the now otherwise quiet Sicilian countryside as the sun once again beat down.

Beyond, on the road to Niscemi, was one of the most horrific sights Johnson had ever seen. Along the river-bed to the left of the road, spread over perhaps 300 yards, were the crushed bodies of forty or fifty Germans – probably Hauptmann Weber's grenadiers. 'Rifles, canteens, packs and helmets are mixed with the flesh,' noted Johnson, 'and the whole has been flattened into a horrible, gory mess.'

Meanwhile, the Americans pushed on. The Ponte Olivo airfield was captured around 10 a.m. that day while Comiso, from which Malta had been so grievously battered the previous year, was also taken – by men of the 179th Infantry, part of the US 45th 'Thunderbird' Division – at around 4.30 p.m. With the latter had come a bounty of 125 Axis aircraft – most of them, it's true, unserviceable – as well as 200,000 gallons of fuel and an arsenal of some 500 bombs: all told, not a bad bag. Soon after there were some more bonuses as first a Ju88 and then two fighters, the pilots not realizing the airfield was now in American hands, landed and were promptly captured. The airfield at Licata was also taken, while Pachino was already in Allied hands. Capturing the airfields, of course, had the double benefit of denying their use to the enemy and gaining it for the Allied air forces. This in turn meant Allied fighters would soon be able to spend more time in the combat area and less time – and fuel – travelling to and from their bases.

It was, by now, only a matter of time before the Luftwaffe were forced to abandon Sicily for good. At Trapani, Major Macky Steinhoff had been woken early that morning by a telephone call and news of a teleprint from Luftflotte II. Reichsmarschall Göring had felt the need to humiliate his pilots further. 'I can only regard you with contempt,' Göring wrote in a memo to all his pilots in the Mediterranean. 'I want an immediate improvement in fighting spirit. If this improvement is not forthcoming, flying personnel from Kommodore downwards must expect to be reduced to the ranks and transferred to the Eastern Front to serve as infantry.' It was an appallingly brutal message, even by Göring's standards. That the fault lay entirely with the war leadership in Nazi Germany and not at all with the overworked, undersupplied, outnumbered men at the sharp end was never going to be accepted by a commander-in-chief whose mind was addled by drugs, hubris and his own waning influence. The loss of airfields and the damage to those still held meant that Axis fighter units on Sicily were now constantly flitting from one landing ground to another, with all the ensuing chaos and disruption that caused in terms of refuelling, rearming and maintenance. Steinhoff doubted whether they would survive the day at Trapani – or at Gerbini, for that matter, to where his latest orders instructed him to fly; he was well aware the situation there would be every bit as dire. 'We would refuel our aircraft by hand-pump,' he wrote, 'rearm and top up with oil. We would leap into slit trenches and shelters and wait for the bomb carpets to unroll over us. And then we would crawl out again, haul the wrecked aircraft to one side, repair any damage and, provided we still had enough machines to make up a modest formation, take off on the next patrol. This was what all these men had had to go on doing day after day. And now I was expected to talk to them about fighting spirit!'

Perhaps predictably, JG 77's day panned out much as Steinhoff had foreseen. General Galland rang to tell him to try not to worry too much about the *Reichsmarschall's* signal, then ordered him to take all available aircraft to Gerbini. He also warned him to get what vehicles he had left ready to move out of Sicily. 'There'll be no transport aircraft,' Galland told him. 'Air corps haven't a Ju left. And once again, don't take that teleprint too seriously. D'you promise me that?'

Then, in their first scramble of the day, from Gerbini, Steinhoff's great friend and II. Gruppe commander, Major Siegfried Freytag, was shot down and wounded. Steinhoff was desolate – completely at the end of his tether. The dashing, confident fighter pilot of the early part of the war had gone. Looking around at his men as they sat down in the heat and shade later that afternoon, he noticed how dishevelled they'd become. Too tired to speak, they all looked filthy, their shirts and trousers covered in grime and stained with oil. Dust was everywhere – in their hair, on their faces, on their boots. Covering their aircraft, too.

It was still quite early when Steinhoff took off to attack Gela. He only had nine Me109s behind him – all that remained serviceable from II. Gruppe and his own headquarters flight. They flew into a brief thunderstorm that hammered his cockpit with rain; then the clouds parted and there ahead were the long beaches of Gela, with tanks, trucks and other vehicles stacked up on the roads leading from them. Lining up, Steinhoff swooped down and opened fire, through a curtain of tracer arcing towards him. A couple of seconds, men leaping off the road, and then he was past, hurtling on at well over 350 mph as he went into a climbing right-hand turn. He then heard over his R/T the news that enemy bombers were heading to Agrigento, further west along the coast, so led his group to try to intercept them. Up ahead, smudges of flak pockmarked the sky, but while Steinhoff soon spotted the bombers, he couldn't see the fighter escort. Two of the bombers collided, locking together and hurtling downwards, but before they had hit the ground, Steinhoff saw the fighter escort and was soon tussling with P-40s. After firing all his remaining ammunition he managed to break away and, realizing that his fuel was almost out and that he was now in the western part of Sicily, decided to fly into Trapani instead of returning to Gerbini. 'The airfield looked dead and deserted,' he noted, 'as though it had already been abandoned by the group. All at once, I knew that the end had come – irrevocably.'

By afternoon on Monday, 12 July, the Americans had created a bridgehead some 50 miles wide, and had not only linked up the forces from all three landings but were now also ranged alongside the Canadians advancing on Ragusa. The 15th Infantry had reached Canicattì, more than 25 miles inland, with Combat Command A on their left. That day, too, Audie Murphy had killed his first men. On a scouting patrol ahead of the rest of B Company, he and some others had flushed out a couple of Italian officers, who had set off on their horses at a canter. Without pausing for thought, Murphy had dropped to one knee, brought his rifle into his shoulder and shot both of them, seeing them tumble from their saddles. The lieutenant was shocked and berated Murphy.

'That's our job, isn't it? They would have killed us if they'd had the chance,' Murphy answered. 'That's their job. Or have I been wrongly informed?'

The lieutenant conceded the point; but it was a big thing to kill a man, and a number of soldiers faced this moral conundrum when first in action. For Murphy, however, seeing his fellows getting killed – by the shellfire on the first evening and again when storming the railtracks – had hardened him to what he had to do. 'Now I have shed my first blood,' he wrote. 'I feel no qualms; no pride; no remorse.'

Among those who had also more than played their part in the great link-up had been Major Mark Alexander and his 2nd Battalion of the 505th PIR, who had cleared a fair-sized part of the area to the east of the 45th Division's landings. Having quickly established exactly where he was and gathered up 530 of his men, he had been able to keep them together as they worked their way inland, away from the cliffs along the coast, then turned west towards Scoglitti and Gela, clearing Italian resistance as they went. Most of the prisoners they took, they disarmed and then let free. 'It would have been a lot of trouble to take our prisoners with us,' said Alexander, 'and it would have tied up a lot of our men. There wasn't any sense in it.' As they'd neared Scoglitti, they had cut in behind the 45th Division and continued their march towards Gela, in time to witness the disaster unfolding on the 504th's drop. Soon after that, Alexander had made radio contact with General Ridgway. At dawn, they'd reached Ridgway's headquarters, now on the ground near the Gela beaches. It had been an epic journey for the 2nd 505th.

The day's fighting had been a stark lesson for the Axis forces about how quickly the situation could change. Suddenly and dramatically the map had shifted, so that, having been in heavy action that morning, by early afternoon Leutnant Karl Goldschmidt and his two surviving tank crews now found themselves stuck deep behind enemy lines in one of the most bizarre situations experienced since the invasion had begun. A little while after parking up the two battle-scarred Tigers, Goldschmidt had realized that Hahn and Grün had taken far too long to fetch water, and so had headed up to the nearby farmhouse himself, only to hear, as he drew near, voices – both German and English. Opening the front door, he had stepped inside and seen Hahn and Grün sitting there with twelve American paratroopers. He was dumbfounded. Hahn explained that when they'd first approached the house they'd heard English being spoken, so had pulled open the door, pistols at the ready, only to find the American officer inside facing them with his own pistol drawn. Neither side had pulled a trigger; instead, they had talked, shared cigarettes and wine, and the two Germans had filled up their jerry-cans with water. They discovered something in common – the Germans were from the 504. Panzer Bataillon, while the Americans were from the 504th Parachute Infantry Regiment. Also in the house were a number of wounded paratroopers and the American now asked Goldschmidt if he could call for medical aid by radio. He gave him his word he would not try any tricks. Goldschmidt agreed, but only after returning to the Tigers and moving them into a firing position pointing directly at the house.

After an hour an American doctor reached them and, with Hahn – who spoke English – translating, he spoke to Goldschmidt, explaining they must surrender. It was an unusual situation, to say the least: two Tiger tanks, still capable of firing but mechanically disabled, with their two five-man crews, against a dozen and more American paratroopers. Goldschmidt flatly refused to surrender, even when the doctor showed him a map and pointed out that the front line had moved and they were now cut adrift from the rest of their division. Eventually, a six-hour truce was agreed, not least because of the bizarre bond the two sides had struck up. In time, a jeep arrived and took off the wounded men; but when the six hours were up, Goldschmidt still had no intention of throwing in the towel. By now it was dusk, night was falling rapidly and most of the Americans were drunk on the wine they'd found in the house. Goldschmidt had already ordered his men to start slipping away from the building, the first two given the task of blowing up the Tigers. In the hiatus caused by the blasts, all ten men managed to flee into the shadows, and head north to safety.

Earlier that day, Eisenhower had visited Sicily, coming ashore then later heading back on board the *Monrovia* and cruising up the coast off Licata. The sea had been filled with ships, and he had been mesmerized by the sight of landing craft hurrying back and forth and the amount of supplies being unloaded. 'I must say,' he wrote to General Marshall, 'the sight of hundreds of vessels, with landing craft everywhere, operating along the shoreline from Licata on the eastward, was unforgettable.' At around the same time, a little way inland, General von Senger had been touring the front; pausing on some high ground to look down on Licata and the sea beyond, he saw what Eisenhower had seen, and even used the same word to describe it. 'Unforgettable it was,' he recalled; but while for Eisenhower the sight had convinced him the invasion had already been a success, for the German general it confirmed what he'd already feared. That Sicily, and even the war, was lost.

PART III

The Race to Catania

CHAPTER 19

Taking Stock

A MONG THOSE NOW FIGHTING in Brigade Schmalz was Unteroffizier
Bruno Kanert, one of a number of men in the HG Division brought
in from the army rather than from a flying unit of the Luftwaffe –
although, in an indication of the hasty and unsystematic way in which
the division had been flung together, he and the others in the III. Bataillon of the Hermann Göring Panzer Regiment had only crossed the
Straits of Messina on 9 July, the day before the invasion. Allied air power
had harried them all the way, although a massive defensive barrage had
been fired as they'd crossed the narrow waters and the bombers appeared
to drop their bombs wide. Then, as they'd passed Catania, that city had
been hit too. That night, as they'd set up camp in a wood, they had been
briefed properly for the first time; then the following morning, as the
invasion was taking place, they had hastened off towards Syracuse with
the rest of Brigade Schmalz to meet the enemy.

The battalion was equipped with assault guns and a mixture of
tracked, self-propelled artillery. Most platoons were equipped with Sturm-
geschütze, known as StuGs – Mk III panzers with a fixed howitzer or
Pak 40 75mm anti-tank gun, although Kanert was in the Heavy Platoon
of the 11. Heavy Batterie equipped with the Sturmhaubitze or StuH 42 –
a hybrid designed the previous year, also on a Panzer III chassis, but
with a 105mm howitzer mounted on top. They had only recently been
sent to fighting units, and most had been sent to the Eastern Front; yet
the HG Division had managed to get hold of some too. Regardless of the
state of its personnel, the HG Division was the best-equipped Axis unit
on Sicily.

Attacked several times from the air as they rumbled south, they had reached the town of Villasmundo, 8 miles west of Augusta, at around four in the morning on 11 July; here they finally halted and waited for further orders. Kanert's platoon was commanded by Stabswachtmeister – staff sergeant – Grethe, one of the most experienced men in the entire battalion and a veteran assault gun commander with the German Cross in Gold to his name. Grethe now ordered them into firing positions in the hills overlooking the Bay of Augusta, although at that time in the morning Augusta itself lay shrouded in mist. 'In the course of our "inspection of the terrain",' noted Kanert, 'we found an Italian clothing store, where we outfitted ourselves with black shirts and field jackets.' That they needed to take these Italian uniforms was another reminder of just how hastily this division had been assembled.

Kanert and his comrades were some 18 miles north of Syracuse, so on the 11th were yet to come face-to-face with the British pushing up from the south; but on this eastern side of the island Eighth Army had had two very successful days, the Italian coastal divisions disintegrating in front of them as they pressed northwards and the Divisione Napoli not show-ing much appetite for a fight. The Airlanding Brigade's role was over, however; Lieutenant-Colonel George Chatterton, having finally reached Ponte Grande on the morning of D plus 1 and found the area strewn with wrecks of gliders, had soon afterwards been hailed by General Hoppy Hopkinson passing by in a jeep. Wearily, Chatterton had clam-bered in beside him and they had sped off into Syracuse. Chatterton, exhausted, distraught at the loss of so many of his men, but also relieved to still be alive himself, ended up having a long and drunken lunch with the brigade second-in-command and a beautiful American lady in a fine villa owned by her Italian husband. 'I don't know how many bottles of Chianti we drank,' he noted, 'or how much spaghetti we ate, but it was a very, very good lunch.'

The SRS, meanwhile, reached Syracuse that same morning, to find the town almost deserted and, Peter Davis thought, looking in a very sorry state. They did not stay long, however, but headed to the harbour where they embarked in landing craft that took them back to the *Ulster Monarch*, waiting for them offshore, unsure whether they would be needed again.

The bulk of Eighth Army had been advancing up the south-east of Sicily, the Canadians and the 51st Highland Division meeting very little opposition and the Malta Brigade swiftly capturing Noto and then pushing on north too. The closest troops to the vital Catania Plain, however, were those that had landed furthest north, the 5th and 50th Divisions; but here, after the great success of the first day, opposition started to stiffen.

Lieutenant David Cole and the 2nd Inniskillings had been part of 13th Brigade's advance towards Floridia, about 8 miles west of Syracuse. At dawn on the 11th, they'd headed off towards this new objective and had soon come under attack from a battalion of the 75° Reggimento of the Divisione Napoli. Mortars began to whine down and explode around them; over to Cole's right, a Sicilian woman screamed hysterically as a mortar shell exploded near to where she and several other civilians were sheltering behind a wall. A short while later, the air thick with smoke, a messenger, crouching as he ran, delivered to Cole the news from the adjutant that one of their tracked carriers had been hit and Captain Graham Turnbull, one of Cole's friends in the battalion, had been killed. 'I felt stunned,' he wrote. 'It seemed only a few hours ago that Graham Turnbull had been nonchalantly spreading out his maps in our cabin.'

Some Sherman tanks from the County of London Yeomanry, unloaded early to support the infantry advance, now clanked and squeaked their way forward down the road only for the lead one to be knocked out by an 88mm anti-tank gun fired by the Brigade Schmalz. Right in the centre of the narrow road, it burned fiercely, billowing smoke, as a few of the Skins tried to drag one of the crew clear. It was also now blocking the road, although the 91st Field Regiment were not far behind and were hastily hurried forward. All of this took time; but once the British artillery opened up, the enemy anti-tank gun swiftly pulled back and after that a number of Italians began raising their hands in surrender. At the same time another company of Inniskillings, warned by a Sicilian farmer, worked their way to the flank of the Italian position and then attacked, charging them with Bren machine guns, Tommy guns and grenades.

By noon the battle was over, and Cole and his signals platoon moved forward, up the road past the still smouldering Sherman, its turret split and blackened, and on into orchards where the battalion was to 'consolidate' and allow another to pass through them and then attack Solarino a couple of miles further on. They had taken some four hundred prisoners, who shuffled forward in a long column followed by their officers and commander, a tall, immaculately dressed, grey-haired fellow with a drawn expression. When they were halted, he turned to his officers and addressed them with a catch in his voice, whereupon they all clasped each other's hands. Cole, watching this, thought it all a bit theatrical; it was certainly not how he and his fellow stiff-upper-lipped officers would have reacted to surrendering.

The Inniskillings' fight with the Napoli near Floridia was a foretaste of hardening resistance: Oberst Wilhelm Schmalz and his enlarged brigade had reached the front and were now beginning to enter the fray. Schmalz was operating on the assumption he could no longer expect any help whatsoever from the Italians; if any showed up, then all well and good, but he certainly wasn't going to hang around waiting for them. Vaguely aware that the bulk of the HG Division had been in action near Gela, he knew that he and his brigade were effectively on their own, and that meant making their own decisions. The key, he realized, was to delay the Allied forces for as long as possible on the way to the Plain of Catania. If the counter-attacks against the Americans were successful then so much the better, but if not, he needed to buy time to allow both the rest of the HG Division and the 15. Panzer Grenadier to pull back into a line that cordoned off the entire north-east of the island. Having already begun to establish defensive positions at the foot of Etna and overlooking the Catania Plain, he was well aware that this was ground that offered good opportunities for defence. What he could not allow to happen was for the British to hustle their way to Catania and then forge on to Messina before the rest of the German forces in Sicily had had a chance to get back in line. That meant these delaying actions were vital to the entire course of the battle for Sicily.

The task for his men was to lie in wait for the advancing British, on ground of their own choosing, hold them as long as possible without sustaining serious casualties of their own, and then pull back. This still involved some very difficult decisions. Augusta, for example, like Syracuse, lay on a limb of land curling out into the sea. It would, he knew, be easy for too many of his still rather meagre forces to get sucked into a battle there, with no clear way of easily pulling back. Far better, he reasoned, to focus on the main roads further inland that ran north to Lentini and then the Catania Plain. What's more, on the evening of 11 July he had seen with his own eyes that warships were massing off the coast at Augusta and that a British landing would inevitably be made there. In fact, these were warships with which Admiral Troubridge was planning a *coup de main* operation to take Augusta that night.

The combination of the warships massing out at sea and the

abandonment of Augusta by Schmalz – except for the men of 3. Bataillon HG Panzer Division, who remained in position overlooking the harbour – was enough to prompt another wave of panic and mass desertions such as had happened at Syracuse. Troubridge's naval forces, including HMS *Tartar*, attacked as planned early on the morning of 12 July. The StuH assault guns in the hills overlooking the bay, which had a range of just over 8 miles, opened fire on the ships; the British warships' guns did likewise, and soon naval shells were screaming over towards Kanert and his companions, getting closer and closer with every salvo. 'We sneaked back across a rickety bridge over a deep gorge,' recalled Kanert. 'Once on the other side we breathed a sigh of relief.' It was not only the assault guns that were firing at the naval force, however, but also the commander of the coastal fortress area, Ammiraglio Leonardi himself, who, with two members of his staff, took on the role of gunners in place of a crew that had deserted. This combined effort was enough to make Troubridge think twice and call off the assault for the time being.

Schmalz's troops were already proving very effective, having held up 17th Brigade at Priolo, halfway between Syracuse and Augusta, where they knocked out several Shermans and forced the Allies to pause and wait for artillery, and to prepare a plan that involved the use of fighter-bombers early the following morning, 12 July. This all took time – half a day and a night, in fact, which was just the kind of delay Schmalz wanted. Then, under cover of darkness, his forces pulled back into the hills beyond the town of Melilli on the main Lentini road, where they linked up with the assault gun battalion.

During this time, Schmalz himself barely stood still. 'At times I was with the troops,' he wrote, 'then again at Lentini to choose the most suitable positions for defence and giving advice, then a jump to the Augusta area, then Melilli, back to the command post to try and get a connection with other German and Italian units.' There seemed to be so much to consider. The supply of food and ammunition required careful planning, as his base supply area was back in the hills around Misterbianco, to the west of Catania, yet fuel and trucks were limited and the roads were dangerous places to be in daylight with the constant threat of attack from the air and, closer to the front, from offshore naval guns. And all the time the sun bore down, the blazing heat sapping energy. Flies swarmed around the men, feeding off their sweat, and malarial mosquitoes were an ever-present menace. There were also dressing stations to set up, the inquisitiveness of the local civilians and refugees clogging the roads to deal with. And questions – endless questions: What was the situation at the front? Where was the Divisione Napoli? 'Anyone who has not personally experienced such hours and days,' he observed, 'cannot imagine the variety of events and the demands on mind and body.'

'This morning, the Scirocco ripped both window shutters out of my hand,' jotted Hanns Cibulka in his diary on Monday, 12 July. 'Now it chases the grains of sand around the room like shotgun shells.' He found it curious that such a strong wind should sweep over across the Mediterranean from Africa and yet the sky still be a rich deep blue without a cloud in sight. Despite the invasion, his flak battalion had not moved, and the headquarters remained at the farmhouse at the edge of Catenanuova. This meant that Cibulka, even though a mere wiring man, was able to pick up news more readily than others. Word was out that morning that the HG Division had failed to push the Americans back into the sea – and, worse, that apparently Allied naval gunfire had done for them, carving up the coast all the way between Gela and Licata. It was estimated that 80,000 American troops had landed either side of Gela already; this was actually a bit less than the true total, but none the less an alarming number. Although Cibulka still felt a safe distance from the fighting, the battalion were not entirely secure from death where they were; early that very morning, one of their drivers collapsed at the wheel. 'In vain the paramedic had looked for a wound,' noted Cibulka, 'and had finally discovered a small iron splinter in the neck.' It seemed the man had been driving without a helmet. Three hours later, bombs fell on the town, killing two children who had been outside playing. 'The dead,' he added, 'are increasing.'

Receiving reports in Rome that morning, Feldmarschall Albert Kesselring had to accept that not only were the numbers of dead on Sicily increasing, but so too were those of the wounded and, especially, those being taken into captivity. Even someone disposed always to look on the bright side could not conclude that the first two days of the invasion had gone well. Clearly, more troops were needed – German troops; and so he ordered the deployment of the 1. Fallschirmjäger Division to Sicily, even though in doing so he was encroaching badly on Generale Guzzoni's authority. These paratroopers were some of the best fighting men in the Wehrmacht, in a different league from any of those already on the island. Having fought superbly on the Eastern Front, they had been among those already withdrawn with an eye to their being sent to the Southern

Front. They were now to be sent in stages: 3. Fallschirmjäger Regiment would be parachuted in first, followed by elements of 1. Fallschirmjäger, who would be landed, rather than dropped, at Catania, with the rest crossing the Straits later.

Even so, with telephone and radio communications still patchy, to say the very least, Kesselring realized he needed to fly urgently over to Sicily and see the situation for himself. It was a risky course with Allied aircraft now marauding almost freely; but he landed safe and sound and immediately sped off to see von Senger and Guzzoni in Enna.

By this time, both of them had concluded the best they could achieve was to delay the Allies for as long as possible and then evacuate their forces on Sicily to the mainland. Kesselring, while broadly agreeing, still wanted to see the current state of play with his own eyes, so set off, with von Senger in tow, on a whirlwind tour of the front, even heading over to Lentini and down the road towards Melilli, where he met with Oberst Wilhelm Schmalz and told him of the failed counter-attack at Gela. Kesselring agreed with Schmalz's current plan of action: not to counter-attack but to delay the British advance. The C-in-C South tried to sound positive. More German troops were on their way, he told Schmalz, and would be under his command.

For all his encouraging words to Schmalz, Kesselring had been shocked by what he'd discovered on Sicily. The collapse of many of the Italian units had been a particularly heavy blow, as with this disintegration the agreed defence plan had already fallen apart at the seams. Clearly, the west of the island would now have to be abandoned – as Guzzoni had already ordered – and the HG Division brought back inland. The issue now was what reinforcements to bring over. A second *Fallschirmjäger* division was also on standby, two further panzer-grenadier regiments were ready and waiting to move in Reggio di Calabria, in the toe of Italy, and there was also the entire 29. Panzer Grenadier Division in southern Italy. These were not insubstantial forces – and they were all in a different league of training and combat standard from the bulk of the ill-trained HG Division and even the flung-together 15. Panzer Grenadier Division.

Both von Senger and Guzzoni, now thoroughly despondent about future prospects, were opposed to such reinforcements, however, especially to bringing in the whole 29. Panzer Grenadier Division. Guzzoni feared that if more men were brought to Sicily and the enemy broke through the Catania Plain, there would be a risk of overcrowding on the road to Messina and a greater likelihood of losing even more Axis troops before they had a chance to get back across the straits. This, though, was the kind of appreciation Kesselring simply didn't want to hear. As far as he was concerned, there was still something to fight for, and he had already ordered not only the 1. Fallschirmjäger Division but also two panzer-grenadier regiments to Sicily; these would be subordinated to Brigade Schmalz, the only formation in which he had much faith, and the one that was now defending the most critical part of Sicily – Catania, the plain and the road to Messina. This meant Schmalz's force had rapidly grown into a division-strength formation. What's more, it was now decently equipped and soon to contain some fine – and fresh – troops. It was also clear to Kesselring that the Italians had shot their bolt. 'My flight to Sicily,' noted Kesselring, 'yielded nothing but a headache.'

The headaches of the Axis forces in general were not being alleviated by the continued lack of effective communications between army, corps, divisions and disparate units. That same afternoon of the 12th, Conrath had reported to von Senger that his men were firmly holding the road south of Niscemi and south of the Acate valley, when in reality there was nothing left of those forces but piles of dead Germans and a number of smouldering tanks, half-tracks and other vehicles. His highly valuable company of Tigers had also been effectively destroyed during the past two days' fighting. Despite this pointless sacrifice – the result of his orders – Conrath was fuming about the performance of his cobbled-together division. 'I had the bitter experience,' he wrote in a communiqué to all his unit commanders that day, 'to watch scenes, during the last day, which are not worthy of a German soldier, particularly not a soldier of the Panzerdivision Hermann Göring. Persons came running to the rear, hysterically crying, because they had heard the detonation of a single shot fired somewhere in the landscape.' His anger and contempt were spat on to the page. 'Panic, "Panzer fear" and the spreading of rumours', he continued, 'are to be eliminated by the severest measures. Withdrawal without orders, and cowardice are to be punished on the spot, and, if necessary, by the use of weapons.' He was certainly not mincing his words. But what did he expect from a division flung together in haste with far too little training and almost no inter-unit cohesion?

Brigade Schmalz, on the other hand, were showing no signs of panic or hysteria, and were going about the business of delaying the British advance with growing effectiveness by covering both roads heading north towards Lentini. Oberst Schmalz had awoken that morning,

12 July, at his command post in Lentini to the thunder of distant cannons and machine guns. He had few concerns about the quality of his fighting men, having chosen the NCOs and officers carefully to make best use of men with substantial experience – as far as he could; but the staff officers he'd been allocated were air force men new to ground combat, and had to learn on the hoof the many tasks of fighting while constantly on the move, from supplying troops with rations, ammunition and fuel to getting the wounded into field hospitals and a host of other tasks which really required training and specialist knowledge. This meant his first task of the day was ensuring his new staff were doing their jobs and had the most important issues in hand. Then he had to go through the mass of incoming reports and work out which required his most immediate attention. 'As soon as this is done,' noted Schmalz, 'the gathering of personal impressions of what is happening on the battlefield begins; the best and clearest messages can never replace what one sees oneself.'

Around him Schmalz had gathered a trusted team who had been with him for much of the war. These included his driver, known simply as 'Schumacher'; his accompanying NCO, Unteroffizier Busch; and his ordnance officer, Oberleutnant Klein. Then there was his personal servant, Karl Widhahn, who, with Schumacher, had been with him since before the war. Together, these men had served with Schmalz in Poland, France, the Balkans, Russia – and now Sicily. 'Cities, plains, mountains, heat, ice and snow and rivers,' reflected Schmalz, 'and shelling, machine-gun fire, air raids, bombs, beautiful quarters or rainy and silty holes and ditches. We have experienced everything together.'

As they sped off on the morning of 12 July, the sun was already beating down, the heat roasting. Dust clouds swirling around them, they passed a gun battery, then a field kitchen. Pause, chat, check all OK. On to an aid post, then to a battalion CP. Schmalz always tried to bring some cigarettes and chocolate to hand out; it was always appreciated. From there he went by foot to an observation post. The men looked dusty but in good heart. 'Behind us is Melilli, in front of us Priolo,' he noted; 'to the right a rocky plateau rises, to the left a barely overgrown plain that slopes down to the sea.' Earlier, Allied fighter planes had strafed coastal artillery around Priolo and Melilli; now, out to sea, Schmalz saw British warships – and then they opened fire, the orange flashes from their guns seen long before they could be heard. Then the missiles were screaming over, smashing into Melilli.

The town followed age-old Sicilian tradition in being perched high on the ridge of hills overlooking the coast. The idea was that up here, inhabitants would be safe from attack from the sea, and that might have been the case in days of yore – but no longer, as the Royal Navy now demonstrated with an awesome display of fire-power that flattened nearly the entire town and cut off the water supply. Some fifteen civilians were killed and many more injured, buried in the rubble of their homes. Already, in respect of the effects on the local population, Sicily was proving very different from North Africa and even northern Tunisia.

The Allied way of war that had been developing was increasingly based on heavy fire-power. Both Britain and America had entered this war determined to use science, technology, mechanization and their enormous global reach to the maximum, in order to get as much as possible of the hard graft done by machines rather than men. Infantry and armour were still needed, but the enemy could be ground down first with immense amounts of fire-power – from bombers, from fighter planes, from growing arsenals of ever more powerful artillery that could hurl shells more than 10 miles, and from the sea as well as on land. This was the tri-service brotherhood that General Alexander identified as key to successful modern warfare; but while it was unquestionably a far more efficient way of fighting a war in terms of casualties to their own side, it exacted a huge cost from anyone who got in the way. In North Africa, especially in the desert regions, for the most part the only ones on the receiving end were the Axis forces; but to some extent in northern Tunisia and especially now, here in Sicily, where an immense typhoon of steel surrounded a civilian population of millions, the collateral damage – to use a more recent phrase – was enormous, as the wrecked and ruined cities of Messina, Catania and Palermo – and even tiny Catenanuova, where Hanns Cibulka was based – could already testify. So too, now, could Melilli.

Melilli served as a vivid demonstration of the Allies' 'steel not flesh' strategy. After the naval bombardment, 15th Brigade was sent in to attack later that afternoon, the assault led by the 1st Green Howards, including Major Hedley Verity's B Company. Defending the town were elements of the Divisione Napoli; the garrison surrendered with barely a casualty. So the destruction of Melilli was good for 15th Brigade, but very bad for the Sicilians living there. This exemplified a moral conundrum the Allies were increasingly facing as the war progressed. Britain, the British Dominions such as Canada, and America perceived the war as a moral crusade: Nazism and Fascism had to be crushed because they embodied an evil that had no place in the modern world; and yet to defeat them, hard choices had to be made. The war had to be won as quickly as possible with as few casualties as possible, especially among the Allied combatants. National interests came first, so if destroying cities in the Ruhr, or even little Melilli, meant the war would be over more quickly and at less overall cost, then that was justifiable – in the minds of the Allied planners, at any rate. None the less, the morality of the crusade the Allies were on was beginning to blur a little.

A few miles to the west of Melilli, advancing up the left-hand road from Floridia towards Sortino, were 50th Division, led by 69th Brigade. Just before it reached Sortino, the road wound its way through hills and up and down narrow valleys that led towards the coast. It was here, as the road climbed, that Schmalz's men set up one of their delaying positions. As the 6th and 7th Green Howards advanced, the Germans opened fire with mortars, machine guns and anti-tank weapons. Already the attacking infantry were exhausted, having marched more than 40 miles already since the landings, in oven-like heat and with very little sleep. Despite this, they pressed on and eventually forced the Germans to pull back. 'My pal, Charlie Lee, was missing,' noted Bill Cheall of the 6th Green Howards. 'Jack Ramsden and all his section were blown to pieces.' Another pal, Jack Betley, was also killed in the attack. And even once the Germans had pulled back, they still had to contend with a web of mines and booby-traps that had been hastily laid.

Later that evening, Paddy Mayne's SRS were ordered to attack Augusta, landing in LCAs from the *Ulster Monarch*. As they neared the port they came under fire, but naval gunfire from their escort – a cruiser, a destroyer and two motor gun boats – returned it tenfold. Bullets ripped the ground as Lieutenant Peter Davis and his men in No. 2 Troop leaped out of the LCA and on to the beach and made it to a small, narrow street where he and his section paused. The frontal fire was soon silenced, and before long Mayne was seen walking down the main street with his hands in his pockets as though he were on a Sunday afternoon stroll. Once again, casualties had been very light, underlining the point yet again that amphibious operations such as this and at Capo Murro di Porco were considerably more effective than airborne ones on coastal targets in Sicily.

No one had been hurt in Davis' section, for example. Splitting into subsections, Davis and his men began clearing the town, a place that looked eerie in the evening half-light. 'It was soon obvious that the town was completely deserted,' wrote Davis, startled by the lack of civilians: 'not even a stray cat was to be seen, let alone a human being.' The only real trouble came as No. 3 Troop pushed on towards the railway station and got involved in quite a heavy firefight; but at 4 a.m. on Tuesday, 13 July, the lead elements of 17th Brigade arrived and the town was secured. In all, the SRS had lost two killed and eight wounded, and the Allies now had their second significant port.

That same night the Allies bombed Enna, another ancient hilltop town, now home to an army headquarters as well. Generale Guzzoni had been at his desk at midnight when the thunder of aircraft rumbled over and the whistle of falling bombs could be heard. Several hit his HQ, badly damaging the buildings and knocking out all communications other than some portable radios. Clearly, this meant evacuation, not least because the Allies now knew where the Axis HQ was; but although Guzzoni himself was lucky to escape with his life, the experience seemed to cause something in him to snap, because when the raiders had passed he began ranting about insisting on staying put with his men. It took all the powers of persuasion of his chief of staff and von Senger to convince him the headquarters really did need to move. In the meantime, this disruption merely threw another spanner in the works of the already inadequate Axis communications network.

It was clear that a critical moment had arrived in the battle for Sicily. Late in the day on 12 July and on into the 13th, a series of decisions were made that were to give shape to the rest of the campaign. General Montgomery had been delighted by the softness of Italian resistance and was quite open about admitting he'd overestimated how tough a fight the invasion was going to be. This still didn't mean acknowledging his thought processes or earlier caution had been at fault – far from it – but after three days of rapid advance against limited opposition, and with the Americans having given the German HG Division a bloody nose, he recognized there was a golden opportunity to move rapidly into the Plain of Catania, get across it and then push on to Messina. Speed was key, however; he was well aware that the opportunity to wrap up the campaign in a matter of days was a fleeting one and had to be taken before the Germans could pull back into an organized defensive position. The gateway was the Primosole Bridge, at the southern edge of the plain, where the roads heading north all converged. During the planning phase this had been highlighted and earmarked for an airborne operation. Operation FUSTIAN was now to take place, carried out by the 1st Parachute Brigade, on the evening of Tuesday, 13 July, while a Commando assault from the sea was to capture the Malati Bridge, on the same road but a few miles to the south, just to the north-east of Lentini.

Monty's hope was that the paratroopers and Commandos could take the bridges intact, so that the infantry and armour could then quickly pass through after dawn on the morning of 14 July; his leading units were, after all, only between 15 and 20 miles away. To achieve this they would need a fair wind behind them and a dollop of good fortune, but it was certainly doable. 'My battle situation very good,' Monty signalled to Alexander at 10 p.m. on Monday, 12 July from his temporary tactical HQ at General Sir Oliver Leese's XXX Corps headquarters. 'Intend now to operate on two axes. 13 Corps on CATANIA and northwards. 30 Corps on CALTAGIRONE–ENNA–LEONFORTE. Suggest AMERICAN DIV at COMISO might now move westwards towards NISCEMI and GELA.' He then pointed out that the road network and current supply and maintenance situation would not allow two different armies to carry out offensive operations at the same time in the same south-eastern part of the island, and proposed that Seventh Army should instead hold a line and block the Axis forces to the west to prevent them getting away. By pushing XXX Corps and the Canadians wide using Highway 124, he intended to cut the Axis forces in two, deny them the main routes through the centre of the island and block any attempt by them to effectively withdraw into a coordinated defensive position in the north-east around the south and south-west of Etna. He also hoped that XXX Corps would drive on to the north Sicilian coast at Santo Stefano.

Alexander accepted Monty's suggestion and the following day visited Patton at his new CP up on the Capo Soprano at the western edge of Gela. He arrived with Mary Coningham at around 1.10 p.m., just as Patton was having a spot of lunch. 'I had to quit eating and see them,' he noted in his diary. 'They gave us the future plan of operations which cuts us off from any possibility of taking Messina.' Patton was annoyed not to see any Americans accompanying Alex – not even his US deputy chief of staff, Major-General Clarence Huebner, a personal friend of Patton's. Patton was always prickly – and perhaps especially so that day because he'd been admonished by Eisenhower during a visit the previous day for not sending him enough progress reports, and then had received a signal that morning from Ike 'cussing him out' over the tragic fiasco of the 504th's drop and demanding a formal investigation.

Alexander then toured the American front and left satisfied that all concerned were quite happy with this new plan. 'I spent all yesterday with American Seventh Army at Gela,' he wrote in a signal to General Brooke on 14 July. 'They have done well and are in good heart and show lots of enterprise.' Later on the 13th he issued new orders on the lines suggested by Montgomery and discussed with Patton.

What Alexander did not know at this point, however, was that Kesselring's reinforcements had already begun to reach Sicily. On the evening of 12 July, three battalions of the 3. Fallschirmjäger Regiment – some 3,200 men, commanded by Oberst Ludwig Heilmann – were dropped near Lentini during a break in Allied fighter cover, the Germans having by now worked out that this was very regular, offering opportunities to take advantage of gaps. They landed on target with spectacular efficiency and without any casualties, bar the odd sprained ankle. The two panzer-grenadier regiments from the toe of Italy were also now on their way to further bolster Schmalz's force. On the morning of 13 July, moreover, Kesselring had conferred with Hitler, who that day had decided to call off ZITADELLE, the offensive at Kursk on the Eastern Front; his forces had barely broken through two of the seven defensive lines built by the Red Army, and had run out of steam. Losses were considerable, but Hitler accepted that at this moment the threat to his southern front, so much closer to Germany than Kursk, was strategically greater than that to the east. Hitler also agreed that the 29. Panzer Grenadier Division would be sent to Sicily too, no matter what von Senger or Guzzoni thought.

To tie all these new troops together also required a new and highly experienced German commander, and to that end Hitler approved the appointment of Generalleutnant Hans-Valentin Hube, one of his most favoured and experienced generals, to take over command of the reconstituted XIV Panzer Korps and with it all German troops on Sicily.

The defence of the island had suddenly taken on an entirely different complexion. Italian troops were increasingly being written out of the campaign's script. Early on the morning of 13 July, British troops managed to break through a gap in the Italian line and captured the command post of the Divisione Napoli near Solarino, taking prisoner most of its staff and its commander, the grandly titled General Count Giulio Cesare Gotti-Porcinari. One battalion of infantry and some artillery then attached themselves to Schmalz's brigade, but that was the end of the Napoli as a separate entity.

To all intents and purposes, the Divisione Livorno had gone as well. Of the 11,400 men and officers in the division on 10 July, more than 7,200 had been lost; some 214 of Tenente Livio Messina's fellow officers had been killed, wounded or taken prisoner. Not a single coherent combat unit could now be formed. Messina himself had managed to get a ride back to their camp at Mazzarino, only to discover it had been pillaged by locals from the town. His camera, photos, books and family letters had all been stolen. Still weak from his fever and ordeal at Gela, he fell in with the Gruppo Livorno, the division's remnants, who overnight on 13 July were moved by truck towards the centre of the island.

There were still, however, plenty of Italian troops in the western half of the island, even though the US 3rd Division was doing a good job of reducing their number. It was here that Lieutenant Max Corvo and his OSS team intended to get to work, infiltrating the remaining coastal divisions, the Assietta and Aosta divisions and much of XII Corpo, and then encouraging them to rise up against the Nazi–Fascist beast. Much to Corvo's frustration, however, so far nothing much had gone according to plan. He had left the United States on 20 May, but the plane had developed engine trouble, which had meant a delay of a week in Dutch Guiana getting it repaired. He eventually reached Algiers on 28 May. This in itself wasn't too much of an issue, and he spent the next six weeks getting his team of agents ready under the overseeing eye of Colonel William Eddy, head of the OSS in Algiers.

On 8 July, Eddy, Corvo and Captain Frank Tarallo, another OSS operative, headed to Bizerte to catch a ride with the invasion fleet, carrying radio equipment, false documents, civilian clothes and everything else they'd need for life behind enemy lines in western Sicily. Reaching the port on the afternoon of the 9th, they reported in, expecting to be told what berth they would be given, only to learn the invasion fleet had already sailed and that they'd missed the boat. Literally. Corvo was understandably distraught. The whole point had been to land with the first wave of troops, get inland quickly and start fermenting insurrection. These plans had been approved at the highest level. 'It was incomprehensible to me that the OSS should have been given such meagre information,' wrote Corvo. 'It was particularly difficult to understand in view of the fact that we had the only pool of manpower and expertise in the US Army which was familiar with both the language and terrain and that our planning was so advanced.' Corvo wasn't entirely correct about this. There were others willing to help, but these – Sicilian gangsters in America like Lucky Luciano – had connections with the Mafia, and Corvo had steadfastly refused the suggestion from those further up the chain that he make contact with these men, even though they still had powerful connections in Sicily.

Desperate to get on with the task and tearing his hair out in frustration at the time being wasted – vital time in which he might be helping the Allied cause – Corvo, with Tarallo and Eddy, finally boarded an LST at Bizerte on the afternoon of 13 July with a grudging assurance that, once ashore, they would be given a chance to talk to General Terry Allen. No one, it had to be said, seemed very interested in Corvo's team or his plans to start an insurrection in Sicily.

CHAPTER 20

Primosole Bridge

T HE ORDER TO EVACUATE reached Major Macky Steinhoff early on Tuesday, 13 July. All serviceable aircraft were to fly to the mainland. 'So, it had been decided,' noted Steinhoff. 'It amounted in fact to an admission by the high command that yet another battle had been lost.' Oddly, he didn't feel demoralized; on the contrary, the decision gave him a sense of hope. They had escaped after all. A little while later, as the first Me109s were taxiing, Steinhoff made a last tour of the airfield, supervising the destruction of anything they could not take with them. The hangars and old administrative buildings were already utterly wrecked. Charred remains of aircraft littered the perimeter. Now men were setting fire to the workshops; tents were going up in a mass of flames. Chairs, camp beds, telephones, desks, tools – everything was being flung on to the conflagration. 'There was,' thought Steinhoff, 'something orgiastic about this dance around the fire.'

Not long afterwards, he took off with his headquarters flight and climbed up over Monte Erice for the last time. Flying along the north coast, he saw Etna looming up, an ever-present sentinel over the island – and then he was over the Straits of Messina. 'My mission here was over,' he wrote. 'The burden of responsibility had suddenly been lifted from me.' He now felt a deep shame and anger that so much had been asked of him and his men – so much more than they had ever been able to perform. But it was over. The last of the Luftwaffe on Sicily were leaving. There was still a battle to be fought on the ground, but in the air the Allies had won.

*

'This country is absolutely foul,' wrote Lieutenant Farley Mowat in a letter to his parents. It was hot as hell all day and icy cold at night. 'Towns are few and scruffy, always perched on hills like ravens' nests and the stink has been collecting in them since Year One.' The locals were shockingly poor and filthy. 'Eyetie' soldiers were crack troops, he wrote – they cracked every time they saw them. Progress had been fantastic, he added, but might now slow down. 'The rumour is,' he added, 'that Jerry is moving south to meet us, and he is a horse of another colour.'

Mowat and his fellows in the Hasty Ps, as part of the 1st Infantry Brigade, had been working their way north, finally pausing on the western flank of Eighth Army some miles north of Giarratana, another deserted town stinking of effluent. It had been midnight on 12 July when they arrived; they were now at the lip of a high plateau around a dozen miles south of Vizzini, and by mid-morning on the 13th would be just a stone's throw from the most easterly leading elements of the US 45th Division, the 'Thunderbirds'. Mowat and his men were utterly fed up. The initial excitement and relief of successfully landing and capturing their first Italians seemed like a lifetime ago. Since then they had marched the best part of 50 miles on foot; not enough transport had yet landed, and even though Syracuse and now Augusta too had fallen to the Allies, almost all maintenance and supply were still coming in through the beaches. DUKWs, especially, had proved invaluable; but even on the fourth day in, only 1,104 tons were being unloaded on the Canadian beaches each day – even with the help of a mass of Italian POWs – and this then had to be driven increasing distances to the troops on the road.

Long miles of marching in such stultifying heat during daylight hours were sapping everyone's energy. Flies and mosquitoes were a constant menace; they all sweated terribly, which meant they had to drink more, and water was one of the scarcest commodities of all. Dust covered everything, getting into their eyes and ears and up their noses and sticking in their throats. 'The sun became an implacable enemy,' recalled Mowat, 'and our steel helmets became brain furnaces. The weight of our personal equipment, together with weapons and extra ammunition, became almost intolerable.' He had begun to wish he had been a fighter pilot and had looked up enviously at any he'd seen. Then two Me109s had swooped down early one morning, spraying the road with bullets and cannon shells before flying into a mass of light anti-aircraft fire. One of the pilots flew straight into a hill at more than 350 mph, while the second, also hit, was last seen disappearing over a distant ridge trailing smoke. Mowat promptly changed his mind about wanting to fly.

While the 1st Infantry Brigade had paused, 5th and 50th Divisions were still pushing north towards Lentini and the Catania Plain. Major Hedley Verity and the 1st Green Howards had remained in the ruins of Melilli as their fellow battalions in 15th Brigade pushed on down Highway 114 to the next town en route to Lentini, Villasmundo. A couple of miles out from Melilli, the road wound its way down a comparatively steep gorge perhaps 400 yards wide, crossed over a small bridge, then climbed up again towards the plateau beyond. Accompanied by Shermans of the County of London Yeomanry, the 1st Battalion of the York and Lancaster Regiment – the Yorks and Lancs – had just begun descending into the ravine when one of Schmalz's blocking positions opened fire with really well-sighted anti-tank guns, machine guns and a few mortars. The entire force was no more than fifty men, but quickly knocked out several carriers, half-tracks and Shermans, and brought the whole of 5th Division's advance north down Highway 114 to a grinding halt. With every yard of the road into the gorge covered, there was nothing 15th Brigade could do. All day the Yorks and Lancs and then the King's Own Yorkshire Light Infantry – KOYLI – tried to work their way down into the ravine and up the other side but made little progress. Artillery was brought up and pounded the German positions. In the evening, the 1st Green Howards moved up as well, and it was agreed they should move across country and try to get over the ravine further to the southwest. Off they set, Hedley Verity leading his men in B Company on a time-consuming trek across patchy scrub and brittle, rocky ground. As it happened, as dusk fell, the Germans pulled back to Lentini on Schmalz's orders, their mission more than fulfilled; the Battle of the Gorge had held up the British advance for more than twenty-four hours and it wasn't until 2 a.m. on the 14th that the 1st Green Howards finally reached Villasmundo.

Earlier on that Tuesday, 13 July, Oberst Schmalz had been dashing around trying to see his troops and deploy them ready for the battle for the Primosole Bridge which he knew was to come. The trouble was, the rest of the HG Division had still not closed up; there was now a big gap of around 15 miles separating his brigade from the rest of the division between Lentini and Vizzini to the south-west, and the British were advancing up every single artery there was. Ludwig Heilmann's 3. Fallschirmjäger Regiment had arrived not a moment too soon, and a battalion was hurriedly sent to Francofonte, another hilltop town halfway between Lentini and Vizzini. Schmalz knew that 'to hold this place was vital'. If the British broke through and prevented a linking up of the division that would isolate all Axis forces to the west. Another blocking position was established south of Monte Pancali, a few miles south of Lentini, while Heilmann's other two battalions and Schmalz's assault guns, Bruno Kanert's battery included, were brought back into the hills north-east of Lentini to cover the five miles from there to the coast. By this time, Lentini was already being shelled by British artillery several miles to the south.

Messages had been reaching Schmalz from Guzzoni's headquarters, but he had steadfastly ignored them, absolutely disgusted by the Italian leadership – so disgusted, in fact, that he'd even found time to write a report on the Italian abandonment of Syracuse and send it direct to Kesselring, who in turn forwarded it to the OKW. What Schmalz really wanted to know at this moment was what was going on with the rest of the HG Division and 15. Panzer Grenadier. As far as he was concerned, the defence of Sicily was now in the hands of the Germans, and that meant pulling back to a joined-up defensive line at the southern foot of Etna. He'd already identified this position as the *Hauptkampflinie* – main line of defence – before he'd moved his men south to meet the invasion, and had not only begun constructing defences there but had left some of his troops behind to continue doing so.

Not until the afternoon of 13 July did he finally succeed in getting through to HG Division headquarters. In a brief telephone call, his suggestion of falling behind the *Hauptkampflinie* running from Catania through to Gerbini and on to Leonforte to the north of Enna was agreed. He was to hold out where he was then pull back behind the new line by dawn on the 15th. 'We had thus been pushed into the last possible position that existed before the Catania line,' he noted, 'and had to hold it under all circumstances even on 14 July, otherwise there would have been a catastrophe. Directly behind us now is the plain. Will the Englishmen take the opportunity to land there and cut us off? This concern weighed on me very much.' As he was well aware, right now there were almost no troops at all protecting Catania.

Further help was on its way, however, with the 1. Maschinengewehr – Machine-Gun – Bataillon and a signals company from 1. Fallschirmjäger Division flying south to Catania. Leutnant Martin Pöppel, commanding 2. Platoon of 1. Kompanie in the MG battalion, was feeling a little tense as they flew down over Messina towards the airfield at Catania. Some men looked apprehensive but others were sleeping; Pöppel always found the rhythmic drone of the engines rather soporific. It had been a hectic few days. From their temporary base in Avignon in southern France, the company had been flown to Pogliano, near Naples, not in the usual Junkers 52 transports, but in converted bombers, Heinkel 111s. They then had an anxious wait to find out whether there would be enough fuel to get them to Catania; once it had arrived, just in time, they took off – at 6 a.m., amid so much dust the sun was entirely blotted out.

Now, coming into land at around 8.15 a.m., Pöppel saw three other He111s of their wing turning in for the final approach. As they touched down soon after, he spotted two aircraft ablaze on the airfield. 'Has there been a raid just before we got here?' he wondered. 'If so, our tired old crate has brought us luck after all.' Their Heinkel hadn't even stopped moving before a truck was speeding towards them. As they clambered out of the aircraft with their equipment, they were barked at to be quick – British fighters had just been over and shot up the airfield and there might well be more. Then they were off, trundling 5 miles south through yet more swirling dust to their assembly point, south-west of the Primosole Bridge in the hills that rose up behind and around the crossing. 'We pass a sentry on the road, then we soon see our commander, Major Schmidt,' he noted. 'Short instructions and directions to the bivouac area, and we're there.' In theatre, and soon to go into combat once more.

Under the blazing sun, they lugged what weapons and ammunition they had off the trucks – the sum of what they'd been able to fly in earlier. It wasn't a huge amount, none the less; neither machine guns nor their ammunition were lightweight, which meant they had landed with these weapons but nothing more substantial. Then, while they were still unloading, four-engine Fortresses thundered over and bombed the airfield from which they'd just come. Pöppel hoped those men still there had managed to take some cover in time as the shock waves reached them, sending violent pulses through the ground and blast waves rushing over them. Huge rolling columns of smoke rose and spread out, covering every part of the airfield. When the survivors arrived some time later, they learned they had taken a number of casualties, while two transport aircraft were missing altogether. 'Appalling casualties before the bloody operation has even begun,' noted Pöppel, 'and all because they sent the formation off without any fighter escort. What kind of people have we become?'

Pöppel was twenty-three years old and from near Neubiberg in Bavaria. As a teenager he'd fancied joining the navy, and had even been part of the marine section of the Hitler Youth. He'd changed his mind, however, when he'd learned that in joining the Kriegsmarine he would have been committed for four years – this was still before war had broken out – so he'd applied to join the Luftwaffe instead, only to find the story was the same: four years and not a day less. Then he'd seen an article about the paratroopers and discovered he only had to commit two years with them. So he applied to the *Fallschirmjäger*, who accepted him as part of the first intakes, training at the new school at Stendhal.

Since then, Pöppel had fought pretty much everywhere the 1. Fallschirmjäger had seen action, from Norway and the Low Countries back in 1940, to the mayhem of Crete, to the Eastern Front. Singled out as officer material early on, he had been promoted early to *Oberjäger* and then to *Leutnant*, and was now one of only two officers commanding ninety men in 1. Kompanie of the division's machine-gun battalion. *Fallschirmjäger* were volunteers, and like American and British airborne troops, they were highly motivated and extremely well trained; every unit contained a hard core of men with huge combat experience, of which Pöppel was just one. The difference between a young junior officer like Pöppel and his Italian equivalent, such as Livio Messina, could hardly have been greater. However easy it might have been to brush aside Italian coastal divisions and even the Napoli, the British were about to face enemy troops of an entirely different calibre.

While Pöppel and his men continued to dig in, their battalion commander, Major Werner Schmidt, had headed off to Lentini to report to Schmalz, his new superior. Schmalz was delighted to see him – Schmidt's appearance at his CP was like a gift. 'Watch out,' Schmalz warned him. The enemy, he felt certain, would try something that night. 'Either from the sea or from the air, the Englishman will land there with the intention of cutting us off and taking possession of the Catania Plain.'

He was, of course, absolutely right: heading towards them that evening were 1,856 British paratroopers of the 1st Parachute Brigade commanded by Brigadier Gerald Lathbury. The Red Berets, as they were known, had been loaded up ready to go the previous evening but then, much to their frustration, found their move cancelled at the last moment because XIII Corps' advance was not as far forward as the commanders would have liked; it was key to the entire operation that the Red Berets would quickly grab the bridge intact in a *coup de main* operation and then soon after be relieved by the advancing infantry and armour. Some 116 C-47s of the US 51st Troop Carrier Wing were available along with nineteen gliders, which would be bringing in ten 6-pounder anti-tank guns and seventy-seven glider-borne gunners. The first C-47 took off at 7.01 p.m. with the aim of arriving at the drop zones at around 10 p.m., while the gliders were to take off a little later, at 9.45 p.m., and land around 1 a.m.

All the conditions that had caused so many problems to the airborne forces over Sicily earlier were in place once again. It was another night-time drop, near the coast, approached from the sea, over naval warships and anti-aircraft guns. By contrast, Heilmann's 3. Fallschirmjäger Regiment had landed in clear daylight the previous evening – as it happened, on precisely the same DZs as had been earmarked for the 1st Parachute Brigade's 2nd Parachute Battalion – and, despite total Allied air superiority and offshore naval guns, they had landed with complete success. Admittedly, the German drop had been within their own lines; but even so, it wasn't going to take the enemy long to twig an Allied airborne operation was under way once C-47s came over and men started parachuting, whether it was day or night; and they were already well aware how crucially important the Primosole Bridge was. So the benefits of an accurate daylight drop would surely outweigh the potential pitfalls of attempting it by night – pitfalls that had already been amply demonstrated, with tragic consequences.

The three battalions of the 1st Parachute Brigade were each given different objectives. The 2nd Battalion, commanded by Lieutenant-Colonel John Frost, was aiming for three knolls – which Frost had immodestly code-named Johnny I, II and III – on the hills north of Lentini, overlooking the Catania Plain and the road from the south running down to the Primosole Bridge itself. Their drop zones were in fields just below those hills on the flat southern edge of the plain. Meanwhile, the 3rd Battalion was to land 1,000 yards north of the bridge to block the road running south towards it, while Lieutenant-Colonel Alastair Pearson's 1st Battalion was to take and hold the bridge itself.

Among those in Frost's 2nd Battalion was Sergeant John Johnstone, an NCO who had joined the 1st Airborne back in 1941 because he thought it would be more exciting and interesting than the stultifying coastal watch duty he'd been doing up to then. Serving under Frost in Algiers and Tunisia, he'd emerged from the ranks to become platoon sergeant and had by now seen enough action to make him a better soldier but also aware of the reality of modern warfare. The most senior rank on his C-47, Johnstone was beside the fuselage doorway and so would be the first to jump; and since it was open the whole way, he was able to look out from time to time and, in between times while it was still light, to try to read a Penguin paperback. By around 10 p.m. they were approaching the coast, and Johnstone warned the lads to get ready to jump. He was absolutely weighed down with his pack, the platoon No. 38 radio set, extra Bren and Sten magazines, and his own Sten stuck through the webbing across his chest. Outside, a glimpse of a beach and then they turned, the milky moonlight revealing a monochrome world beyond. First the red light went on, and he stood up with the rest of the men; then the green light, a quick shout of good luck and he was out. In what seemed like no time, he hit the ground with a wallop, lay still for a moment with the radio uncomfortably under his chest, then eased himself up and released his harness.

For a few minutes he felt incredibly alone, because there was no sign at all of the rest of his stick, but then Sergeant Fisher and several of his section joined him and they began moving along to where the designated forming-up area was supposed to be. A burst of fire up ahead made them all hit the deck. Johnstone levelled his Sten and pulled the trigger but nothing happened. Cocking it again, he squeezed a second time and still it didn't fire, prompting him to curse as he recalled having picked up a new issue weapon the day before without testing it first. They could hear German voices, which was not what they had been expecting, and then suddenly away to their left and slightly behind them a haystack crackled and burst into flames.

Unbeknown to Johnstone, or indeed Lieutenant-Colonel Frost, Johnnies I, II and III were the very same positions being held by the 1. Fallschirmjäger Maschinengewehr Bataillon. Leutnant Martin Pöppel had eased off his boots and been sleepily watching the moon shining down brightly on the trees when aircraft had suddenly begun thundering over. 'German paratroopers!' someone shouted. 'But shit! Shit!' jotted Pöppel in his diary. 'When the signal flares light up the eerie darkness we can see yellow and red parachutes. In an instant we all realise what's going on! British airborne troops overhead!' Pöppel grabbed his submachine gun and, with no time to get his boots back on, joined his men in opening fire on the descending paratroopers. A number of Tommies landed among them and were swiftly taken prisoner. Nearby wheat fields caught fire, tinder-dry in the summer heat, while tracer from the MGs criss-crossed the sky. The noise was immense: machine guns, other small arms, the roar of the C-47s' flak.

Now flying over the coast was 28-year-old Lieutenant-Colonel Alastair Pearson, a former baker from Glasgow who'd served in France in 1940 with the Highland Light Infantry before joining the Parachute Regiment a year before in August 1942. In Tunisia, he'd won first a Military Cross and then a Distinguished Service Order twice over, and at twenty-seven had been promoted to command the 1st Parachute Battalion. It had been quite a meteoric rise, all the more impressive given that along the way he'd been demoted from major to captain for going on a massive bender and had had to work his way back up again. His fearlessness, imperturbability and natural leadership skills, however, had marked him out and, as with others such as Hard Nose Gorham, these had trumped his youthfulness.

Like John Johnstone, Pearson had been quietly reading a book on the flight over, while most of the other men in his C-47 chattered with one another above the drone of the engines. Suddenly, there was a clatter of machine-gun fire and, looking out, he saw to his horror that their own ships were once again firing at them, even though he had been promised this would not happen again. Soon the firing settled down – but then it became clear they were over Mount Etna, some distance from their DZ. Realizing he urgently needed to speak to the pilots and navigator, he unclipped his parachute and headed towards the cockpit. By the time he got there, he saw they had turned and were now heading back to sea. 'The DZ's down there,' Pearson said. 'What are we doing?'

At this point, the co-pilot put his head in his hands and told him they couldn't go down there. Pearson looked out of the cockpit and could see blobs of fire on the ground. In fact, these were the haystacks now blazing, but the pilots had assumed they were aircraft that had been shot down.

'There's nothing for it, boy,' Pearson told the pilot. 'We've got to do it. If your co-pilot's no good I've no hesitation in shooting him,' and he pulled out his revolver.

'You can't do that,' the pilot replied. 'Who'd fly the aeroplane?'

Pearson told him one of his men behind him was a trained pilot.

'Yeah, but he won't know how to land it!'

'No one asked him to land the bloody thing!' Pearson replied, pointing out they were all paratroopers and would jump. At this, the pilot banked and turned back towards the drop zone and Pearson went back to his parachute. But by the time the lights went on they were going too fast, diving too low, and it seemed to Pearson that no sooner had he jumped and his parachute blossomed than he was hitting the ground. 'I'd gone out number ten,' said Pearson, 'my knees hurt but I was all right. My batman at number eleven was all right, but the remainder of the stick all suffered serious injuries or were killed. I was very angry.'

They were, at least, on the DZ. Despite the friendly fire and enemy flak, thirty-nine C-47s dropped their troops on or near the DZs, while forty-nine did not and many were scattered to the four winds. Of the rest, three turned back almost immediately after taking off, twelve never found Sicily and eleven returned with all their troops still on board. In all, eleven transports were shot down, eight after the drops had been made, and many more damaged. Of the gliders, eleven came down on or near the landing zones, four crashed badly on landing, three were lost at sea and one crashed during take-off so never left Tunisia. It hadn't been a total disaster, but the losses were still significant – and, yet again, most of them had been caused by friendly fire.

Meanwhile, John Johnstone and his small party of troopers had taken temporary shelter in a bomb crater, all feeling woefully underarmed with not a single Bren machine gun among them. The haystack near them was burning fiercely, and the moment they clambered out and tried to move, they would be silhouetted against it. A little way to the south of their position, Johnstone could see a number of men moving about with what appeared to be the same helmets and jump smocks, and was about to shout out the identification words but something stopped him – there was something unfamiliar about the way they were moving in column. He was right to be cautious, as these were in fact men from the 1. Fallschirmjäger Maschinengewehr Bataillon; while all the American paratroopers wore the US M1 helmet, the British and Germans had adapted theirs to the point where the differences between them were minimal. German paratroopers wore a longer jump smock than the British Denison but, like the Tommies, were also issued with short ankle boots. It was not surprising the two sides were confusing one another.

Once the enemy platoon had passed by and with no more German troops to be seen, Johnstone got his men moving towards the assembly point once more, increasingly perturbed not to hear greater sounds of battle. The aircraft had gone and while there was shooting, it was by now sporadic and lacking any intensity. Sergeant Fisher reckoned the whole drop must have been a massive cock-up. They pressed on – startled at one moment by the sudden sound of a vehicle nearby they were quite unable to identify – then a while later were eventually challenged by a paratrooper emerging from the shadows. It turned out to be the brigade major, who told them to head for the Johnnies, where Frost was assembling – so on they went, following a road but on the other side of the wall that ran alongside it.

Despite Johnstone's concerns about the lack of noise, by around 2.15 a.m. some fifty men of Pearson's 1st Battalion had stormed the bridge from the north, capturing fifty or more Italian troops who, rather than the Germans, had been defending the crossing itself. The bridge itself was sizeable: some 120 yards long, made of a box-like lattice of steel girders mounted on concrete struts. It stood about 8 feet off the River Simeto in a coastal plain that was flat as a board except for a series of raised dykes and ditches for irrigation. Reeds rose up from the river-banks, while on the flat ground either side were wheat fields, olive groves and citrus plantations. Here, mosquitoes thrived in abundance, especially in this high summer heat.

Lieutenant-Colonel Pearson reached the bridge with a hundred or so men not long afterwards; by around 4 a.m. the demolition fuses had all been cut, and his men were dug in around defensive positions protecting each end. By 6.30 a.m., they even had three of the 6-pounder anti-tank guns in place, along with a captured Italian gun that had also been pressed into service. None the less, FUSTIAN had been another disappointing operation. Barely two platoons of the 3rd Battalion were now with 1st Battalion at the bridge: the rest had all landed in enemy territory and a large number had promptly been taken prisoner. At least, though, the Red Berets' commander, Brigadier Gerald Lathbury, whose thirty-seventh birthday it was, had managed to make his way to the bridge, albeit wounded in the arm by a grenade splinter. Setting up his CP on the south side of the bridge, he had just one working radio – but was not able to get through to XIII Corps and let them know the bridge was in their hands.

By early morning, the situation was beginning to become clearer. Lathbury and Pearson realized that while they held the bridge, they were none the less sandwiched between German paratroopers to the north and to the south in the hills where Frost's 2nd Battalion were supposed to be. Relief by the infantry and armour from the south was becoming increasingly urgent with every passing hour, because there was a limit to what lightly armed paratroopers could do if the enemy started to bring to bear some heavy fire-power of their own.

For their part, after the confusion of darkness and dawn, the Germans were trying to establish in what strength the British had landed and where they were now positioned, a task complicated by the objective of Frost's 2nd Battalion being the same as that of 1. Maschinengewehr Bataillon. From interrogating the prisoners they'd taken, Martin Pöppel and his comrades had a much clearer idea of what they were up against. Pöppel was not impressed by the quality of British weapons, reserving particular derision for the Sten submachine gun. 'The guns look pathetic,' he noted, 'reminding us of Russian weapons. Simply knocked together.' There were certainly few submachine guns better made and balanced than the MP40 Pöppel was using. Beautifully finished, with no appreciable recoil, it was accurate, reliable and wonderfully engineered. It was also incredibly expensive, costing ten times as much to manufacture as a Sten, which was simply soldered together and cheap as chips. But at the 20–30 yards or so which was the limit of their effective range, there really wasn't much to choose between the two. It was not Pöppel's place, however, to worry about production costs; it was the finished article he was interested in. Now, looking at the Brits' weapons, and the Denison smock – which reminded him of the kind issued to motor vehicle drivers – and considering how many had allowed themselves to be captured, he was getting a clear impression of Tommies whose fighting capability had deteriorated a fair bit since he'd last come up against them on Crete. That a handful of Red Berets half the number of his company had captured the bridge intact did not alter this view. 'They have deteriorated,' he jotted, 'in every respect.'

Just below Johnny III, John Johnstone and his small band had rested up in a vineyard. Earlier, Johnstone had taken a pill – Benzedrine: amphetamine, or 'speed' – which he now regretted because, as its effects wore off, he felt utterly exhausted, both physically and mentally. He must have dozed off, because he was jolted awake by the sound of rapid enemy machine-gun fire not far away on the rocky hill a bit further up. It was immediately answered by more methodical Bren fire, followed by the swish and crump of mortars. Moments later there was movement close by and then a German paratrooper appeared and told them to raise their hands. Johnstone was about to raise his Sten when, seeing this, Sergeant Fisher said, 'Not now, Johnno.' Johnstone lowered his weapon. It was around 6.30 a.m. As they were marched away, he apologized to his men, his mind whirring about what had happened and whether he should have acted differently. For him, Sergeant Fisher and the others, however, the war was over.

In fact, Lieutenant-Colonel Frost had managed to gather around 140 men on Johnny I, most from Dicky Lonsdale's A Company. For Frost, the night had been one of frustration. He'd hurt his knee badly on landing, he couldn't find lots of key men – including his second-in-command and adjutant – and every time he tried to issue orders, small arms or artillery seemed to blot out his words. The Germans had control of Johnny II and were firing bursts from MGs and mortars. A fighting patrol was sent to try to silence the machine gun, but was driven back. Then the long grass below them caught fire, which quickly spread and shrouded the entire group of hills in smoke, allowing the Germans to strengthen their hold further. And there was still no word on when the relief might be expected.

While these chaotic events were taking place around the Primosole Bridge, General Montgomery was visiting the Canadians. Lieutenant Farley Mowat and his men were not at all happy to have to scrub up and specially clean their weapons. They'd not seen Montgomery before, but suddenly there he was, driving past them in his open-topped car as they stood to attention. Inspection over, he told them to gather round. Standing in the back of the car, his trademark black beret on his head and whisking a fly swatter, he assured them they were all first-rate troops who'd done very well so far.

'But there's a big task ahead, my lads,' he told them. 'The Eyeties are packing it in but Jerry is determined to hold on to Sicily. Our job is to toss him out! We'll do it . . . yes, we'll do it! See him off, by Heavens! So keep up the good work, lads. I'll have my eye on you, never fear. Eighth Army always looks after its own!'

For a moment, the men absorbed this, then someone at the back shouted, 'Where the hell's our beer ration, then?'

Monty merely grinned. First things first, he told them. 'And while I'm on the subject, I strongly advise all of you to leave the Eyetie wine alone. Deadly stuff! Can make you blind, you know.'

Soon after, he was off again. 'As a result of this stirring experience,' it was written in the battalion war diary, 'all ranks were imbued with much added enthusiasm and an increased respect for this great commander.' Mowat was surprised to find himself rather agreeing with this sentiment.

As it happened, Eighth Army's advance was already slowing dramatically, with XXX Corps held up at Vizzini and south of Lentini, and XIII Corps pushing forward only slowly to relieve the Red Berets at Primosole. Yet Montgomery's plans for the future course of the campaign remained in place, having been decided the day before on the back of conclusions drawn on the evening of the 12th.

That Wednesday morning, 14 July, General Bradley visited Patton's CP, finding the Seventh Army commander wreathed in cigar smoke and poring over a map.

'We've received a directive from Army Group, Brad,' Patton told him. 'Monty's to get the Vizzini–Caltagirone road in his drive to flank Catania and Mount Etna by going through Enna. This means you'll have to sideslip to the west with your 45th Division.' The main road between Vizzini and Caltagirone was part of Highway 124, identified before the invasion as the agreed boundary line between Eighth and Seventh Armies; however, that part of the road, before it continued its winding way through the hills towards Enna, had been allocated to US II Corps.

Bradley whistled at hearing this. 'This will raise hell with us,' he replied. 'I had counted heavily on that road. Now if we've got to shift over, it'll slow up our entire advance.' He asked Patton whether he could use Highway 124 first, before the Canadians did, just in order to shift to the far side of 1st Division.

'Sorry, Brad,' Patton told him, 'but the change-over takes place immediately. Monty wants the road right away.'

At the time, Middleton's Thunderbirds were almost at the road, which pretty much cut across them at right angles, running east–west. Also, by this time, the Canadians were pretty exhausted and could certainly have allowed the 45th to use the road to skip across the top of the Big Red One rather than turning around, heading back on themselves, and crossing westwards by using Highway 115, the coast road between Vittoria and Gela. There is no record of anyone in Seventh Army requesting this; but it was this inconvenience and the consequent unnecessary slowing of II Corps' advance that really annoyed Bradley, rather than being instructed to remain on Eighth Army's flank. Historians over the years have repeatedly levelled the harshest criticism at Alexander's orders, arguing that they were a slight against the Americans, and one that showed a total lack of grip on his part and excessive deference to his hubristic Eighth Army commander. That view, however, takes too much account of later reputations and not enough of the situation as it stood at the time, and really does need knocking on the head.

Alexander had quite deliberately given no detailed orders beyond the initial HUSKY invasion plans of getting ashore, securing a bridgehead and capturing key airfields and ports. The overall aim had always been then to get to Messina as quickly as possible; but there was no point issuing detailed orders on how this was to be done before those initial objectives had been taken, because it was impossible to know what the landscape would be like and how the Axis forces would be reacting. This wasn't woolly thinking, it was common sense. By the evening of 12 July, the situation was starting to look clearer. Eighth Army had always been given the lead role in the HUSKY plan, and understandably so, both for geographical reasons – their launch base in Egypt – and because of their undoubted greater experience. It cannot be stressed enough that when the plans were agreed back in early May, neither Patton nor his army had the experience to justify their taking the lead role. There was absolutely no shame in this whatsoever. It was just the way things were.

Also, by the evening of 12 July, Eighth Army had made more ground than Seventh Army, with the exception of Truscott's 3rd Division. This was entirely because resistance in the south-east so far had been considerably less than in the central south; Eighth Army had not had to face a counter-attack on the scale of that faced by II Corps. Although the Americans had seen off this counter-attack, it had cost them – the 16th, 26th and 180th Regimental Combat Teams, especially, had been hit hard. On the morning of the 13th, Patton had also been worried about the Big Red One. 'I am not too pleased with progress of 1st Division,' he noted. 'They had halted just north of Ponte Olivo airport, waiting for 16th Inf Regt to catch up. I ordered them to keep moving.'

In other words, with Eighth Army in the driving seat on the eastern side of the island, and with the pre-invasion expectation that they'd take the lead in any case, Alexander's orders were quite reasonable at the moment they were issued. Furthermore, in his instructions for HUSKY issued back on 19 May, he'd given instructions to Seventh Army – then Force 343 – to capture Ponte Olivo, Comiso, Biscari and the port of Licata, and make contact with Eighth Army at Ragusa. This had all been achieved. 'Subsequently,' Alex had written, they were 'to prevent enemy reserves moving eastwards against the left flank' – that is, Patton's men were to prevent a drive by the enemy into the side of Eighth Army. In other words, the orders, as far as Seventh Army's role was concerned, had not changed, except that Eighth Army now had use of Highway 124.

What's more, Alex had had no indication at all that Patton had been unhappy about these plans. The Seventh Army commander hadn't even particularly groused to his diary, his usual means of venting any frustrations he might be feeling.

There was also an issue of infrastructure and roads. As the US II Corps advanced north, it did so veering slightly to the east, while as the Canadians and XXX Corps pushed north, they did so veering slightly to the west. In other words, the two forces were beginning to converge around the town of Vizzini. From here, one road – which had always been in Eighth Army's zone – continued north, while Highway 124 turned broadly westwards, cutting right across the axis of the American advance. So, no matter what the orders, a general shift west would have had to take place, because it would have been impossible to fit two divisions along the same road, except sequentially.

There was, however, certainly an argument for taking a different approach. The Canadians could have slipped into reserve, leaving XXX Corps to continue pushing north using minor roads and tracks and staying closer on XIII Corps' left flank. That would have allowed II Corps to retain Highway 124 and to use their greater number of vehicles to speed on towards Enna; but it would have meant units from two different armies operating side-by-side on the same offensive operation and with two different commanders. That was possible, although not ideal; but with II Corps having just had a very active and also costly first few days of the campaign, it was understandable that Alexander should consider it Eighth Army's turn to take up the main impetus on the drive north. What's more, the whole point of the Anglo-US war strategy was to limit the number of casualties among their troops. If Eighth Army was prepared to undertake the lion's share of the fighting in the next phase of the campaign, that was surely a good thing for the young men of Seventh Army. Patton, Bradley and even young commanders like Gavin might have been chomping at the bit to get their men into action and drive for glory, but the vast majority of the men under their command were only too happy to have an easier time of it for a while and get through the campaign alive. So, although there were certainly valid arguments for giving II Corps a greater role, including priority on Highway 124, there were plenty of good reasons for following the plan as suggested by Montgomery and agreed by Alexander.

Whatever the arguments, the course of action decided upon, and Alex's orders of 13 July, were both reasonable and justified at the time. It is also unlikely it would have made a huge amount of difference even if Bradley had kept Highway 124 and his II Corps had been given the lead to press up towards Enna and Leonforte, because a substantial realignment of US troops would have to have taken place in any case, and that would have taken precious time. The big difference came with the decisions being made by Kesselring, with Hitler's backing: that Sicily should be substantially reinforced with quality German troops and that their own commanders should now take back control.

CHAPTER 21

Shooting

G ENERAL GEORGE PATTON HAD been given permission by Alexander to press west to capture Agrigento, one of the greatest classical sites anywhere on Sicily but also, and more importantly for Seventh Army, offering a potentially valuable further port at Porto Empedocle. So, on the morning of 14 July, he spent time plotting out future plans. A unit of French colonial troops, known as Goums, had arrived and been attached to Seventh Army. The 39th Combat Team from the 9th Division, which had remained in North Africa, was also due in, and so it occurred to him to create a new corps under his deputy at Seventh Army and trusted friend, Major-General Geoffrey Keyes, incorporating also the 3rd Division and a composite division of the 82nd Airborne and 39th Combat Team. They could take Agrigento and then press on to Palermo; it wasn't the great prize of Messina, but it was Sicily's largest city, familiar to millions of Italian-Americans, and so its capture would undoubtedly make a big splash back home. At the same time, Bradley's II Corps could drive north and cut off the whole of the west of Sicily. 'I will bring this question up with Alexander,' he jotted in his diary, 'when the time is ripe.'

Patton, with General Lucas in tow, then set off to Licata to see Truscott and to tell him to get moving towards Agrigento and Porto Empedocle. The navy were to help with fire from their warships, and Patton and Truscott both agreed the port could be taken with few casualties. In the meantime, Seventh Army had been pushing forward and expanding their rapidly enlarging bridgehead. Sergeant Al Altieri and the Rangers, with the aid of some extra artillery and assault guns, had pushed into the hills beyond the Gela Plain and captured Butera, while Breezy Griffin and the 41st Armored Infantry Regiment had advanced along with the rest of Combat Command A to capture the town of Canicattì, around 20 miles north-west of Licata. Even so, mortar and sniper fire was still coming from the surrounding hills, and the 41st Armored were given the task of clearing them out.

Griffin's HQ Company of the 2nd Battalion, given one of the hills to clear, fired a barrage of white phosphorus shells on to it and then waited; but with no return fire it was hard to know whether their mortaring had done the trick or not. Someone needed to scout ahead and see, and Griffin and his pal Herb Queen drew the short straw. They were already on a slight rise, a broad valley sweeping away from them then climbing towards the wooded knoll at the top of the hill they'd been aiming at. Griffin and Queen were told to walk straight up. 'We want you to draw fire,' the lieutenant told them, 'so we can see where they're firing from.' Neither man was at all happy. To Griffin, it felt like a suicide mission.

Off they went. There was no cover at all, apart from long grass, but they'd gone roughly halfway to the knoll without being shot at when suddenly half a dozen Italian troops rose up out of the grass. Griffin had the shock of his life, but the Italians were more scared than he was and immediately put their hands on their heads in surrender and stood there shaking. The two Americans could hardly take them with them, so motioned to them to head towards company HQ's lines then continued on their way, tension mounting with every step. Reaching the wood, still without being shot at, they tentatively moved from tree to tree until they reached the remains of the Italian gun position, complete with trenches and machine-gun emplacements. Griffin felt sickened. The guns lay wrecked while around them lay the remains of ten dead Italians, body parts strewn about. 'The dead were all blackened and burned to a crisp,' he noted. 'There were cooking and eating utensils scattered around. Evidently our white phosphorus shells had hit while they were eating.' Griffin prayed he would never find himself on the receiving end of white phosphorus.

Griffin and his fellows might have treated Italian prisoners reasonably and in line with the Geneva Conventions, but not all Allied troops did. On the morning of 14 July, Companies A and C of the 1st Battalion, 180th Infantry, part of the 45th Thunderbirds Division, had been attacking the airfield at Biscari, a little way north of the town. The men had been in action since D-Day and casualties were mounting. The Italian troops at the airfield, stiffened by a number of Germans of the HG Division, had put up a fight, but by around 7.30 a.m., the Americans had won the battle and the defenders began to surrender. By this time, both companies were down to half strength. Bodies lay strewn around the airfield along with wrecked aircraft, shattered hangers and knocked-out tanks and weapons.

At about 8 a.m., some forty-six prisoners were handed over to Sergeant Horace T. West of Company A, who was told to take them away from the road to a place where the POWs could not observe any troop movements. Selecting some of his men to be guards, West marched the prisoners in a column of twos along a track away from the airfield. The 1st battalion XO, Major Roger Denman, seeing West and his handful of guards, told him to treat the prisoners well so long as they behaved. Most of the POWs were Italian but three were German, and all had had their shirts and boots taken to discourage them from attempting to escape. After marching them a little way off the road, West announced to one of his men that he was going to shoot 'these sons of bitches' because these were his orders, and took a Tommy gun from Sergeant Brown. He told the others that if they didn't want to see it, they should walk away. Then he opened fire. Those not shot immediately began begging for mercy. 'They were sort of shouting,' said one witness, 'and yelling "no, no!" in Italian.' Unmoved, West kept firing until his magazine was empty and just three men were left standing. When they began running for their lives, some of the other guards opened fire and shot them too; then West, having fitted another clip, walked down the row of dead and dying men, shooting any who still seemed to be alive.

West, by all accounts, had earlier treated prisoners well and had been a highly regarded NCO. He had, though, been involved in bitter hand-to-hand fighting, and earlier that morning had witnessed a scene that seemed to tip him over the edge. Two Americans had been captured and he saw them being taken into a blockhouse. Determined to save them, he'd scampered up the slope towards it and, without being spotted, had risked a peek through a slit hole. The two Americans were already dead – and one still had blood gushing from throat and chest. Standing over them were three German soldiers. Rushing round to the entrance, West had lobbed a grenade through and killed all three. 'It was the damnedest feeling I ever had in my life,' West said. 'I knew they killed them after taking them prisoners. One thing it seemed to me was to take every living soul up there.' Whatever the reasons, West was not the only one in a killing mood that day: around 1 p.m., Captain John T. Compton, commander of Company C, organized a makeshift firing squad and executed a further thirty-six prisoners.

Violence was, of course, the very fabric of war; but losing friends and comrades was hard to take. That same morning, the 18th Infantry of the Big Red One had been at San Cono, 20 miles north of Gela. They were now into the relentlessly hilly and mountainous centre of the island, and faced with taking one hilltop town after another. San Cono had at least provided some rich pickings: Lieutenant Frank Johnson and his men in 3rd Platoon, Cannon Company, had come across an Italian supply depot that looked as if it had been left in a hurry. Trucks, bicycles, rifles, howitzers, officers' baggage, medals and even paymasters' boxes had all been abandoned in the rush for flight. By midday, Johnson had a personal booty that included an Agfa camera, a trench knife, a 105mm howitzer sight, a handful of medals and ribbons and – his favourite – an officer's dress sword. He'd also purloined a Moto Guzzi Trialce three-wheeled motorbike. 'To me,' he noted, 'possessed of only a clumsy truck and a pair of very sore feet for reconnaissance, the silly old tricycle looks like a fine carryall and recon vehicle.'

He and his men had therefore been feeling pretty pleased with themselves as they'd begun moving out towards their next objective, the town of Mazzarino, where Dante Ugo Leonardi and his men had been based on the eve of the invasion. Then someone brought the news to Johnson that Dick Koehler was dead. Johnson could not believe it. They had been best friends since childhood, their fathers colleagues; he and Dick had been to college together and had both joined the 18th Infantry. Struggling to process the terrible news, he told himself over and over it simply could not be true. But it was – Koehler had been killed returning from a recce mission when his jeep had hit a mine. 'For me, like others who lose a buddy,' wrote Johnson, 'the day Dick is killed is when the war gets personal, and my hatred of our enemy becomes a continual gnawing thing.' Many shared such feelings; they were not, of course, either a reason or an excuse for cold-bloodedly mowing down more than eighty prisoners.

Meanwhile, just to the north of Lentini, No. 3 Commando under Colonel John Durnford-Slater, some four hundred strong and arriving by sea, had had considerably better fortunes than the British 1st Parachute Brigade, proving yet again that in assaulting targets close to the coast, amphibious operations were better in every respect than the hugely more haphazard option of a parachute drop. Coming ashore on the beach north of Agnone around 10.30 p.m. the previous night, 13 July, they had moved inland some 7 miles to the Malati Bridge, where Highway 114 crossed the San Leonardo River just to the north of Lentini. Having driven off the Italian defenders, they took the bridge intact and by 4 a.m. had removed the demolition charges. Durnford-Slater had been told by General Dempsey that if 50th Division hadn't reached them by morning, he was to pull back and try and get back to friendly lines. However, neither Dempsey nor Durnford-Slater knew that the bridge was in the area between Lentini and the sea held by two battalions of Heilmann's 3. Fallschirmjäger Regiment; and when the Germans learned what had happened, they were determined to win the bridge back, aware they still needed it intact in order to pull back across the Catania Plain.

Some 8 miles to the north, the British paratroopers were still holding on to Primosole Bridge. The German paratroopers were firmly established on Johnny II and III, however, which was a problem for Frost's lightly armed men, because Johnny I was in between the two. None the less, help was on hand from the Royal Navy. Around 7 a.m., a forward observation officer from the 1st Airlanding Light Regiment showed up at Lathbury and Pearson's CP near the bridge and managed to make contact with HMS *Newfoundland*, a cruiser lying off the coast. A little while later, at around 10 a.m., *Newfoundland*'s 6-inch guns opened fire and hammered Martin Pöppel and his fellows on Johnny II and III, forcing them to pull back and allowing Frost's men a much-needed breather. Two of Pöppel's best men were killed. 'It's a bloody mess,' he cursed in his diary. 'Those dogs out there in their tubs can fire just like they're on manoeuvres and we're just sitting targets.'

What the beleaguered Red Berets really needed, however, was relief from XIII Corps advancing from the south, with both infantry and the armour and fire-power of the 4th Armoured Brigade. At 9.30 a.m., a radio link to the 4th Armoured was made – but only fleetingly and then, once again, contact was lost.

Sniping and shelling and machine-gun fire continued around the Primosole and Malati bridges all that day. Despite Dempsey's personal instruction to pull back in the morning if there was no sign of the relief, Colonel Durnford-Slater had kept his No. 3 Commando holding on through into the afternoon. A Brigade Schmalz Panzer Mk IV had been brought up to give Heilmann's *Fallschirmjäger* some extra fire-power and had repeatedly shelled the Commandos, while heavy mortars and MG fire rained down on them without let-up. All the Commandos had in reply were small arms, PIAT – an anti-tank charge, which did not have the range to hit the panzer – and their wits. Eventually, however, having taken a steady flow of casualties all day, Colonel Durnford-Slater finally ordered his men to fall back: it was either that or risk losing his entire force.

By now, however, 50th Division were beginning to punch their way through, although it had been a hard slog for them in the broiling heat and with the men only now starting to get some motor transport, while the 4th Armoured Brigade, landed at Augusta, had hurried northwards and been thrown straight in to the fray. 'Good roads were few and far between,' noted Bill Cheall, part of 50th Division's drive from Sortino towards Monte Pancali and Lentini, 'and whenever we had the opportunity to use transport great clouds of dust, particularly from the Bren carriers, were created along the winding roads.' They were all beginning to get frustrated by the German roadblocks and delaying actions. 'It was very time-consuming having to dislodge them,' he added, 'and the enemy was retreating faster than we could advance.'

Unteroffizier Bruno Kanert was now at Lentini, commanding two StuH assault guns, with the task of protecting the roads leading out of the town. Positioning one on a roundabout at the northern edge of town, facing down the road towards the Malati Bridge and the Catania Plain, he then moved his own on the road heading east to Agnone on the coast. Around 3.30 p.m., an Italian assault gun squeaked and rumbled its way towards them. The English were on their way, the Italian captain told Kanert, who then asked him to stay and help defend the town. 'The Italian refused to comply,' said Kanert, who had drawn his pistol to add pressure. 'He simply drove on and we weren't about to shoot him.' Around an hour later his other assault gun appeared, along with the news that the British were entering the town to the south, having broken through the last Brigade Schmalz delaying position. A few minutes later, two anti-tank gun crews joined them with their Pak 40s and told Kanert he should follow them to the coast and then north towards Catania. Kanert's StuHs were short of fuel, but he remembered there was a fuel store in Lentini; so with his loader in tow, he set off to try and find it.

They found the store, but no sign of any fuel, despite looking high and low throughout the warehouse. As they emerged, they were shot at by a hidden machine-gunner; running and crouching and weaving through orange and olive trees, they managed to get away, but were then strafed by marauding fighter aircraft. Taking cover behind some rocks, they survived this new threat, only to see a long line of British armour and troop-carrying trucks behind them rumbling through the town. Still some 900 yards from their assault gun, they ran for their lives, making the comparative safety of their StuH just as the leading British tanks appeared. Although the StuH was a howitzer designed to lob shells as far as possible rather than with the high velocity of an anti-tank gun, they fired anyway and, much to their relief, managed to knock out the lead British tank. While the column halted, Kanert and his two assault guns quickly got moving again, with at least enough fuel to get to safety.

The British column of infantry and armour pushed on through Lentini and managed to reach the Malati Bridge soon after Heilmann's paratroopers had taken possession of it but not before they could refix charges and blow it. As the *Fallschirmjäger* hastily pulled back over the bridge and melted away to the north, the British were able to cross and press on towards the Primosole Bridge. It was touch and go, though, as to whether the Red Berets would be able to hang on until the men of 50th Division reached them. Earlier, around midday, a Luftwaffe staff officer from Brigade Schmalz base HQ at Misterbianco, Hauptmann Franz Stangenberg, had driven down towards Primosole Bridge himself to see what was going on and, as he neared, had been fired on by Tommy paratroopers dug in around the north side of the bridge. Recognizing the importance of destroying the bridge and aware the next batch of *Fallschirmjäger* were not due to arrive until that evening, he hurried back to Misterbianco and began gathering all the troops he could, including men of the 1. Kompanie, 1. Fallschirmjäger Nachrichten – Signals – Bataillon, which had landed the previous day, as well as a number of service troops and, crucially, a heavy flak battery of 88mm dual-purpose anti-aircraft and anti-tank guns, big 4-ton beasts that could hurtle a shell vertically or horizontally some 28,000 feet in less than six seconds.

By early afternoon, Stangenberg, with a tactical flair that had been so sorely lacking in many of the HG Division's attacks around Gela, had amassed a force of some 350 men and had his 88s banging away and making very short work of the Italian pillboxes protecting the northern end of the bridge, which the Red Berets had been using.

Suddenly a comparatively stable situation for Lathbury's men had become an untenable one. After an afternoon being attacked from the north, with the Maschinengewehr Bataillon still harassing them from the hills overlooking the bridge to the south, and with ammunition now running dangerously low, at 5.05 p.m. Lathbury ordered all men north of the bridge to pull back to the southern side. Even there they were becoming increasingly exposed, completely cut off from contact with Frost's men and still with no sign of the relief force, and now with Stangenberg's 88s systematically destroying the bunkers on that side as well. Heavy fire-power really was the enemy of lightly armed shock troops such as paratroopers.

At around 6.30 p.m., Lathbury told Pearson he was going to order everyone back under the cover of darkness to join Frost and his men on and around Johnny I. Pearson disagreed, but Lathbury was the boss and orders were orders. None the less, Pearson had a gut feeling he'd be back there before too long so, before pulling back, he took his sergeant, 'Panzer' Manser, and his batman, Jock Clements, and made a thorough recce of the river-bank. 'It was stinking,' he said, 'and the mosquitoes were there in their millions.' About 200 yards to the west of the bridge the Simeto was joined by the River Gornalunga – narrower and just a trickle, but impassable to vehicles because of the high banks of the dykes either side. Just the other side of the Gornalunga was a stretch where Pearson had forded the Simeto the night before. Beyond, on the far side of the northern bank, were vines and then a sunken track and then, a little further to the west, a dried-up oxbow where the Simeto had once run. Certainly, there were places where infantry could get across and into the flat plain beyond – whether from the south or north, whether friend or foe.

Oberst Schmalz, meanwhile, was trying to work out how to get his entire brigade back across the Catania Plain without the British realizing what was going on. There was only one route he could feasibly send his men and that was to the north-west of Lentini, where a single dirt road ran down to the plain, over the dried-up Gornalunga and trickle of the Dittaino and then across the single bridge in the central part of the plain at Passo di Fico that spanned the Simeto. Schmalz had already abandoned Lentini and got the main body of his troops moving, while his last blocking position holding up XXX Corps was at Francoforte, to the south-west of Lentini. His troops there were to fall back under cover of darkness and then, if necessary, hold Scordia, a few miles to the north-west, to buy time. 'This nightly backward movement,' he noted, 'was actually the greatest test of nerves. Will it be possible to reach the new positions at the northern edge of the plain undisturbed on the one existing road and bridge, with all our vehicles and guns?' The key, he knew, was to conceal his intentions at the front for as long as possible. The British must not realize what was afoot too early.

By Wednesday, 14 July, Axis air forces had been driven from Sicily and the number of enemy aircraft now seen over the island had been reduced to a scattered few. It had been a phenomenal effort by the Allied fliers. 'The invasion has, of course, gone far better than any one of us here had dared to hope,' jotted Air Commodore Tommy Elmhirst. 'The German air force might have ruined the whole show. There were literally thousands of ships as a target on their front door step.' Enemy naval gunners were still taking pot-shots at Allied aircraft, which had forced fighters to operate higher than they would have liked; but there was no longer any need to provide fighter cover over the beaches, and now only the ports were being protected. Six airfields on Sicily were in Allied hands, and fighter control facilities were being set up at several of them. The RAF's 244 Wing had begun flying into Pachino the day before, and on the 14th it was 324 Wing's turn. Wing Commander Cocky Dundas flew over from Malta with a sponge-bag and pyjamas stuffed into his cockpit beside him and, after completing a combat patrol over the battlefront, touched down on Sicilian soil ninety minutes later. 'It was a moment to remember and treasure,' he noted, 'as I taxied cautiously in, guided by an airman who had run out and jumped up to sit on my wing.' He was thrilled to see so many enemy aircraft littering the periphery, some smashed and broken but others seemingly in pretty mint condition, including several Me109Gs – an aircraft Dundas was determined to have a go at flying.

By dawn on 15 July, Schmalz's men had safely made it across the plain, in what had been a truly epic withdrawal operation. The only ones missing were Heilmann's 3. Fallschirmjäger. The night before, Schmalz had asked all units to acknowledge receipt of his orders, and each one had – except Heilmann, who instead sent a runner with a message for Schmalz. 'Wherever *Fallschirmjäger* are,' Heilmann said, 'there will be no retreat.' Not for nothing was this undoubtedly courageous but equally vain and arrogant commander known as 'King Ludwig' after Mad King Ludwig of Bavaria. Such sentiments were no help to Schmalz, or to the German cause; Heilmann's men were needed behind the *Hauptkampflinie*, not stuck behind enemy lines with rapidly depleting rations and ammunition. In any case, it made Schmalz look as though he had lost control of a subordinate, and that didn't help either. 'I had to give my report to

Kesselring,' he noted, 'that we were in our new position but without 3. Fallschirmjäger Regiment. Very embarrassing!'

His new command post was at Misterbianco, a small town to the north-west of Catania on the lower slopes of Etna. Schmalz was utterly exhausted after a night of no sleep at all on top of several nights of only snatched moments of rest, and hoped he might now be able to have a brief nap. It was not to be, however, as a procession of people arrived asking for orders. 'I could not rest,' he noted, 'but I finally had a roof over my head and a reasonably cool room. The panorama from here was both scenically and militarily overwhelmingly beautiful.' Behind him was Etna; to the east, Catania and the sea – still dotted with British warships; and in front lay the plain: the battlefield to come, spread before him. From here, he would be able to see every movement, every artillery strike. Brigade Schmalz might have their backs to the wall, but as a defensive position, his new *Hauptkampflinie* was about as good as it got.

Meanwhile, at the Primosole Bridge, further help had arrived in the form of the 1. Fallschirm-Pionier Bataillon of combat engineers, who had been dropped the previous evening. Among them was Oberfeld-webel Josef 'Jupp' Klein, who had originally trained as a pilot and had ended up flying air–sea rescue missions rather than fighters; craving a bit more adventure, he had volunteered for the *Fallschirmjäger*, and since he'd been a young carpenter in civilian life back in the Moselle region of western Germany, he had been posted to the engineers. With dark hair, a strong chin and fierce, pale blue eyes, Klein had natural authority and had quickly risen from the ranks to NCO status. He had not only proved himself to be a highly competent and quick-thinking soldier; he was also lucky. His first posting had been to the Eastern Front, and his first time in action the Germans had been attacked by thousands of Red Army troops. 'You had to shoot them, of course,' he said. 'It was terrible and a deep shock.' Soon afterwards, the Russian guns had opened up and he had dived into a foxhole with two other men, one either side of him. When the barrage lifted, he realized both his comrades had been killed but he'd not received so much as a scratch. By the time his company were withdrawn, he found that he was one of only two still standing; all the rest had been killed or wounded. He couldn't understand why he'd been spared; why he'd had so much luck.

For most of the flight to Sicily, he'd been on edge for fear of being shot down en route, but they had made it, jumping into the Catania Plain unmolested. He'd been shocked, though, by the scenes of carnage and huge numbers of abandoned aircraft around the airfield as they assembled and moved south. As soon as they neared the Primosole Bridge they took over from the Nachrichten Kompanie, and Hauptmann Heinz-Paul Adolff, the 1. Pionier Bataillon commander, sent two companies to the south side, keeping Jupp Klein and the 2. Kompanie to the north. Major Schmidt's Maschinengewehr Bataillon, meanwhile, were brought back across the Simeto and positioned along the northern banks behind the dyke to the west of the bridge, while an Italian Blackshirt Commando company was brought in on the eastern side. Suddenly, the Primosole Bridge was looking very well defended indeed.

German paratroop engineers were not the only fresh forces arriving at the Primosole Bridge. At around 7.45 p.m., the first tanks of the 4th Armoured Brigade reached Frost's 2nd Parachute Battalion, and by midnight the infantry of 151st Brigade had begun to arrive too. This brigade was unusual in that all three of its infantry battalions, each of 845 men, were from the same regiment, the Durham Light Infantry or DLI: the 6th Battalion, to which Lieutenant David Fenner belonged, and the 8th and 9th. Despite their origin in one of the smallest cities and counties in England – and one of the poorest, its main industry the back-breaking work of colliers in the abundant coal seams – the Durhams had been in the firing line since the war began. Wherever Britain's army had been fighting, the DLI were usually to be found.

And now it was the 9th DLI who were to be thrown into the battle at Primosole Bridge. Overnight, two regiments of artillery – each with sixteen 25-pounder field guns – had arrived. Their opening barrage at 7.30 a.m. on Thursday, 15 July, was followed by the 9th Durhams advancing from behind Johnny I some three-quarters of a mile towards the bridge – where they were cut to pieces by machine-gunners, most of whom had survived the artillery barrage from their foxholes dug into the soft clay soil of the plain. The 9th DLI lost more than a hundred casualties, including thirty-four dead – the kind of figure that decimated the lead company – while three tanks were also knocked out. None the less, the Durhams had secured a foothold on the north bank and unexpectedly, the commander of the 1. Kompanie of Fallschirmjäger engineers, believing he had been left isolated and having lost contact with the battalion, pulled his men back across to the north side of the bridge. It was a small silver lining for the British in what had otherwise been a disastrous attack. But Eighth Army was no closer to getting across the plain, while with every passing hour more German troops were digging in behind the *Hauptkampflinie*.

Lieutenant Max Corvo, Colonel William Eddy and Captain Frank Tarallo had finally come ashore at Gela on 14 July and were immediately directed to a bivouac area. No one there, however, seemed to know where Seventh Army headquarters were. The following morning they were told to make for Licata, which was where Patton was headed that day; so, having been given a jeep to use, they set off in that direction. On the way they spotted a magnificent old castle, situated on a small headland that jutted out to sea. Although it had clearly been used by Italian coastal troops, there was no one there now but a caretaker, who showed them around and took them up to the battlements, from where the views up and down the coastline were spectacular. The castle, it turned out, was called Falconara and was owned by the Bordonaro family. Corvo thought it would be ideal for his purposes; so 'I decided to requisition the castle and set up the first OSS headquarters in Italy'. Why he, a mere lieutenant, was making such decisions in the presence of a captain and colonel is not clear.

Leaving Tarallo in charge at Falconara, Corvo and Eddy drove on to Licata. The town looked neglected and battered. Dust coated everything. In the main square, there were already signs declaring the presence of the Allied Military Government of Occupied Territories – or AMGOT – put up by the advance party of Colonel Charles Poletti's team. Poletti, an Italian-American and, the previous year, briefly the governor of New York, was now the designated Head of Civil Affairs for Palermo and the western half of Sicily. A barber's shop was open, so Corvo decided to have a quick trim, then managed to find Colonel Oscar Koch, G-2 – staff officer in charge of intelligence – for Seventh Army. Corvo and Eddy had been expecting an audience with Patton himself, but that was clearly not going to happen. Koch, showing little enthusiasm for what they had to say, told them that whatever intelligence-gathering operation they planned, it would have to be carefully and closely coordinated with each of the divisions. Corvo now suggested he head east, to Eighth Army's area, to try to recruit some native Sicilians to help; since his own family were from Melilli, he had better contacts there. Jumping at this chance to get them out of his hair, Koch quickly fixed up a note of introduction to Montgomery and sent them on their way. Back at Gela they eventually found their boss, head of the OSS General William 'Wild Bill' Donovan, who had landed on D-Day and who now told them it was unlikely their mission could achieve very much – which was putting it mildly.

Clearly, no one in Seventh Army was the remotest bit interested in the Corvo mission. It was hard to take them seriously in any case; for intelligence officers, they didn't seem to have a particularly keen grasp of intelligence. They'd been delayed getting to Sicily; when they got there, they hadn't been able to find Seventh Army HQ; they'd requisitioned possibly the most conspicuous property on the south coast; and then they'd stopped for a haircut. Now Corvo was planning to head east, where there were no Italians in any position to start an insurrection. And yet he had been encouraged to do so. It was as though someone higher up the chain was trying to get him and his team out of the way.

While Corvo and his colleagues had been driving back and forth between Licata and Gela, an American fighter plane had swooped in low over the quiet town of Villalba, home to Don Calò Vizzini. The previous day, the pilot had dropped a small nylon bag over the house of Monsignor Giovanni Vizzini, a priest and one of Don Calò's brothers; but, rather than falling into his hands, it had been picked up by a young Carabinieri officer. Now, on the morning of Thursday, 15 July, a second bag was dropped – this time right in front of Don Calò's own house outside town, where it was picked up by Carmelo Bartolomeo, one of Vizzini's servants. Written on the bag was 'Zu Calò' – Uncle Calò – and inside was a yellow-gold handkerchief with the letter 'L' stitched on to it, rather like the one Don Calò had sent some years earlier to his friends in New York when he spirited away the young mafioso Lottò, although whether the 'L' stood for 'Lottò', 'liberty' or some other name, such as 'Luciano', was not clear.

That evening, another of Don Calò's men, nicknamed Mangiapane, set off by horse to Mussomeli, some miles' ride away, with a message for Giuseppe Genco Russo, second in the Mafia hierarchy to Vizzini. It read:

> Turi, the farm bailiff, will go to the fair at Cerda with the calves on Thursday 20th. I'll leave on the same day with the cows, cart-oxen, and the bull. Get the faggots ready for making the cheese, and provide folds for the sheep. Tell the other bailiffs to get ready. I'll see to the rennet.

This was, of course, in code – the warning signal to start the plan which had been hatched months before through links to the New York Mafia.

*

Across in the east of Sicily the 6th Durhams, last in line in the 151st Brigade, were moving up towards the Primosole Bridge. The previous evening, Lieutenant David Fenner and his men had passed Monte Pancali, the site of one of Brigade Schmalz's delaying actions. Here was the debris of battle – a number of charred Carriers reeking of burnt flesh and paint, and dead bodies, including several Germans. One, without his boots, was lying there with a Tommy gun and a pile of bloodstained British webbing beside him. Fenner wondered what violence had been seen at that spot. Burying the dead in the slit-trenches the men had dug while still alive, the 6th Durhams then pressed on, the all-covering dust clinging to them, and the sound of small arms crackling in the distance as dusk fell.

The following morning they reached the front near the Primosole Bridge, marching on down the hill as the road cut through the Johnnies and past what had already been dubbed 'dead horse corner', where the twisted, bloated and disembowelled bodies of mules and donkeys lay rotting in the morning heat, flies swarming around them. The stench was horrific. 'Fighting was going on just in front,' noted Fenner. 'It was an unpleasant place full of unpleasant sights and smells.'

More troops were arriving on both sides as this bottleneck and gateway to the plain was now becoming the site of an epic battle. Already, the area was starting to take on a hellish form with shell craters pockmarking the landscape, burnt grass and wheat blackening the ground and the unburied dead bloating and beginning to stink badly in the relentless hundred-degree heat. Flies had joined the mosquitoes in their millions. The German Nachrichten Kompanie had returned, having decided they were not sufficiently strong to make much difference if the Allies attacked Catania from the sea and so might as well head back to the bridge where they could actually be some help. Since most of the Italian coastal defences had already disappeared, this left the city almost entirely undefended. There was an argument for making another amphibious landing, and that was being considered. Back on the *Ulster Monarch*, the SRS men were even briefed for such an attack, designated Operation CHOPPER. There were big problems with such a plan, however. The few hundred men of the SRS would almost certainly have been enough to get into the city, but whether they could then hold it, with the *Hauptkampflinie* growing in strength, was another matter entirely. There was an argument that their intrusion would have forced the Germans at the bridge to fall back, but whether the follow-up forces could then bludgeon their way through and relieve Mayne's men in time was questionable. There was also a suggestion of sending in the Commandos as well; but the bigger the attacking force, the more organization and, especially, shipping would have to be diverted – shipping that was still performing vitally important work bringing in an endless stream of much-needed supplies. By the time any such operation could be mounted, the situation at Primosole would most likely have changed in any case as British forces built up overwhelming strength there. On board the *Ulster Monarch*, the SRS men were game to go in if ordered, but hardly enthusiastic. 'Even before we knew the full facts of the situation,' noted Peter Davis, 'grave doubts milled through our minds.'

The 50th Division commander, Major-General Sidney Kirkman, had reached the CP at Johnny I mid-morning and had immediately ordered another assault for that afternoon. The pressure to push on and get into the plain quickly that same day, Thursday, 15 July, was immense; and yet there was no reason to suppose this second push would fare any better than the first attack that morning. Field artillery and mortars were only effective against dug-in defenders if a shell landed directly in a foxhole, and in the soft ground much of the blast effect was absorbed. The Germans had their 88s to take on the British Shermans, and everyone knew that machine guns could rip infantry to shreds. *Fallschirmjäger* had double the number of machine guns and submachine guns wielded by ordinary infantry, and Jupp Klein and his fellows had been told to wait as long as possible before opening fire on the attacking infantry so as to cause the maximum amount of casualties before the enemy had a chance to pull back.

The surviving paratroopers had become bystanders; but Lieutenant-Colonel Alastair Pearson had been called into the Durham Brigade's command post and had listened to the plan of attack for that afternoon with mounting horror. 'If you want to lose another battalion,' he said, 'you're going the right way about it.' For a moment, no one spoke; the collected commanders, including Brigadiers John Currie of the 4th Armoured and R. H. Senior of 151st Brigade, both gave him a long stare at his outspoken insolence. Fortunately, Lathbury was also present, having had his wounded arm patched up, and urged them to listen to what Pearson had to say.

'All right, Pearson,' said Senior, 'what do you want?' He meant what kind of fire support, but that was not what Pearson had in mind.

'Two thousand yards of white tape,' he replied – and then proposed a silent night-time attack with the infantry crossing the stretch of the Simeto he knew was fordable. He suggested using two companies – a couple of hundred men – with the rest of the infantry and armour ready and waiting to move.

Axis aircraft might have become significantly rarer beasts over the skies of Sicily, but there was no let-up for the Allied air forces, whose role now was to help the troops on the ground by hammering enemy traffic and transport. It was in this role that the 1st Fighter Group, equipped with P-38 Lightnings, were given the target of an Axis motor park at Randazzo, at the foot of the northern slopes of Mount Etna. As the Axis air forces became increasingly depleted, so the Allied air presence in the Mediterranean was growing, and this meant new Allied pilots were entering the fray. Among them was Lieutenant Robert A. 'Smoky' Vrilakas, who had reached North Africa in early June and been assigned to the 94th Fighter Squadron, part of the 1st Fighter Group. The son of a Cretan father and an American mother, Vrilakas had been raised in the country in Proberta, Northern California, and although he had initially been drafted into the army back in early 1941, he had ended up as a typist at 7th Infantry Division Headquarters. Not at all happy at leaving his infantry buddies to become a pen-pusher, he began thinking about applying for a transfer to the Air Corps. He hadn't held out much hope, though, assuming it wasn't the kind of thing that happened to farm boys like him. However, he had two years of college under his belt, ticked all the right boxes, and to his surprise and delight was accepted. A year later, he was heading to the Mediterranean.

While new pilots in the Luftwaffe were necessarily flung straight into action, in the USAAF, even in Tunisia, bomber and fighter groups had the opportunity to train up their new charges some more. Flying and combat flying were two very different skills, and if new boys were to have a chance of making the cut and surviving it was vital they could fly their aircraft as though it were second nature, allowing them to focus on the business of combat rather than the technicalities of how to trim, fly in formation or perform any other manoeuvre. So it was not until 15 July, by which time he had some three hundred hours in his logbook and a further ninety-eight on the Lightning alone, that Vrilakas was finally cleared to fly his first combat mission.

The P-38, a twin-boom fighter with a central cockpit, though robust and forgiving to fly, was not really designed for dog-fighting against more nimble single-engine fighters; but it was quick, capable of flying at over 400 mph, had much better range than a single-engine fighter – which made it very useful in the Mediterranean – and packed a big punch, with one 20mm cannon and four .50-calibre machine guns, all in the nose, which meant all a pilot had to do was point and fire. It could also carry 2 tons of bombs, as much as a Heinkel 111, for example, which meant it could be used in a variety of roles: traditional fighter, fighter-bomber or night-fighter. For Smoky Vrilakas, it had been love at first flight. 'It flew beautifully,' he enthused. 'The pilot's seat in a P-38 is in the centre of the wings and that position gave the pilot a feeling of being part of the airplane, with the wings an extension of the arms.'

Now, on the morning of 15 July, he was about to test the Lightning in action for the first time. Having been told the night before, at their base in Mateur, northern Tunisia, that they would be flying the next day, the pilots had now gathered in the briefing tent where they were told the target, timings, routes, altitudes, alternative targets and expected ground and air opposition. Since it was his first mission, Vrilakas was to fly as wingman to his flight commander, which was the safest position for a rookie.

Take-off was around 2 p.m., and Vrilakas taxied out following the squadron leader closely. At the end of the runway they paused for final checks, then they were off, gunning the throttle and speeding one after the other down the runway until, at around 90 mph, Vrilakas felt himself leaving the ground. Sticking to his leader like glue, he climbed and they all headed north, now in formation as three flights of four aircraft. Under the wings of each plane were two 500-pound bombs, and although Vrilakas had never dropped a live bomb before, he had been assured that if he did exactly what his squadron commander told him, he would be just fine. On they flew, up to the north coast of Sicily, then east towards Messina before beginning to dive down towards Randazzo around half-past three. Only now was radio silence broken: the squadron were told to arm their bombs, which was done by a simple electrical connection from the cockpit. Fires and smoke could be seen on the ground from where the first squadron of the group had already attacked, and then suddenly they were diving, Vrilakas gripping the control column as the Lightning screamed. 'Drop bombs – now!' he heard over his headset, and did so, the P-38 immediately feeling lighter as it was freed of its load. Now his ears were full of radio chatter as they climbed once more, formed up and turned for home through a few clouds of black but harmless flak.

Vrilakas landed, delighted to have successfully chalked up his first mission, and clambered out of the cockpit as a jeep beetled up to whisk him away for the debrief. Only then did he learn that two pilots in another flight of their squadron had collided over the target and both been killed. 'The loss of a pilot on any mission,' noted Vrilakas, 'was a difficult matter to accept and emphatically brought home the tragic and sad consequences of war.'

CHAPTER 22

Slaughter at the Bridge

O N THE MORNING OF Thursday, 15 July, General Bradley had visited
Patton in something of a state with the news of the massacres at
Biscari. 'A captain in the 180th,' noted Patton, 'had taken my instructions to kill all those who resisted after we got within 200 yards too
literally.' Before the invasion, Patton had given this exhortation to all the
officers and troops he'd addressed, as part of his attempt to add some fire
to their bellies. Now, confronted by what had happened, Patton told
Bradley the report was probably an exaggeration, and that in any case it
was best to say the dead men were snipers or had attempted to escape,
otherwise it would only cause a stink in the press and make the local
civilians mad. 'Anyhow,' he jotted, 'they are dead so nothing can be done
about it.' With that, the appalling massacres at Biscari were firmly
parked – for the time being.

Patton's mind was whirring with possibilities, not least that of swiftly
taking Palermo, which had now become lodged very firmly in his head.
That afternoon Tedder's deputy, Air Marshal Philip Wigglesworth,
arrived at Gela and Patton bet him a bottle of whisky against a bottle of
gin that Seventh Army would take Palermo by midnight on 23 July. Certainly, the American war machine was evolving with immense efficiency
and demonstrating just how a modern, supremely well-equipped and
supplied army in the field could operate. The US Army might still be
comparatively new to front-line combat in this western, European theatre, but the apparatus they were bringing to the show was leaving all
other combatant nations behind, even the British. A map depot had
already been set up at Gela and was producing fresh maps, while a water

pump, to provide that most precious of commodities, had been established near the town with a capacity of 25,000 gallons per day. Bulldozers, graders and heavy trucks had been brought over and were already at work clearing rubble and repairing airfields, while vast supply dumps had been set up. Landing ships and DUKWs were also delivering supplies directly to the beachheads at a rate not expected by the pre-invasion planners. The war reporter Ernie Pyle found watching the build-up of supplies from his perch on the *Monrovia* absolutely mesmerizing. Waking up one morning to find the sea almost empty of ships, when he looked again after lunch it was once more covered with vessels – big and small. 'Every one was coated at the top with a brown layer like icing on a cake,' he wrote. 'When we drew closer, the icing turned out to be decks crammed solid with army vehicles and khaki-clad men.'

Big freighters, anchored offshore, would soon be surrounded by a mass of DUKWs and landing craft swarming to ferry the constant procession of supplies to the beaches and ports. Coming ashore, Pyle walked on the steel pontoons that had been so swiftly set up; it felt a bit as though half of America had arrived in Sicily. And it occurred to him then that he was witnessing the long-heralded power of America's industrial and manufacturing might. 'The point was', he added, 'that we on the scene knew for sure that we could substitute machines for lives and that if we could plague and smother the enemy with an unbearable weight of machinery in the months to follow, hundreds of thousands of our young men whose expectancy of survival would otherwise have been small could someday walk again through their own front doors.'

This was the 'steel not flesh' strategy of the United States and Britain, the effective implementation of which depended crucially on exceptionally well-developed operational systems and skills. It wasn't just weaponry that could overwhelm enemy forces, but trucks and jeeps and half-tracks, gargantuan amounts of fuel and medical supplies – and Camel cigarettes and bottles of Coca-Cola, all of which were constantly arriving and being funnelled straight to the front-line troops. Already, by 15 July, Patton now had some 203,204 troops under his command. The predominantly Italian forces left in the western half of Sicily looked likely to be crushed by a breathtaking and war-winning combination of weight of numbers and modernity. Palermo by 23 July was more achievable than Air Marshal Wigglesworth might have appreciated.

While the 45th Division were moving, as were the 82nd Airborne, now largely brought back together at last, 3rd Division with the help of the 3rd Battalion of the Army Rangers were pushing on towards Agrigento. The Rangers had moved up to Favara, a small hilltop town 4 miles from Agrigento. Their plan was to advance through the night round the north of Agrigento itself, which was the objective of the 7th Infantry, and sweep down to the coast to capture Porto Empedocle. Trained for night operations and with combat experience from North Africa, Colonel Herman W. Dammer's men weren't at all fazed by such a challenge and set out just after midnight on the morning of 16 July. Their advance was met by some artillery fire, but it was scattered and inaccurate and no one was injured, so they made good progress until faced with an Italian roadblock. After a swift reconnaissance, the Rangers went in and within an hour had cleared the block and captured 160 enemy troops.

By first light, they were west of Agrigento and less than 3 miles from the port when they suddenly spotted an Italian column of ten motorcycles and two trucks of troops heading towards the town. Swiftly moving on to high ground above the road, they waited for the column to draw near and then opened fire, killing a number of men and stalling the column in its tracks. A further forty prisoners were taken. On they pressed over a hill that looked down on to Porto Empedocle and four Italian coastal batteries. Using their 60mm mortars along with machine guns and small arms, they opened fire then attacked down the hill towards them. It was at this point that Lieutenant Bing Evans was hit in the head by a bullet, just above his left eye. Collapsing to the ground with blood gushing down his face, he thought he was going to die – but after a few moments realized that not only was he alive, he was still in full command of his faculties too. Taking off his helmet, he saw the bullet hole on the outside and then a scored line running round the inside. Clearly, the bullet had hit him a glancing blow, then lost potency as it screwed around between the steel shell and liner of the helmet, but still causing enough damage to cut a long surface wound around his head. 'I was bleeding like a stuck hog,' he said. 'I could hardly believe I was still alive.' Hurrying over to him, a medic hastily applied sulfa and wrapped bandages around his head. 'Lieutenant Evans,' he said, 'you sure are a lucky SOB.'

Evans then put his helmet back on and kept going. Later that day, the Rangers took Porto Empedocle, while by nightfall the 7th Infantry were almost in Agrigento. Night-time shelling by naval guns added the finishing touches and by the morning of 17 July, Colonnello de Laurentiis, the garrison commander, had surrendered Agrigento. Another port was now in American hands.

Meanwhile, many of those who had been caught up in the opening battles of the campaign had faced long journeys. It had taken Melino Barbagallo a couple of days to reach Catania, driving mostly under the cover of darkness. At the barracks in Piazza Giovanni Verga he reported with his men and the radio equipment they'd brought from the airfield at Ponte Olivo, but had then been grilled by the Carabinieri over whether they had deserted. Barbagallo, who was both exhausted and fed up, showed them his uniform and weapons. 'I am not a deserter!' he shouted. 'I just want to see my family and then I will continue with the mission.' After this he was given a pass, joined his family in Catania for just one night, and then continued his journey north to Messina along with two pilots who, like him, were headed for the airfield at Bari in southeast Italy.

By the 16th, Tenente Livio Messina had reached the upper Dittaino valley between Enna and Leonforte. He was now with just two companions, having one night lost contact with the rest of the Gruppo Livorno. Movement had been slow, sometimes by truck but usually on foot. That morning, resting by the side of the road, they had been spotted by a priest who'd approached them offering absolution. No sooner had he administered the rite than three trucks pulled up and the Italian troops inside them jumped out, shouting a warning that enemy planes were bearing down upon them.

Messina, suddenly hearing the noise of the aircraft, cowered in the ditch to the side of the road. Moments later, they roared over, cannons and machine guns blazing, swooping so low he felt a gust of hot air as they passed. Then he had a strange out-of-body experience, as though he were looking down on himself; his dead uncle, killed in Albania, was with him, and so too St Anthony. An ammunition truck exploded but the Spitfires were gone and Messina was back in the ditch, shaking. Getting to their feet, he and his fellow officers hugged and kissed one another, relieved to have survived once again, but Messina could not stop shaking. His experiences, his fever, the shame of defeat and retreat were proving too much. He was still a young man, but he was broken.

The same could certainly not be said of Leutnant Karl Goldschmidt, who had reached Caltagirone with his small band of Tiger crewmen the previous evening only for a bridge into the town to be blown up as they approached. Clambering over the wreckage as they forded the river, Goldschmidt was seething. 'You stupid idiots!' he yelled at the *Unteroffizier* in charge on the far side. 'Why did you blow the bridge ahead of us? You could have killed us!' To his shock and surprise, the NCO now ordered his men to arrest them, accusing Goldschmidt and his crews of being Americans. Goldschmidt was incandescent, but not even pay books and other ID could persuade the sergeant and he ordered them to line up against a wall. 'Our own troops,' noted Goldschmidt, 'mistook us for a Commando and almost shot us.' Still furiously protesting their innocence, Goldschmidt insisted on speaking to the *Unteroffizier*'s superior. Their identity was then swiftly confirmed, and Goldschmidt and his men continued on their way to report to HG Division headquarters.

While the 3rd Rangers and 7th Infantry were attacking Agrigento, the Big Red One were continuing their advance north, the 45th Thunderbirds Division having successfully switched over to their left flank. Now attached to the 1st Division's 26th Infantry was the 70th Light Tank Battalion, a veteran unit from Tunisia. Commander of the 1st Platoon in Company B was Sergeant Carl Rambo. Originally from Tennessee in the Deep South, when he'd been drafted he had been working as a caterpillar driver in a construction firm in Pennsylvania. Like all of the others in the founding draft of the 70th, he'd joined as a high-school graduate; and like almost all of them, he already had experience of driving, operating and maintaining heavy equipment. Smart, quick-witted and good with his hands, Rambo had proved himself to be a highly competent tank commander, determined to use his wits and assimilated experience to the best possible effect both to do his duty and to keep himself and his crews alive. As he had swiftly learned, however, operating tanks could be a lethally dangerous occupation.

Their first action on Sicily, on 16 July, was supporting the infantry's attack on Barrafranca, another hill town some 10 miles to the south of Enna. Both infantry and tanks had pushed north from Mazzarino and now came up against Oberst Karl Ens's *Kampfgruppe* of 104. Panzer Grenadier Regiment, part of 15. Panzer Grenadier Division and now hurriedly trying to move east to reach the *Hauptkampflinie*. With the Americans pressing on his heels and with the hilltop town of Barrafranca lending itself to defence, Ens turned some of his forces towards the Americans in an effort to push them back and buy time.

The Germans greeted the American assault with artillery and

mortars from their Nebelwerfers, rockets that fired six-barrelled 210mm warheads whose whining noise as they came over had led to their having been swiftly renamed 'moaning minnies' – or 'meemies' – by the Allied troops. Then a number of Panzer Mk IVs began trundling down the road out of town to meet them. Like so many central Sicilian towns, Barrafranca stood on the summit of a hill, from which the land sloped down into the plain below before rising towards the next ridge. The 70th Light Tank Battalion was equipped with M5 tanks, known as 'Stuarts' – named, like the Sherman, after a Civil War commander, Confederate General J. E. B. Stuart – which, although more thinly armoured than a Sherman or a Panzer Mk IV, were armed with a 37mm and three .30-calibre machine guns and were both quick and nimble. The tank men now used their Tunisian experience to great effect, with Company A on one side of the road and Company B on the other. 'We would run up to the crest of a hill,' said Carl Rambo, 'fire a shot or two, back off, then go to the right or left, run up again and fire another shot.' The German tank crews, with their hatches down because they were in close action, did not have enough visibility to be able to respond quickly enough, and soon the Stuarts were running rings around them and, at close range, starting to knock out the panzers. Before long, five Panzer Mk IVs were left disabled and burning. 'We never lost a tank,' said Rambo, 'and shot them up pretty good.'

With their armour taking a beating, and with American artillery knocking out three more panzers as well as pounding the Germans in deadly concentrations, eventually the enemy began to pull back north from the town. By nightfall they had gone, allowing the US 16th Infantry to pass through the 26th and continue pressing northwards towards Enna.

Meanwhile, in the east, the Durhams launched their second attack on the Primosole Bridge at 1 a.m. on Friday, 16 July, with Alastair Pearson of the 1st Parachute Brigade, his trusted sidekick Panzer Manser, batman Jock Clements and several more of his men leading the way. As they crept across the open ground and over the already taped mine-cleared crossing of the Gornalunga, the commander of the DLI asked who was out front laying the tape. 'My bloody batman, I hope!' Pearson replied. Suddenly, one of his paratroopers fired his rifle, killing the man in front stone dead; he'd had his rifle loaded and ready, and accidentally squeezed the trigger. Quite apart from the tragedy of it, Pearson worried the single shot in a still night would rouse a terrible response from the Germans, but all remained calm.

When they reached the banks of the Simeto, he saw Jock Clements standing there, waiting, so ordered him to get moving.

'What, me sir?' Clements replied.

'Aye, you, yes,' Pearson told him and handed him his torch. 'If you see anything give it a wee wave. If there's anyone on the other side you'll soon know about it.'

Fortunately, there was no torch-waving nor any sudden flurry of shots, and Pearson and the Durhams successfully forded the river and gained their toehold. Fighting soon broke out as the German defenders woke up to what was happening, but the attackers managed to get to the north end of the bridge. Pearson now suggested to the Durhams' commander that they fan out either side of the bridge because the Germans were bound to counter-attack at first light; then a green Very light was fired, which was the signal for the armour and the rest of the infantry to thunder swiftly across the bridge. His mission complete, Pearson took his men and worked his way back along the northern bank of the Simeto, forded the river once more and set off back to the CP, by which time dawn was creeping over the Plain of Catania. 'I expected to see the Durhams go into action,' he said, 'streams of jeeps and tanks. The only person I met was a War Office observer on his bike.'

In fact, it wasn't until a little while later that the armour and infantry got moving. Not for the first time in a coordinated night-time attack of this kind, the Very signal was not seen because of early morning fog, radio messages did not get through immediately, and in the dark, with lots of different groups of men and vehicles to organize, the main assault was slow to get going. As the first tanks began crossing the long metal bridge, so the German 88s opened fire, knocking out the first and then the second; the burning remains blocked the way to the other vehicles trying to get through and the attack stalled. Meanwhile, the Durhams dug in on the northern side found themselves caught in a vicious fight with Jupp Klein and his comrades in among the reeds, vines and citrus groves.

With the 8th Durhams managing to cling on to their small bridgehead around the northern end of the bridge, another attack was planned for that night. During the day the 1st Parachute Brigade were pulled out, and trucks arrived to take them south. Lieutenant-Colonel Pearson was asleep in the front of a truck waiting to move when Clements shook him awake. General Dempsey had come up to the front and also the boss himself, General Montgomery. Expecting to receive a rocket for being asleep, Pearson instead found himself being taken to one side by Monty and congratulated on his men's effort at the bridge. The general then walked with Pearson down the road a little way. Behind them, one of his ADCs was handing out packets of cigarettes, so that when the two officers walked back up towards them, the paratroopers were all awake, smoking and cheering their C-in-C. 'There he was,' said Pearson, 'lapping this all up – all the cheers. It was very, very clever – a great morale raiser.' Soon after, the Red Berets were on their way, their part in the Sicily battle over. In fact, that was the end of all airborne operations on Sicily, as General Alexander called a halt to any further plans until considerably more inter-service training could be carried out. Just twelve officers and 280 other ranks of the 1st Parachute Brigade had fought at Primosole, which amounted to just 16 per cent of the force that had set off from North Africa – the rest had been flung to the four winds and had taken no part in the battle. Of those who'd fought at the bridge, more than a third had become casualties, including seventy-eight wounded, twenty-seven killed and a further ten missing. At Primosole, as at Gela, Ponte Grande and elsewhere, Allied airborne troops had achieved some important and significant results – but the cost to some of the very best troops in the US and British armies had been far too high.

Generalleutnant Hans-Valentin Hube, commander of XIV Panzer Korps, now deployed to Sicily, had been in Italy since mid-June, moving to Reggio di Calabria, in the toe, as soon as the Allies invaded, and finally flying over to Sicily on the morning of 16 July. Later, Kesselring also flew in; having left Sicily on the 12th in a state of shock at the dire situation, he had since recovered his normal positive outlook and now felt it might be possible to hold the north-east corner of the island indefinitely, especially since the rest of 1. Fallschirmjäger and the 29. Panzer Grenadier Division were already on their way. General Jodl, the OKW Chief of Staff, was less optimistic, however, and told Hube he was to defend Sicily for as long as possible but should not, under any circumstances, risk the loss of three German divisions.

On the 16th, Kesselring, Hube and von Senger met with Guzzoni, who felt very keenly the poor showing of his Italian troops and had clearly been crushed by the entire experience of commanding on Sicily. He had, though, had enough spirit left to object to von Senger over the placement of the 15. Panzer Grenadier Division. As the bulk of the HG Division had begun moving east to link up behind the *Hauptkampflinie*, so another widening gap had developed between the two German panzer divisions. Guzzoni had wanted to keep the 15. Panzers where they were, in reserve in the centre, but von Senger, backed up by Hube, overruled him and insisted they start moving east too. Now Guzzoni was also told that Hube was to take over formal command of all German troops the following day. The message was heard loud and clear by the Italian commander: effectively, he was now out of the running and the defence of the island was no longer an Italian show in any way. The Germans had always been the dominant partner, and now in Sicily they were asserting that dominance.

Kesselring was mightily relieved to have Hube in charge, and for good reason. By 1943, the quality of both German troops and their senior commanders was hugely variable, generally far more so than among their Allied equivalents. This could even be seen within the HG Division, as reflected in their performance since the invasion – for while they had been poor in their fight against the Americans, those operating under Schmalz had been much more competent, which was precisely why Kesselring had given the latter so much responsibility.

Hube was a class act. Fifty-two years old, with a solid face and pale, humorous eyes, he exuded calm imperturbability. He was a career soldier: having lost his right arm at the Battle of Verdun in 1916, a wound and handicap that would have done for a lesser man, he became the only one-armed officer in the massively reduced German army of the 1920s. A deep thinker and a modernist, during the 1930s he had embraced motorized warfare and gradually climbed the ranks, first to command the infantry school and then, in 1936, to become the commandant of the Olympic Village at the Berlin Games – a position that put him in direct contact with Hitler. After war broke out again he commanded a division in France in 1940 and repeatedly proved himself on the Eastern Front, so that by the autumn of 1942 he was commanding XIV Panzer Korps, part of General Paulus' Sixth Army. In January 1943, as German forces were becoming trapped at Stalingrad and it was increasingly obvious that Sixth Army was going to be destroyed there, Hitler ordered Hube to fly out. Hube replied by radio that he would either lead his men out of the Red Army encirclement or die with them – directly and defiantly disobeying the Führer's orders. Two days later, on 18 January, a transport landed at the airfield within the German pocket. On board were four SS men ordered by Hitler to grab Hube at pistol point and take him back to Berlin. The other senior commanders at Stalingrad, Paulus included, were left to their fate.

Clear-headed, courageous and a master of armoured warfare, Hube was also a general who looked after his men, and was universally admired and liked by those who served under him. It was for this reason he was known simply as 'der Mann'. And now the Man was here, on Sicily, commanding an entirely new XIV Panzer Korps rebuilt after its terrible destruction at Stalingrad six months earlier. With his arrival, a degree of measured calm spread over the German leadership, for Hube had brought with him a level of competence that had been missing from the cobbled-together hotch-potch of German units that had so far been fighting the invasion. At a stroke, the arrival of Hube and XIV Korps had brought German forces back under one umbrella and under one very competent and vastly experienced commander.

With the British airborne troops now out of the fray, it was left to the 151st Brigade of the DLI to finish the battle at Primosole Bridge once and for all. The next attack was to be launched at 1 a.m. on the morning of Saturday 17 July, a week after HUSKY D-Day. By the evening of the 16th General Kirkman, the 50th Division commander, had amassed six field regiments and one of medium artillery, furnishing him with 159 guns in all, including ninety-five 25-pounders and forty-eight 5.5-inch guns. It was a massive amount of fire-power for such a narrow front; but it was still the infantry and the tanks of the County of London Yeomanry who would have to do the hard graft, prising the German defenders from the ditches, vineyards and other nooks and crannies of this now blighted corner of Sicily.

Lieutenant David Fenner learned that the 6th DLI would be fording the Simeto to the west of the bridge, and advancing forward to the sunken track now renamed 'Spandau Alley' after the Allies' nickname for German machine guns. The capture of this track was seen as the key to unlocking the German defences. The 9th Battalion would follow behind, then push to the right towards the bridge. The tanks would then attack across the bridge as there was no alternative route over the river for them. No one expected it to be easy.

A rum ration had been issued before the men set off, and then they were on their way, Fenner and his men walking in single file up to the Gornalunga, now a dry ditch. Evidence of the earlier fighting was everywhere, from the burned vegetation to the blackened bodies starkly visible in the moonlight. One of the dead was sitting upright in the Gornalunga river-bed, staring sightlessly at each of them as they struggled past. Harassing machine-gun fire from their own side cut through the night, but otherwise the only sound came from the bullfrogs croaking in the reeds. As they approached the fording point across the still-flowing Simeto river, they paused to let the lead company cross and to fix bayonets. Then they were sliding down the bank and into chest-high water, guiding themselves across by a wire that had been strung from one side to the other.

So far, so good. They were across the Simeto and had moved into three companies abreast for their advance. At zero hour, 1 a.m., they still hadn't been given the signal to move and nervous voices began to say, 'What are we waiting for?' and 'Let's get stuck in.' Then the gunners opened up. They'd been firing all day, softening up the enemy, and were now shooting on fixed lines as they couldn't see their own troops in the dark. Enemy machine guns opened up, bullets and tracer fizzing and zipping past at knee height. Men were falling, but the Durhams kept pushing forward through the vines, a hundred yards, then two hundred, towards the sunken alley until they caught up with the artillery shells, which were crashing around them and blasting earth, grit, stone and shards of shrapnel. 'When I get out of this,' shouted Ben Dickinson, one of Fenner's fellow officers, 'I'll do those bloody gunners!' Fenner thought this was a little optimistic, given the intensity of their own shells falling all around them, but then the barrage lifted and they moved forward once more; the infantry had simply got ahead of themselves in the dark.

The air was thick with the stench of rotting bodies, explosives, smoke – and lemons, the citrus scent heavy from the shredding the groves had received. On the Durhams went, through a cactus hedge, and then they were down and into the sunken road itself. 'There was a lot of shooting,' noted Fenner; then 'suddenly it was over and we had taken about eight prisoners, all but two wounded.' What remained of the company was hastily formed into a defensive position either side of Spandau Alley and the men began furiously digging in: Fenner noticed that those who had sensibly taken German entrenching tools were making a far better fist of it. All around them the ground was littered with corpses, abandoned and knocked-out machine guns and belts of ammunition. Meanwhile, a fierce battle raged on their right where the 9th Battalion was going in.

By first light, all contact with battalion HQ had been lost, and as dawn crept over the carnage they realized there were still plenty of German paratroopers around with fight left in them. Snap-shooting broke out as heads popped up, fired and ducked down again. Eventually, two Shermans appeared, but with hatches closed and so with no means of communicating. One officer jumped on to the back of one but was promptly shot through the hip; still, just the appearance of the tanks encouraged the *Fallschirmjäger* in front of them to start pulling back in small groups, and during another firefight Fenner's men captured fifteen more men, including two officers. As they searched them they found several tickets for brothels in Marseilles, and suddenly all of them were laughing, Tommies and Jerries alike.

Further to the west, Leutnant Martin Pöppel had witnessed less of the action as his company had been ensuring safe crossings of the Simeto for stragglers of Brigade Schmalz. In any case, he was now struggling with a fever. 'I felt sick as a dog,' he noted, 'aching limbs, headache, dry throat, the whole works.' Later that day they were ordered to pull back, part of a staged withdrawal to the *Hauptkampflinie*. By this time, Pöppel was so ill he could no longer walk by himself.

By the Primosole Bridge itself, the fighting had been brutal. Jupp Klein's men had one machine gun and a submachine gun every 10 yards, which in the close-quarters fighting taking place was an incredible weight of fire through which the Durhams had been expected to advance. Dead and wounded littered the ground on and either side of the bridge and the sunken road, to the point where a ceasefire was agreed to allow both sides to pull out their wounded. British and Germans alike had suffered horrifically: the 6th DLI had lost 120 men, about one in three of those attacking – 100 of them from the 9th Battalion alone – while the *Fallschirmjäger* had lost around 300 dead and a further 155 taken prisoner. The Nachrichten Kompanie had just seventeen men left. 'It was terrible,' said Jupp Klein. 'And the stench – in the heat the dead soon began to rot.'

Such losses had devastated the *Fallschirmjäger* defending the bridge, who by early afternoon had no choice but to pull back. Before they did so, however, Jupp Klein and his fellows loaded several trucks full of shells and – in an act of immense courage – drove the first one on to the bridge, past the burnt-out Shermans, intending to explode it and destroy the bridge in the process. The first attempt failed, however; then so did a second and finally a third. In the process, Klein's battalion commander, Hauptmann Adolff, was shot and killed. And all for nothing. 'It was a

very brave act,' said Klein, 'and a huge loss. We were also very disappointed when we were told we would have to withdraw. It had been
drummed into us that paratroopers never retreated.'

By evening, the battle was over and the bridge was finally in British
hands – for good. But the carnage was appalling. Everywhere lay abandoned weapons, scattered ammunition boxes, bloodied uniforms and
the dead, rapidly blackening in the heat. On the road north to Catania,
the 88s that had caused so much trouble stood abandoned and broken;
on the bridge, the burnt-out shells of Shermans smouldered. Flies
swarmed; mosquitoes hung over the battlefield in clouds. Primosole
Bridge had become a hellish place indeed.

On 15 July the Canadians had got moving again, pushing on through
Vizzini, which had been cleared by the 51st Highland Division the day
before. They were now in trucks, which sped them up a bit. Even in vehicles, though, with the breeze of movement in their faces, it was still
blisteringly hot. Lieutenant Farley Mowat had gazed out at the sun-
beaten landscape through the swirls of dust kicked up by their column.
On the summits of many of the hills stood lonely and desolate small
towns, while in the fields scrawny peasants straightened their backs to
pause and watch as they rumbled by.

They knew they were on the tails of the HG Division, and there was a
tingle of excitement and apprehension that they might meet them at any
moment. When they did, however, it was initially something of an anti-
climax – just two German privates in a ration truck who had taken a
wrong turn and who quickly flung up their hands in panicky surrender.

Further on, however, things got more serious. As they approached
Grammichele they came under fire: the lead Sherman travelling with
them was hit and brewed up, and then a mixture of cannons, 88s, 105mm
howitzers, mortars and machine guns was flung at them – Mowat was
pleasantly surprised to find he recognized all the different weapons the
Germans were using – causing them to leap hurriedly from their trucks.
Soon, though, their own mobile artillery was firing back, and although
two Shermans had been hit, the Germans could not keep the advancing
Canadians far enough away to prevent the tanks, hurrying forward,
from quickly overrunning the enemy positions. The 2nd Brigade then
had a tough fight at the next town on Highway 124, Piazza Armerina,
where they came up against the 15. Panzer Grenadier Division for the
first time before eventually forcing their way through.

All the roads heading north in the eastern part of the island were now being used by Eighth Army. On the 17th, the 51st Highland Division bashed their way through a blocking position in the very centre of Eighth Army's front and crossed the Gornalunga some 20 miles inland from the coast, after which they continued to push north towards the Gerbini airfields. Away on their left, between the Highlanders and the Canadians, the Malta Brigade also crossed the Gornalunga that same day, so that along all the routes north Monty's men were making broadly similar progress, bumping into enemy rearguards but still pushing forward along the dusty, mountainous roads of eastern Sicily.

On Friday, 16 July, General Alexander had set about preparing a new directive for Patton and Montgomery, now that Eighth Army was within spitting distance of Catania. It was already clear that the German forces, at any rate, were beginning to regain their balance as they gathered behind the new defensive line at the southern foot of Etna. He was also concerned about the problem posed by the Messina peninsula, which stretched out north-east like a long, mountainous isosceles triangle, dominated by the mass of Mount Etna. Here the Axis forces could gradually retreat in stages because, as the peninsula tapered to its tip, so they would have shortening lines to defend – and in terrain that helped the defender and hindered the attacker, the mountains offering good positions for both observation and the direction of artillery and small-arms fire. Such terrain also worked against the materiel-rich attacker because there was less room for manoeuvre and, crucially, the roads were very limited and not of great quality for the heavy trucks, guns and tanks of a massive industrialized army.

Alexander felt that Eighth Army was best placed to take the lead in the assault on Messina, using three main lines of attack around Etna, not least because it would be difficult to fit a second army into this narrow space with its poor infrastructure. Seventh Army's role, in Alex's new directive, was to continue to protect Eighth Army's back and to cut off and secure the main roads that ran across the island. A few days earlier, in a signal to General Brooke back in London, he had also made clear his intention to send Seventh Army west to take Trapani and Palermo as well, but his directive did not mention these objectives; it was concerned only with the axes of attack towards Messina for Eighth Army and the Americans' role in that assault.

Patton received Alex's new directive just before midnight, and by morning had determined to go and visit him in person, even though that meant flying to Army Group Headquarters back in Tunis. He was right to do so, because resentment was rapidly growing within the American command – to the point where Patton's own private mutterings were by no means the harshest criticisms of Alexander being voiced. At any rate, this mounting tension needed resolving, and quickly. 'I am sure,' jotted Patton, 'that neither he nor any of his staff has any conception of the power of mobility of the Seventh Army, nor are they aware of the political implications latent in such a course of action.'

When Patton had briefly commanded II Corps in southern Tunisia, Alexander had been warned beforehand that he was a firebrand and would need careful watching. Alex had taken a nurturing role, determined that Patton's impetuosity should not lead to him overextending and incurring a second bloody nose like that of Kasserine, and so had issued no fewer than six specific orders to him as the situation had evolved in an effort to keep him on a fairly tight leash. It had worked, too, because Patton had indeed wanted to strike harder and more quickly than his men or supply lines allowed. Now, and a mere four months later, Patton was in command of a vast army four times the size II Corps had been in Tunisia. There was no doubt that Alexander rated him highly, but if there was a note of caution in that regard it was surely unsurprising. Even so, that was not the main reason for giving Seventh Army the secondary role, which remained the same as it had always been: that Eighth Army was in the east, closest to Messina, and so had always been intended to play the main role. A week on since the invasion, there was no real reason to change that.

Patton arrived in Tunis at ten past one that Saturday after an hour's flight from Ponte Olivo and went straight to see Alex, accompanied by Major-General Albert Wedemeyer, who was visiting Sicily at the time as General Marshall's representative. Clearly, Alexander was somewhat embarrassed and nonplussed by the strength of Patton's feelings – not least because neither Eisenhower nor Major-General Huebner, Alex's deputy chief of staff and an American, had raised any concerns over Seventh Army feeling sidelined. This, however, was because they were not aware of it either – largely because, up to this point, Patton had not raised the matter. For all his thundering and martial rhetoric, Patton always obeyed orders from above, which was very much the American way, even though at a junior level the relationship between ordinary troops and officers could be very informal, even casual by British standards. It was the British custom, however, for directives from above not to be necessarily taken without question; if those on the ground felt important issues needed to be raised or had an alternative view, then it was expected they would voice their concerns.

Patton explained his plans for taking Palermo and Trapani, and these, Alexander told him, chimed with his own thoughts. So long as Patton assured him he could secure the key central roads through Caltanissetta up to the town of Petralia, which blocked the entire central axis through the island, then he was happy for the US commander to unleash his forces and secure the western half of the island. 'If I do what I am going to do,' scribbled Patton, 'there is no need of holding anything, but it's a mean man who won't promise so I did.' With this ruffle smoothed over, Patton flew back to Ponte Olivo, happy he could now send II Corps north towards Petralia and on to the north coast, and his new Provisional Corps, under Major-General Geoffrey Keyes, west and north-west to clear the rest of the island, secure Trapani and capture Palermo. Barring his way were still a lot of Italian troops, including the Aosta and Assietta divisions as well as the coastal divisions, but Patton was not much concerned about them from what he'd seen of Italian troops so far. That night, he wrote to his beloved wife Bea, telling her of his trip to Tunis to see Alex. 'It was all settled in a nice way,' he told her, 'and we can keep on attacking. If we halt, we should lose momentum.'

CHAPTER 23

The Bloody Plain

DAWN, SUNDAY, 18 JULY 1943. In the hilly country to the south of Valguarnera, the sun rising over the rugged countryside swiftly banished the night's chill with a soothing warmth. Lieutenant Farley Mowat and the men of A Company of the Hasty Ps were digging in on a dome-shaped hill with terraced slopes about a mile south of the hilltop town, their next objective. Their journey there had begun the previous evening, and frankly it was something of a miracle they'd got to within a stone's throw of their objective. Just north of Piazza Armerina the road forked, left towards Enna and right to Valguarnera. It had been the intention of Major-General Guy Simonds, the youthful 1st Canadian Division commander, to push on and take Enna that evening, but a big spanner had been thrown into those plans when they first came across a blown bridge and then discovered that a battalion of Oberst Ens's 104. Panzer Grenadier Regiment, part of the 15. Panzer Grenadier Division, was firmly on top of Monte della Forma, the 2,700-foot-high mountain that overlooked the road as it approached the fork. The Germans had very sensibly realized that while they held Monte della Forma, the Canadians weren't going to be using either road in a hurry.

Sure enough, the Canadian 3rd Brigade soon found itself caught up in a difficult battle; and so a plan was hatched to send the Hastings & Prince Edward Regiment on a cross-country march around the back of the German blocking position, in a neat side-step. Lieutenant-Colonel Bruce Sutcliffe, the CO of the Hasty Ps, reckoned his men were equal to the challenge, but it was none the less a tall order – their maps were woefully inaccurate, there appeared to be precious few trails of any kind, and the low mountain ahead of them looked forbidding, to put it mildly.

Undeterred and loaded to the gunwales with ammunition, grenades, cartons of 2-inch mortar bombs and ration packs – none of them carrying less than 60 pounds – they had set off, Alex Campbell's A Company leading. Although the moon rose clear and bright, they had soon found themselves tramping over low cliffs and across a network of stony, scrubby gullies, and in no time had lost contact with the other companies following behind. Campbell had repeatedly stopped, looked at his map with a hooded flashlight, cursed and then tramped on. After a while they had given up on the map and used a compass and dead reckoning instead.

Eventually, they came across a mountain hovel, where their debonair escort, Lieutenant Pat Amoore from the British Intelligence Corps – a fluent Italian speaker – banged on the door to ask directions. The old woman of the house began screaming like a banshee, while her husband, stark naked, pleaded for their lives. None the wiser, they hastily left – only to run straight into C Company, whom they'd earlier lost. More time passed, and then they found a track, realized it was heading north in the right direction and, before dawn, reached a road on which they saw tank tracks, which told them it had been recently used by military traffic of a German variety.

Across the road was the domed hill, its terraces looking likely to offer good concealment and all-round defence, and a place from which they could command the road in both directions. With the first light of dawn now creeping up from the horizon, they were further surprised to find a number of Sicilian refugees sheltering there. Pat Amoore learned they had fled from the fighting further down the road to the west – where 3rd Brigade had become embroiled. At least they knew they were in the right place, even if they had found it by luck as much as anything.

Lieutenant Mowat had just closed his weary eyes for a moment, letting the warming sun bathe him, when he was snapped alert again by the sound of machine-gun and rifle fire. Rapidly getting to his feet, he saw that the road was no longer empty: six enemy trucks coming from the east were grinding to a halt below them. The lead vehicle pulled over to the side of the road and German troops started to spill out hurriedly. Yelling at his men to get up and start firing, he then turned to see Captain Campbell charging down the slope towards the road, a Bren tucked under his arm, firing short, sharp bursts and with another magazine clenched between his teeth. Watching this open-mouthed, Mowat and the rest of the company momentarily lost concentration, and suddenly it was Alex Campbell, a giant of a man physically, and now, it seemed, metaphorically too, against 150 enemy, who had clearly travelled through the night to reinforce the battle down the road and had now been caught napping. In his fury, he almost single-handedly killed every man in the first truck, while the rest of A Company, their temporary trance over, poured fire on to the rest.

It was all over in a matter of minutes – the entire column, dead, wounded or hands aloft and surrendering. Hurrying down the slope, Mowat found himself carrying out the grisly task of counting the slain and the maimed and looking through *Soldbücher* – pay books – and other documents. It wasn't the dead that troubled him so much as the wounded, and one sight in particular: 'the driver of a truck hanging over his steering wheel and hiccupping great gouts of cherry-pink foam through a smashed windscreen, to the accompaniment of a sound like a slush-pump sucking air as his perforated lungs laboured to expel his own heart's blood . . . in which he was slowly drowning'.

One of the A Company officers suggested it might be better to put some of the worst wounded out of their misery, but Campbell had snarled at him and warned that none of them should even think about shooting prisoners. If they did, he growled, he'd see they were put on a murder charge. 'The anomaly of hearing such sentiments voiced by a man who had just butchered twenty or thirty Germans,' noted Mowat, 'did not strike me at the time.' But wartime was not normal time. Ordinary, peaceful, law-abiding young men were trained to kill other young men – and so they did. Violence and brutality and even indifference to these horrors had become a new kind of normal.

Unbeknown to Able and Charlie Companies, Dog and Baker had also cut the road, further to the west, after which they had knocked out a couple of enemy guns and entrapped the German troops facing 3rd Brigade. But they had stirred up a hornet's nest in Valguarnera as well, and before long mortars began falling around Able and Charlie; then they saw armoured cars heading their way; and moments later, just for good measure, 105mm shells started screaming over. The refugees fled and Alex Campbell recognized it was time for them to pull back too. Charlie Company pulled back first, then Able. When Mowat and his platoon made their dash back across the road, he felt as though he had winged feet and only stopped, breathless, once high on a rocky knoll some 200

yards from the road. Once C Company had set off back across the mountain with the POWs, Campbell told his men they would stay where they
were for as long as they could. The biggest immediate problem was thirst;
all their bottles were dry and their mouths were as parched as sand.
Eventually, Pat Amoore went off with a couple of men and returned a
while later laden with dripping water bottles, having surprised and killed
several Germans on the way.

Around 2 p.m. the Germans on the top of the mountain began to
launch their assault. Campbell decided the time had come for them
to pull back further, a platoon at a time; Mowat's men were to be the last
to leave, covering their retreat. As soon as 9 Platoon made a dash for it,
an MG42 began spraying bullets towards them, but by chance Mowat
saw the gun barrel flash. Sergeant Mitchuk, beside him with the Bren,
handed him the machine gun.

'You take 'em, Junior,' he said.

Pulling the butt into his shoulder and wrenching back the cock,
Mowat squeezed the trigger and felt the solid, reassuring and rapid pump
of bullets spewing from the muzzle. The Bren had half the rate of fire of
an MG42 and was magazine-fed not belt-fed, but it was accurate and
reliable and could keep firing so long as there were magazines to keep
punching into the top of the breech.

'Give 'em another!' said Mitchuk. 'You're on to the fuckers good!'

Mowat wasn't sure – he couldn't actually see any enemy – but mortar
shells were whistling over and a Panzer Mk III was firing its main gun
towards them too. He was itching to be on the move, but knew they
could not leave until the rest of the company had gone. Eventually, low
on ammo and with three men wounded – albeit not seriously – he fired
the signal flare and moments later a smoke mortar shell dropped and
then another. With white smoke now covering their path, Mowat
screamed, 'Get the hell out of here!' and they all ran for their lives. By
good fortune, all made it safely; and so began the return journey,
although, much to their relief, this time still in daylight.

The Hasty Ps might have pulled back, but most of the 1st Canadian
Division had been sucked into the battle for the road junction that had
begun the previous day and, as the afternoon had worn on, had captured
the key Monte della Forma overlooking the main road to Enna. Fearing
that both this road and the one heading north from Valguarnera were in
danger of being cut off, and with them his means of escape, overnight
Oberst Ens ordered his men to pull back towards Enna, Leonforte and

Assoro, which – though the Canadians did not know it – was the western edge of the *Hauptkampflinie*.

While in the first days of the invasion it had been the Americans who had faced the toughest fighting, with Eighth Army having a comparatively easy ride, the bitter and bloody battle for the Primosole Bridge had changed all that. Already, Montgomery was lagging behind his own timetable and the chance to snatch Catania swiftly and charge on up to Messina had gone. Three of Eighth Army's divisions were now in the line – 5th and 50th were on the southern side of the Catania Plain, the 51st Highland were driving northwards towards Gerbini, and even the independent Malta Brigade had been committed, shoved into the line on a route north between the Highlanders and the Canadians on the left. Against them were now three German divisions, together under a single – and hugely competent – commander, and on territory that favoured the defender. For all the advantages Eighth Army had in terms of fire-power and air superiority, it looked likely they might be in for a bruising time. A bloody, grinding battle of attrition appeared to be on the cards, and while this was a situation with which Monty was very familiar, on this occasion there was no reserve to punch through and then exploit. There was another division – the 78th – but it was not yet in Sicily. So, what was in the line on 18 July was all there was.

Montgomery, well aware the Germans were now hurriedly forming their *Hauptkampflinie*, had still not given up hope of bursting through it; this was why he had his different thrusts all attacking at the same time. The 51st Highland Division, for example, had got within spitting distance of the Gerbini airfield complex, having crossed the second of the three rivers that flowed into the Catania Plain, the Dittaino, and then climbed up a long ridge that overlooked both the airfields and the railway at the small town of Sferro. Beyond lay another ridge of hills and the upper Simeto valley, then beyond that another series of peaks to the north and the mass of Etna to the north-east. From their ridgeline, the Highlanders could look out and see the entire length of the *Hauptkampflinie* and the battlefield to come spread out before them – the rolling farmland of the wide, open valleys, the hilltop towns twinkling in the sunlight in the distance. It was a forbidding sight, and yet Major-General Douglas Wimberley's men had every reason to feel optimistic.

What they couldn't see from their own positions, however, were the guns lying in wait behind the next line of hills, or the forward positions of mortars and machine guns. At Monty's urging, the Highlanders attacked before the division had enough fire support and were promptly dealt a bloody nose; bulldozing their way through rearguards was one thing, but smashing a strong defensive line was quite another.

After the British had fallen back, a brace of assault guns from 11. Batterie, III. Bataillon HG Panzer Regiment had been sent forward to scout the situation at Gerbini, one of them manned by Bruno Kanert and his crew. Reaching the airfield, they saw no sign of life. Around the field were smashed, blackened and abandoned aircraft, broken hangars and badly damaged barracks. Anxiously pressing forward, they paused by the barracks and clambered out to have a look around; seeing nothing, they turned back, crossing the bridge over the Dittaino to meet the fuel and ammo truck that had been sent forward in case they needed it. There, behind the truck, on the far side of the road, Kanert spotted a Horch Kfz 15 command car and realized it belonged to Oberst Schmalz.

'He's waited for you here,' the truck driver told him, 'to learn the results of your reconnaissance.'

Jumping down, Kanert walked over, suddenly feeling conspicuous in his sneakers, Italian black shirt and tropical shorts. Reaching the Horch, he did his best to straighten himself and saluted.

'The airfield is deserted,' Kanert reported.

'Go back to the truck,' Schmalz replied. 'I've left cigarettes and chocolates for you with the driver. He will give them to you. And thank you, Kanert!'

Suddenly one of the men shouted, 'Look out, tank!'

They now saw a wheeled armoured car on the Gerbini side of the bridge, which had somehow appeared without them noticing. A shot rang out, which missed them all; then it disappeared again. Schmalz immediately gave chase. 'All due respect!' remarked Kanert. 'How many other commanders would have done this?'

Further east, the British capture of the Primosole Bridge had not opened any kind of floodgates for Eighth Army. To start with, the bridge itself had been zeroed by guns now dug in on the Etna foothills around Misterbianco and shells screamed over at regular intervals, making crossing it a hazardous operation. A fresh brigade had passed through the exhausted Durhams only to find the *Fallschirmjäger* had pulled back as far as a wide dyke, the Fosso Bottaceto, which cut across the road to the south of the airfield. When they attacked, they were cut to pieces.

The Primosole Bridge had been seen as crucially important because the main road north passed over it – but also because it was here that the Gornalunga flowed into the Simeto, as the River Dittaino did a couple of miles further west. All three rivers ran down from the mountains into the plain, and then the Simeto, swelled by the other two, flowed on across the plain in a winding but diagonal route from the north-west to the south-east and into the sea. The British now needed to get across to the northern side of the Simeto and attack across the plain towards the lower slopes of Etna, where the Germans were digging in behind the *Hauptkampflinie*.

Lieutenant David Cole and the 2nd Inniskillings had reached the edge of the Catania Plain the previous evening and had been rewarded by a magnificent view across this fertile strip of land towards the rising vastness of Mount Etna. Through his field glasses, Cole had seen the snaking River Simeto and the two tributary and now dried-up river-beds. Catania lay away to the north-east, shimmering in the golden evening light. It would have been rather lovely had it not been for the dull explosion of shells, the distant chatter of machine guns and repeated puffs of black smoke. Here before them was their next battleground, a daunting prospect, because the Germans would be able to see their every move.

The following day, Monday, 19 July, 13th Brigade were ordered to capture a crossing about 5 miles west of Primosole where a small, narrow and generally unremarkable concrete bridge had been discovered still intact. This was the route that had been used by Brigade Schmalz as they'd pulled back across the plain, now renamed 'Lemon Bridge' by the British. Lemon was given to the 2nd Inniskillings, while the 2nd Wiltshires found a fordable crossing point a little way to their right just before the junction of the dried-up River Dittaino with the Simeto. The plan was for the 2nd Skins and 2nd Wilts to get across and form a bridgehead through which the rest of 5th Division could pour and rapidly establish a hold on the Catania Plain.

Cole had moved down towards the bridge on foot that afternoon along with the CO, Lieutenant-Colonel O'Brien Twohig, and the rest of battalion HQ, feeling uncomfortably exposed the whole way. The entire journey was littered with parachute silk and debris, while away to their left were the shattered remains of a satellite landing ground. The wrecked and blackened skeletons of aircraft, one standing on its nose, reminded Cole of a painting by Dali. As they finally neared the bridge, bullets began fizzing and mortars crashing just up ahead: C Company, in the lead, had taken the small pocket of Germans defending the crossing by surprise. Not long after, however, the fighting died down and word reached them that C Company was now across the bridge and trying to dig in on the far side.

Dusk was falling and the light fading rapidly as they reached the river a few hundred yards to the right of the bridge. Here it was quite thickly bordered by bushes and trees, but they hurried forward, crouching as they did so and passing a wounded German lying in the grass, groaning and clutching his stomach. Cole hoped their stretcher-bearers would take care of him but was conscious they might well all have a very busy night ahead.

At the bridge, however, they were able to get across and confer with Major Owen Meade, the C Company commander. The darkness was increasing all the time now, and even while they were talking visibility dropped from 100 yards to a few feet. Suddenly, they all stopped. Up ahead there was noise, indistinct at first and then unmistakable: tracked vehicles, and coming towards them. Enemy tracked vehicles. Panzers. And between them and the rumbling was nothing but flat grassland, which, Cole thought, might not have been quite as flat as Lord's Cricket Ground, but was perfect for the murderous fire of tanks. Then came the jingling and clink of infantry moving about, and suddenly a voice called in strange English, 'Don't fire, it's the Jocks.' No one was fooled; but even so, someone called out the password, to which, of course, there was no reply, except the pulling back of bolts on weapons. Cole was terrified and wondered whether this would be it; that he'd found his corner of a foreign field.

Then the firing started – a deafening clatter of weapons, tracer criss-crossing the night air. Cole and the men around him all hit the ground. 'These bullets were not haphazard Italian ones,' noted Cole, 'they were methodical Teutonic ones really striving to kill us.' Then, just as suddenly, the shooting subsided and it seemed the tanks up ahead had halted. The CO, with Cole in tow, now scuttled back across the bridge to the newly established Advance HQ where O'Brien Twohig issued his orders. A company was to be in reserve at an abandoned farmhouse some 300 yards behind them, along with the one 6-pounder anti-tank gun they had so far managed to get across the dried-up Dittaino, set up to hit any panzer that tried to cross the bridge. D Company was to dig in on the left of the bridge and B company to the right, using the slit-trenches dug earlier by the Germans, both ready to attack anything that moved up ahead. Major Meade's C Company would remain on the northern side of the river.

The second attack was not long in coming. Once again the night was torn apart by the sudden, deafening and head-jarring hammer of machine guns and small arms. Flares shot into the air and crackled as they burst, casting an eerie silvery light on the scene below. Cole saw one of their own men knocked backwards by a stream of bullets hitting him square in the chest. 'I bent over him,' wrote Cole. 'His shirt and equipment were soaked with blood and out of his pale face, his eyes stared up at me, through the dark, wide-open and blind. He was absolutely dead.' Cole, who had not seen a man killed right in front of him before, was shocked and angry.

The panzers were now approaching and, in the light of the flares, Cole saw the lead beast emerge, squat, dark and menacing, its gun and turret swivelling towards them. More tanks could be heard coming up behind and Cole felt a renewed wave of cold terror. Then a single, massive explosion burst open the night with a blinding flash of light erupting from the tank and simultaneously silhouetting a mass of enemy soldiers. The panzer had hit a Hawkins anti-tank mine, one of a number that had been hastily thrown down on the road leading up to the bridge. To the uneducated eye, one of these mines looked like a small tin of oil; but in fact each one contained 2 pounds of TNT or ammonal, and when it was driven over, the crushing cracked a chemical igniter, leaking acid on to a sensitive chemical, which then detonated the explosive. By luck – or misfortune, depending on perspective – the explosion had clearly hit a weak spot in the tank and then ignited fuel or ammunition. Whatever it was, the panzer was now engulfed in an angry ball of fire, while the Brens now easily picked off the Germans caught in the light of the flames. This caused the enemy attack to stall so that D Company could be pushed across the bridge, a second tank being hit by one of them using a PIAT, a hand-held anti-tank mortar that required the user to be almost suicidally close for it to have any effect.

A period of calm descended. Cole, like his fellows, was being bitten to pieces by the mosquitoes as they dive-bombed him, buzzing in his ear – just one more ingredient in the deeply disturbing business of fighting in the dark. Night battles were a terrible assault on the senses – confusing, disconcerting, disorientating. Cole really had no idea what was going on even at Lemon Bridge, let alone further down the river at the 2nd Wilts' sector. Just after midnight the enemy shelling began, both artillery and smaller mortars. Silence one moment, deafening noise the next, the ground pulsing as though an earthquake was rippling through it. At one moment, both Cole and O'Brien Twohig were knocked off their feet by the blast of an exploding mortar; they were unhurt, but a nearby fusilier was killed by shrapnel, torn so badly that even in the dark Cole had to turn his eyes.

Then, as suddenly as it had started, it stopped again, so that all that could be heard were the cries and groans of the wounded. The air was heavy with the rasping stench of cordite. It was, of course, only a brief respite before the HG men launched yet another attack; and while the Inniskillings fought back with small arms and grenades, it was only when the artillery, that backbone of Allied fire-power, began to offer the beleaguered infantry some support that the enemy attack was once again beaten back. Now B Company was sent over the bridge; as the commander, Captain Bob Alexander, passed Cole he said to him, with a smile, 'It's suicide.' Alexander had played rugby and cricket for Ireland and had toured South Africa with the 1938 British Lions alongside Paddy Mayne. He was a hero to many in the battalion and a much-loved officer. 'He was a really fine man,' wrote Cole, 'down-to-earth, good-humoured, courageous and honourable in every way.' Tragically, as he predicted, he was cut down along with the men he was leading.

As dawn cast its grey light, the scene that emerged was a shocking one: cratered landscape, shredded vegetation, bloodied corpses, still smoking panzers. Shadowy figures and the sound of engines warned of yet another onslaught – and so it proved, shells and mortars raining down as part of the terrible prelude. Cole was knocked over again by a mortar blast, and for a second time was fortunate not to be hurt. Now the CO ordered the men on the far side of the Simeto to pull back. Captain Tom McCabe, acting commander of C Company, after Owen Meade was wounded, was killed, as was another of Cole's friends, Lieutenant Basil Fenton.

Back on the south bank, the fusiliers kept firing; but again, it was the artillery that broke the enemy's assault. 'It came like a monsoon,' wrote Cole, 'a few big, slow drops first, and then a deluge. The first few shells whooshed lazily over our heads, each a separately identifiable projectile, to crash here and there in front. Then their numbers grew and grew and grew until the air immediately above us vibrated with their tumultuous and crowded passage and, all along the front, the ground shuddered with the seismic upheaval of their explosions.'

It was the end of the battle for Lemon Bridge. Prisoners were brought in and confessed the artillery was worse than anything they had experienced in Russia. Three tanks lay smouldering on the far side among the dead and dying. Clearing the slain was a grim business and the numbers increased when a Carrier went forward and was promptly blown to bits by a single 88. 'The only Germans who got to the bridge throughout,' noted Colonel O'Brien Twohig, 'were prisoners and the bridge was handed over in the same state (less minefield) as we found it.' That was true up to a point – although few glancing at the carnage around the bridge would have claimed so – and while no one could doubt 13th Brigade's heroic effort both there and at a similarly hard-fought-for stretch where the Wiltshires had also crossed, their defence of the Simeto had fallen significantly short of the complete breakthrough of the German line that Montgomery and Dempsey had been hoping for. For now, though, 13th Brigade was pulled back into reserve; another attempt would be made that night, but this time, it would be 15th Brigade leading the charge.

On that same Monday, 19 July, General Keyes' Provisional Corps jumped off for the drive west. The 82nd Airborne Division were to use the southern coastal road, Highway 115, as their axis of advance. Setting off at 5 a.m., they sped forward, the 504th Parachute Combat Team in the lead, Gavin's 505th taking a back-seat role. By nightfall, they'd taken Ribera and pushed on to the airfields at Sciacca, where Macky Steinhoff's I. Gruppe had been based, and which had been so brutally and repeatedly smashed by Allied bombers. Elsewhere, Seventh Army made rapid gains, the hardest fighting being on the road to Enna, where the 16th Infantry were fighting another battlegroup of Ens's 104. Panzer Grenadier Regiment. That they were attacking Enna at all was the result of the decision by the Canadians, after their battle at the road junction around Monte della Forma, to side-step Enna and head directly towards Leonforte to the north-east. This had left Enna in enemy hands, potentially threatening the rear of the Big Red One's strike north. Bradley had quite rightly accepted it needed to be captured, even though that meant a diversion of effort.

Generale Guzzoni might have lost any authority over German troops, but the Italians were still under his command, and so, hearing on Sunday 18th of the fall of Agrigento the day before, had already ordered his XII Corpo, in the west of the island and protecting Palermo, to cut their losses and head east, first along the northern coast road and then on Highway 120, which ran parallel to the coast around 20 miles inland, through Petralia, Gangi and Nicosia. It was this road that Alexander was so anxious Bradley's II Corps should sever at Petralia before the Italian Aosta and Assietta divisions managed to escape.

On Tuesday, 20 July, the 16th Infantry took Enna, Guzzoni's former headquarters, and the Americans pushed further west and north. Heading down Highway 121, the asphalted road that led from Enna directly to Palermo, were the men of the 180th Infantry, 45th Thunderbirds Division. That morning, just a couple of miles or so from Villalba, they hit a roadblock held by the Gruppo Mobile A of the Divisione Assietta, which held them up briefly. Heading for the town that same morning was a jeep bearing a large yellow-gold pennant emblazoned with a black 'L'. Nearing the town, the driver took a wrong turning and was fired on by Italian troops. One of the Americans inside was hit and fell out; the jeep then turned around and drove off again.

Later, in the afternoon, three Shermans reached the town, one of them flying the same yellow pennant with a black 'L'. An officer with an American-Sicilian accent looked down from the turret to the crowd gathering around and asked someone to fetch Don Calogero Vizzini. Not long after, the man himself appeared, wearing his trademark short-sleeved shirt, a cigar in his mouth and a cap pulled almost down to his tortoiseshell spectacles. Reaching the lead tank, he pulled out a yellow handkerchief with a black 'L' embroidered on it and then, with the help of one of his nephews, Damiano Lumio, who had only recently returned from the United States, clambered up on to the back of the tank. Before moving off, Don Calò told his man Mangiapane to ride back to Mussomeli and tell Genco Russo what had happened. Then the tanks trundled off out of the town and disappeared, and with them, Don Calò and Damiano Lumio.

While these curious events had been taking place, the British 5th Division had been planning another assault across the Plain of Catania to try to break through the *Hauptkampflinie*. For all the Allies' military hardware and materiel, and the enormous mechanized support they were able to give their fighting troops, it was still down to the foot-sloggers and tank crews physically to take ground from the enemy. This was incredibly dangerous, because human bodies are soft and huge damage can be caused by bullets, explosives and shrapnel. A front-line infantryman in the war had almost no chance of getting through it unscathed – in fact, the chances of survival were as bad as, if not worse than, those of his predecessor twenty years earlier during the First World War. What's more, in essence, the method of attack hadn't much changed since then. Enemy positions were usually softened up with air and artillery barrages, and then the infantry advanced out across the open – a leap of faith in which they were extremely vulnerable.

During the 19th, 15th Brigade had pushed out and expanded the bridgehead created by the Inniskillings, Wiltshires and men of 50th Division from Primosole Bridge. They now had a good swathe of the Catania Plain in their hands and Catania itself, away to their north-east, seemed close enough almost to touch. Another attack towards Misterbianco, supported by a massive nine artillery regiments, could – it was hoped – bludgeon a way through the German defences.

There were two schools of thought about how to conduct night-time attacks. The first was to infiltrate as silently as possible and strike in the first glimmer of dawn. The other – adopted for this occasion – was to go in during the hours of darkness with artillery blazing – a heavy barrage of enemy positions followed by a creeping barrage behind which the infantry would advance. The advantage of the latter was that it meant the enemy were cowering – or, even better, being blown to bits – while the infantry began moving forward. It also sat well with the overriding principle of Allied tactics, which was to use overwhelming fire-power as much as possible. The flip side, however, was that the enemy knew an attack was coming.

As always in a brigade attack, one of the three battalions would be held in reserve, as would one of the companies of each battalion. This meant that although a brigade might amount to some 3,500 men in total, in an infantry brigade-strength attack there would be only 1,200 men at most. On this occasion, the assault was to be shared by the 1st Green Howards on the right and the 1st Yorks and Lancs on the left; and in the former, it was B Company who were up front, which meant that Major Hedley Verity was leading the Green Howards' attack. They had been moved up to their starting position by lorry at around 10 p.m., and then before the attack the barrage had opened up.

Officers had to lead by example, as had been demonstrated during the Inniskillings' battle around Lemon Bridge, particularly when they were company commanders leading an attack. The noise, as the men moved up towards the planned start line, was deafening. Shells hurtling over, screaming as they sped through the air. Explosions up ahead. This was Verity's first taste of combat. Nearly four years of training had come to this moment. Heart pounding. Adrenalin coursing through him. B Company crossed the road behind the barrage at around 2 a.m. on Tuesday, 20 July, still struggling across open ground crossed with ditches and watercourses.

When the barrage finally ended, B Company were well ahead of the other companies but still some distance away from the enemy, which meant they were both exposed and isolated. After the deafening barrage, the abruptness of artillery silence was startling. Ahead were fields of corn which gave comparatively good cover, but night attacks – especially for those who hadn't experienced them before – were incredibly confusing and disorientating. Spandaus opened up from another dyke, the Massa Carnazza, which curved in a bulge ahead of them. A mound perhaps 12 feet high, this dyke gave the enemy the ideal place from which to fire at any attackers, while behind the dyke mortar teams were protected. Flares now rose into the sky with a hiss, then a crackle as they burst and slowly descended, lighting up the ground briefly as clear as daylight.

As Verity and his men advanced towards this dyke, at first mistakenly thinking it was the railway line that ran behind it, bursts of rapid machine-gun fire continued to streak across the open fields of corn – high to begin with, but soon adjusted, the machine-gunners now firing at waist height. Men began to get hit, and then the stabs of tracer started to set the corn on fire. The key was to keep moving and keep firing their own machine guns too. German MG42s could only fire short, sharp bursts, otherwise they soon overheated and lost any accuracy, and rarely would a Bren and an MG42 be firing at the same time; one side would fire a burst then duck, then the other side would do the same.

Progress was slow and, with mortars falling as well, casualties were rising. Lines of criss-crossing tracer, shells exploding, flares rising and falling, dramatic light, then shadows once more, smoke and fire. Verity urged his men on, but the fire in the trees and corn behind them was starting to silhouette them just as the HG men had been silhouetted the previous night when they'd attacked the bridge; the tables had been turned. Verity, desperately trying to take stock and think clearly, recognized that with their limited resources – a few light machine guns, grenades, submachine guns and rifles – the key immediate objective had to be a farmhouse he could see just to the left of the bulge in the dyke; so he ordered one platoon round towards the farmhouse and another to give covering fire. No sooner had he done so than he was hit in the chest by a piece of flying shrapnel. Still leading his men, he continued to shout, 'Keep going! Get them out of the farmhouse and me into it!'

A moment later, Verity's second-in-command, Lieutenant Laurie Hesmondhalgh, was hit and killed outright; beside the wounded Verity was his batman, Private Tom Rennoldson. The rest of the company was still struggling to make headway, and it was clear that unless they were quickly relieved by A and D Companies, they were going to be trapped. In fact, the other two companies were desperately trying to help their stranded colleagues, but were being pegged back by the same withering machine-gun and mortar fire that was decimating B Company.

By 4.30 a.m. it was all over, 15th Brigade's attack a failure. B Company, without their commander and second-in-command, began to fall back, as did A and D Companies, so that by the time dawn broke Verity, with Rennoldson still beside him, was stuck firmly behind enemy lines. As the sun began slowly to rise, smoke hung over the battlefield while the dead and wounded lay where they had fallen. Verity and Rennoldson were soon captured. The Germans brought a broken mortar carrier from the farm and, packing it with sheaves of corn, lifted Verity on to it and took him, with Rennoldson still in tow, to their field hospital a mile or so further back to the north. It was a farmhouse – nothing more.

That afternoon, Verity underwent an emergency operation in a stable at the farm. As he was lifted on to a table, a grenade fell from his shirt. After a moment of panic, Rennoldson was ordered to unprime it, which he did. He remained with Verity until that evening, when the major was taken away. It was the last time he saw him. As darkness began to fall again, the makeshift hospital came under British artillery fire. It had clearly already been hit – there were holes in the roof and the windows were glassless. As Verity was recovering from his operation, a German ambulance was hit and exploded, killing all on board. Two doctors worked ceaselessly on the wounded through the night.

News that he'd been wounded and was missing spread quickly. Lieutenant David Cole was not alone in feeling utterly shocked. Verity had been one of his schoolboy heroes; such losses, and those of men like Bob Alexander, had a profound effect on the men. Nor was morale improved by finding themselves up against the brick wall of the *Hauptkampflinie*, stuck in a mosquito- and fly-infested plain in broiling heat and with the enemy's eyes on their every move.

*

It has long been a widely accepted axiom that the first thing to fall by the wayside in any battle is the plan, which is one of the reasons why, before the invasion, General Alexander had not wanted to look too far beyond the broad-brush aims of the campaign. The landings had gone far better than anyone had hoped, and it was also quickly clear that the German forces on Sicily were understrength, undercooked and in the wrong places; so it was no wonder Montgomery had got his hopes up for a quick dash to Catania and beyond. However, once the Germans had rapidly reinforced the eastern side of the island with some of their better troops, Allied hopes of a rapid victory had become illusory. Had Eighth Army got past Primosole Bridge more quickly, events might have turned out differently; but that hadn't happened, and so plans had had to be adjusted. Montgomery has been repeatedly criticized for the predicament in which he now found himself; but still, collectively, the two Allied armies had driven the German forces on Sicily into the narrow north-east corner, while the Americans were now conquering vast swathes of the western part of the island – and all this in just ten days. By anyone's reckoning that was good going. On the other hand, the German forces opposing Eighth Army were now reasonably well equipped, pulled together, well led, in superb defensive country – and about to be reinforced with the rest of 1. Fallschirmjäger and 29. Panzer Grenadier Divisions. That made them a very tough nut to crack.

His detractors have also accused Montgomery of faulty tactics, of overcommitting his forces and of generally being too hubristic in his approach. All too often, however, historians have conflated their personal dislike of his less appealing character traits with his abilities as a general, when the two things do not necessarily go hand-in-hand; Montgomery certainly wasn't the only general in the war to seem a little too pleased with himself on occasion.

The real problem lay in trying to fight a large-scale modern, mechanized and technologically advanced war in the narrow confines of an island of many hills and mountains and not many roads or much other modern infrastructure. Of course, it would have been wonderful to charge into the Catania Plain with two divisions at once, side-by-side, with two more following immediately behind, as has been suggested by some historians, but there simply wasn't the space; there was a limit, and quite a severe one, to how much infantry, armour and artillery could pass down any one road. Infantry battalions, mostly made up of conscripts, who had walked a large part of the many miles it took simply to get to the Catania Plain, could not be expected to attack day after day, night after night, without respite; and nor could they be expected to take the kind of casualties a German or Soviet infantry battalion might be willing to expend. Allied commanders were better men, too, for understanding that; as it was, Primosole Bridge and the fighting so far in the plain had proved as brutal and bloody and difficult as anything Eighth Army had yet faced in the war. A very delicate balance had to be struck in pushing forward as aggressively as possible in order to win as quickly as possible – but not at too great a price. 'Always at the back of my mind when I make plans,' General Alexander said some years later, 'is the thought that I am playing with human lives. Good chaps get killed and wounded and it is a terrible thing.'

The failure to capture Catania quickly did force Alexander to think again about how the final phase of the campaign might develop, however. He was increasingly worried that the narrow north-east triangle of Sicily now occupied by the Germans could turn into the modern-day Lines of Torres Vedras built by General Wellington nearly 140 years earlier, which had effectively protected Lisbon indefinitely. He shared these concerns with Eisenhower. 'Neither Alexander nor I,' Ike wrote to the Allied Combined Chiefs of Staff on 18 July, 'contemplate any prolonged resistance in the west of Sicily but owing to the very difficult nature of the country in the northeast of the island and particularly in the Mount Etna region, we should not overlook the possibility of some delay in capturing Messina – possibly until mid-August.' It was an entirely reasonable appreciation.

On 19 July, Alexander signalled Montgomery suggesting the new German front might be hard for Eighth Army alone to pierce. He was now confident Patton's forces would swiftly fold up the rest of the island and with it the port of Palermo. 'And if the Germans are then too strong for you,' he wrote, 'Seventh Army can take over a sector in the north from S. Stefano to Troina.' Santo Stefano lay on the coast north of Enna, Troina about 20 miles to the south-east.

Montgomery had swiftly signalled back that he had four strong thrusts all attacking at the same time, but agreed some American help might be a good idea. The next day, as Hedley Verity was undergoing a rudimentary operation in a German field hospital and Don Calò Vizzini was clambering aboard a Sherman tank, Alexander was in Sicily, visiting Montgomery's tactical HQ. In the shaded grove where Monty's caravans had been set up, Alexander again pressed his desire to use the Americans in the northern drive towards Messina, and Montgomery agreed it was a sound decision. 'Intention,' Alex signalled to Brooke that night, 'is to base Seventh Army on Palermo so as they can operate against the Germans north of Eighth Army in the final thrust for Messina.'

The final phase of the Sicilian campaign was about to begin.

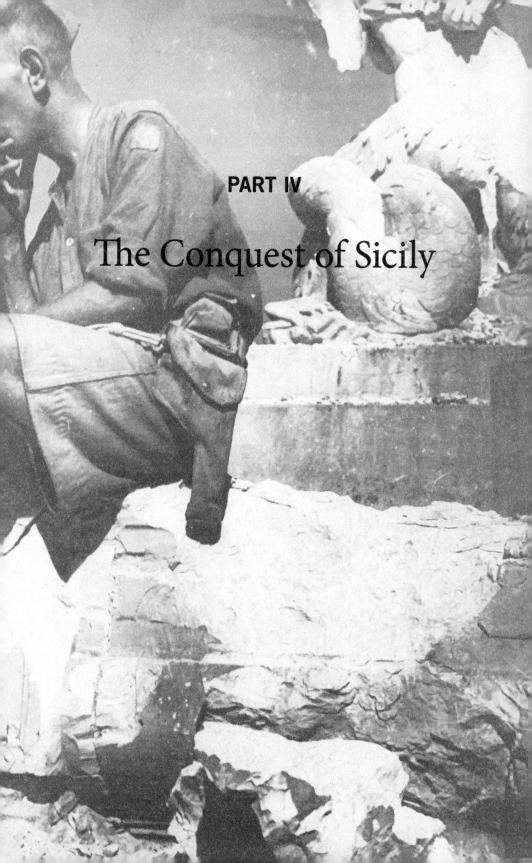

PART IV

The Conquest of Sicily

CHAPTER 24

Assoro

T HE XIV PANZER KORPS command post stood within a sheltered almond grove near the town of Linguaglossa on the north-east edge of Etna. It was very much the modern way of war to eschew the more ostentatious trappings of high command, but General Hube and his staff were hardly slumming it, despite the tented and caravan accommodation. Here was one of the loveliest spots in all of Sicily, Etna towering above them, mountains lush with vineyards and groves stretching over the folds all around and beneath them, and breathtaking views across north-east Sicily and the Straits of Messina to Reggio di Calabria and the toe of Italy's boot. Sheltered, and almost impossible to see from the air, it was a corps field headquarters that had been chosen well.

Among the staff as chief medical officer was Oberstarzt – Colonel Doctor – Wilhelm Mauss, forty-four years old, bespectacled, and a man who had seen front-line action as both a soldier and a doctor, serving in Berlin and then on the Eastern Front, where he'd even won an Iron Cross. Arriving in Italy in June, he had joined Hube's headquarters at Cassino, 60 miles south-east of Rome, and so had been well placed to hear what was happening in Sicily. 'All in all,' he'd noted in his diary on 13 July, 'a rather gloomy picture.' At dinner he had discussed with Hube and his staff whether XIV Panzer Korps should even be sent to Sicily if the island was already effectively lost. Hube had pointed out that the decision was not theirs, but the Führer's, whom he talked about 'in warm tones of praise'. The discussion had rapidly expanded to consider the nature and meaning of the whole war, and had continued deep into the night. 'In the end,' noted Mauss, 'we concluded with the statement that it was not so much a discussion of worldviews that stood in the foreground, but the simple stark necessity of creating more living space. Only a German people who renounce any future could live on forever in the shackles of the past. In order to guarantee the lives of many millions in the future, several millions must now sacrifice themselves. May the future Germany always be mindful of this.'

Packing up and setting off towards Sicily the following day, Mauss had been reminded of the start of the campaign in the west in May 1940 and then of the attack on the Soviet Union back in June 1941; peaceful days before, then suddenly a big stride forward into the unknown. As he set off, he couldn't help thinking about his family back in Germany – his wife and three sons. They would accompany him in spirit. Travelling south by train, his journey was a long one, and it wasn't until late on the 17th that he finally reached the command post near Linguaglossa. En route, he'd passed smashed-up airfields in the toe of the mainland, and found Messina almost completely destroyed – the city had been hit heavily yet again on the 14th, this time by 179 bombers. On he'd driven, down the coast road before climbing up into the hills around Etna and stopping at the Luftwaffe Medical Park Catania, in Linguaglossa itself. It was in a pitiful state; the man in charge was clearly not up to the job, and they did not have enough supplies of essential drugs. Medical supplies were a constant problem for Germany by this stage of the war as they struggled to maintain supply lines that were being constantly pounded by Allied air forces. The HG Panzer Division's field hospital thankfully appeared to be in better order, but by the time he finally reached the Korps CP, he had a pretty clear picture of just how precarious the situation really was. 'Nowhere is one safe from English aircraft that fly both high and low,' he noted. 'They have almost completely destroyed Randazzo. Many camps, also well camouflaged, seem to be betrayed to them and then offer a welcome destination for their planes. None of the natives can be trusted here.'

Allied air power was certainly continuing to menace Axis efforts on the ground right across the island. Bombers were now targeting the main Axis communication centres – Randazzo, Messina, Palermo and Catania had been particularly hard hit – while fighters were split between escort duties and ranging across the island shooting up any enemy movement they saw. By 17 July, there were sixteen Allied fighter squadrons operating from Sicily, although Flying Officer Hap Kennedy was not in any of them – yet. He reckoned he'd been flying from base in

Malta at least twice a day and now, having been on ops for six months, on 21 July he became tour expired, which meant leaving 249 Squadron. He wasn't happy about it. 'I didn't feel the need of a rest at all,' he noted. 'I just wasn't keen on the idea of going back to England to instruct.' He'd learned a huge amount while based on Malta, and felt in the prime of his combat flying life. Confident, competent and still enthusiastic for the excitement of daily flying, he decided not to sit back and accept his lot, but instead borrowed his old Spit and flew over to Comiso, formerly an Me109 base but now home to 324 Wing. Landing and taxiing, he clambered out and asked to see Group Captain Sheep Gilroy.

He was pointed in Gilroy's direction and found him standing in the sun outside his tent.

'What can I do for you?' Gilroy asked him. An ace four times over, Gilroy was much revered among pilots – and still only twenty-nine.

'I've completed a tour in Malta, sir,' Kennedy told him, 'and now I've been posted back to the UK. I was wondering if you had any use for a good pilot?'

Gilroy was rather taken by Kennedy's spirit and immediately offered him a place in either 72 or 111 Squadron. Since he'd known George Hill, the treble-one commander, Hap opted for the latter. So it was agreed, just like that, and Kennedy flew back to Malta to get his belongings. 'I was very happy,' he wrote. 'We had a job to do. Living in a tent would be just fine. This was the place to be right now.'

Smoky Vrilakas, meanwhile, was soon back in action too, although he didn't fly his second combat sortie until 20 July, five days after his first. American fighter squadrons had an abundance of pilots, in recognition that combat flying could be a mentally as well as physically exhausting exercise. This meant pilots had proper rest between combat sorties, but also the time to practise and hone their skills. At Mateur, life was pretty good. There were trips into Bizerte to visit the bars, there were games of cards and volleyball, and, of course, there was flying. Vrilakas was also learning that missions were not confined to operations over Sicily as the Allied air forces began to cast their net increasingly further afield in the effort to grind down enemy lines of supply. Thus it was that on 20 July he found himself on a fighter sweep to Naples.

The heavy bombers were also pushing further afield as air power was being harnessed not only for its destructive power but for its psychological impact too. The Italians, it was believed, were wilting, and heavy bombing might be just the extra push they needed to get them out of the war; and so on three nights RAF Bomber Command sent Lancasters from England to hit industrial targets in northern Italy. Then, on 19 July, the decision was made to bomb the railway marshalling yards at Rome; it was not just all roads that led to Rome but all rail routes too, and the railway yards there were a vital network hub. The raid was to be a big effort by Spaatz's Mediterranean Allied Strategic Air Force, with some 149 Fortresses on the mission, a number of medium bombers hitting the airfield at Ciampino and a further 125 B-24 Liberators targeting the Littorio marshalling yards nearby. Including the escorting P-38s, more than five hundred aircraft were involved, making it the largest daylight bombing raid yet mounted in the war. It was quite deliberately a show of immense strength over the Italian capital, and designed for its psychological impact as much for its destructive power.

The prospect caused a fair bit of nervousness among the aircrews involved. At their base at Navarin, near the north-east coast of Algeria, Lieutenant Jimmy Bruno and his fellow officers of the 99th Bomb Group were listening to the briefing especially carefully, aware there was very little margin for error in an attack on the capital city of Italy, with its densely populated streets, ancient monuments and, of course, the Vatican. Hitting the Holy City didn't bear thinking about. 'The moral and political repercussions,' wrote Bruno, 'would be on our shoulders. It was a sobering responsibility to all of us.'

Fortunately, they pulled it off – and Bruno, for one, felt mightily relieved his crew had dropped their bombs within the target zone. Certainly, no bombs threatened the Vatican or the Colosseum, although the Basilica of San Lorenzo was badly damaged. Huge damage was caused to rolling stock, and bombs hit the tracks no fewer than forty-five times. Ciampino and Littorio were also severely damaged, as were the Fiat and Bianchi works in the San Lorenzo district. Some seven hundred people were killed and sixteen hundred wounded – while in response, the Axis air forces shot down just two aircraft.

Over Sicily, meanwhile, Allied fighters and bombers continued to roam freely and now with almost total impunity; they were especially effective in the west, responding to clouds of dust and shooting up Italian columns whenever they tried to move. On the ground, the Provisional Corps continued to surge west, opposition melting away. The 505th had now taken the lead in 82nd Airborne's advance, and had been moved inland to cut across towards Trapani. 'It was a strange affair,' noted Lieutenant-Colonel Jim Gavin. 'It did seem like a road march, but suddenly a machine-gun or

anti-tank weapon would open up, and then the white flags would appear.'
On the 21st, X Force entered the drive west, still led by Colonel Darby, who had been offered the command of a regiment in the 45th Division by Bradley but had preferred to stay with his Rangers. That day they took the town and airfield of Castelvetrano, then pressed on to Mazara del Vallo. For Al Altieri in the 4th Ranger Battalion, the surge west hurtled by in something of a blur, as they thundered past shell-pocked fields, through blackened and still-burning Italian guns and knocked-out tanks. He noticed that now the Sicilians were suddenly cheering them whenever they entered a town. 'For the most part,' he noted, 'our main job was rounding up prisoners and herding them in barbed wire enclosures.'

On Thursday, 22 July, the 505th were climbing up towards the summit of Monte Erice, overlooking Trapani and the western coastline of Sicily. On the far side, beneath the sheer rock face, was the old Luftwaffe operations room, but it was on the strange, flat-topped summit that the village of Erice had been built – and also an impressive Norman castle. There were some Italian guns firing from the bastions, rather as their medieval predecessors would have done, and as Mark Alexander's 2nd Battalion climbed up towards the summit one trooper was killed and another wounded. Alexander reckoned quick and decisive action could silence the guns in short order and was just briefing Captain Neal L. McRoberts, the F Company commander, when an Italian shell landed between them. Looking down, they saw a hole in the ground – but there had been no blast.

'That must have been a dud,' said Alexander.

'Yeah, I think it was,' replied McRoberts, the colour drained from his face.

Realizing that the closer his men got to the castle walls, the harder it would be for the Italians to lower the barrels of their guns enough to hit them, Alexander's plan was to get as near as they could without being seen and then charge; but Gavin, who now joined them, felt it would be better to bring up some of their own fire support and mount a larger-scale attack. This, though, would take time and hold them up. 'Sir,' said McRoberts to Gavin, 'if we don't go now, we could lose a lot of men.'

Gavin relented, F Company went in as planned, and before they'd even reached the castle the white flag went up. Alexander was seething. 'It was frustrating,' he admitted, 'because they killed one of our men and we were not given a chance to retaliate.'

*

'So far,' noted Lieutenant Frank Johnson, 'this campaign has been more pursuit than battle, almost pleasant compared with Tunisia.' It was true the 18th Infantry had had a comparatively easy time of it since the battles around Gela – they'd not even had to take Enna, which had been the task of the 16th. He knew, though, that it couldn't possibly last. They were due to join the drive north to the coast, and then, under Alexander's latest directive, they would be turning east, part of the northern drive towards Messina.

This was exactly what General Bradley had hoped for a few days earlier, having identified the same possible axes of advance for Seventh Army as Alexander had done. The worry for Bradley now, however, was the delay caused by the diversion to capture Enna, a fight and an objective that had been thrust upon him by the Canadian side-step through Valguarnera. 'Originally, our time table called for us to reach the sea by today,' noted his aide Captain Chet Hansen, 'but this was disrupted by the Enna incident and by the reappearance of German units before the advance of 1st Division.' It had been a nuisance, although Enna's capture had brought with it some prestige; after all, it was an ancient capital, standing at the very heart of the island, and had been the headquarters of Axis forces on Sicily.

Even so, Bradley had sent a terse note to Leese, the commander of XXX Corps, about unexpectedly throwing him this extra task, and stiffly asking whether he minded if the Americans now used the road to Enna after all. 'Leese replied so promptly and apologetically,' noted Bradley, 'that I regretted my brusque note.' Of course Bradley must use those roads, Leese insisted, and confessed it was an error of staff work and that no slight was intended at all. Accompanying the message were two bottles of Scotch. Now, on 21 July, Leese visited him at II Corps' grand new HQ in Caltanissetta, where, to show there were absolutely no hard feelings, Bradley had tea served up using a china tea-set embossed with the crest of the House of Savoy, an occasion which, it seems, was enjoyed by all.

While Seventh Army was busy clearing the western half of the island, Eighth Army was continuing to hammer at the *Hauptkampflinie*. The line now extended along the northern edge of the Catania Plain just south of the city itself, curving slightly north-west towards Gerbini and Sferro and then climbing out of the western edge of the plain, after which it was anchored by a series of mountaintop towns. With the fall of Enna, the westernmost of these were Leonforte and Assoro; now, though, the 15. Panzer Grenadier Division were starting to extend their position northwards towards Nicosia, ten miles north of Leonforte, and southwards from just west of the coastal town of Santo Stefano, as the remains of the Assietta and Aosta divisions staggered through and the newly arriving 29. Panzer Grenadier Division began moving in, to create a single, curving defensive line that neatly isolated the entire north-eastern peninsula of the island.

The defensive line wasn't a single entity; rather, the Germans were making good use of the terrain. Their positions on the lower slopes of Etna gave them eyes on anything that moved in the plain, while inland, the hilltop towns provided what they had always provided – amazing views, not least of anyone approaching. The mountainous interior of Sicily was not rich in dense vegetation; rather, between the hills and craggy outcrops were sweeping open valleys. Even out of view an advancing enemy could be seen from the swirls of dust caused by an army on the march. This was why the towns had been built on these mountains in the first place, and why so many of them were topped off with castles; over the centuries, arrows and spears had been replaced by cannons, and now by powerful modern artillery and high-velocity anti-tank guns, but the principle remained the same. Connecting these settlements and strongpoints was a fragile network of dusty roads and bridges. The latter could be blown up, the former easily blocked and laced with mines. Anyone advancing would have to pick their way round these blown bridges, or through these minefields; and as they did, Germans on the hills above could look down and direct mortar and artillery fire on to them. It didn't require a huge number of guns, or mortars, or machine guns to hold up quite a major Eighth Army attack. In Sicily, anyone attacking a half-determined and organized enemy well dug in on the high ground was going to have a very big headache indeed. It was as simple as that.

Since Leonforte and Assoro were at the westernmost part of the *Hauptkampflinie*, and the Canadians were on the left flank of Eighth Army, it was their task to clear these hilltop towns and begin the process of crumbling the German defences. Both were in the hands of Oberst Karl Ens's 104. Panzer Grenadier Regiment, already becoming a rather too familiar foe. Since Leonforte and Assoro were so close together, and separated by a narrow, plunging valley, Ens had split his forces. On Assoro were about a hundred men, a handful of Panzer Mk IIIs and his artillery observers, while on and around Leonforte and the ridge to the north of both were most of his artillery, the 33. Artillerie Regiment and 315. Army Flak Bataillon – about fifty guns in all, which was quite a lot.

While the 2nd Canadian Brigade were to attack Leonforte, the assault on Assoro fell to the 1st Brigade – and, specifically, the Hasty Ps. On 19 July, the battalion was resting up after their battle and exertions at Valguarnera, and that afternoon Major Campbell sent Farley Mowat up to battalion HQ with the casualty list. There, under a large canvas canopy extending from the side of a truck, Mowat met with Lieutenant Battle Cockin, who was busily marking up known enemy dispositions on a map. Valguarnera, he explained, had been the opening phase of a battle to break the German line – what Monty was referring to as a 'left hook'. 'We must swing eastwards now, you see,' Cockin told him. 'But first we have to crack the hinge of Jerry's defence line on the other side of the Dittaino. Here.' Cockin was pointing to Assoro. It was, Cockin told him cheerfully, a very tough nut to crack. The castle, built by Roger II of Normandy in the eleventh century, was thought to have been impregnable back in the day. 'Shouldn't wonder, eh?' Cockin chuckled. 'Need a goat with wings to scale that bloody thing.'

Overnight, the Loyal Edmonton Regiment managed to secure a foothold over on the northern side of the Dittaino, which allowed the rest of the brigade to move up and, for the first time, see the mighty crag they were to assault. In fact, Assoro had been a strongpoint long before Roger II had ever laid eyes on the place, and had been defended by Greeks, Romans, Byzantines and Arabs before the Normans showed up on Sicily. According to Cockin and the learned second-in-command, Major Lord John Tweedsmuir, it had never once been successfully assaulted.

Since they did not possess a winged goat, Cockin and the Hasty Ps' CO, Lieutenant-Colonel Sutcliffe, moved up around mid-morning on the 20th to have a look at how they might possibly crack this seemingly impregnable spot, perched some 2,000 feet above them with only a single, winding road of hairpins leading up to it. Peering through their binoculars, they made the fatal error of doing so with the sun still ahead of them. With the glass glinting, moments later there was a rapid whoosh as an 88mm shell hit the ground lethally close. Sutcliffe was killed outright and Cockin mortally wounded, which left Lord Tweedsmuir as the new commander of the Hasty Ps.

Tweedsmuir was the son of the adventure writer John Buchan, who in 1935 had been ennobled on his appointment as Governor-General of Canada. On Buchan's death in 1940 his son, also John, had become second Baron Tweedsmuir. Brought up in Scotland and educated in England, Tweedsmuir was tall, fair-haired and softly spoken, but a young man who had done his best to live up to the reputation of his father's literary hero, Richard Hannay. A keen fly fisherman, expert stalker and devoted outdoorsman, he had kept a kestrel at Oxford, and later headed overseas to work in the Colonial Service in Africa. After getting amoebic dysentery and hearing the locals start to make his coffin, on recovering he had decided he was finished with Africa and headed to Canada to join his family, joining the Hudson Bay Company. Over the winter of 1938–9, Tweedsmuir had then driven a dog-sled some 3,000 miles to the remote Cape Dorset in Baffinland. On the outbreak of war, he had immediately volunteered and had been among the very first Canadian troops to reach Britain.

He had only joined the Hasty Ps at the last minute in June 1943, however, when the previous second-in-command had got injured in a motor accident. He had spent much of the journey out desperately trying to learn everyone's names, although sharing a cabin with Sutcliffe had led to the two men forging an immediate and close friendship. Now, though, that friend was dead and Tweedsmuir – 'Tweedie' to the men – had unexpectedly had command thrust upon him, and with it the mission to attack an historically impregnable fortress.

Battle Cockin had still been alive when they brought him back, and although in terrible pain insisted on speaking to Tweedsmuir, who hurried over. Cockin grabbed his wrist and said, 'John, for God's sake, don't go up that road.' Tweedsmuir was equally convinced such an approach would be suicidal and, after a recce of his own with his new second-in-command, Major Bert 'Ack Ack' Kennedy, reckoned there was a possible alternative route. To the east of the small town was a trackless gully that, below the town, plunged out of view of anyone up above. It started away to the right of the road leading up to Assoro, and then looped round to a precipitous and rocky cliff that could, if climbed, take them directly to the summit of Assoro and to the castle ruins – which, in their commanding position on the highest point, stood sentinel over the town and the country all around. It was not entirely clear whether the climb would be too steep or too difficult to tackle both in silence and at night; but Tweedsmuir reckoned it was their best chance.

Having been given reluctant permission to make the attempt by Brigadier Howard Graham, that evening Tweedsmuir called his officers together for an 'O' group – orders group – in an old cowshed and outlined his plan. He wanted the whole battalion to move up to the base of the cliff, at which point a special assault company of just twenty men and an officer from each of the rifle companies would tackle the climb first. Alex Campbell was to lead this group; these men were to carry nothing but weapons and ammunition, and must get rid of anything that might unnecessarily make a noise. If they could secure the summit, then the rest were to follow. Once the brief was over, Tweedsmuir felt as though he and his men were part of a great modern crusade. 'And gentlemen in England now abed,' he said to them, citing Shakespeare's *Henry V*, 'Shall think themselves accursed they were not here, And hold their manhoods cheap whiles any speaks that fought with us.' Looking around, he felt they all straightened their backs a little at this.

Afterwards, Alex Campbell returned to his own men and told Farley Mowat he was picking him for the assault company. Mowat had absolutely no idea why he'd been chosen but was pleased as punch, so much so that one of his fellow officers reckoned he was as swollen-headed 'as a frog full of fart'. At dusk the battalion moved out, the assault company having shed their kit bags and haversacks. Mowat thought that as warriors they didn't look particularly intimidating; after eleven days on the march they were all dirty, dusty and threadbare, their boots cracked and coming apart at the seams.

Bren carriers took them as far as possible, but that wasn't very far – across the Dittaino and a few hundred yards further on until they reached the steep-sided gully that led all the way up to the eastern side of the town. Out they jumped and continued on foot. It was now around 9 p.m.; they had a lot to do, and not very much time in which to do it. There was the scent of sage on the air and not a breath of wind as they marched along the gully, keeping as quiet as they could. 'We were tensely fearful of discovery,' noted Mowat. 'It seemed inconceivable that the Germans would not at least have listening posts in this exposed flank, no matter how secure they felt.'

It took an age to reach the foot of the cliff. At one point, they all halted at the sound of stones being disturbed and then the click of cocking bolts on a weapon; but it was just a Sicilian youth with his goats, and he passed them without uttering a word. Mowat found the hike through the ravine absolutely exhausting, made worse by a stick that had worked its way through the cracked sole of his boot. Wishing he had a Benzedrine tablet to hand, by 4 a.m. he felt almost beaten, but at that point they had only reached the base of the 1,000-foot cliff that would take them to the summit. This was the moment of truth: before they had set off, Tweeds-muir had had no real idea whether the cliff would prove possible for five hundred men to climb. Pausing there at the cliff's foot, gazing up the forbidding dark mass rising above them, he remembered an old stalker's trick taught him by his uncle of gauging the angle of a slope by holding his walking stick against it then holding it up without tilting his arm. Not having a walking stick, Tweedsmuir now used a rifle. 'I felt that all eyes were on my face at this moment of decision,' he recalled. Relieved to find the slope not so severe as first he'd feared, 'I handed back the rifle. I said, "We're on!" And away we went.'

It was certainly too late now to beat a hasty retreat; no matter how exhausted they were, there was no alternative to hauling themselves up, ledge by ledge, rock by rock. Mowat thought he would collapse, but with mutual cajoling and helping hands when needed, finally, 100 feet from the summit, they reached a set of stone terraces. After clambering up several, Mowat reckoned he was just about finished. Then Private Archie 'A. K.' Long from his platoon heaved himself over the next ledge, caught Mowat's hand and pulled him up. Dawn was now spreading, its faint yellow glow from the east creeping over the mountains and the pinnacle of Agira a few miles away. Long jumped up on to the last terrace then disappeared. A moment later came the bark of a Tommy gun shattering the dawn peace. Mowat had never been more scared in his life, but forced himself to climb over the lip of the last terrace – and there, ahead of him, were the crumbling wall of the castle, A. K. Long down on one knee pointing his Tommy gun, and three stupefied Germans standing beside a tripod-mounted telescope, a fourth man dead at their feet.

'The crazy bastard,' said Long, 'went for his damn gun.'

At the same time, Tweedsmuir, who had been leading the rest of the battalion to the right of the assault company, had heard the shots, but had none the less felt compelled briefly to admire one of the most spectacular views in all of Sicily. He could see Etna, a coral-pink cloud above its volcanic summit, while away to the south-west was Enna. As he'd paused, it had occurred to him that King Roger must have gazed on the very same scene all those centuries earlier. 'Then,' he wrote, 'all question of historical soliloquy terminated.'

There was a small plateau around 200 yards long and 30 wide right at the foot of the castle walls and now Tommy-helmeted men were all clambering up on to it. While one of the assault platoons hurried to clear the castle, Mowat led his men towards the shelter of a low stone wall, expecting firing to break out any moment. But there was no reaction at all. Clearly, believing Assoro to be impregnable from the eastern cliffs, the Germans had posted no one at the top apart from the artillery observation team – now dead or captured. If anyone else had heard the Tommy gun, they'd not thought anything of it.

Inching forward, Mowat and his men were able to reach the southern edge of the plateau and look down on the terracotta roofs of the town, thin curls of smoke rising from some of the chimneys. Beyond, along a narrow road that snaked its way up into the town, clusters of Germans were emerging from the night, some stripped to the waist, stretching, another shaving, while anti-aircraft gunners prepared their breakfast. A motorbike puttered past, seemingly without a care in the world. A convoy of trucks was now working its way up to the town, rumbling in low gear.

'Shit a brick!' muttered Sergeant Bates. 'Will you look at that! Let's clobber the sons of bitches quick!'

Before Mowat could say another word, a Bren gunner in a different platoon opened fire; then suddenly there were a dozen of them spraying bullets on to the ambushed enemy below. Trucks were hit, several bursting into flames. The light flak gunners quickly traversed their 20mm barrels and began to shoot, while Mowat spotted a couple of cooks leaving their field kitchen and picking up rifles. Further to the south, more trucks began moving off, the men firing rifles and submachine guns as they did so and driving up to the rescue until halted by burning wreckage on the road. Three half-tracks then veered up the verges until they could climb no more, at which point men leaped out and began setting up their 81mm mortars. That was ominous enough; but then artillery from behind and around Leonforte began to open up. Mowat had just moved his platoon further down the slope to a more protected position when suddenly the air was filled with an immense cacophony of sound as shells screeched over, smashing on to the slopes around them. The entire plateau, on which most of Tweedsmuir's five hundred men were crowded, disappeared in a pall of smoke and dust. Most of the shells were falling to the north of them, but Mowat felt almost paralysed save for the urge to frantically try to dig himself a hole with his tin hat. The noise, the smoke, the dust, the pounding of the ground were so intense he could barely take in what was happening; he was unware that several of his platoon had already been wounded and that two more, Sharon and Robinson, had been obliterated.

Help, however, was at hand, because someone now remembered the optics that had been captured earlier and, dodging the shell bursts, retrieved the crucial piece of kit and hurried over to the goat shed in the shelter of the north slope where Tweedsmuir and Major Kennedy had set up a command post. There they had set up a large, long-range No. 46 radio set, insisted upon by Tweedsmuir because at Valguarnera their back-pack radios had been so ineffective. At 24 pounds, the long-range set was too heavy for a man – or even several men – to carry, so they had fixed it to the back of a mule, which had miraculously made it to the summit before keeling over and dying of exhaustion. This animal sacrifice meant the battalion was now in contact with the artillery far away behind hills on the far side of the Dittaino valley; and, thanks to the German optics, Major Kennedy was able to start pinpointing enemy positions and directing the counter-battery fire.

No matter how formidable the enemy artillery, Allied fire-power was greater, and with Kennedy expertly directing fire the enemy gun positions began to be knocked out while others moved back to positions of better safety. Yet although the Hasty Ps were not now being shelled so heavily, they still had only what they'd carried up with them. The sun bore down relentlessly, water bottles soon ran dry, and with no well at the top of the town, the Canadians soon began to feel parched. Nor was it clear where the Germans now were. Alex Campbell sent Mowat on a recce down into the town. He took Long with him, and the pair of them crept through the narrow, winding and empty streets, dodging several bursts of small-arms fire, until Mowat saw an arm beckoning him from a doorway. It turned out to belong to a smiling Italian captain who had deliberately got himself and the best part of fifty men 'lost' in Assoro only for the Germans to move in. They'd been hunkering down in cellars ever since.

'We are finished with this war,' he told Mowat. 'It is the Germans' business, so let the Germans have it. Barbarians they are! Now we happily surrender to you Britishers who are our liberators.' Mowat pointed out they were actually Canadians and told them to stay where they were; fifty POWs up at the summit were hardly going to help. Mowat did learn from the Italian captain, however, that Germans had moved up into the town itself and were already in the houses at the bottom of the same street. 'They just came up,' the Italian told him. 'Many of them. Very well armed. Perhaps you should bring down a few more of your men?'

Hurrying back up to the plateau, Mowat reported his findings only to learn that Baker Company, attacking down a different set of streets, had just been pushed back, which meant they were now isolated on the summit and with no obvious chance of getting any more supplies of ammunition, food or water. A shallow well discovered near the castle offered only a small amount of fetid and muddy water. Now a Nebelwerfer barrage screamed down upon them. For Mowat, it was a terrible experience. 'Although I had experienced spasms of fear during the previous few days,' he recalled, 'what I now felt was undiluted terror.' Repeated salvoes crashed around the men as they did their best to flatten themselves against walls and in scrapes in the ground as blast waves swept over them. Fortunately, the assault did not last long, and by midafternoon a lull had descended on the battle.

Taking the chance to check on his men, Tweedsmuir found them all looking like ghosts, covered from head to toe in white rock dust. It seemed hard to tell the living from the dead until he realized the dead had flies crawling all over their skin, whereas the living did not. The sun continued to beat down oppressively. 'Our heads were swimming with heat and exhaustion,' he wrote. 'We lay and suffered in that heat. The rocks were too hot to touch, and so was the metal of our weapons. We had practically no water, and we hadn't eaten for more than 30 hours, or slept, other than occasional nodding and dozing.' Later, when he was back at his CP and beside the No. 46 set, a jagged piece of shrapnel suddenly hissed and landed between Tweedsmuir and the radio operator. Another close call.

Three men who might have been fighting with Oberst Ens's men but were not were Werner Stappenbeck and his two comrades, Gerhard Dybeck and Gerhard Preller. They were still where they had been on 10 July, out west in Salemi, waiting for transport to come and pick them up along with all the stores and supplies left under their command. As the days had passed, they had begun to get increasingly worried they had been abandoned entirely. The three had formed an uneasy alliance with the local Italians, who would pilfer a few things in return for food, although at times Stappenbeck had had to warn them off when too many appeared; he had kept his rifle with him at all times. 'Every day,' he jotted, 'I had twenty, thirty, even more visitors. They got on my nerves with their questions.' Snatches of news reached him from the locals, none of it good. There was a rumour the Americans had landed at Trapani and then that Castelvetrano had been taken. Then the locals began trying to steal weapons, something Stappenbeck could not countenance. Seeing two thieves, he aimed a single tracer round at a haystack as the two men passed and set it on fire; the two men scuttled off, and later, when some food was brought to him, they begged him not to set their homes on fire with his miracle weapon.

Then the Americans appeared. Before he could be spotted, Stappenbeck ran for his life to Dybeck and Preller, who had set themselves up in a different tent a little way away, only to find it had been abandoned. Hearing them call to him, he joined them in some nearby bushes where they were hiding. Plans were quickly discussed; none of them wanted to be taken prisoner. 'We remained loyal to the Wehrmacht,' insisted Stappenbeck, 'but we had to find our way to them. But that meant facing danger and considerable privations and we had no idea where our units stood.' The two Thuringians had discovered a cave-like crevice in the rock of a craggy hill that rose up behind them. By swinging from the branches of the tree covering its entrance, it was possible to get inside. This, they agreed, should be their new hideout. With a bit of luck they could wait there a few days, by which time their injured feet – which had been afflicting them since before they got to Sicily – would be properly healed at long last. Then they could finally set out for their own lines.

Meanwhile, only a couple of miles away from Assoro, the Canadian 2nd Brigade was preparing to attack Leonforte, a larger town occupied by more of Oberst Ens's regiment. The attack had been due to jump off at 4 p.m. on the afternoon of 21 July with an assault by the Seaforth Highlanders, but as they were holding their 'O' group in their farmyard CP, they were shelled and thirty officers and men were wounded or killed. While the Highlanders desperately tried to reorganize themselves, Brigadier Chris Vokes ordered the Loyal Edmontons to attack instead, behind an artillery barrage under cover of darkness a few hours later, at 9.30 p.m. Once they reached the town, however, they were on their own, their isolation made worse by the Germans' smoke bombs. From down in the valley below, Leonforte disappeared behind a cloud of smoke; the fog of war had literally descended.

Up in the town, the Edmontons cleared much of the town in vicious street-fighting but then were heavily counter-attacked by panzer-grenadiers, tanks and assault guns. With no heavy weapons themselves, they fell back in disarray. Hearing the battle from south of the Dittaino river, but having lost all radio contact, Brigadier Vokes feared the worst and warned General Simonds that the Edmontons might well have been destroyed. In fact, the Edmontons' CO, Lieutenant-Colonel Jim Jefferson, was holed up in a cellar in the town, from where he offered a ten-year-old boy, Antonio Giuseppi, what was an eye-watering amount of money for a young Sicilian boy to get a message to the Canadian lines saying he and his men could hold on until anti-tank gun artillery and armour could be brought up. Managing to get his way through the German positions, the boy was taken to see Vokes and there handed over his message – which was received with immense relief.

That night the River Dittaino was crossed by the first ever Bailey bridge to be built under fire. Designed by a British civil servant, Donald Bailey, these bridges were ingenious because they could be transported in prefabricated sections that could be simply bolted together and pushed across a river or ditch without any need for lifting cranes. A column of infantry, Shermans and 6-pounder anti-tank guns was forced back by enemy fire at the first attempt, but by 9 a.m. on 22 July was across, after which it was soon able to get into the town and begin forcing the Germans back.

Back on Assoro, the Hasty Ps' situation had improved dramatically overnight. Two men had headed back down the eastern cliffs at dusk and reached battalion headquarters, where the Royal Canadian Regiment immediately offered to organize a resupply mission. Now the route was known and a better climb up the cliffs had been worked out, the journey was simpler and quicker than it had been the previous night, and D Company of the RCR had been able to deliver ammo and rations and return to battalion HQ by 6 a.m. Also overnight, the 48th Highlanders of Canada had scaled the heights and begun fighting the panzer-grenadiers and clearing the streets. The battle was now all but over and Ens's men were pulling out; but even so, the Hasty Ps on the summit had been greeted at their second dawn on Assoro with a further barrage of 'moaning minnies' as Nebelwerfer shells screamed down once more. When the smoke had cleared, the mangled remains of four more men were strewn across the rocks. 'It was a bitter way', noted Mowat, 'to learn that battles end but war goes on.'

The Canadians at Leonforte had captured the summit around 3.20 that same afternoon, Thursday, 22 July, and with that the panzer-grenadiers began pulling back out of the town towards Agira, 8 miles to the east as the crow flies. In all, the 2nd Brigade suffered 276 casualties for the capture of Leonforte and Assoro; incredibly, the Hasty Ps lost just eight men dead, though the number wounded was never recorded; following the battle, Farley Mowat was out of action for a couple of days with dysentery and a fever. The 104. Panzer Grenadier Regiment came off far worse, with losses of more than six hundred. A rumour was soon circulating that the Canadians in Leonforte had shot a number of German prisoners, apparently witnessed by forward artillery observers. 'News of this incident', wrote General Eberhard Rodt, the divisional commander, 'quickly spread through the division and served to raise defensive determination.' There is, however, no evidence at all of this actually having taken place.

Leonforte and Assoro had been significant victories for the Canadians, especially given that less than two weeks had passed since their first taste of combat. Yet this, and the other first battles at the *Hauptkampflinie*, had shown Eighth Army that there would be no rapid and dramatic smashing of the German lines. They would have to slog it out, one bloody mountain after another.

CHAPTER 25

Overthrow

T O THOSE IN ROME and those running Nazi Germany, the fight raging in Sicily was not just a battle; it was the inevitable end of an alliance. The OKW knew it and had already been planning for what might happen should Italy crumble; Hitler, on the other hand, although convinced of Italian treachery, refused to accept that Mussolini would fail him. Il Duce, meanwhile, increasingly ill, felt trapped by his inability to stem the rot yet terrified of the retribution that would inevitably follow if he was toppled and Italy collapsed. And for fear of the consequences, all parties were wary of making the first move.

On 13 July Mussolini had written to Hitler urging him – not for the first time – to conclude a peace with the Soviet Union and focus Germany's military effort on the south, and on saving Italy. Hitler – also not for the first time – ignored his appeal. There could be no peace on the Eastern Front; that was a life-and-death struggle that defined Nazism and Hitler's rule. Mussolini was desperately hoping that German military might and a reversal of Axis fortunes in the Mediterranean would save him from the terrible predicament in which he found himself; he was, though, clutching at straws.

For those trying to plot Italy's way out of its predicament, the Allied invasion of Sicily had clarified matters. If Mussolini was deposed, then perhaps time could be bought in which to put out clandestine peace feelers to the Americans and British. That way, German retribution might well be blunted by the clearly impressive military and industrial might of the western Allies. On 14 July Generale Ambrosio, still head of the Comando Supremo, had visited the King to ask him to agree to the arrest of Mussolini. A small cabal of plotters had formed around three men: Maresciallo Pietro Badoglio, former head of the Comando Supremo; Ivanoe Bonomi, the last pre-Fascist prime minister; and Duc Pietro d'Acquarone, minister of the Royal Household. Ambrosio had already broached the matter with King Vittorio Emanuele once, five days before the invasion; then the King had thought such a move both premature and dangerous, but now he agreed, although did not give a date for Mussolini's political decapitation.

The opportunity arose when three leading Fascists went to see Mussolini two days later, 16 July, to urge him to call the Grand Council. This body had been set up by Il Duce back in 1923 as a means of bringing the Fascist Party under state control. It had always been separate from, and higher in authority than, the Council of Ministers and the two houses of parliament, and its twenty to thirty members were all chosen by Mussolini. On paper it was the executive board of the Fascist state, with Il Duce as chairman. In reality, Mussolini rarely called it, and even when he did, its members had little say; Mussolini would listen to their views then make his own decisions. It was Giuseppe Bottai, a dedicated Fascist who had always been devoted to Mussolini, who now appealed to him to call the Grand Council – not, he said, to undermine Il Duce's power but so they might help share his immense responsibilities. Mussolini reluctantly agreed and then the next day, 17 July, signalled Hitler asking for an urgent meeting. 'I believe, Führer,' he wrote, 'that the time has come to examine closely together the situation, so as to reach conclusions conforming to the common interests of each country.'

It was arranged that the two should meet at a grand villa near Feltre, outside Venice on the morning of 19 July. The German contingent, including Feldmarschall Keitel and General Warlimont, flew to Berchtesgaden to meet Hitler on the 18th and then on to Treviso the following morning, landing at 9 a.m. There followed a further two hours by car, train and then car again before they arrived at the ornate villa that Mussolini described as 'a crossword puzzle frozen into a house'. Once there, the two parties assembled in the summerhouse – and then Hitler began talking. The only moment he paused for breath was when a phone was brought to Mussolini with the news Rome was being bombed by the Allied air forces. 'Hitler took no notice of this news,' noted Warlimont, 'and after a pause of only a second or two his flow of words continued.' The nub of this long, rambling discourse was the Führer's plan to send more German units to Sicily, which would ultimately enable the Axis to take the offensive once more. And then they broke for lunch.

Mussolini ate with Hitler alone, but before he did was collared by Ambrosio, who warned him that unless he told the Führer Italy must sue for peace with the Allies, he would call on the Italian armed forces to lay down their weapons in fifteen days' time. Mussolini turned on him. Did Ambrosio think he was not aware of this terrible problem? 'It's easy to say it,' he told him, 'disengage from Germany. What reaction would Hitler have? Do you believe perhaps that he would permit us freedom of action?' During their lunch, Hitler talked of new secret weapons that would turn the tide and of a renewed U-boat offensive, trying to stiffen Mussolini's resolve. There seems to have been no mention on the latter's part of any break in the alliance. Instead, when Mussolini could get a word in edgeways, he returned to an old theme – a German peace with the Soviet Union.

Lunch over, the summit broke up. Warlimont had hoped Hitler would stress a theme that both he and Jodl had tried to impress upon him and, in turn, Mussolini and the Italians: that of unity of command. That would allow them to send Rommel into Italy now with more divisions and, in a nutshell, start running the military show in the Mediterranean entirely. But Hitler didn't mention this to Mussolini, nor did Keitel to Ambrosio. Rather, the Führer felt he'd achieved what he'd set out to do, which was to bring his old Fascist friend and ally back on track. He'd done nothing of the sort. As for Mussolini, he had been the only person in Italy who had even the remotest chance of persuading Hitler to agree to a separate Italian peace, and he'd failed even to mention it – not least because he'd known the Führer would never in a million years agree. But Mussolini's failure went further: he had lost his own last chance of survival. In Rome, the vultures were circling.

While the Canadians had been battling Kampfgruppe Ens at Leonforte and Assoro, the Big Red One had been driving northwards towards Petralia. The German *Hauptkampflinie* had now developed from a long line running roughly east–west into an almost continuous curve reaching northwards towards the coast. Holding this north-western stretch was another battlegroup of the 15. Panzer Grenadier Division, centred on Oberstleutnant Fritz Fullriede's 129. Panzer Grenadier Regiment. Like Karl Ens, Fullriede was a vastly experienced battlefield commander who had seen action pretty much everywhere the Wehrmacht had been fighting; he'd been in Poland, France, on the Eastern Front, in North Africa. He'd fought in the snow and in the desert, had been awarded the Iron Cross first and second class and won a Knight's Cross to boot. Full-riede was a tough, uncompromising, tactically astute and determined commander of a totally different calibre from any of the Italians Keyes' Provisional Corps had come up against.

For his part, General Terry Allen had assembled a pretty strong battle-group of his own around the 26th Infantry, with the Shermans of the 753rd Tank Battalion as well as the Stuarts of the 70th, the 1st Engineer Battalion, the 26th's Cannon Company and forward observers of the 33rd Field Artillery Battalion. All told, this task force had quite a lot of fire-power with which to bludgeon its way through.

To the south of Petralia lay the towns of Alimena and Bompietro. At Alimena Allen's force ran into the Italian Gruppo Schreiber, which was on its last legs and in no mood to fight, but as they neared Bompietro the advancing Americans, led by the 70th Tank Battalion, were pulled up by a blown bridge, and as they ground to a halt waiting Nebelwerfers and anti-tank guns beyond opened fire. Among the first to be hit was Sergeant Carl Rambo's tank, a Nebelwerfer round blowing off the periscope. With the driver unable to see, the tank slewed off the road, one track becoming caught on a pipeline that ran in a ditch alongside. The blast had also perforated the fuel tank, and so Rambo ordered his men to get out, and quickly. Just as they jumped clear, a line of fuel caught fire and ran up to the gasoline tank and the whole thing blew up. 'We were all out and got away,' said Rambo, 'but the screaming meemies kept coming in.'

Not until the following day was the bridge repaired so that the Americans could get going again; in this close, mountainous country the roads really were the only artery of advance, especially for an armoured battlegroup. That same day, Lieutenant Frank Johnson's Cannon Company platoon in the 18th Infantry, waiting behind to pass through the 26th, also came under its first Nebelwerfer attack – and before they'd had a chance to dig in. Frank Johnson had never experienced anything like it. 'Helpless without holes,' he wrote, 'our bodies try to melt into the soil like worms, as shrapnel, splinters of truck chassis and limbs of human beings fly crazily through the air.' Ammunition began to explode, while the dust and smoke temporarily blinded the men and the noise deafened them. In the lull that followed, Johnson quickly ordered his platoon to get into their vehicles and get moving; but in just that first salvo, three of his anti-tank gunners were killed, two men stupefied with shell-shock and two others wounded. The remaining three trucks sped out through the burning wreckage, along with Johnson on his Moto Guzzi. A short distance on, however, he turned a sharp bend too fast, lost control and crashed. Fortunately, he and his passengers were unhurt, but it was the end of the road for the trike. All in all, 22 July was not a good day for Johnson and his platoon.

Later, however, having brought the full weight of American fire-power to bear, the 26th Infantry's task force pushed forward again as outposts of Kampfgruppe Fullreide pulled back. At 7 p.m. on 22 July Bompietro was finally taken; that night, Johnson and the rest of the 18th Infantry passed through and by 9.00 the following morning they had taken Petralia.

Meanwhile, away to the west, the Provisional Corps' forces had closed in on Palermo, the 2nd Armored homing in from the south-west and the 3rd Division from the south-east, with the 180th Infantry Regiment of the Thunderbirds not far behind until diverted east for Seventh Army's drive towards Messina. By the afternoon of 22 July, both divisions were massed on the hills overlooking the island's capital and braced, finally, for a fight. How big a part had been played by Don Calò Vizzini's machinations and networking in the Honoured Society is not clear, but certainly the opposition had been minimal – not much more than occasional pot-shots, broken bridges and mines as the largely Sicilian coastal divisions had simply put down their arms and either surrendered in droves or disappeared. There were, however, occasional acts of defiance. As the 2nd Armored Division reached the southern end of the Portella della Paglia Pass, its axis of advance through the mountains, the leading tank was hit by a single anti-tank gun, fired by Tenente Sergio Barbadoro, a 23-year-old artillery officer in the 25° Reggimento di Artiglieria of the Divisione Assietta. Although he knew Palermo was lost, Barbadoro was determined to make one last show of defiance for the sake of the army's lost pride. Having told the rest of his men to leave, he loaded the gun himself, knocked out the lead tank and held off the column. Soon after, an American reconnaissance aircraft flew over, circling like a hawk. His position was accurately fed back to those on the ground, at which point it was plastered with shells and the heroic Barbadoro was killed.

With the pass cleared, the American 2nd Armored pushed on to the edge of the city. Generale Giovanni Marciani, commander of the 208°

Divisione Costiera, came forward to rally his troops only to run straight into a forward patrol from Combat Command A, and was promptly taken prisoner. Later that evening, Generale Giuseppe Molinero, commander of Porto Difesa – Port Defence Force – 'N', greeted another American patrol and, recognizing the utter hopelessness of the situation, offered to surrender the city. The offer was relayed to Keyes, who accepted; and so, with Molinero in the back seat of their command car, General Keyes and Major-General Hugh Gaffey, the 2nd Armored commander, entered Palermo to streets already lined with civilians and drove straight to the Palazzo dei Normanni where, at 7 p.m., the surrender was formally signed.

General Patton, who had left for the front at 2 p.m. that day, soon caught up with the rear elements of the Provisional Corps. His car passed one knocked-out Italian light tank, covered in blood, and a number of 105mm guns. Road discipline had been good and he'd been pleased to be cheered by 2nd Armored troops as he'd passed by, the pennant on the car fluttering in the wind. By dusk they had reached 2nd Armored's CP, where Colonel Redding F. Perry, the divisional chief of staff, offered to take the general into the city, heading through the pass where Tenente Barbadoro had made his lone stand. Looking at the mountains rising either side, Patton thought it one of the strongest defensive positions he'd ever seen and wondered how his men could have forced it so easily. They passed through Monreale, where people were out in the streets shouting, 'Viva America!' and 'Down with Mussolini!', and then reached the city, by which time it was nearly 10 p.m. and night had fallen. 'It is a great thrill,' Patton noted in his diary later that night, 'to be driving into a captured city in the dark.' By the time he reached the Palazzo, Keyes and Gaffey had already gone to bed, but they got up and together the commanders had a drink from a small flask. Later, Patton received a signal from Alexander. 'This is a great triumph,' ran the message. 'Well done. Heartiest congratulations to you and all your splendid soldiers.'

That evening, the men of the 41st Armored Infantry had not been among those heading into the capital but had instead been stopped in the hills overlooking Palermo. Breezy Griffin and his pal Herb Queen were told to go and guard one of the main aqueducts that ran from the hills into the city. Alone on their hilltop spot, they could see Palermo stretched out before them and, beyond it, the sea. Both men were filthy after their days on the road and, after following the water pipe for 100 yards, noticed there was a maintenance door on one side before it began heading underground. Opening the door, they discovered a metal-runged ladder that led down to an underground stream. Grabbing a bar of soap from their packs, they quickly undressed and jumped in, giving themselves a refreshing and much-needed bath. 'If the folks in Palermo thought their drinking water tasted a bit soapy next morning,' noted Griffin, 'they were probably right.'

The following day, 23 July, Colonel Gavin and the 505th took Trapani, while Darby's X Force moved in on Marsala, location of Trapani's satellite airfield and another port. The 39th Infantry were first into the town, following covering fire laid down by the artillery, and entered the port without a shot being fired. In the lead as they pulled into the central Piazza del Popolo was Lieutenant Charlie Scheffel in his jeep, followed by the 1st Battalion troops in trucks. After being directed to the town hall, Scheffel called on the Italian port commander to make the formal surrender. Scheffel was surprised to find an elderly man with a trim white beard still wearing a nightgown and old-fashioned night cap. The man looked confused at first, then straightened up and asked permission to get himself dressed and into uniform. Scheffel agreed. When he hadn't reappeared after twenty minutes, Scheffel pushed open the door and walked into the hallway, up two marble steps and on into the foyer. There he saw the old man, wearing his dress uniform, complete with black boots and ceremonial sword. He had hanged himself from the second-storey balustrade.

The west had been won, and for the paltry cost of 272 casualties in the Provisional Corps, of which only 57 had been killed. In return, the Americans had captured a staggering 53,000 Italians and killed and wounded a further 2,900. Added to the bag were 189 guns, 359 vehicles and 41 tanks. It was an extraordinary achievement, and while it was true the opposition had not been up to much, the victory should in no way be belittled. One of the reasons why so many Italians gave up the fight was because of the awesome superiority demonstrated by the Americans in terms of weaponry, machinery and discipline, but especially their astounding operational skill. These forces had required phenomenal levels of organization as they rapidly surged forward, spreading their tentacles with immense efficiency across all the major arteries of the western half of the island. Despite the blazing heat, and despite the extent of the territory covered, the Provisional Corps had totally conquered a third of the island in just four days since beginning its surge west.

Too often, historians have judged armies largely on tactical flair at the coal-face of war, when every bit as important is an army's ability to maintain its effort. The better supplied and equipped and maintained an army is, the better are its chances of performing on the battlefield. On Sicily in 1943, maintenance of the effort was absolutely crucial; and to keep two entire corps in ammunition, fuel, food, water and other essential supplies as they moved across difficult terrain, over such a wide area and at such speed, was immensely impressive. It was also one of the reasons why any concerns Alexander might have had before HUSKY about the combat readiness of the Americans had long since been dispelled. The value of Patton's sweep around the west, to the US Army as well as to the Allied campaign, cannot be stressed enough; this vital four-day operation allowed his men to test much of what they'd trained to do and the logistical systems they had put in place. By its conclusion, his soldiers had had valuable combat experience, had learned a great deal, and were now ready to be tested against stiffer opposition. It had also been a terrific public relations exercise, because people back home in the States and around the free world were now being shown maps with arrows reaching across great swathes of Sicily, along with photographs and film footage of vast columns of American materiel might and of Patton strutting around Palermo. No matter how disgruntled he, General Lucas and others might have been at playing second fiddle to the British, Seventh Army had had a lot of gain for not very much pain over the past few days.

Even though Eighth Army had been stalled by the Germans, now behind the *Hauptkampflinie*, across the whole Allied front a great deal had already been learned during the campaign. The logistics involved were breathtakingly complex, and much of this work was being tested for the very first time – by the British and Canadians as well as the Americans, for although the British had been fighting the Axis longer, an operation of this scale was something new for them too.

It had always been reckoned that for the first two weeks of the campaign, the Allied forces would have to be maintained through the beaches. Even once they had captured ports, the time it would take to repair damage and get them operating at full capacity again could only be guessed at. Huge amounts of supplies could be shuttled over from Tunisia, Algeria and Egypt, but new methods had to be developed to deliver these from ship to lighter, from lighter to beach, from beach to transport and from transport to beach maintenance area. Supplies also had to be shipped not just for the armies, but also for the air forces now operating from Sicily. 'Beach groups' were one such development, the core of each group consisting of fifteen naval officers and 150 ratings who handled signals and the handling, repair and maintenance of boats. On shore, each component of the army then provided men of its own who would be temporarily attached to a beach group – an infantry battalion for the infantry, a field company for the engineers, one heavy and one light anti-aircraft battery for the artillery – and whose task it would be to get supplies to the beach maintenance area. Teams of RAF personnel were similarly allocated to move their share of supplies.

Between 13 and 23 July, on XXX Corps' beaches alone, some 4,364 vehicles and 73,000 tons of supplies were unloaded, while between 15 and 24 July, a further 4,741 vehicles and 25,272 tons of supplies were unloaded through Syracuse and Augusta. Yet while this was undoubtedly impressive, it fell some way short of the Americans' unloading miracle. On Seventh Army's beaches, 8,286 vehicles and 22,000 tons of supplies had been unloaded in the first four days alone, while up to 31 July, 104,000 tons would be unloaded through both the beaches and the ports of Licata and Porto Empedocle, which had been rapidly developed with increased capacity – in itself no mean feat. That was a rate of nearly 5,000 tons per day – an incredible amount. Before HUSKY had been launched, it was reckoned the two armies together would need 6,000 tons per day; this figure was being surpassed long before Palermo was captured and without Catania. And while the beach group structure was being used for both armies, it was the Americans who were unquestionably showing the way. By 23 July, for example, Eighth Army had around 30 per cent of its normal vehicle allotment, while by that stage Seventh Army had almost all of its transport.

It was because of the shortfall of vehicles in Eighth Army that, by this last week in July, XIII Corps, on the east of the line, had twice had to have its ammunition expenditure cut – which in turn had put paid to any further offensive operations until supplies had been built up once more. The Canadians, meanwhile, at the western end of Eighth Army's line, had the longest supply lines, with a 225-mile round trip. On inadequate roads and with a shortage of vehicles, they had, to a large extent, overcome the problem by creating a shuttle service, with relays of drivers, 'while you wait' pit crews, and vehicles that ran all day and all night. Trucks would reach the front, a bevy of troops would unload them, and they would be on their way again. The transport shortage, however, was also the reason why so many of Eighth Army's soldiers now lined up against the Germans on the *Hauptkampflinie* had ended up walking most of the way there from their invasion beaches. If they were exhausted and in need of a pause, it was hardly surprising. Yet it has to be remembered that on 23 July the campaign was not even two weeks old, and in that time the Allies had conquered four-fifths of one of the most challenging environments imaginable in which to fight a rapid war. It really was a remarkable achievement.

For the most part, the Allies had been rather shocked by the condition of Sicily, even though they'd been warned to expect a land that was considerably poorer and less developed than the United States, Canada or Britain. Even during the battle for Assoro, Farley Mowat had noticed the great poverty of the town in which he found himself. 'The squalid stone houses hunkering against the slope seemed rooted in windows of filth,' he wrote, 'which had built up since the last heavy rain and would continue to accumulate until a new deluge washed the offal and excrement down the reeking streets.' The stench had been terrible, and not just from smoke and cordite but from the effluent discarded outside in the road.

Frank Johnson had found Gela as filthy and poverty-stricken as the *Soldier's Guide* had warned, and the civilians he encountered showed little sign of enthusiasm for Mussolini or Fascism, despite the Fascist slogans painted on dozens of walls. Captain Chet Hansen was surprised, having passed through the shattered town of San Cataldo near Caltanissetta, to read in reports about the civilian reaction to this destruction that most local people continued to blame the Germans and the Fascists for the bombing of their town rather than the Allies. Generally, most Sicilians seemed antagonistic towards Fascism and nearly all wanted the war to end. Hansen was also dismayed by the haggard appearance of so many of the Sicilian women, and deeply unimpressed by the dishevelled and undernourished appearance of most Italian troops, who were small by the hulking standards of the well-fed and muscular Americans. 'The Italian soldier,' he noted with a contempt felt by most Allied soldiers, 'is a slothful creature poorly disciplined.'

One day, a tiny Italian soldier was brought before General Bradley. The man was wearing civilian clothes; he had been home on furlough when the invasion began and so had remained there, hoping to keep his head down and avoid notice. Young men were a rarity, however; Bradley had already noticed that a lot of crops were ripening in the fields without the manpower to harvest it. 'Villages had long ago been stripped of all but aged men,' he noted, and were populated largely by 'their worn-looking women, and children.' He realized that in putting Sicilian prisoners of war into cages and then shipping them to North Africa, they were achieving nothing but a costly hassle, while at the same time depriving the impoverished Sicilians. The prisoner brought before him had been scared witless, and simply wanted to be out of the war and left alone. Bradley told the man he could go home, and then instructed Colonel Monk Dickson, his chief intelligence officer, to spread the word that any Sicilians wanting to desert could go home without fear of being picked up. At Caltanissetta, Dickson called on the local bishop to ask his help, and soon enough the bush telegraph had encouraged thousands to emerge from the surrounding hills and give themselves up. After processing, they were sent home.

That men like Bradley were acting with both pragmatism and compassion did not, however, lessen the destruction being visited on many of the towns the Americans were now fighting through. Captain Chet Hansen was shocked by the carnage that had been brought to the town of San Cataldo. As he'd passed through, he had seen civilians gazing at the remains of their homes, and others picking through the debris trying to find the dead. 'Morgue is now crowded with approximately 300 bodies, most of them unrecognisable,' he recorded in his diary. 'The city is a thorough shambles.' Near Catenanuova, Hanns Cibulka had one day heard what he'd thought at first was strange singing before he realized it was a dirge. 'What kind of woman is this,' he'd wondered, 'screaming out her pain like an animal into the landscape?' Then a door had opened and a child's coffin had been brought out.

After the Allied bombing of Rome on 19 July, the King had gone to visit the damage and had handed out money. 'We don't want your dirty money,' someone had shouted, 'we want peace!' Vittorio Emanuele had been shaken by this, and was finally convinced the time had come to rid Italy of both Mussolini and the war. Since the ill-fated meeting at Feltre, the Italian capital had been a hotbed of plotting and double-dealing, but two principal schemes had emerged, one led by the military and supported by the King, the other promoted by leading Fascists. Mussolini finally called the Grand Council for Saturday 24 July and although there were three separate motions to be tabled, only one was discussed – that proposed by Dino Grandi, former Ambassador to Great Britain in the early 1930s and one of the most duplicitous and scheming of all the

Fascists, which was saying something. Grandi's suggestion was that Mussolini should share power with the various organs of state and hand over authority of the armed forces to the King. Both Grandi's motion and Mussolini's calling of the Grand Council rather disconcerted the military plotters, who feared that Mussolini might be overthrown only to be replaced by another Fascist. On the 22nd, at Mussolini's usual Thursday morning audience with the King, Vittorio Emanuele had strongly suggested – although not explicitly stated – that it was time for him to go. Mussolini told him he intended to extricate Italy from the war by 15 September and left believing he still had the King's support – which rather underlined both how much the King had minced his words and how far Mussolini was interpreting what was being said to suit his own purposes. In fact, the King had decided to arrest Mussolini on 26 July regardless of the outcome of the Grand Council, and to replace him with Badoglio. On the morning of 24 July, before the Grand Council met, Ambrosio and d'Acquarone visited Badoglio to tell him he was to be the next political leader of Italy; none of them seemed at all queasy at the hypocrisy of their gathering at Badoglio's luxurious villa outside Rome, a gift from Mussolini for victory in Abyssinia, where the marshal had authorized the use of lethal gas. Ambrosio had also taken the precaution of forming a corps of three motorized divisions based outside Rome, ready to defend the capital from either Germans or Fascists.

Mussolini, having left home that afternoon with his wife, Rachele, warning him of treachery – rather as Caesar's wife had done on the Ides of March – and urging him to arrest all the plotters, made his way to the Palazzo Venezia, his office at the heart of Rome. It was from the balcony here that he'd declared war to the enthusiastic crowds below back in June 1940; now it was here, in the Sala del Pappagallo, that the Grand Council meeting finally convened. At 5.14 p.m. Mussolini walked in and, rather as Hitler had done at Feltre, spoke non-stop for around two hours. Eventually, Grandi's motion was put forward and a vote was taken. Nineteen of the members voted for it, seven against, and one abstained. It was now 2.40 a.m. on Sunday, 25 July. So the vote had been passed; but what it meant, exactly, wasn't clear, although Mussolini had been told to present the result to the King the following day.

That Sunday afternoon, Mussolini was driven to the Villa Savoia, the King's official residence, arriving just a few minutes before 5 p.m. Meeting the King in the drawing room, Mussolini told him of the vote and assured him it carried no constitutional weight – but at this point the

King interrupted him. Italy was on its knees, he told Mussolini, and the army's morale was broken. No one wanted the fighting to continue. It was time for a different leader, and the man for the current situation was Badoglio.

'Then, everything is finished?' said Mussolini.

'I am sorry, I am sorry,' replied Vittorio Emanuele, 'but there was no other solution.' The King assured Mussolini, as his friend, that he need not worry about his personal safety, and shook his hand as he left. Mussolini was promptly arrested by the Carabinieri and taken away in an ambulance. It was over. Mussolini had fallen; and with him, so too had Fascism.

Initially, the dramatic fall of Mussolini and Fascism looked as though it might stop the war in Sicily in its tracks. The first whiff of what was going on reached the Führer's headquarters at Rastenburg in East Prussia during the midday conference that Sunday, 25 July. Later that evening and into the following morning, more details arrived, throwing Hitler into a towering rage. 'Basically,' noted Warlimont, 'he was yelling for revenge and retribution.' Badoglio, Hitler railed, was their bitterest enemy. Clearly, this meant the Italians were going to lay down their arms immediately. 'They say they'll fight,' ranted Hitler, 'but that's treachery! We must be quite clear: it's pure treachery!' Urgent plans needed to be made. German troops in Sicily had to be pulled out right away. Rommel, who was on an inspection tour of Salonika, was to be recalled and was to take over active command of Army Group B. Hitler even thought of sending 3. Panzer Division to take Rome and arrest the King, Badoglio and other leading 'traitors'. For Hitler, whose alliance with Italy and entire Mediterranean strategy had been based on his paranoia about the threat to the Reich's southern flank, it was essential the Alpine passes should be secured without delay. 'Under all circumstances we must rescue the people here,' he said, pointing to the map of Sicily. 'They're no good here. They must cross, particularly the paratroops and the Göring Division. The equipment doesn't matter a damn, they must blow it up or destroy it. But we must get the men back.' All 70,000 of them.

After the initial shock, calmer thinking took hold once more, especially as Rome continued to insist there was no plan to sue for peace with the Allies. Clearly, that was now only a matter of time; still, in the German camp it was realized they should tread carefully and not give the Badoglio government an excuse to renounce the alliance in a hurry.

Rather, they needed to buy time to make the best of a bad situation. Various plans had already been drawn up for the inevitable collapse of Italy, and these were now to be swiftly accelerated; they included the withdrawal of German troops from Sicily and Sardinia, and preparing German troops to sweep into Italy, the Balkans and Greece to disarm the Italian armed forces. To this end, Rommel was to be on standby in Bavaria ready to take command in Italy itself, while several divisions were to be withdrawn from the Eastern Front, even though that would weaken the already stretched forces there who were currently battling the Red Army offensive around Orel.

Hitler still harboured plans to mount a coup in Rome, a scheme to which Kesselring and Jodl were deeply opposed, but in the meantime the Sicilian campaign was to continue. 'If ever there was an obligation for us to stay calm and keep our nerves,' jotted Dr Mauss at XIV Korps headquarters, 'it is now, at this moment.' German forces were engaged in heavy fighting, pressed on all sides by the Allies' huge strength in materiel, their constant harassment from the air and the presence of naval forces that threatened the possibility of a landing being launched behind their lines at any moment. And then had come the bombshell of Mussolini's overthrow! Mauss and his fellows struggled to know what it meant. Badoglio had promised the Italians would fight on, but would they really? As it was, most Italian troops on Sicily had stopped fighting already. Mauss wondered whether Italy was about to stab them in the back or whether it was really just a palace coup, Mussolini being replaced by another military dictator in Badoglio. Rumours were rampant. 'There is a big question mark over everything,' he added. 'Our thoughts turn to the future, which is still dark before us.' Mauss prayed that God might yet save the German Fatherland. 'For us now we must unite ourselves even more firmly than before as Germans under our General and trust him firmly,' he continued in his diary. 'We are not lost yet, and we also have the hope that we will not be lost in the future.'

Despite the overthrow of Il Duce, and despite the frantic response at Führer HQ, Hube continued to hold his line and prepare further defensive positions behind it through the narrowing peninsula. Although the Assietta and Aosta divisions had largely avoided any action so far, what useful units remained – especially artillery – were pushed into the line alongside German units, especially the newly arriving 29. Panzer Grenadier Division in the north of the *Hauptkampflinie*. Back in Sicily, too, was Oberst Ernst-Günther Baade, who had been Kesselring's choice to become Kommandant of the Straits of Messina. It was Baade's job to start getting ready for the evacuation. Until that moment arrived, the German forces in Sicily were to hold the Allies for as long as possible. But there was no further talk of holding out indefinitely. Sicily was finished – it was now a matter of when, not if; that was clear and accepted. Before that time came, though, bitter and bloody battles remained to be fought under the broiling heat of the Sicilian sun.

CHAPTER 26

The Bloody Mountains

A LITTLE AFTER 9 A.M. on Friday, 23 July, Major-General Troy
Middleton signalled Bradley at II Corps headquarters to tell him his
Thunderbird Division had reached the northern shore of Sicily at Termini
Imerese, a town 30 miles east of Palermo. With Petralia in the hands of 1st
Division and 45th on the coast road, the time had come to pivot 90 degrees
and start heading east. Bradley's biggest concern was the flow of supplies,
which, so brilliantly managed for the Provisional Corps in their drive
west, had not given equal priority to II Corps as it forged on to the north.
Bradley had repeatedly badgered Patton about this; but worrying about
logistics didn't really interest the Seventh Army commander who, while
unquestionably a highly charismatic leader and an inspired tactician, was
not much interested in paperwork. He wanted to know that his troops
were superbly well equipped, but how that happened was of little interest
to him. 'In war as Patton knew it then,' Bradley remarked later, 'there was
little time for logistics in the busy day of a field commander.'

Now, though, with the western half of Sicily wrapped up, and Keyes'
Provisional Corps out of the line and being rested on occupation duties,
on 23 July Alexander instructed Patton to throw the full weight of
Seventh Army's extraordinary logistical support behind Bradley's men
and their drive east; and while supplies were for the present still being
directed through the south coast, the intention was to make Palermo the
main logistical base for Seventh Army just as soon as possible. 'In order
to bring about the rapid collapse of the German forces left in Sicily,' Alex
signalled, 'it is imperative that you exert strong pressure in their northern flank and maintain pressure continuously.'

To begin with, the Thunderbirds came up against only light resistance. Ahead of them was Kampfgruppe Ulich, named after Oberst Max Ulich, a commander in the newly arriving 29. Panzer Grenadier Division, who first bumped into the Americans near the coastal town of Campofelice. Thereafter, for the next three days, the Germans pulled back, leaving a trail of blown bridges and roads, mines and other delay-inducing hazards and disruptions before finally falling behind the Tusa river and on to the long, mountainous Tusa Ridge immediately to the east, which ran across the Thunderbirds' advance. It was a formidable defensive position. The Americans had hit a brick wall.

To the south, the 1st Division – the Big Red One – now found themselves facing similar conditions to those of XXX Corps in Eighth Army, canalized along inland narrow and mountainous roads, separated from other thrusts – so without any mutual support on the flanks – in terrain that favoured the defender in every respect. Initially, they came up only against remnants of the Divisione Aosta, and quickly reached the hilltop town of Gangi; but thereafter they hit Kampfgruppe Fullriede once more, and from then on, the going became dramatically tougher.

On Sunday, 25 July, General Alexander flew over to Sicily to confer with Patton and Montgomery at Syracuse. Up until now, he had felt the amounts of supplies, vehicles and equipment that would be needed to house and operate 15th Army Group HQ on the island could not be justified; but with the pause in operations and the supply situation improving significantly with each passing day, he now planned to move his HQ permanently to Sicily in a few days' time, which would certainly make him better placed to oversee the command of his two armies as the final drive for Messina got under way.

Before that, however, new plans needed to be confirmed. Alex arrived at Syracuse with his new American deputy chief of staff, Brigadier-General Lyman L. Lemnitzer, who had been working on Eisenhower's staff but now filled a role left open by the dismissal of Huebner – allegedly moved on for hiding one of Alexander's orders from Patton. That departure had caused Patton some consternation, as he believed Huebner had been dismissed only because he had stuck up for American interests at Alexander's HQ. It was, though, very much Patton's way to see every single aspect of his life as a competition, in which he, first, and then the United States, had to come out on top. Perceived snubs, slights, or restraints on his own convictions and ambitions were framed in terms of mirror images of his own competitiveness and nationalism. If he didn't like an order that reached him, it was because the British were looking down their noses at him and his fellow Americans.

As it happened, Huebner had that very day passed on to him copies of signals Monty had sent Alexander at the start of the campaign, when it had looked as if Eighth Army would burst into the Catania Plain before the Germans regained their balance. Huebner, however, clearly feeling sore, was merely fanning the flames of Patton's easily provoked sense of outrage. Only ten days ago, Patton reflected, Monty had wanted Seventh Army to play second fiddle; now they wanted the Americans' help. Well, he reckoned that had his men been left with Highway 124 they would have nearly reached Messina by now. He had absolutely no grounds whatsoever on which to make this claim. 'Now the British have given me 117 and 120 and are damned glad we are there,' he groused in his diary. 'The Canadians never took Enna, and lost 700 men trying; then they took three days to take Leonforte. The rest of the Eighth Army has not gained a foot and the Seventh Army has taken most of the island.' Really, it was the kind of schoolboy one-upmanship usually left on the playground – and precisely the kind of attitude Eisenhower and others had worked so hard to stamp out. On the other hand, although Patton was happy to grumble to Lucas, Huebner and other senior commanders, for the most part the worst of his griping was confined to his diary. So long as it remained there, he could grouse all he liked.

Now that the German defences had stiffened, it made sense to bring in Seventh Army to help, especially since they had performed so magnificently in the campaign to date. Monty had acknowledged this, and so too had Alexander, who had been very quick to give credit where credit was due. In other words, Patton, flush with his success of the previous week, could afford to feel a little more magnanimous towards his superiors and coalition partners.

On the morning of the 25th, Patton set off in a C-47 from Palermo, escorted by two Spitfires, and reached Syracuse around 10.20 a.m. Montgomery was already there ahead of Alexander and Eisenhower's chief of staff, Walter Bedell Smith. Monty suggested to Patton they look at a map and unfolded one on the bonnet of his car. The only debate was over the road between Randazzo and Linguaglossa, but Montgomery agreed it should be used by both armies. 'He agreed so readily,' noted Patton, 'that I felt something was wrong, but have not found it yet.' That was because there was nothing to find; insufferable Monty could unquestionably be at times, but he did not share Patton's paranoia.

Montgomery also offered Patton the use of all of Highway 117 north and south of Enna, and by the time Alexander and Bedell Smith joined them, the two had largely agreed their plans for the final offensive. These were very much along the lines Alex had suggested two days earlier. Aware the Germans were creating a secondary defensive line around the base of Etna, the Allied commanders hoped the *Hauptkampflinie* could be broken, opening the way for a joint renewed and all-out offensive against the Etna Line – as the Allies were now calling it – on 1 August, which would drive the Axis forces from Sicily for good. By the end of July, both armies would have brought up fresh supplies and forces; the US 3rd Division would join Bradley's II Corps, while Montgomery had already ordered the British 78th Division, still in North Africa, to be shipped to Sicily.

In the meantime, several preliminary operations would be carried out in order to crack the *Hauptkampflinie*, the Americans continuing their drive to Nicosia and Santo Stefano, while the Canadians – with the Malta Brigade attached – would take Agira and Regalbuto. Once 78th Division had reached the front, they and the 51st Highland would swiftly secure a bridgehead over the Dittaino at Gerbini.

Patton also asked for some landing craft for outflanking amphibious operations on the north coast, and for some warships. Alex agreed to try with the landing craft and said he would see he got the warships. 'I doubt if he does,' noted Patton, entirely without foundation. Why he was feeling so particularly peevish that day was unclear. Soon after that, the meeting broke up and they all went their separate ways, Patton taking further umbrage because Montgomery did not offer him any lunch. 'I want to assure you,' Alex told him as they parted company, 'that 15th Army Group is completely Allied in mind and favours neither Army.' Everything he had said and done over the past week supported this statement; and no matter what anyone thought of Alexander, honesty and a sense of honour were his watchwords. Yet Patton recorded in his diary later, 'I know this is a lie.'

The Allied air forces still had a vital part to play in the campaign, and while Spaatz's strategic air forces were to continue to range further, on 21 July Coningham's tactical air forces were given fresh priorities. Disruption of the enemy's supplies was high on the list, to be pursued by dive-bombing and strafing sea links and, especially, roads and rail lines. They were also to continue to give direct support to the troops on the land, and provide fighter protection by day and night. On 19 July the 99th Fighter Squadron had moved to an airfield near Licata, their ground support all transported from North Africa in C-47s under escort by their own fighters. By the following morning, Charlie Dryden and the rest of the squadron were straight into the action, dive-bombing and strafing German columns and positions. Dryden soon got used to his new surroundings. It was hot all right, but then it had been in Tunisia too. 'The living was easy at Licata,' he noted. 'We were bivouacked a short distance from the beach and could get a cool dip in the sea after a hot day in the cockpit.'

Canadian Hap Kennedy was also now in Sicily, with 111 Squadron at Pachino – and very relieved to have secured another operational tour. Being in Sicily hadn't changed his flying duties a great deal, although his targets now were no longer airfields but stubborn German positions. 'We lay in the shade under the wings of Spitfires,' he noted, 'eating luscious handfuls of blue grapes off the vine, ready to jump as soon as we saw the bomber formation approaching from the south.' As the bombers approached, they would make one circle overhead, which would give the fighter boys time to get into their kites, tear off in a cloud of dust, climb up above them and head north.

By now, with Allied air superiority almost complete over Sicily, Coningham's fighters were rarely seeing any enemy aircraft over the island itself. Sunday, 25 July, however, was to prove an exception. That morning, while Patton and Alexander were flying towards Syracuse, New Zealander Colin Gray, commander of 322 Wing, was leading his three squadrons on a fighting sweep over the north-east of the island. Earlier, intelligence had been picked up on Malta that a number of transport aircraft were planning to carry out an air drop of supplies on the beach at Capo di Milazzo, just down the north coast from Messina. So confident were the RAF fighter pilots by this stage that most were desperate to fly whenever given the chance and quite a heated argument had developed over whether Gray or his immediate superior, Piet Hugo, would lead the wing. In the end, Hugo was ordered to stay put in case something else came up and Gray got the job. As it was, he had been given precious little time to prepare, and his three squadrons took off without even being properly briefed. Taking off from Malta at around 9.45 a.m., they skimmed over the hills and the front line before any enemy below had a chance to fire and crossed the coast at sea level – just in the nick of time, as a gaggle of two dozen Junkers 52 transports were circling prior to landing directly on the beach. Quickly glancing around, Gray saw a number of escorting Me109s at around 3,000 feet; among these were several from I. Gruppe of Macky Steinhoff's JG 77, now based in southern Italy.

Gray ordered 81 Squadron, with their new and more powerful Spitfire Mk IXs, to climb up and tackle the 109s, while 242 and 152 Squadrons pounced on the transports. Leading the wing, he made straight for the lead Junkers 52, got in good and close, opened fire and saw it burst into flames. Exactly the same happened to the second Junkers. 'From the spectacular results,' noted Gray, 'it looked as if they must have been carrying petrol.' Pulling up, he climbed to discover quite a melee going on with more than thirty fighters tussling. By this time, he couldn't see a single transport still flying, and it looked as though every enemy fighter had a Spitfire on its tail. Finally spotting a lone Messerschmitt heading back to Italy, he applied boost and set off in hot pursuit. After a few minutes, however, he was still not in range and fuel was getting low, so he turned and headed back to Lentini, getting a fairly hostile reception from the flak gunners as he passed the Straits of Messina.

In all, they had destroyed nine out of ten Junkers, along with five Me109s, one of which belonged to Oberleutnant Gerhard Strausen of Steinhoff's HQ flight. Strausen managed to bail out and was safely picked up; but it had been a slaughter, and another indication – if any had been needed – of the dominance of the Allies in the air. It made such a colossal difference to the chances of those operating on the ground. At his flak battalion, Hanns Cibulka saw Allied aircraft overhead every day, including three Spitfires that flew over at 8.00 each morning; it was unnerving that the enemy had eyes on them like this. Up near Etna at XIV Panzer Korps HQ, Wilhelm Mauss was cursing with the rest of the staff at the lack of any Luftwaffe. 'One can be sure when something roars in the air,' he noted, 'they are English but not Germans.' This Allied command of the skies was, he admitted, having a growing psychological effect. 'Randazzo is a popular target,' he added, 'it is being attacked several times daily and from there the enemy air force always hunts individual German vehicles in low-level flight.'

The plans drawn up by Alexander, Patton and Montgomery on 25 July had sounded straightforward enough, although privately Alex had warned Eisenhower it might still take another month to finish the job. This wasn't what Ike had wanted to hear, but Alex had been looking at the terrain, the shortage of decent roads and a landscape that made it very difficult for the Allies to manoeuvre. That tapering peninsula, with Etna slap bang in the middle and Messina right on the tip, was a gift to the defenders; and, as he was well aware, those defenders now included some very decent enemy troops who were disciplined, determined, equipped with some half-decent weaponry and highly unlikely to throw in the towel too readily. It was important to be positive; but it was also better to err on the side of caution rather than promise what might prove difficult to deliver. Alex was also mindful that despite the vast air fleets available, the naval warships offshore and the immense amount of materiel support that could be given to the two armies, it was still the infantry, especially, and the armour that were going to have to do the hard work; and that under the blazing heat and in the choking dust of July and August, they were expecting a lot from their mostly conscript troops.

The battles for Nicosia and Agira were two cases in point. By dawn on 25 July, the Big Red One's 26th Infantry were 8 miles from Nicosia and holding Hill 937, a key feature overlooking the road. Early the following morning, however, Kampfgruppe Fullreide's motorized artillery pummelled the hill, the infantry holding it – just a platoon – pulled back and the Germans retook it. This prompted the deployment of no fewer than six American artillery battalions, all of which took time to get organized; by late afternoon, the hill was once more in the hands of the 26th Infantry, who then pushed on. In all, the division had advanced just 2 miles in twenty-four hours.

The 26th started their advance again the following morning, only to receive a second ferocious counter-attack, and were thrown back once more. That night, the Germans pulled back yet again and the Americans also took the high ground again. By now it was 27 July, and it seemed the 26th had been stopped dead; but General Terry Allen was urging his men on, and now all three regimental combat teams were brought into line, the 18th Infantry to the north and, to the south, the 16th, along with the Stuarts of the 70th Light Tank Battalion. Carl Rambo and his crew had been given a replacement for the tank they'd lost a few days earlier and were among those in B Company leading the assault that evening. 'We were told to go in, shoot everything and come back out,' said Rambo. 'It was quite dark, and we had no lights on. So we went in, everything ablaze.' Very quickly a big firefight developed, with mortars, tanks, machine guns all blasting away and tracer zipping every which way. One of the tanks behind Rambo's was hit, and then the one in front stopped – and, instead of manoeuvring around it, Rambo stopped his tank too. It was to prove a fatal error: moments later, the entire tank shook and Rambo was blown through the hatch on his turret. When he came to, he was hanging over the edge of the tank. Quickly kicking himself loose, he ran round to the front looking for his crew. The assistant driver was out, and so too was the gunner – and he was on fire. Rambo frantically looked for Glenn Griffin, his driver, but he was already burned to death. He now jumped on Cecil Lauderdale, his gunner, rolled him into the ditch to extinguish the flames, and managed to get him swiftly evacuated on the back of another tank. Suffering himself from burns to his hand, arm and face, Rambo found himself shipped back to Tunisia the very next day, his time on Sicily over. Lauderdale did not make it.

To the north of Nicosia, another key high point, Monte Sambughetti, was captured by a battalion of the 18th fighting alongside the French Goums attached to the division, and the Italians of the Aosta, on Fulliede's right, were thrown back. This, combined with news that Allied warships had been spotted off the north coast of Sicily, persuaded General Hube it was time for the 15. Panzer Grenadier Division to withdraw from Nicosia. Overnight, Fullreide's men pulled back to the next delaying position. The following morning, the 18th Infantry passed through the 26th Infantry and into the town. Frank Johnson was amazed at the welcome they got from the mayor, the chief of the Carabinieri, and hundreds of locals, who bombarded them with kisses, bottles of wine and flowers. 'The priest blesses us for saving the town,' Johnson wrote, 'for saving the town from Mussolini and the Tedeschi [Germans].' This brief moment of celebration, however, was soon over: they had to press forward again, in blazing heat, down the next dusty road, down another hill, up the next and on towards Troina.

To the south, meanwhile, Agira was the next mountaintop target for the Canadians. It could be seen clearly from the top of Assoro, the distant town perched upon a pointed peak; but it didn't look real – more like a picture from a folk story or an illustration of Middle Earth. It was part of a long ridge, curving slightly but running roughly west–east, that began at Leonforte and continued across to the town of Paterno, nestling on the south-west slopes of Etna. Below this ridge to the south snaked the Dittaino valley. It was no wonder the Germans thought this such a good position for the *Hauptkampflinie*.

The battle plan for the Canadians was to take Agira in chunks, demarcated by a series of imaginary lines on the map and code-named Lion, Tiger and, finally, Grizzly. Unfortunately for them, as they were forming up to attack Lion on the night of 22 July, Kampfgruppe Ens's artillery opened up and caught them as they began their advance, forcing the infantry back with heavy machine-gun fire. The 1st Canadian Brigade attacked again on the 24th, this time supported by no fewer than seven artillery regiments – more than 160 guns – and also more than a hundred Kittyhawk fighter-bombers. The advancing infantry took the town of Nissoria, halfway to Agira and just before the Lion objective, but then became bogged down. What followed was a slow and costly slugging match. The Hasty Ps, brought in on the southern flank of the advance, could not repeat their incredible success at Assoro. In the course of their attempt, Alex Campbell was hit by a bullet that made a glancing blow on his tin helmet and scored his cheek, while Major Tweedsmuir suffered a shrapnel wound in the leg; brought into brigade headquarters on a stretcher, he reported their failure to Brigadier Howard Graham, then passed out.

Both Angus Duffy, the Hasty Ps' regimental sergeant-major, and Lieutenant Farley Mowat had already been evacuated to a field hospital in a former nunnery in Valguarnera when the wounded from the attack on the Lion line on 25 July began coming in.

'You'd best get up,' Duffy told Mowat, appearing by his stretcher. 'There's been a balls-up at the front. Five loads of our lads have already come in and there's more on the way.' Duffy reckoned it was time he and Mowat discharged themselves and got back to the front to help. Mowat was certainly over the worst of his dysentery; though still feeling pretty ropey, he felt the RSM was right and so twenty minutes later they were on an ambulance heading back north. The journey took most of the afternoon in sweltering temperatures, and when they eventually reached the battalion's command post, they were shocked to learn just how badly it had been mauled. 'The colonel's wounded and gone down the line,' Dickie Bird, the adjutant, told him. 'Kennedy's hit and half delirious. There's *nobody* left to clear up the mess!' It was, he told Mowat, a massacre. Among those severely wounded was A. K. Long from Mowat's platoon; a mortar had done for him, smashing his legs and filling his guts with shrapnel.

Back at the nunnery-cum-hospital in Valguarnera, Tweedsmuir found himself lying on a stretcher with a statue of the Virgin and Child staring down at him and a row of others, all filthy and dusty, their khaki blotched with blood. 'No one complained,' he wrote. 'The badly wounded men smoked stoically, others talked or slept. We were all so dog-tired that few can have felt pain.' That day, the Hasty Ps lost five officers and seventy-five men – the worst casualty figures for any single Canadian unit in the entire Sicilian campaign. As a result, they were, for now, withdrawn from the line.

Among the many others who saw the inside of a field hospital in Sicily was Ernie Pyle, who had come down with a fever and aches and pains and been sent to the 45th Division's clearing station. This was a kind of flag stop for the wounded – here men would be patched up and made as secure as possible; then, assuming they hadn't died, they were sent on to a regular hospital or put on a ship back to Tunisia or Malta. Pyle noticed that some men were furious about their wounds, others more stoic. Others clearly weren't going to make it. Several dying men were brought into Pyle's tent, their death rattles making those who were going to live feel thoughtful. One of those who died haunted Pyle for a long time afterwards. A chaplain came in and knelt down beside the man, who was still semi-conscious, and offered a prayer that he might get well, even though it was obvious that was not going to happen. The dying man tried to repeat the words and then the chaplain said, 'John, you're doing fine, you're doing fine.' And then he got up and dashed off, presumably to attend another man.

'The dying man was left utterly alone,' wrote Pyle, 'just lying there on his litter on the ground, lying in an aisle, because the tent was full. Of course it couldn't be otherwise, but the aloneness of that man as he went through the last few minutes of his life was what tormented me. I felt like going over and holding his hand while he died, but it would have been out of order and I didn't do it. I wish now I had.'

Hedley Verity was dying too. He and the other wounded – British and German alike – had survived that first night of 20 July and the next day had been taken to Misterbianco, put on to open railway trucks and ferried up through Sicily. At Messina, they had been put on a ship and taken across the Straits to Reggio di Calabria on the southern tip of Italy. Bundled off again and put into more trucks, Verity and his fellow wounded had been taken to a hospital in Reggio and then the next day placed on another goods train, on straw, to begin a slow journey north to Naples, which had taken two whole days. All this to-ing and fro-ing and being lifted on and off, with little water and little food, had not helped the wounded. By the time Verity reached Naples he was very ill indeed – feverish, with his wound becoming infected.

Nor was his journey over yet. From Naples he was taken by truck to the Italian military hospital at Caserta, a few miles to the north. There he met Corporal Henty, another wounded Yorkshireman, who recognized him. Word soon spread among the wounded British troops that the great English bowler was there with them. Verity talked to Henty, showing him photographs of his wife and sons, Douglas and Wilfred. He was in increasingly terrible pain as the wound began to fester badly, and also because a part of one rib was broken and pressing against his lung. Eventually, three days later, on 31 July, he was operated on again and part of his rib removed, using only a local anaesthetic.

At first, the operation appeared to have been a success, but then he suffered the first of three haemorrhages. He remained conscious to the end, talking about his repatriation, and getting home again once the war was over – but he was in a bad way. The haemorrhage could have been caused by a Curling's ulcer – a gastric ulcer brought on by extreme stress – or by a break in one of the blood vessels caused by the operation, which would have caused bleeding into his lung and would have been very distressing and frightening indeed. Whatever the precise circumstances, later that night, one of England's great cricketers died.

Back on Sicily, the grinding slog of fighting in the mountains continued. The taking of Agira and then Regalbuto had been supposed to be a comparatively straightforward mopping-up operation, but it was not until 28 July that the first of these towns finally fell to the exhausted Canadians, and then only with the aid of the Malta Brigade, who had eventually arrived and taken key hills to the east and south-east of the town. Among those involved had been James Donaldson and his mortar platoon of the 2nd Devons. Their task had been to cut the road east in coordination with the Canadians' attack; but although they attacked and crossed the road several times, each time, under heavy mortar attack, they were forced back again. Agira had ended up costing the Canadians 438 casualties and the Malta Brigade some 300 – a lot from three infantry battalions. With Agira finally taken, however, they now both faced the prospect of attacking yet another town on the long ridgeline: Regalbuto, which was also perched on a hill and surrounded by more hills and plunging valleys. However, no matter how bad the previous few days had been for the Canadians, they had been twice as bad for the Germans, who were in retreat, being hit by considerably greater fire-power than they were sending over themselves, and being harassed by Allied air forces as well. Kampfgruppe Ens had been so badly ground down, in fact, that it could no longer function effectively, and had only managed to get away from Agira by taking the northern road to Troina, the sole escape route available.

Down below in the Dittaino valley, meanwhile, the Canadian 3rd Brigade had been pushing east either side of the river and against less opposition. Not until south of Catenanuova and Gerbini did the *Hauptkampflinie* drop down from the ridgeline. This was where Hanns Cibulka and his 31. Flak Bataillon were based, now reinforced by two 88mm dual-purpose anti-aircraft and anti-tank guns, expertly camouflaged so Cibulka himself could not even see them from 200 yards away. A further battery of Flakvierling quadruple cannons had also been positioned in an orange grove in such a way that they could target anything moving in the river valley beneath them or on the next ridge of hills to the south.

They were all braced for action, aware of the roll of artillery fire getting closer with each passing day. Major von Treptow, the battalion commander, had told them starkly that they would not retreat until 50 per cent of the batteries had been destroyed. It had been quite a sobering thought. It was this willingness to sacrifice themselves that was really the difference between Allied and German troops on Sicily. Allied commanders recognized that their troops were largely conscripts – or, in the case of the Canadians, all volunteers – and from democratic countries rather than totalitarian militaristic states. The Allies, as Ernie Pyle had pointed out, were attempting to fight with steel rather than flesh as far as they possibly could, and consciously sought to limit the number of casualties to the bare minimum. The Hasty Ps, after losing two battalion commanders in four days and suffering 100 casualties out of a total strength of 845, had been withdrawn from further front-line action for the time being. German units, on the other hand, like Kampfgruppe Ens, were expected to fight and keep fighting until they were reduced to as little as 20 per cent of their full strength. It wasn't that they were better trained, or better soldiers – many of the German troops on Sicily were considerably less well trained than their Allied counterparts; rather, it was that if they were told to keep fighting to the last man, that was what they would do. To disobey would almost certainly mean being shot for cowardice. If one was going to get killed or wounded, it was better to do so with honour intact.

Hanns Cibulka and his fellows first came under attack on Sunday, 25 July as the 1st Canadian Army Tank Brigade approached from the south. They had so far not been committed, but on the 23rd had moved up to Scordia, west of Lentini, and were ordered north to help with the clearing of Catenanuova. Cibulka watched, fascinated, as the first tanks appeared over the ridge the far side of the Dittaino valley, followed by armoured vehicles. They drove down the slope slowly, as if in a military training area, and then, through his field glasses, he saw the white star on the tanks. Perhaps understandably, he assumed that meant they were American; in fact, the white star was an Allied recognition symbol, not peculiar to Seventh Army but shared across all Allied forces on Sicily.

A dozen tanks now rumbled forward down the road into the valley, infantry spread out either side of them. Suddenly, the 88s opened fire while the Flakvierling cannons also began hammering. 'A firework of tracer,' jotted Cibulka in his diary; 'the bullet paths break out in clusters from the cover. The tracer is magnesium bright. I see how the projectiles hit the target, how the sheaves hit the armoured personnel carriers with full force, here and there shells bounce off the armour plate rising diagonally into the sky.' Two tanks were hit and stopped; he watched men jumping out from another, throwing themselves flat on the ground before their Sherman exploded. Soon after, the Canadians stopped and began pulling back out of danger, leaving five tanks and four armoured scout cars. A few minutes later, two ambulances came down the road and stopped; out got the medics to pick up the wounded and off they all went again.

Not long after, calm returned to the valley and the birds began singing once more. Cibulka's friend Arno warned him the enemy would be back the following day. 'Not on foot, they will plough the positions in the valley with their planes like a field of arable land,' Arno assured him, 'all day long they will fly their missions, throw their bombs, fire their cannons, they will bomb everything that moves in the valley, and only then will they make a new advance.'

It really cannot be stressed enough just how brutal it was trying to fight in Sicily. The terrible heat of the day sapped everyone's energy. Dust got everywhere. Flies and mosquitoes buzzed and whined incessantly. Most men spent much of the day with large dark sweat patches on their shirts and glistening brows, swatting and slapping insects whenever they could. No one got much sleep, especially not when on the move or in combat. Tin helmets became painfully hot, but to be without one was

courting disaster because in this rocky terrain razor-sharp and potentially lethal shards of stone would fill the air space whenever artillery
and mortar shelling began. Allied troops were criticized even at the time
for being too slow, too ponderous, not ruthless enough in following up
success. It was easy to criticize; but it should be remembered that many
of the Allied troops on Sicily had marched much of the way to where
they were now fighting. Even during the Provisional Corps' sweep west,
one battalion of the 3rd Infantry marched 54 miles in thirty-three hours,
partly across country, in intense heat and with limited water rations.
None of the men out here – Paddy Mayne's SRS apart – had trained for
this, and what looked like 3 miles on a map was, by the time men had
marched up a hill and down the other side, invariably almost double that.

In fact, the conditions in Sicily were unlike anything the Allies – or
the Germans, for that matter – had yet experienced. 'The country fought
over was of the roughest kind,' explained an official set of US training
notes from the campaign. 'Its chief features were high, rocky mountains
and hills of volcanic origin, studded and broken with sharp and rugged
outcroppings of rock formations, crossed by tortuous tracks and trails,
and cut by deep and narrow valleys and dry water courses. Such terrain
as this, encountered throughout most of the island, presented difficulties
of movement and transport.' The physical strain of operating in such terrain and in such heat was enormous.

The Allies' aim was to get to Messina as quickly as possible without
the front-line troops suffering the kind of casualties the Germans were
willing to take. As it was, the infantry and armour were suffering appallingly, because for all the immense amounts of fire-power brought to
bear, it was still the infantry, especially, and the tanks who had to push
forward and actually take possession of ground.

The Germans – and Italians – had considerably fewer guns, almost no
air cover, no naval support at all and less of every kind of materiel – but
they did have, and to an increasing extent, enough units to cover their
front – given that the coastline of the area they were defending had
already been reduced from 922 miles to around 80, and would soon,
once the Germans fell back behind the Etna Line, be reduced again to
about 60 miles. Most of the troops were well trained and well disciplined,
and had enough machine guns, mortars and guns to make life very
unpleasant for the attackers. Mines and booby-traps were comparatively
plentiful and offered a lot of bang for their buck. They were also easier to
transport to the front than a lot of other weaponry. Because the Allies

were forced to advance down the limited road system – a network that became progressively more restricted as the terrain became more mountainous, as it did in the north-east of the island – the Germans could sow large numbers of these devices and create untold delays and misery for their enemy.

The hastily prepared defensive lines were nothing like the Westwall protecting Germany or the Atlantic Wall still being developed along the continental coastline of Europe. Hanns Cibulka, who had learned a thing or two about concrete emplacements during his army career, was grateful to have the open sky above him. 'In a bunker you are completely at the mercy of the enemy's firepower,' he wrote; 'the defence line is static, limited to a small room.' The term 'front' was flexible. 'The soldiers no longer stand behind a protective earth wall either,' he added; there was 'no sophisticated trench system, no camouflaged connecting trenches'. Rather, it was a case of carefully choosing ground – of hiding guns in the plentiful groves, or on hills overlooking the roads below. It was about having observers with superb optics watching the enemy advance all too obviously with his trail of dust rising into the air. Towns were useful, because the roads always connected them and because Allied fighter-bombers were less effective there than in the open countryside. There were cellars for protection, taller buildings from which to see, rubble to block roads.

On the 26th, 31. Flak Bataillon was ordered to pull back, and by late afternoon Cibulka and his comrades had dismantled most of the telephone cables and were ready to move. At dusk, a column of the HG Panzer Division moved past them: rumbling and squeaking tanks, half-tracks and armoured cars, the men all filthy and covered in dust, machine guns pointing at the sky. Then it was their turn, heading down a road where a few weeks earlier he'd smelled acacia; this time, he could smell only oil, fumes and dust. They overtook an infantry battalion, the men all looking haggard and exhausted in the moonlight. By 5 a.m. on Wednesday, 28 July, they reached their new destination near Adrano and Cibulka and his friend Arno immediately set to laying cables and linking up the batteries with their vital communications network. Soon, they discovered a bombed-out anti-aircraft battery; as they investigated, they found at their feet a dead soldier, mouth half-open, and a few yards away a young gunner, lying on his back, arms outstretched as though nailed to an invisible cross. A third man lay strewn against a wall like a straw doll. 'It is as if death had struck the temporal out of the faces with a single blow,' he scribbled. 'The bodies are bloated, flies squat on the blood-crusted uniforms.' Seeing the dead, aware they were being steadily pushed back, Cibulka began to wonder whether he would ever get away. From time to time, he was tormented by a vision of himself lying in a ditch with a shot through the lung, bright blood-red froth at the corners of his mouth.

A further debilitating factor about fighting in Sicily was the abundance of disease. Dysentery had disabled Farley Mowat and RSM Duffy and also Livio Messina, although by far the biggest cause of casualties was malaria, which was striking down more men than bullets and shrapnel put together. It had got Audie Murphy during the Provisional Corps' drive west. They'd been marching under the burning sun, clouds of dust swirling as they tramped on towards Palermo. Murphy had begun feeling rough, then gradually worse and worse. 'My brain swam,' he wrote, 'and my internal organs rumbled. Finally, I could take it no longer. I fell out of the ranks, lay down on the roadside, and heaved until I thought I would lose my stomach.' He got up again and somehow managed to keep going, but the following day passed out completely and was packed off to hospital – one of the many thousands knocked out of the fight by malaria.

And, naturally, it afflicted both sides. Martin Pöppel eventually fell prey to malaria in the Catania Plain, and although he did not know it yet, Hanns Cibulka was also beginning to come down with it too. In Bruno Kanert's assault gun battery, several men were already out of the line with the disease. The worst of it was in the interior of the island and especially in the Plain of Catania, so it had taken ten days or so of battle for the effects to really kick home, but by this time some 55 per cent of all casualties were now due to malaria. While that included supply and service troops who would not be expecting to be in the front line, this further affliction, combined with the heat, the terrain and a determined foe, goes a long way towards explaining why the Allies were struggling to burst their way through the enemy defences.

CHAPTER 27

Closing In

E VER SINCE THE BRUTAL battle for the Primosole Bridge, the exhausted
50th Division had remained on the defensive in a situation akin to
the dark days of the First World War. Lieutenant David Fenner and the
6th DLI were rotated into and out of the 'FDLs' – forward defended
localities – with their fellow battalions, the distance between them and
the *Fallschirmjäger* units in front of them varying between 100 and
1,000 yards. Desultory shelling continued. 'Malaria began to make its
appearance felt,' he noted. 'Reinforcements were absorbed, casualties
continued. In the bridgehead, conditions were pretty grim with the millions of flies, mosquitoes and the stench.' Only under cover of darkness
was any kind of movement possible. 'Natural bodily functions,' he wrote,
'were attended to after dark or one used an empty bully beef can.' Bill
Cheall and the 6th Green Howards, reinforced with some fifty replacements, took over from the 8th DLI on 25 July, and almost as soon as
they'd done so, the regimental aid post was hit by a shell, killing the
medical officer, the padre and another soldier. Two more men were killed
by a land mine.

Oberst Wilhelm Schmalz had been grateful for a slightly less frenetic
few days. Much to his relief, the errant Ludwig Heilmann and his
3. Fallschirmjäger had turned up on 18 July, having made an impressive
and daring night-time dash back through British lines to safety. They
had then been packed off to Catenanuova, while 4. Fallschirmjäger held
the airfield and the southern edge of Catania. Getting sufficient artillery
into the line had been a challenge, as they'd lost a number of men and
weapons during the earlier heavy fighting and were not receiving the

replacements the British opposite them had been enjoying. One welcome arrival was a battalion of Italian artillery, which he slotted in close to the coast. 'It turned out after a short time that this artillery unit fired excellently and had very courageous observers who directed their fire in the front line,' wrote Schmalz. 'Both officers and crew made a brilliant impression, and we soon became the best of friends.'

Martin Pöppel and his platoon in the Maschinengewehr Bataillon were also suffering from artillery fire worse than anything they were hurling at the British. One of his best mortar teams had been knocked out on 24 July, with one man killed and three wounded. 'This bloody harassing fire wounds another of our men,' he cursed on 26 July, and two more were wounded on the 27th. They were all finding the heat, and the thousands of flies that buzzed around them constantly, almost unendurable. He'd taken to keeping a towel about him all the time – to roll up and use as a whisk, and to put over his head while eating. On the 28th Hauptmann Laun, the company commander, succumbed to malaria, which meant Pöppel was given command. He hoped he was up to such a responsibility; he was still only a second lieutenant.

Two days later, however, came a shock. 'To our astonishment the commander tells us that we're to withdraw,' noted Martin Pöppel in his diary on 30 July. 'The decision is completely incomprehensible to us all and comes as a real hammer blow.' Later, he heard that Mussolini had fallen and suddenly it seemed to make more sense. In fact, though, they were withdrawing because of what was happening not in Rome but elsewhere along the *Hauptkampflinie*. Both Hube and Schmalz recognized the need to pull back in an orderly way, and so the line needed to be thinned out first, with units being withdrawn to the next line in ordered stages.

Meanwhile, the Allied commanders were gearing up for the assault on the Etna Line, still scheduled for 1 August. On 28 July, Alexander moved his headquarters to Sicily and an encampment near Cassibile, south of Syracuse, and on the same day Montgomery headed to Palermo to see Patton. He flew in his B-17, a gift earlier in the year from Eisenhower, accompanied by his chief of staff, Major-General Francis 'Freddie' de Guingand, and Harry Broadhurst, the commander of the Desert Air Force. They were all very nearly killed on landing because the runway at Palermo wasn't really long enough for a Fortress, forcing the pilot to apply all the brakes on the starboard side and swing around to avoid crashing straight into a hangar. Fortunately, he just made it, but the force of the turn led to the collapse of one side, and Monty's personal aircraft had to be written off. All were unhurt and Montgomery quite unperturbed, although very put out to have lost his beloved Flying Fortress.

In sharp contrast to the informal meeting at Syracuse, Patton pulled out all the stops with a band, guard of honour and lavish lunch in the Palazzo dei Normanii. 'I hope Monty realized,' wrote Patton, 'that I did this to show him up for doing nothing for me on the 25th.' During their subsequent discussion, Montgomery stressed how vital the Americans' part in the drive to Messina would be. 'Monty kept repeating that the move of our 45th Division along the coast was a most significant operation,' Patton scribbled in his diary. 'I can't decide whether he is honest or wants me to lay off 120.' Patton's paranoia and the ever-largening chips on his shoulder really were extraordinary. There was no conspiracy against him and Seventh Army, no desire by the British to show up his men in any way or deny them the fruits of victory. Montgomery most certainly did want the Americans continuing their drive along Highway 120; indeed, he expected the US 1st Division to continue eastwards on that axis and smash through the Etna Line at Troina. Monty also told Patton that if his Eighth Army troops got to Randazzo and then Taormina to the south of Messina first, then it would be useful if they could turn south. In other words, this would leave the Americans on the north coast to take Messina. This objective, so prized by Patton, was simply not one Montgomery felt anything like as competitive about – if indeed he saw it as a matter of competition at all.

If Monty had felt embarrassed for the lack of razzmatazz at Syracuse, he never mentioned it. 'We had a great reception. The Americans are most delightful people and are very easy to work with,' he noted in his own diary without a trace of irony. 'Their troops are quite first-class and I have a very great admiration for the way they fight.' People were allowed to change their minds. Back in March and April, when planning for HUSKY had begun, the American troops in Tunisia were still fresh from the setback at Kasserine and the disastrous command of Lloyd Fredendall, and while II Corps' performance had improved dramatically as the campaign had progressed, it was hardly surprising if the British were a little cautious about how well an entire new American army might perform. But on Sicily the Americans had very quickly shown their mettle, and now neither Alexander nor Montgomery had any cause at all to doubt their fighting capability. Their praise for Seventh Army was heartfelt and entirely sincere.

Monty was also cautiously optimistic about plans for Operation

HARDGATE, XXX Corps' renewed offensive. Some 142,000 shells had been stockpiled for the 264 25-pounders and 88 4.5-inch and 5.5-inch medium guns supporting the corps, which was considered what would be needed just for operations up to the Etna Line from 28 July to 2 August. More and more aircraft were lined up for support, and he had reorganized his front, with 78th Division arriving from Tunisia and moving up and into position. Catania, originally prized as a valuable port and also the key to the route to Messina, was no longer considered such an important objective. Eighth Army was now getting some 4,000 tons a day through Syracuse and a little bit more from Augusta, and landing ships were still shuttling materiel straight on to the beaches at Avola. The supply issue, such a worry during the planning stage and in the first ten days of the campaign, was no longer the headache it had been. So much blood had been spilled to get across the Primosole Bridge and to ensure it was captured and kept intact, and yet now it was barely being used; in fact, it had been repeatedly shelled since all that fighting and had been put out of action twice, only finally reopening for traffic on 29 July.

On the 27th Monty had written to Brooke, telling him of his plans to attack the Etna Line at Adrano; this, he correctly surmised, was the hinge to the German defences, as it stood on the Etna foothills at the curve where the line turned east to Catania and north towards San Fratello on the coast. If both armies put in a big, full-blooded effort, then, Monty reckoned, the end should be in sight – although it was not going to be easy, because the enemy was in ideal defensive country with good-quality German troops. 'We have not done so badly,' he added; 'in two weeks we have got the whole island and pinned the Germans in the NE corner.'

This was nothing less than the truth; and, with eventual victory in Sicily assured, Allied thoughts had already begun turning to what might follow the campaign there. At the TRIDENT conference between American and British chiefs of staff back in May, Churchill had urged an invasion of southern Italy, and while such a suggestion had not been dismissed, it had not been enthusiastically endorsed either. Instead, various tentative follow-up operations were to be looked into, from the invasion of Sardinia and Corsica to an operation in the toe of Italy; depending on how HUSKY went, a decision was to be taken at a later stage. The biggest concern of General Marshall and the US chiefs was the potential diversion of attention and effort from the planned cross-Channel invasion of northern France, now inked in to take place on or around 1 May 1944. However, Marshall did see the benefit of continuing operations in the Mediterranean, so long as they were not open-ended. An assault on Italy would inevitably impose a massive commitment on Germany, which was all to the good. He also recognized that the swift capture of the southern half of Italy would open up the airfield complex at Foggia, where heavy bombers could then be stationed to continue the strategic air campaign against Germany; and Foggia was also a step closer to the Ploesti oilfields in Romania, Germany's only source of natural oil. A continuous tightening of the noose around Germany's neck was part of the agreed Allied strategy. What's more, decrypts of German Enigma-coded signals traffic had already revealed the Nazis' plans to abandon Italy south of the River Po, which runs across the northern plains south of the Alps. This suggested that Rome – and, more importantly as far as Marshall was concerned, Foggia – could be captured relatively easily in a limited campaign that made the best use of the enormous assets now gathered in the Mediterranean theatre.

Eisenhower was rather of the same mind. 'I recommend carrying the war to the mainland of Italy immediately Sicily has been captured,' Ike had cabled the Combined Chiefs on 18 July, 'and request very early approval in order that no time may be lost in making preparations.'

As it happened, two days earlier, Marshall had suggested a new plan to the Combined Chiefs: that Eisenhower should mount an amphibious operation to capture Naples and then drive on as quickly as possible to Rome. The Combined Chiefs swiftly approved Marshall's plan, and Eisenhower was now directed to start making preparations for Operation AVALANCHE alongside other plans for following up completion of the Sicilian campaign. By 27 July, with Mussolini toppled and Fascism gone, Eisenhower reported to the Combined Chiefs that he'd ordered two operations to be prepared: BUTTRESS, an invasion by Eighth Army into the toe of Italy; and AVALANCHE, using Lieutenant-General Mark Clark's Fifth Army, now building and training in North Africa, and incorporating both an American and a British corps. 'The military significance of recent political changes in Italy ought to be revealed during the next few days,' he wrote to the Combined Chiefs that same day, 'and it will then be possible to decide which of the two plans to put into effect. My one concern is speed of action and all our efforts are bent on launching the next operation as soon after the completion of HUSKY as is humanly possible to do so.' The Allies now urgently needed to smash open the Etna Line, burst through and finish the job in Sicily.

*

First on the list of HARDGATE's objectives was the town of Regalbuto, now held by a strong battlegroup of HG Division combat engineers, a company of Heilmann's 3. Fallschirmjäger, a battery of HG artillery, and a handful of tanks and assault guns. However poor the HG Division might have been at Gela, they were learning fast, especially in terms of defensive operations. Perhaps more importantly, they were no longer fleeing when the chips were down but staying and fighting it out with the kind of Teutonic discipline that had won the Germans so much respect as soldiers. At Regalbuto, an order had been issued to each man making it clear the town was to be held at all costs.

It was the job of the 1st Canadian and Malta Brigades to take Regalbuto. The main road from Agira ran along an east–west ridge, and the town itself was surrounded by a number of high hills, all of which would have to be taken in order to unlock the German defence. It was the Dorsets and Hampshires of the Malta Brigade who led the attack on the night of 30 July, the sky soon lit up with flares and a heavy response from machine guns, mortars, artillery and the dreaded Nebelwerfers. Although the Dorsets got a toehold on Monte Serione just to the north of the town, by daybreak the attack had stalled. Brigadier Roy Urquhart, the brigade commander, then sent in the Devons the following night, straight on to the ridge overlooking the road from Agira as it ran into the town. The Devons had had a bloody time at Agira, losing some 200 men; this time, with support from a massive 144 guns, by 2.35 a.m. on 1 August they were able to fire the success signal. The enemy then counter-attacked, pushing them back. Urquhart now arrived on the scene and, bringing forward his reserve company, urged all available men to give it one more effort to clear the ridge a second time. James Donaldson, who had been firing mortars all night, was now out of rounds. 'We were sitting with our backs to a little slope so we'd be out of danger,' said Donaldson. Urquhart then appeared and told them to pick up a rifle, fix bayonets and advance. 'It was the first bayonet charge I'd been in,' Donaldson added, 'and the first time I'd been with a rifle company in action.' They'd not charged so much as walked, picking their way through the prickly-pear cactus plants that seemed to cover the ridge. Canadian artillery was firing shot over their heads as Donaldson picked his way past dead Germans and dead Tommies. 'We had to keep moving all the time,' he said – but they did secure the ridge, and this time for good. In doing so, the Devons lost a further twenty-seven killed and eighty-two wounded.

It was turning into another attritional battle, with the British and Canadian attack chipping away at the enemy defences with a mass of artillery shelling, Kittyhawk fighter-bombers diving in on enemy positions during the day, and then the infantry pushing forward and clearing another hill by night. The Canadian infantry went in on the night of the 31st–1st along the Dorsets' route to the north of Regalbuto, but during the day were pinned down on the shale-littered slopes before the town. That night, the Hasty Ps were also thrown into the fray once again – their fourth battle in a fortnight. With all the casualties they had suffered, it was now a very different-looking unit; Farley Mowat had been made intelligence officer, while Bill Kennedy, despite being wounded at Agira, had insisted on remaining with the battalion and had become the third CO in a week. As it happened, General Conrath, most of whose combat engineers lay slaughtered within the battered town, had decided to pull out that night, so that when the Hasty Ps went in, they were able to make swift progress: first they took Monte Tiglio, a mile to the south, with ease, then crossed the road out of town and took another high point, Monte San Giorgio, to the south-east, and then swung north-west and took hold of what had been named Tower Hill behind Regalbuto. By dawn, the battle was over and Regalbuto was in Allied hands.

As the Hasty Ps lounged on the slopes overlooking the town early that morning, Allied medium bombers came over. Clearly, word of the town's capture had not reached them: as Mowat wrote, 'In leisurely style, they proceeded to churn the already battered streets and houses into heaps of smoking rubble.' Certainly, there wasn't much left of Regalbuto after this latest battle – another Sicilian town blasted into ruins. Yet Sicilians were still living in these places. Vincenza La Bruna and her family had suffered quite enough already in the war; but then one day they'd heard artillery shelling, distant at first and getting ever closer. After Agira, their own town had been next – not that Vincenza had known what was coming their way. 'Suddenly it was hell,' she said. 'Planes arrived, flying over the town, strafing everywhere.' During the bombing on the morning of the 2nd, a neighbour, seeing Vincenza's sister Pridda, offered her refuge in her house. 'But I discouraged,' said Vincenza. 'If we were to die, it was better to die embraced together, in our house.'

When the bombing was over, Vincenza and her family were relieved their house had been spared, although it had suffered blast damage and the front door was in pieces. 'Outside it was a disaster,' said Vincenza. 'Everywhere rubble, debris, fire dust – and corpses.' Among them was the neighbour who had offered shelter to Pridda. They decided to leave and head to Sparacollo, a farmstead to the north-east of the town, picking their way through the debris and past frightened and distressed townspeople, many of whom were looking for dead or missing relatives. It was desperate.

As part of the realigning and reorganization of Eighth Army prior to the launch of the new offensive, 13th Infantry Brigade were ordered up to Sferro and temporarily attached to the 51st Highland Division. The Scots were due to launch an assault across the Dittaino towards the town of Adrano in the Etna foothills, and General Leese wanted a brigade kept at Sferro to form a firm base. First to be sent from the 2nd Inniskillings were B Company and Advance HQ which included David Cole, newly promoted captain after the fighting at Lemon Bridge; advancement could come quickly during a vicious campaign like this one.

Just getting clear of the Catania Plain had involved dodging a few shells but, after safely reaching the rear, Cole and the rest of Advance HQ had embussed and trundled over the network of dusty grit roads until, clearing a ridge and heading down the long, straight route to Sferro, they approached the town just as night descended. Cole had heard nothing but bad things about Sferro, and first impressions didn't change his mind. Up ahead, flames leaped from a burning oil wagon on the railway line. As they drew closer, he saw an entire trainload of wagons shattered, burning and wrecked alongside equally smashed buildings. Cole thought it looked more like a Hollywood film set until they reached this godforsaken spot and he saw real chunks of masonry falling from the signal box as it was hit by a shell. Flames danced angrily and billowing oily smoke rolled into the sky. 'Everywhere the acrid fumes of explosives mingled with the odour of death,' he wrote. 'All this and the rattle of machine guns, with their tracers streaking into the sky, strengthened my feeling that this change of residence was not for the better.'

They had arrived as the Highland Division's artillery was battering the HG Division's positions to the north and the Germans were replying with a heavy barrage of their own right on to the shattered wreck of Sferro. Clambering swiftly out of their trucks, Cole and his men ran over the tracks to find the battalion HQ of the Highland Division unit they were replacing the following day. The signals officer was in a row of dugouts against a wall beyond a shattered goods shed, the makeshift refuge covered with sleepers and sandbags. There he found two signallers, huddled down and dimly lit by a torch bulb. Soon after, B Company men from his own battalion scuttled past carrying machine guns and ammo boxes. A hundred yards further on one of them opened up with a Tommy gun, which was answered by a burst from a German MP40 submachine gun.

Cole survived the night, despite having to undertake some urgent wire repair work and despite the dawn bringing a fresh deluge of mortars down upon them, and when the barrage lifted he was able to look around his blighted surroundings. Sferro stood at the western end of the Catania Plain, with hills to the south rising up to the rear of the British positions, behind which were their own artillery; beyond the narrowing plain to the north was yet another ridgeline from where the enemy were firing, and behind this was the Simeto valley and then the town of Paterno. Sferro stood on the forward *Hauptkampflinie*, as did Catenanuova, 10 miles to the north-west. In fact, the HG Division were on the point of pulling out from this section of the line and now, on the morning of 31 July, all that remained were rearguards. Every house in Sferro was damaged or totally destroyed. The express train still standing on the tracks was gutted, while dead German soldiers were strewn about the place. Some of the Jocks had put up signs. 'All change. The engine's bust,' had been written on the main platform sign for Sferro. 'Do not use while the train is standing at the platform,' another wag had written beside the station's latrine.

Now arriving just up the road at Catenanuova were the 78th 'Battleaxe' Division, which Montgomery planned to throw into the line immediately. Although the division was only a year old, its core had been formed from men who had served with the BEF in France and Belgium back in 1940, and so there was a good layer of experience, further enriched by the campaign in Tunisia. Setting sail in an LST on 27 July, the 17th Field Regiment had reached Avola at 8.30 a.m. on the 29th. 'Unloaded the ship in forty-five minutes,' Major Peter Pettit jotted in his diary, '(sixty-odd vehicles on two decks and 200 souls).' The division was due to go into action the following day, 30 July, so getting them into the line and in position was a challenge, not helped by a freak thunderstorm that broke out as they wound their way north. 'Streets in Vizzini and Palazzolo running like torrents,' noted Pettit. 'Mountains again, bad roads and bends. Heard guns again and smelt the peculiar odour of dead men.'

That same night, the leading elements of 78th Division, on the right of the Canadian 3rd Infantry Brigade, pushed across the River Dittaino and took Catenanuova with barely a shot: Hanns Cibulka's battery and the HG Division's troops had already pulled back to the Etna Line now that Agira had fallen and the old *Hauptkampflinie* had collapsed. The following night the 51st Highlanders, on 78th Division's right, also pushed forward, clearing the ridge beyond and seeing off counter-attacks from the last of the HG men. Gerbini was, at long last, in British hands.

The 39th Infantry had become the lost regiment of Seventh Army, passed first to Colonel Darby, and now attached to Allen's Big Red One. The rest of their 9th Division was on its way, but that day, 31 July, they were out on a limb, literally and metaphorically. They also had a new regimental commander in Harry 'Paddy' Flint, a tough, aggressive, bow-legged 56-year-old who had been in the army all his adult life and was a decidedly unique character within the US Army. A veteran of the First World War in France, since the outbreak of the Second he'd been serving first with the 2nd Armored Division and then on the staff at II Corps headquarters, where he had been badgering Bradley repeatedly for a combat command. When the 39th's commanding officer had broken a leg in a motor accident, he was finally given his chance. 'He expects to be killed,' Patton wrote of him to his wife Bea, 'and probably will be.'

Charlie Scheffel first met Flint a couple of days before the battle for Troina began, when he and other officers were summoned to the regimental CP to meet their new commanding officer. He'd been talking with a few of his fellows when a craggy, lean-faced man wearing cowboy boots and a black bandana round his neck ambled over and introduced himself. Shaking hands with them all, he asked Scheffel where he was from, then told him he'd been stationed near Enid, Oklahoma after the First World War. 'Stayed at the Youngblood quite a few times,' he said. Scheffel smiled; the Youngblood Hotel was notorious as a place to pick up prostitutes.

Then Flint smoothed a bit of ground and with his swagger stick drew AAA-O in the dirt. 'Anybody know what it is?' he asked.

'Looks like a cattle brand,' answered Scheffel.

'That's right, son,' said Flint, then explained. This was triple-A-bar-zero. 'Gentlemen, this is going to be our new motto. It means anything, anytime, anywhere, bar nothing.' Turning to the supply officer, he added, 'By tomorrow morning, I want every helmet in the regiment to have triple-A-bar-zero on both sides, two-inch letters, white paint.' By the next day, it was done, and the regiment pushed forwards down Highway

120 towards Cerami and Troina, in the van of the Big Red One's renewed advance.

Along Seventh Army's front, the Americans were discovering there were no more quick and easy victories to be had, no more mass surrenders to be expected. Rather, they were rapidly learning, as the British and Canadians had been learning, that this bloody mountain fighting against a determined foe was an entirely different kettle of fish from hoovering up browbeaten Italians who had lost the will to fight. On the north coastal road, it had taken the 45th Thunderbirds four days to get over the Tusa Ridge – and even when they did get through, on 29 July, they were heavily counter-attacked 10 miles from Santo Stefano by a reinforced Kampfgruppe Fullreide, and sent back almost all the way to the Tusa Ridge again. Overseeing the fighting here was Generalmajor Walter Fries, the 29. Panzer Grenadier Division's commander: another battle-hardened veteran of multiple campaigns who was still fighting despite having only one arm and one leg. No German troops were going to be giving up the ghost any time soon on his watch.

The counter-thrust made by Fries and Fullreide was eventually halted by American artillery, which took time to be deployed afresh, but also by the arrival of Task Force 88, which Patton had asked for but had suspected Alexander would not ever deliver. Yet Alex had assured him help would be forthcoming and had been as good as his word, as he always was. Task Force 88 included the cruisers *Philadelphia* and *Savannah*, six destroyers and a host of amphibious craft that could, if needed, help mount leap-frogging operations and also move heavy equipment and weaponry up the coast in an effort to ease congestion on the narrow coast road. That same day, 29 July, the Germans pulled back east of Santo Stefano, and the 45th Division finally reached the town the following morning.

Meanwhile, to their south, the Big Red One was approaching Troina, the highest town in all of Sicily. This was a key strongpoint on the Etna Line, perched on a high mountainous outcrop with wide, sweeping crests and folds all around. Up there, it felt like a different world – a high plain with its own valleys, ridges and gullies. There was also a remoteness to it that was almost unique on Sicily. The rest of civilization felt a long way away; the road leading to it wound its way ever higher until, over yet another brow, there it was in the distance, nestling around the shallow cone of a mountain, with Etna, ever-present, looming behind.

General Terry Allen expected Troina to be a pretty straightforward operation. What intelligence they had on the town suggested it was lightly held; and, as if to add to the mood of cautious optimism, Cerami, 8 miles of winding road to the west, was captured with a minimal amount of fuss early on 31 July. As it happened, General Rodt, the 15. Panzer Grenadier Division commander, was so concerned about the state of his troops that he wondered whether it might not be better to retreat further to the east. So far, he'd lost more than 1,600 men, which was a major dent in the front-line strength of his division. Once again, it was Fullreide's and Ens's *Kampfgruppen* who were expected to take on the Americans at Troina, and both units were starting to feel the strain, especially since there had not been any substantial replacements.

However, when Rodt suggested abandoning the town, Hube dismissed the suggestion out of hand. In fact, Der Mann had personally overseen the defence of this high mountain town. Engineers from 15. Panzer Grenadier Division had been sent up there well in advance as part of the preparations for the Etna Line defences. Stone sangers – small defensive positions – were built, scrapes dug, mines laid and fields of fire cleared, while gun, mortar and MG positions were all carefully worked out and made mutually supporting, with troops from the Divisione Aosta roped in to help with the labour. In pretty quick order, Troina had become a mountain fortress.

So it was that instead of the quick and easy victory Allen had hoped it would prove, Troina became a cauldron of bitter violence and destruction. When the 39th Infantry pushed on from Cerami that Saturday, 31 July, the air was suddenly alive with screaming shells and Nebelwerfers, stopping them in their tracks.

'Troina's going to be tougher than we thought,' Terry Allen told Bradley the following morning. 'The Kraut's touchy as hell here.'

CHAPTER 28

Troina and Centuripe

O N THE EVENING OF 31 July, Terry Allen had explained to Bradley that he was now planning a much larger-scale attack on Troina, and had brought up not only the three infantry regiments of the Big Red One but also the Goums, who were being passed around as much as the 39th Infantry. Flint's men were to spearhead the attack again, with the 18th Infantry attacking from the south, the 26th to the north and the 16th in reserve. Supporting them were no fewer than twenty-four artillery battalions – nigh on three hundred guns.

On paper, it was a formidable force that had been assembled; but on that Sunday, 1 August, it wasn't enough. The narrow and limited road network, lined with mines, bridges blown and holed by craters, meant a terrible log-jam of traffic so that much of the artillery simply couldn't get forward. Flint decided to attack anyway, and managed to get his leading companies from Scheffel's 1st Battalion on to a key bit of high ground, Hill 1034, less than 2 miles west of the town, where they came up against the weakened Kampfgruppe Ens. Although it wasn't Flint's place to lead his men into battle in person, he was visibly out in front, and at one point stood up from their cover and, banging his chest, yelled, 'Hey, you fuckers, we're coming to get you!' He might have been at best eccentric and at worst completely mad, but the men loved it. By dusk, however, Oberst Ens had managed to rally his men and they launched a brutal counter-attack, pushing the 1st Battalion back a mile. By midnight, the battalion was down to just three hundred men. They'd been slaughtered.

Allen now tried a double envelopment, sending his men to the north and to the south to try encircling Troina. Getting the men into position and bringing up all the guns took time, so the next day the Americans made little ground; even the Goums to the north, trained to fight in mountains, were unable to get across the Troina river, and in the heat and dust the day's fighting was dominated by an artillery slugging match. Although the 26th Infantry, sweeping around the north, made some progress, it was not until Tuesday, 3 August, when the Big Red One attacked at three in the morning, that another major assault was made. The 18th was to attack from the small town of Gagliano, around 6 miles to the south of Troina. It meant a stiff climb, and their lines of advance took them well clear of any road; so not only was their vast arsenal of motorized vehicles going to be no use to them at all, since they wouldn't be able to get their 105mm howitzers into position, Cannon Company were going to be out of a job. With this in mind, Lieutenant Frank Johnson and the rest of Cannon Company were now attached to the Anti-Tank Company as muleteers. Around fifty emaciated animals were hastily bought from impoverished Sicilian peasants and sent up the trail to the 18th's supply dump at the base of Monte Pellegrino, 3 miles to the south of Troina. There, Johnson and his men improvised saddles and packs and bridles using old ammo bags, blankets and rope, then loaded each of these beasts of burden with some 250 pounds of mortar shells, twelve cases of rations, or several reels of phone wire and radio equipment. This, though, was the easy part. None of them had any experience of handling animals, let alone cajoling laden mules over skyline crags and precipitous cliffs by night on unfamiliar terrain. 'How to make a mule move is still the animal's secret,' wrote Johnson. 'We pull on the reins, to the accompaniment of bites; we push from behind, getting kicked more than once; we gently tap their ears with a club, receiving only a scornful flopping; we even seductively whisper sweet nothings in persuasion, but somehow our charges fail to share our realization of the urgent need of supplies topside.'

Nebelwerfers helped stall the American attack yet again that Tuesday, as did the constant withering fire of machine guns and mortars. General Bradley visited Allen in the morning, joining him in his CP, an empty school-house with the Fascist slogan, 'believe, obey, fight', painted on one of the exterior walls. Bradley knew Allen was well aware of the importance of this battle, but had developed doubts about him. For one thing, he worried he was getting tired; it was also well known that the Big Red One commander liked a drink.

A battalion of twelve 155mm 'Long Tom' howitzers, six-wheeled towed beasts, had been dragged into position behind the school-house and began pounding the enemy, their muzzle blasts rippling the roof tiles.

'Terry,' Bradley said, turning to him, 'could you arrange to have those guns shoot over the building instead of through it?' Allen reached for the field telephone and the guns were moved back a short distance.

So far, II Corps had rarely called on direct air support, but now, at Troina, air support parties on the ground were radioing in target requests directly to controllers, who then passed them on to the fighters. What was needed was ground fighter control units equipped with VHF radio that would enable them to talk directly to the pilots above; that would come, but in early August 1943, the Allies were still feeling their way with close air support operations. Further trials and much refining of methods were needed.

As a result, fighter-bomber operations over the battlefield were at times haphazard. Around Troina, with smoke hampering visibility, ground troops fighting at close quarters and pilots dependent on maps on their knees as they flew, pinpointing targets correctly was difficult, to say the least. A P-40 Kittyhawk, for example, flying over at 340 miles per hour, might have a run-in to its target of as little as half a mile, a mile at most, giving the pilot just five to ten seconds in which to assess wind speed, peg his own speed and establish a stable attitude. Even from 500 feet off the deck, the target itself – a gun battery, for example – would be tiny to the naked eye and, without any kind of weapons guidance system, and only a basic gyro-stabilized gunsight through which to judge release range and account for any crosswind, whether it was hit or not was really a matter of luck. Close air support hammered the town, but inevitably also dropped bombs in the wrong places. A column of American tanks was strafed, while aircraft also narrowly avoided bombing General Allen's CP. All this meant that up there around Troina, close air support was only of limited help.

The key, as always in mountain warfare, was to take the high ground around an objective, because from there observers could pinpoint enemy targets and direct fire. The trouble was, that meant infantry had to emerge from where they were hidden into open ground and get moving. Smoke shells, artillery, their own mortars and suppressing fire could all help. It was recognized on Sicily, for example, that the distinct 'brrrrrp' of the German MG42 and the more solid rapid fire of the .30-calibre or Browning automatic rifle would rarely be heard in the same vicinity at once, because one side would fire then duck down, then the other would have a go. None the less, advancing forward over open ground took guts of steel, along with determined and dogged leadership to keep the men going, and was, needless to say, extremely dangerous – even more so on a mountain where the soil was so thin. Men would advance spaced out, perhaps ten yards apart, but that distance was often hard to maintain, and, in any case, a single mortar shell or two-second burst from a machine gun could easily fell an entire squad of ten men, leaving perhaps two dead, two more severely wounded and the rest hurt enough to be out of the battle. Battalions moved forward in companies, usually eighty or so men at a time, two platoons up front, one behind in reserve, with medics and company HQ attached. Of the four companies in each battalion, no more than three – at most, but usually only two – would be attacking at any one time. This meant a battalion attack generally had around 240 men at the sharp end, and since a regiment would usually only send two battalions forward at a time, an infantry division's attack at any given moment would involve directly about 1,500 men – about 10 per cent of its total strength.

Although Allen's men at Troina were attacking across a 10-mile front, each regiment was doing so with its individual battalions, companies, platoons and squads, and it was very easy for these to become bogged down. A platoon would start taking casualties, men would shelter behind rocks or in the many gullies, or behind crests and ridgelines, and suddenly the attack would be stalled. Shells would be continuing to scream over, mortars crashing, machine guns burping and chattering. The noise would be immense, the ground would shake, and the concussion of heavy shells would ripple over the troops with a blast of wind and debris. Grit, stone and dust would clatter on their helmets, a buddy would get shot or have a leg or arm shattered or his guts ripped out or get blown to smithereens. It was amazing, really, that anyone had the courage to get up and keep going at all.

And this was why assaults against a determined defender equipped with decent weaponry took time. In fact, if the infantry failed to take an objective swiftly, there was really only one way of winning and that was to grind down the enemy by hurling over twice, three, four times as much ordnance at him. One tactic Germans could always be relied upon to use was counter-attack – and that was the moment of vulnerability for them, because the moment they got up out of their own foxholes and sheltered positions, they faced exactly the same problems that confronted the American infantry, only worse.

General Rodt, the 15. Panzer Grenadier Division's commander, had won a defensive victory on 3 August, but the Big Red One had still made ground; they were getting closer. That evening, Oberst Ens's men counter-attacked once more against Hill 1034, where the 16th Infantry had taken over from Flint's men. And once again, American artillery ensured the panzer-grenadiers made only limited gains. Unlike the Americans, the Germans had no reserves at all, and that night Rodt asked Hube again if he could pull back his men. No, was the answer, again. Neither Hitler nor Kesselring had authorized the evacuation of Sicily, and that meant they had to go on holding out for as long as possible. Troina was key to ensuring that.

From down in the Dittaino valley, the town of Centuripe could be seen in the distance, perched impossibly high in the mountains. At certain times of the day when the sun was high, it twinkled and shimmered, a silvery line on the top of a briefly flat crest. The town sat on neither the *Hauptkampflinie* nor the Etna Line, but roughly in between the two, a jutting outpost. However, because of its height, and because it lay on the same ridge as Leonforte, Assoro, Agira and Regalbuto, it stood sentinel to the Etna Line, imperiously guarding the key towns of Paterno and Adrano. If the British could get up on Centuripe, they would be able to stare down at these latter towns and unlock the entire position around the south of Etna – and with it, Misterbianco and Catania. Equally, if the Germans there could hold on, then they could very well frustrate British ambitions for quite some time to come.

Centuripe was one of the most extraordinary towns in all of Sicily. Built on the apex of a number of spurs and ridgelines and then spread along them, from the air it looked either rather like a thick-limbed starfish or a prostrate man, depending on the angle of view. Lying some 2,000 feet above the Dittaino and Simeto valleys, it could be reached only via one winding, narrow road of numerous switchbacks that ran from one valley up to the town and then back down again to the other. All around it were the arms and legs of the ridges that fanned out from its centre, and which plunged precipitously, sometimes in sheer drops, at other places in a series of 6-foot-high terraced walls, elsewhere in banks of loose stone and scree. Guarding Centuripe now were some of the best German troops on the island, men from 'King' Ludwig Heilmann's 3. Fallschirmjäger – the 1. Bataillon and much of the 2. Bataillon – bolstered by some Panzer Mk IIIs, a field artillery battery and an anti-tank troop from the HG Panzer Grenadier Division. *Fallschirmjäger* had double the number of machine guns a normal infantry unit would have – one every five men, rather than one every ten. This meant that every approach up to the town was covered not only by mortars and artillery fire, but also – and especially – by machine guns, whose teams had been placed in such a way that the moment anyone attacking showed their head, they would come within the field of fire.

It was the newly arrived 78th Battleaxe Division who were given the unenviable task of capturing this imposing objective; and, because of the successful capture of Catenanuova more quickly than expected, Major-General Evelegh decided to bring forward his attack by twenty-four hours. As a result, his 36th Brigade were sent in to attack on Sunday, 1 August. The key to their chances of success, as always, was the fire support – even *Fallschirmjäger* couldn't be firing their MGs properly when shells were falling all around them – but Major Peter Pettit and the 17th Field Artillery were struggling to find the right places to set up their batteries of 25-pounders. Excellent field guns though they were, each weighed more than 1½ tons and required a Morris Commercial Quad – or equivalent – gun tractor to tow it, plus an extra ammunition limber. The 17th, like all British field artillery regiments, consisted of three batteries of eight guns, so twenty-four in all – and while they were terrific once in position, the problem in Sicily, particularly when firing at such an oddly shaped and difficult bit of high ground as Centuripe, was successfully getting them into good firing positions in the first place; below the town, there were few opportunities for a 25-pounder, Quad and limber to get off the road and deploy. 'We recce almond groves on steep hillside and move in after dark,' noted Pettit in his diary. 'Very difficult country, rocks, bad roads and worse tracks cratered or landslid.'

Evelegh's 36th Brigade managed to cross the open country before nightfall and then launched its attack that night – but made only limited progress, so that by first light the next day, 2 August, none of the infantry battalions were in the town itself, but rather were pinned down some way short, Centuripe still towering over them up slopes that looked even more precipitous and impossible than they did from the valley floor. During the morning, they continued to try to inch their way further up the slopes; but while progress could be made through the hidden gullies and folds in the land, the moment they emerged into the open, machine-gun bullets scythed through the air and another wave of mortars whistled down.

As the day progressed, however, so the supporting artillery increasingly began to join the fight. In all, there were three field regiments and a further three regiments of medium artillery firing 5.5-inch howitzers, so the best part of 150 guns in support, of which only a fraction had been available the day before. Getting them into position was not at all easy, because the road up was both covered by enemy fire and cratered; the engineers worked ceaselessly to repair it so that the artillery could get into position. Peter Pettit and the 17th FA moved up as close as they could, but the road was a nightmare to climb. 'It is cut out of mountainsides,' he jotted in his diary, 'with hairpin bends galore and steeply terraced almond groves on either side. Go over and you drop for hundreds of feet.'

General Evelegh decided to bring in a second brigade, the 38th Irish, to attack the town again that night; one of its battalions, the 2nd London Irish Rifles, were to climb west of the town and capture three high features, Hills 611, 704 and 703 on their maps, which covered the northwest of the town. From here, the London Irish could give mortar and machine-gun support for an assault by the 1st Royal Irish Fusiliers – or 'Faughs' as they were known – who were to attack the town's cemetery at the end of the western arm of Centuripe's prostrate man. The 6th Royal Inniskilling Fusiliers, meanwhile, were to attack up what had already been dubbed 'Suicide Gully' – the prostrate man's left leg.

In the 6th Skins, 10 Platoon sergeant in A Company was Ray Phillips, a tough soldier who'd fought well in Tunisia. As a rule of thumb, infantrymen – of whatever nationality – could be divided into four rough groups, which for argument's sake could be labelled A, B, C and D. Most fell into Category C – men who were willing to do their bit but didn't want to be there, weren't interested in using their initiative very much, wanted to keep their heads down and prayed they might survive. Category Ds were those who simply couldn't cope at all – who were terrified, and who would most likely crumble in the face of danger or run away. Numbers in Category D were small. Then there were Category As – adrenalin junkies, thrill-seekers, who regarded war as little more than Boy Scouts with guns. These were the most gung-ho and would be the first to join any special forces. There weren't many of these, either. But then there were the Category Bs – men who didn't want to be in the war, would far rather be at home, but would go the extra mile to get the job done and who would selflessly look out for others above themselves. These were comparatively few in number, but there were enough of them to keep the armies going. Typically, they were company commanders or sergeants. They were the backbone of any infantry unit, the glue around which the Category Cs could function. Sergeant Ray Phillips was one such man.

The battalion had moved up the previous day, 1 August, marching through cleared minefields, over blown bridges, on through Catenanuova and past what had been the HG Division command post. All around them they had seen a lot of abandoned equipment and transport, as well as plenty of dead. 'The pioneer battalion had gone on ahead,' noted the battalion diarist, 'and had buried most of the dead Boche by the time the main body arrived so the stench wasn't too bad, but the hum of a dead mule wasn't too pleasant.'

Orders to push on up and take over from 36th Brigade were received and they were told to be ready to move at 3.30 the following morning, 2 August. They moved out at 4 a.m., heading up the slopes for the best part of 2 miles, which entailed a climb of nearly 2,000 feet along tracks so bad even the mules couldn't cope; there was nothing for it but to hump everything themselves, including the No. 22 radio set, which weighed more than 16kg, plus spare batteries. They had been expecting to climb straight into the town, but when mortars started falling nearby it became clear that 36th Brigade had not managed to take the peaks and that they would have to do that first. They paused on a knoll marked on their maps as Point 640, hidden from view from the summit, and began sending out patrols, while B Company moved across a gully to Point 664, in order to attack up the right leg of the prostrate man. The heat, as ever, bore down. Exhausted after their climb, they were short of water and energy, so Brigade HQ decided they should not launch their attack until later that afternoon.

The battalion was briefed for attack at 3 p.m., by which time mortars and Nebelwerfers were screaming over and they started to take casualties. In A Company alone, two men were killed and eleven injured. They set off at 4.30, with C Company leading behind heavy artillery fire. Their first objective was Point 709, on which stood a large church, Santa Nicola, at the end of the left leg. Following behind were A Company, led off by 10 Platoon. Sergeant Phillips had listened carefully to the briefing; there was no alternative to Suicide Gully; they could expect MG42s to fire on them, and there were lots of Jerry paratroopers about. The situation, Phillips thought, looked pretty hopeless. They were also told to carry their rations as well as ammo and the men began to grumble. Phillips wasn't having it. 'The damn job's got to be done,' he told them, 'so let's do it.' Phillips had a new platoon commander, Lieutenant Morrow, who he thought was a grand chap, but who was about to go into action for the first time. As they got moving, the air was soon filled with zipping bullets and fizzing shards of shrapnel and Morrow was hit in the head, so Phillips took over command.

Up ahead, C Company had somehow managed to get into the edge of the town, but there were still plenty of enemy firing at Phillips and his men as they scaled an almost sheer 100-foot-high rock face. 'God, what a job,' he wrote. 'It seemed impossible with all the arms, ammo and weight of food etc., still, bashed on we did, it was child's play for Jerry to pick us off as we were climbing, still he was a hell of a poor shot and only got 4 of my boys, the bastard.' On they went, and Phillips managed to clamber up on to the road that ran around and beneath the Church of Santa Nicola, the rest of the platoon following. Then one of his best men lost his footing, stumbled and fell backwards on to a mine which blew him sky high; tragic as it was, Phillips was all too aware they might well have all suffered the same fate. Ahead was a small shack, so he charged it and smashed down the door, but found no enemy inside. It provided a good place for his men to pause and get their wind back, so while they rested, Phillips went for a look around. Shocked by the state of the shacks the townspeople called home, he saw the church at the end of the promontory about 200 yards away so decided that should be their next objective.

He was now joined by Major George 'Hobo' Crocker, the A Company commander, only recently back in the line, having been wounded in Tunisia. Phillips wondered where the rest of his company was, but it seemed Crocker had lost them in the climb and his wireless set was out of order. There were only twenty-four men now in 10 Platoon, most of them in fact not Irish at all but Welshmen – a not uncommon situation by this stage of the war, as regional regiments were filled with whoever arrived from the training depots. Phillips had also lost his mortar team and his PIAT man, wielding the only anti-tank weapon they had as infantrymen. This was not a time for dilly-dallying, however; Phillips knew they had to get on, and so, having made a quick appreciation, he got his section commanders together – all three corporals he knew he could rely on – and told them the plan. They were going to make a dash for the church. There would be small arms firing at them, but it couldn't be helped; this was a key objective, overlooked the advance of the rest of the battalion following behind, and had to be secured. And there was only one thing for it: to run as hard as they could. Phillips led 1st Section, and although four of his men were mown down the others reached the church and stormed inside, fortunately finding it empty. With the remainder of the platoon safely in and around the church he took a quick roll-call and discovered he had only thirteen men left, although all three of his NCOs were still standing. No sooner had they had a brief pause to catch their breath again than the Germans counter-attacked, in what looked like company strength. 'We gave them hell,' he wrote, 'fired everything we had into the swines, killed a hell of a lot, good show.'

Being holed up in the church now didn't seem such a good idea after all, so he told his men they were going to simply charge the enemy. Out they went, shouting and firing Bren guns and Tommy guns from the hip. The startled Germans turned and ran, and Phillips and his men followed right into the heart of the town, to a small triangular piazza. He'd had in mind to push on round to Point 709, which was B Company's objective on the prostrate man's right leg, but the town was now swarming with more Germans, who had recovered their balance. Taking cover, they fired back, but more of his men were getting hit. Phillips himself was nicked on the arm and, having had it bandaged up, tried to see if he could get any help, but it was hopeless – they were effectively surrounded. Back with his men, he told them there was nothing for it but to give the enemy hell for as long as possible. With luck, the rest of the battalion would join them. 'We were in a tight corner,' he noted, 'but Jerry had to come and get us and he didn't dare, for as soon as one poked his head out, he had it.'

They were still holed up as dusk descended. Elsewhere, the sounds of battle could be heard, although from the piazza it was hard to tell from what direction. In fact, by 9 p.m. the London Irish had managed to secure all three of their objectives, the high points to the north-west of the town, while the Faughs had also got on to Point 711, the town's cemetery, at the end of the left arm of the prostrate man. By now, Phillips had just eight men left – and then his two best Bren gunners, Beer and Dackin, were hit, a big blow. At this point an Italian tank rumbled into a street 150 yards away; Phillips knew he couldn't allow it to get into the fight, so, grabbing one of the Brens, he let it get within 100 yards then opened up with the machine gun, emptying some thirteen magazines at it. Fortunately, it did the trick: the tank reversed and disappeared out of sight.

With darkness, Phillips took two of his remaining men and went out on a recce to see just how many Germans were still about, so that he could judge whether to make a break for it. There seemed to be far too many for comfort and so, getting back to what was left of his platoon, he led them down into a coal cellar where he hoped they could hide until reinforcements arrived. Outside, they could hear the enemy troops talking and searching for them, but eventually it seemed to quieten down and so, telling his men to stay put, he ventured out again, and this time found the rest of the battalion who had begun clearing the town. Hobo Crocker had been wounded and so was sent off to an RAP; and at daylight, Phillips began the search for those of his men who had been killed. 'Found 3,' he noted, 'and as I was going to one I found an Itie taking the boots off the body. I shot the swine dead.' At roll-call, he had just four men still standing from a platoon of thirty-seven. 'Too bad,' he added, 'but we won the day.' The Germans, who had already begun thinning out in the town early the previous evening, had now pulled back. The Battle-axe Division had taken Centuripe; and once again, it was the infantry who had had to claw their way forward, and at a terrible cost. For the survivors, there would be more fighting to come; but for the time being, Phillips and the rest of A Company were able to enjoy some hot tea and breakfast and then a chance to sleep for the rest of the day, before loading up on to trucks and moving on, down the winding hairpins amid clouds of dust and on towards Adrano on the Etna Line, their next objective. 'Goodbye Centuripe,' wrote Phillips, 'you ghost town of the heavens.'

A little way to the north, at Troina, the battle continued to rage. On the night of 3 August, Frank Johnson and his men were attempting to lead their first mule train up on to Monte Pellegrino. They'd not gone far, however, when the lead mule stopped and nothing would make it move again. Everyone was cursing furiously when they heard a shell whistle in; all the men ducked, but the mule stood where it was and was hurled off into the chasm below. 'Although we have lost his twelve cases of chow,' noted Johnson, 'our path is clear and for once I am glad to see the enemy make a hit.'

The following morning, Wednesday 4 August, the fighting was just as vicious as on the previous one. By now, eighteen artillery battalions were pummelling the German positions. Waves of fighter-bombers, operating in fighter groups and wings, flew over, and whether they were accurate or not, Charlie Scheffel, for one, was both very pleased to see them and impressed with the results. As they thundered over, the American artillery fire slackened and the Kittyhawks began diving down; and as the bombs exploded, so Troina itself disappeared behind rolling clouds of smoke and dust. 'They swept into Troina,' he wrote, 'engines screaming over the gunfire and dropped their bombs right on the target. The town erupted in explosions as the planes pulled up in a steep climb, fell into a quick sideways turn and roared back across the town on a low strafing run.' Among those flying that day were Charlie Dryden and the 99th Fighter Squadron; whether reducing Troina to rubble was helping their compatriots' cause, though, was another matter. It certainly didn't particularly help the infantry assaults that day, and especially not to the north of the town where Oberst Fullreide's men carried out numerous local counter-attacks. One was launched by the Italians of the Aosta's 5° Reggimento di Fanteria, who managed to capture around forty Americans from the 26th Infantry.

Ernie Pyle was up at the front line to see the Troina battle for himself, and noticed that a lot of the men he saw looked utterly exhausted. He was not surprised. 'I believe the outstanding trait in any campaign is the terrible weariness that gradually comes over everybody,' he noted. 'Soldiers become exhausted in mind and in soul as well as physically.' The men of the Big Red One had been on the go since 10 July almost without let-up, walking, fighting, clambering into trucks, getting out again – repeatedly. Pyle had been at the divisional CP when a breathless runner arrived and went up to one of the captains.

'"I've got to find Captain Blank right away," he said. "Important message."

"But I am Captain Blank," the officer replied. "Don't you recognise me?"

The runner looked at him and said again, "I've got to find Captain Blank right away," and then dashed off again.'

Pyle had seen enough of war by this stage to understand fully the plight of these men. 'It's the perpetual, choking dust, the muscle-racking hard ground,' he wrote, 'the snatched food sitting ill on the stomach, the heat and the flies and dirty feet and the constant roar of engines and the perpetual moving and the never settling down and the go, go, go, night and day, and on through the night again. Eventually, it all works itself into an emotional tapestry of one dull, dead pattern – yesterday is tomorrow and Troina is Randazzo and when will we ever stop and, God, I'm so tired.'

Again, on the 5th, the American advance was stopped before Troina; but with the 9th Division now arriving and being thrown into the battle alongside Flint's men, II Corps was biting out ever larger chunks of enemy ground and inching ever closer, although still having to fend off repeated local counter-attacks. On Monte Basilio, 2 miles to the north of the town, Company I of 3rd Battalion, 26th Infantry, had just seventeen men still standing. As Fullreide's men counter-attacked the hill yet again, Private James W. Reese moved his mortar squad to where he could get at the enemy and kept a steady stream of shells raining down on them. When his own position came under fire, he told his squad to pull back, picked up his mortar, moved again and, with the three remaining shells he had left, took out an enemy MG team. Grabbing a discarded rifle, he then carried on firing until eventually he was cut down and killed. Reese was posthumously awarded the Congressional Medal of Honor for what he did that day.

By now, the 18th Infantry had taken all of Monte Pellegrino and were not going to be pushed off it again by Oberst Ens's exhausted battle-group. Forward observers could now see where the Germans were firing from, and were able to knock out at least ten enemy gun positions. Over the previous six days, the Battle of Troina had become a terrible, bloody slugging match; and while it was inevitable that eventually the Americans would chew up the defenders so badly they would no longer be able to carry on, every act of astonishing heroism from the Americans had been matched by the Germans, whose units were all horrendously depleted.

Saturday, 7 August was another sunny day of clear blue skies. As the 16th Infantry began their latest advance up the steep slopes towards the shattered remains of Troina, for the first time there was no return fire. Overnight, it seemed, Rodt had finally pulled his men back. The brutal battle for Troina was over.

CHAPTER 29

The Etna Battles

Away from the battlefields of Sicily, many high-level conversations were going on behind closed doors. After the fall of Mussolini, Kesselring had visited Badoglio, who assured the field marshal he had had nothing to do with the coup and had known nothing about it, but had felt honour bound to answer the call when the King had asked him to take up the reins. This, of course, was a whopping lie. He fully intended to continue the alliance, he told Kesselring – which, curiously enough, wasn't quite the fib it at first seemed. The German C-in-C South then visited Ambrosio, still head of the Comando Supremo, who, like Badoglio, stressed Italy's determination to continue fighting. On the basis of these meetings, he then reported to Hitler and the OKW that he believed the professed Italian intentions were sincere and thought it would be a mistake to pursue the plot to capture the Italian leadership in Rome, as the Führer had vowed to do. However, he also reckoned German troops would be able to occupy and hold Italy and the Balkans if sufficient numbers were sent in. The 3. Panzer Grenadier Division was already in Italy, and, as it happened, the 2. Fallschirmjäger Division had now arrived as well, ready to help carry out the planned coup; Kesselring had explained away their presence as reinforcements for Sicily, which Badoglio and Ambrosio accepted. Nor did the Italians appear to object in principle to German units moving into the north of Italy to protect the southern flank of the Reich and the Alpine passes.

On 28 July, the plan for the immediate capture of the King and the Italian leadership was dropped, in part because of Kesselring's report, in part because Jodl was strongly against it, and largely because by that time Hitler had calmed down a little after his initial fury and accepted that a longer game needed to be played with the Italians. Kesselring visited him in person on 29 July, and the Führer and OKW agreed instead to try to keep the alliance going for as long as possible, certainly until they were ready to carry out Operation ALARICH – now renamed, with brilliant irony, ACHSE, or AXIS in English – which would see German troops sweep in, swiftly disarm the entire Italian military and occupy the country by force. Rounding up the King and the Italian leadership would be part and parcel of this operation.

This meant no sudden and hurried evacuation of Sicily lest it alarm the Italian leadership. Even so, Kesselring knew his men had to be prepared; there were now significant numbers of German troops on the island, and they were not to be lost as their compatriots had been in Tunisia. Evacuation plans needed to begin, and on 28 July Hube had ordered Oberst Hans-Günther Baade to start making a viable and efficient plan to get as many German troops out of Sicily as possible. Whether it was a matter of days or weeks, when the time came the Germans needed to be ready to act, and act fast. Initially, Kesselring rather hastily told Hitler that German forces would be sent across the Straits of Messina over three nights. On 2 August, however, Hube submitted a different plan, code-named Operation LEHRGANG, which was based on an evacuation over five nights.

A measured, efficient five-night crossing, Hube believed, would give his troops a much better chance of successfully getting off the island with as much equipment as possible; three nights was simply too rushed and, he believed, not necessary. Geography and infrastructure greatly favoured his exit plan, because the narrowing of the Messina peninsula allowed him to create ever shorter defensive lines. As his men fell back, so fewer troops would be needed to maintain each narrower line, which would allow the bulk of his forces to get across the Straits before the last line was overrun. The Allies could pound their positions with as many aircraft as they liked, but Baade was already assembling an astonishingly large number of anti-aircraft and other guns either side of the Straits, while the narrowing of the peninsula and the limited road network would constrain the numbers of ground troops the Allies could throw at them. Keeping a cool head in the days to come was going to be vital, and Hube had one of the coolest around; he wasn't Der Mann for nothing.

By the evening of 5 August, however, Hube had realized that the Etna Line had been smashed wide open. The loss of Centuripe, the pressure on Adrano and Paterno, and the battering 15. Panzer Grenadier had taken at Troina had persuaded him the time had come to pull back to the next defensive line, and the last one that ran south of Etna – what Guzzoni had termed the Tortorici Line. It meant abandoning all those towns, and, at last, Catania too, but uppermost in his mind was the need to ensure that his units were not surrounded, cut off and taken prisoner; the moment one part of the line crumbled, the risk of that happening became just too great. Maintaining balance, and pulling back with as much cohesion as possible, was vital.

Meanwhile, on 31 July, Generale Guzzoni had received a directive from the Comando Supremo in Rome telling him to hand over all remaining Italian troops on Sicily to the command of Hube and XIV Panzer Korps. In truth, Hube had barely paid him lip service since arriving on the island, but at midday on 1 August Guzzoni formally relinquished the reins; he still maintained his Sixth Army headquarters, however, feeling that, until ordered to the contrary, he had to remain at his post, no matter how impotently. The withdrawal of Guzzoni's authority rather left von Senger twiddling his thumbs as well – although he too remained on Sicily, pending any instructions to the contrary. At this point he was encamped in a wood high in the mountains halfway between the northern slopes of Etna and Milazzo on the north-east coast. This ensured he was close to Hube and Guzzoni but also within easy reach of Baade, who visited him frequently to talk through his evacuation plans and get his advice. 'Both of us had the feeling of having left the stage,' wrote von Senger, 'in order – as Baade expressed it – to watch this cosmic event from the box.' Even up there, though, von Senger was hardly safe; every time he drove anywhere, he was at risk of attack by Allied aircraft. Then, in early August, he was forced to move his camp when an enemy plane was shot down and crashed into the trees nearby, setting them alight. In between his duties and dodging Allied aircraft, however, von Senger found time to head to the coast and bathe in the sea; and on these occasions, for a short while, the endless fighting and destruction would disappear as he immersed himself in the cool and twinkling azure blue of the Mediterranean.

On several evenings he dined with Guzzoni, of whom he had become fond. He respected the general's honesty and sympathized with him over the invidious situation in which he found himself. It was clear to both men that the King and Badoglio wanted out, but Guzzoni was not part of any plotting or even privy to what was going on back in Rome, and he believed he should continue as he'd been ordered to do until those instructions changed. Both men knew the war was already lost. Both wished it could all be over. 'Naturally,' noted von Senger, 'the mood in the dining caravan was gloomy.' He noticed that while Guzzoni still had a portrait of the King on display, the frame where Mussolini's image had once been on show stood empty, a symbol of the hiatus that existed now that Il Duce and Fascism had fallen.

And a hiatus did indeed exist. Badoglio really had intended to be true to his pledge to continue the alliance, although he hoped to try to persuade Hitler and Nazi Germany to make a joint effort for peace. It was, of course, a vain hope, just as Mussolini's entreaties to Hitler to make peace with Stalin had been the stuff of fantasy; Badoglio was clutching at straws every bit as much as his predecessor. Even before Mussolini's fall, trust between the two allies had evaporated, and now neither the Italians nor the Germans believed a word of what the other was saying. Part of Operation ACHSE was the plan to get as many troops into Italy as possible before the Italians quit, and although Ambrosio, as chief of the Comando Supremo, had already sanctioned the movement of some German divisions before Mussolini's fall, the Germans were now stipulating that two more be sent down through the Alps. This, they explained, was to help protect Italy against an Allied invasion; but increasingly the Italians were seeing the move for what it really was, so that when the 44. Division tried to move through the Brenner Pass in the Alps, it was halted at the Italian border. For a couple of days an uneasy impasse ensued, until eventually, after much soothing from Kesselring, Ambrosio relented; after all, while Italy was still Germany's ally, he had no choice, because to deny the entry of 44. Division would be to admit that he suspected the Germans of ulterior motives.

Hitler interpreted Ambrosio's relenting as indicating that the Italians had already made peace overtures to the Allies but had been rebuffed. In fact, only half of this was true – the first half. Because Hitler had dismissed Badoglio's suggestion of making a joint peace, the new Italian prime minister had felt he had no choice but to then turn to the Allies. On 31 July, the Crown Council authorized a tentative approach. These plans, though, would take time to develop; and so, for the time being, the charade continued. As did the battle in Sicily.

Air operations continued without let-up, although most of the Spitfire squadrons' work now was escorting bombers, and they were not required

to dive-bomb in the same way that the Kittyhawk and Mustang squadrons had been doing, with all the risks that low-level flying incurred. Nor
were the Spitfires expected to follow the bombers all the way to the more
distant bombing targets. On the evening of Sunday, 1 August, Wing
Commander Cocky Dundas had been sitting outside his tent at Pachino,
smoking a 'V' cigarette – which he thought vile – and drinking a cooling
bottle of beer when he saw a big four-engined B-24 bomber appear overhead at very low altitude, circle, then approach to land. 'The idea of a
Liberator', Dundas wrote, 'trying to land on our little dust patch was in
direct contravention of all known theory of flight.' He watched expect-
antly, waiting for the pilot to realize his error, open the throttles and
pull up, but instead the big beast touched down, shot across the landing
strip and kept going until it finally came to a halt in the vineyard beyond
with an explosion of dust and the grating sound of rending metal.
Dundas closed his eyes, but no explosion came. Then, to his mounting
horror, more appeared, each landing more spectacular than the one
before as each pilot had not only to land but then to swerve to avoid the
growing number of Liberators already halted among the vines. Dundas
thought they looked like elephants lost and far from home. Jumping
into his jeep, he beetled off to see if he could help in any way. Most of the
emerging crews were in a state of shock. 'They had evidently been subjected to exceptional and excessive strain,' noted Dundas. 'Some of the
planes were pockmarked with bullet holes, some of the crewmen were
wounded.'

These visitors at Pachino were Liberators of the US Ninth Air Force,
based in the Middle East. That day, with two extra bomb groups that had
been earmarked for the Eighth Air Force in England, they had mounted
Operation TIDAL WAVE from Libya, a long-distance raid to bomb the
oilfields at Ploesti. General Hap Arnold, C-in-C of the USAAF, had been
pushing for one such raid on Ploesti and Spaatz, who agreed that hammering German fuel supplies was sound strategy, had concurred. In all,
some 177 bombers were sent to attack Ploesti, and although they inflicted
heavy – but not decisive – damage, it had been costly. In all, fifty-four
bombers had failed to return and 532 aircrew had been killed or taken
prisoner.

On average, nearly 1,500 Allied aircraft were operating over Sicily and
the Mediterranean every single day from 29 July, a huge number. It was
no wonder that even von Senger in his wooded mountain retreat was
having to take cover. Hap Kennedy was now usually flying twice a day,

while Smoky Vrilakas was adding to his tally of combat missions. On 5 August he and the rest of 94th Fighter Squadron were escorting B-17s to bomb Messina, a particular target during that week now that Allied planners had picked up on Axis plans to prepare for an evacuation. Already, the flak there was intensifying, and Vrilakas in his Lightning did not envy the bomber crews having to fly through it. 'It would explode in a large puff of black smoke,' he noted, 'and when concentrated the smoke from them seemed to cover the entire sky around the bombers. You could see the bursts tracking the bomber formation and the adjustments being made by the enemy gunners.' Vrilakas had already worked out that he only needed to worry about flak if he could hear the burst in his cockpit – that meant shrapnel would almost certainly hit the aircraft. On this occasion, he was well clear – although as they turned back after the bomb run, fifteen Me109s appeared; the Lightnings immediately pounced, diving down on them and preventing the German fighters from attacking the Fortresses.

Messina was now being hit around the clock – in the day by American bombers, in the night by the British. The flak, though, was also doing its work; for although bomber losses were comparatively light, it was increasingly difficult to hit targets at low altitude, and the higher they were when they dropped their loads, the less accurate they could be. It was also very hard to know exactly what effect these attacks were having; but undoubtedly, with every passing day Baade's defences around the Straits were getting stronger.

Max Corvo and his OSS team had managed briefly to get behind enemy lines in Caltanissetta just before the town had fallen on 18 July. There they had captured some documents and arrested an Italian officer who was in charge of food supplies for the area. When they questioned him, it became clear he had already established a black market operation with some local bandits. Corvo made the officer open up the stores and distribute the food to the local population. That was one good deed ticked off; but after that there was little else the Corvo mission could do. 'The speed of the Sicilian campaign', they signalled from the Falconara castle back to the OSS in Algiers, 'has made our plans redundant and infiltrations are almost impossible. Patton's troops are moving too fast for even our efficient intelligence techniques.' Just how efficient they had been after all that careering around and sight-seeing was a moot point, but there was now little more he could do other than get some of the documents he'd recovered translated. At least, though, he and his team had a fine castle by the sea from which to carry out this work.

Then, on 27 July, Don Calò Vizzini arrived back in Villalba. Exactly what he'd been doing in the week since he had disappeared on the back of a Sherman tank wasn't clear, although he claimed he'd helped encourage Sicilian troops to lay down their arms to the Americans. Certainly, he had been to Palermo during that time. Now, in the Carabinieri barracks of his home town, Vizzini was formally appointed mayor of Villalba by Lieutenant Beher, an American civil affairs officer, acting on the authorization of Colonel Charles Poletti. A number of people had gathered outside the barracks to cheer Vizzini as he emerged; they included his two priest brothers and another priest, Father Piccillo, from Caltanissetta, by way of underlying the good connections between the Vizzini family and the Catholic Church in Sicily. Others from Don Calò's household were also there, along with some locals. Also watching was Michele Pantaleone, a local resident and left-wing political activist who loathed Don Calò, and all that he and the Mafia stood for, with a passion. To his horror, as Don Calò emerged, the crowd started cheering, 'Long live the Mafia!'

Just how much Don Calò and his fellows in the Onorata Società encouraged local Sicilian troops to lay down their arms is impossible to gauge, though it is likely that chronically bad morale, poor leadership, woeful equipment and the sight of vast numbers of self-evidently superior troops hurtling towards them in mechanized columns and with flashing aircraft leading the way in the skies above had more to do with it. The episode of the yellow pennant and Don Calò's trip on the Sherman tank have entered a kind of Mafia folklore; and although the tale has been questioned by some, there were a number of witnesses to the episode – not least Michele Pantaleone, who had absolutely nothing to gain from elevating a man he despised into a cult hero. Nor was there any chance that an elderly, overweight Sicilian would have been given a ride on a tank unless the crew had been authorized to do so.

Nor is there any doubt at all that Colonel Charles Poletti appointed Don Calò as the local mayor. Poletti was the senior civil affairs officer – CAO – for Seventh Army's area of AMGOT, the Allied Military Government of Occupied Territories. AMGOT had been planned in advance of the invasion at Eisenhower's suggestion, because he quite sensibly believed it was vital there should be a single Allied policy for the exercise of civil and military authority once they had occupied the island.

Under this unified system, Sicily was to be divided into different provinces, each with a senior CAO and a team of officers working underneath him. These people would be responsible for legal and financial matters, as well as supplies for civilians, especially of food and public health. Needless to say, the challenges on an island that had been half-starved, and whose towns and cities had been partially or totally flattened, were many.

Charles Poletti had formerly been a lawyer in New York and lieutenant governor of the city, and had briefly served as governor, too. The son of Italian immigrants and an Italian speaker himself, he had made broadcasts in Italian urging Italians to overthrow both Mussolini and Hitler. Another Italian-American New Yorker helping with the war effort was the gangster Lucky Luciano. Although locked up in prison in upstate New York, Luciano still had his hand firmly on the controls of his business empire and, recognizing his influence, the Office of Naval Intelligence had contacted him in 1942 to ask for his help in protecting New York harbour from any enemy sabotage. It was help that Luciano was both able and willing to provide. Later, in May 1943, several ONI agents – all of whom could speak Italian with flawless command of Sicilian dialects – were sent to North Africa and then on to Sicily, where – unlike the Corvo team – they were landed immediately at Licata and Gela and began making contact with the local mafiosi. They were able to do so through a network of Italian-American gangsters who had been deported from the States for various crimes and misdemeanours, but who had been put in touch with the ONI either directly through Luciano or on his say-so. Luciano may have been in prison, but he still wielded huge influence in the criminal world and was, as the post-war Herlands Report revealed, working for the ONI. What's more, it was suggested to Corvo as he was preparing his OSS mission that he could and should make contact with Luciano. Corvo had turned this offer down, but the ONI had not. It made sense, after all. Luciano had helped the ONI in New York, and was Sicilian by birth, having been born in Lercara Friddi near Palermo back in 1897; he still had plenty of links with the Old Country, and, more to the point, with members of the Onorata Società.

It was quickly arranged between Don Calò, other mafiosi and Charles Poletti that this network would be used to help establish order and cooperation now that the Americans occupied the western half of the island. The price would be the reinvigoration of the Mafia, an organization that had been rendered almost dormant under the long years of Fascist rule.

*

In the Plain of Catania, the front was finally about to move once more after over a fortnight of stasis on either side of battle lines redolent of the First World War. General Dempsey, XIII Corps commander, had begun to realize from the patrol reports he was receiving that the Germans were starting to thin out their line in preparation for a withdrawal. With this in mind, he decided to attack with both 5th and 50th Divisions, going in on the night of Tuesday, 3 August. Earlier that day, Lieutenant David Fenner and his men in 13 Platoon, 6th Durhams, had had a brief exchange with some Germans in the Fosso Bottaceto just north of the Primosole Bridge. They'd lobbed over some mortars as Fenner had been dozing quietly at the bottom of their ditch. In reply, Fenner and several of his men decided to throw some mortars back and to give the line a spray with the Bren. Honour salvaged, they'd returned to their ditch. Then word had reached him that he was to mount a patrol to see whether the Fosso up ahead was empty of enemy troops, as intelligence seemed to think they'd gone. Fenner explained what had happened earlier and this was fed back to battalion HQ. 'It made no difference,' recalled Fenner, 'we were told to get on with it.' He felt as though he'd been handed a death sentence, and was amazed when two of his men volunteered to go with him. His plan was simple. They'd each take a Tommy gun. Sergeant Connell would shoot up the Fosso with the Bren, and they'd run like hell, climb up over, have a look and hope for the best. They were just about to go when the patrol was cancelled because the company commander had been shot in the leg – which was bad news for him, but rather proved Fenner's point.

That night, Bill Cheall and the men of the 6th Green Howards were among those in 50th Division moving forward at last, advancing at around 8 p.m., then digging in for the night before jumping off the following morning. Cheall was in his slit-trench at 5.30 a.m. on Wednesday, 4 August, when the artillery opened up behind them with a thunderous barrage. The screaming of shells passing overhead was music to his ears; then he heard the distinct rumble and clanking of tanks also coming from behind; and then they were being ordered to get up out of their positions and advance. Men were falling, but the attackers were making ground.

Also attacking that morning were David Fenner and the men of the 6th DLI, who were following the 8th Durhams out across the Plain. Nebelwerfers, mortars and an 88 were all firing, and one mortar shell landed directly on one of the 3-tonners carrying the brigade support company's 4.2-inch mortar section, causing the ammunition to explode along with the truck and everyone on it. C Company were caught by the Nebelwerfers, with a number of the new boys in 13 Platoon catching the worst of it. Then they passed the bodies of their anti-tank gunners who had been killed back on 16 July and, much to their disgust, had not been buried by the Germans. Fenner couldn't understand it; they'd been most careful to bury all the dead in their area, no matter what their nationality. By afternoon they had advanced some 4 miles, the enemy fire lessening as the rearguards pulled out, and by dusk Fenner and his men were on the outskirts of Catania. 'The locals were busy looting the stores and shops,' he wrote, 'and didn't pay much attention to us.'

Overnight, in accordance with Hube's orders, Schmalz ordered his men to pull back. By morning, Catania – and Misterbianco – had been emptied of German troops. At first light on Thursday, 5 August, the 9th Durhams reached the seafront and port of Catania without firing a shot; and on the same day British troops entered Misterbianco. One of Montgomery's first objectives had finally been taken.

On 28 July, at around 10.30 p.m., Werner Stappenbeck and his two colleagues, Dybeck and Preller, left their cave near Salemi in the western part of the island and set out on foot for Messina. Since they had been forgotten – or rather, simply abandoned – their only chance of escape was to use their wits, trust to some good fortune and get walking now that their injuries had healed. Wearing civilian clothes and suitably tanned after long weeks on the island, they looked passable as Sicilians, although Stappenbeck worried about the military boots. Little did they realize that thousands of Sicilians were now wearing Allied boots, stripped with ruthless pragmatism from the many dead soldiers. On the first night they were nearly caught by two American sentries, but managed to evade them and keep moving. They avoided roads as a matter of principle, which made the going even tougher. 'Sicily is a mountainous island,' wrote Stappenbeck, 'not a country for walking. Stones, hedges, ditches, fences stood in the way.'

A rhythm developed: walk by night, rest up by day. They were carrying packs with food supplies they'd stockpiled before setting off, so although the weight was an added burden, at least they weren't starving. Then they learned a curfew had been imposed, so they decided they had better march in the heat of the day instead and sleep by night. As they discovered, however, while the midday sun was broiling it could get very cold at night, and they had nothing in which to wrap themselves. On 4 August, they bathed in a cool mountain stream, but were then shot at by locals: one of the bullets knocked off Preller's cap and grazed his brow, though the wound wasn't serious. Stappenbeck reckoned some forty shots had been fired at them, but they managed to get away. In their flight, though, they had had to abandon their packs, so that now they had nothing – no food, no water, no weapons. From Allied leaflets they picked up, they discovered there was a bounty of £50 on offer for every German reported; so perhaps it was no wonder they had been shot at.

From this point, each of them carried a sturdy club, which at least helped protect them from dogs, who were generally wary of and aggressive towards any strangers. Water they snatched from streams whenever they could find them, and food they bought from farmers – they had money with them. They also picked fruit, which wasn't always ripe. So, all-in-all, they were surviving, even if their diet was not especially nutritious. Stappenbeck had begun the trek with a toe that was still suppurating, but as he began to run out of bandages his foot miraculously began to stop weeping rather than worsen. Eleven days on, they were near Enna, a major confluence of roads but also of troops. Only by taking numerous detours through vineyards, over fields, under fences and over ditches did they get round the town undetected. Using map, compass and binoculars they kept going, driven on by the constant worry that they were rapidly running out of time.

One man who did manage to get away early was Hanns Cibulka. On 30 July, he'd staggered to the medical tent, hot and feverish, and was examined by the doctor. It was malaria. After collecting his things and saying farewell to his friend Arno, Cibulka was sent up to a field hospital, where his temperature began to rise further and he started to hallucinate. The following day he was put on a truck, sitting with his back to the cab and next to an NCO who would barely speak and whose legs were full of shrapnel splinters. Another man had been shot through the lung. 'Others are sitting there quite restlessly,' he noted, 'slipped down, each with a bullet in his body, a splinter. One shot more, one shot less, and still one shot too many.'

Among the snatches of conversation, often a little nervous, Cibulka heard several men mutter how glad they were the war was over for them. He drifted in and out of sleep as the flat-bedded wooden-planked back of the truck jolted them up and down over the rough roads. 'I see a fighter bomber approaching, hear the howling of the engine,' he jotted, 'it turns off, it must have seen the white flag with the red cross. I look up into the sky, above us a fleeing sun.' The chills were now subsiding as he began to sweat. He tried not to worry. Soon he would be on a hospital ship, taken not across the Straits but up the Italian coast to Livorno. He would have a bed with white sheets, and be far away from the war.

Cibulka had left Sicily behind, but the endgame still had to be played. On 4 August, Montgomery issued new instructions. XXX Corps was to continue its drive towards Adrano and then head off up the left, western side of Etna to Bronte, a town and ducal fiefdom that in 1799 had been gifted to Admiral Nelson by Ferdinand III, monarch of what had then been the Kingdom of the Two Sicilies. History was never far away in Sicily, not that most of the men fighting there had much opportunity or inclination to appreciate it. With plans for the invasion of mainland Italy now under way, Monty also had to start withdrawing troops in preparation for that next phase of the war in the Mediterranean. The Canadians were to be pulled out of the line once Adrano had fallen, 5th Division after the fall of Belpasso. In any event, the narrowing of the north-east of the island meant that only limited numbers of troops could make their way through the network of tiny mountain roads.

General Leese now gave the 78th Battleaxe Division a particularly brutal assignment. From Centuripe, they were to get across the River Salso down the far side of the mountain, cross the Simeto the next night, then attack Adrano the night after that, with the 51st Highlanders protecting their right flank and the Canadians their left. For Peter Pettit and the gunners of 17th Field Artillery, this was a truly punishing schedule, especially coming on the back of the Centuripe battle – not to mention that they'd been on the go ever since their arrival. First, on 4 August, Pettit had to work out how they were going to get down from the town; this meant a recce on foot with the second-in-command from the 57th Field Artillery. The only possible route for all their guns, Quads and limbers was by the winding road, which was in full view of the enemy, now on the slopes overlooking the Simeto valley below Adrano. Halfway down, a large part of the road had been destroyed, but it was too dangerous for the sappers to repair in daylight; it would have to wait until dark. Further beyond the break in the road were almond and orange groves. 'No cover worth the name for vehicles,' noted Pettit. Later, at dusk, he went down again with the battery recce parties and showed them where he reckoned they should deploy the gun. That night, they dumped 6,000 rounds of ammo; then the convoy of thirty Quads and guns rumbled down, inched over a diversion round the blown bit of road and finally got in position for first light. Pettit, having snatched two and a half hours' sleep, then hurried around trying to get the guns into place and camouflaged as much as possible before the sun began to rise far enough to show their every movement. By this time, he was both hot and exhausted. Three lorries were hit by enemy shelling and exploded as a further convoy of sixty came down the road.

The infantry attack across the Simeto went off that night as planned; then, after Pettit's men had finished firing, they had to pack up and get moving again. 'We could not afford to have the column on the road at daylight or there really would be trouble,' he noted, breathlessly. 'Behind the ammo lorries were a Brigade HQ and the transport of two or more battalions who had to get down and through the river at the bottom in darkness.' Somehow, the long convoys managed to push on over the Simeto. The enemy had pulled back again so there was no contact, although plenty of shelling.

It was now Friday, 6 August, and the division was to attack Adrano that night. Yet again the guns were deployed ready for firing early in the morning. They shelled the town all morning while Pettit watched squadrons of fighter-bombers circling and dive-bombing enemy positions around Adrano. 'The whole town seems to jump up in smoke and dust and nothing is seen but the huge dust cloud for some minutes,' he jotted. 'The amazing thing is that when it clears away, the whole town is still there and looks from this distance just the same as before.' In the afternoon, word reached the gunners that the recce regiment ahead were already in Adrano, so they swivelled the guns and began pounding Bronte instead. Later, it then turned out the recce regiment wasn't in Adrano after all, and so they changed the fire plan once again. Then Pettit was summoned by an officious intelligence officer to the division HQRA – the artillery headquarters. Off he went on what was a shockingly difficult drive in the dark. Getting back at 9.20 p.m., he was immediately plunged into preparations for the infantry attack on Adrano – zero hour midnight. Fire plans were as follows: concentrated fire for 170 minutes before the attack, then 180 minutes to accompany the infantry, moving their aim forward 100 yards every five minutes. The medium guns – the 5.5-inch – would also fire for 195 minutes on the back of the town from midnight.

Incredibly, the Battleaxe Division had managed to keep to Leese's timetable. By the morning of Saturday, 7 August, the infantry were in Adrano, their objective taken, and the gunners were packing up, loading up and moving out once again – straight into a log-jam as traffic from Regalbuto converged with their own convoys. They had to be ready to provide fire support just as soon as possible, although this was easier said than done. 'Thick orange groves, walls, narrow gates and lava all over the area made it very difficult to find gun positions,' Pettit acknowledged, 'but we did after much head-scratching.' Craters in the road hardly helped, and the maps they'd been issued with didn't seem to bear much relation to the reality on the ground. Supper that night was eaten on the go, by heating up a tin of M&V – meat and veg – in his Humber's radiator, where it fitted neatly if they took out the filter.

The next day, Sunday 8 August, Pettit and his gunners passed through Adrano on their way up to Bronte, part of the western thrust of XXX Corps around the edge of Etna. 'Adrano is a sort of Guernica,' he noted, 'bodies still on the pavements, ruins everywhere and they had to use bulldozers to clear a way through for wheels.' That a bulldozer was even in Adrano was impressive, yet these sturdy machines were rapidly becoming as essential a piece of Allied equipment as any tank, truck or artillery piece, such was the level of destruction being caused. Quite simply, without bulldozers there could be no advance.

They pushed on again in the heat, stopping repeatedly because of craters in the road. Here the country was much closer, the wide-open valleys of the island's centre long gone. It was greener, too, a place of myriad groves and vineyards, but still more winding, narrow roads. Pettit spent much of his time wondering where on earth they were going to place their guns. 'This is,' he lamented, 'the most awful artillery country.' Which was a problem when the Allied way of war so heavily depended upon it; but such was the gunner's exhausting, stressful and exceptionally demanding lot. No wonder that at times, this highly mechanized army appeared to take its time. In fact, given the circumstances and the conditions in which they found themselves, they were progressing with extraordinary speed.

CHAPTER 30

The Straits of Messina

Now that Catania and Misterbianco had fallen, 5th and 50th Divisions were advancing side-by-side in Dempsey's XIII Corps as the Germans fell back towards the Tortorici Line. It was scrappy, difficult fighting, in which the advancing troops were being squeezed down roads that either hugged the coast or wound their way through the foothills of Etna. With so little room for manoeuvre, everyone felt cramped. David Fenner, for one, found the experience deeply unpleasant. The 50th Division, especially, was hemmed in along the coast, which meant brigades moving up one at a time and, invariably, battalions advancing one at a time. Companies, taking it in turns to lead, would push ahead cautiously, waiting for the inevitable ambush. The officers, especially, were taking a hammering. 'The platoon officer would be with the point section,' noted Fenner, 'the company commander with the lead platoon. The ambush would get the lot. Machine-guns, mortars and 88mm guns were all used.' There would also be mines, booby-traps and snipers. The Germans were proving to be masters of the slow retreat, not least because they were disciplined enough to hold ground until the last.

Martin Pöppel and his *Fallschirmjäger* proved Fenner's point with lethal efficiency on 6 August. 'Another day's hard fighting for us,' wrote Pöppel in his diary that day. He and his company were in the foothills north of Catania near the town of Mascalucia, acting as rearguards to slow the British advance. The day's activity began at 7 a.m. when they met some British forward patrols, with another burst again an hour later. At around 10.30 a.m., Pöppel and his men had been resting among the trees on the slopes overlooking the main road north to Nicolosi and

Pedara, the last line of towns at the foot of Etna. A short distance down the road they had set up a roadblock and an anti-tank gun. 'Tommies on our left!' came a shout, at which Pöppel and his men grabbed their weapons and headed for the anti-tank gun at breakneck speed, jumping from the stone wall right on top of the startled enemy. 'There's some fierce close combat,' he noted, 'before we drive them off and get time for a well-earned cigarette. But they almost caught us in our combat post in this broken countryside, damn it.' In this small action, they killed several men, took six prisoners and spotted a number of blood trails heading back down the road. Pöppel and his men suffered no casualties at all, which, he reckoned, just went to show that when one attacked hard and courageously one got the best results.

Not long afterwards, another British section probed forward. One of Pöppel's men was about to light a cigarette when he saw them and, raising his submachine gun, killed two, including a lieutenant. Another four wounded Tommies were brought in and valuable maps discovered. Later, when trying to use a captured 2-inch mortar, two of his men accidentally fired it into a tree and were wounded in the process. Then fifty or sixty Tommies were discovered moving on their right flank, so they opened up with machine guns and felled a number of those. The fighting went on into the evening, his company picking off the British infantry who had been probing forward without the usual artillery support because it was still battling its way through rubble-strewn streets and log-jams of traffic.

At 10.20 p.m. on the nose they pulled back again, leaving only the anti-tank gun crew behind briefly to cover their backs, and marched through Tremestieri, San Giovanni La Punta and then north to Viagrande, through engineers busily mining the roads, preparing bridges for demolition and installing all manner of other booby-traps. By the time they reached the new assembly area it was 3 a.m. on Saturday, 7 August; they were now in line with the rest of Brigade Schmalz along the base of Etna, strung out between Nicolosi, Pedara, Trecastagni, Viagrande and Acireale on the coast.

The remnants of 504. Heavy Panzer Bataillon, meanwhile, had been fighting in the hills around Paterno and Belpasso, where they had been facing 5th Division. On 5 August, Leutnant Karl Goldschmidt had taken over as company commander after Leutnant Heim had been wounded, first at Paterno and then again when a hand grenade exploded nearby, and had had to be evacuated. They still had four Tigers left but the rest of the men had been turned into an infantry platoon. It was all a bit desperate.

They were now at Trecastagni in the last line of settlements before the slopes of Etna became too steep for habitation. So, too, that morning of 6 August, were Jupp Klein and his fellow *Fallschirmjäger* engineers, who had been busy laying mines and explosive charges at significant points, including two houses opposite one another at a narrow place in the middle of the town on the main road that led north towards Messina. This had involved ordering the civilians to leave their homes and get clear. Unsurprisingly, the inhabitants were far from happy, and a crowd soon gathered. Some were crying; others began threatening the *Fallschirmjäger* with old rifles and shotguns. 'The spectre only came to an end when our platoon sergeant had a group of machine-gunners with an MG42 set up on the market square,' noted Klein, 'and made it clear to the insurgents that if they continued to obstruct their tasks he would have them shoot without consideration.'

Once teamed up with Goldschmidt's Tigers, Klein had agreed the engineers would concentrate on laying mines and booby-traps, while the tank men kept watch. Later, though, after it got dark, Klein realized he should have set up his own guards, because they were attacked in the ground-floor apartment where they were holed up for the night and one man was wounded; whether it was a British patrol or angry locals, Klein couldn't be sure, for their assailants ran before they could respond.

The following morning, 7 August, it was most certainly the British attacking. Goldschmidt led his four Tigers in a counter-attack. Shells were soon falling around them and even hitting them, but while Goldschmidt's tank kept firing and moving forward, Feldwebel Uhlig's started burning when the exhaust armour was shot off and a fuel line began to leak. Jumping out of his own panzer, Goldschmidt rushed over and helped put out the flames. Against all the odds, Uhlig's tank was still able to run so, pulling back, they headed north, the damaged Tiger still running under its own steam. After an hour, however, there was a second explosion from it as the machine-gun ammunition inside started to blow up. Goldschmidt again hurried over and personally pulled the driver up out through the hatch, although not before he'd suffered severe burns. They now had a big problem on their hands, because the stricken Tiger had come to a halt diagonally across the road, which had walls either side. 'All attempts to move it to the side of the road failed,' noted Goldschmidt. 'Ambulances and other vehicles soon piled up.' Then a small miracle occurred: suddenly the Tiger began to burn more brightly, and as it did so, it jerked forward. All watched aghast as there was no one inside, but the tank was rolling forward into the wall, where it burrowed itself in and halted again – and now there was room to pass. 'Two hours later,' noted Goldschmidt, 'I was at General Hube's. Thank God this was a man who knew a lot about panzers and understood our problems.' Hube now ordered Goldschmidt to go back, collect his men, and get himself and whatever tanks and equipment could be saved back across the Straits.

Goldschmidt reached his company staging area at around 2.00 the next morning, 8 August, only to find that two of his mechanically temperamental Tigers had suffered gearbox problems during the last counter-attack, and one of those had then burned out its engine trying to salvage the fourth; the lesson from the Acate valley back on the second day of the invasion had clearly not been learned. With no possible chance of repairing them, Goldschmidt had no choice but to blow up these two Tigers, leaving him with just one from the entire company of seventeen that had first headed to Sicily back in May.

Throughout the 7th fierce fighting had continued in the Etna foothills, and not just in 504. Bataillon's sector. It was turning into a bloody and violent business, and XIII Corps were in danger of becoming bogged down. This was the day when 13th Brigade, who had been in transit through wrecked and deserted towns, passing burnt-out British armoured cars and a host of other battle debris, arrived at the front, having been hurriedly brought forward into the fold of 5th Division. Captain David Cole and the 2nd Skins reached Pedara that evening with instructions to attack and capture three volcanic hills known as Tremonti a couple of miles north of the town the following day, Sunday, 8 August. These conical pimples had emerged back in 1669 during one of Etna's worst eruptions and looked beautifully green compared with the bleached central plains and mountains. All around, the land was considerably more verdant here, with patches of bushes, undergrowth and plentiful trees. The volcanic hills themselves were steeply terraced; spreading away from them on the slopes running down to Pedara were vineyards and a maze of paths, while the road running towards them was, like most in the area, lined with stone walls. After the bare, wide-open Dittaino valley, this was dramatically close country.

Supported by the Canadian Tank Brigade, artillery and mortars, the infantry once again had to take the leap of faith and venture forward – and no sooner had they all raised their heads than German machine guns opened up, tracer bullets whipping past and a cluster of mortar bombs crashing among them. Captain Cole and his wiring party were following behind D Company, and now quickly hurried forward to join D Company HQ and hastily install a field telephone. 'There we were able,' wrote Cole, 'from behind a stone wall, to observe with the occasional distraction of random bullets zipping past us, the beginning of the attack.'

Forward went the D Company men, ducking, dodging, occasionally sprinting then diving, until they reached the foot of the Tremonti – where they ground to a halt. British mortars now drenched the three hills, while the heavy Vickers of the 7th Cheshire Machine-Gun Battalion continued to pour in relentless fire and the Shermans banged off shell after shell. The cacophony was deafening, the hills shrouded in swirling smoke and debris and dust – and then the infantry began climbing up the first of them, terrace by terrace. Just at the point where they were about to crest and take the summit, the Germans counter-attacked in time-honoured fashion. Cole watched it all open-mouthed. 'With the two sides so closely intermingled, there was nothing we could do to help,' he wrote. 'A bloody scrap followed in which we saw our own men falling, as well as theirs, amidst the sunlit smoke drifting through the undergrowth.' Grenades were hurling through the air, shots ringing out along with shouts and screams, and Lieutenant Roy Hingston's platoon were falling back. By the time they reached the bottom again, he had just nine men left from the thirty or so who had begun the attack. Clearly, it was going to take more than a single company to capture Tremonti; but this would involve bringing up more men, more fire support, more ammunition – and so would take more time. After consulting with brigade HQ, it was decided to try again the following morning at dawn, with two battalions attacking. In the meantime, fighting patrols would be sent up the forward slopes of Tremonti to keep the enemy both on his toes and awake.

At first light on Monday, 9 August, the 2nd Inniskillings attacked again, this time with A Company in the lead and the rest of the battalion following behind. Despite some initially heavy MG fire, their objectives were quickly taken as the enemy scurried away and disappeared down the slopes, mortars and bursts of machine-gun fire following them. A number of dead were found, both their own and the enemy's. That evening, after dealing with prisoners, burying the dead and gathering themselves back together, the brigade moved out, heading forward again into Trecastagni and on to the road that led straight to Messina. From there, the next day, Tuesday, 10 August, they moved on once more, to the town of Fleri. This was still some 50 miles from the Straits, but the 2nd Royal Inniskilling Fusiliers had now fought their last in Sicily. News reached them on the 11th that they were being pulled back to a rest area near Paterno, to fatten them up for the next big battle – the invasion of Italy itself.

While Eighth Army was battling its way north either side of Etna, Seventh Army was continuing to push hard from the east. The glory days of the drive to Palermo, when the Americans had been able to make the most of their vast mechanized might, had already passed into ancient history as they too struggled with the coastal and mountain roads – or rather, the lack of them. Neither in North Africa nor in the first couple of weeks of the Sicily battle had they been so hemmed in and crammed for space. On the north coast, General Truscott's 3rd Division had taken over the frustrating and bloody drive along the coastal Highway 113, with the Thunderbirds pulled out of the line for a much-needed rest.

The division had crawled forward through seemingly endless demolitions, blown bridges and liberally scattered mines. Only the procurement of a number of mules enabled them to make much progress at all, so that by the afternoon of 3 August they had reached the Furiano river – forward outpost of the 29. Panzer Grenadier Division's San Fratello position. San Fratello, nearly 60 miles from Messina, marked the northern end of the Etna Line, and was well defended, so that when the leading troops of the 3rd Division tried to hustle their way through they were stopped dead. Audie Murphy, now a corporal and recovered from his bout of malaria, was back with the 1st Battalion, 15th Infantry, just in time for the attack. As they tried to cross the dried-up and mined Furiano, they were caught by a barrage of artillery and mortar fire. 'The earth shudders,' he noted, 'and the screaming of shells intermingles with the screaming of men.' They fell back, at which point one of the men in Murphy's platoon broke down, bawling 'I can't take any more', and was taken away to the rear. Murphy was disgusted; he had no time for such histrionics and thought them weak and cowardly.

The following morning, by which time more artillery had been brought up, they tried again – and once again they hit a brick wall. Patton, frustrated, now called up Task Force 88 and ordered an amphibious outflanking operation. This option had been on the cards from the outset; the SRS and Commandos had earlier been poised for a landing at Catania, and there had been an argument for using them again in Eighth Army's area in an effort to speed the advance to Messina from the south. The problem was that in the first two weeks of the campaign landing craft were still being used to unload supplies, and now most had been withdrawn for urgent repairs and refitting before the planned invasion of mainland Italy. The other snag was that with only a handful of landing craft available and a fluid situation on the ground, there was always going to be a high risk that not enough troops would be landed with not enough fire-power and support for a slightly uncertain operation. It wasn't quite the same as landing to take a fixed position like a gun emplacement or a particular bridge.

Patton, however, was always willing to take more risks than most, and despite TF88 having only enough landing craft to support a single battalion, he ordered the operation to go ahead. Truscott chose Colonel Lyle Bernard's 2nd Battalion of the 30th Infantry Regiment and told them to get ready. On land, meanwhile, the 3rd Division attacked the San Fratello position yet again on 6 August, with exactly the same result. Colonel Bernard's force was now ordered to land behind the position the following day, but just after midday on the 6th four Junkers 88s appeared, bombing and strafing the small amphibious force just before loading had begun. Although two of the planes were shot down by American anti-aircraft fire, one of the LSTs was badly damaged. Since this vessel was vital to the entire operation, the landing had to be postponed by twenty-four hours. So, four days after the 3rd Division had reached the San Fratello position, they still hadn't broken through. The new timetable meant the amphibious operation would be launched on the night of the 7th and the land attack would go in early the following day, Sunday, 8 August.

On the morning of Saturday 7th, Patton drove to the front, accompanied by Truscott, and up to an observation post in the mountains, using a 5-mile road that had been built in less than twenty-four hours by American engineers – a quite extraordinary feat. It was hazy up there, but through his binoculars Patton could see shells hitting enemy positions and also the little white puffs of the Germans' 60mm mortars. Machine-gun fire could also be heard, and the cracks of individual rifles. Later that afternoon, another four Junkers 88s attacked the landing vessels as they loaded up, but this time missed. There would be no more delays; and that evening, when the 3rd Division attacked with the full weight of American fire-power and offshore naval guns, they took the key Hill 673 overlooking San Fratello. Audie Murphy had been among those ordered to stay behind and guard a machine-gun emplacement and so, from his vineyard vantage point – where he'd eaten more grapes than was good for him – he'd had a grandstand view. As always, the Germans furiously counter-attacked, an assault in which Murphy's company commander was killed; but the Americans were not to be budged. Defending was considerably easier than attacking in Sicily.

General Fries accepted it was now time to abandon the position and pull back. At the same time, in the early hours of 8 August, Colonel Bernard's men landed at Sant' Agata, just after a shell from one of the American destroyers, aimed at the retreating enemy, had hit a bridge already wired for demolition. The shell detonated the explosives, blew the bridge, and although the river-bed beneath was dry, it had also been mined. There was now something of a log-jam: as Bernard's men came ashore, they were able to surprise the enemy stuck there, knock out several panzers, and kill and capture some 350 enemy troops, a considerable bag. When Fries had pulled out, he'd also abandoned the Italian troops from the Divisione Assietta who had been supporting their ally on the left flank. That morning, 8 August, they surrendered in droves. Audie Murphy had had only a bit part in this battle, but it had been his first time fighting the Germans and he'd learned much. 'I acquired a healthy respect for the Germans as fighters,' he wrote, 'an insight into the fury of mass combat; and a bad case of diarrhea. I had eaten too many grapes.'

While these desperate battles were going on, Oberst Ernst-Günther Baade was overseeing an extremely well-planned evacuation operation. He'd been given considerable authority as Kommandant, Straits of Messina. In fact, he had been given carte blanche to gather together as many guns and men as he could, and to take command of a special ad hoc force that included army, navy and air force troops. Luftwaffe and Kriegsmarine flak batteries came under his command, including more than seventeen hundred naval gunners, as did a number of highly competent naval commanders – among them Fregattenkapitän Gustav von Liebenstein, commander of the 2. Landung Division. It certainly helped that Baade had been appointed well in advance of the evacuation: even by 1 August, he and von Liebenstein had amassed some 140 vessels of all kinds, including 76 motor boats, 33 naval barges, 7 MFPs – 163-foot-long beaching craft – 13 further smaller landing craft and 12 Siebel ferries, each of which was a kind of double-ended motorized raft that could carry 450 men or ten loaded trucks.

Back in the 1930s, Nazi Germany had very sensibly set up the world's first combined services general staff, the OKW; but Hitler had then used it more as his mouthpiece than for its proper purpose of tri-service planning. Rarely, in fact, had there been much close cooperation between the three arms of the Wehrmacht, even during the glory years of the Blitzkrieg when the Luftwaffe had been spearheading great panzer thrusts on the ground. For the sole and particular purpose of Operation LEHRGANG, however, Baade had been given the authority to create a unified command; and with this, and with von Liebenstein's cooperation, he had very effectively and efficiently set up new systems for roll-on, roll-off loading and unloading, ensuring that all crews were thoroughly trained in such procedures, all while frequently changing the embarkation and disembarkation points so as not to give the Allied air forces any firm targets. Baade had also amassed a staggering 333 guns either side of the Straits, making them one of the most heavily fortified stretches of coastline anywhere in the world. He had worked out, too, a very clear and efficient system of four distinct routes that would be used, with two more developed as back-up if necessary. The first route across the Straits would begin at the northernmost tip of the island, where 15. Panzer Grenadier Division were to embark. The second route, a little to the south, would be for 29. Division. The third route, a little longer, began just on the northern edge of Messina and would take XIV Panzer Korps headquarters, while the fourth route, starting close by and also a little to the north of the town, would ferry the HG Division, including the 1. Fallschirmjäger Division under Schmalz. Traffic controllers and engineers were assigned to each route, while assembly points were linked to ferry sites by telephone so that there would be no traffic build-up on the water's edge as a juicy target for Allied air forces. Each assembly area was also camouflaged.

Hube gave clear instructions to both Baade and his divisional commanders. No troops would be ferried across the straits by day, only by night. Weapons and equipment, however, could cross by day at Baade's discretion, with anti-tank weapons, artillery and assault guns taking priority, in that order. Discipline was to be maintained at all times, and any sign of panic was to be dealt with immediately and with the severest measures – offenders were to be shot or clubbed to death. Hube, in turn, had been getting a series of messages from Hitler, including one in which he insisted Hube should not tell his men of the evacuation plans until they reached the crossing points. This Hube sensibly ignored, aware that many of his men feared a second Tunisgrad. He wasn't ready to pull the plug on Sicily yet, but by the start of the second week of August, plans for LEHRGANG looked to be in good fettle. Baade and von Liebenstein had done well. Nothing, it seemed, had been left to chance.

Meanwhile, bitter fighting continued, not least on the north coast, where Truscott's 3rd Division were still trying to bludgeon their way forward as Patton became increasingly nervous that Montgomery's Eighth Army would beat him to Messina. No one on Sicily wanted Seventh Army to be first in Messina more than he did. 'This is a horse race, in which the prestige of the US Army is at stake,' he had told General Middleton before the Thunderbirds' push had begun. 'We must take Messina before the British.' This was, of course, nonsense; the US Army's stock had risen considerably in Sicily, and would not suffer now no matter whose troops reached Messina first. Patton was not to be foiled, however, and to ensure his men got there ahead he demanded another amphibious outflanking manoeuvre to help get past the next major defensive position of 29. Panzer Grenadier Division at Brolo. Both Bradley and Truscott objected, but Patton overruled them. Now they were so close to southern Italy, the Luftwaffe was more in evidence than it had been, and once again a vital landing vessel was hit, necessitating another frustrating twenty-four hour delay. None the less, Truscott's 3rd and 15th Infantry both attacked on the night of 10 August, and in the early hours of Wednesday 11th, Colonel Lyle Bernard's battalion once again made an amphibious land- ing. The key to unlocking the town was Monte Cipolla, a big, sickle-shaped massif, and this was Colonel Bernard's objective.

To begin with, everything that could go wrong did. The five tanks accompanying Bernard's men either became bogged down or were dam- aged, while thirteen of his fifteen mules were then killed in an ambush as they neared the summit. Notwithstanding these setbacks, his men stayed glued to the ridge all morning, despite rapidly depleting stocks of ammu- nition, and by just after 2 p.m. the Germans below, covering the wide beach and the mouths of the Zappulla and Naso rivers, had been pushed back all the way to the town of Brolo. With the warships offshore, guns at the ready, here was a golden chance to finish off 29. Panzer Grenadier once and for all. Fate, though, now played a hand: at the crucial moment, with Colonel Bernard on the summit of Monte Cipolla ready to direct naval artillery fire on to the retreating Germans, he lost his radio link with the ships. Despite frantic and repeated efforts, a connection couldn't be re-established; and, not wanting to risk hitting fellow Americans, the navy had no choice but to withdraw. To make matters worse, Allied fighter-bombers from Ponte Olivo then roared over and accidentally bombed Colonel Bernard's positions, killing and wounding nineteen men.

Overnight, Fries pulled back his forces once more and by 7.30 a.m. the Americans were in Brolo. Colonel Bernard's men were relieved from their tenuous hold on Monte Cipolla; but his 2nd Battalion had lost ninety-nine men killed and missing and a further seventy-eight wounded. The truth was, one battalion was not enough for the objective they'd been given. Amphibious operations needed to be better prepared and on a bigger scale to be truly effective; they needed to be done prop-erly, or not at all.

While Truscott's men were hammering their way along the coast, the 9th Division had pushed on beyond Troina towards Randazzo, having taken over from the 1st. The Big Red One had certainly earned a break, having seen more action since arriving in North Africa the previous November than any other American unit in the western theatre. It had also been given a change of command, with Terry Allen and his deputy, Teddy Roosevelt Jr, both relieved. The loss of their familiar and well-regarded chief had caused consternation among many of the troops; but, good though Allen was, Bradley felt he was getting tired – and there was also a nagging concern that he drank too much and had created an atmosphere within the division that didn't quite sit comfortably in the new and increasingly professional US Army; encouraging his men to go on an unconstrained drunken frenzy in Oran before HUSKY hadn't helped. Bradley had suggested the change and Patton had required little persuading. Clarence Huebner, a trusted friend of Patton's, took the helm of the Big Red One in his place.

The town of Randazzo, nestling beneath the northern slopes of Etna, was another key objective for the Allies because it stood halfway between the north and east coasts, and the last lateral road in the peninsula that ran from coast to coast passed through the town. If it could be taken, Hube's men would be cut in half, each part isolated from the other, and while he had prepared three more defensive phase lines, the fall of Ran-dazzo would really seal the fate of the island; with Randazzo gone, Hube could not hope to hold out for much longer. So the Allies were attacking in strength, with both the 78th Battleaxe Division and the 9th converging on this already bomb-blasted, shattered shell of a town. The 9th took Cesarò on 8 August and by the 11th were getting close, having finally crossed the upper reaches of the River Simeto; but, as always, German rearguards of the 15. Panzer Grenadier Division continued to fight hard.

After Troina, the 39th Infantry were exhausted. Because of the losses there, sergeants had taken over platoons and officers had had to be moved to plug gaps elsewhere. Charlie Scheffel had been given temporary command of B Company; then the commander had returned and so he'd headed back to his S-3 job. Since Troina, they'd been in reserve, but now the 39th Infantry was once again to take the lead, this time in the drive to take Randazzo and back where it should be in the US 9th Division; and, as S-3, it was Scheffel's task to suggest which troops did what in the attack that would be launched early the following morning, Friday, 13 August.

That evening he briefed the company commanders, and by midnight was in his foxhole trying to get some much-needed sleep. Soon after, he was roused by the commander's runner and told to report to the CO. Stiff, exhausted and miserable, he dragged himself to the command post, where he was told he would be taking over command of A Company; the current commander had bust his ankle and could no longer walk.

In the dark, he followed the communication wire up to A Company, getting there around 1 a.m. Dog-tired, he then tried to get his head down for a couple of hours; 3 a.m. came around all too soon and, although it was still pitch dark, he forced himself up and gathered the four platoon leaders around him. Two of the platoons were temporarily commanded by a couple of sergeants, one of the others by a lieutenant he knew from Tunisia, the other by a lieutenant he'd never properly met. Scheffel now turned to the one officer he did know.

'We're taking Randazzo this morning,' he said. 'You lead the attack with first platoon.'

'I'm weapons platoon,' he replied.

'We'll sort that out later,' Scheffel told him. 'Right now, I need you in the lead. I'll be right behind you, then the other—'

'Why the fuck are you trying to get me killed?' the lieutenant snapped.

'Look,' snarled Scheffel. 'I'm in command here, and you're the only guy I know.'

The lieutenant protested again, and Scheffel just stared at him for a moment. No one else said a word. Then, touching the lieutenant's arm, he said, 'Look, I need you at point. I'll be right there.' That was the end of it. Scheffel knew the lieutenant was a good officer; he also knew they were all exhausted, and at times tempers flared. It was to be expected.

At dawn they attacked Randazzo, unsure what to expect; but after thin, sporadic firing, they entered the town and found it abandoned. The Germans had gone.

On the 14th, Major Peter Pettit reached Randazzo to find a long column of US troops heading into the town from the west. Gridlock ensued, and Pettit got out of his jeep and continued on foot. 'Walked on nine miles,' he wrote. 'No sign of enemy at all. US pouring through, very slowly with many halts. Our battle obviously over.' Apparently it was mines and demolitions that were causing the log-jam, and certainly casualties were coming back, while a rumour soon reached him that a man had reached for some grapes only to be blown up by a booby-trap. Orders now arrived forbidding any more fruit-eating.

While the Etna battles raged, Werner Stappenbeck and his two comrades continued their epic journey across Sicily. As the three of them neared the volcano, they began to hear the distant sounds of artillery fire. Now they had to work out how they were going to get through Allied lines; they reckoned their best chance was to climb high up on to the volcano where they knew there could be no fighting. First, though, they had to get beyond the British, and that was nearly their undoing. As they crossed a road, a British officer drove towards them in a jeep, stopping just a couple of yards from them. Fortunately, he barely glanced at them; they walked on past and, once out of sight, clambered over a wall, then another, and thought they had got clear away – only to discover they'd stumbled into the rear area of an artillery battery. Another big detour set them back but then, at last, they were clear to cross high over Etna. The higher they climbed, however, the less water there was, and soon they were parched. 'Here we were all alone,' he wrote. 'Where there is no water, no man can live. After using up our few supplies, we had to go down again and had done 24 km for nothing.' On they pressed, tramping over the lava, then through an oak forest, until they were within touching distance of their own lines. That night, however, the lines moved back and they found themselves in no man's land. It was Friday, 13 August.

General Guzzoni had evacuated his surviving troops ahead of XIV Panzer Korps; typically, Italian and German plans were completely different, entirely independent and carried out without any cooperation whatsoever. The Italians were unable to lift much heavy equipment but, starting on 3 August, and using mainly two train ferries, began taking troops across the straits south of Messina straight away. Guzzoni finally left Sicily on 10 August; von Senger, his work done, had left two days earlier.

The Allies were aware the Axis were preparing to evacuate, and on 3 August Alexander signalled both Admiral Cunningham and Air Chief Marshal Tedder, warning them the exodus might begin any day. 'We must be in a position to take immediate advantage of such a situation,' he wrote, 'but using full weight of Navy and Air Power. You have no doubt co-ordinated plans to meet this contingency.' As it happened, they hadn't; but they did confer after receiving Alex's signal. The Allied air forces had already been hammering Messina and the straits and continued to do so, but the geography was in the Axis' favour. At their narrowest, the straits were a little over a mile wide, and most of Baade's routes were 3–5 miles end to end, which was no great distance at all. It was a very confined space, closed in further by steep cliffs on either side. Added to these constraints was the mass of the more than three hundred guns assembled there in defence, which made hitting shipping very difficult indeed. Bombers were pounding the straits day and night – some 532 aircraft struck Messina in the first week of August alone – but mostly from height. Over 170 fighter-bombers dive-bombed Messina and the straits, but the intensity of flak made dive-bombing the narrows a lethal proposition with small chance of much reward. Even at a few thousand feet a barge looked tiny; from 20,000 feet, it looked like a pin-prick. Despite these difficulties, on 5 August alone two merchant ships, one of Baade's precious Siebel ferries and twenty-one barges were destroyed by air power. Mary Coningham, one of the most aggressive of Allied air commanders, feared there was little that could be done to prevent an evacuation. 'The difficulty of operating naval surface forces in the narrow part of the strait', he wrote to Broadhurst on 4 August, 'is obvious and I do not see how we can hope for the same proportion of success as at Cap Bon.'

For his part, Cunningham sent up motor torpedo boats – MTBs – on fast, in-and-out raids, but there was not the remotest chance of warships successfully venturing into such heavily defended narrows, especially not with a follow-up invasion of mainland Italy to come in which every vessel in the Mediterranean would be needed. 'A ship's a fool to fight a fort,' Nelson had once said, and – despite having himself attacked Copenhagen from the sea – he had a point. Warships passing a very heavily defended coastline in front of more than three hundred guns was simply not an option, especially not along straits as narrow as those of Messina.

General Hube had given the order to begin Operation LEHRGANG on the afternoon of 10 August, three days before Randazzo had fallen, and the evacuation began on the night of the 11th. Even before then, however, a number of troops had already been sent back, among them Dr Wilhelm Mauss. Corps headquarters had been transferred to the toe of Italy on the 9th, and the bulk of the staff began moving right away. 'The Sicilian adventure comes to an end,' noted Mauss. 'The achievements of the German troops were above all praise.' Then he added, 'We can leave the island; this retreat never was a defeat!' The following morning, 10 August, he was on the mainland.

Bruno Kanert and the III. Bataillon of the HG Panzer Regiment had also left. After the fighting around Nicolosi and Trecastagni, they had been ordered up to Messina. Kanert had boarded a Siebel ferry on 8 August and had been immensely impressed by the calm efficiency with which the thirty-minute crossing had been conducted, without any shouting or fuss. A bomber formation had approached while they were on the water but, as he said, 'Our anti-aircraft guns opened fire from both sides of the strait. The exploding flak shells in the sky above us formed a dense screen into which the enemy dared not fly.' He reckoned the bombs that were dropped disturbed no one but the fish.

The Allied air forces continued to come over, but with limited effect. On the nights of 8–9 and 12–13 August, Wellington night bombers dropped more than 800 tons of bombs on Messina and the crossing points, while by day medium bombers flew 576 sorties – individual flights – and the fighter-bombers 1,883. All that effort resulted in just thirteen craft sunk and three damaged. Heavy bombers were also in the skies, but their primary targets remained further afield, pounding enemy lines of communication, industry and ports in Italy.

Meanwhile, Martin Pöppel and his small band of brothers were still fighting. By the evening of 8 August, his company had been reduced to just twenty-three men; since then, they'd been on the move continuously, pausing only to fire, covering the engineers as they laid more mines and booby-traps, then moving on again. Jupp Klein was among those laying many of these 'devil's gardens'. 'We had an abundance of explosives at our disposal,' he recalled, 'and we really made the most of that. I can't remember any object not being professionally and thoroughly destroyed due to lack of mass.' In this way comparatively few German troops, in the narrow confines of the Sicilian coastline, were able to slow down the Allied advance pretty effectively. No Allied commander expected his troops to simply plunge on over minefields and booby-traps. 'Tommy is meeting constant resistance, is unsure of our strength and is therefore cautious about advancing,' Pöppel noted. 'All the same, I'm bound to admit that this broken countryside is easy to defend but difficult to attack. Even when weak forces are overrun, they still have a good chance to make it back to their own lines.'

He and his men reached Messina on 13 August, a month to the day after reaching Sicily. They'd arrived on 13 July, now they would be leaving on the 13th, too, and a Friday to boot, although he hoped no ill wind would prevent them getting across. Against Hube's rule forbidding crossing in daylight, they set off over the straits at 3 p.m. and made it safely to the far side. Pöppel was glad they had been able to do their duty well, even though it turned out to be in a lost cause. He tried not to think of home. 'Oh, it would be wonderful to be there,' he thought, 'but we're soldiers, the Führer's best troops, and there's no such thing as leave in times as turbulent as these. We need just a little time to recover, then we'll be ready for action again.'

The following day, Saturday, 14 August, Werner Stappenbeck and his two comrades walked from six in the morning until ten-thirty at night with only three half-hour breaks. All three felt utterly broken. Then, at long last, as they trudged on, they saw the straits and their spirits rose once more. Finding a last ounce of energy, they headed down to the port where they were first stopped but then, after producing their papers, allowed to pass. They were quite a sight with their tattered, filthy clothes and beards. At one of the crossing points there were stocks of food. 'And what a hunger we had!' wrote Stappenbeck. 'A good month without a single piece of meat fibre and without a knife point of fat, with many hundreds of kilometres of walking at all altitudes up to over 1,000 metres, over ditches, fences, walls, through areas of gangs of bounty hunters, ragged, chased by dogs – that is how we now faced the German troops!' It was Sunday, 15 August, and after eighteen days of the most extraordinary epic journey, the three men had made it. They crossed the straits that day – three more German soldiers who had successfully got away from Sicily.

The last of the Italians were also getting across to the mainland. Even though they had begun their evacuation earlier, the loss of the 932-ton ferry *Villa*, which had caught fire on 12 August, had slowed things down. Their crossing points to the south of Messina had been longer too, so more time-consuming. Livio Messina had reached his namesake town around midday on the 16th, after a trek almost as long as Stappenbeck's. Unshaven, thin and broken, he and his few men had joined a further eight hundred on the quayside waiting to cross. The air was foul: nearby a warehouse had collapsed, crushing a number of people to death, and the bodies were smelling terrible in the midday heat. Messina prayed all the way across the water, reciting the words his parents had taught him. 'My Lord, save me,' he mouthed. 'Holy Mary, help me. Let the souls of my dead relatives pray to the Lord for me.' Whether protected by his prayers or the gunners either side of the straits, Messina did reach the other side. His long ordeal was over.

Meanwhile, back on the island, the final battles were taking place, frustration hounding the Allies to the last. On 12 August, Ernie Pyle had moved along the northern coastal highway to see 3rd Division's progress. After Brolo, the Americans had ground their way through yet more detonations and mines until they'd reached the tunnel that ran under Capo Calavà. The retreating Germans had not blocked the tunnel, but they had blown a large 120-yard section of the road the far side, most of which now lay at the foot of the cliffs below. It was possible for individual troops to pick their way across the scree, but the way was utterly impassable for vehicles. The 10th Engineer Battalion was hurried forward, and Pyle watched in awestruck amazement as they set to work at around four o'clock that afternoon. Bulldozers, winches, jackhammers – all seemed to appear by magic, while men scurried about, stripped to the waist and glistening with sweat, each of them looking completely on top of what he was supposed to be doing. Overnight they drilled and blasted two holes into the side of the cliffs, while pneumatic drills helped create ledges at either end on to which abutments of wood were bolted. By morning, uprights were being lowered into the drilled holes as struts on to which cross-beams were then attached. Pyle watched one man, 'doing practically a wire-walking act', edge out over the timber and, with a pneumatic bit, bore a long hole down through two timbers. Into this was hammered a steel rod, joining them up. Others added more bracing, sledge-hammering huge spikes into the timbers. The whole thing was bound together with steel cables, tightened by a mechanical winch. By 11 a.m.

on the 13th, just nineteen hours after work had begun, General Truscott himself rolled over in a jeep. More strengthening work continued, and by afternoon heavy vehicles were crossing and the division was rumbling forward once more. Pyle was bowled over by what these engineers had achieved. 'They had built a jerry bridge, a comical bridge, a proud bridge,' he wrote, 'but above all the kind of bridge that wins wars.' He was not wrong.

After the collapse of the Tortorici Line and the beginning of the evacuation, Hube's men fell back in carefully staged phases, each position defending a line narrower than the one before. When the Allies reached the first on 13 August, Eighth Army on the east coast was closer to Messina than Seventh on the north, which prompted Patton to order yet another amphibious operation on the night of 15–16 August. That same night, No. 40 Commando, led by Lieutenant-Colonel 'Mad' Jack Churchill, landed some 15 miles south of Messina along with elements of the 4th Armoured Brigade. Churchill was known for his cut and dash, but even his assembled forces couldn't cut or dash their way forward in a hurry here. On 15 August the Germans fell behind the last phase line, and overnight on the 16th–17th the evacuation was completed – with Jupp Klein, who had been carrying out demolitions with his platoon to the last possible moment, among the final men to be taken across.

At first light, leading British troops from Eighth Army reached Tremestieri, a couple of miles south of the town, but were then halted by a blown bridge, while at 7 a.m. an American patrol entered the town and the Italian mayor formally surrendered. It had been a close-run thing, but Patton had won his race after all, and in the nick of time. The Sicilian campaign was over.

Postscript

SURPRISINGLY LITTLE HAS BEEN written about the Sicilian campaign, and narratives of the battles that took place there in that blisteringly hot summer of 1943 are few and far between. That's odd, because this campaign came at a fascinating turning point in the war in the west, and so much of what was learned there was carried forward into future operations and campaigns. It's also curious because it's such an incredible story – one of extraordinary characters, machiavellian machinations and skulduggery, daring special forces raids, barely credible mountain ascents, stunning air battles, phenomenal naval operations, and two of the most famous Allied commanders of the entire war.

What's more, those historians who have paid attention to the campaign have not been especially kind to the Allies' conduct of it, to such an extent that there has remained something of a black mark against it. The criticisms run deep, and probably would have been less harsh had the German evacuation, especially, been averted. In all, the Italians evacuated 62,182 men, although most of their equipment was left behind – just 41 guns and 227 vehicles were saved, not really enough to worry anyone on the Allied side. The Germans, on the other hand, evacuated 39,569 men, along with 9,605 vehicles, 94 guns and 47 tanks. Having said that, while getting nearly 40,000 men out meant a decent number of troops available for more fighting, only 25,669 of them were ferried across the straits during LEHRGANG, the formal evacuation operation from 11 to 16 August. Although some of those taken off earlier – men such as Bruno Kanert, for example – were fighting troops, most of those lifted before LEHRGANG got under way were odds and sods, casualties, staff and service troops. The fighting, combat troops evacuated numbered less than 30,000, barely enough to make up two complete full-strength divisions and, in the grand scheme of things, hardly enough to make a dramatic impact one way or the other in the future Italian campaign. Even had the Allies managed to halt the evacuation, they would have still faced the German troops moving into Italy in readiness for Operation ACHSE; by the end of October there would be some nineteen German divisions in Italy, and by the following March twenty-four, so the numbers that escaped from Sicily were in no way decisive. In any case, the four divisions that did escape had been badly mauled and were under-strength, the HG Division and 1. Fallschirmjäger especially so; 15. Panzer Grenadier received reasonable numbers of replacements at the end of the campaign but had been in dire straits by the time Troina was over, as testified by the losses to units such as Pöppel's machine-gun battalion or Karl Goldschmidt's Tiger tank company. In other words, the number of German troops that managed to cross the straits was not quite so big a deal as historians have tried to claim.

It's also worth considering other evacuations during the war. Few people deny that the German sweep across western Europe in May and June 1940 was a massive victory, and yet they allowed 338,000 British and Allied troops to escape at Dunkirk – and all those thousands of troops got away across a far larger and less well protected stretch of sea in far more difficult circumstances. One of the reasons was that even over skies where almost no flak threatened them, German dive-bombers found it very hard to hit a moving vessel such as a cross-Channel ferry or Royal Navy destroyer, which from 6,000 feet looked like a tiny pencil; but from that height a Siebel ferry in the Straits of Messina was barely a dot on the water. It's true that most British equipment was left behind, but it was the troops that Hitler was most anxious to save from Sicily, not his tanks and guns, and the 40,000 that did escape fell some way short of the 70,000 he demanded be saved after the fall of Mussolini. The vast majority of British troops managed to escape Greece in April 1941; two-thirds of those on Crete were evacuated a month later. Perhaps the biggest evacuation of the war, and one that still lay ahead in August 1943, was Operation HANNIBAL, when a staggering two million Germans, mostly civilians but also some troops, were evacuated from East Prussia in the final stages of the war, using old and barely functioning ships and with almost no artillery, air or naval protection at all. The message from wartime evacuations is clear: most were extremely successful, which suggests they were very hard to stop. Cunningham, Tedder and Coningham have all been heavily criticized for not doing more to stop the Axis evacuations, but this seems unfair and reflects a lack of proper understanding of the campaign in Sicily, the very heavy defences protecting the straits, and the wider context of evacuations during the Second World War. Operation LEHRGANG was pretty much impossible to stop.

Another criticism has been that the Allied approach was over-cautious; but it has to be remembered that HUSKY was planned at a time when it was not at all clear what the strength of the defence would be, and on the back of a stiff battle in Tunisia in which Italian units for the most part had fought well. In fact, the loss of North Africa had marked the end of Italy's commitment to the war. With that, the will to fight had gone and morale had collapsed; and armies that have lost morale are armies waiting to be defeated. But that was apparent only later.

While a great deal of time and thought has been devoted to the interplay between the Allies within the Anglo-US coalition, less attention has been paid to that between Italy and Germany within the Axis; but the contempt with which the Germans dealt with their ally almost beggars belief. The two states had never been natural or obvious bedfellows, and the Pact of Steel had been signed in 1939 on the understanding that neither side would get intimately involved in the foreign affairs of the other. From Hitler's perspective, Italy was supposed to protect Germany's southern flank and not much more; yet the Italians had dragged the Germans into the Mediterranean theatre, with disastrous consequences. Culturally and temperamentally the two nations were radically different, and by July 1943 whatever suspicions German commanders had had of their battlefield ally had been confirmed, even exacerbated, by the abject material poverty and crushed morale of Mussolini's Italy. 'The Italian soldier was tired, aimless and undisciplined,' wrote Max Ulich, one of the 29. Division's regimental commanders. 'Consequently, Italians only rarely constituted an asset in combat, and for the most part proved to be a liability.' Ulich's views were widely shared among his compatriots. Schmalz thought the Italian command was rotten to its core and that Guzzoni was defeatist from the outset. Even before the invasion of Sicily, he had absolutely no faith or trust whatsoever in Germany's ally. Nor did General von Richthofen of Fliegerkorps II, who was incensed that Guzzoni had been given command of any German troops at all. 'Although the unreliability of the Italian Armed Forces and of the Italians in general had been clearly demonstrated by the African campaign, with its tragic outcome and its military and political consequences,' he wrote on 17 July, 'control of defensive operations was once again placed in the hands of the Italians at a time when the Allied attack on Europe was immediately imminent.' Von Richthofen simply hadn't been able to understand it; after all, everyone knew the fighting value of the Italians was low, to put it mildly.

Only when the Germans were back in charge and able to fight on their own terms did the defence of Sicily begin to coalesce. Once it had, from 15 July onwards, they had fought very effectively and, using all the many advantages Sicily's terrain and geography held for the defender, became an extremely tough nut to crack. This change in authority, and its conse-quences, should not be underestimated, and the Allies deserve to be saluted for conquering Sicily in a mere thirty-eight days. HUSKY was the first major contested amphibious operation mounted during the war, put into action by two coalition partners very much feeling their way, and it took Allied troops back into Axis-controlled Europe. Nothing on this scale had been mounted before, not during this war, not in all of history; maintaining two armies, not to mention air forces, on a mountainous island such as Sicily from across the Mediterranean Sea was immensely difficult and immensely challenging. The Allied achievement really does deserve far greater appreciation. It was also a major stepping stone in the conduct of the war overall, one in which the Allied way of war really began to develop – a mechanical, highly technological war of aircraft, immense naval guns, tanks, high-velocity guns, half-tracks, bulldozers and jackhammers. It was a new kind of warfare, one that harnessed air, land and naval power together.

Many lessons were to be learned from Sicily, and fed back into the evolution of this great Allied fighting machine. Notably, in Italy in the months to come, techniques of close air support would be developed fur-ther. Sicily had also taught the Allies much about preparing for major operations. When it came to planning the invasion of Normandy the following year, those commanding would no longer be expected to fight one campaign and plan for another at the same time. By the end of 1943, many of those who had shaped and fought through the Sicily campaign would have left the Mediterranean behind to take charge of preparing for the greatest amphibious operation of them all: OVERLORD, the D-Day landings, which would take place on 6 June 1944. Eisenhower,

Montgomery, Bradley, Patton, Dempsey, Tedder, Coningham, Spaatz, Ramsay, Huebner, Doolittle and others would all play major roles in that campaign and the long battles in north-western Europe that followed. It is interesting, for example, that on 10 July 1943 Dempsey's XIII Corps managed to take Syracuse, an objective just 10 miles from the invasion beaches. Less than a year on, Dempsey would be commanding British Second Army, and one of the objectives on that D-Day would be the city of Caen, 10 miles from the invasion beaches. On 6 June 1944, it would prove an objective too far; but on Sicily, the capture of a city 10 miles from the landing beaches had been successfully achieved.

Important lessons were also learned from the costly airborne operations, although arguably not enough of the right ones. Hopkinson, the messianic glider man, was killed in Italy in September, shot by a sniper, but although the Allies never quite managed to solve the problem of how most effectively to send some of their best-trained troops into battle, the British and Americans certainly improved the standard of glider and tug training. Among those leading the tugs to capture vital bridges on D-Day was Flight Lieutenant Tommy Grant, while on 6 June 1944 Jim Wallwork, who over Sicily had ended up miles off course, landed a glider perfectly at Pegasus Bridge, contributing to its capture in a matter of minutes.

Air power certainly paved the way for victory on the ground. As HUSKY got under way, arguments rumbled on about whether the air forces were providing enough support for those below, but the gripes of Patton and others should be largely discounted because they were viewing air power only from the narrow prism of what they could see with their own eyes directly over their part of the front, and not as part of the bigger picture. Arguments have also raged over just how many Allied aircraft were destroyed over Sicily itself, when actually it's how many were destroyed in the wider theatre that really mattered. In all, some 322 Axis bombers and 268 fighters were destroyed on the ground between 6 July and 19 October 1943 – figures that also include the start of the Italian campaign that followed – while a further 207 bombers and 700 fighters were destroyed in the air and some 1,000 aircraft captured: so, some 2,500 in all. It was enough, at any rate, to gain the Allies air superiority in the theatre, which in turn allowed amphibious operations to take place and those on the ground to have the comfort of air support over their heads.

The air war did, however, cause a huge amount of destruction, and would continue to do so in Italy as the Allied typhoon of steel rolled up the long, mountainous leg. Cassino and the destruction of the Benedictine monastery above the town would become bywords for the terrible carnage wrought on Italy, but many more Cassinos were utterly destroyed by mostly Allied bombs and shells in that devastated country. Tragically for the Italians, the end of their war did not bring about the end of the war. Neither Mussolini nor the King nor Badoglio nor any other leading Italians had worked out how to extricate themselves cleanly from the tragic mess into which they'd got themselves, and that was largely because the task was impossible. Eisenhower had finalized plans for Fifth Army's invasion at Salerno and for Eighth Army's across into the toe of Italy on 16 August, the day before the Sicilian campaign ended. Two days later these were accepted, and at the same time it was also agreed to open formal talks with the Italians, who had been tentatively sending out peace feelers since the beginning of the month. Proposals were put to the Italians on 19 August, to which they eventually agreed on 1 September, according to which they would be co-belligerents, not allies, against Germany. But although the armistice was signed on 1 September, it was not announced until the 8th; and while Eighth Army had already landed in the toe by then, the main landing, that of Mark Clark's Fifth Army, did not assault Salerno until 9 September, by which time Operation ACHSE had been put into action with clinical efficiency. Italian barracks were overrun, the King, Badoglio and the royal government fled Rome for Bari in the south, and across Italy, the Balkans and Greece, some fifty-six Italian divisions were immediately dissolved. By February 1944, some 617,000 former Italian troops had been interned and transported to Germany, where they worked as forced labourers.

No one had a very good time in Italy over the next eighteen months. The Allies had planned their campaign there under the baking heat of the summer sun, but although the prime objective, capturing the Foggia airfield complex, was achieved in pretty quick order, the campaign itself soon got bogged down as the Allied armies in Italy had to contend not only with too many mountains, not enough roads, and endless rivers, mines and demolitions, but also rain and mud. Because building up the strategic air forces had been the initial priority, Alexander's armies never quite had enough supplies delivered soon enough to drive home their advantage. Nor had the Germans retreated to the north. Instead, after Kesselring's impressive defence against the Salerno landings, Hitler changed his mind – as he was wont to do – and decided his troops there should fight for every bitter yard. The long, brutal and bloody campaign in Italy did not end until 2 May 1945. When it did, though, it brought the first total surrender of German forces in the war. Not only Alexander himself, but many of those who had fought in Sicily slugged it out in mainland Italy too, including many on the German side.

Alexander, who has had an unfair press for Sicily, achieved the Allies' greatest land victory in the war to that date when, on 4 June 1944, his armies finally captured Rome at the end of a superbly fought battle against two German armies. By then Montgomery was back in England – as was Patton, whose Seventh Army had not been part of the plans for Italy. After what had been unquestionably a triumph for the Americans in Sicily, Patton rather blew matters for himself over a couple of incidents that took place before the campaign ended. On 3 August, he visited the 15th Evacuation Hospital in Nicosia, where he had found a soldier from the 26th Infantry with no obvious wound. When the patient confessed he was suffering from battle exhaustion, Patton flew into a rage, slapped him across the face, picked him up and threw him out of the tent. He then sent a note to his senior commanders warning against such malingerers. 'Such men are cowards,' he wrote, 'and bring discredit on the Army and disgrace to their comrades.' He wanted such men arrested and put before courts martial for cowardice in the face of the enemy. On 10 August, he was making another such visit, this time to the 93rd Evacuation Hospital, and came across a second man suffering from shell-shock, huddled in his bunk and shivering. When questioned by Patton, the soldier said, 'It's my nerves.' Patton again blew his top. 'Your nerves, Hell, you are just a goddamned coward, you yellow son of a bitch!' he yelled. 'You're a disgrace to the Army . . . You ought to be lined up against a wall and shot. In fact, I ought to shoot you myself, right now, Goddam you!' Reaching for one of his pearl-handled pistols, he waved it in the man's face before striking him across the cheek with his other hand. Colonel Currier, the doctor in charge, then had to intervene. It turned out the patient was also suffering from malaria.

News of this second incident, especially, soon got around. An account of it even reached the press camp at Allied Forces HQ. Several journalists claimed there were fifty thousand men on Sicily prepared to shoot Patton themselves. Others thought the Seventh commander must have gone insane. Inevitably, word eventually reached Eisenhower, who reprimanded Patton severely and seriously considered relieving him of his command. His punishment was to apologize in person to both men, and publicly – which, to be fair to him, he did. Patton always obeyed orders. His reputation for poor judgement and hot-headedness, however, did not disappear, and it wasn't improved when Sergeant Horace T. West and Captain John T. Crompton were court-martialled for the unlawful killing of prisoners at Biscari. Both claimed they were merely obeying the instructions of Patton, who before the campaign had exhorted his men not to take prisoners. That Patton said such things was not in dispute, and although the defence of both men was thrown out, the episode further tarnished his reputation. West was convicted of murder and sentenced to life imprisonment, but was released in November 1944 and served in the infantry until the end of the war, when he was given an honourable discharge. Incredibly, Crompton was acquitted; transferred to the 179th Infantry, he was killed in action in Italy on 8 November the same year, 1943. No one much remembered this case when, after the war, German soldiers were accused of war crimes. It is interesting to note that between them, West and Crompton killed around the same number of Italians as the Americans shot by Kampfgruppe Peiper in December 1944 during the Battle of the Bulge.

Patton was certainly not directly responsible for West's and Crompton's actions at Biscari, but whether they would have still shot those men had Patton not made such pre-battle speeches is an interesting point for discussion. At the very least, it was surely less likely to have happened. There is no doubt, however, that Patton was a highly driven and charismatic commander, and he would successfully lead Third Army in Normandy and beyond until the end of the war. He was, though, a strange beast, to say the least, and because of his obvious shortcomings, never commanded more than an army. That was, however, still quite an achievement, and one shared by comparatively few men.

Whether the population of Sicily was any less downtrodden after the Allied conquest of the island is debatable, for although civilian casualties were comparatively light, many of the island's towns and much of its infrastructure lay in ruins, and most of its people were as impoverished as ever. When General Patton had entered Messina on the morning of 17 August, he had been shocked by what met his eyes; it was the worst destruction of any town he'd seen, and by that stage he'd seen a fair few. Reports reached him that five thousand civilians had been discovered living in a cave for more than a week. 'I do not believe that this indiscriminate bombing of towns is worth the ammunition,' he wrote in his diary, 'and it is unnecessarily cruel to civilians.'

In the weeks and months to come, Sicily would also become a hotbed of corruption and a resurgent Onorata Società. Don Calò Vizzini, for example, grew even richer and more powerful in the aftermath of the Allied victory. Given two trucks and a tractor by AMGOT to help clear rubble in the area, he used them to deliver food supplies stolen from various Allied and Italian military warehouses. Before long, Vizzini had a considerable racket going, which seemed only to enhance his wider reputation. By early 1944 the OSS in Palermo, now headed by Joseph Russo, was heavily dependent on Don Calò and the Mafia for intelligence – to the extent that Russo met with the Don at least once a month.

Perhaps one of the most unpleasant characters to move in on Sicily, however, was Vito Genovese, who managed to inveigle his way into Colonel Charles Poletti's AMGOT set-up in Palermo almost as soon as the campaign was over. Genovese was another hood who had fled back to Italy in 1937 from New York, where he was wanted for murder. Clever, ruthless, manipulative but also charming, Genovese had quickly ingratiated himself with a number of leading Fascists and others of the Roman elite, not least Count Galeazzo Ciano and his wife Edda, Mussolini's daughter. He had also further won favour by arranging the murder of Carlo Tresco – editor of an anti-Fascist paper – in New York through his contacts still over there.

With Mussolini gone and the Allies ruling the roost in Sicily, he wasted no time in getting himself over to Palermo, where he managed to land himself a job as Charles Poletti's right-hand man, translating, guiding and acting as his go-between and even driver. Back in New York, moreover, he had once been Lucky Luciano's number one man; and before he had to make a run for it back to Italy, he had even managed Luciano's business interests when the latter was first in prison. Later, after the war, Luciano described Poletti as 'one of our good friends'. The Poletti–Genovese racket continued well into 1944, by which time Poletti was head of AMGOT in Naples and Genovese was one of the biggest gangsters in town, having sewn up the black market, thereby adding considerably to the misery of first Sicilians and then southern Italians. In essence, the Mafia quickly filled a power vacuum on Sicily, and because of the tactical endorsement of their activities by the occupying authorities, particularly in the western half of the island, their power and influence grew rapidly. Once almost snuffed out by Cesare Mori, from 1943 they ruled the roost once more. They have never gone away.

*

Battlefield casualties in the Sicilian campaign were 4,678 German dead and a further 4,583 missing; for the Italians, 4,325 dead and 40,655 missing. Most of the German missing were probably killed, whereas the Italian missing were predominantly Sicilian and most likely simply went home. British and Canadian dead together amounted to 2,721, and Americans, 2,811. On average, this worked out at 237 Axis troops and 146 Allied troops – at least – killed every day. On one level, that might not sound like too many, but for the Axis it equated to almost two infantry companies per day, while for the Allies it meant a little more than one company per day. As a proportion of fighting strength, that was quite a lot. The figures for wounded were roughly three times those killed, while 5,532 Germans and 116,681 Italians were taken prisoner. A total of 11,590 British troops and 9,892 Americans (and much the same numbers of Germans) caught malaria. That is, more Allied troops suffered from malaria than were killed or wounded.

As a proportion of the troops on Sicily the number of casualties seems, at first glance, comparatively low; however, the vast majority of battlefield casualties were in the infantry, which made up only around 15 per cent of Allied troops in Sicily; more than 40 per cent were service troops, for example. That I have focused so heavily on the infantry in this narrative does give a slightly lopsided view of the Allied armies at this time; yet it was those men who were responsible for getting off their backsides and actually taking ground, and for them, Sicily was brutal – as it was for the Axis troops caught up in the heaviest fighting.

The Hasty Ps were withdrawn from the fighting after Regalbuto, but before leaving the mountains Farley Mowat felt compelled to try to discover what had happened to one of his men, Archie 'A. K.' Long, who had been so badly wounded at Nissoria just after the battle for Assoro. Borrowing Bill Kennedy's jeep, he and Corporal Hill, a friend of Long's, set off to see if they could find out. Along they drove towards Agira, over pockmarked and cratered roads, past vineyards and olive groves desecrated by battle. They stopped by a temporary graveyard where those killed had been roughly buried before their eventual disinterment and reburial in a more permanent cemetery that would be built and maintained by the Imperial (later, Commonwealth) War Graves Commission. It was pretty rough and ready, graves marked by thin white crosses stuck in the red earth with identity tags draped over them. 'The transient bodies were shallowly buried and the heat was oppressive,' wrote Mowat. 'The ripe stench of decay filled our nostrils as we worked our way up and down the line of crosses.' There were several Hasty Ps there, but no sign of A. K.

They made their way up a long, bare slope where just ten days earlier Able Company had advanced. Debris lay strewn everywhere. A ripped shirt behind a bush; unravelled dressings, black with dried blood. Steel helmets, rifles, split bandoliers. Webbing that had been discarded, and a carton of 2-inch mortar bombs. There were blackened craters, too, and paper – lots of paper – fluttering in the hot and gentle breeze. Then they came to a gully where Long had been lain down after being wounded, and Hill spotted a gnarled and twisted tree where he'd quietly read as he awaited his fate. They both approached, somehow expecting to find the book Long had been reading lying there. But they found nothing, except long lines of ants and a single lizard on the tree. 'For the first time during the Sicilian campaign,' wrote Mowat, 'I experienced heartfelt pain at the loss of a comrade . . . which was passing strange, for I had never been his chum, had never really known the man. An enigma, he had lived among us for a while, then vanished from us . . . but I had felt for him . . . would feel for him in the years ahead.'

A. K. Long is in fact remembered not in Sicily at all but on the memorial at Cassino. Picked up by the Germans, he suffered much the same fate as Hedley Verity, although somewhere along the line he had died and his body had been dumped so that he was never given a proper grave. Perhaps it doesn't matter, but it seems tragic all the same, especially since so many of his fellows are buried in one of the loveliest Commonwealth War Graves Commission cemeteries anywhere in the world. Just below Agira, on an outcrop just off the road, lie the graves of some 490 men, mostly Canadians, who fought in those terrible ridgeline battles, and who are now shaded by sweet-smelling poplars in a way that was denied them during those blisteringly hot days of fighting. From here there are views out over a lake, created some years after the war to provide much-needed water supplies, and towards Regalbuto, long ago rebuilt from the ruins of the fighting.

Mowat himself went on to fight in Italy, survived the war and returned home to Canada, where he became a much-loved writer and naturalist. Alex Campbell, his company commander, was killed in Italy on Christmas Day later that year. Lord Tweedsmuir, another survivor, continued to be an adventurer and environmentalist, and was made CBE in 1964 for his work for the British Schools Society. David Cole also fought in Italy and later became a diplomat; in the 1970s he was the British

Ambassador to Thailand. In the honours stakes he did one better than Tweedsmuir, awarded a knighthood. James Donaldson fought in Normandy, as did Bill Cheall, who was wounded but, after recovering, returned to Europe as a member of the Regimental Police of the East Lancashire Regiment. He finished the war in Hamburg, was discharged in 1946 and returned to the family grocery business. David Fenner also landed on D-Day and, like Cheall, was wounded in Normandy and invalided home. He remained in the army and eventually retired to Dorset. Peter Pettit also later fought in north-west Europe and survived to the end of hostilities, returning to post-war civilian life as a solicitor.

Of the British airborne troops, George Chatterton was largely responsible for retraining the glider pilots in advance of their D-Day and subsequent operations; he too survived the war, later writing his memoirs. Dennis Galpin was another who flew on D-Day and also made it through the war. Peter Davis remained with the SRS when it reverted to its original title as the SAS, fought in France and won an MC in Germany. Later he moved to South Africa, where he was tragically murdered in March 1994 in a case that has never been solved. Alastair Pearson won his third DSO for his actions in Sicily and commanded the 8th Parachute Battalion on D-Day; he fought through the campaign but later had to hand over command owing to ill health. Resigning his commission, he then returned to his bakery in Scotland, although he remained in the Territorial Army. Later he became a farmer and was also, in the late 1950s, aide-de-camp to the Queen. Sergeant John Johnstone remained a POW until the end of the war; what happened to him and James Donaldson after the war, I'm not sure, but both lived to old age.

Of the Americans, Mark Alexander and James Gavin both landed on D-Day, by which time the latter was commander of the 82nd Airborne and the youngest general in the US Army. Alexander was badly wounded during the Normandy campaign and invalided back home, but Gavin took part in Operation MARKET GARDEN and continued to have a long and very distinguished career in the army long after the war was over. Breezy Griffin also survived the war, as did Frank Johnson, who landed on Omaha Beach with the Big Red One on D-Day but was later wounded in Normandy and sent home. Charlie Scheffel too fought in Normandy and kept going until wounded during the Siegfried Line battles. So many who fought in the infantry tended to get wounded somewhere along the line, which rather underlines just how tough their role was. Audie Murphy also fought in Italy, then in southern France and

on into Germany. By the war's end he had become the single most decorated American soldier of the war, with a Congressional Medal of Honor,
Distinguished Service Cross, two Silver Stars, the Legion of Merit, two
Bronze Stars and three Purple Hearts for wounds sustained in combat.
He later became a film star and even played himself in a film of his wartime career, but tragically died in a plane crash when still only forty-five
years old.

Chet Hansen remained as Bradley's aide and headed back to England
when the latter – rather than Patton – was given command of First Army
for Normandy. When Bradley took charge of Twelfth Army Group on
1 August 1944, he became Patton's boss. Ernie Pyle went to Italy and
then to Normandy and followed the American troops across the European Theater of Operations. In April 1945 he was killed by a Japanese
machine-gunner while covering the terrible Battle of Okinawa. Max
Corvo went on to Italy and helped run the OSS there – with somewhat
more success than he'd had in Sicily.

Of the naval men, Douglas Fairbanks Jr returned to Hollywood
after the war, while Philip Mountbatten married Princess Elizabeth,
later Queen Elizabeth II, and became Duke of Edinburgh, later Prince
Philip. Peter Hay remained in the navy and rose to the rank of commander. All the fliers featured here survived, too. Smoky Vrilakas
returned home after his tour was over, as did Charlie Dryden. The 99th
Fighter Squadron later grew into the 322nd Fighter Group and the
Tuskegee Airmen – among the most legendary flying formations of the
war, with a reputation for always ensuring the bombers they escorted got
home safely. Jimmy Bruno also successfully completed his tour and was
sent home. Hap Kennedy flew in Italy and then headed back to the UK
before returning to Europe as commander of 401 Squadron in Normandy.
Shot down in late July 1944, he was helped by the Maquis to get back to
Allied lines and continued flying. After the war, he returned to Canada
and became a successful doctor. Cocky Dundas went on to serve in Italy,
where he became the youngest group captain in the RAF. After leaving
the RAF in 1947, he first worked for Beaverbrook Newspapers and later
became chair of Thames Television before finally retiring in 1987.

Livio Messina made it home to Naples and later became an interpreter
for the Allies. After the war was over, he trained as a lawyer and enjoyed
a long and successful life. Dante Ugo Leonardi eventually made it back
to Italy and later built a memorial to his men at the Castelluccio di Gela,
which is still there to this day. Of the civilians, Mario Turco still lives in

Gela, where Giuseppe Bruccoleri too remained in his family home and lived to an old age. Vincenza La Bruna remained in the rebuilt Regalbuto, while Michele Piccione lived the rest of his long life in Syracuse. Melino Barbagallo remained in the air force and, at the time of writing, is living in Catania.

Hanns Cibulka survived the war and became a distinguished poet. Karl Goldschmidt made it through too, as did Bruno Kanert. Martin Pöppel fought in Italy and then in Normandy, where he was wounded but survived to the end. So did Jupp Klein, but only after a long and difficult campaign in Italy, where he was eventually captured. Released after the war, he married, took over his father-in-law's building business and became one of the co-founders of the Monte Cassino Foundation, an organization set up to promote peace and reconciliation. Werner Stappenbeck also survived the war, although I have no idea what happened to him; his account of his extraordinary time on Sicily, together with a long letter to his parents, was left at the Tagebuch Archiv in Emmendingen in the Black Forest. Wilhelm Schmalz took over command of the HG Division in Italy, where he continued his extremely distinguished combat career; although later tried for war crimes, he was acquitted. Frido von Senger commanded XIV Panzer Korps in Italy, including – very successfully – at Cassino. Hans-Valentin Hube became commander of 1. Panzerarmee in October 1943, but after being awarded the Knight's Cross with Diamonds by Hitler was killed when the plane taking him from Salzburg crashed. Dr Wilhelm Mauss remained in Italy until the war's end, surviving and returning to Hessen, where he continued as a doctor until his death aged only fifty-four.

Macky Steinhoff somehow managed to keep going and survive the war, flying the Me262 jets with Adolf Galland, and later had the courage to challenge the authority of Göring over the plight of the Luftwaffe's pilots. Shortly before the end of the war his Me262, failing to take off properly, crashed and caught fire. Steinhoff suffered horrific burns and was disfigured for life, although he served in the post-war West German air force and later served as Acting Commander Allied Air Forces Central Europe in NATO and as Chairman of the NATO Military Committee.

Sicily is a wonderful place to visit, whether just for fun or to explore its incredible heritage. It's a place of staggering beauty; but there's also a roughness to it that emphasizes its sense of being a place apart from the rest of Italy, not just physically but culturally too. Today, as throughout history, it sits very much on the edge of Europe, and has struggled in recent years with the massive numbers of migrants coming across the Mediterranean.

While there are plenty of relics of the island's ancient past, the brief days of the battle for Sicily in the summer heat of 1943 have also left their mark. It is still possible to walk over the remains of the gun batteries on Capo Murro di Porco and explore the bunkers. One bunker overlooking the beach where Hedley Verity came ashore gets closer to falling into the sea every time I visit; another, to the south of Syracuse, has been neatly sliced in half with the construction of a roundabout where once it guarded a simple junction. The Ponte Grande has been replaced, as has the Primosole Bridge, but both places are much the same in essence. It's certainly not hard to imagine what it must have been like there back in 1943. The exact spot where Hedley Verity was mortally wounded is now shrouded by a high fenced-off citrus plantation rumoured to be Mafia-owned, but it's quite possible to see the jump-off positions of the 1st Green Howards on that disastrous night attack, which have barely changed at all since then. All along the east and south coasts, bunkers remain – including the gun positions at Ponte Dirillo at the edge of the Acate valley. Even the Casa dei Priolo, the villa where Sayre's paratroopers attacked soon after landing, still stands on the ridgeline south of Niscemi, although it is empty and derelict, with bullet holes pockmarking the outer plaster.

To clamber to the top of Assoro and stand on the plateau where Tweedsmuir's men assembled, or to drive up to Troina or Centuripe, is to marvel at what those men – on both sides – went through. From each of these high towns, Etna seems to bear down, somehow mystical with its puff of volcanic cloud on top, and it's impossible not to be awed by the scale of the island, the awfulness of having to fight here, or amazed by the endless series of mountaintop towns that had to be climbed up to and down from and fought over. It's still not a fast or easy place to get around, and travelling across the island it is all too easy to understand why manoeuvring highly mechanized and industrialized armies through this terrain was so difficult. The Allies have often been accused of being too slow, too stodgy, too risk-averse. These criticisms, are, for the most part, misplaced. Britain and America – rightly – decided to use mechanization as much as possible, but rarely were they able to use their might in mechanized materiel to its very best advantage. Not on Sicily, anyway: perhaps following the end of the Normandy campaign in late August 1944, or after crossing the River Po in northern Italy in April 1945, but certainly not here, where they found themselves canalized by geography and by too many small roads unsuited to the scale of operations they were mounting. It's no wonder it took time to advance on occasion. It is impossible not to conclude that conquering this extraordinary island in a mere thirty-eight days was a very impressive performance indeed. Having studied this campaign – and the wider war – in great detail, I simply do not understand why historians have been so grudging about what was achieved here.

While I was researching this book, I took my then twelve-year-old daughter with me on one of my numerous trips to the island. There were some places I hadn't seen before that I wanted to see, and some people I hadn't met before that I wanted to meet. It was half-term and she gamely agreed to come along for the ride. We drove up to Troina, where a still ruined church stands as a memorial to how the town suffered, and how so many combatants suffered, in that epic battle. We also made a detour to Villalba, where the locals chuckled wryly when we asked them about Don Calogero Vizzini. He's certainly still remembered there, even though he died, a very rich man, back in 1954.

And we also visited Trapani, where Macky Steinhoff and his brave band of pilots battled so courageously against the odds. Using Steinhoff's diary to guide us, we climbed the winding road until, a few kilometres from the top, we saw a sheer rock face and, before it, a small plateau, just as he'd described it – and, lo and behold, there was the remains of a compound, with several derelict stone buildings and even a metal-runged ladder leading to a cave in the rock face: the very air-raid shelter that was being constructed during Steinhoff's visits there. This was the Monte Erice operations base for the fighters, long since abandoned, overgrown and forgotten. But a real, palpable link to those burning summer days of 1943.

We looked around, and I paused and gazed out to the flat plain below, to the white buildings of Trapani and towards the airfield and the wide, deep Mediterranean beyond. The sun shone down from the cloudless blue sky and I realized I was looking at exactly the same view that Steinhoff had looked at all those years before. Half-closing my eyes, it was not hard at all to picture him standing where I was standing, a young man exhausted by war, and by the huge responsibilities on his shoulders, and I couldn't help feeling a little wistful.

Overlooking Paterno

Glossary of Terms and Abbreviations

AA	anti-aircraft
ACHSE	code name for German invasion of mainland Italy
AMGOT	Allied Military Government of Occupied Territories
ammiraglio	admiral (It.)
artiglieria	artillery (It.)
AVALANCHE	code name for Allied invasion of mainland Italy at Salerno
AVM	Air Vice-Marshal
BAR	Browning Automatic Rifle (light machine gun)
Bataillon	battalion (Ger.)
battaglione	battalion (It.)
BEF	British Expeditionary Force (1940)
CAO	civil affairs officer
capitano	captain (It.)
carri armati	tanks (It.)
cavalleria	cavalry (It.)
CCA	Combat Command A
CIC	Counter Intelligence Corps (US)
CIGS	Chief of the Imperial General Staff (Br.)
C-in-C	commander-in-chief
CO	commanding officer
Comando Supremo	Italian high command
compagnia	company (It.)
CORKSCREW	code name for Allied operation to capture Pantelleria
costiera	coastal (It.)
CP	command post
DFC	Distinguished Flying Cross
DLI	Durham Light Infantry
DSC	Distinguished Service Cross

DSO	Distinguished Service Order
DUKW	(pronounced 'duck') modified amphibious truck by General Motors using the company's nomenclature: D = designed in 1942; U = utility; K = all-wheel drive; W = dual-tandem rear axles
DZ	drop zone
FA	Field Artillery
Fallschirmjäger	paratrooper(s) (Ger.)
fanteria	infantry (It.)
FDLs	forward defended localities
Feldmarschall	field marshal (Ger.)
Feldwebel	sergeant (Ger.)
FS	fighter squadron
FUSTIAN	code name for Allied operation to take Primosole Bridge
Geschwader	a Luftwaffe unit of three *Gruppen* – groups – each with an establishment of 36 aircraft
Gewehr	rifle (Ger.)
GI	US soldier/airman
HAC	Honourable Artillery Company
HARDGATE	code name for renewed offensive by XXX Corps from 29 July
Hasty Ps	Hastings & Prince Edward Regiment
Hauptkampflinie	German main line of defence
HG Division	Hermann Göring Panzer Division
HMT	hired military transport (ship)
HQ	headquarters
HQRA	Headquarters, Royal Artillery
HUSKY	code name for Allied invasion of Sicily
Jabo	*Jagdbomber* or fighter-bomber (Ger.)
Jafü	fighter commander (Ger.)
Jagdflieger	fighter pilot (Ger.)
JG	Jagdgeschwader (Fighter Wing: Ger.)
Ju	Junkers
Kampfgruppe	battlegroup (Ger.)
KOYLI	King's Own Yorkshire Light Infantry
Kriegsmarine	German navy
Kübelwagen	light German military vehicle
LADBROKE	code name for Allied airborne landings on Sicily, 9 July
LCA	landing craft, assault
LCF	landing craft, flak
LCG	landing craft, gun
LCI	landing craft, infantry
LCS	landing craft, support

LEHRGANG	code name for German operation to evacuate Sicily
LST	landing ship, tank: 100 yards long, capable of carrying 18 tanks, 350 men or 2,100 tons of supplies
Luftwaffe	German air force
LZ	landing zone
MAC	Mediterranean Air Command
maresciallo	field marshal (It.)
Maschinengewehr	machine gun (Ger.)
MC	Military Cross
Me	Messerschmitt
MG	machine gun
MGB	motor gun boat
MT	motor transport
MTB	motor torpedo boat
NAAF	Northwest African Air Forces
NCO	non-commissioned officer
OKW	Oberkommando der Wehrmacht, the German combined services general staff
ONI	Office of Naval Intelligence (US)
Onorata Società	Honoured Society (It.)
OP	observation post
OSS	Office of Strategic Services (US), founded 1942
OVERLORD	code name for Allied cross-Channel invasion, planned for 1944
Pfc	private first class
PIAT	projector, infantry, anti-tank: hand-held anti-tank weapon
Pionier	engineer (Ger.)
PIR	parachute infantry regiment
point section	in a British infantry platoon, the ten-man unit in the lead
pom-pom	quick-firing 40mm cannon
POW	prisoner of war
Pz	panzer
RAAF	Royal Australian Air Force
RAF	Royal Air Force
RAP	regimental aid post
RAuxF	Royal Auxiliary Air Force
RCAF	Royal Canadian Air Force
RCT	regimental combat team
reggimento	regiment (It.)
Regia Aeronautica	Italian air force
Regia Marina	Italian navy
ROTC	Reserve Officer Training Corps (US)
RSM	regimental sergeant-major

R/T	radio transmitter
SAAF	South African Air Force
sapper	engineer
SAS	Special Air Service
SBS	Special Boat Squadron
Schwerpunkt	the main impact and concentration of force, literally 'heavy point'
Skins	Inniskillings
snafu	situation normal, all fouled/f****d up
SOE	Special Operations Executive (Br.)
SRS	Special Raiding Squadron
Staffel	squadron (Ger.)
stonk	heavy barrage of artillery fire
tenente	lieutenant (It.)
tenente-colonnello	lieutenant-colonel (It.)
TF	task force
USAAF	United States Army Air Forces
USNR	United States Naval Reserve
XO	deputy commander
ZITADELLE	German offensive to reduce Kursk salient in the Soviet Union

Appendix 1:
Allied and Axis Forces

ALLIED FORCES

Allied Forces Headquarters – *Mediterranean*

Supreme Commander: *General Dwight D. Eisenhower*

ALLIED 15TH ARMY GROUP

Commanded by General Sir Harold Alexander

- US 9th Infantry Division, commanded by Major-General Manton S. Eddy
  - 39th Infantry Regiment
  - 47th Infantry Regiment
  - 60th Infantry Regiment
  - 26th Field Artillery Battalion
  - 34th Field Artillery Battalion
  - 60th Field Artillery Battalion
  - 84th Field Artillery Battalion
  - 15th Engineer Combat Battalion
  - 42nd Anti-Aircraft Battalion
  - 9th Reconnaissance Troop

- US 82nd Airborne Division, commanded by Major-General Matthew Ridgway. The independent 509th Parachute Infantry Battalion was held in reserve and never saw action in the Sicily campaign.
  - 504th Parachute Infantry Regiment
  - 505th Parachute Infantry Regiment
  - 325th Glider Infantry Regiment
  - 376th Parachute Field Artillery Battalion
  - 456th Parachute Field Artillery Battalion
  - 319th Glider Field Artillery Battalion
  - 320th Glider Field Artillery Battalion
  - 307th Airborne Engineer Battalion
  - 80th Airborne Anti-Aircraft Battalion

- 46th British Infantry Division, commanded by Major-General H. A. Freeman-Attwood
  - 128th Infantry Brigade
  - 188th Infantry Brigade

- 139th Infantry Brigade
- 46th Royal Artillery Brigade
- 46th Royal Engineer Brigade

US SEVENTH ARMY

Commanded by Lieutenant-General George S. Patton

- 1st Ranger Battalion
- 3rd Ranger Battalion
- 4th Ranger Battalion
- 70th Tank Battalion
- 753rd Tank Battalion
- 601st Tank Destroyer Battalion
- 813th Tank Destroyer Battalion – two platoons
- 39th Engineer Regiment
- 540th Engineer Shore Regiment
- 5th Armored Artillery Group
  - 58th Armored Field Artillery Battalion
  - 62nd Armored Field Artillery Battalion
  - 65th Armored Field Artillery Battalion
- 17th Artillery Regiment
- 36th Artillery Regiment
- 77th Artillery Regiment
- 178th Artillery Regiment
- Free French 4th Moroccan Tabor

US II CORPS

Commanded by Lieutenant-General Omar Bradley

- US 1st Infantry Division, commanded first by Major-General Terry Allen, then from 7 August by Major-General Clarence Huebner
  - 16th Infantry Regiment
  - 18th Infantry Regiment
  - 26th Infantry Regiment
  - 5th Field Artillery Battalion
  - 7th Field Artillery Battalion
  - 32nd Field Artillery Battalion
  - 33rd Field Artillery Battalion
  - 1st Engineer Combat Battalion
  - 1st Reconnaissance Troop
- US 45th Infantry Division, commanded by Major-General Troy H. Middleton
  - 157th Infantry Regiment
  - 179th Infantry Regiment
  - 180th Infantry Regiment
  - 158th Field Artillery Battalion
  - 160th Field Artillery Battalion
  - 171st Field Artillery Battalion

- 189th Field Artillery Battalion
- 645th Tank Destroyer Battalion
- 120th Engineer Combat Battalion
- 45th Reconnaissance Troop

US Provisional Corps
Commanded by Major-General Geoffrey Keyes

- US 2nd Armored Division, commanded by Major-General Hugh Gaffey
  - Combat Command A
  - Combat Command B
  - 41st Armored Infantry Regiment
  - 66th Armored Regiment
  - 67th Armored Regiment
  - 14th Armored Field Artillery Battalion
  - 78th Armored Field Artillery Battalion
  - 92nd Armored Field Artillery Battalion
  - 17th Armored Engineer Battalion
  - 82nd Armored Reconnaissance Battalion

- US 3rd Infantry Division, commanded by Major-General Lucian Truscott
  - 7th Infantry Regiment
  - 15th Infantry Regiment
  - 30th Infantry Regiment
  - 9th Field Artillery Battalion
  - 10th Field Artillery Battalion
  - 39th Field Artillery Battalion
  - 41st Field Artillery Battalion
  - 10th Engineer Combat Battalion

British Eighth Army
Commanded by General Sir Bernard Montgomery

The British 46th Infantry Division formed a floating reserve, but did not participate in the Sicily campaign.

ARMY TROOPS

- 2nd Special Air Service
- No. 3 (Army) Commando
- No. 40 (Royal Marine) Commando
- No. 41 (Royal Marine) Commando
- Three companies of 2/7th Battalion, Middlesex Regiment
- 2/4th Battalion, Hampshire Regiment
- 1st Battalion, Argyll and Sutherland Highlanders
- 2nd Battalion, Highland Light Infantry
- 1st Battalion, Welch Regiment
- 7th Battalion, Royal Marines

BRITISH XIII CORPS

Commanded by Lieutenant-General Miles Dempsey

- 105th Anti-Tank Regiment, Royal Artillery
- 6th Army Group Royal Artillery
  - 24th Field Regiment, Royal Artillery
  - 98th (Surrey & Sussex Yeomanry Queen Mary's) Field Regiment, Royal Artillery
  - 111th Field Regiment, Royal Artillery
  - 66th Medium Regiment, Royal Artillery
  - 75th (Shropshire Yeomanry) Medium Regiment, Royal Artillery
  - 80th (Scottish Horse Yeomanry) Medium Regiment, Royal Artillery

- XIII Corps Troops Royal Engineers
  - 56th Field Company, Royal Engineers
  - 576th Corps Field Park Company, Royal Engineers
  - 577th Army Field Company, Royal Engineers
  - 578th Army Field Company, Royal Engineers

- 5th Infantry Division, commanded first by Major-General Horatio Berney-Ficklin, then from 3 August by Major-General Gerard Bucknall
  - 13th Infantry Brigade
      2nd Battalion, Cameronians (Scottish Rifles)
      2nd Battalion, Royal Inniskilling Fusiliers
      2nd Battalion, Wiltshire Regiment
  - 15th Infantry Brigade
      1st Battalion, Green Howards
      1st Battalion, King's Own Yorkshire Light Infantry
      1st Battalion, York and Lancaster Regiment
  - 17th Infantry Brigade
      2nd Battalion, Royal Scots Fusiliers
      2nd Battalion, Northamptonshire Regiment
      6th Battalion, Seaforth Highlanders
  - 91st (4th London) Field Regiment, Royal Artillery
  - 92nd Field Regiment, Royal Artillery
  - 156th (Lanarkshire Yeomanry) Field Regiment, Royal Artillery
  - 52nd Anti-Tank Regiment, Royal Artillery
  - 18th Light Anti-Aircraft Regiment, Royal Artillery
  - 5th Reconnaissance Regiment, Reconnaissance Corps
  - 7th Battalion, Cheshire Regiment (machine-gun battalion)
  - 5th Divisional Engineers
      38th Field Company, Royal Engineers
      245th Field Company, Royal Engineers
      252nd Field Company, Royal Engineers
      245th Field Park Company, Royal Engineers

- 50th Infantry Division, commanded by Major-General Sidney Kirkman
  - 69th Infantry Brigade
      5th Battalion, East Yorkshire Regiment
      6th Battalion, Green Howards

7th Battalion, Green Howards
- 151st Infantry Brigade
6th Battalion, Durham Light Infantry
8th Battalion, Durham Light Infantry
9th Battalion, Durham Light Infantry
- 168th Infantry Brigade
1st Battalion, London Irish Rifles
1st Battalion, London Scottish
10th Battalion, Royal Berkshire Regiment
- 74th Field Regiment, Royal Artillery
- 90th (City of London) Field Regiment, Royal Artillery
- 124th Field Regiment, Royal Artillery
- 102nd (Northumberland Hussars) Anti-Tank Regiment, Royal Artillery
- 25th Light Anti-Aircraft Regiment, Royal Artillery
- 2nd Battalion, Cheshire Regiment (machine-gun battalion)

• 50th Divisional Engineers
- 233rd (Northumbrian) Field Company, Royal Engineers
- 501st (London) Field Company, Royal Engineers
- 505th Field Company, Royal Engineers
- 235th (Northumbrian) Field Park Company, Royal Engineers

• British 78th Infantry Division, commanded by Major-General Vyvyan Evelegh
- 11th Infantry Brigade
2nd Battalion, Lancashire Fusiliers
1st Battalion, East Surrey Regiment
5th (Huntingdonshire) Battalion, Northamptonshire Regiment
- 36th Infantry Brigade
5th Battalion, Buffs (Royal East Kent Regiment)
6th Battalion, Queen's Own Royal West Kent Regiment
8th Battalion, Argyll and Sutherland Highlanders
- 38th (Irish) Infantry Brigade
6th Battalion, Royal Inniskilling Fusiliers
1st Battalion, Royal Irish Fusiliers
2nd Battalion, London Irish Rifles
- 56th Reconnaissance Regiment, Reconnaissance Corps
- 17th Field Regiment, Royal Artillery
- 132nd (Welsh) Field Regiment, Royal Artillery
- 138th (City of London) Field Regiment, Royal Artillery
- 64th (Queen's Own Royal Glasgow Yeomanry) Anti-Tank Regiment, Royal Artillery
- 49th Light Anti-Aircraft Regiment, Royal Artillery
- 1st Battalion, Kensington Regiment (Princess Louise's) (machine-gun battalion)
- 78th Divisional Engineers
214th Field Company, Royal Engineers
237th Field Company, Royal Engineers
256th Field Company, Royal Engineers
281st Field Park Company, Royal Engineers

- British 1st Airborne Division, commanded by Major-General George Hopkinson
This unit did not participate as a division.
  - 1st Airlanding Brigade
      1st Battalion, Border Regiment
      2nd Battalion, South Staffordshire Regiment
      9th Field Company, Royal Engineers
  - 1st Parachute Brigade
      1st Battalion, Parachute Regiment
      2nd Battalion, Parachute Regiment
      3rd Battalion, Parachute Regiment
      16th (Parachute) Field Ambulance
      1st Airlanding Anti-Tank Battery, Royal Artillery
      1st (Airborne) Divisional Provost, Corps of Military Police

- British 4th Armoured Brigade
  - 3rd County of London Yeomanry (Sharpshooters)
  - 44th Royal Tank Regiment
  - A Squadron, 1st (Royal) Dragoons

BRITISH XXX CORPS

Commanded by Lieutenant-General Sir Oliver Leese

- 73rd Anti-Tank Regiment, Royal Artillery
- 5th Army Group Royal Artillery
  - 57th (Home Counties) Field Regiment, Royal Artillery
  - 58th (Sussex) Field Regiment, Royal Artillery
  - 78th (Lowland) Field Regiment, Royal Artillery
  - 7th Medium Regiment, Royal Artillery
  - 64th (London) Medium Regiment, Royal Artillery
  - 70th Medium Regiment, Royal Artillery
  - 11th Regiment, Royal Horse Artillery (Honourable Artillery Company)
  - 142nd (Royal Devon Yeomanry) Field Regiment, Royal Artillery

- 1st Canadian Infantry Division, commanded by Major-General Guy Simonds
  - 1st Canadian Infantry Brigade
      The Royal Canadian Regiment
      1st Battalion, The Hastings & Prince Edward Regiment
      1st Battalion, 48th Highlanders of Canada
  - 2nd Canadian Infantry Brigade
      Princess Patricia's Canadian Light Infantry
      1st Battalion, The Seaforth Highlanders of Canada
      1st Battalion, The Loyal Edmonton Regiment
  - 3rd Canadian Infantry Brigade
      Royal 22e Régiment
      1st Battalion, The Carleton and York Regiment
      1st Battalion, The West Nova Scotia Regiment
  - 1st Field Regiment, Royal Canadian Horse Artillery
  - 2nd Field Regiment, Royal Canadian Artillery
  - 3rd Field Regiment, Royal Canadian Artillery

- 1st Infantry Division Support Battalion (The Saskatoon Light Infantry) (machine-gun battalion)
- 1st Anti-Tank Regiment, Royal Canadian Artillery
- 2nd Light Anti-Aircraft Regiment, Royal Canadian Artillery
- 4th Reconnaissance Regiment (4th Princess Louise Dragoon Guards)
- No. 1 Defence and Employment Platoon (Lorne Scots)
- 1st Field Company, Royal Canadian Engineers
- 3rd Field Company, Royal Canadian Engineers
- 4th Field Company, Royal Canadian Engineers
- 2nd Field Park Company, Royal Canadian Engineers

- 1st Canadian Tank Brigade
  - 11th Army Tank Regiment (The Ontario Regiment (Tank))
  - 12th Army Tank Regiment (Three Rivers Regiment (Tank))
  - 14th Army Tank Regiment (The Calgary Regiment (Tank))

- British 51st (Highland) Infantry Division, commanded by Major-General Douglas Wimberley
  - 152nd Infantry Brigade
    5th Battalion, Queen's Own Cameron Highlanders
    2nd Battalion, Seaforth Highlanders
    5th Battalion, Seaforth Highlanders
  - 153rd Infantry Brigade
    5th Battalion, Black Watch
    1st Battalion, Gordon Highlanders
    5/7th Battalion, Gordon Highlanders
  - 154th Infantry Brigade
    1st Battalion, Black Watch
    7th Battalion, Black Watch
    7th Battalion, Argyll and Sutherland Highlanders
  - 126th (Highland) Field Regiment, Royal Artillery
  - 127th (Highland) Field Regiment, Royal Artillery
  - 128th (Highland) Field Regiment, Royal Artillery
  - 61st Anti-Tank Regiment, Royal Artillery
  - 40th Light Anti-Aircraft Regiment, Royal Artillery
  - 1/7th Battalion, Middlesex Regiment (machine-gun battalion)
  - 7th Battalion, Royal Marines (under command 19–29 July)
  - 274th Field Company, Royal Engineers
  - 275th Field Company, Royal Engineers
  - 276th Field Company, Royal Engineers
  - 239th Field Park Company, Royal Engineers

- British 23rd Armoured Brigade – 23rd Armoured Brigade HQ fought as Arrow Force in mid-July with 2nd Battalion, Seaforth Highlanders (from 152nd Brigade) under command together with elements of 50th Royal Tank Regiment and 11th Regiment, Royal Horse Artillery (Honourable Artillery Company), as well as an anti-tank battery and a machine-gun company
  - 50th Royal Tank Regiment
  - 46th (Liverpool Welsh) Royal Tank Regiment
  - 40th (The King's) Royal Tank Regiment
  - 11th (Queen's Westminsters) Battalion, King's Royal Rifle Corps

- British 231st Infantry Brigade
  - 2nd Battalion, Devonshire Regiment
  - 1st Battalion, Dorsetshire Regiment
  - 1st Battalion, Hampshire Regiment
  - 165th Field Regiment, Royal Artillery
  - 300th Anti-Tank Battery, Royal Artillery
  - 352nd Light Anti-Aircraft Battery, Royal Artillery
  - 295th Field Company, Royal Engineers
  - 200th Field Ambulance, Royal Army Medical Corps

ALLIED MEDITERRANEAN NAVAL COMMAND
Commanded by Admiral of the Fleet Sir Andrew Browne Cunningham

COVERING FORCE (TO PREVENT ITALIAN NAVY FROM ATTACKING THE INVASION FORCES)

Eastern Naval Task Force (transported Eastern Task Force (British Eighth Army) and provided naval gunfire support)

Western Naval Task Force (transported Western Task Force (US Seventh Army) and provided naval gunfire support)

- 8th US Amphibious Force, commanded by Vice-Admiral Henry Kent Hewitt
  - 80.2 Escort Group
    DesRon 7
    - USS *Plunkett* (DD-431), Destroyers Flag
    - DesDiv 13
      - USS *Niblack* (DD-424)
      - USS *Benson* (DD-421)
      - USS *Gleaves* (DD-423)
    DesRon 8
    - USS *Wainwright* (DD-419), Flag
    - DesDiv 16
      - USS *Mayrant* (DD-402)
      - USS *Trippe* (DD-403)
      - USS *Rhind* (DD-404)
      - USS *Rowan* (DD-405)
  - Shark Force
    Dime Force, Task Force 81, commanded by Rear-Admiral John L. Hall, USN:
    landed US Army 1st Division (reinforced) and attached units near Gela
    Cent Force, Task Force 85, commanded by Rear-Admiral Alan G. Kirk, USN:
    landed US Army 45th Division (reinforced) and attached units near Scoglitti
  - Joss Force, Task Force 86, commanded by Rear-Admiral Richard L. Conolly, USN:
    landed US 3rd Division (reinforced) and attached units near Licata

Task Force Organization
- • 86.1 Cover and Support Group, commanded by Rear-Admiral Lawrence T. Dubose, USN
  - – Cruiser Division 13
  - – Destroyer Squadron 13
  - – Nine LCG(L) British
  - – Eight LCF(L) British
- • 86.2 Landing Craft Group, commanded by Commander L. S. Sabin, USN
  - – LST Group Two
  - – LST Group Three
  - – LST Group Six
  - – LST Division Seven (less LSTs 4 and 38)
  - – LCI Flotilla Two
  - – LCI Flotilla Four
  - – LCT Group Thirty-one
    Less LCTs 80, 207, 208, 214
    Plus LCTs 276, 305, 311, 332
  - – LCT 12 British LCTs
  - – HMS *Princess Astrid*
  - – HMS *Prince Leopold*
- • 86.3 Escort Group, commanded by Commander Block, USNR
  - – USS *Seer* (AM-112)
  - – USS *Sentinel* (AM-113)
  - – 7 PCs
  - – 26 SCs
  - – 6 YMS
- • 86.4 Joss Assault Force, commanded by Major-General Lucian Truscott, US Army
  - – US Army 3rd Division (reinforced) and attached units
- • 86.5 Train
  - – USS *Moreno* (AT-87)
  - – USS *Intent*
  - – USS *Evea* (YT-458)
  - – USS *Resolute*
- • 86.6 Force Flagship
  - – USS *Biscayne* (AVP-11)
- • 86.9 Joint Loading Control, commanded by Captain Zimmerli, USN
- – Kool Force (Floating Reserve)

ALLIED AIR FORCES

At the time of Operation Husky, the Allied air forces in the North African and Mediterranean theatres were organized as the Mediterranean Air Command (MAC) under the command of Air Chief Marshal Sir Arthur Tedder of the British Royal Air Force (RAF). The major subdivisions of the MAC included the Northwest African Air Forces (NAAF) under the command of Lieutenant-General Carl Spaatz of the US Army Air Forces, the American 12th Air Force (also commanded by General Spaatz), the American 9th Air Force under the command of Lieutenant-General Lewis H. Brereton, and units of the RAF.

Also supporting the NAAF were the RAF Middle East Command, Air Headquarters Malta, RAF Gibraltar, and the No. 216 (Transport and Ferry) Group, which were subdivisions of MAC under the command of Tedder. He reported to the Supreme Allied Commander, Dwight D. Eisenhower, for the NAAF operations, but to the British chiefs of staff for RAF Command operations. Air Headquarters Malta, under the command of Air Vice-Marshal Sir Keith Park, also supported Operation HUSKY.

The 'Desert Air Task Force', consisting of American B-25 Mitchell medium bombers (the 12th and 340th Bombardment Groups) and P-40 Warhawk fighter planes (the 57th, 79th and 324th Fighter Groups) from the Ninth Air Force, served under the command of Air Marshal Sir Arthur Coningham of the Northwest African Tactical Air Force. These bomber and fighter groups moved to new airfields on Sicily as soon as a significant beachhead had been captured there.

In the MAC organization established at the Casablanca Conference in January 1943, the Ninth Air Force was assigned as a subdivision of the RAF Middle East Command under the command of Air Chief Marshal Sir Sholto Douglas.

MEDITERRANEAN AIR COMMAND (ALLIED)

Commanded by Air Chief Marshal Sir Arthur Tedder
Headquarters in Algiers, Algeria

Northwest African Strategic Air Force
Commanded by Major-General James Doolittle
Headquarters in Constantine, Algeria

- 5th Bombardment Wing (Heavy)

Northwest African Coastal Air Force
Commanded by Air Vice-Marshal Sir Hugh Lloyd
Headquarters in Algiers

- No. 242 Group RAF, commanded by Air Commodore Kenneth Cross
  - No. 323 Wing, RAF
    No. 73 Squadron, Spitfire fighters
    No. 255 Squadron, Beaufighter fighter-bombers
    No. II/5 Escadre (French Air Force), P-40 Warhawk fighters
    No. II/7 Escadre (French Air Force), Spitfires
    No. 283 Squadron, Walrus Air–Sea Rescue planes
    No. 284 Squadron, Walrus Air–Sea Rescue planes
  - No. 328 Wing, RAF
    No. 14 Squadron, B-26 Marauder medium bombers
    No. 39 Squadron, Beaufort bombers
    No. 47 Squadron, Beauforts
    No. 144 Squadron, Beaufighters
    No. 52 Squadron, Baltimore light bombers
    No. 221 Squadron (detached), Vickers Wellington medium bombers
    No. 458 Squadron (RAAF), Wellingtons

British Units

- RAF Units
  - No. 13 Squadron, Blenheim bombers
  - No. 614 Squadron, Blenheims
  - No. 36 Squadron, Wellingtons
  - No. 253 Squadron, Hurricane fighters
  - No. 274 Squadron, Hurricanes
  - No. 313 Squadron, Hurricanes
  - No. 500 Squadron, Hudson light bombers
  - No. 608 Squadron, Hudsons
  - No. 1575 Flight, Halifax and Ventura bombers
- Royal Navy Fleet Air Arm Units
  Torpedo Spotter Reconnaissance
  - 813 NAS (detached), Swordfish torpedo planes
  - 820 NAS, Albacore c
  - 821 NAS, Albacore n
  - 826 NAS, Albacore r
  - 828 NAS, Albacore r
- Bone, Algeria Sector:
  - No. 32 Squadron, Hurricanes
  - No. 87 Squadron, Hurricanes
  - No. 219 Squadron, Beaufighters
- 2nd Air Defence Wing:
  - No. 153 Squadron, Beaufighters

American Units

- 52nd Fighter Group, commanded by Lieutenant-Colonel James Coward
  - 2nd Squadron, Spitfires
  - 4th Squadron, Spitfires
  - 5th Squadron, Spitfires
  - 414th Night Fighter Squadron, Beaufighters
  - 415th Night Fighter Squadron, Beaufighters
- 81st Fighter Group, commanded by Lieutenant-Colonel Michael Gordon
- Oran, Algeria Sector:
  - 92nd Squadron, P-39 Airacobra fighters
- 1st Air Defense Wing:
  - 91st Squadron, P-39 Airacobras
  - 93rd Squadron, P-39 Airacobras
- 350th Fighter Group, commanded by Lieutenant-Colonel Marvin McNickle
  - 345th Squadron, P-39 Airacobras
  - 346th Squadron, P-39 Airacobras
  - 347th Squadron, P-39 Airacobras
- 480th Antisubmarine Group, commanded by Colonel Jack Roberts
  - 1st Squadron, B-24 Liberator patrol planes
  - 2nd Squadron, B-24 Liberators

Northwest African Tactical Air Force
Commanded by Air Marshal Sir Arthur Coningham
Headquarters in Hammamet, Tunisia

For Operation HUSKY, No. 242 Group, originally (February 1943) a component of the Northwest African Tactical Air Force, was assigned to the Northwest African Coastal Air Force. At the same time, Air Headquarters, Western Desert became known as the Desert Air Force. All the fighter units of Desert Air Force formed No. 211 (Offensive Fighter) Group, commanded by Air Commodore Richard Atcherley, on 11 April 1943 in Tripoli. The 99th Fighter Squadron was assigned to XII Air Support Command on 28 May 1943, and later made a part of the 33rd Fighter Group.

Desert Air Force
Commanded by Air Vice-Marshal Harry Broadhurst

- 7 Wing, South African Air Force
  - 2 Squadron SAAF, Spitfires
  - 4 Squadron SAAF, Spitfires
  - 5 Squadron SAAF, P-40 Kittyhawks
- 239 (Fighter) Wing RAF, P-40 Kittyhawks
  - 3 Squadron RAAF
  - 112 Squadron RAF
  - 250 Squadron RAF
  - 260 Squadron RAF
  - 450 Squadron RAAF
- 244 (Fighter) Wing RAF, Spitfires
  - 1 Squadron SAAF
  - 92 Squadron RCAF
  - 145 Squadron RAF
  - 417 Squadron RCAF
  - 601 (County of London) Squadron RAuxF
- 322 (Fighter) Wing RAF, commanded by Wing Commander Colin Gray, Spitfires
  - 81 Squadron RAF
  - 152 (Hyderabad) Squadron RAF
  - 154 (Motor Industries) Squadron RAF
  - 232 Squadron RAF
  - 242 Squadron RAF
- 324 Wing RAF, Spitfires, commanded by Wing Commander Hugh Dundas
  - 43 Squadron RAF
  - 72 Squadron RAF
  - 93 Squadron RAF
  - 111 Squadron RAF
  - 243 Squadron RAF
- 57th Fighter Group (USAAF), commanded by Colonel Arthur Salisbury
  - 64th Squadron, P-40 Warhawks
  - 65th Squadron, P-40 Warhawks
  - 66th Squadron, P-40 Warhawks

- 79th Fighter Group (USAAF), commanded by Colonel Earl Bates
  - 85th Squadron, P-40 Warhawks
  - 86th Squadron, P-40 Warhawks
  - 87th Squadron, P-40 Warhawks
- 285 (Reconnaissance) Wing RAF
  - 40 Squadron SAAF (detached), Spitfires
  - 60 Squadron SAAF, Mosquito fighter-bombers
  - 1437 Flight RAF, P-51A Mustang fighters
- No. 6 Squadron, Hurricane ground attack

XII Air Support Command
Commanded by Major-General Edwin House

- 27th Fighter-Bomber Group (USAAF), commanded by Lieutenant-Colonel John Stevenson
  - 522nd Squadron, A-36 Mustang ground attack aircraft
  - 523rd Squadron, A-36 Mustangs
  - 524th Squadron, A-36 Mustangs
- 86th Fighter-Bomber Group (USAAF), commanded by Major Clinton True
  - 525th Squadron, A-36 Mustangs
  - 526th Squadron, A-36 Mustangs
  - 527th Squadron, A-36 Mustangs
- 33rd Fighter Group (USAAF), commanded by Colonel William W. Momyer
  - 58th Squadron, P-40 Warhawks
  - 59th Squadron, P-40 Warhawks
  - 60th Squadron, P-40 Warhawks
  - 99th Squadron (detached), P-40 Warhawks
- 324th Fighter Group (USAAF), commanded by Colonel William McNown
  - 314th Squadron, P-40 Warhawks
  - 315th Squadron, P-40 Warhawks
  - 316th Squadron, P-40 Warhawks
- 31st Fighter Group (USAAF), commanded by Lieutenant-Colonel Frank Hill
  - 307th Squadron, Spitfires
  - 308th Squadron, Spitfires
  - 309th Squadron, Spitfires
- 111th Tactical Reconnaissance Squadron, P-51A Mustangs

Tactical Bomber Force
Commanded by Air Commodore Laurence Sinclair

- 3 Wing SAAF
  - 12 Squadron SAAF, Boston light bombers
  - 21 Squadron SAAF, Baltimores
  - 24 Squadron SAAF, Bostons
- 232 (Light Bomber) Wing RAF
  - 55 Squadron RAF, Baltimores
  - 223 Squadron RAF, Baltimores

- 33rd Fighter Group (USAAF), commanded by Colonel William W. Momyer
  - 58th Squadron, P-40 Warhawks
  - 59th Squadron, P-40 Warhawks
  - 60th Squadron, P-40 Warhawks
  - 99th Squadron (detached), P-40 Warhawks
- 326 Wing RAF
  - 18 Squadron RAF, Bostons
  - 114 Squadron RAF, Bostons
- 47th Bombardment Group (USAAF), commanded by Colonel Malcolm Green, Jr
  - 84th Squadron, A-20 Havoc fighter-bombers
  - 85th Squadron, A-20 Havocs
  - 86th Squadron, A-20 Havocs
  - 97th Squadron, A-20 Havocs
- 31st Fighter Group (USAAF), commanded by Lieutenant-Colonel Frank Hill
  - 307th Squadron, Spitfires
  - 308th Squadron, Spitfires
  - 309th Squadron, Spitfires
- 12th Bombardment Group (USAAF), commanded by Colonel Edward Backus
  - 81st Squadron, B-25 Mitchell medium bombers
  - 82nd Squadron, B-25 Mitchells
  - 83rd Squadron, B-25 Mitchells
  - 434th Squadron, B-25 Mitchells
- 340th Bombardment Group (USAAF), commanded by Lieutenant-Colonel Adolph Tokaz
  - 486th Squadron, B-25 Mitchells
  - 487th Squadron, B-25 Mitchells
  - 488th Squadron, B-25 Mitchells
  - 489th Squadron, B-25 Mitchells
- 225 Squadron RAF, Spitfires
- 241 Squadron RAF, Hurricanes

Northwest African Troop Carrier Command
Commanded by Brigadier-General Paul Williams
Headquarters in Tunisia

- 51st Troop Carrier Wing, commanded by Brigadier-General Ray Dunn
  - 60th Troop Carrier Group, commanded by Lieutenant-Colonel Frederick Sherwood
    10th Squadron, C-47 Skytrains
    11th Squadron, C-47s
    12th Squadron, C-47s
    28th Squadron, C-47s
  - 62nd Troop Carrier Group, commanded by Lieutenant-Colonel Aubrey Hurren
    4th Squadron, C-47s
    7th Squadron, C-47s

        8th Squadron, C-47s
        51st Squadron, C-47s
    – 64th Troop Carrier Group, commanded by Colonel John Cerny
        16th Squadron, C-47s
        17th Squadron, C-47s
        18th Squadron, C-47s
        35th Squadron, C-47s
- 52nd Troop Carrier Wing, commanded by Colonel Harold Clark
    – 61st Troop Carrier Group, commanded by Colonel Willis Mitchell
        14th Squadron, C-47s
        15th Squadron, C-47s
        53rd Squadron, C-47s
        59th Squadron, C-47s
    – 313th Troop Carrier Group, commanded by Colonel James Roberts, Jr
        29th Squadron, C-47s
        47th Squadron, C-47s
        48th Squadron, C-47s
        49th Squadron, C-47s
    – 314th Troop Carrier Group, commanded by Colonel Clayton Stiles
        32nd Squadron, C-47s
        50th Squadron, C-47s
        61st Squadron, C-47s
        62nd Squadron, C-47s
    – 316th Troop Carrier Group, commanded by Colonel Jerome McCauley
        36th Squadron, C-47s
        44th Squadron, C-47s
        45th Squadron, C-47s
- RAF Detachment
    – 38 Wing, commanded by Air Commodore William Primrose
        No. 295 Squadron RAF (detached), Halifaxes
        No. 296 Squadron RAF, Albemarle bombers

To help carry out transport and supply operations for Operation HUSKY, in mid-1943 the American 315th Troop Carrier Group (34th and 43rd Squadrons) had been flown from England to Tunisia. There it was assigned to the Mediterranean Air Transport Service, another subdivision of the MAC.

Northwest African Photographic Reconnaissance Wing
Commanded by Colonel Elliott Roosevelt
Headquarters at La Marsa, Tunisia

- 3rd Photographic Group, commanded by Lieutenant-Colonel Frank Dunn
    – 5th Combat Mapping Squadron, P-38 Lightnings
    – 12th Photographic Reconnaissance Squadron, P-38 Lightnings
    – 12th Weather Detachment
    – 15th Photographic Reconnaissance Squadron, B-17 Flying Fortresses
    – 13th Photographic Reconnaissance Squadron photo intelligence squadron
- 60 Squadron SAAF (detached), Mosquitoes

- 540 Squadron RAF (detached), Mosquitoes
- 680 Squadron RAF, Spitfires
- 2/33 Groupe (French), P-38 Lightnings (F-5 reconnaissance planes)

Northwest African Air Service Command
Commanded by Brigadier-General Delmar
Headquarters in Dunton, Algiers

Northwest African Training Command
Commanded by Brigadier-General John K. Cannon

Air Headquarters Malta
Commanded by Air Vice-Marshal Sir Keith Park
Headquarters in Valletta, Malta

- 248 (Naval Co-operation) Wing
  - 69 Squadron RAF, Baltimores
  - 108 Squadron RAF, Beaufighters
  - 221 Squadron RAF, Wellington bombers
  - 272 Squadron RAF, Beaufighters
  - 683 Squadron RAF, Spitfires
- Spitfire fighter plane units
  - 40 Squadron SAAF
  - 126 Squadron RAF
  - 185 Squadron RAF
  - 229 Squadron RAF
  - 249 Squadron RAF
  - 1435 Flight RAF
- Other units
  - 23 Squadron RAF, counter-night-intruder operations with Mosquito fighter planes
  - 73 Squadron RAF Detachment, Hurricanes
  - 256 Squadron RAF Detachment, Mosquitoes
  - 600 Squadron RAF, Beaufighters
  - 815 Naval Air Squadron Detachment (Fleet Air Arm), Fairey Albacores

No. 216 (Transport and Ferry) Group
Commanded by Air Commodore Whitney Straight
Headquarters at Heliopolis, Egypt

- 17 Squadron SAAF, Junkers 52
- 28 Squadron SAAF, Ansons
- 117 Squadron RAF, Hudsons
- 173 Squadron RAF, Lodestars, Proctors, Hurricanes
- 216 Squadron RAF, Douglas Dakotas
- 230 Squadron RAF, Short Sunderlands
- 267 Squadron RAF, Hudsons

RAF Gibraltar
Commanded by Air Vice-Marshal Sturley Simpson
Headquarters in Gibraltar

- 48 Squadron RAF, Hudsons
- 179 Squadron RAF, Wellingtons
- 202 Squadron RAF, Catalinas
- 210 Squadron RAF, Catalinas
- 233 Squadron RAF, Hudsons
- 248 Squadron RAF, Beaufighters
- 544 Squadron RAF, Spitfires
- 813 Naval Air Squadron (Fleet Air Arm), Swordfish torpedo planes
- 1403 (Meteorological) Flight Hampden, Gloster Gladiators

Middle East Command
Commanded by Air Chief Marshal Sir Sholto Douglas
Headquarters at Cairo, Egypt

No. 201 (Naval Co-operation) Group
Commanded by Air Vice-Marshal Thomas Langford-Sainsbury
Headquarters at Alexandria, Egypt

- 235 Wing
  - 13 Squadron (Royal Hellenic Air Force), Blenheim bombers
  - 227 Squadron RAF (detached), Beaufighters
  - 454 Squadron RAAF, Baltimores
  - 459 Squadron RAAF, Hudsons
  - Naval Air Squadron (Fleet Air Arm), Swordfishes
- 238 Wing
  - 16 Squadron SAAF, Beauforts
  - 227 Squadron RAF, Beaufighters
  - 603 Squadron RAF, Beaufighters
  - 815 Naval Air Squadron (Fleet Air Arm), Swordfishes
- 245 Wing
  - 15 Squadron SAAF, Blenheims and Baltimores
  - 38 Squadron RAF, Wellingtons
  - 1 General Reconnaissance Unit, Wellingtons
- 247 Wing
  - 38 Squadron RAF, Wellingtons
  - 203 Squadron RAF, Baltimores
  - 227 Squadron RAF, Beaufighters
  - 252 Squadron RAF, Beaufighters

No Wing assignment: 701 Naval Air Squadron (Fleet Air Arm), Walrus Air–Sea Rescue

Air Headquarters Air Defences Eastern Mediterranean
Commanded by Air Vice-Marshal Richard Saul

- No. 209 (Fighter) Group, commanded by Group Captain R. C. F. Lister
  - 46 Squadron RAF (detached), Beaufighters

- 127 Squadron RAF, Hurricanes and Spitfires
- No. 210 (Fighter) Group, commanded by Group Captain John Grandy
  - 3 Squadron SAAF, Hurricanes
  - 33 Squadron RAF, Hurricanes
  - 89 Squadron RAF, Beaufighters
  - 213 Squadron RAF, Hurricanes
  - 274 Squadron RAF, Hurricanes
- No. 212 (Fighter) Group, commanded by Air Commodore Archibald Wann
  - 7 Squadron SAAF, Hurricanes
  - 41 Squadron SAAF, Hurricanes
  - 80 Squadron RAF, Spitfires
  - 94 Squadron RAF, Hurricanes
  - 108 Squadron RAF (detached), Beaufighters
  - 123 Squadron RAF, Hurricanes
  - 134 Squadron RAF, Hurricanes
  - 237 Squadron RAF, Hurricanes
  - 1563 Meteorological Flight, Gladiators
  - 1654 Meteorological Flight, Gladiators
- No. 219 (Fighter) Group, commanded by Group Captain Max Aitken
  - 46 Squadron RAF, Beaufighters
  - 74 Squadron RAF, Hurricanes
  - 238 Squadron RAF, Hurricanes
  - 335 Squadron RAF, Hurricanes
  - 336 Squadron RAF, Hurricanes
  - 451 Squadron RAAF, Hurricanes

US Ninth Air Force
Commanded by Major-General Lewis H. Brereton
Headquarters in Cairo, Egypt

- IX Advanced Headquarters, Tripoli, Libya
- IX Fighter Command Headquarters, Tripoli
- IX Bomber Command Headquarters, Benghazi, Libya
  - 98th Bombardment Group, B-24D Liberator II
    343rd Squadron, Lete Airfield, Libya
    344th Squadron, Lete Airfield
    345th Squadron, Benina Airfield, Libya
    415th Squadron, Benina Airfield
  - 376th Bombardment Group, B-24D Liberator II, Berka, Libya
    512th Squadron
    513th Squadron
    514th Squadron
    515th Squadron

AXIS FORCES

ARMED FORCES COMMAND

Commanded by Generale d'Armata Alfredo Guzzoni

GERMAN

- 15th Panzer Grenadier Division, commanded by Generalmajor Eberhard Rodt from 5 June. One-third of the division (a reinforced infantry group) was attached to Italian XVI Corpo and the rest to Italian XII Corpo until the activation of XIV Panzer Korps on 18 July.
  - 215. Panzer Bataillon – 17 Tiger I tanks
  - 104. Panzer Grenadier Regiment
  - 115. Panzer Grenadier Regiment
  - 129. Panzer Grenadier Regiment
  - 33. Artillerie Regiment
  - 315. Anti-aircraft Bataillon
  - 33. Pionier Bataillon

- Luftwaffe Hermann Göring Panzer Division, commanded by Generalmajor Paul Conrath. Attached to Italian XVI Corpo until the activation of XIV Panzer Korps on 18 July.
  - 1. Hermann Göring Panzer Grenadier Regiment
  - Hermann Göring Panzer Regiment
      1. Hermann Göring Panzer Bataillon
      2. Hermann Göring Panzer Bataillon
  - Hermann Göring Panzer Reconnaissance Bataillon
  - Hermann Göring Panzer Artillerie Regiment
  - Hermann Göring Panzer Pionier Bataillon
  - Hermann Göring Anti-aircraft Regiment
- 382. Panzer Grenadier Regiment
- 926. Fortress Bataillon

XIV PANZER KORPS

Commanded by General der Panzertruppe Hans-Valentin Hube

- German 1. Fallschirmjäger Division, commanded by Generalleutnant Richard Heidrich
  - 3. Fallschirmjäger Regiment
  - 4. Fallschirmjäger Regiment
  - 1. Fallschirmjäger Maschinengewehr Bataillon
  - I/1. Fallschirmjäger Feld-Artillerie Regiment
  - 1. Fallschirmjäger Pionier Bataillon
- German 29. Panzer Grenadier Division, commanded by Generalmajor Walter Fries
  - 129. Panzer Bataillon
  - 15. Panzer Grenadier Regiment
  - 71. Panzer Grenadier Regiment

- 29. Artillerie Regiment
- 313. Anti-aircraft Bataillon

ITALIAN

SIXTH ARMY
Commanded by Generale d'Armata Alfredo Guzzoni
German Army Liaison Officer: Generalleutnant Fridolin von Senger und Etterlin

XII Corpo
Commanded by Generale di Corpo d'Armata Mario Arisio; from 12 July 1943, Generale di Corpo d'Armata Francesco Zingales

- 26° Divisione Fanteria da Montagna Assietta, commanded by Generale Francesco Scotti; from 26 July by Generale Ottorino Schreiber
  - 29° Reggimento di Fanteria
  - 30° Reggimento di Fanteria
  - 17° Legione 'Camicie Nere'
  - 25° Reggimento di Artiglieria
  - CXXVI° Battaglione Mortaio
  - Engineer battalion
- 28° Divisione Fanteria Aosta, commanded by Generale Giacomo Romano
  - 5° Reggimento di Fanteria
  - 6° Reggimento di Fanteria
  - 171° Legione 'Camicie Nere'
  - 22° Reggimento di Artiglieria
  - XXVIII° Battaglione Mortaio
  - Engineer battalion
- 202° Divisione Costiera
  - 124° Reggimento di Fanteria Costiera
  - 142° Reggimento di Fanteria Costiera
  - 43° Gruppo Artiglieria (26 batteries, ad hoc regiment)
- 207° Divisione Costiera
  - 138° Reggimento di Fanteria Costiera
  - 139° Reggimento di Fanteria Costiera
  - 51° Gruppo Artiglieria (12 batteries, ad hoc regiment)
- 208° Divisione Costiera
  - 133° Reggimento di Fanteria Costiera
  - 147° Reggimento di Fanteria Costiera
  - 28° Gruppo Artiglieria (6 batteries, ad hoc regiment)
- 136° Reggimento di Fanteria Costiera
- Palermo Harbour Garrison
- 10° Reggimento Bersaglieri
- 177° Reggimento Bersaglieri
- Corpo Artiglieria
  - 30 batteries
- 1° Tank Company 'Fiat 3000' (Fiat 3000 tanks), static defence at airfields
- Gruppo Mobile 'A', initially at Paceco, commanded by Tenente-Colonnello Renato Perrone

- XII° Battaglione di Carri Armati 'L' Headquarters
- 4° Compagnia, CII Battaglione di Carri Armati 'R35' (Renault R35 tanks)
- 1° Compagnia, CXXXIII° Battaglione Semovente '47/32' (Semovente 47/32)
- Coastal infantry company (motorized)
- Artillery battery (75/27 mod. 06 guns)
- Anti-aircraft artillery section (20/65 mod. 35 anti-aircraft guns)
- Gruppo Mobile 'B', initially at Santa Ninfa, commanded by Tenente-Colonnello Vito Gaetano Mascio
  - CXXXIII° Battaglione Semovente (47/32) Headquarters
  - 6° Compagnia, CII° Battaglione di Carri Armati 'R35' (Renault R35 tanks)
  - 3° Compagnia, CXXXIII° Battaglione Semovente '47/32' (Semovente 47/32)
  - Two companies of coastal infantry (motorized)
  - Bersaglieri platoon, on motorcycles
  - Artillery battery (75/27 mod. 06 guns)
  - Anti-aircraft artillery section (20/65 mod. 35 anti-aircraft guns)
- Gruppo Mobile 'C', initially at Portella Misilbesi, commanded by Tenente-Colonnello Osvaldo Mazzei
  - CII° Battaglione di Carri Armati 'R35' Headquarters
  - 5° Compagnia, CII° Battaglione di Carri Armati 'R35' (Renault R35 tanks)
  - Coastal infantry company (motorized)
  - Anti-tank company (47/32 mod. 35 anti-tank guns)

XVI Corpo
Commanded by Generale di Corpo d'Armata Carlo Rossi

- 4° Divisione Fanteria 'Livorno' (initially held as Army Reserve), commanded by Generale Domenico Chirieleison
  - 33° Reggimento di Fanteria
  - 34° Reggimento di Fanteria
  - 28° Reggimento di Artiglieria (3 AA batteries; the standard was 2)
  - IV° Battaglione Semovente '47/32' (Semovente 47/32)
  - Engineer battalion
  - Assault battalion
- 54° Divisione Fanteria 'Napoli', commanded by Generale Giulio Cesare Gotti Porcinari
  - 75° Reggimento di Fanteria
  - 76° Reggimento di Fanteria
  - 173° Legione 'Camicie Nere'
  - 54° Reggimento di Artiglieria
  - Engineer battalion
- 206° Divisione Costiera
  - 122° Reggimento di Fanteria Costiera
  - 123° Reggimento di Fanteria Costiera
  - 146° Reggimento di Fanteria Costiera
  - 44° Gruppo d'Artiglieria (14 batteries, ad hoc regiment)
  - CXXXIII° Battaglione Semovente '47/32' (Semovente 47/32)

- 213° Divisione Costiera
  - 135° Reggimento di Fanteria Costiera
  - Catania Harbour Garrison
  - 22° Gruppo d'Artiglieria (12 batteries, ad hoc regiment)
- XVIII Brigata Costiera
  - 134° Reggimento di Fanteria Costiera
  - 178° Reggimento di Fanteria Costiera
  - 9 artillery batteries
- XIX Brigata Costiera
  - 140° Reggimento di Fanteria Costiera
  - 179° Reggimento di Fanteria Costiera
  - 4 artillery batteries
- Corpo d'Artiglieria
  - 19 batteries
- Gruppo Mobile 'D', initially at Misterbianco, commanded by Tenente-Colonnello Massimino d'Andretta
  - CI° Battaglione di Carri Armati 'R35' Headquarters
  - 3° Compagnia, CI° Battaglione di Carri Armati 'R35' (Renault R35 tanks)
  - Infantry company
  - Machine-gun company, on motorcycles
  - Anti-tank company (47/32 mod. 35 anti-tank guns)
  - Artillery battery (75/18 mod. 34 howitzers)
  - Anti-aircraft artillery section (20/65 mod. 35 anti-aircraft guns)
- Gruppo Mobile 'E', initially at Niscemi, commanded by Capitano Giuseppe Granieri
  - 1° Compagnia, Battaglione di Carri Armati 'R35' (Renault R35 tanks)
  - Coastal infantry company
  - Machine-gun company, on motorcycles
  - Anti-tank company (47/32 mod. 35 anti-tank guns)
  - Artillery battery (75/18 mod. 34 howitzers)
  - Anti-aircraft artillery section (20/65 mod. 35 anti-aircraft guns)
- Gruppo Mobile 'F', initially at Rosolini
  - 2° Compagnia, Battaglione di Carri Armati 'R35' (Renault R35 tanks), minus 1 platoon
  - Coastal infantry company
  - Machine-gun company, on motorcycles
  - Anti-tank company (47/32 mod. 35 anti-tank guns)
  - Artillery battery (75/18 mod. 34 howitzers)
- Gruppo Mobile 'G', initially at Comiso
  - Battaglione delle 'Camicie Nere' Headquarters
  - 1 platoon of 2° Compagnia, Battaglione di Carri Armati 'R35'
  - Anti-tank company (47/32 mod. 35 anti-tank guns)
  - Artillery battery (75/18 mod. 34 howitzers)
- Gruppo Mobile 'H', initially at Caltagirone, commanded by Tenente-Colonnello Luigi Cixi
  - 131° Reggimento di Fanteria di Carri Armati Headquarters
  - 2° Compagnia di Carri Armati 'Fiat 3000' (Fiat 3000 tanks)

- Anti-tank company (47/32 mod. 35 anti-tank guns)
- Artillery battery (75/18 mod. 34 howitzers)
- Mortar platoon (81/14 mod. 35 mortars)

Navy Garrison
Commanded by Generale Guzzoni, Italian Navy and Chief of Joint Command

- Augusta–Syracuse Harbours
  - 121° Reggimento di Fanteria Costiera
  - Naval battalion
  - Air force battalion
  - 24 artillery batteries (coastal and AA batteries included)
- Trapani Harbour
  - 137° Reggimento di Fanteria Costiera
  - 12 artillery batteries (coastal and AA batteries included)
- Messina–Reggio di Calabria Harbours
  - 116° Reggimento di Fanteria Costiera
  - 119° Reggimento di Fanteria Costiera
  - Legione di 'Camicie Nere'
  - Cavalry battalion (on foot)
  - 55 artillery batteries (coastal and AA batteries included)

Among wreckage
in Messina

Appendix 2:
Number of Times Sicilian Towns and Cities Hit by Allied Bombers

(All those listed were hit three times or more.)

Acireale	5
Agrigento	17
Augusta	43
Avola	3
Caltanissetta	6
Catania	87
Comiso	12
Gela	12
Ispica	3
Lentini	3
Licata	19
Magnisi	3
Marsala	16
Messina	58
Palermo	69
Porto Empedocle	21
Pozzallo	12
Ragusa	27
Sciacca	10
Syracuse	36
Trapani	41

Spitfires at Lentini

Timeline,
January–September 1943

January

17 JANUARY

Decision to invade Sicily made during the Casablanca Conference

23 JANUARY

Directive issued to Eisenhower

April

24 APRIL

Montgomery sends his 'dog's breakfast' signal criticizing the proposed HUSKY plan

---

May

3 MAY

Plan for HUSKY agreed

13 MAY

Surrender of all Axis forces in North Africa with the loss of 250,000 troops taken prisoner

20 MAY

Hitler and his commanders meet at Wolfschanze

June

1–2 JUNE

Allied bombing of Pantelleria begins

7 JUNE

Continued Allied bombing of Pantelleria

9 JUNE

Naval bombardment of Pantelleria

11 JUNE

Pantelleria falls to the Allies

15 JUNE

3. Panzer Grenadier, 16. Panzer, 26. Panzer and 29. Panzer Grenadier Divisions plus XIV and LXXVI Panzer Korps warned for movement to Sicily

20 JUNE

Hermann Göring Panzer Division begins move to Sicily

26 JUNE

Kesselring's last conference with Guzzoni before the Allied invasion

---

July

SATURDAY 3 JULY

Second phase of HUSKY air plan begins, focused on attacking Axis airfields on Sicily

MONDAY 5 JULY

Operation ZITADELLE launched by Germans against Kursk salient on Eastern Front

Big Allied bombing raids on Gerbini and Comiso

FRIDAY 9 JULY

Peak of Allied air attacks on airfields on Sicily

1 p.m. Glider pilots briefing for Operation LADBROKE

6.48 p.m. First gliders take off

8.15 p.m. 505th Parachute Combat Team airborne

10.45 p.m. Glider 133 on the ground near Ponte Grande

11.45 p.m. First Italian counter-attack at Ponte Grande

11.55 p.m. Ceremony aboard *Monrovia* to activate Seventh Army

SATURDAY 10 JULY

D-Day for Operation HUSKY – Allied landings on Sicily

1.25 a.m. First C-47s of 52nd Troop Carrier Wing back in Tunisia

2.45 a.m. Allied assault begins

2.50 a.m. 3rd Ranger Battalion land near Licata

3.30 a.m. SRS land at Capo Murro di Porco

3.35 a.m. X Force hit beaches at Gela

4.30 a.m. SRS fighting over

6 a.m. SRS leave Damerio farmhouse

6.20 a.m. Last C-47s of 52nd Troop Carrier Wing back in Tunisia

9 a.m. Rangers have cleared Gela

9 a.m. 26th RCT nearing Gela

12 noon Pachino airfield falls

3.30 p.m. South Staffs abandon Ponte Grande

4 p.m.   Ponte Grande recaptured by British

SUNDAY 11 JULY

German and Italian counter-attack at Gela

8.45 a.m. Patton orders 504th PIR drop for that night

12 noon Axis counter-attack defeated

5 p.m. *Robert Rowan* blows up

6.30 p.m. Loaded LST hit by bomb at Gela

7.30 p.m. Attacks by Luftwaffe

9.50 p.m. Luftwaffe attack against Seventh Army beaches

10.15 p.m. Ju88s arrive over US beaches

10.45 p.m. 504th PIR drop begins

MONDAY 12 JULY

10 a.m. Ponte Olivo airfield captured

12 noon Last counter-attack by HG Division at Gela defeated

SRS back aboard *Ulster Monarch*

Kesselring on Sicily

4.30 p.m. Comiso airfield captured

TUESDAY 13 JULY

4.00 a.m. Augusta falls

Eighth Army starts drive on Catania

Battle of the Gorge – 5th Division against Brigade Schmalz

Operation ZITADELLE halted on Eastern Front

Operation FUSTIAN – 1st Parachute Brigade assault on Primosole Bridge

WEDNESDAY 14 JULY

1st Parachute Brigade hold on to Primosole Bridge

Biscari massacre

14–15 JULY

1st Parachute Brigade fall back south of Primosole Bridge

Schmalz orders retreat to *Hauptkampflinie*/Santo Stefano Line

THURSDAY 15 JULY

Yellow handkerchief dropped on Villalba

Guzzoni orders withdrawal of all Axis forces to Santo Stefano Line

9th DLI attacks Primosole Bridge. Attack fails by 9.30 a.m.

Schmalz sets up HQ in Misterbianco and links up with rest of HG Division

FRIDAY 16 JULY

1 a.m. 8th DLI attack Primosole Bridge

By dawn both 8th and 9th DLI across bridge with small bridgehead

Alexander considers new directive

SATURDAY 17 JULY

Agrigento in US hands by morning

1.30 a.m. Renewed assault north of Primosole Bridge

Patton flies to Tunis to see Alexander

45th Division now in place on left of 1st Division

Hube takes over command of all German troops on Sicily

17–18 JULY

Further attacks by 50th Division beyond Primosole Bridge

SUNDAY 18 JULY

Agrigento port open

MONDAY 19 JULY

US Provisional Corps begins drive west

Hitler and Mussolini meet at Feltre

Allied bombing of Rome

82nd Airborne Brigade advances 25 miles

Canadians capture Valguarnera

Alexander issues new directive

Tuesday 20 July

5th Division attack across Catania Plain

16th US Infantry take Enna

Wednesday 21 July

Hasty Ps' attack on Assoro begins

Attack on Leonforte begins

Montgomery changes plan

Castelvetrano falls

4,000 Italian prisoners captured

Thursday 22 July

Palermo falls to US Provisional Corps

Canadians capture Assoro and Leonforte

82nd Airborne Brigade reach Santa Margherita

15. Panzergruppe and HG Division link up

Bompietro falls to US 1st Division

Friday 23 July

US troops occupy Palermo; end of first phase of campaign

505th Parachute Combat Team take Trapani

1st Division takes Petralia

9 a.m. 45th Division reaches north coast

Primosole Bridge hit and damaged and out of action for two days

Saturday 24 July

Fascist Grand Council meets

Canadians attack Agira

Sunday 25 July

Mussolini overthrown

Fighting continues at Agira

Alexander holds conference with senior commanders at Syracuse

Monday 26 July

Primosole Bridge damaged again

Fighting continues at Agira

Tuesday 27 July

Allied planning for invasion of Italy – Operation AVALANCHE – begins

Palermo port open

Germans withdraw to San Fratello Line

Fighting continues at Agira

Wednesday 28 July

Nicosia falls to Seventh Army

Agira falls to Canadians

Alexander moves headquarters to Cassibile

German planning for evacuation of Sicily begins

Thursday 29 July

Primosole Bridge reopened

Operation HARDGATE launched by XXX Corps

1st Canadian Brigade and Malta Brigade at Regalbuto

45th Division get past Tusa Ridge

Friday 30 July

Palermo port operating at 60 per cent

45th Division take Santo Stefano

Saturday 31 July

Italian Crown Council decides to seek peace

Operation ACHSE, the German invasion and occupation of Italy, ready

Primosole Bridge hit again

Battle for Troina begins

Canadians and Malta Brigade assault Regalbuto

August

SUNDAY 1 AUGUST

Battle for Troina continues

Battle for Centuripe begins

Regalbuto falls

MONDAY 2 AUGUST

German Army Group B starts moving into Italy through the Brenner Pass

Battle for Troina continues

Battle for Centuripe continues

TUESDAY 3 AUGUST

General Alexander asks air and navy to seal Messina Straits

Centuripe falls to Eighth Army

Renewed attack in 5th Division's area

Battle for Troina continues

First Patton slapping incident

WEDNESDAY 4 AUGUST

Montgomery issues new instructions

THURSDAY 5 AUGUST

Battle for Troina continues

Etna battles

Axis withdrawal to Tortorici Line

Catania falls to Eighth Army

FRIDAY 6 AUGUST

Troina falls to Seventh Army

SATURDAY 7 AUGUST

78th Division takes Adrano

3rd Division attempt to cross Furiano River

NIGHT 7–8 AUGUST

US amphibious landings at San Fratello

SUNDAY 8 AUGUST

Cesarò taken by 9th Infantry

78th Division attacks Bronte

5th Division at Tremonti

MONDAY 9 AUGUST

5th Division takes Tremonti

TUESDAY 10 AUGUST

Second Patton slapping incident

Generale Guzzoni leaves Sicily

General Hube orders Operation LEHRGANG, the German evacuation of Sicily, to begin the following day

WEDNESDAY 11 AUGUST

Battle for Monte Cipolla

US landing at Brolo

General Hube starts Operation LEHRGANG

THURSDAY 12 AUGUST

US 9th Infantry Division nearing Randazzo

FRIDAY 13 AUGUST

39th Infantry take Randazzo

SATURDAY 14 AUGUST

British and American forces link up at Randazzo

SUNDAY 15 AUGUST

Taormina falls to Eighth Army

MONDAY 16 AUGUST

Eisenhower finalizes Allied plans post-HUSKY

TUESDAY 17 AUGUST

General Hube reports evacuation of Sicily complete

Allies reach Messina

Short-term basis for Italian surrender agreed with Allies

QUADRANT Conference starts in Quebec

WEDNESDAY 18 AUGUST

Allied post-HUSKY plans agreed

September

1 SEPTEMBER

Italian armistice signed

8 SEPTEMBER

Italian armistice announced

9 SEPTEMBER

Operation AVALANCHE begins with Fifth Army landings at Salerno

Notes

Abbreviations used in notes

BA-MA	Bundesarchiv-Militärarchiv, Freiburg
CCA	Churchill College Archives, Churchill College, Cambridge
DDE	*The Papers of Dwight D. Eisenhower*, ed. Chandler
DTA	Deutsches Tagebucharchiv, Emmendingen
EPL	Dwight D. Eisenhower Presidential Library, Abilene, KS
FMS	Foreign Military Studies, USAHEC
IWM	Imperial War Museum, London
LHCMA	Liddell Hart Centre for Military Archives, King's College London
LoC	Library of Congress, Washington DC
NARA	National Archives and Records Administration, College Park, MD
TNA	The National Archives, Kew, London
USAHEC	United States Army Heritage and Education Center, Carlisle Barracks, PA

Prologue: The Burning Blue

3   'A day seems very long . . .': Steinhoff, *Messerschmitts over Sicily*, p. 22
3   'I want to be here . . .': ibid, p. 22
3   'Today's your big chance . . .': ibid, p. 24
3   'For God's sake . . .': ibid, p. 24
4   'Yes, but how's it all . . .': ibid, p. 25
5   'Odysseus One to Eagle . . .': ibid, p. 33
5   'Pantechnicons withdrawing . . .': ibid, p. 33
6   'Odysseus turn on to . . .': ibid, p. 34
6   'Odysseus, steer two-eight-zero . . .': ibid, p. 34
6   'Pantechnicons right beneath us!': ibid, p. 35
7   'I pulled up my M-E . . .': ibid, p. 37
7   'Nothing, absolutely nothing . . .': ibid, p. 38

8   'That was a gorgeous balls-up . . .': ibid, p. 39
8   'But I told you . . .': ibid, p. 40
9   'Was there really . . .': ibid, p. 40
9   'I'll be accountable . . .': ibid, p. 40
9   'But, my God . . .': ibid, p. 41

1 The Long Path to HUSKY

14   'We realised that we . . .': Cheall, *Fighting Through from Dunkirk to Hamburg*, p. 71
15   'I imagined the faces . . .': ibid, p. 66
16   'Training from 0600 . . .': cited in Jones, *Battles of a Gunner Officer*, loc. 1465
16   'Gun drill for . . .': cited ibid, loc. 1472
17   'He said he planned . . .': cited ibid, loc. 1480
17   'He got right under . . .': cited ibid, loc. 1480
18   'We love and respect . . .': Johnson, *One More Hill*, p. 77
19   'After the aide signals . . .': ibid, p. 78
19   'Sir, it is my duty . . .': TNA WO 214/10

2 A United Front

32   'All of a sudden . . .': Scheffel, *Crack! And Thump*, p. 11
33   'We had no time . . .': ibid, p. 15
33   'A surge of patriotism . . .': ibid, p. 15
33   'If you're an officer . . .': ibid, p. 28
33   'I think we got the . . .': ibid, p. 28
35   'We sat there giving . . .': ibid, p. 70
35   'You're an American?': cited ibid, p. 70
35   'I want you to remember . . .': cited ibid, p. 71
37   'As calm and serene . . .': Gunther, *D Day*, p. 71
37   'I had great respect . . .': Scheffel, *Crack! And Thump*, p. 71
38   'We were impressed . . .': Hansen Diary, 28 March 1943, USAHEC
38   'By a brilliant piece . . .': cited in Jackson, *Alexander of Tunis as Military Commander*, p. 204
39   'I do not allow, ever . . .': cited in Ambrose, *The Supreme Commander*, p. 205
39   'In his current efforts . . .': Butcher Diary, 7 March 1943, EPL

3 The Problem of Planning

44   'Army, Air Force and Navy must become a brotherhood': cited in Gunther, *D Day*, p. 80
45   'It was strongly defended . . .': TNA WO 32/13255
47   'I think we are on a good wicket . . .': Alexander to Brooke, 3 April 1943, Alanbrooke Papers, LHCMA
48   'We are doubtful . . .': TNA WO 32/32257
48   'The month of February . . .': TNA WO 32/32257

49   'dog's breakfast': cited in Tedder, *With Prejudice*, p. 431
49   'I'm afraid Montgomery . . . ': cited ibid, p. 432
50   'Planning so far . . . ': TNA WO 32/32257
51   'It must be remembered . . . ': TNA WO 32/32257
52   'It is an impressive . . . ': TNA WO 32/32257

4 Hitler's Gamble

55   'In the coastal waters . . . ': Cibulka, *Nachtwache*, p. 12
55   'So this is what death . . . ': ibid, p. 13
56   'Italy without Sicily . . .': cited ibid, pp. 13–14
58   'almost more dangerous . . . ': cited in Warlimont, *Inside Hitler's Headquarters*, p. 318
60   'Do you think . . . ': cited in Dönitz, *Memoirs*, p. 363
61   'more important purposes': cited in Heiber and Glantz, *Hitler and His Generals*, p. 33
61   'Well, my Führer . . . ': cited in Warlimont, *Inside Hitler's Headquarters*, p. 320
61   'Personally, in so far as . . . ': cited in Heiber and Glantz, *Hitler and His Generals*, p. 134; Warlimont, *Inside Hitler's Headquarters*, p. 322
63   'From October 1942 I had . . . ': Mussolini, *Pensieri, pontini e sardi*, p. 105
64   'The ways which Providence . . . ': Ciano, *Ciano's Diary*, 5 Feb. 1943, p. 587
64   'A few days ago . . . ': cited in Farrell, *Mussolini*, p. 493

5 Air Power

68   'Tiger Green One . . . ': Kennedy, *Black Crosses Off My Wingtip*, p. 49
69   'Green One. The three . . . ': ibid, p. 50
69   'Green Two . . . ': ibid, p. 52
69   'We were rubbing it in': ibid, p. 53
70   'What about sharing even . . . ': ibid, p. 53
70   'Our bombing of ports and railways . . . ': Tedder, *With Prejudice*, p. 439
76   'We parted friends': Patton Diary, 4 April 1943, LoC

6 CORKSCREW

77   'Following the loss . . . ': TNA AIR 20/10659
79   'I was really passionate . . . ': Melino Barbagallo, interview with Elio Chisari
79   'I had never been there . . . ': cited in Heaton and Lewis, *The German Aces Speak*, p. 166
79   'I knew him . . . ': cited ibid, p. 166
80   'Let me just say . . . ': cited ibid, p. 168
80   'Steinhoff, do your men know . . . ': ibid, p. 168
80   'Sir, the group is no longer . . . ': Steinhoff, *Messerschmitts over Sicily*, p. 13
81   'But be quick about it . . . ': cited ibid, p. 15
82   'Well, fuck 'em all . . . ': Dundas, *Flying Start*, p. 143
82   'You know Broadie . . . ': cited ibid, p. 144

83   'as critical points . . .': Spaatz, 7 May 1943, Box 12, Spaatz Papers, LoC
83   'A high degree of destruction . . .': Spaatz, 7 May 1943, Box 12, Spaatz
       Papers, LoC
83   'Aviation is in its infancy . . .': Bruno, *Beyond Fighter Escort*, p. 3
84   'This particular mission . . .': ibid, p. 41
85   'I want to make . . .': cited in Davis, *Carl A. Spaatz and the Air War in
       Europe*, p. 229
85   'They were men who were learning . . .': cited ibid, p. 232
85   'In so far as the task . . .': Spaatz, 7 May 1943, Box 12, Spaatz Papers, LoC
86   'My situation was saved!' Elmhirst Papers, pp. 83–4, CCA
86   'Lieutenant-Colonel Davis . . .': Spaatz, 19 May 1943, Box 12, Spaatz
       Papers, LoC
87   'My heart was racing so fast . . .': Dryden, *A-Train*, p. 63
88   'Only then did I tweak a bit': ibid, p. 124
88   'When I saw the swastikas . . .': ibid, p. 126
88   'It was a perfect dawn . . .': Hay, 7 June 1943, IWM 4171
89   'There were literally hundreds . . .': ibid, 8 June 1943
89   'At first our shots . . .': ibid, 8 June 1943
90   'a hurricane of fire and smoke': cited in Mitcham and von Stauffenberg,
       The Battle of Sicily, p. 43
90   'We could distinctly . . .': Hay, 11 June 1943, IWM 4171
90   'Pantelleria was the first . . .': Tedder, *With Prejudice*, p. 441.

7 Man of Honour

91   'The Island has a long . . .': *Soldier's Guide to Sicily*, p. 1
93   'I had a good childhood . . .': Mario Turco, interview with author
93   'During the war . . .': Mario Turco, interview with author
93   'People used to move on . . .': Mario Turco, interview with author
94   'At home, but there was also . . .': interview with Vincenza la Bruna in
       Comune di Regalbuto, *Viaggio nella memoria*, p. 78
94   'We were barefoot . . .': ibid, p. 78
94   'The insanitary condition . . .': *Soldier's Guide to Sicily*, p. 12
97   'Your Excellency has carte blanche . . .': cited in Petacco, *Il prefetto di
       ferro*, p. 190
101   'I explained to Brennan . . .': Corvo, *Max Corvo*, p. 22
102   'How could we not . . .': Garra, *Il Nonno Racconta*, p. 25
102   'There was only one radio . . .': Mario Turco, interview with author
102   'And do you know . . . ?: Mario Turco, interview with author
102   'My son, you don't realise . . .': cited in Follain, *Mussolini's Island*, p. 9
104   'The conditions on Sicily . . .': Leonardi, *Luglio 1943 in Sicilia*, p. 37
104   'For example, the Battaglione 435 . . .': ibid, p. 45
107   'This appreciation . . .': von Senger, *Neither Fear Nor Hope*, p. 126
107   'I detested him . . .': ibid, p. 126
108   'All this revealed . . .': ibid, p. 128

8 The Glitch in the Plan

109   'We are sweating . . .': Gavin Diary, 13 June 1943, USAHEC
110   'No one hit . . .': ibid, 13 June 1943
110   'Said he was going to be . . .': ibid, 6 July 1943
116   'I was full of foreboding . . .': cited in Peters, *Glider Pilots in Sicily*, p. 24
116   'American gliders?': Chatterton, *The Wings of Pegasus*, pp. 41–2
117   'An oil leak . . .': TNA AIR 20/6040
119   'His form seemed to fill . . .': Davis, *SAS*, p. 32
119   'It hardly mattered . . .': ibid, p. 37
120   'The attack was an outstanding . . .': ibid, p. 65
121   'I feel quite certain . . .': Gavin Diary, 8 May 1943, USAHEC
122   'More bad judgement . . .': ibid, 22 June 1943
122   'It really put pressure on me . . .': cited in Alexander and Sparry, *Jump Commander*, p. 69
122   'The loneliest sight . . .': Gavin Diary, 6 July 1943, USAHEC

9 Crescendo in the Air

123   'What do you do at night?': cited in Follain, *Mussolini's Island*, p. 33
124   'Palermo has things . . .': de Grada, *Giornale del tempo di guerra*, p. 168
125   'These kinds of happenings . . .': Piccione Papers
125   'Take no action . . .': Steinhoff, *Messerschmitts over Sicily*, p. 44
125   'One pilot . . .': cited in Shores et al., *A History of the Mediterranean Air War*, Vol. 4, p. 110
125   'Well, well, let's drink to that . . .': Steinhoff, *Messerschmitts over Sicily*, p. 51
126   'Discussed the whole fighter . . .': cited in Shores et al., *A History of the Mediterranean Air War*, Vol. 4, p. 110
128   'Campbell, break right . . .': Dryden, *A-Train*, p. 131
129   'Twisting and turning . . .': ibid, p. 136
129   'Needless to say . . .': ibid, p. 136
130   'In this way . . .': Dundas, *Flying Start*, p. 149
130   'Hold on . . .': ibid, p. 151
130   'Thanks, sir . . .': ibid, p. 152
131   'It was unbearably hot . . .': Steinhoff, *Messerschmitts over Sicily*, p. 95
131   'This complex of airfields . . .': ibid, p. 97
131   'One time . . .': ibid, p. 98
132   'How's it all going to end . . .': ibid, p. 102
133   'Under no circumstances . . .': Bruno, *Beyond Fighter Escort*, p. 49
133   'I do not know what thoughts . . .': ibid, pp. 51–2
133   'Give us a course . . .': ibid, p. 53
133   'He can do 400 miles per hour . . .': ibid, p. 54
134   'If we had any battle . . .': ibid, p. 66
135   'And suddenly . . .': Steinhoff, *Messerschmitts over Sicily*, p. 110
136   'Long before . . .': Bruno, *Beyond Fighter Escort*, p. 70
137   'We were tired . . .': Steinhoff, *Messerschmitts over Sicily*, p. 124

10 Countdown

138   'But of all these . . .': Mowat, *And No Birds Sang*, p. 41
138   'It is my great pleasure . . .': ibid, p. 41
140   'Oddly, I don't feel the least . . .': ibid, p. 33
140   'The whole valley . . .': Cibulka, *Nachtwache*, p. 23
141   'If the Italians had shown . . .': Stappenbeck, 'That's How It Was', p. 68, DTA
142   'Now a tug of war began . . .': Goldschmidt, BA-MA MSG2/6303
144   'The fact is . . .': von Senger, *Neither Fear Nor Hope*, p. 133
144   'Was the island's crew . . .': Stappenbeck, 'That's How It Was', p. 71
145   'A lot of fuel . . .': ibid, p. 73
146   'If you mean to go for them . . .': Kesselring, *The Memoirs of Field-Marshal Kesselring*, p. 161
147   'Victory at Kursk . . .': cited in Bellamy, *Absolute War*, p. 577
147   'So far as Italy . . .': TNA HW 1/1846
149   'I cannot help remembering . . .': Brown, *To All Hands*, p. 76
150   'If you don't get all the news . . .': ibid, pp. 85–6
150   'It is obvious now . . .': Hay, 6 July 1943, IWM 4171
150   'Alex seems to have . . .': DDE, Vol. 2, No. 1096, p. 1236
152   'Looking at that chart . . .': Cunningham, *A Sailor's Odyssey*, p. 548
152   'It is hard to describe . . .': ibid, p. 548
152   '3. Batterie reports . . .': Cibulka, *Nachtwache*, p. 125
152   'The things we did . . .': Steinhoff, *Messerschmitts over Sicily*, p. 129

11 Airborne Assault

158   'a clenched fist . . .': Butcher Diary, 6 July 1943, EPL
158   'It is no small event . . .': ibid
158   'So with rather fearful hearts . . .': Cunningham, *A Sailor's Odyssey*, p. 550
159   'I could not find . . .': Lucas Diary, 9 June 1943, USAHEC
160   'We have a pro-British . . .': Patton Diary, 22 May 1943, LoC
161   'I don't, I look forward . .': ibid, 8 July 1943
162   'Why have we not been attacked . . .': Lucas Diary, 9 July 1943, USAHEC
162   'It was a tense moment . . .': Chatterton, *The Wings of Pegasus*, p. 71
163   'Stretching back . . .': ibid, p. 72
165   'Its pieces of concrete . . .': Piccione Papers
165   'I couldn't sleep . . .': Piccione Papers
165   'bloody glider': Peters, *Glider Pilots in Sicily*, p. 151
166   'Can you see . . .': Chatterton, *The Wings of Pegasus*, p. 73
166   'It's no good staying . . .': ibid, p. 74
167   'I lay there . . .': ibid, p. 74
167   'This was a great help . . .': cited in Peters, *Glider Pilots in Sicily*, p. 181
168   'The searchlight followed . . .': cited ibid, p. 182
172   'Get back, dammit!' Alexander and Sparry, *Jump Commander*, p. 73

172   'He sure as hell did!' ibid, p. 73
172   'I could have brought charges . . . ': ibid, pp. 75–6
173   'I wrapped a bandage . . . ': ibid, p. 77
173   'I still had some doubt . . . ': Gavin, *On to Berlin*, p. 25
174   'We anticipate . . . ': von Senger, *Neither Fear Nor Hope*, p. 133
174   'This battalion . . . ': cited in Follain, *Mussolini's Island*, p. 73
174   'I stood still . . . ': Piccione Papers

12 Early Hours of D-Day

176   'I looked at the electric light . . . ': Cole, *Rough Road to Rome*, p. 18
177   'At least only . . . ': Hay, 10 July 1943, IWM 4171
178   'You don't get off that easy!': Mowat, *And No Birds Sang*, p. 54
178   'My bowels . . . ': ibid, p. 56
178   'Standing in the bows . . . ': ibid, p. 58
178   'A great wave . . . ': Brown, *To All Hands*, p. 118
179   'Apprehension now . . . ': Hansen Diary, 10 July 1943, USAHEC
179   'And still no enemy . . . ': ibid, 10 July 1943
179   'The Navy is requesting . . . ': cited at http://www.beachjumpers.com/History/theinception.htm
180   'I said I thought . . . ': Fairbanks, *A Hell of a War*, p. 183
181   'A terrible explosion . . . ': Hansen Diary, 10 July 1943, USAHEC
182   'Right, sir!': Altieri, *The Spearheaders*, p. 212
182   'Hey, Al . . . ': ibid, p. 213
183   'We couldn't restrain ourselves': . . . ibid, p. 213
183   'It's against Ranger . . . ': ibid, p. 215
185   'The uncertainties . . . ': Davis, *SAS*, p. 72
187   'The sound of this voice . . . ': ibid, p. 77
188   'It was unpleasant . . . ': ibid, p. 81
188   'They were a poor lot . . . ': ibid, p. 80
189   'Heavens, they were . . . ': ibid, p. 84
190   'any subsequent action': TNA WO 218/99

13 Landings

191   'Italians, c'mon . . . ': Piccione Papers
191   'Thankfully, God saved us . . . ': ibid
192   'I then took a firm line . . . ': Fenner, p. 2, IWM 3854
193   'We should have been . . . ': ibid, p. 3
195   'They started belting away . . . ': Donaldson, IWM 22357
195   'We're fucking well lost . . . ': Mowat, *And No Birds Sang*, p. 59
196   'Somebody blow that wire!' ibid, p. 64
197   'Cor! You chaps . . . ': ibid, p. 66
198   'The rising sky of dawn . . . ': Johnson, *One More Hill*, p. 84
199   'I couldn't take any more . . . ': Altieri, *The Spearheaders*, p. 227
200   'Put your hands up . . . ': Angela Bruccoleri, interview with author

201   'You don't know fear . . .': Bing Evans, interview with author
202   'And there, with the help . . .': Gavin, *On to Berlin*, p. 27
202   'My father drove the buggy . . .': Garra, *Il Nonno Racconta*, p. 34
203   'At this point . . .': Bergengruen, C-087b, p. 3, FMS, USAHEC
203   'Things were very confused . . .': Goldschmidt, BA-MA MSG2/6303
204   'And so the Tigers . . .': ibid
205   'I would have laughed too . . .': Leonardi, *Luglio 1943 in Sicilia*, p. 122
206   'Lieutenant, sir! . . .': Follain, *Mussolini's Island*, p. 88
206   'Don't worry . . .': ibid, p. 88
207   'These are the commander's . . .': Schmalz, BA-MA MSG2/13109

14 Foothold

209   'There were the usual . . .': Steinhoff, *Messerschmitts over Sicily*, p. 129
209   'It's probably one . . .': ibid, p. 130
209   'We were out . . .': ibid, p. 131
210   'For a long time . . .': ibid, p. 133
210   'The entire sea . . .': cited in Eriksson, *Alarmstart South and Final Defeat*,
       p. 125
212   'The absence of Alexander . . .': Tedder, *With Prejudice*, p. 449
213   'We expect to help . . .': Dryden, *A-Train*, p. 139
214   'There was an unforgettable . . .': Dundas, *Flying Start*, p. 153
214   'Beneath us . . .': ibid, p. 154
218   'Get the hell out of here . . .': Lucas Diary, 10 July 1943, USAHEC
218   'Sir! Thank God . . .': Fairbanks, *A Hell of a War*, p. 186
219   'All right . . .': Altieri, *The Spearheaders*, p. 232
220   'We cheered wildly . . .': ibid, p. 233
220   'We used some of our . . .': cited in Chatterton, *The Wings of Pegasus*,
       p. 84
221   'Why on earth did you do that?' ibid, pp. 92–3
222   'They were firmly . . .': Davis, *SAS*, p. 86
222   'Needless to say . . .': Mortimer, *Stirling's Men*, p. 118
222   'There was no more trouble . . .': Chatterton, *The Wings of Pegasus*,
       p. 93
223   'His eyes were open . . .': Mowat, *And No Birds Sang*, p. 71
224   'Where are Mussolini's . . .': Cole, *Rough Road to Rome*, p. 23
224   'If the landing . . .': Murphy, *To Hell and Back*, p. 1
225   'I was not overjoyed . . .': ibid, p. 8
225   'Amazingly, our LCI . . .': Eugene Griffin, Veterans Questionnaire, p. 41,
       USAHEC

15 Night Attack

226   'And that's when I saw . . .': Mario Turco, interview with author
226   'All that pride . . .': Mario Turco, interview with author
226   'Everyone in Gela . . .': Mario Turco, interview with author

227   'There was a lot of confusion . . .': Melino Barbagallo, interview with Elio Chisari
228   'The young panzer regiment . . .': Bergengruen, C-087b, FMS, p. 14, USAHEC
229   'He could hardly . . .': Bergengruen, C-087b, FMS, p. 15, USAHEC
231   'It was not long . . .': cited in Chatterton, *The Wings of Pegasus*, p. 84
232   'Our organisation on shore . . .': Pyle, *Brave Men*, p. 29
232   'The Americans worked . . .': ibid, p. 29
233   'They wouldn't have stopped . . .': ibid, p. 29
233   'Still no enemy . . .': Hansen Diary, 10 July 1943, USAHEC
234   'Breaking into the breakers . . .': ibid
234   'When they pointed a gun . . .': Piccione Papers
235   'What had looked . . .': Cole, *Rough Road to Rome*, p. 27
235   'I asked him to find out . . .': Schmalz, BA-MA MSG 2/13109
236   'The planned counter-attack . . .': ibid
237   'C-in-C of Italian . . .': von Senger, *Neither Fear Nor Hope*, p. 134
237   'All that was certain . . .': Stappenbeck, 'That's How It Was', p. 73
238   'On a day like this . . .': Cibulka, *Nachtwache*, p. 128
238   'We had Spitfires . . .': Hay, 10 July 1943, IWM 4171
239   'We carried on firing . . .': ibid
239   'We passed many . . .': Hansen Diary, 10 July 1943, USAHEC
239   'Crawl in slit trench . . .': ibid
240   'They really formed . . .': Hay, 10 July 1943, IWM 4171
240   'With a crackling . . .': ibid

16 Counter-Attack at Gela

243   'So far the operation . . .': DDE, Vol. 2, No. 1115, p. 1255
244   'General situation . . .': TNA WO 214/12
244   'I was wrong': cited in Hamilton, *Monty*, p. 298
245   'Some are solid flame . . .': Johnson, *One More Hill*, p. 84
246   'We do not know . . .': ibid, p. 86
246   'The enemy could have . . .': Leonardi, *Luglio 1943 in Sicilia*, p. 142
248   'Tomorrow, I will be . . .': cited in Follain, *Mussolini's Island*, p. 112
248   'In these situations . . .': Leonardi, *Luglio 1943 in Sicilia*, p. 148
249   'The ground was vomiting fire . . .': ibid, p. 150
249   'Must be a hundred . . .': Altieri, *The Spearheaders*, p. 235
250   'How do you like that?' ibid, p. 236
250   'Tenente-Colonnello, what good . . .': cited in Follain, *Mussolini's Island*, p. 130
251   'The crucial moment . . .': Leonardi, *Luglio 1943 in Sicilia*, p. 151
252   'We looked at each other . . .': ibid, p. 160
253   'It's all right, Hap . . .': cited in D'Este, *Patton*, p. 507
254   'Kill every one . . .': cited in Garland and McGaw Smyth, *Sicily and the Surrender of Italy*, p. 168

254   'I knew I was about to witness . . .': Altieri, *The Spearheaders*, p. 239
255   'The beachhead, at least . . .': Johnson, *One More Hill*, p. 90
256   'I'm glad to shed blood . . .': cited in Leonardi, *Luglio 1943 in Sicilia*, p. 166
256   'The Italian advance . . .': Patton Diary, 11 July 1943
257   'No one was hurt . . .': Patton Diary, 11 July 1943, LoC
258   'We've got to move . . .': cited in Follain, *Mussolini's Island*, p. 136

17 Fightback at Gela

260   'We weren't about . . .': Gavin, *On to Berlin*, p. 28
261   'Refugees simply pass the dead . . .': Hansen Diary, USAHEC, 11 July 1943
262   'The sirocco started . . .': cited in Steinhoff, *Messerschmitts over Sicily*, p. 163
262   'I'd better have a word . . .': ibid, p. 163
263   'At first we waved . . .': Goldschmidt, BA-MA MSG2/6303
265   'We were going to have . . .': Gavin, *On to Berlin*, p. 29
265   'A Tiger tank . . .': ibid, p. 31
266   'We are staying . . .': cited in LoFaro, *The Sword of St Michael*, p. 99
267   'Better watch your step . . .': cited in Bradley, *A Soldier's Story*, p. 131
267   'Chet, be careful . . .': ibid, p. 131
269   'A wave of new hope . . .': Leonardi, *Luglio 1943 in Sicilia*, p. 169
270   'I decided it was time . . .': Gavin, *On to Berlin*, p. 33

18 Expanding the Bridgehead

271   'When you get the signal . . .': Murphy, *To Hell and Back*, p. 9
272   'Did they get the machine gun? . . .': ibid, p. 10
272   'Boy, we were glad . . .': Griffin, Veterans Questionnaire
274   'But before they could . . .': Steinhoff, *Messerschmitts over Sicily*, p. 178
275   'There are Italian . . .': ibid, p. 178
275   'We would certainly . . .': ibid, p. 179
275   'The event confirmed . . .': Leonardi, *Luglio 1943 in Sicilia*, p. 173
276   'No. Officers must never . . .': cited in Follain, *Mussolini's Island*, p. 144
276   'It's up to you . . .': cited ibid, p. 145
276   'Leaving those positions . . .': Leonardi, *Luglio 1943 in Sicilia*, p. 174
277   'Went to office . . .': Patton Diary, 11 July 1943, LoC
278   'So at dawn . . .': Leonardi, *Luglio 1943 in Sicilia*, p. 179
279   'We were leaving ideals . . .': ibid, p. 186
280   'The Sherman tank is about . . .': Goldschmidt, BA-BA MSG 2/6303
281   'We roar into the area . . .': ibid
281   'Finally, the idiots . . .': ibid
282   'Rivets fly around . . .': ibid
282   'It looks bad . . .': ibid
282   'Only now do we realize . . .': ibid
283   'Rifles, canteens . . .': Johnson, *One More Hill*, p. 92

283   'I can only regard . . .': cited in Shores et al., *A History of the Mediterranean Air War*, Vol. 4, p. 184
284   'We would refuel . . .': Steinhoff, *Messerschmitts over Sicily*, p. 182
284   'There'll be no transport . . .': ibid, p. 187
285   'The airfield looked . . .': ibid, p. 208
285   'That's our job . . .': Murphy, *To Hell and Back*, p. 11
286   'Now I have shed . . .': ibid, p. 11
286   'It would have been . . .': Alexander and Sparry, *Jump Commander*, p. 85
287   'I must say . . .': DDE, Vol. 2, No. 1118, p. 1258
287   'Unforgettable it was . . .': von Senger, *Neither Fear Nor Hope*, p. 15

19 Taking Stock

292   'In the course of our . . .': cited in Kurowski, *The History of the Fallschirmjägerkorps Hermann Göring*, p. 195
292   'I don't know . . .': Chatterton, *The Wings of Pegasus*, p. 96
293   'I felt stunned . . .': Cole, *Rough Road to Rome*, p. 33
295   'We sneaked back across . . .': cited in Kurowski, *The History of the Fallschirmpanzerkorps Hermann Göring*, p. 196
295   'At times I was with . . .': Schmalz, BA-MA MSG 2/13109
296   'Anyone who has not . . .': ibid
296   'In vain the paramedic . . .': Cibulka, *Nachtwache*, p. 133
296   'The dead are increasing.': ibid, p. 133
298   'My flight to Sicily . . .': Kesselring, *The Memoirs of Field-Marshal Kesselring*, p. 163
298   'I had the bitter . . .': Conrath, NARA RG 407/427/95-AL1-2.6
299   'As soon as this is done . . .': Schmalz, BA-MA MSG 2/13109
299   'Cities, plains, mountains . . .': ibid
299   'Behind us is Melilli . . .': ibid
301   'My pal, Charlie Lee . . .': Cheall, *Fighting Through from Dunkirk to Hamburg*, p. 73
302   'It was soon obvious . . .': Davis, *SAS*, p. 101
303   'My battle situation very good . . .': cited in Molony, *The Mediterranean and Middle East*, Vol. 5, p. 88
303   'I had to quit eating . . .': Patton Diary, 13 July 1943, LoC
304   'cussing him out': ibid
304   'I spent all yesterday . . .': TNA WO 214/12
305   'It was incomprehensible . . .': Corvo, *Max Corvo*, p. 65

20 Primosole Bridge

307   'So, it had been decided . . .': Steinhoff, *Messerschmitts over Sicily*, p. 231
307   'There was something . . .': ibid, p. 237
307   'My mission here was over . . .': ibid, p. 240
308   'This country is . . .': Mowat, *And No Birds Sang*, pp. 81–2
308   'The sun became . . .': ibid, p. 73

310   'to hold this place . . .': Schmalz, BA-MA MSG 2/13109
310   'We had thus . . .': ibid
311   'Has there been a raid . . .': Pöppel, *Heaven and Hell*, p. 120
311   'We pass a sentry . . .': ibid, p. 121
311   'Appalling casualties . . .': ibid, p. 121
312   'Watch out . . .': Schmalz, BA-MA MSG 2/13109
314   'German paratroopers!': ibid, p. 122
315   'The DZ's down there . . .': cited in Arthur, *Men of the Red Beret*, p. 82
315   'There's nothing for it . . .': ibid, p. 82
316   'I'd gone out number ten . . .': ibid, p. 82
318   'The guns look pathetic . . .': Pöppel, *Heaven and Hell*, p. 123
318   'They have deteriorated . . .': ibid, p. 123
319   'But there's a big task . . .': Mowat, *And No Birds Sang*, p. 80
319   'As a result . . .': ibid, p. 80
320   'We've received . . .': Bradley, *A Soldier's Story*, pp. 135–6
321   'I am not too pleased . . .': Patton Diary, 13 July 1943, LoC
321   'Subsequently, to prevent . . .': cited in Molony, *The Mediterranean and Middle East*, Vol. 5, p. 89

21 Shooting

324   'I will bring this question . . .': Patton Diary, 14 July 1943, LoC
325   'We want you to . . .': Griffin, 'Memoirs of World War II', p. 43
325   'The dead were all blackened . . .': ibid, p. 44
326   'these sons of bitches': Biscari incident collected papers, NARA
326   'They were sort of . . .': ibid
326   'It was the damnedest feeling . . .': ibid
327   'To me, possessed . . .': Johnson, *One More Hill*, p. 98
327   'For me, like others . . .': ibid, p. 98
328   'It's a bloody mess . . .': Pöppel, *Heaven and Hell*, p. 124
329   'Good roads were . . .': Cheall, *Fighting Through from Dunkirk to Hamburg*, p. 74
329   'It was very time-consuming . . .': ibid, p. 74
329   'The Italian refused . . .': cited in Kurowski, *The History of the Fallschirmpanzerkorps Hermann Göring*, p. 197
331   'It was stinking . . .': Pearson, IWM 12151
331   'This nightly backward . . .': Schmalz, BA-MA MSG 2/13109
332   'The invasion has . . .': Elmhirst Papers, CCA
332   'It was a moment . . .': Dundas, *Flying Start*, p. 156
332   'Wherever *Fallschirmjäger* are . . .': cited in Schmalz, MA-BA MSG 2/13109
332   'I had to give my report . . .': Schmalz, BA-MA MSG 2/13109
333   'I could not rest . . .': ibid
333   'You had to shoot them . . .': Jupp Klein, interview with author
335   'I decided to requisition . . .': Corvo, *Max Corvo*, p. 70

336   'Turi, the farm bailiff . . . ': cited in Pantaleone, *The Mafia and Politics*, p. 55
337   'Fighting was going on . . . ': Fenner, p. 6 IWM 3854
338   'Even before we knew . . . ': Davis, *SAS*, p. 110
338   'If you want to lose another . . . ': Pearson, IWM 12151
338   'All right, Pearson . . . ': cited ibid
340   'It flew beautifully . . . ': Vrilakas, *Look Mom – I Can Fly!*, p. 9
341   'The loss of a pilot . . . ': ibid, p. 81

22 Slaughter at the Bridge

342   'A captain in the 180th . . . ': Patton Diary, 15 July 1944, LoC
342   'Anyhow, they are dead . . . ': ibid
343   'Every one was coated . . . ': Pyle, *Brave Men*, p. 35
343   'The point was . . . ': ibid, p. 36
344   'I was bleeding . . . ': Bing Evans, interview with author, p. 133
344   'Lieutenant Evans . . . ': ibid, p. 133
345   'I am not a deserter!': Melino Barbagallo, interview with Elio Chisari
346   'You stupid idiots!' cited in Follain, *Mussolini's Island*, p. 176
346   'Our own troops . . . ': Goldschmidt, BA-MA MSG 2/6303
347   'We would run . . . ': cited in Jensen, *Strike Swiftly!*, p. 83
347   'We never lost . . . ': cited ibid, p. 83
347   'My bloody batman . . . ': Pearson, IWM 12151
348   'What, me sir?': cited ibid
348   'I expected to see . . . ': Pearson, IWM 12151
349   'There he was . . . ': ibid
352   'When I get out of this . . . ': cited in Fenner, IWM 3854
352   'There was a lot . . . ': ibid
353   'I felt sick as a dog . . . ': Pöppel, *Heaven and Hell*, p. 125
353   'It was terrible . . . ': Jupp Klein, interview with author
353   'It was a very brave act . . . ': ibid
356   'I am sure that . . . ': Patton Diary, 17 July 1943, LoC
357   'If I do what . . . ': ibid
357   'It was all settled . . . ': Blumenson, ed., *The Patton Papers*, p. 292

23 The Bloody Plain

360   'the driver of a truck . . . ': Mowat, *And No Birds Sang*, pp. 99–100
360   'The anomaly . . . ': ibid, p. 100
361   'You take 'em, Junior': cited ibid, p. 104
361   'Give 'em another!': cited ibid, p. 104
361   'Get the hell . . . ': ibid, p. 105
363   'He's waited for you . . . ': Kurowski, *The History of the Fallschirmpanzerkorps Hermann Göring*, p. 200
363   'All due respect!': ibid, p. 200
365   'These bullets were . . . ': Cole, *Rough Road to Rome*, p. 49

366   'I bent over him . . .': ibid, p. 50
367   'It's suicide . . .': ibid, p. 54
367   'It came like a monsoon . . .': ibid, p. 56
368   'The only Germans . . .': TNA WO 169/10233
372   'Keep going! . . .': cited in Hill, *Hedley Verity*
374   'Always at the back . . .': *The Times*, 17 June 1969
374   'Neither Alexander nor I . . .': DDE, Vol. 2, No. 1119, p. 1261
374   'And if the Germans . . .': cited in Molony, *The Mediterranean and the Middle East*, Vol. 5, p. 120
375   'Intention is to base . . .': TNA WO 214/12

24 Assoro

379   'All in all . . .': Mauss Diary, 13 July 1943, Mauss and de Rijke, *The War Diary of Dr Wilhelm Mauss*
379   'In the end . . .': ibid, 13 July 1943
380   'Nowhere is one safe . . .': ibid, 17 July 1943
381   'I didn't feel the need . . .': Kennedy, *Black Crosses off my Wingtip*, p. 69
381   'I was very happy . . .': ibid, p. 71
382   'The moral and political . . .': Bruno, *Beyond Fighter Escort*, p. 83
382   'It was a strange affair . . .': Gavin, *On to Berlin*, p. 45
383   'For the most part . . .': Altieri, *The Spearheaders*, p. 251
383   'That must have been . . .': Alexander and Sparry, *Jump Commander*, p. 93
383   'Sir, if we don't go . . .': cited ibid, p. 94
383   'It was frustrating . . .': ibid, p. 93
384   'So far, this campaign . . .': Johnson, *One More Hill*, p. 102
384   'Originally, our time table . . .': Hansen Diary, 21 July 1943, USAHEC
384   'Leese replied so promptly . . .': Bradley, *A Soldier's Story*, p. 143
386   'We must swing eastwards . . .': cited in Mowat, *And No Birds Sang*, p. 108
387   'John, for God's sake . . .': cited in Tweedsmuir, IWM 779
388   'And gentlemen in England . . .': ibid
388   'as a frog full of fart': Mowat, *And No Birds Sang*, p. 113
389   'I felt that all eyes . . .': Tweedsmuir, IWM 779
389   'The crazy bastard . . .': cited in Mowat, *And No Birds Sang*, p. 116
389   'Then all question . . .': Tweedsmuir, IWM 779
390   'Shit a brick!': cited in Mowat, *And No Birds Sang*, p. 118
391   'We are finished . . .': cited ibid, p. 124
391   'They just came up . . .': cited ibid, p. 125
392   'Although I had experienced . . .': ibid, p. 126
392   'Our heads were swimming . . .': Tweedsmuir, IWM 779
392   'Every day . . .': Stappenbeck, 'That's How It Was', p. 75
393   'We remained loyal . . .': ibid, p. 77
394   'It was a bitter way . . .': Mowat, *And No Birds Sang*, p. 130
395   'News of this . . .': Rodt, C-077, FMS, USAHEC

25 Overthrow

397   'I believe, Führer . . . ': cited in Farrell, *Mussolini*, p. 386

397   'a crossword puzzle . . . ': Mussolini, *Pensieri, pontini e sardi*, Vol. XVI, p. 123

397   'Hitler took no notice . . . ': Warlimont, *Inside Hitler's Headquarters*, p. 339

398   'It's easy to say it . . . ': cited in Farrell, *Mussolini*, p. 387; Deakin, *The Brutal Friendship*, p. 445

399   'We were all out . . . ': cited in Jensen, *Strike Swiftly!*, p. 93

399   'Helpless without holes . . . ': Johnson, *One More Hill*, p. 103

401   'Viva America!': Patton, *War As I Knew It*, p. 66

401   'It is a great thrill . . . ': Patton Diary, 22 July 1943, LoC

401   'This is a great . . . ': ibid

402   'If the folks in Palermo . . . ': Griffin, Veteran's Questionnaire, p. 48, USAHEC

405   'The squalid stone houses . . . ': Mowat, *And No Birds Sang*, p. 124

405   'The Italian soldier . . . ': Hansen Diary, 21 July 1943, USAHEC

405   'Villages had long ago . . . ': Bradley, *A Soldier's Story*, p. 142

406   'Morgue is now crowded . . . ': Hansen Diary, 21 July 1943, USAHEC

406   'What kind of woman . . . ': Cibulka, *Nachtwache*, p. 135

406   'We don't want . . . ': cited in Farrell, *Mussolini*, p. 388

408   'Then, everything is finished?' Mussolini, *Pensieri, pontini e sardi*, Vol. XVIII, p. 101

408   'Basically, he was yelling . . . ': Warlimont, *Inside Hitler's Headquarters*, p. 343

408   'They say they'll fight . . . ': cited ibid, p. 334

408   'Under all circumstances . . . ': cited ibid, p. 345

409   'If ever there was . . . ': Mauss Diary, 26 July 1943, Mauss and de Rijke, *The War Diary of Dr Wilhelm Mauss*, p. 694

409   'There is a big . . . ': ibid, p. 695

26 The Bloody Mountains

411   'In war as Patton knew it . . . ': Bradley, *A Soldier's Story*, p. 146

411   'In order to bring . . . ': Alexander dispatch, Alexander Papers, App. C-5, TNA

413   'Now the British . . . ': Patton Diary, 24 July 1943, LoC

413   'He agreed so readily . . . ': Patton Diary, 25 July 1943, LoC

414   'I doubt if he does.': ibid

414   'I want to assure you . . . ': ibid

415   'The living was easy . . . ': Dryden, *A-Train*, p. 141

415   'We lay in the shade . . . ': Kennedy, *Black Crosses off My Wingtip*, p. 71

416   'From the spectacular . . . ': cited in Shores et al., *A History of the Mediterranean Air War*, Vol. 4, p. 244

416   'One can be sure . . .': Mauss Diary, 26 July 1943, Mauss and de Rijke, *The War Diary of Dr Wilhelm Mauss*, p. 315

416   'Randazzo is a popular . . .': ibid, 26 July 1943, p. 315

417   'We were told . . .': cited in Jensen, *Strike Swiftly!*, p. 95

418   'The priest blesses us . . .': Johnson, *One More Hill*, p. 107

419   'You'd best get up . . .': cited in Mowat, *And No Birds Sang*, p. 131

419   'The colonel's wounded . . .': cited ibid, p. 132

420   'No one complained . . .': Tweedsmuir, IWM 779

420   'John, you're doing fine . . .': cited in Pyle, *Brave Men*, p. 50

420   'The dying man . . .': ibid, p. 51

423   'A firework of tracer . . .': Cibulka, *Nachtwache*, p. 157

423   'Not on foot . . .': cited ibid, p. 158

424   'The country fought over . . .': Training notes from the Sicilian campaign, NARA RG 407/112/427

425   'In a bunker . . .': Cibulka, *Nachtwache*, p. 152

425   'It is as if . . .': ibid, p. 163

426   'My brain swam . . .': Murphy, *To Hell and Back*, p. 12

27 Closing In

427   'Malaria began . . .': Fenner, IWM 3854

428   'It turned out . . .': Schmalz, BA-MA MSG 2/13109

428   'To our astonishment . . .': Pöppel, *Heaven and Hell*, p. 133

429   'I hope Monty realized . . .': Patton Diary, 28 July 1943, LoC

429   'Monty kept repeating . . .': Patton Diary, 28 July 1943, LoC

429   'We had a great reception . . .': Montgomery Diary, 28 July 1943, Montgomery Papers, IWM

430   'We have not done so badly . . .': Montgomery to Brooke, cited in Hamilton, *Monty*, p. 342

431   'I recommend . . .': DDE, Vol. 2, No. 1119, p. 1262

431   'The military significance . . .': ibid, No. 1141, p. 1292

432   'We were sitting . . .': Donaldson, IWM 22357

432   'We had to keep moving . . .': ibid

433   'In leisurely style . . .': Mowat, *And No Birds Sang*, p. 138

433   'Suddenly it was hell . . .': Vincenza la Bruna, in Comune di Regalbuto, *Viaggio nella memoria*

433   'Outside it was a disaster . . .': ibid

434   'Everywhere the acrid fumes . . .': Cole, *Rough Road to Rome*, p. 63

435   'Unloaded the ship . . .': Jones, *Battles of a Gunner Officer*, loc. 1561

435   'Streets in Vizzini . . .': ibid, loc. 1569

436   'He expects to be killed . . .': Patton Papers, Box 18, LoC

436   'Stayed at the Youngblood . . .': cited in Scheffel, *Crack! And Thump*, p. 109

436   'Anyone know what it is?' cited ibid

436   'That's right, son . . .': cited ibid, p. 110

438   'Troina's going to be tougher . . .': cited in Bradley, *A Soldier's Story*, p. 149

28 Troina and Centuripe

439   'Hey, you fuckers . . .': cited in Scheffel, *Crack! And Thump*, p. 111
440   'How to make a mule . . .': Johnson, *One More Hill*, p. 110
441   'Terry, could you arrange . . .': Bradley, *A Soldier's Story*, p. 150
444   'We recce almond groves . . .': Jones, *Battles of a Gunner Officer*, loc. 1590
445   'It is cut out of . . .': ibid, loc. 1590
446   'The pioneer battalion . . .': TNA WO 169/10234
447   'The damn job's got to be done . . .': WO 169/10234
447   'God, what a job . . .': TNA WO 169/10234
448   'We gave them hell . . .': TNA WO 169/10234
448   'We were in a tight . . .': TNA WO 169/10234
449   'Goodbye Centuripe . . .': TNA WO 169/10234
449   'Although we have lost . . .': Johnson, *One More Hill*, p. 110
450   'They swept into Troina . . .': Scheffel, *Crack! And Thump*, p. 111
450   'I believe the outstanding . . .': Pyle, *Brave Men*, p. 84
450   'I've got to find . . .': ibid, pp. 84–5
450   'It's the perpetual . . .': ibid, p. 85

29 The Etna Battles

454   'Both of us . . .': von Senger, *Neither Fear Nor Hope*, p. 155
455   'Naturally, the mood . . .': ibid, p. 156
456   'The idea of a Liberator . . .': Dundas, *Flying Start*, p. 159
457   'It would explode . . .': Vrilakas, *Look Mom – I Can Fly!*, p. 88
457   'The speed of the Sicilian . . .': Corvo, *Max Corvo*, p. 82
460   'It made no difference . . .': Fenner, IWM 3854
461   'The locals were busy . . .': ibid
461   'Sicily is a mountainous . . .': Stappenbeck, 'That's How It Was', p. 81
462   'Others are sitting . . .': Cibulka, *Nachtwache*, p. 167
462   'I see a fighter bomber . . .': ibid, p. 168
463   'No cover worth the name . . .': Jones, *Battles of a Gunner Officer*, loc. 1607
464   'We could not afford . . .': Jones, *Battles of a Gunner Officer*, loc. 1638
464   'The whole town . . .': ibid, loc. 1638
465   'Thick orange groves . . .': ibid, loc. 1638
465   'Adrano is a sort of . . .': ibid, loc. 1659
465   'This is the most awful . . .': ibid, loc. 1659

30 The Straits of Messina

466   'The platoon officer . . .': Fenner, IWM 3854
466   'Another day's hard fighting . . .': Pöppel, *Heaven and Hell*, p. 135
467   'Tommies on our left!': ibid, p. 135
468   'The spectre only came . . .': Klein, *Fallschirmjäger*, p. 37
468   'All attempts to move it . . .': Goldschmidt, BA-MA MSG 2/6303
470   'There we were able . . .': Cole, *Rough Road to Rome*, p. 75
470   'With the two sides . . .': ibid, p. 76

471 'The earth shudders . . .': Murphy, *To Hell and Back*, p. 13
473 'I acquired a healthy respect . . .': ibid, p. 15
475 'This is a horse race . . .': cited in Blumenson, ed., *The Patton Papers*, p. 306
477 'We're taking Randazzo . . .': Scheffel, *Crack! And Thump*, p. 115
478 'Walked on nine miles . . .': Jones, *Battles of a Gunner Officer*, loc. 1731
478 'Here we were all alone . . .': Stappenbeck, letter to parents, 29 Aug. 1943
479 'We must be in . . .': cited in Morison, *History of United States Naval Operations in World War II*, p. 213
479 'The difficulty of operating . . .': cited in Orange, *Coningham*, p. 166
480 'The Sicilian adventure . . .': Mauss Diary, 10 Aug. 1943, Mauss and de Rijke, *The War Diary of Dr Wilhelm Mauss*, p. 320
480 'Our anti-aircraft guns . . .': cited in Kurowski, *The History of the Fallschirmpanzerkorps Hermann Göring*, p. 201
480 'We had an abundance . . .': Klein, *Fallschirmjäger*, pp. 44–5
481 'Tommy is meeting . . .': Pöppel, *Heaven and Hell*, p. 141
481 'Oh, it would be wonderful . . .': ibid, p. 144
481 'And what a hunger . . .': Stappenbeck, 'That's How It Was', p. 96
482 'My Lord, save me . . .': cited in Follain, *Mussolini's Island*, p. 290
482 'doing practically . . .': Pyle, *Brave Men*, p. 70
483 'They had built a jerry bridge . . .': ibid, p. 71

Postscript

486 'The Italian soldier . . .': Ulich, D-004, FMS, USAHEC
486 'Although the unreliability . . .': TNA AIR 20/10658
490 'Such men are cowards . . .': cited in Garland and McGaw Smyth, *Sicily and the Surrender of Italy*, p. 427
490 'It's my nerves . . .': cited ibid, p. 428
491 'I do not believe . . .': Patton Diary, 17 Aug. 1943, LoC
492 'one of our good friends': cited in Krüger, *The Great Heroin Coup*, p. 25
493 'The transient bodies . . .': Mowat, *And No Birds Sang*, p. 140
494 'For the first time . . .': Mowat, *And No Birds Sang*, p. 142

Selected Sources

PERSONAL TESTIMONIES

Interviews by the Author

Bowles, Henry D.
Bowles, Tom
Bruccoleri, Angela
Burbridge, Ralph
Colston, Bryan
Costain, Hank
Crawford, Michael 'Tubby'

Ellington, Edward 'Duke'
Evans, Warren 'Bing'
Renzo, Guglielmino
Klein, Jupp
Turco, Mario
Virgilio, Pietro

Interviews by Elio Chisari

Barbagallo, Melino
Frattini, Mario

Imperial War Museum, London

Cummings, John
Donaldson, James
Lumsden, Jim

Pearson, Alastair
Vaughn, Odell
Wiseman, John

Interview by Mario Orsini

Sardo, Lea

National World War II Museum, New Orleans

Chaisson, Roland
Dumas, Floyd
Griffenhagen, George

Peterson, Carl
Pierce, Wayne
Riddle, Clinton

Rutgers, The State University of New Jersey

Johnson, Franklyn A.

US Air Force Historical Research Agency, Maxwell, Alabama

Quesada, Elwood R. 'Pete'

US Army Heritage and Education Center, Carlisle, Pennsylvania

Bonesteel, Charles H.
Gay, Hobart

UNPUBLISHED REPORTS, MEMOIRS AND PAPERS

Bundesarchiv-Militärarchiv, Freiburg

Goldschmidt, Karl: MSG 2/6303
Schmalz, Wilhelm: MSG 2/13109

Churchill College Archives, Cambridge

Elmhirst, Thomas: Papers
Lewin, Ronald: Papers

Deutsches Tagebucharchiv, Emmendingen

Stappenbeck, Werner: Memoir ('That's How It Was'), Letters

Dwight D. Eisenhower Presidential Library, Abilene, Kansas

Bedell Smith, Walter: Papers
Butcher, Harry C.: Diary 1943

Eton College Library, Eton

Henderson, John: Diary, Papers, Photographs

Ike Skelton Combined Arms Research Library, Fort Leavenworth, Kansas

70th Tank Battalion, 3663

Imperial War Museum, London

Ball, G. M.: Papers

Carpenter, J. M. V.: Papers

Fenner, David: Papers

Hay, Peter: Midshipman's Journal

Lovett, P. J.: Papers

Mitchell, Gordon: Papers

Montgomery, Bernard: Diary, Papers

Neville, H. C.: Papers

Scollen, J. B.: Papers

Tweedsmuir, Lord: Papers

Library of Congress, Washington DC

Patton, George S.: Diary, Papers

Spaatz, Carl 'Tooey': Papers

Liddell Hart Centre for Military Archives, King's College, London

Alanbrooke, Lord: Papers

Davidson, F. H. N.: Papers

Howson, John: Papers

Kirkman, Sidney: Papers

National Archives, Kew

War Diaries

1st Airlanding Brigade

2nd Battalion, Devonshire Regiment

17th Field Regiment, Royal Artillery

1st Battalion, The Green Howards

6th Battalion, The Green Howards

1st Battalion, Parachute Regiment

2nd Battalion, Parachute Regiment

3rd Battalion, Parachute Regiment

2nd Battalion, Royal Inniskilling Fusiliers

6th Battalion, Royal Inniskilling Fusiliers

2nd Battalion, South Staffordshire Regiment

Special Raiding Squadron

RAF Operational Record Books

45 Squadron
74 Squadron
111 Squadron

249 Squadron
324 Wing

Documents

Alexander, Harold: Papers
HUSKY Enemy situation reports
HUSKY Enemy situation reports supplement
JG 77, Operations in the Mediterranean
Luftwaffe reports, Sicily
North Africa Tactical Air Force, Report on operations
Order of battle, Sicily
Seventh Army narrative, the Sicilian campaign
Sicilian campaign: administrative lessons and training notes
Ultra decrypts, Sicily

National Archives and Records Administration, College Park, Maryland

1st Infantry Division Operations and Reports
2nd Armored Division Operations and Reports
3rd Infantry Division in Sicily, Report on operations
15th Infantry Regiment in Sicily
45th Infantry Division Operations and Reports
Allied Airborne Operations in Sicily
Biscari incident, Collected papers
Captured German documents, Sicily
Operations, Circulars and Memoranda
Training notes from the Sicilian campaign
US wire monitoring
Weekly intelligence summaries

Naval History and Heritage Command, Washington DC

US Naval ships, reports and operations
US Navy narratives, the Sicilian campaign

US Air Force Historical Research Agency, Maxwell, Alabama

Galland, Adolf: Interview, Papers

US Army Heritage and Education Center, Carlisle, Pennsylvania

Memoirs

Dabinett, John T.: Papers
Dickson, Benjamin, 'G-2 Journal: Algiers to the Elbe' (Memoir)
Dillon, William T., 'Pearl Harbor to Normandy & Beyond' (Memoir)
Gavin, James M.: Diary, Papers
Gay, Hobart: Diary
Griffin, Eugene 'Breezy': Veteran's Questionnaire, Memoir
Hansen, Chester 'Chet': Diary
Hooper, Vincent: 'My Favourite War'
Kunz, William J.: Veteran's Questionnaire, Memoir
Lucas, John P.: Diary, Papers
Maffei, Norman: Papers
Moses, Russell T.: Papers
Ridgway, Matthew B.: Diary, Papers
Valenti, Isadore: Veteran's Questionnaire, 'Combat Medic' (Memoir)

Foreign Military Studies

C-087b, Bergengruen, Hellmuth, Battle of the Panzer Division Hermann
   Göring in Sicily
C-087d, Bergengruen, Hellmuth, Hermann Göring Division, Questionnaire
D-041, Fries, Walter, 29th Panzer Grenadier Division, June–July 1943
D-112, Fries, Walter, 29th Panzer Grenadier Division
C-014, Kesselring, Albert, Concluding Remarks on the Mediterranean
   Campaign
C-015, Kesselring, Albert, Italy as a Military Ally
C-077, Rodt, Eberhard, 15th Panzer Grenadier Division in Sicily
D-090, Seibt, Conrad, Stockpiling Supplies for Sardinia and Sicily
D-004, Ulich, Max, Sicilian Campaign – Special Problems and Their Solutions
D-089, Ulich, Max, Reconnaissance in the Battle of Sicily

CONTEMPORARY PAMPHLETS, BOOKLETS AND TRAINING MEMORANDA

Army Life, War Department Pamphlet 21-13, US Government Printing
   Office, 1944
Basic Field Manual: First Aid for Soldiers, FM 21-11, US War Department, 1943
*The Battle of the Atlantic: The Official Account of the Fight Against the U-Boats,
   1939–1945*, HMSO, 1946
By Air to Battle: The Official Account of the British Airborne Divisions,
   HMSO, 1945

Combat Instruction for the Panzer Grenadier, by Helmut von Wehren (Eng. trans. John Baum), 1944

Company Officer's Handbook of the German Army, Military Intelligence Division, US War Department, 1944

The Development of Artillery Tactics and Equipment, War Office, 1951

Der Dienst-Unterricht im Heere by Dr jur. W. Reibert, E. S. Mittler & Sohn, 1941

Field Service Pocket Book, various pamphlets, War Office, 1939–1945

German Infantry Weapons, Military Intelligence Service, US War Department, 1943

The German Squad in Combat, Military Intelligence Service, US War Department, 1944

German Tactical Doctrine, Military Intelligence Service, US War Department, 1942

German Tank Maintenance in World War II, Department of the US Army, June 1954

The Gunnery Pocket Book, 1945, Admiralty, 1945

Handbook of German Military Forces, TM-E 30-451, US War Department, 1945

Handbook on the British Army with Supplements on the Royal Air Force and Civilian Defense Organizations, TM 30-410, US War Department, Sept. 1942

Handbook on the Italian Military Forces, TME-30-240, Military Intelligence Service, US Army, August 1943

Infantry Training, Part VIII – Fieldcraft, Battle Drill, Section and Platoon Tactics, War Office, 1944

Infantry Training: Training and War, HMSO, 1937

Instruction Manual for the Infantry, Vol. 2, *Field Fortifications of the Infantry*, H.Dv. 130/11 (Eng. trans. John Baum), 1940

Instruction Manual for the Infantry, Vol. 2a, *The Rifle Company*, H.Dv. 103/2a (Eng. trans. John Baum), 1942

Instruction Manual for the Infantry, Vol. 3a, *The Machinegun Company*, H.Dv. 130/3a (Eng. trans. John Baum), 1942

Logistical History of NATOUSA & MTOUSA, US War Department, 1945

On the German Art of War: Truppenführung, ed. Bruce Condell and David T. Zabecki, Stackpole, 2009

Pilot's Notes General, Air Ministry, 1943

The Rise and Fall of the German Air Force (1933 to 1945), Air Ministry, 1948

Der Schütze Hilfsbuch, 1943, by Oberst Hasso von Wedel and Oberleutnant Pfafferott, Richard Schröder Verlag, 1943

Shooting to Live, by Capt. W. E. Fairbairn and Capt. E. A. Sykes, 1942

The Soldier's Guide to Sicily, Middle East Forces, 1943

Statistics Relating to the War Effort of the United Kingdom, HMSO, Nov. 1944

Tactics in the Context of the Reinforced Infantry Battalions, by Generalmajor Greiner and Generalmajor Degener (Eng. trans. John Baum), 1941

TEE EMM: Air Ministry Monthly Training Memoranda, Vols I, II, III, Air Ministry, 1939–45

What Britain Has Done 1939–1945, Ministry of Information, 1945

OFFICIAL HISTORIES

American Battle Monuments Commission, *American Armies and Battlefields in Europe*, US Government Printing Office, 1938

Aris, George, *The Fifth British Division 1939 to 1945*, The Fifth Division Benevolent Fund, 1959

Behrens, C. B. A., *Merchant Shipping and the Demands of War*, HMSO, 1955

Cosmas, Graham A., and Cowdrey, Albert E., *United States Army in World War II: Medical Service in the European Theater of Operations*, Historical Division, Department of the Army, 1992

Craven, Wesley Frank, and Cate, James Lea, *The Army Air Forces in World War II*, Vol. 2, *Europe: Torch to Pointblank*, University of Chicago Press, 1947

Duncan Hall, H., and Wrigley, C. C., *Studies of Overseas Supply*, HMSO, 1956

Echternkamp, Jörg, ed., *Germany and the Second World War*, Vol. IX/I, *German Wartime Society 1939–1945: Politicization, Disintegration, and the Struggle for Survival*, Clarendon, 2008

Fairchild, Byron, and Grossman, Jonathan, *United States Army in World War II: The Army and Industrial Manpower*, Office of the Chief of Military History, 1959

Garland, Albert N., and McGaw Smyth, Howard, *Sicily and the Surrender of Italy* (United States Army in World War II), Center of Military History, United States Army, 1986

Hancock, W. K., and Gowing, M. M., *British War Economy*, HMSO, 1949

Harris, C. R. S., *Allied Military Administration of Italy, 1943–1945*, HMSO, 1957

Hinsley, F. H., *British Intelligence in the Second World War*, HMSO, 1993

Howard, Michael, *Grand Strategy*, Vol. 4, *August 1942–September 1943*, HMSO, 1972

Hurstfield, J., *The Control of Raw Materials*, HMSO, 1953

Institution of the Royal Army Service Corps, *The Story of the Royal Army Service Corps 1939–1945*, G. Bell & Sons, 1955

Knickerbocker, H. R., et al., *Danger Forward: The Story of the First Division in World War II* (United States Army in World War II), Society of the First Division, 1947

Militärgeschichtliches Forschungsamt, *Germany and the Second World War*, Vol. 5, Part 1, *Organization and Mobilization of the German Sphere of Power: Wartime Administration, Economy and Manpower Resources, 1939–1941*, Clarendon, 2000

—*Germany and the Second World War*, Vol. 5, Part 2B, *Organization and Mobilization of the German Sphere of Power: Wartime Administration, Economy and Manpower Resources, 1942–1944/5*, Clarendon, 2003

—*Germany and the Second World War*, Vol. 6, *The Global War*, Clarendon, 2001

—*Germany and the Second World War*, Vol. 8, *The Eastern Front 1943–1944: The War in the East and on the Neighbouring Fronts*, Clarendon, 2017

Molony, C. J. C., *The Mediterranean and the Middle East*, Vol. 5, *The Campaign in Sicily 1943 and the Campaign in Italy 3rd September 1943 to 31st March 1944*, HMSO, 1973

Morison, Samuel Eliot, *History of the United States Naval Operations in World War II: Sicily–Salerno–Anzio, January 1943–June 1944,* Castle, 2001

Naval Historical Branch, *Invasion Europe,* HMSO, 1994

Nicholson, G. W. L., *Official History of the Canadian Army in the Second World War,* Vol. 2, *The Canadians in Italy, 1943–1945,* Edmond Cloutier, 1957

Otway, T. B. H., *Airborne Forces of the Second World War 1939–45,* HMSO, 1951

Palmer, Robert R., Wiley, Bell I., and Keast, William R., *The Procurement and Training of Ground Combat Troops* (United States Army in World War II), Historical Division, Department of the Army, 1948

Parker, H. M. D., *Manpower: A Study of War-Time Policy and Administration,* HMSO, 1957

Pogue, Forrest, *The Supreme Command* (United States Army in World War II), Historical Division, Department of the Army, 1954

Postan, M. M., *British War Production,* HMSO, 1952

Postan, M. M., Hay, D., and Scott, J. D., *Design and Development of Weapons,* HMSO, 1964

Rapport, Leonard, and Northwood, Arthur, *Rendezvous with Destiny: A History of the 101st Airborne Division,* 101st Airborne Association, 1948

Richards, Denis, *Royal Air Force 1939–1945,* Vol. 2, *The Fight Avails,* HMSO, 1954

—*Royal Air Force 1939–1945,* Vol. 3, *The Fight is Won,* HMSO, 1954

Risch, Erna, *The Technical Services: The Quartermaster Corps – Organization, Supply, and Services,* Vol. 1 (United States Army in World War II), Historical Division, Department of the Army, 1953

Rissik, David, *The D.L.I. at War: The History of the Durham Light Infantry 1939–1945,* The Depot, Durham Light Infantry, no date

Roberts Greenfield, Kent et al., *The Organization of Ground Combat Troops* (United States Army in World War II), Historical Division, Department of the Army, 1947

Scott, J. D., and Hughes, Richard, *The Administration of War Production,* HMSO, 1955

Wardlow, Chester, *The Transportation Corps: Movements, Training, and Supply,* (United States Army in World War II), Office of the Chief of Military History, 1956

Warren, John C., *Airborne Missions in the Mediterranean, 1942–1945,* USAF Historical Division, 1955

—*Airborne Operations in World War II, European Theater,* USAF Historical Division, 1956

EQUIPMENT, WEAPONS AND TECHNICAL

Barker, A. J., *British and American Infantry Weapons of World War 2,* Arms and Armour, 1969

Bidwell, Shelford, and Graham, Dominick, *Fire-Power: British Army Weapons and Theories of War 1904–1945,* Allen & Unwin, 1982

Bouchery, Jean, *The British Soldier*, Vol. 1, *Uniforms, Insignia, Equipment*, Histoire & Collections, no date

—*The British Soldier*, Vol. 2, *Organisation, Armament, Tanks and Vehicles*, Histoire & Collections, no date

Brayley, Martin, *The British Army 1939–45 (1), North-West Europe*, Osprey, 2001

—*British Web Equipment of the Two World Wars*, Crowood, 2005

Bruce, Robert, *German Automatic Weapons of World War II*, Crowood, 1996

Bull, Dr Stephen, *World War II Infantry Tactics*, Osprey, 2004

—*World War II Street-Fighting Tactics*, Osprey, 2008

Chamberlain, Peter, and Ellis, Chris, *Tanks of the World*, Cassell, 2002

Chesneau, Roger, ed., *Conway's All the World's Fighting Ships 1922–1946*, Conway Maritime, 1980

Dallies-Labourdette, Jean-Philippe, *S-Boote: German E-Boats in Action 1939–1945*, Histoire and Collections, no date

Davis, Brian L., *German Combat Uniforms of World War II*, Vol. 2, Arms & Armour, 1985

Doyle, David, *The Complete Guide to German Armored Vehicles*, Skyhorse, 2019

Enjames, Henri-Paul, *Government Issue: US Army European Theater of Operations Collector's Guide*, Histoire & Collections, 2003

Falconer, Jonathan, *D-Day Operations Manual*, Haynes, 2013

Farrar-Hockley, Anthony, *Infantry Tactics 1939–1945*, Almark, 1976

Fleischer, Wolfgang, *The Illustrated Guide to German Panzers*, Schiffer, 2002

Forty, George, and Livesey, Jack, *The Complete Guide to Tanks and Armoured Fighting Vehicles*, Southwater, 2012

Gander, Terry, and Chamberlain, Peter, *Small Arms, Artillery and Special Weapons of the Third Reich*, Macdonald & Jane's, 1978

Gordon, David B., *Equipment of the WWII Tommy*, Pictorial Histories, 2004

—*Uniforms of the WWII Tommy*, Pictorial Histories, 2005

—*Weapons of the WWII Tommy*, Pictorial Histories, 2004

Grant, Neil, *The Bren Gun*, Osprey, 2013

Griehl, Manfred, and Dressel, Joachim, *Luftwaffe Combat Aircraft: Development, Production, Operations, 1935–1945*, Schiffer, 1994

Gunston, Bill, *Fighting Aircraft of World War II*, Salamander, 1988

Hart, S., and Hart, R., *The German Soldier in World War II*, Spellmount, 2000

Hogg, Ian V., intr., *The American Arsenal: The World War II Official Standard Ordnance Catalog of Small Arms, Tanks, Armored Cars, Artillery, Antiaircraft Guns, Ammunition, Grenades, Mines, Etcetera*, Greenhill, 1996

—*The Guns 1939–1945*, Macdonald, 1969

Jowett, Philip, *The Italian Army 1940–45 (1)*, Osprey, 2000

—*The Italian Army 1940–45 (2)*, Osprey, 2001

—*The Italian Army 1940–45 (3)*, Osprey, 2001

Kay, Antony L., and Smith, J. R., *German Aircraft of the Second World War*, Putnam, 2002

Konstan, Angus, *British Battlecruisers 1939–45*, Osprey, 2003

Lagarde, Jean de, *German Soldiers of World War II*, Histoire & Collections, no date

Lavery, Brian, *Churchill's Navy: The Ships, Men and Organisation 1939–1945*, Conway, 2006

Lee, Cyrus A., *Soldat*, Vol. 2, *Equipping the German Army Foot Soldier in Europe 1943*, Pictorial Histories, 1988

Lepage, Jean-Denis G. G., *German Military Vehicles*, McFarland & Co., 2007

Lüdeke, Alexander, *Weapons of World War II*, Parragon, 2007

McNab, Chris, *MG 34 and MG 42 Machine Guns*, Osprey, 2012

Mason, Chris, *Soldat*, Vol. 8, *Fallschirmjäger*, Pictorial Histories, 2000

Ministry of Information, *What Britain Has Done, 1939–45*, HMSO

Mundt, Richard W., and Lee, Cyrus A., *Soldat*, Vol. 6, *Equipping the Waffen-SS Panzer Divisions 1942–1945*, Pictorial Histories, 1997

Musgrave, Daniel D., *German Machineguns*, Greenhill, 1992

Myerscough, W., *Air Navigation Simply Explained*, Pitman & Sons, 1942

Ruge, Friedrich, *Rommel in Normandy*, Macdonald & Jane's, 1979

Saiz, Augustin, *Deutsche Soldaten*, Casemate, 2008

Spayd, P. A., *Bayerlein: From Afrikakorps to Panzer Lehr*, Schiffer, 2003

Stedman, Robert, *Kampfflieger: Bomber Crewman of the Luftwaffe 1939–45*, Osprey, 2005

Suermondt, Jan, *World War II Wehrmacht Vehicles*, Crowood, 2003

Sumner, Ian, and Vauvillier, François, *The French Army 1939–1945 (1)*, Osprey, 1998

Sutherland, Jonathan, *World War II Tanks and AFVs*, Airlife, 2002

Trye, Rex, *Mussolini's Soldiers*, Airlife, 1995

Vanderveen, Bart, *Historic Military Vehicles Directory*, After the Battle, 1989

Williamson, Gordon, *Gebirgsjäger*, Osprey, 2003

—*German Mountain and Ski Troops 1939–45*, Osprey, 1996

—*U-Boats vs Destroyer Escorts*, Osprey, 2007

Windrow, Richard, and Hawkins, Tim, *The World War II GI: US Army Uniforms 1941–45*, Crowood, 2003

Zaloga, Steven, *Armored Thunderbolt: The US Army Sherman in World War II*, Stackpole, 2008

—*Sicily 1943: The Debut of Allied Joint Operations*, Osprey, 2013

—*US Anti-Tank Artillery 1941–45*, Osprey, 2005

MEMOIRS AND BIOGRAPHIES

Alanbrooke, Field Marshal Lord, *War Diaries, 1939–1945*, Weidenfeld & Nicolson, 2001

Alexander, Field Marshal Earl, *The Alexander Memoirs 1940–1945*, McGraw-Hill, 1962

Alexander, Mark J., and Sparry, John, *Jump Commander*, Casemate, 2012

Altieri, James, *The Spearheaders*, Popular Library, 1960

Ambrose, Stephen E., *Eisenhower: Soldier and President*, Pocket, 2003

—*The Supreme Commander: The War Years of Dwight D. Eisenhower*, University Press of Mississippi, 1999

Arneson, Paul S., *I Closed Too Many Eyes: A World War II Medic Finally Talks*, self-published, no date

Badoglio, Marshal, *Italy in the Second World War*, Oxford University Press, 1948

Baker, David, *Adolf Galland: The Authorised Biography*, Window & Greene, 1996

Binder, L. James, *Lemnitzer: A Soldier for His Time*, Brassey's, 1997

Blumenson, Martin, ed., *The Patton Papers, 1940–1945*, Da Capo, 1974

Booth, T. Michael, and Spencer, Duncan, *Paratrooper: The Life of General James M. Gavin*, Casemate, 2013

Bosworth, R. J. B., *Mussolini*, Arnold, 2002

Bradley, Omar N., *A Soldier's Story*, Henry Holt, 1951

—and Blair, Clay, *A General's Life*, Simon & Schuster, 1983

Bradner, Liesl, *Snap Dragon: The World War II Exploits of Darby's Ranger and Combat Photographer Phil Stern*, Osprey, 2018

Brown, John Mason, *To All Hands: An Amphibious Adventure*, Whittesley House, 1943

Bruno, James F., *Beyond Fighter Escort*, Ken Cook, 1995

Burgwyn, H. James, *Mussolini Warlord: Failed Dreams of Empire 1940–1943*, Enigma, 2012

Butcher, Harry C., *Three Years with Eisenhower*, William Heinemann, 1946

Caddick-Adams, Peter, *Monty and Rommel: Parallel Lives*, Arrow, 2012

Chandler, Alfred D., Jr, ed., *The Papers of Dwight David Eisenhower: The War Years*, Vol. 2, John Hopkins University Press, 1970

Chatterton, George, *The Wings of Pegasus*, Macdonald, 1962

Cheall, Bill, *Fighting Through from Dunkirk to Hamburg*, Pen & Sword, 2011

Ciano, Galeazzo, *Ciano's Diary 1937–1943*, Phoenix, 2002

Cibulka, Hanns, *Nachtwache: Tagebuch aus dem Kriege Sizilien, 1943*, Mitteldeutscher Verlag, 1989

Clarke, Rupert, *With Alex at War*, Pen & Sword, 2000

Cole, David, *Rough Road to Rome: A Foot Soldier in Sicily and Italy 1943–44*, William Kimber, 1983

Corvo, Max, *Max Corvo: OSS in Italy, 1942–1945*, Enigma, 2005

Costanzo, Ezio, *La Guerra in Sicilia 1943: Storia Fotografica*, Le Nove Muse Editrice, 2009

Cunningham, Admiral of the Fleet Viscount, *A Sailor's Odyssey*, Hutchinson, 1951

Darby, William O., with Baumer, William H., *Darby's Rangers*, Ballantine, 2003

Davis, Peter, *SAS: Men in the Making*, Pen & Sword, 2015

Davis, Richard G., *Carl A. Spaatz and the Air War in Europe*, Center for Air Force History, 1992

Deakin, F. W., *The Brutal Friendship: Mussolini, Hitler and the Fall of Italian Fascism*, Pelican, 1966

de Grada, Magda Ceccarelli, *Giornale del Tempo di Guerra*, Il Mulino, 2011

Deniston, Dale R., *The Memoirs of a Combat Fighter Pilot*, self-published, 1995

D'Este, Carlo, *Patton: A Genius for War*, Harper Perennial, 1996

Dönitz, Grand Admiral Karl, *Memoirs: Ten Years and Twenty Days*, Da Capo, 1997

Doolittle, James H. 'Jimmy', *I Could Never Be So Lucky Again*, Bantam, 1992

Dryden, Charles W., *A-Train: Memoirs of a Tuskegee Airman*, University of Alabama Press, 1997

Dundas, Hugh, *Flying Start*, Penguin, 1990

Durnford-Slater, John, *Commando: Memoirs of a Fighting Commando in World War Two*, Greenhill, 2002

Eade, Philip, *Young Prince Philip*, Harper, 2012

Eisenhower, Dwight D., *Crusade in Europe*, William Heinemann, 1948

Fairbanks, Douglas, Jr, *A Hell of a War*, St Martin's, 1993

Farrell, Nicholas, *Mussolini: A New Life*, Phoenix, 2004

Forman, Denis, *To Reason Why*, Pen & Sword, 2008

Frost, John, *A Drop Too Many*, Buchan & Enright, 1982

Galland, Adolf, *The First and the Last*, Fontana, 1971

Garra, Giacomo, *Il Nonno Racconta*, Le Nove Muse, 2005

Gavin, James M., *On To Berlin: Battle of an Airborne Commander, 1943–1946*, Viking, 1978

Gorle, Richmond, *The Quiet Gunner at War: El Alamein to the Rhine with the Scottish Divisions*, Pen & Sword, 2011

Gunther, John, *D Day*, Hamish Hamilton, 1944

Hamilton, Nigel, *Monty: Master of the Battlefield 1942–1944*, Hamish Hamilton, 1983

Hargreaves, Harry, *It Wasn't All Mayhem: The Musings of a Matelot*, Compaid Graphics, 2005

Hill, Alan, *Hedley Verity: A Portrait of a Cricketer*, Kingswood, 1986

Hirshson, Stanley P., *General Patton: A Soldier's Life*, HarperCollins, 2002

Jackson, W. G. F., *Alexander of Tunis as Military Commander*, Batsford, 1971

Johnson, Franklyn A., *One More Hill*, Bantam, 1983

Jones, John Philip, *Battles of a Gunner Officer: Tunisia, Sicily, Normandy and the Long Road to Germany*, Praetorian, 2014

Kays, William M., *Letters from a Soldier: A Memoir of World War II*, Wimke, 2010

Kemp, Nick, *Ever your own, Johnnie – Sicily and Italy, 1943–45*, Nick Kemp, 2016

Kennedy, Squadron Leader I. F., *Black Crosses off my Wingtip*, General Store Publishing House, 1995

Kershaw, Ian, *Hitler: 1936–1945 – Nemesis*, Penguin, 2001

Kesselring, Albert, *The Memoirs of Field-Marshal Kesselring*, Greenhill, 2007

Klein, Joseph, *Fallschirmjäger*, self-published, 2008

Leonardi, Dante Ugo, *Luglio 1943 in Sicilia*, Società tipografica modenese, 1947

Mansfield, Angus, *Barney Barnfather: Life on a Spitfire Squadron*, History Press, 2008

Mauss, Hans-Jörg, and de Rijke, Roger, *The War Diary of Dr Wilhelm Mauss*, Mook wi, 2016

Meon, Marcia, and Heinen, Margo, *Heroes Cry Too*, Meadowlark, 2002

Miller, Victor, *Nothing Is Impossible*, Pen & Sword, 2015

Millers, Lee G., *The Story of Ernie Pyle*, Viking, 1950

Montgomery, Field Marshal the Viscount, *El Alamein to the River Sangro*, Hutchinson, 1944

—*Memoirs*, Collins, 1958

Mowat, Farley, *And No Birds Sang*, Douglas & McIntyre, 2012

Murphy, Audie, *To Hell and Back*, Picador, 2002

Mussolini, Benito, *Pensieri, pontini e sardi: Scritti e discorsi*, Ulrico Hoepli Milano, 1940

Nicolson, Nigel, *Alex: The Life of Field Marshal Earl Alexander of Tunis*, Weidenfeld & Nicolson, 1973

Orange, Vincent, *Coningham: A Biography of Air Marshal Sir Arthur Coningham*, Center for Air Force History, 1990

Origo, Iris, *War in Val d'Orcia*, Flamingo, 2002

Patton, George S., *War as I Knew It*, Pyramid, 1966

Petacco, Arrigo, *Il prefetto di ferro: L'uomo di Mussolini che mise in ginocchio la mafia*, Mondadori, 2004

Peyton, John, *Solly Zuckerman*, John Murray, 2001

Pinkham, John H., *Jack's Memoirs*, self-published, 2008

Pöppel, Martin, *Heaven and Hell: The Wartime Diary of a German Paratrooper*, Spellmount, 1988

Pyle, Ernie, *Brave Men*, Henry Holt, 1944

Richardson, Robert L., *The Jagged Edge of Duty: A Fighter Pilot's World War II*, Stackpole, 2017

Ridgway, Matthew B., *Soldier: The Memoirs of Matthew B. Ridgway*, Harper & Brothers, 1956

Ross, Hamish, *Paddy Mayne*, History Press, 2004

Samwell, H. P., *Fighting with the Desert Rats: An Infantry Officer's War with the Eighth Army*, Pen & Sword, 2012

Scheffel, Charles, with Basden, Barry, *Crack! And Thump – With a Combat Infantry Officer in World War II*, Camroc, 2007

Senger und Etterlin, Frido von, *Neither Fear Nor Hope*, Presidio, 1989

Shockley, Orion C., *Random Chance: One Infantry Soldier's Story*, Trafford, 2007

Smith, Albert H., *Recollections of an Infantry Company Commander*, Society of the First Infantry Division, 2001

Smith, David A., *The Price of Valor: The Life of Audie Murphy, America's Most Decorated Hero of World War II*, Regnery History, 2015

Steinhoff, Johannes, *Messerschmitts over Sicily*, Pen & Sword, 2004

Tedder, Marshal of the Royal Air Force Lord, *With Prejudice*, Cassell, 1966

Tobin, James, *Ernie Pyle's War*, University of Kansas Press, 1997

Toliver, Raymond F., and Constable, Trevor J., *Fighter General: The Life of Adolf Galland*, AmPress, 1990

Truscott, Lucian K., *Command Missions*, Presidio, 1990

Ullrich, Volker, *Hitler: Downfall, 1939–45*, Bodley Head, 2020

Vrilakas, Robert 'Smoky', *Look Mom – I Can Fly!*, Amethyst Moon, 2011

Warlimont, Walter, *Inside Hitler's Headquarters 1939–45*, Presidio, 1962

Warner, Oliver, *Cunningham of Hyndehope: Admiral of the Fleet*, John Murray, 1967

Winton, John, *Cunningham: The Greatest Admiral since Nelson*, John Murray, 1998

GENERAL

Air Ministry, *The Rise and Fall of the German Air Force 1933–1945*, 1948

Arthur, Max, *Men of the Red Beret*, Hutchinson, 1990

Atkinson, Rick, *The Day of Battle: The War in Sicily and Italy, 1943–1944*, Abacus, 2007

Baedeker, Karl, *Southern Italy and Sicily*, Baedeker, 1912

Baumer, Robert W., with Reardon, Mark J., *American Iliad: The 18th Infantry Regiment in World War II*, Aberjona, 2004

Bekker, Cajus, *The Luftwaffe War Diaries*, Corgi, 1972

Bellamy, Chris, *Absolute War: Soviet Russia in the Second World War – A Modern History*, Macmillan, 2007

Black, Robert W., *Rangers in World War II*, Ballantine, 1992

Blok, Anton, *The Mafia of a Sicilian Village 1860–1960*, Polity, 1975

Bosworth, R. J. B., *Mussolini's Italy: Life under the Fascist Dictatorship, 1915–1945*, Penguin, 2005

Carafano, James Jay, *GI Ingenuity: Improvisation, Technology and Winning WWII*, Stackpole, 2006

Champagne, Daniel, *Dogface Soldiers: The Story of B Company, 15th Regiment, 3rd Infantry Division*, Merriam, 2003

Citino, Robert M., *The German Way of War*, University Press of Kansas, 2005

—*The Wehrmacht Retreats: Fighting a Lost War, 1943*, University Press of Kansas, 2012

Comune di Regalbuto, *Viaggio nella memoria*, Le Nove Muse, 2007

Costanza, Ezio, *The Mafia and the Allies*, Enigma, 2007

Cull, Brian, with Malizia, Nicola, and Galea, Frederick, *Spitfires over Sicily*, Grub Street, 2000

d'Este, Carlo, *Bitter Victory: The Battle for Sicily 1943*, William Collins, 1988

Dickie, John, *Cosa Nostra: A History of the Sicilian Mafia*, Hodder, 2007

Dickson, Paul, *The Rise of the GI Army, 1940–1941*, Atlantic Monthly, 2020

Dinardo, R. L., *Germany and the Axis Powers: From Coalition to Collapse*, University of Kansas Press, 2005

—*Germany's Panzer Arm in WWII*, Stackpole, 1997

Doherty, Richard, *Clear the Way! A History of the 38th (Irish) Brigade, 1941–47*, Irish Academic, 1993

Duggan, Christopher, *Fascist Voices: An Intimate History of Mussolini's Italy*, Bodley Head, 2012

Edgerton, David, *Britain's War Machine*, Penguin, 2012

—*Warfare State, Britain 1920–1970*, Cambridge University Press, 2006

Eriksson, Patrick G., *Alarmstart South and Final Defeat*, Amberley, 2019

Fennell, Jonathan, *Fighting the People's War*, Cambridge University Press, 2019

Fitzgerald-Black, Alexander, *Eagles over Husky*, Helion, 2018

Follain, John, *Mussolini's Island*, Hodder, 2005

Ford, Ken, *Battleaxe Division*, Sutton, 2003

Fraser, David, *And We Shall Shock Them: The British Army in the Second World War*, Cassell, 1999

Garvey, James, *Operation Husky: The Untold Story of the Logistics of the Sicily Invasion*, Farm Publications, 2019

Gavin, James M., and Lee, William C., *Airborne Warfare*, Infantry Journal, 1947

Gooderson, Ian, *Air Power at the Battlefront: Allied Close Air Support in Europe, 1943–45*, Frank Cass, 1998

Gregory, Barry, *British Airborne Troops*, Macdonald & Jane's, 1974

Harrison Place, Timothy, *Military Training in the British Army, 1940–1944*, Frank Cass, 2000

Harris Smith, Richard, *OSS: The Secret of America's First Central Intelligence Agency*, Lyons, 2005

Haulman, Daniel L., *The Tuskegee Airman Chronology*, New South, 2017

Heaton, Colin D., and Lewis, Anne-Marie, *The German Aces Speak*, Zenith, 2011

Heiber, Helmut, and Glanz, David, *Hitler and His Generals: Military Conferences 1942–1945*, Enigma, 2002

Holland, James, *Heroes: The Greatest Generation and the Second World War*, Harper Perennial, 2007

—*Italy's Sorrow: A Year of War 1944–45*, Harper, 2008

Howard, Michael, *The Mediterranean Strategy in the Second World War*, Greenhill, 1993

Irving, David, *The Rise and Fall of the Luftwaffe: The Life of Luftwaffe Marshal Erhard Milch*, Weidenfeld & Nicolson, 1973

Jackson, W. G. F., *The Battle for Italy*, Harper & Row, 1967

Jensen, Marvin, *Strike Swiftly! The 70th Tank Battalion from North Africa to Normandy to Germany*, Presidio, 1997

Joseph, Frank, *Mussolini's War*, Helion, 2010

Knox, MacGregor, *Hitler's Italian Allies*, Cambridge University Press, 2000

Krüger, Henrik, *The Great Heroin Coup: Drugs, Intelligence and International Fascism*, Trine Day, 1980

Kurowski, Franz, *The History of the Fallschirm Panzerkorps Hermann Göring*, J. J. Fedorowicz, 1995

Lewis, Norman, *The Honoured Society: The Sicilian Mafia Observed*, Eland, 1984

LoFaro, Guy, *The Sword of St Michael: The 82nd Airborne Division in World War II*, Da Capo, 2011

Lopez, Jean, et al., *World War II Infographics*, Thames & Hudson, 2019

McGaw Smyth, Howard, *Secrets of the Fascist Era: How Uncle Sam Obtained Some of the Top-Level Documents of Mussolini's Period*, Southern Illinois University Press, 1975

Macintyre, Ben, *Operation Mincemeat*, Bloomsbury, 2010

—*SAS: Rogue Heroes – The Authorized Wartime History*, Viking, 2016

Mead, Richard, *Churchill's Lions: A Biographical Guide to the Key British Generals of World War II*, Spellmount, 2007

—*The Men Behind Monty*, Pen & Sword, 2015

Mitcham, Samuel W., Jr., and von Stauffenberg, Friedrich, *The Battle of Sicily: How the Allies Lost their Chance for Total Victory*, Stackpole, 1991

Mortimer, Gavin, *Stirling's Men: The Inside History of the SAS in World War II*, Cassell, 2005

Mule, Nuccio, *Nel Corso della Battaglia di Gela*, self-published, 2018

—*Sbarco Americano a Gela*, Gela, 2008

Newark, Tim, *The Mafia at War: Allied Collusion with the Mob*, Greenhill, 2007

Norwich, John Julius, *Sicily: A Short History from the Ancient Greeks to Cosa Nostra*, John Murray, 2016

O'Brien, Phillips Payson, *How the War Was Won: Air–Sea Power and Allied Victory in World War II*, Cambridge University Press, 2015

Owen, James, *Commando: Winning World War II Behind Enemy Lines*, Abacus, 2012

Pantaleone, Michele, *The Mafia and Politics*, Chatto & Windus, 1966

Peters, Mike, *Glider Pilots in Sicily*, Pen & Sword, 2012

Roskill, Stephen, *The Navy at War 1939–1945*, Wordsworth, 1998

Saliger, Mark, *The First Bridge Too Far: The Battle of Primosole Bridge 1943*, Casemate, 2018

Seth, Ronald, *Lion with Blue Wings*, Panther, 1959

Shores, Christopher, Massimello, Giovanni, et al., *A History of the Mediterranean Air War 1940–1945*, Vol. 4, *Sicily and Italy to the Fall of Rome, 14 May 1943 – 5 June 1944*, Grub Street, 2018

Spick, Mike, *Luftwaffe Fighter Aces*, Greenhill, 2003

Stargardt, Nicholas, *The German War: A Nation under Arms, 1939–45*, Bodley Head, 2015

Steinhoff, Johannes, Pechel, Peter, and Showalter, Dennis, *Voices from the Third Reich: An Oral History*, Da Capo, 1994

Thompson, Julian, *Ready for Anything: The Parachute Regiment at War 1940–1982*, Weidenfeld & Nicolson, 1989

Todman, Daniel, *Britain's War: Into Battle, 1937–1941*, Allen Lane, 2016

—*Britain's War: A New World, 1942–1947*, Allen Lane, 2020

Tooze, Adam, *The Wages of Destruction: The Making and Breaking of the Nazi Economy*, Penguin, 2007

Weal, John, *Jagdgeschwader 53 'Pik-As'*, Osprey, 2007

Whiting, Charles, *Hunters from the Sky*, Cooper Square, 2001

Zuehlke, Mark, *Operation Husky: The Canadian Invasion of Sicily, July 10 – August 7, 1943*, Douglas & Macintyre, 2010

PERIODICALS, JOURNALS, MAGAZINES AND PAMPHLETS

After the Battle, No. 77

Exercise SPRING HUSKY Study Guide, 2017, Defence Infrastructure
  Organisation

Exercise SUMMER HUSKY Study Guide, 2016, Department of Manning
  (Army)

Exercise VIKING HUSKY Study Guide, 2015, 1st Battalion, The Royal Anglian
  Regiment

Historical Museum of Military Landing in Sicily 1943, guide, Provincia
  Regionale di Catania, 2004

Life, 30 Aug. 1943

Picture Post, 'Sicilian Victory', 21 Aug. 1943

GIs at Brolo

Acknowledgements

To complete this book I was, as is always the case with such projects, dependent on the help of a lot of people. I'm going to start with Sicily itself, where I found extraordinary generosity and kindness at every turn, and genuine willingness to see a new book on the campaign being published. In Syracuse, Roberto Piccione got the ball rolling and not only gave me copies of his father's testimony but put me in touch with others, showed me around former gun batteries and bunkers, and bent over backwards to do all he could. He also put me in touch with Elio Chisari, who has become a firm friend and who drove me around, set up interviews with veterans, introduced me to the historian Mario Orsini, and conducted two interviews with veterans on my behalf. He also gave me and my daughter, Daisy, a ride in his wonderful wartime German BMW motorcycle and sidecar. His son, Leonardo, has also been a brilliantly efficient translator, so to both of you and your family, *grazie mille* for all your immense help.

I am also incredibly grateful to my old university pal Roddy Bassett, who now spends some of his time living in Sicily and who followed up on leads, broke through red tape, and also acted as companion and translator at various times. It was a memorable time we had in Sicily, and Roddy, huge thanks, my friend. I would also like to thank Filippo Spadi, who does great work conserving the Gothic Line in the Apennines and who put me in touch with Nuccio Mulè in Gela. Nuccio not only gave me some of his own books on the subject but introduced me to several veterans, including Angela Bruccoleri, Mario Turco and Guglielmino Renzo, who also gave their time and memories freely and whom it was fascinating to meet. I am also hugely grateful to Pietro Virgilio for giving up an afternoon to talk to me, and to Melino Barbagallo and Mario Frattini for sharing their memories of those times. I would also like to thank Giovanni Galavotti in Bologna for his huge help in translating various materials for me.

My great friend Dorothee Schneider has been tireless in poring over scores of German documents and helping me to bring the testimonies of Wilhelm Schmalz, Karl Goldschmidt, Hanns Cibulka, Werner Stappenbeck and others into the narrative of the book. Thank you, Dorothee, for all your enormous work on this. Thanks, too, to the staffs at the Tagebucharchiv in Emmendingen and at the Bundesarchiv-Militärarchiv in Freiburg for their help.

In the United States, various friends and colleagues helped along the way, not least John McManus, Rob Citino and Mike Neiberg, and also Conrad Crane and the staff at the United States Army Heritage and Education Center at Carlisle Barracks, Pennsylvania. I'd particularly like to thank Tom Buffenbarger, John Giblin, Steven Bye and Rodney Foytik, who are among the most friendly, helpful and cooperative archive staff I've ever had the pleasure to work with. I'd also particularly like to thank Guy Nasuti at the United States Naval History and Heritage Command in Washington DC, and the staffs at the National Archive and Records Administration in College Park, Maryland, and at the Library of Congress. In the States I would also like to thank another great pal, Chaz Mena, who kept me company in Washington and who was recruited at the last minute as Chief Research Assistant at NARA and the Library of Congress. Thanks, Old Sport.

In the UK, I would particularly like to thank Joseph Quinn for all his help at the National Archives in Kew, as well as his numerous colleagues, and the staff of the Imperial War Museum, London. At the National Army Museum, I am indebted to Justin Maciejewski and his team, and especially to Peter Johnston for all his valuable help with maps, photographs and much more besides. At the brilliant Tank Museum in Bovington, huge thanks to David Willey, and also to Richard Smith, Roz Skellorn and the team there.

There are a large number of other people who have helped along the way, including Jon Baker, Neil Barber, Adam Berry, Paul Davis, Simon Fletcher, John Follain, Adrian Freer, Richard Moore, Richard O'Sullivan, Ray Polidano and Brigadier Jim Tanner, who have all willingly shared documents and research of their own. Thank you. To Laura Bailey and Lalla Hitchings, for all your help, huge thanks, as always. I have also been able to call upon a circle of trusted and highly valued friends. Mike 'Chalky' Peters has been brilliant and a companion on a number of trips to Sicily. Lieutenant-Colonel Graham Goodey has given me some contemporary military perspectives, has been another excellent travelling companion in Sicily, and has shared a number of documents and thoughts. Matt Doncaster, a former fast-jet pilot in the RAF, is another friend who has painstakingly talked me through some of the finer details of combat flying, as well as heroically proofreading the entire text, and for both parts of his contribution to this book, I am enormously grateful. Professor Peter Caddick-Adams is an old friend, a travelling companion over the Sicilian battlefields, a person with whom I can always chew the historical cud and an unfailingly helpful sounding board. Ditto Stephen Prince, Head of the Naval Historical Branch, with whom a conversation on any aspect of the war is never wasted.

Thanks, too, to the *We Have Ways* podcast gang: Al Murray, Tony Pastor, Jon Gill, Harry Lineker and Joey McCarthy, who are great fun to be with and work with, and who have willingly let me prattle on about Sicily over the past year or so.

Ultimately, it's publishers who ensure what is tapped away at on a keyboard eventually becomes a physical book, and I am incredibly lucky to be looked after by such a brilliant bunch of people – colleagues but, over the years, firm friends too. In New York, I am indebted to Morgan Entrekin at Grove Atlantic and also to the brilliant George Gibson, whose enthusiasm, encouragement and terrific judgement know no bounds. Here in the UK, Gillian Somerscales has bravely taken on the mantle of copy-editing – a big undertaking and a task that has been done with immense skill, patience and kindness – thank you. To John Ash and Margaret Halton and PEW Literary, thank you for all your enormous help and for being so wonderful. At Bantam Press, Phil Lord, Vivien Thompson, Sophie Bruce, Tom Hill, Larry Finlay and all the team there have been as brilliant as always, and I am immensely grateful that they have all been so wonderful during what has been a particularly challenging time for them and publishing as a whole. I am especially grateful to Eloisa Clegg for all her incredible attention to detail, patience and kindness at every turn – thank you. Finally, huge thanks, as always to Bill Scott-Kerr, Publisher at Bantam, and Patrick Walsh, my agent – I truly could not wish to have two better people guiding me along the way, and for your friendship, help and support, I am for ever in your debt.

To my parents for accompanying me on my very first visit to Sicily, thank you for all your support and for being my travelling companions. And to my long-suffering family, thank you – for Ned, for also coming along on that first trip, for Daisy for coming with me on the last, and for

Rachel for always being there for me. I don't what I'd do without you, I'm not going to lie. And finally, to my oldest of friends, Giles Bourne, my brilliant pal of well over forty years, all I can say is this: thank you for being such a fabulous chum, but you better bloody well read this book after the fuss you have made about the dedication.

Picture Acknowledgements

All photographs have been kindly supplied by the author except those listed below. Every effort has been made to trace copyright holders; those overlooked are invited to get in touch with the publishers.

Section 1

Page 1, bottom left
Pantelleria under attack: © Imperial War Museum CNA 902.

All other images on page 1: Courtesy National Archives and Records Administration, USA

Page 2, top left
Me109 partially hidden beneath olive trees: Büschgens/Bundesarchiv, bild: 101I-421-2070-21

Page 2, upper right
One of JG77's Me109s at Trapani: Büschgens/Bundesarchiv, bild 101I-421-2070-10

Page 2, middle left
American P-38 Lightning: Courtesy US Air Force Historical Research Agency

Page 2, middle right
Two destroyed Me109s: Supplied by author

Page 2, bottom
Abandoned and captured Luftwaffe Messerschmitts and Regia Aeronautica Macchis: Courtesy National Archives and Records Administration, USA

Page 3, top
The allied commanders for HUSKY: © Imperial War Museum CNA 1075

Page 3, middle left
Mussolini: AP/Shutterstock

Page 3, middle right
Kesselring and von Senger: Supplied by author

Page 3, bottom left
RAF operations room in underground Lascaris bunker complex on Malta: Fondazzjoni Wirt Artna (The Malta Heritage Trust)

Page 3, bottom right
British troops loading LSTs for Operation HUSKY: National Army Museum

Page 4, top left
Rows of LSTs line up at Bizerte as US troops march aboard: Courtesy National Archives and Records Administration, USA

Page 4, top right
The invasion fleet under sail: National Army Museum

Page 4, middle left
British glider-borne troops load up in Tunisia: © Imperial War Museum CNA 1002

Page 4, middle right
US paratroopers aboard a C-47: Courtesy National Archives and Records Administration, USA

Page 4, bottom
A Horsa glider en route to Sicily: Malta Aviation Museum

Page 5, top left
Very rough seas off Licata on D-Day: Courtesy National Archives and Records Administration, USA

Page 5, top right
The British XIII Corps invasion, with the high escarpment looking down on the invasion beaches: National Army Museum

Page 5, middle left
British Tommies coming ashore: Supplied by author

Page 5, middle right
A near miss sends a fountain of water high into the air near Avola: National Army Museum

Page 5, bottom
The 231st Malta Brigade coming ashore on D-Day: National Army Museum

Page 6, top left
LST 313 destroyed at Gela: Courtesy National Archives and Records Administration, USA

Page 6, top right
Destruction of Liberty ship *Robert Rowan*: Courtesy National Archives and Records Administration, USA

Page 6, middle left
Jam-packed transport vessels: Courtesy National Archives and Records Administration, USA

Page 6, middle right
Light cruiser *USS Brooklyn*: Naval History Heritage Command

Page 6, bottom
British troops move through Cassibile: National Army Museum

Page 7, lower right
The destroyer HMS *Tetcott* firing on Augusta: National Army Museum

Page 7, bottom right
Canadian infantry push inland: © Imperial War Museum NA 4491

All other images on page 7: Courtesy National Archives and Records Administration, USA

Page 8, bottom
The landscape around Mount Etna: National Army Museum

All other images on page 8, with the exception of middle left (Don Calogero Vizzini): Courtesy National Archives and Records Administration, USA

Section 2

Page 9, top left
Melilli after its bombardment from the sea: National Army Museum

Page 9, top right
The Italian strongpoint at Ponte Dirillo: Courtesy National Archives and Records Administration, USA

Page 9, middle left
One of the mighty Tigers of 2. Kompanie, 504. Heavy Panzer Bataillon: Esselborn/Bundesarchiv, bild 183-J14953

Page 9, middle right
Well-positioned German machine-gunners: Dohm/Bundesarchiv, bild 183-J14874

Page 9, bottom left
US infantry moving forward: Courtesy National Archives and Records Administration, USA

Page 9, bottom right
Monty addressing Canadian troops: National Army Museum

Page 10, top right
German *Fallschirmjäger* (paratroopers) moving forward: Novak/Bundesarchiv, bild: 101I-634-3899-02A

Page 10, bottom
British paratroopers of the 1st Parachute Brigade: Airborne Assault Museum

All other images on page 10: National Army Museum

Page 11, top left
Captured British paratroopers and Tommies: Funke/Bundesarchiv, bild: 101I-303-0558-22

Page 11, top right
An American half-track struggles through the narrow Sicilian streets: Courtesy National Archives and Records Administration, USA

All other images on page 11: National Army Museum

Page 12, top left
German machine-gunners well camouflaged: Dohm/Bundesarchiv, bild: 101I-303-0559-27

Page 12, top right
A German *Kubelwagon* needs a change of wheel as a Sicilian boy watches: Grund/Horst/Bundesarchiv, bild: 101I-303-0559-27

Page 12, middle left
The Allies captured tens of thousands of prisoners: Courtesy National Archives and Records Administration, USA

Page 12, middle right
Germans of the Herman Göring Division talk to their captor: Courtesy National Archives and Records Administration, USA

Page 12, bottom left
A Spitfire comes into land: © Imperial War Museum CAN 1098

Page 12, bottom right
A British sapper clears one of the many mines the Germans left: National Army Museum

Page 13, middle left
British tanks of the County of London Yeomanry cross the Plain of Catania: National Army Museum

All other images on page 13: Courtesy National Archives and Records Administration, USA

Page 14, bottom
A *Fallschirmjäger* anti-tank gun crew: Haas/Bundesarchiv, bild: 101I-567-1515-32

All other images on page 14: National Army Museum

Page 15, top left
Major-General Vyvyan Evelegh and Colonel George R. Smith meet on the road to Randazzo: Courtesy National Archives and Records Administration, USA

Page 15, middle right
The astonishing bridge-building effort by American 10th Engineer Battalion at Capo Calavà: Courtesy National Archives and Records Administration, USA

Page 15, bottom left
US troops enter the wreckage of Messina: Courtesy National Archives and Records Administration, USA

All other images on page 15: National Army Museum

Page 16, top
The view from Assoro: © Mike Peters

Page 16, top left
Centuripe – the prostrate man: 4Corners images

All other images on page 16: Supplied by author

Integrated Pictures

Page xiii
Operations room in Malta: © Imperial War Museum NA 4094

Page xxii
SRS men with captured Italian gun: Paul Davis

Pages xxxix–xl
Supplied by the author from various sources where known: Airborne Assault Museum, Angela Bruccoleri, Max Corvo, Paul Davis, Charles Dryden, Robin Dundas, Imperial War Museum, National Archives UK, National Archives and Records Administration USA, Roberto Piccione.

Pages 288–9
Part 3 opener: 'The Race to Catania': © Imperial War Museum NA 4666

Index

ABOUT THE AUTHOR

James Holland is a historian, writer and broadcaster. The author of a number of bestselling histories including *Battle of Britain*, *Dam Busters* and, most recently, *Normandy '44*, he has also written nine works of historical fiction, including the Jack Tanner novels.

He is currently writing the final volume of an acclaimed new history of the Second World War, *The War in the West*. He has presented – and written – a large number of television programmes and series for the BBC, Channel 4, National Geographic, and the History and Discovery channels.

James is co-founder of the Chalke Valley History Festival and of WarGen.org, an online Second World War resource site, and presents the Chalke Valley History Hit podcast. He also presents *We Have Ways of Making You Talk*, a podcast with Al Murray in which they discuss the Second World War. A fellow of the Royal Historical Society, he can be found on Twitter and Instagram as @James1940.

A three-part documentary series based on his bestselling book *Normandy '44* can be found on Normandy44.info and Amazon Prime under the same title.

US infantryman